P9-EDZ-447

Country Music, U.S.A.

SECOND REVISED EDITION

Country Music, U.S.A.

By Bill C. Malone

SECOND REVISED EDITION

To Dix Bruce,
Thanks for the great
music and good
friendship. I hope you
like my version of
American folk culture.

University of Texas Press, Austin

Bill Malone

Second revised edition, 2002

Requests for permission to reproduce material from this
work should be sent to Permissions, University of Texas
Press, Box 7819, Austin, TX 78713-7819.

Library of Congress Cataloging-in-Publication Data
Malone, Bill C.
    Country music, U.S.A. / by Bill C. Malone.—2nd rev. ed.
        p.   cm.
Includes bibliographical references (p.   ), discography,
(p.   ), and indexes.
    ISBN 0-292-75262-8 (pbk. : alk. paper)
    1. Country music—History and criticism.   I. Title:
Country music, USA.   II. Title.
ML3524 .M34   2002
781.642′ 0973—dc21   2002004792

⊗ The paper used in this book meets the minimum
requirements of ANSI/NISO Z39.48-1992 (R1997)
(Permanence of Paper).
ISBN 0-292-75262-8

Contents

Illustrations

Preface

It has been forty-five years since the little Philco battery radio came into our farmhouse in East Texas (a little community, now vanished, called Galena—about twenty miles west of Tyler), bringing a touch of the outside world, along with the music of the Chuck Wagon Gang, the Stamps Quartet, the Shelton Brothers, the Callahan Brothers, Cowboy Slim Rinehart, and the many performers of the *National Barn Dance* and the *Grand Ole Opry*. For me it was the beginning of a love affair that has never ceased. It has been even longer than that since I first heard my mother singing such old-fashioned sentimental songs as "The East Bound Train" and "Prisoner at the Bar," or pouring out her soul in religious tunes like "Farther Along" and "Leave It There." My older brothers, Wylie and Kelly, began trying out their voices on country music when they were about fourteen or fifteen years old, strumming on a cheap guitar which Wylie, however, had obtained in a trade with neighbor Thomas Starr (he plowed for him for about a week). Through my brothers, and through the voices that sang to us over the battery radio, such songs as "The Last Letter" and "It Makes No Difference Now" moved into my consciousness alongside the gospel and sentimental parlor pieces learned from my mother.

I sang country music all my life, but made no serious attempts to learn the guitar until my graduate days at the University of Texas in Austin. Until I learned my first chords, such friends as Tom Crouch and Willie Benson wore out their fingers playing accompaniment for me as I sang at parties and beer busts in the Austin area. I eventually discovered Thread-gill's, a now-famous bar in North Austin, where I sang a couple of times a week in the informal jam sessions that prevailed around the big wooden tables. It was my notoriety as an amateur country singer that led to the writing of this book. In December 1960, I traveled to Houston with a few graduate student friends and my supervising professor, Joe B. Frantz, to see the Texas Longhorn football team play in the Bluebonnet Bowl. We sang songs all the way to Houston, with Dr. Frantz requesting song after song, and that evening during dinner he suggested that I choose as a doctoral dissertation a business history of Nashville music publishing. Once the work was begun, I expanded the topic to its present limits with his blessings. I will always be thankful that in a conservative discipline, history, Dr. Frantz exhibited such tolerance for an unorthodox subject. The dissertation eventually became *Country Music, U.S.A.*

When I began my research, Austin had not yet become a hotbed of live music performance. I was far removed from people who did serious collecting or scholarship in the field of country music and was largely unaware of their existence. The two country music repositories, the John Edwards Memorial Foundation and the Country Music Foundation, did not exist when I began my research in 1961 and were still in their infancy by the time the book was published in 1968. Resource material was extremely limited. In the sixteen years that have passed since the original publication there has been an explosion of scholarship, and new writers, both academic and popular, have entered the field, bringing new information and fresh perspectives. Country music itself, as a dynamic and ever-changing facet of American popular culture, has burgeoned since the late sixties. The careers of some musicians have faded, while others have blossomed; others will have bloomed and faded by the time this revised edition appears.

My own perspectives have changed as my knowledge has deepened. I no longer agree with some of my earlier points of view, and some of my original statements were flatly wrong. The reader is invited to compare the two editions to find out where differences exist. I also expended too much energy defending country music as an art form and asserting its folkness. While those battles have not been completely won, they no longer merit the kind of extensive, and often defensive, attention I devoted to them.

I believe that *Country Music, U.S.A.* has done its part to tell country music's story around the world, while also lending some respectability to the serious academic treatment of the subject. Country music courses are now taught in many colleges and universities; theses and dissertations assay the field in a variety of scholarly disciplines; and academic papers dealing with country music are occasionally presented at conventions and symposia. A milestone of sorts was reached in my own discipline in November 1977, when I gave a lecture-concert on country music, accompanied by a bluegrass band, at the opening session of the Southern Historical Association convention in New Orleans. This was a considerable advance, indeed, for an organization which had previously ignored country music at its convention sessions and in its journal, and which had once had as a president an eminent historian of the South who referred to the "hillbilly rabble" of radio. The millennium, though, clearly has not arrived. Country music scholars still have far to go in demonstrating the cultural relevance of their subject.

Historians of the South, with a few striking exceptions such as Tom Connelly, Jim Cobb, and John Rumble, still ignore the music of their region's working people. It is still not sufficiently understood that country music is not merely a facet of southern culture, but is also southern culture's chief industry. Passing references in southern history surveys to Elizabethan balladry, Appalachian dulcimers, or the *Grand Ole Opry* hardly do justice to the institution that country music has become. General or monographic histories of the United States also rarely discuss country music. Accounts of the Great Depression, the era of the "common man's" rediscovery, say virtually nothing about the music of the plain folk, except for a few brief references to Woody Guthrie or the Library of Congress' Archive of American Folk-Song. But almost every radio station in the nation during those perilous years harbored a cowboy balladeer, a gospel quartet, or a hillbilly string band. Cultural analyses of the sixties, to cite still another example, properly emphasized the centrality of music in American youth culture while also demonstrating the role played by rock and popular musicians in counterculture protests. But not one word is uttered in these accounts about country music's burgeoning growth during those years, or about the appeal it exhibited to a very large slice of the American people (including the "silent majority").

My perspective as both a historian and a fan of country music hopefully works to assure balance, although my biases have no doubt affected my perceptions and interpretations. Still, I have striven for objectivity and have attempted to be fair to those styles that I do not like. My personal preferences clearly lean toward hard-core country, and to singers with individuality whose sounds and styles reflect their rural or working-class origins—whether they are "down-home" stylists like the Blue Sky Boys, Molly O'Day, the Bailes Brothers, and Ralph Stanley, or honky-tonk performers like Ernest Tubb, George Jones, and Merle Haggard. Country music is now being inundated by musicians whose sounds suggest neither regional, rustic, nor blue-collar nativity, but are instead rooted in the homogenizing and mass-consumption-oriented media establishment. That is why it is so gratifying to hear new country musicians, like Ricky Skaggs and Tony Rice on the one hand, or Gene Watson and Moe Bandy on the other, who effectively fuse modernity and tradition, affirming that such a reconciliation not only is possible, but also can be commercial. I feel that I am not alone in my desire for honest, unpretentious, and down-to-earth entertainment. The unprecedented popularity of Garrison Keillor's *Prairie Home Companion* on National Public Radio—a half-serious, half-comic recreation of barn-dance Americana broadcast from St. Paul, Minnesota— indicates that there is a large audience hungry for simple, home-style fare and therefore grateful to find something palpable rather than plastic. May there always be such a public to keep these impulses alive.

My debts are many, and I hope they have been properly acknowledged in the bibliographical essays. As I noted in the first edition, the real sources of this book are the many musicians, professional and amateur, who have captivated my interest since I was a child. While I can, neither name nor repay all of them, I can at least acknowledge the profound impact they have had upon my life. Among the many non-musicians who have provided both friendship and research support, I feel the need to single out three individuals: Bob Pinson, Archie Green, and Jo Walker-Meador. Bob Pinson, now Director of Acquisitions for the Country Music Foundation Library, sought me out during the early stages of my dissertation research (when he was a private collector in Southern California) and has ever since been unselfish in his aid and encouragement. Bob knows more than the rest of us, but has written less. Archie Green is known and revered by every student of American vernacular music. One of the greatest folklorists, Green is a model of indefatigability, limitless ideas, and insatiable curiosity. He is an inspiration to all who know him. Jo Walker-Meador, the Executive Director of the Country Music Association, has been with that organization since its beginnings and has been a prime force in its remarkable expansion. Without her help back in 1961 in arranging interviews and providing contacts, my first research trip to Nashville might very well have proved fruitless.

Finally, I wish to dedicate this book to the memory of my mother and father, Maude and Cleburne Malone, and to my wife, Bobbie. My parents bequeathed to me the culture of which country music is a part as well as a special love and respect for that music's primacy in their lives. Bobbie came to me with little knowledge of or experience with country music, but in the few short years since our marriage began she has become an accomplished mandolin player and a good country singer. Her immersion in my "redneck culture" has not kept her from making a more thorough commitment to her own culture; she became a "bat mitzvah girl" at the age of thirty-nine. Above all, she has given me a special love that I never believed possible. In the words of the Ricky Skaggs song, "I wouldn't change a single thing."

B.C.M.
1985

Introduction to the Revised Edition of 2002

Over thirty years have passed since *Country Music, U.S.A.* was first published, and more than sixteen years have elapsed since its last revision. Commercially, the music has prospered beyond anyone's dreams or expectations. A musical culture that always yearned for acceptance in mainstream American life has won at least grudging respect, if not universal approbation. When Toby Keith triumphantly sang "How Do You Like Me Now?," his award-winning song and video of 2000, he was gloating about his personal success to a woman who had rejected him when both were in high school. In a sense, though, his message can be taken as an anthem for country music as a whole, an art form that too long has suffered from low self-esteem but, like the singer's songs, is "living in your radio" throughout the world.

While country music has prospered, its look and sound have changed dramatically in the past sixteen years. Many veteran performers moved on to Hillbilly Heaven during those years. The partial list that follows suggests the magnitude of the loss: Roy Acuff, Rex Allen, Jimmy Arnold, Charline Arthur, Bob Atcher, Chet Atkins, Gene Autry, Walter Bailes, Earl Bolick (of the Blue Sky Boys), Cliff Bruner, Archie Campbell, Wilf Carter (Montana Slim), Jerry Clower, Dick Curless, Ted Daffan, Johnny Darrell, Jimmie Davis, John Duffey, Arlie Duff, Stoney Edwards, Dale Evans, Tennessee Ernie Ford, Wally Fowler, Lonnie Glosson, Stuart Hamblen, John Hartford, Bobby Helms, Doc Hopkins, Harlan Howard, Shot Jackson, Waylon Jennings, Grandpa Jones, Rose Carter Karnes (of the Chuck Wagon Gang), Bradley Kincaid, Pee Wee King, Lily May Ledford, Leon McAuliffe, Laura Lee McBride, O. B. McClinton, Rose Maddox, Benny Martin, Roger Miller, Minnie Pearl, Bill Monroe, Patsy Montana, Clyde Moody, Molly O'Day, Hank Penny, Webb Pierce, Wayne

Raney, Charlie Rich, Roy Rogers, Johnny Russell, Leon "Pappy" Selph, Bob (Attlesey) Shelton, Hank Snow, Buddy Starcher, Wynn Stewart, Nat Stuckey, Al Terry, Justin Tubb, Townes Van Zandt, Conway Twitty, Keith Whitley, Chubby Wise, Tammy Wynette, and Faron Young. Still others have found themselves excluded from Top Forty radio airplay in order to make room for the rash of young entertainers who have emerged in staggering numbers. The period, in short, witnessed a changing of the guard in country music, the virtual disappearance of the last generation of musicians whose music, with a few exceptions, reflected southern blue-collar origins.

I hope that this book has contributed to both an acceptance and an understanding of country music. My affection for the music has never been hidden, and, for good or ill, that emotional attachment has colored my scholarship. I still submit that the music emerged from southern working-class culture, and I remain persuaded by the evidence that it long carried the marks of those origins in its sound, themes, and perspectives. Although no one can any longer convincingly demonstrate such bonds between southern working-class life and the music that now flows out of Nashville, the precise moment when those cords were severed cannot be dated. Furthermore, public perceptions of country music around the world are still clearly influenced by visions of southern mountaineers, cowboys, or Celtic minstrels, and even the most intelligent performers are still prone to assertions of romantic nonsense concerning their music's alleged Celtic or Appalachian ancestry.

Although some passages in the original text call for correction or improvement, and a few areas exist where I have changed my mind, I have chosen to concentrate largely on the years following 1985. Making sense of those years is as daunting a task as I wish to undertake. I am a poor prophet and have been surprised but pleased by the revivals of hard country music that have periodically occurred within a general context of incessant homogenization, so I will make no predictions. I will instead argue, as I have reaffirmed in the text, that country music exists in many forms outside the Nashville mainstream and those forms can be found if people search for them. If Top Forty country music offends, vibrant alternatives can be enjoyed.

My contention that country music actually comes from the people who write and perform it may be little more than a romantic conceit, but my emphasis continues to be on singers, songwriters, musicians, and the music they have made, and not on the large and complex industry that produces, advertises, and markets the music. While I will not apologize for my perspective, I will readily acknowledge that the industry sorely needs its chroniclers. Now that Bill Ivey, the former head of the Country Music Association, has retired from his post as director of the National Endowment for the Arts and has expressed his wish to write some overdue books, perhaps he will give us the study of music industry producers for which he has long called. And others may write about the most overlooked music industry people of all, the "sidemen" who make the singers sound good and who, like Bill Monroe's Blue Grass Boys of the late forties and Ray Price's great Cherokee Cowboys of the late fifties and early sixties, fuel country music's most significant innovations.

Again, I wish to acknowledge those people who gave me invaluable support and advice back when this book was in its formative stages: the late Joe B. Frantz, who supervised my doctoral dissertation; the late Bill Pool, who introduced me to Frank Wardlaw, director of the University of Texas Press when the manuscript was being considered for publication; the fine editors at the Press who labored to convert my academic jargon into readable prose; and Archie Green (my favorite folklorist), Bob Pinson (onetime director of acquisitions for the Country Music Foundation Library), and Jo Walker-Meador (former executive director of the Country Music Association), each of whom unselfishly aided my research and writing in many ways. None of them of course are responsible for the mistakes and errors of judgment that may have intruded into the text.

Finally, I wish to dedicate this book to all the folks who have made good bluegrass and old-time music with me down at the Green Room, the Copper Grid, Dudley's Bar, the Speedway Bar, and other jamming venues in Madison, Wisconsin, each Monday night for the past six years, to all the patrons and friends of WORT-FM (89.9) who keep my program "Back to the Country" on the air each Wednesday morning, and of course to my parents, Maude and Cleburne Malone, who introduced me to country music and southern working-class life, and to my wife Bobbie who still sustains me with her love, radiant smile, intelligent counsel, and mandolin playing. The words of one of Ricky Skaggs' most popular songs still sums up my attitude toward her and our relationship: "I wouldn't change a single thing."

Bill C. Malone
2002

Country Music, U.S.A.

SECOND REVISED EDITION

Left to right, Al Hopkins, John Hopkins, Tony Alderman, John Rector, Uncle Am Stuart, Fiddlin' John Carson. Photographed at old-time fiddlers' convention, Mountain City, Tennessee, 1925. Courtesy of Bob Pinson.

1. The Folk Background before Commercialism

Country music is no longer simply an American cultural expression; it is now a phenomenon of worldwide appeal. Nevertheless, it defies precise definition, and no term (not even "country") has ever successfully encapsulated its essence. It is a vigorous hybrid form of music, constantly changing and growing in complexity, just as the society in which it thrives also matures and evolves. It was introduced to the world as a southern phenomenon, and in the sixty years or more since it was first commercialized it has preserved, to a remarkable degree, the marks of that origin. The music is nonetheless older than the South itself, and the massive commercialization it has undergone is merely a facet of that larger technological and communications revolution which has so radically transformed American popular tastes and steadily worked to pull the rural, socially conservative South into the homogenizing mainstream of American life.

Hillbilly music (a once universal designation for country music) evolved primarily out of the reservoir of folksongs, ballads, dances, and instrumental pieces brought to North America by Anglo-Celtic immigrants. Gradually absorbing influences from other musical sources, particularly from the culture of Afro-Americans, it eventually emerged as a force strong enough to survive, and even thrive, in an urban-industrial society. British folk culture of course came to all regions of English-speaking North America, and pockets of tradition still persist in such places as rural New England and Canada's Maritime Provinces. It was only in the southern United States, though, that dynamic folk cultural expressions, black and white, evolved into viable commercial forms in our own time.

The social conservatism that encouraged the preservation of older values and institutions in the South was a product of geography, economics, religion, and politics. Climate and topography conspired to create an environment favorable to productive agriculture, or one where people could live in relative freedom and security, as did the herders and stockdrovers, by exploiting the abundant resources of the public domain. While some people accumulated great wealth from agriculture, the majority embraced such a livelihood, or professed to do so, because of the supposed nonmaterial blessings that came from cultivation of the soil: independence, self-fulfillment, health, and virtue. This beneficent vision of agriculture and the rural life which surrounded it did not really begin to dim until after the Civil War. When tenantry and sharecropping became fastened upon the land, and as farmers of all kinds became enmeshed in an impersonal system of credit and marketing demands, much of the old sense of freedom began to diminish, and people began to feel imprisoned by agriculture.[1] It is only then that we begin to see the first stirrings of what would become a mass exodus from the farms.

Whether rural life promoted independence and virtue is an arguable point, but that it fostered isolation would seem to be a certainty. In the South people were separated, not only by social class, but also by great distances and by rugged terrain which hindered easy communication. Cities grew slowly, while most villages and small towns remained mere appendages of the surrounding agricultural areas. European immigration, for the most part, flowed into the northern states, forsaking the South because of the lack of cities, the scarcity of jobs, and the competition of slavery. Slavery, which lay at the base of the South's socioeconomic system, contributed even more virulently to the region's isolation as white southerners from all social classes banded in defense of white supremacy and in opposition to the growing chorus of worldwide hostile criticism. Thus, the defense of slavery and the racial hierarchy which derived from it lay at the core of the South's belief system, a system militantly dedicated to the preservation of the status quo. Increasingly cut off from the currents of change in a nation rapidly succumbing to the blandishment of urbanism and industrialization, responding to the rhythms of agriculture, and clinging to an evangelical Protestantism that encouraged Bible literalism and orthodoxy, southerners adhered to that which was familiar and comfortable, and to the maintenance of traditions which had once been the common property of Americans everywhere.

1. For an amplification of this view of southern abundance, see Frank Owsley, *Plain Folk of the Old South* (Baton Rouge: Louisiana State University Press, 1949). Grady McWhiney and Forrest MacDonald make some of the same points, while also stressing the freedom promoted by the open and abundant southern range, in "The Antebellum Southern Herdsman: A Reinterpretation," *Journal of Southern History* 41, no. 2 (May 1975): 147–167. A brilliant exposition of the emergence of market capitalism among southern small farmers, and the consequent spawning of rural radicalism, is Steven Hahn, *The Roots of Southern Populism: Yeoman Farmers and the Transformation of the Georgia Upcountry, 1850–1890* (New York: Oxford University Press, 1983).

The South, then, was a folk culture. And while the reliance on the familiar was a trait that cut across social and economic lines, it was strongest among the poorer classes, black and white. The plantation owners might know "Barbara Allen" or "Lord Lovel," and they very well might have fond memories of kicking up their heels at a country dance, but it was their yeoman and poor white cousins who preserved these kinds of musical diversions. Regardless of where they lived, in mountains or flatlands, the common people of the South shared a passionate commitment to music. Furthermore, since they shared similar cultural traditions, they preserved the same songs and styles. Arthur Palmer Hudson argues that "not only was the singing habit a widely and perhaps equally diffused one in the South as a whole; the songs sung over the South are much the same, irrespective of locality."[2]

The socially ingrown rural South, from the tidewater of Virginia to the pine barrens of East Texas, encompassed a population that, in its commitment to and preservation of traditional cultural values, should be considered a distinct family unit. This immense region, so incredibly diverse in its topography, is what two scholars have called "the fertile crescent of country music."[3] Following the lure of King Cotton, which forever demanded fresh land and a suitably long growing season, or otherwise seeking a temperate climate similar to that which they had left, southern migrants moved southwestward across the mountains and toward the potential cotton-producing regions of Arkansas, Louisiana, and Texas. As the frontier receded steadily westward, the southern musical culture moved with it. A poor Georgian entering a small farmer's cabin in East Texas would have felt very much at home. The architecture of the house, the food on the table, the dress and speech patterns of the hosts, and even the theology of the local church would have been reassuringly familiar. And more than likely there would have been a fiddle over the mantel, and in the general area a multitude of musical reminders of the old homestead: a shape-note singing school, a Sacred Harp convention, and house parties galore.

Of course, the folk music heard in East Texas would not have been precisely identical to that heard in North Georgia, just as the music cherished on the southern frontier was not exactly like that found in the British Isles. British immigrants to the United States brought a great storehouse of lore and song, but three thousand miles of ocean and radically different historical experiences wrought a similar divergence in musical expression. It is now next to impossible to determine the exact ethnic origin of a particular song or style dating from the British experience. English, high-

2. Arthur Palmer Hudson, "Folk Songs of the Southern Whites," in *Culture in the South*, ed. W. T. Couch (Chapel Hill: University of North Carolina Press, 1934), p. 520.
3. Richard A. Peterson and Russell Davis, "The Fertile Crescent of Country Music," *Journal of Country Music* 6, no. 1 (Spring 1975): 19–25.

land Scots, Scotch-Irish, Catholic Irish, and Welsh elements intermingled on the southern frontier, as they had previously done in the British Isles. The backcountry South may very well have been Celtic, as two eminent historians have argued,[4] but cultural intermixing had occurred so frequently and for such a long period of time that white folk culture should most appropriately be called "British."

Whatever the specific source of the British tunes, rural southerners did not rely exclusively upon them. As soon as the American experience began, colonists began creating songs based upon their new lives here, and they borrowed songs from other cultural groups with whom they came in contact. With the passage of time the country people built up a body of songs of American origin which sang, not of knights and fair English damsels, but of scenes and events in their own purview. Similarly, the ancient British ballads underwent, in terms of structure, subject matter, and melodic contour, a measure of Americanization. American names and places sometimes replaced those of British origin, and words from the American vocabulary replaced the sixteenth- and seventeenth-century terms that no longer had meaning. American ballads still spoke of "wee pen knives," "milk white steeds," and fair maidens with "lily-white hands," but the Robin Hood ballads and songs of witchcraft rarely survived the Atlantic transit. British folk culture remained most dramatically evident in the most inaccessible areas, such as the Appalachian and Ozark mountains. Many of the songs discovered by Cecil Sharp and other collectors in the early twentieth century were in the modal scale of an older musical culture, that is, restricted to five or six tones and characterized by melodies that sound incomplete to modern ears.

British folk culture did not survive intact in the southern wilderness, nor should one expect it to have done so. The folk music of the South was a blending of cultural strains, British at its core, but overlain and intermingled with the musical contributions of other ethnic and racial groups who inhabited the vast southern region. As they inched their way across the southern frontier, British migrants came in contact with other peoples, whom they often fought, traded, and worked with, made love to, and sang and danced with: the Germans of the Great Valley of Virginia; the Indians of the backcountry; Spanish, French, and mixed-breed elements in the Mississippi Valley; the Mexicans of South Texas; and, of course, blacks everywhere. Southern folk music was touched and energized by the contributions of all of these people, and country music still bears the marks of these influences. Of all the southern ethnic groups, none has played a more important role in providing songs and styles for the white country musician than that forced migrant from Africa, the black. Nowhere is the peculiar love-hate relationship that has prevailed among the southern

---

4. McWhiney and MacDonald, "The Antebellum Southern Herdsman."

races more evidenced than in country music. Country music—seemingly the most "pure white" of all American musical forms—has borrowed heavily from the black. White Southerners who would be horrified at the idea of mixing socially with blacks have nonetheless enthusiastically accepted their musical offerings: the spirituals, the blues, ragtime, jazz, rhythm-and-blues, and a whole host of dance steps, vocal shadings, and instrumental techniques.

Black-white contact began so early and was so omnipresent in American life that it is virtually impossible to know who profited most from the resulting musical exchange. From the time they first saw them on slave ships, white observers have commented frequently on blacks' alleged penchant for music. In the four hundred years that have passed, white musicians have continually drawn on black sources for rejuvenation and sustenance. Anywhere that blacks and whites mingled in the United States, in field, factory, or mine, on railroad section gangs, in juke joints or taverns, at camp meetings or in church, at county fairs or on street corners, the potential existed for mutual cultural transmission. The mountains were no more immune to this kind of musical interchange than were the flatland regions. Blues records, of course, began making their way into the mountains in the mid-twenties, but even before then black folk musicians had been seen and heard on street corners or in work camps. Both the guitar and the blues form may have ventured into the mountains with black laborers who followed the highways and railroads as they gradually inched their way up the Appalachian ridges. Such early country singers as Dock Boggs from Virginia and Frank Hutchison and Dick Justice from the West Virginia coal fields performed both songs and styles which they learned from local black musicians. A long list of country musicians, from Jimmie Rodgers through Bob Wills and Hank Williams to Charlie Rich and Razzy Bailey, provide testimony of the unending appeal of black music.

If southern white folk music was neither pure white nor "Anglo" in origin or manifestations, neither was it exclusively rural or noncommercial. Folk isolation was never complete. No southern area (nor any other American area for that matter) has ever been totally isolated from the world at large. The currents of change that have swept over the United States, making it the most advanced, industrially oriented nation in the world, have also moved across the South. The South, though changing slowly, and often with dogged resistance, has indeed changed.

The southern pockets of rural folk culture—whether mountain, hill country, delta, bayou, or flatland—have never been completely immune to the forces of technological or social change. Scarcely a rural community in the decades before 1920 remained unvisited at one time or another by some kind of peripatetic agent of the world outside who brought news, business, religion, education, or amusement. It might be the Methodist circuit rider braving the flooded streams or frozen wilderness to bring not only the gospel but gossip from the towns and cities. It might be the singing-school teacher boarding with farm families until the shape-note method had been learned by the entire community. Or it might be any number of salesmen or agents of mercantile houses, the "rider" sent out by the general store to see if the farmers' crops would enable them to meet their credit obligations, or the Yankee or Jewish peddler in a horse-drawn wagon carrying a valuable cargo of needed items—which might even include a musical instrument.

Neither have our rural areas—prior to the coming of radio, television, and rural electrification—been totally immune to the musical trends emanating from the cities. The popular music originating in Tin Pan Alley or on the vaudeville stages of northern cities entered the rural districts in a variety of ways. The city could most effectively transport its musical ideas to the country through the medium of the traveling show. Circuses with their singing clowns and brass bands, puppet shows with their fiddlers, and the brown chautauqua tents whose variety entertainment might include anything from Swiss yodelers to Hawaiian string bands, all did their part to broaden the horizons of isolated rural dwellers. Perhaps the most common of the traveling shows, but one as yet inadequately documented, was the medicine show. The "physick" wagon, with its glib-talking "doctor" and cargo of patent medicines, was a familiar phenomenon to rural Americans as late as the 1930's, and even in 1984 "Doc" Tommy Scott (best known to country music fans for his 1950's recording of "Rosebuds and You") still tours with a show throughout the United States and Canada performing variety entertainment and selling a bottled liniment which is appropriately named "Snake Oil." Nearly all of the medicine shows employed an entertainer—often blackface—to warm up the crowd by singing, cracking jokes, or playing an instrument. Not only were songs introduced to rural America in this manner, but the medicine shows also provided an early commercial outlet for country musicians, who were often employed by the traveling shows. On the physick wagons, country entertainers gained invaluable show business experience which would later serve them well when they set out on their professional careers. The list of country entertainers who learned in this manner is extensive and includes Uncle Dave Macon, Jimmie Rodgers, Roy Acuff, Gene Autry, Lew Childre, Clarence Ashley, and Hank Williams.

On a larger scale, and almost as common as the medicine show until the 1930's, was the traveling tent operation—often called the "tent repertory" show. The tent-rep show brought to rural America a touch of vaudeville, including everything from magicians, acrobats, and trained bears to Irish tenors, Swiss yodelers, and dancing girls. These organizations, transported by horse-drawn wagons in the early days, would move into a rural community, stake out their tents, hold nightly shows that might run as long as a week, and then move on to another excited community. The communities visited, it is clear, often included the smallest villages imaginable. My father remembered a tent show which, just before World War I, lingered for a week in his rural home community of Galena, an East Texas village near Tyler so small that it could not be located on the map. Practically every man, woman, and child attended the show—night after night—spending money if they had it, but just as often bartering eggs, vegetables, or canned goods for the price of admission.

Although the traveling shows were important vehicles for transmitting urban culture to the rural regions, a more common, and obvious, means was the movement of country people to and from the town. As long as the city has existed, it has beckoned the rural dweller. Often pictured in American myth, story, and song as the center of vice, corruption, and lost innocence, the city has more often exerted a contrary pull on the rural mind. Country youth have traditionally seen the city in many different lights: as a place of employment, a means of escape, and a source of amusement. More accurately, then, country people have responded ambivalently to the city and its charms. They have often sought the city's advantages while at the same time attacking its values and longing for the rural life which they readily extol but to which they would not return. The catalogue of country music is filled with songs extolling the farmer, and the whole scheme of rural values (from "The Farmer Is the Man," to "Blackland Farmer," to "Thank God I'm a Country Boy"), and with scores of others describing the innocent ruralite lost in the big city and at the mercy of the city slicker (the classic piece in this genre is "Stay in the Wagon Yard"). But, attacked and ridiculed as the city may have been, the statistics of the past hundred years reveal the irresistible appeal the city has had for rural Americans.

Burdened by the rigors of farm work and by the social isolation of country life, southern country boys and girls have traditionally longed for the bright lights of the city that lay somewhere down the road or beyond the mountains. By the thousands they have ventured into such cities as Louisville, Memphis, Nashville, Atlanta, New Orleans, and Houston. Many went only for temporary employment, later going back to the farm, but the great majority remained as part of the swelling ranks of the urban lower-middle class. In the decades before 1920 the city was never too far away for the country boy whose dreams and longings were intense enough. By foot, by wagon, by horseback, by flatboat or steamboat, the trip to the city was made. Increasingly after the Civil War another agent of industrial change—the railroad—played its powerful role in uniting city and farm. The railroad was among the earliest, and certainly the most dramatic, examples of the industrial process that would ultimately transform the rural South, shatter its façade of isolation, and weaken the hegemony of agriculture over its people. No other industrial phenomenon has held such a magnetic and romantic fascination for Americans, and it is doubtful that any ever again will, even though the automobile has had a greater impact on the breaking down of regional barriers. The railroad provided employment apart from agriculture, it offered the means of escape from unpleasant or unwanted responsibilities, and it in fact could and did transport people to alternative and presumably better economic opportunities. Even those people who were bound to the land, and who had no realistic expectations of leaving it, could experience a vicarious satisfaction in identifying with this great symbol of industrial energy and with the tough, unfettered men who had mastered it. No one can document the number of people who have lain awake in quiet and darkened farmhouses listening to the lonesome wail of a distant freight train or have seen it belching smoke as it thundered down the mountainside and longed for the exciting world that the iron monster seemed to symbolize.

So off they went to the textile mills of the Carolina piedmont, the coal mines of eastern Kentucky, the dockyards of New Orleans and Galveston, the railroad shops of Atlanta and Richmond, and, in this century, to service installations, oil fields, defense plants, and industrial and clerical jobs all over the United States. Many of those who roamed had no particular destination in mind but were part of that nameless throng of drifters and homeless men that has always been such a visible part of American life. Whether they came to visit or stay, they were exposed to a multitude of musical influences that in time would be taken back to their rural homes.

In the mid-nineteenth century one of the more popular urban musical sources was the blackface-minstrel show, which contributed a brand of humor and stage patter, banjo styles, and very popular songs and instrumental pieces—such as "Old Zip Coon," "Blue-Tailed Fly," "Yellow Rose of Texas," and "Old Dan Tucker"—that have endured in the rural tradition. The minstrel troupes were made up primarily of northern-born song-and-dance men who were skillful interpreters of folk-derived or folk-like material. While there may be some doubts about the authentic folk origins of this material, there is no question that songs, dance steps, instrumental styles, and jokes performed by minstrels made their way freely among the southern folk, where they have remained ever since. Blackface humor, for instance, remained a staple of country music stage shows on up to the 1950's. A duo called Jamup and Honey headlined a popular *Grand Ole Opry* tent show as late as the early post–World War II years, and J. E. Mainer and his Mountaineers performed a skit for their Carolina audiences called "Sambo and Liza" right on into the days of racial integration in 1965.

Following in the wake of the minstrel performance was the vaudeville show, a variety extravaganza which began to assume a national identity in the last decades of the nineteenth century, and which flourished until the burgeoning popularity of motion pictures in the 1920's. Like the earlier minstrel show, to which it was much indebted, vaudeville inspired the emergence of a professional song-writing class, and it developed highly sophisticated means of circulating their songs around the nation. Vaudeville troupes played in most of the southern cities, but songs introduced by them made their way into the smaller towns and villages on sheet music, in stereopticon slide shows, on piano rolls and cylinder recordings, and in the performances of tent-rep actors. Northern-composed "pop" tunes were not the only items utilized and circulated by the vaudeville shows. The shows occasionally employed rural talent. Long before the coming of radio, several country entertainers—one of them Uncle Dave Macon—toured the southern theater circuits: Loew's, RKO-Pathe, Keith-Orpheum. During the 1930's Al Hopkins and his band, Asa Martin, Jimmie Rodgers, Otto Gray, the Weaver Brothers and Elviry, and a host of other country performers continued to travel the vaudeville circuits.

The city held a thousand attractions, and not all of them were of the "legitimate" vaudeville variety. Nearly every southern city had its "sin street"—Beale Street in Memphis, Basin Street in New Orleans, Fannin Street in Shreveport, for example, a thoroughfare where gambling, drink, and prostitution thrived and where blues, ragtime, and jazz were learned. Sounds heard there would eventually find their way into the repertories of almost all country musicians from Jimmie Rodgers and Milton Brown to the Delmore Brothers and Hank Williams. Or it might be a street like "Deep Elm (Ellem)," Dallas' notorious red-light district, which lured East Texas farm boys until the 1930's. Here one could find amusement in the white taverns or black juke joints, or listen to street singers—both white and black—who could be heard with frequency in any southern city in those days before ordinances drove them from the streets.

If what was heard was appealing, the country folk were sure to take the song or style back home. It might be a song learned from a Tyrolean yodeler, the latest tune from the pen of a Tin Pan Alley songwriter, a sentimental melody introduced by a touring Hawaiian string band, a rousing march played by a brass band in the city park on the Fourth of July, maybe even an exotic "oriental" piece danced to by some Little Egypt at a state fair, or a ragtime, blues, or jazz melody learned from black performers. Regardless of the origin or style, once a song was introduced into a rural community the folk esthetic began to assert its process of natural selection and the song or style was either accepted or rejected. More important, through some kind of musical chemistry, even the most urban songs and styles were radically transformed into country songs. That is, melodies were altered to fit the tastes of an audience that had little formal musical training and was accustomed to learning songs orally rather than from printed scores. Complex chords were eliminated, melodies were flattened, and words were often forgotten or unconsciously changed. As the years passed, the social conservatism of the rural South not only influenced the modification of urban song structure, it also encouraged the preservation of such songs and styles long after they were forgotten or scorned elsewhere.

Few country music fans know or care that such beloved songs as "Little Rosewood Casket," "I'll Be All Smiles Tonight," "Letter Edged in Black," and "Wildwood Flower" were written by professional songwriters who aimed them at a northern, urban, middle-class audience. As far as the casual observer can tell, the songs not only are "country" but always have been.

It is difficult to know the precise models used by southern folk singers when they reshaped borrowed songs to fit their community esthetic standards. The sentimental songs of Tin Pan Alley origin bear little resemblance to the Old World ballads and love songs that were part of the singers' cultural inheritance. Religious music on the other hand, which was central to rural southerners' existence, may very well have been a source for both the shaping and the performance of secular songs. Country music has been subjected to no greater influence than southern religious life, which affected both the nature of songs and the manner in which they were performed. Country music evolved in a society where religion was pervasive and where the church and its related functions touched the individual's life in a hundred different ways. Rural southerners generally learned to sing in church, or in a milieu that stressed religious music, and they absorbed values in the same settings that colored the lyrics and the performance of even the secular songs they sang.

Rural southerners were heirs to the great tradition of British religious dissent. While the Church of England became established along the Atlantic Coast, the conservative and dissenting sects pushed into the backcountry. Even before the American Revolution, Scotch-Irish Presbyterians moved down the Appalachian valleys as far as Georgia, while German Lutherans and pietistic groups paralleled their movements only a few miles to the east. Meanwhile, Baptist and Methodist congregations, who would soon conquer the whole interior south, steadily made their way from the east into the piedmont regions and from there on into the trans-Appalachian regions.

The phenomenon that did most to deliver the South into the hands of the Methodists and Baptists was also the vehicle that served mightily to transform the music of southern Protestants: the Great Revival of the early 1800's. Beginning with the Kentucky camp meetings of 1799–1800, the fire of evangelical revivalism swept across the South spreading its democratic message of the availability of universal salvation for those who would seek it. Once the fires had cooled, Methodist and Baptist congregations became the main beneficiaries of the mass wave of conversions, along with such new sects as the Cumberland Presbyterians and Disciples of Christ who rose to prominence in the wake of the revivals. The simplicity of the evangelists' message and the emotional urgency with which it was couched were powerful sources of the revivalists' appeal. But music may have been even more important. The stirring congregational music which swept across the old camp grounds, belted out by farmers and frontier people who felt the rapturous relief from the release of sin, must have been one of the most dramatic spectacles of the whole camp meeting experience. Throughout the colonial era, psalm-singing had been the norm in the churches of Protestant America, but during the years of the American Revolution, the hymns of Isaac Watts and the songs of British Methodism began to compete for the favor of American religious singers. Camp meeting music, then, built upon a tradition of musical change that had begun many years before. Camp meeting song leaders usually chose song texts that were familiar to the singers and set them to folk or popular melodies that were equally familiar (responding to the popular dictum: "Why should the Devil have all the good tunes?"). Since few songbooks were available, the leader often resorted to a time-honored practice well known by British-Americans: lining the hymn, a procedure in which the verses are declaimed, usually two lines at a time, to the congregation, which then sings them. Other methods were devised in order to encourage rapid memorization and to lend variety to old hymns. Choruses were added to venerable hymns: after the verses of a song such as "On Jordan's Stormy Banks," people were encouraged to sing "I am bound for the promised land," etc. Repetitive phrases were incorporated in songs ("Say, brother, will you meet me?" "Say, sister . . ." "Say, mother . . .") to the point that even the most illiterate participant could sing with gusto. Camp meeting songs or songs inspired by them began to appear in books soon after the earliest Kentucky revivals, and both their theology and their structure have endured as part of the fabric of southern religious music and country music. Simple, singable melodies and song texts characterized by choruses, refrains, and repetitive phrases have always been obvious characteristics of country music.

As the southern frontier gave way to a more settled, agricultural existence, the drama and emotional fervor of the camp meetings subsided. Camp meeting ritual became institutionalized and, in fact, became largely identified with the Methodist Church. Nevertheless, the revival became a permanent and venerated feature of most southern Protestant churches. All rural and small-town southerners grew up accustomed to the "protracted meetings" that individual churches held, usually on an annual basis, and generally when crops were "laid by." In rural areas church people often moved out of their hot, steaming churches and held their services under a protective canopy of brush and limbs. These "brush arbor meetings," marked by the emotion of the service and by the swarms of insects that gathered around the kerosene lanterns, are bittersweet memories that many southerners can warmly recall.

The music that flowed into the southern country churches in the middle and last years of the nineteenth century, then, flowered from many roots: from traditional British hymnody, from American revivalism, from anonymous folk composers, from Negro sources, and, most important, from the gospel composers of post–Civil War America. Gospel music, so-called for the first time in Ira Sankey and P. P. Bliss's *Gospel Hymns*, published in 1875, was obviously indebted to the camp meeting music that had preceded it. Gospel music, though, profited from a vigorous interchange between British and American revivalists and songwriters and was disseminated largely through the big-city revivals of the late nineteenth century. Famous evangelists such as Dwight L. Moody, Gypsy Smith, and Billy Sunday all had songleaders such as Ira Sankey, Charles Alexander, and Homer Rodeheaver who soothed or cajoled the crowds, or whipped them into an emotional euphoria much the way a contemporary cheerleader works at a football game. The urban revivals, along with such organizations as the YMCA, the Sunday School Union, and the Salvation Army, provided a huge market for religious songs which a large body of commercial writers were ready to provide. Such writers as George F. Root, P. P. Bliss, Charles Gabriel, and Fanny Crosby contributed an immense number of songs that even yet appear in American songbooks and still reside in the repertories of gospel and country singers. This was a music strongly allied with the popular music of the day, and several writers wrote for both genres. Often filled with the martial imagery of missionary Protestantism ("Onward Christian Soldiers," "Keep on the Firing Line," and the like), the music was more often gentle, bucolic, nostalgic, and sentimental, just as the popular music of the late nineteenth century often was. The Savior was perceived as a shepherd tending his flock, or as a loving father watching over his sometimes-erring family. Heaven was sometimes described as a city of gold, but more often as an abundant Beulah Land traversed by flowing rivers and fragrant with the aroma of eternally blooming flowers. In keeping with an urbanizing society that was becoming more prosperous and secure, the songs tended to be more optimistic and complacent than older religious songs. Nevertheless, blood still stained the "Old Rugged Cross" and the vision of a suffering Jesus remained as a central image. And as a rural American society slowly gave way to an urban society of fragile family and human relationships, songs equating rural life with Christian virtue proliferated, as did the number of songs evoking the memory of mother and the old home place or bewailing the fate of the son or daughter who had ventured into the big city.

These songs moved with great frequency into the repertories of southern singers, being circulated by the thousands in the little paperback hymnals published by the southern shape-note publishing houses. The themes favored by the northern composers also found acceptance in the South, but the southern writers seemed more informed by the folk theology that underlay the religion of their region and by a tragic vision of life that had only been reinforced by Civil War defeat and by the poverty that followed it. As in the case of earlier camp meeting song theology, southern gospel songs perceived Heaven as a land devoid of earth's limitations (a land "Where We'll Never Grow Old" and "Where the Roses Never Fade"). Song after song described the Christian as a pilgrim in an unfriendly world, and the world as a dying, unchangeable, but temporary abode. Death could not be ignored, and the soul's combat with it did not always have a happy ending (as described in "Conversation with Death"). Although a folk fatalism that their British ancestors had shared colored the lyrics of southern gospel songs, influencing the popular view of reform and political change, a strong strain of antimaterialism, and even inchoate class consciousness, appeared in many of the songs (such as "This World Is Not My Home," "Farther Along," and "What Would You Give in Exchange for Your Soul?"). Above all, the nostalgic evocation of home as a bastion of virtue and security in a world of ceaseless change is almost the central theme of southern gospel music. A song like "Precious Memories," for example, where "precious father, loving mother, fly across the lonely years," has been long cherished by white and black southerners alike.

The "folkness" of southern religious music was reinforced by the Holiness-Pentecostal revival at the turn of the century. This movement, which was begun principally by dissident Methodists in the 1870's as an effort to restore a sense of piety and emotional urgency to their church, led directly to the emergence of sects and denominations which responded to the call of "holiness." The Holiness movement in turn gave rise to groups who stressed the need for a gift beyond sanctification, the baptism of the Holy Spirit as first witnessed on the Day of Pentecost, and evidenced by "speaking in tongues" (glossalalia). Pentecostalism was not exclusively a southern phenomenon, but it flourished in the South among both poor whites and blacks, and its most bizarre offshoot, the snakehandlers, reside in the southern mountains. Pentecostalism was a genuine folk religious movement, with mostly untrained, itinerant ministers who preached to poor people like themselves. The Pentecostal groups and the Holiness bands which preceded them restored an emotional vitality to a southern Protestantism that had become lukewarm and respectable. They also reinvigorated congregational singing (as opposed to choirs) and, ironically, they seized upon the Devil's music with great passion and converted it to heavenly uses. Giving vent to a freedom that was not always open to them in secular society, Pentecostal singers tended to be freewheeling in style, with open-throated, expressive voices. Instrumentally, they were even more liberated. In the almost one hundred years since the Pentecostal faith first began to spread, its adherents have utilized virtually every secular music style available, from folk tunes to ragtime and jazz. Furthermore, no instrument has been taboo in Pentecostal churches, and anything from a tambourine and rhythm guitar to an electric steel guitar or a retinue of horns can be heard in their joyous services. The Pentecostal and Holiness evangelists, along with their brethren in other evangelistic sects, were receptive to the songs of the paperback hymnals and to other songs of popular origin. But they also produced their own songs. Itinerant evangelists, street preachers, ballad hawkers, and other anonymous balladeers contributed such songs as "When the Saints Go Marching In," "The Great Speckled Bird," "Something Got Ahold of Me," and "Tramp on the Street" to the southern songbag. The singing of such songs has been virtually mandatory for country singers ever since.

Therefore, when country music began its commercial development in the 1920's, a large and diverse repertory of songs, religious and secular, southern and nonsouthern, folk and popular, was available to musicians. At the core of country repertory, however, was the store of traditional songs, both British and American. Love songs, children's songs, nonsense songs, and even a few bawdy songs endured in the repertory of the southern folk. Many of the traditional items were ballads; that is, narrative, impersonal songs that told a story. A large store of British ballads survived the trek across the Atlantic, some in long, extended versions, but many in only fragmentary form. Some verses floated freely from song to song just as did "the mournful dove that flies from pine to pine." Some ballad fragments even took on a life of their own. The beautiful verse beginning with "Who will shoe your pretty little feet?" came from the Scottish ballad "The Lass of Roch Royal." It is now universally sung as a lyrical love song in one of several versions that have no relation to the original ballad.

The old songs were neither consciously preserved nor consciously discarded; they were merely maintained as part of an inheritance that was familiar and comfortable, and they were forgotten when they no longer had meaning or when alternative entertainment forms became available. In a sense, with their tales of seduction, rape, murder, retribution, and revenge, the old ballads were the soap operas of their day. They did not document the news of the time (although many were based on actual historical events), but instead brought emotional release in the same way that fairy tales do. Rural southerners loved the drama and excitement of such ballads as "Little Matty Groves" or "Lord Randall," and they could easily identify with the suffering or romance of the protagonists. But they could not easily accept the overt sexuality conveyed in many of the old British songs. The Puritanism fed by southern revivalism encouraged a bowdlerization of texts. Consequently, graphic or explicit details were sometimes omitted, and moral injunctions were often tacked on at the end. American listeners were generally left to wonder why Willie had killed his sweetheart with "the dark and roving eye," and they were almost always warned to avoid a similar fate.

Southerners gradually forgot the ballads of their ancestors, but they did not soon abandon the ballad form. They adopted songs from other regions such as the cowboy ballads, or political assassination songs like "The Ballad of Charles Guiteau," and they also composed their own. Train wrecks, murders, mountain feuds, fires, mine disasters, labor disputes, bad men, lovers' quarrels, war experiences were only a few of the topics that appealed to the ballad makers. The identities of most of these bards must forever remain unknown, but a few remained active as late as the early commercial period in the 1920's. Blind men, for example, sometimes followed the trade that had been open to them since the Middle Ages, that of ballad hawking. A few of them, such as J. W. Day, Charlie Oaks, and Dick Burnett (all from Kentucky), made the transition to commercial country music. Day wrote "Rowan County Troubles" about a famous feud in Eastern Kentucky, and later found himself immortalized as Jilson Setters of Lost Hope Hollow by festival promoter Jean Thomas. Oaks and Burnett both made phonograph recordings in the 1920's, and both had toured through the Upper South in the early years of the twentieth century circulating broadsides of their own compositions. Anyone who visited a county fair, county court day, religious revival, or public hanging, or who traveled by railway in the days before World War I, was likely to see a lonesome blind fiddler or banjo player hawking songsheets or small pocket songbooks.

The subject matter of southern ballads and songs ran the gamut from the ridiculous to the tragic—from "Froggie Went a-Courtin'" to the "Fatal Flower Garden" (an American adaptation of "Sir Hugh, or the Jew's Daughter"). No one has ever tried to document the precise percentage of themes and moods favored by the southern folk in their music, but the predilection for the mournful would certainly rank very high. In part, this inclination was a legacy from the British tradition, because many of the British songs dealt with somber themes and were cast in modal patterns which evoked melancholy responses in the minds of the singer and listener. The religion of the southern backwoods, with its otherworldly stance and depiction of the world as a vale of sorrow, also contributed to the mood of sadness. The average rural dweller needed few reminders from the Bible or any other source to know that life was indeed tragic—a brief period filled with unrewarded labor, sadness, and disappointment and ending in death.

As filled with death as the old ballads might be, there was nevertheless a major difference between them and the sentimental songs which became predominant in the nineteenth century. The ballads were seldom deliberately contrived to evoke sadness in the listener. They were tragic rather than pathetic. The sentimental songs, on the other hand, often sought sadness for its own sake. These songs, often described as "parlor songs" because they were designed for performance in such a setting and because they commemorated the virtues of domesticity, were written primarily by northern composers who aimed them at an urban middle-class audience. The rapidly urbanizing America of the late nineteenth century still contained a population that had not yet come to terms with city life and still yearned nostalgically for the departed farm and village. Improved material comfort brought not only a piano and sheet music into the parlor, but also a heightened awareness of what death could do to shatter such a tenuous hold on security. The Civil War had touched thousands of American homes where a "vacant chair" was the most poignant memorial to that tragic struggle. Bernard Weisberger notes of late nineteenth-century Americans that "parting and death were real terrors to that generation. The sentimentality which overflowed in the short stories of both the popular and religious presses, however mawkish it might be, had a foundation in real anguish."[5]

Although there were parlor songs so genteel in tone and rhetoric that they never had a life beyond polite upper-middle-class soirées, many of them received a wide hearing throughout America, and a very large percentage found a seemingly permanent home in the rural South. These songs moved into the repertories of folk singers right alongside the venerable ballads, and they constituted one of the single largest categories of songs found on country records in the early 1920's. Many of the writers were obscure even in their own day, but a few achieved fame as composers or publishers: Henry Clay Work ("The Ship That Never Returned," "Father, Dear Father, Come Home," "Grandfather's Clock"), Gussie Davis ("The Fatal Wedding," "Maple on the Hill," "The Baggage Coach Ahead"), Edward B. Marks ("My Mother Was a Lady"), Paul Dresser ("Just Tell Them That You Saw Me," "I Believe It For My Mother Told Me So"), Will S. Hays ("Molly Darling," "We Parted by the Riverside," "The Little Old Log Cabin in the Lane," "Nobody's Darling on Earth," "I'll Remember You, Love, in My Prayers"). Hays, a Louisville newspaperman and riverboat pilot, may have been the quintessential "southern" writer with his songs of rural nostalgia, gentle (but often broken) love, and pastoral retreats. Rural southerners responded affectionately to songs which reaffirmed the values of home, family, mother, and God, and they took to their hearts songs about dying orphans, neglected mothers, blind children, maidens who died of broken hearts, and eastbound trains that carried penniless children to see their poor blind convict fathers.

Although the sad, lonesome tunes may have been preferred, the more joyful, boisterous tunes were also a cherished part of the rural musician's repertory. The frolic traditions of "Merrie Olde England" had endured despite the Puritan Revolution, and a large body of dance tunes, instrumental pieces, and bawdy songs had survived the journey to America. From the southerners' Celtic forebears, and from their black neighbors, came a legacy of jigs, reels, hoedowns, and frolic pieces. Much material that might ultimately have had a folk origin actually came from professional

5. Bernard Weisberger, *They Gathered at the River: The Story of the Great Revivalists and Their Impact upon Religion in America* (Boston: Little, Brown and Company, 1958), p. 217.

song-and-dance men, black-face minstrels who recreated steps or tunes picked up from grassroots sources, vaudeville performers, nimble equestrian entertainers, to mention only a few. Today, all country fiddlers play hornpipes, but probably few now know that a hornpipe was a solo quick-step dance and that the tunes were used to accompany it. Probably only a few know, too, that such presumed country folk dances as the Virginia Reel and the square dance were originally upper-class dances which somehow made their way out among the rural poor who made them their own.

The instrument most favored by rural folk, and for a long time virtually the defining instrument of country music, was the fiddle. The fiddle came with the earliest colonists, was soon mastered by nearly every folk group in North America, from the French *habitants* of Acadia to the blacks of the South, and was taken to the farthest reaches of the frontier. Inheriting an old British folk myth that the fiddle was the Devil's instrument, many southern Christians, black and white, repudiated both the instrument and the tunes it played. But even the most devout Christians could scarcely keep their feet still when the fiddle began its work, an indication perhaps that the Devil works in insidious ways. Nowhere does one find the moral dichotomy of the rural South, with what W. J. Cash describes as the contest between hedonism and Puritanism,[6] more strongly displayed than in the controversies swirling around religion and music. The rural South's reputation as the home of both corn whiskey and Prohibition, and the land of hell-raising good old boys and God-fearing fundamentalists, is reflected in the music of the region.

The fiddle appeared at all social, and even political, occasions, but it was most favored at the rural house party, one of the great seedbeds of country music. The description that A. B. Longstreet gives of a country dance in Georgia in 1835[7] is remarkably similar to that given of other dances in other states almost one hundred years later. Once the word was given out that a dance was to be held in some farmer's house, a room or two was stripped of furniture and a fiddler was hired to keep the dancers moving. Often a fiddler worked alone for hours with no rhythmic accompaniment, but on occasion someone might beat the straws against the fingerboard of the instrument in order to achieve a kind of percussive effect. Sometimes two or more fiddlers might alternate or even play a tune together. Depending on the place and time, other instruments might join in to form a rudimentary string band: a harmonica or even a piano or parlor organ, but more often a five-string banjo or guitar.

Most fiddlers had to be content with playing part-time at house parties or community social functions, and a fiddler was generally nothing more than a farmer or laborer who made music when his neighbors called upon

6. W. J. Cash, *The Mind of the South* (New York: Alfred A. Knopf, 1941).
7. Augustus Baldwin Longstreet, *Georgia Scenes* (Atlanta: Cherokee Publishing Company, 1971; originally published in Augusta, Georgia, 1835), pp. 12–22.

his services. But in the activities of the fiddlers, probably to a greater degree than the street musicians or the ballad hawkers, we begin to see the first faint traces of the professionalism that would evolve into country music. Fiddlers often played at political events, and some politicians, such as the Taylor Brothers (Bob and Alf) in Tennessee and Tom Watson in Georgia, were fiddlers themselves. Fiddlers also took their talents to county fairs and other public gatherings, and into medicine shows, showboats, carnivals, minstrel shows, circuses, and Punch and Judy shows. Music has no doubt always been associated with advertising, and fiddlers were sometimes employed to drum up business. The eccentric Mason "Parson" Weems, the inventor of the George Washington cherry-tree myth, roamed up and down the Atlantic seaboard in the early 1800's, selling books from his horse-drawn wagon and playing his fiddle to attract an audience. He was probably not unique.

Many of the formats, such as the medicine show, that were available to fiddlers in the eighteenth and nineteenth centuries have, of course, disappeared. One venerable institution, though, which has survived, and which has shown a remarkable resurgence since the 1950's, is the fiddlers' contest. Fiddle contests have been documented in what is now the United States as early as 1736, when fiddlers competed for prizes in Hanover County, Virginia. The early contests appear to have been held in conjunction with county fairs or similar events. In the late nineteenth and early twentieth centuries the contests became increasingly associated with Old Settlers' Days and Confederate reunions. Even at this early date, then, there seemed to be a recognition of fiddling as both an "old-time" art and a southern phenomenon as well as a community enterprise, and a means by which the "New South" justified itself through an act of reverence for the old society that was passing away. Atlanta, the "Queen City of the South" and the capital of the banking and business interests that were struggling to dominate the region, was the site of a large fiddlers' convention annually from 1913 to 1935. City officials and local business leaders recognized the powerful political and economic potential of nostalgia, and everyone smiled as thousands of people poured in to the city each year to see the old-time rural art.

Though their art might be a very old one, fiddlers in general did not confine themselves to hoary and age-encrusted melodies. "Old-time" fiddlers were indeed eclectic in their song preferences. Many of the fiddle tunes, of course, were genuine folk melodies whose authorship had been lost or forgotten many years before. Some of them, such as "Soldier's Joy," "Irish Washerwoman," "Patty on the Turnpike," "Old Molly Hare," or "Molly, Put the Kettle On," were of British origin. Others, presumed to be American, such as "Flop-Eared Mule," "Fire on the Mountain," and "Leather Breeches," probably drew on British airs. Many tunes grew out of the frontier experience, referring to specific places such as "Cumberland Gap,"

"Cripple Creek," "Sourwood Mountain," or "Natchez-under-the-Hill," or referring to occupations like "Mississippi Sawyer" or "Tennessee Wagoner." A few fiddle tunes commemorated historical events, such as "Bonaparte's Retreat" or "Eighth of January" (a celebration of Andrew Jackson's victory over the British at New Orleans in 1815).

Fiddle tunes, though, did not come solely from the white folk experience. Black fiddlers, for example, were omnipresent in the South in the nineteenth century. Slave fiddlers were mentioned often in the literature of the antebellum period, and therefore their presence could not have been unknown to white rural musicians. Unfortunately, the precise debts to black fiddlers have not been documented, and some tunes ascribed to black sources may in fact have been derived from minstrel or "coon-song" performers. Black-face minstrelsy contributed some of the most venerated fiddle tunes, such as "Old Dan Tucker," "Listen to the Mockingbird," "Old Zip Coon" (better known as "Turkey in the Straw"), and "Cotton-Eyed Joe" (a much-recorded tune now at the center of the urban cowboy craze), while tunes like "Whistling Rufus" and "Bully of the Town" probably came from the "coon-song" era at the end of the nineteenth century. Other tunes came from the broad panoply of popular and vaudeville styles available to musicians, some, like "Arkansas Traveler," dating to the antebellum period, but most coming from the period dated roughly between 1890 and 1915: "Ragtime Annie" and "Dill Pickle Rag," "Chicken Reel," "Red Wing," "Snow Deer," "Rainbow, My Pretty Rainbow," and many others. If the country fiddler heard a good tune, he made it his own, whether it came from his own immediate experience, was a legacy from his ancestors, or moved into his consciousness from a foreign source. "Over the Waves," which is still probably the most popular country waltz, was originally written as "Sobre las olas" by the Mexican composer Juventino Rosas. "Fisher's Hornpipe" was the brainchild of German composer Johann Christian Fischer (1733–1800), while "Under the Double Eagle," long one of the most popular instrumentals among country musicians, was originally a march tune commemorating the ruling house of Austria-Hungary, by the Austrian composer J. H. Wagner.

We are gradually gaining an understanding of where early country music found its songs, but we are not nearly so knowledgeable about the styles in which they were performed. We have a storehouse of old 78 rpm records from the twenties and a cache of field recordings from that period and the mid-thirties, but we cannot know how much earlier history is represented in those collections. Our speculations about "Celtic" or "Anglo" origins, or about "black" influences, are frankly guesses based upon the most limited of data. The recording of the first southern voices and instrumental sounds in the 1920's came about two hundred years after the first white immigrants had pushed into the southern backcountry, and even longer after their shifting ethnic strains had begun to mix with each other and with the black elements that moved in their midst. If Old World traits were blunted by centuries of American existence, they were not totally obliterated, and neither was southern folk culture molded into one homogeneous whole. Musically, there is not one southern folk style, but many. Southern fiddlers share a common repertory, but they differ markedly from state to state, and even within states, in the way they note with their left hands and the way they move their bows. Southern singers betray their regional origins in their drawls, dialects, vocal inflections, and pronunciations, and they reveal a strong social kinship in their attitudes toward religion, politics, and life itself. Nevertheless, they do not all move from note to note in a song in precisely the same way.

In folk societies, where contacts with outsiders are limited, and where audiences tend to be small and socially ingrown, performance styles change slowly. But they do change, often unconsciously and imperceptibly. A folk style is in fact more tenacious in its persistence than is a song. Songs may be forgotten, but the manner in which they are performed can persist through time and societal changes. Alan Lomax argues that a musical style is "one of the most conservative of culture traits" because it is so deeply interwoven in the security framework of the community, symbolizing for the singer "the place where he was born, his earliest childhood satisfactions, his religious experience, his pleasure in community doings, his courtship and his work." And, adds Lomax, "an entirely new set of tunes or rhythms or harmonic patterns may be introduced; but, in its overall character, a musical style will remain intact."[8]

In the days before radio and recording made it possible for folk musicians to professionalize their art, most performances were carried on in rather restricted, localized formats. D. K. Wilgus and Norm and Anne Cohen point out that there was a "domestic tradition" (music performed at home and usually vocal-oriented) and an "assembly tradition" (music performed at public gatherings, which generally had an instrumental component).[9] The music of the home, it has been suggested, was usually performed by women either as part of their normal workaday activities (while sewing, cooking, cleaning, rocking the baby, etc.) or during quiet periods for the edification of the family or for a few guests. The predominance of women in home singing may help to explain why some male singers sang in a "womanish" tone, that is, in a high register with a rigidly pitched and constricted voice. Of necessity much home singing was performed without the benefit of instrumental accompaniment; consequently, the voice

8. Alan Lomax, "Folk Song Style," *American Anthropologist* 61, no. 6 (December 1959): 929–930.

9. D. K. Wilgus, record reviews in various issues of *Kentucky Folklore Record* and *Journal of American Folklore*; Norm and Anne Cohen, "Folk and Hillbilly Music: Further Thoughts on Their Relation," *John Edwards Memorial Foundation Quarterly* 13, no. 46 (Summer 1977): 50–57.

set its own pitch, pace, and rhythm, altering melody and time to fit the words of the song. Our knowledge of the "pure" folk style is actually limited, because most early descriptions of it came from outside observers who usually saw performances in unnatural settings. The folklorist with pad and pencil in hand, or armed with recording apparatus, saw stiff, often embarrassed, performances, and thought they were the norm. Among their own kind, and not under the scrutiny of an outsider, the singers may very well have cut loose with a natural flair that would have astounded the observer.

Folk singing was often characterized by group performance, but only rarely by harmony embellishments. Country singers are now famous for their harmony singing, and it is virtually taken for granted that this is an art as natural with family singers as is eating and drinking. Close, precise harmony, though, is something that developed only gradually in the years after country music was commercialized. Harmony-singing models, of course, were not unavailable to American audiences in the nineteenth century. In 1839 the Tyrolese Rainer Family, a group of "Alpine" Swiss singers, toured the United States, thrilling large audiences with their "close harmony and clear enunciation." Their paths were soon followed by a number of American disciples who stressed close harmony: the Bakers, Ordway's Aeolians, Father Kemp's Old Folks, and, most famous of all, the Hutchinson Family of New Hampshire. Minstrel troupes also occasionally featured singing by two or more people, as did vaudeville acts toward the end of the nineteenth century. Southern country people could not have been totally unaware of such singers, nor of the barbershop and popular quartets that began to appear on recordings at about the same time.

A more immediate inspiration for harmony singing, though, came from the world of religion. Country church singing, well into the twentieth century, was not necessarily harmonized. Singers sang in unison or just let their voices follow their own undisciplined routes. But the extent to which harmony did exist, in the church or elsewhere, was probably a product of the southern gospel quartets and of the four-part emphasis of the shape-note singing schools. Pioneered by J. D. Vaughan, a successful publisher of shape-note hymnals in Lawrenceburg, Tennessee, the publishing-house quartets toured widely through the rural South in the early twentieth century. Hawking songbooks as they toured, the Vaughan quartets, along with those employed by the Hartford Company in Arkansas, the Trio Music Company in Waco, Texas, and the Stamps-Baxter Company in Dallas, popularized their style of harmony (usually first tenor, second tenor, baritone, and bass) in country churches, at singing schools, at schoolhouse concerts, and at the famous all-day-singings with dinner on the grounds. The latter were usually held at the county courthouse or some other central meeting place and were described as "singing conventions." People thronged to the conventions as much to gorge themselves on the sumptuous feasts laid out on the ground or on picnic tables as they did to sing gospel songs with their neighbors.

The gospel quartets were much influenced by the popular music currents surrounding them, but they were intimately associated with, and were often instructors in, the shape-note singing schools. In the early twentieth century the schools became progressively identified with the shape-note publishing houses, but they grew out of the activities of the indefatigable singing masters who had earlier roamed through the backwoods of America taking their brand of culture to the masses. The itinerant singing-school master played a profound role in the shaping of southern musical style and in the enlargement of the southern song bag. The masters taught a method known as the "shape-note" system, in which the pitch of musical notes was indicated by their shapes independently of the lines and spaces of the staff. Originating in New England in about 1800, the shape-note singing school entered the South from Philadelphia and eastern Pennsylvania. From the Shenandoah Valley of Virginia, where Joseph Funk initiated the first shape-note activity at the little community of Singer's Glen (near Harrisonburg, Virginia), the method eventually penetrated as far west as Texas and Oklahoma. This style of musical instruction, along with religious songs which embodied it, were popularized in such books as William Walker's *Southern Harmony* and B. F. White's *Sacred Harp.* It was a rare southerner indeed whose life was not at some point touched by shape-note activity in the long period from the mid-nineteenth century and on virtually to the beginning of World War II, and those who went to the ten-day or two-week singing schools learned the rudiments of part-singing and were introduced to the beauties of harmony by their instructors or by the professional gospel singers who sometimes appeared at closing ceremonies.

When Wilgus and Cohen refer to the "assembly" or "frolic" tradition, they concentrate on its instrumental or dance components. There is really no reason, though, to exclude gospel performance from the assembly tradition, and when we recall the activities of the publishing-house quartets, for example, we find that they were as predominantly masculine as playing for dances was. Public performances of *all* kinds were dominated by men, and the physically aggressive skills of fiddling, banjo playing, and the like were felt best confined to male participants, particularly when displayed at such rowdy events as country dances or fiddle contests. Women certainly played banjoes, fiddles, and other instruments at home (and some of them, such as Samantha Bumgarner and Eva Davis, even appeared as instrumentalists on early commercial recordings), but few men were eager to compete against the ladies in any kind of public arena, and the women were encouraged to keep their talents noncompetitive and at home. These facts help to explain why men almost monopolized early commercial country music, and why string band music prevailed on early records, radio, and barn dances.

Like the vocal arts, folk instrumentation exhibited a peculiar blend of conservatism and receptivity to innovation. Fiddlers, for example, were conservative in that they generally tried to recreate a song the way they first heard it. But few fiddlers were resistant to innovation, and change often came unconsciously. As in the case of songs, styles were picked up from nonrural musicians: minstrel fiddlers, traveling show entertainers, vaudevillians, and even brass band musicians. We know that from the 1920's on, country fiddlers have borrowed extensively from blues and jazz musicians, particularly from the stylings of Stéphane Grappelli, Django Reinhardt, and the Hot Club of France.

Since fiddling was a Celtic art, some modern aficionados strain to establish a direct relationship between Celtic styles and southern renditions. Richard Nevins,[10] for example, asserts that "it is likely that all the countless variations in southern fiddling are traceable to seven or eight different styles brought over to America by predominantly Celticly cultured immigrants from various sections of northern Ireland, southern Scotland, and to a lesser degree parts of England." Nevins describes Eck Robertson's famous 1922 rendition of "Sallie Gooden" as an "example of a particular American style that most likely was unchanged by even a hair from the time it got off the boat." It is, he says, "probably the oldest extant Celtic fiddle style preserved anywhere." While some listeners maintain they hear the echoes of Irish or Scottish pipe players in Robertson's music, others hear only the superb improvisations of a fiddler who learned from his American experiences. Robertson played about fourteen separate melodic variations of this basically simple tune, a practice encouraged, some say, by his constant appearances at fiddle contests where the fierce competition inspired novel, and winning, techniques. Public performances of any kind, including the house parties, where the repetition of tunes was necessary, encouraged improvisation and melodic variation. Popular fiddlers also resorted to physical and instrumental tricks to win the favor of their audiences. Long before the commercial period began, fiddlers had begun transforming the sentimental minstrel tune "Listen to the Mockingbird" into a novelty piece complete with bird imitations and woodpecker rappings.

Fiddle styles varied from state to state, and even within states. Individual fiddlers differed in the ways they held the instrument, the emphases which they devoted to noting, and the manner in which they bowed. A few fiddlers accompanied their own singing, playing a unison response to the

10. Richard Nevins, notes to *Old-Time Fiddle Classics, vol. 2: 1927–1934* (County 527).

vocal lines. Some fiddlers stuck resolutely to the melody, while others improvised freely or employed syncopated techniques. Some musicians played single-string style; others used double-stops (the playing of two strings). Some shuffled their bows, while others used a long, flowing bow movement and depended on their left hands to produce intricate note changes. Fiddlers in close geographical proximity learned from each other; consequently, one hears a North Georgia style, a Mississippi style, a Texas style, and so on. The generalizations are sometimes confounded, however, because fiddlers sometimes journeyed to other states where they picked up ideas, and they appeared in contests against each other. The long-bow technique, to cite one example, is identified with the fiddlers of Texas, but it is certainly not confined to musicians from that state.

Fiddlers of necessity often played alone, but they were joined by other musicians when they were available. The minstrel format of banjo, fiddle, and such rhythm instruments as tambourine and bones provided a model for country musicians to follow, but we do not know when the first country string bands took shape. They did, however, precede the era of radio and recording. Visual evidence provides examples of the combining of instruments by folk musicians at least as early as the 1870's. *Scribner's Monthly*, for example, carried an engraving in 1873 of a fiddler and a guitarist playing for a boisterous dance in Denison, Texas. The fiddle and guitar combination appears to have been the most common coupling of instruments in the South as a whole and was the immediate ancestor of many of the most important commercial bands of the 1920's and 1930's. The guitar had been present in America since the colonial period, but was originally perceived mainly as a polite upper-class instrument. It seems to have moved into the hinterlands very slowly. Virginia mountain folk singer Hobart Smith told Alan Lomax that he saw his first guitar about the time of World War I when a black construction gang laid rails into Saltville, Virginia. Cajun musicians tell a similar story about their section of the country, asserting that guitars did not appear in southwestern Louisiana until about World War I. The guitar seems to have been a flatland phenomenon long before it ventured into the mountains or other less accessible regions of the nation. The "classical" styles favored by urbane guitar lovers seem to have been rejected everywhere in the rural South. Instead, the most crucial innovations in rural guitar playing came from black musicians who contributed a retinue of finger-picking styles that have forever intrigued white musicians.

The basic instrumental combination of the southern mountains was the fiddle and five-string banjo. The banjo's identification as a rural white instrument is rather curious in that it was presumably brought to this country from Africa and was long associated with American slaves. Its earliest appearance cannot be documented, but the instrument that Thomas Jefferson referred to in 1781 as a "banjar" was probably still similar to the gourdlike device found much earlier in West Africa. Blackface minstrels introduced their modified version of the banjo to an international public in the three decades before the Civil War. Originally a four-stringed, fretless instrument, the banjo was "revolutionized" in the early 1830's by the addition of a shorter fifth, or drone, string which made it more adaptable and flexible. The invention of the five-string banjo is generally attributed, without proof, to a minstrel entertainer from Virginia, Joel (Joe) Walker Sweeney. While Sweeney's claim cannot be authenticated, he at least did popularize the instrument on tours in this country and in the British Isles.

Banjos remained fretless until the 1880's when important manufacturers such as the S. S. Stewart Company began producing their special lines. Hereafter, rural musicians played both homemade banjos and those which they purchased from the manufacturers. Rural styles were also a compound of folk and city-bred traits. A few banjoists experimented with the "classical" style popularized by Fred Van Eps and others (a finger-style technique borrowed from parlor guitar playing), but more learned from the blackface minstrels who traveled extensively through the South. Uncle Dave Macon, the first star of the *Grand Ole Opry*, featured a variety of techniques presumably learned from old-time song-and-dance men, while the frailing style (sometimes called the stroke style) is believed to have been a product of the minstrel stage. The banjo circulated widely in nineteenth-century America, from the popular stage to the cow camps of the Southwest, and its four-string version became a central feature of early Dixieland and jazz music. The five-string banjo, on the other hand, became almost synonymous with the mountain music of the Southeast, and in the hands of skillful rural musicians, this highly adaptable instrument could lend pathos to a lonely lament or give driving excitement to the wild hoedown and breakdown. The banjo was destined to play a leading and crucial role in the country music history that was soon to unfold.

Although the fiddle, banjo, and guitar were the dominant instruments of southern rural music, other instruments made frequent appearances among folk musicians. Dulcimers have become common and widely desired since the revival of interest in folk music in the 1950's, but they never played a very prominent role in rural string bands. The instrument's origins are clouded in mystery. It may have come into the South with the German immigrants from Pennsylvania, or it may have ventured into the southern hills with English settlers who moved in from the East. Principally a solo instrument, the dulcimer beautifully complemented the singing of the lonesome ballads and love songs, but its delicate, fragile sound made it unsuitable for inclusion in hard-driving string bands.

Other instruments were borrowed from other forms of music, or were obtained through mail-order catalogues. As the frontier South gave way to a society dotted with settled farms and stable towns and villages, rural southerners began to acquire the trappings of middle-class civilization.

Like Americans elsewhere in the nineteenth century, southerners bought, when they could afford it, that visible and audible symbol of middle-class culture and respectability, the piano. Stationed prominently in the front room (or parlor if there was one) and decorated with the newest, brightly illustrated sheet music, the piano lent dignity to a household and brought enjoyment to family gatherings. Many pianos, of course, were merely decorative or displayed for status; others provided instruction for future musicians who went into church or pop music, while others provided accompaniment for dances at country house parties. When country music began its commercial existence in the 1920's, it was not unheard of for pianos to appear on radio barn dances or on commercial hillbilly recordings.

In households where pianos were financially prohibitive, the little parlor organ made a most appealing substitute. Farm families could much more readily afford it, and they could more easily move it, even by wagon, if necessity forced a move to another homestead. Actually, those who wanted to make instrumental music found no real deterrents. Comb-and-paper would suffice if nothing else could be found, and kazoos, Jew's harps, or harmonicas (usually called French harps) could easily be found at the general store or purchased through mail-order catalogues. For those who had only minimal musical talent, an autoharp could be obtained through the same sources. Invented by Karl August Gütter in the early 1880's, the autoharp became a popular parlor instrument in late Victorian America. Designed for children, who merely had to press a lettered key bar and then strum the strings to obtain a musical sound, it was soon taken up by adults and pressed into the services of musical home entertainment. Eventually, though, ingenious musicians learned how to "pick" the instrument (that is, to play melodies note-for-note with finger picks), and the autoharp evolved into a complex instrument of great subtlety.

Finally, some instruments became known to folk musicians through their appearances in chautauqua or vaudeville performances, or in urban music clubs which flourished at the turn of the twentieth century. Some of these instruments had a foreign, and therefore exotic, aura about them. Hawaiian musicians began appearing in the United States shortly after the Islands became part of the American empire. After World War I such troupes took the country by storm, popularizing Hawaiian melodies and introducing the ukelele and steel guitar to American audiences. Fretted with a steel bar, the Hawaiian steel guitar emitted a melodious, but crying sound that has thrilled generations of country listeners. Southern rural audiences may have been preconditioned to enjoy the whining sounds of the steel guitar, having heard similar sounds produced by black guitarists using knife-blades, bottle necks, and similar devices.

The mandolin seems to have been brought to this country by both Italian immigrants and concert musicians. Virtuoso musicians introduced it at polite middle-class soirées, and by 1900 the mandolin had become the rage throughout urban America. Everywhere, but particularly on college campuses, mandolin, banjo, and guitar clubs flourished. Entire mandolin orchestras gave concerts composed of popular and semiclassical airs, and smaller string combos performed the equivalent of chamber music or specialized in ragtime or syncopated pop music. The mandolin made its way out into the rural areas by a variety of methods, but most often, one would assume, through the Sears-Roebuck and Montgomery Ward catalogues. Its early "tater bug" construction (a bulging, striped back) may have inhibited both its sound and the ability of musicians to hold it comfortably, but when Lloyd Loar fashioned his slim, finely crafted F5 for the Gibson Company in 1919, he devised an instrument that fit readily into the string bands of the day. Although it appeared earlier in rural string bands, the heyday of the mandolin in country music did not come until the 1930's.

At the dawn of the 1920's, southern folk music remained largely unknown to the outside world. Generally ignored and unobserved by others, it was left to develop on its own. The songs of the southern region, however, were gradually being presented to Americans at large through the publication of various folksong compilations such as those by John Lomax and Cecil Sharp. Sharp's collection of English folksongs found in the southern mountains, *Folksongs from the Southern Appalachians* (1917), constituted the first attempt to include the musical notation as well as the lyrics for the South's traditional store of songs. But nothing had been done as yet to publicize the singers themselves, and since Sharp ignored some of the basic categories of musical expression (such as religious and instrumental music), little was known of the total musical culture that folk southerners had created.

An understanding of southern rural music was hampered by the reluctance of both folk scholars and high-art exponents to see it as it really was: that is, a thoroughly hybrid form of music which shared Old World and American traits, and which revealed itself as both a commercial and a folk expression. More important, it was difficult for such observers to see southern rural culture as it really existed: a culture that was neither static nor pure. Folk music was too often perceived as nothing more than a survival of British culture, or as a static or rarefied expression of a dying peasantry, an art form that could not survive the industrializing process. Consequently, folklorists collected specimens of it before it vanished; high-art people sometimes utilized its songs for artistic purposes; and commercial-music people generally ignored it on the mistaken assumption that it would not sell. No group apparently saw any merit in the performance of the music by the folk themselves.

Rural music was an inchoate phenomenon, existing in a thousand different communities and performed by fiddlers, banjoists, balladeers, songsheet hawkers, family gospel groups, and occasional string bands. Performed usually at home or at a community social function, but occasionally in a paying situation, such as on the medicine show stage, the music was as commercial as its socioeconomic context would permit it to be. Now that we have reached the period of commercialization, it might be useful to build a social profile of a "typical" southern folk musician in, say, 1920. Such composite theorizing has its obvious pitfalls, but a hypothetical case might tell us much about the folk music that prevailed at the end of World War I and about the "hillbilly music" that was soon to be presented to the world at large.

First of all, our hypothetical folk musician who was just about to become a hillbilly was more than likely a man. He and other men predominated in the early commercial music because women in their culture were not supposed to assume the role of entertainer. Nevertheless, he was a man whose musical perceptions had been shaped by women, first by the mother who had lullabied him to sleep and who, perhaps, had taught him his first musical instrument. Furthermore, his songs were often consumed by the theme of male-female relations, and the insecurities that plagued his life as a poor, unfulfilled worker or farmer often worked themselves out in songs of unrequited love, guilt, or self-pity, or in macho songs such as "Black Jack David."

He was also white—but probably not the "Anglo-Saxon" that romanticists theorize about. He may have been "Celtic," or German, but most likely was a composite of forgotten European groups, with a bit of Indian thrown in (at least he liked to romanticize himself as part Indian). His music was just as eclectic, being a composite of instrumental and vocal styles and songs, heavily indebted to the various ethnic groups of the South, and particularly to the blacks from whom his ancestors had borrowed since the beginning of American life.

He was Protestant Christian, but in a very general, almost cultural, sense. He was much influenced, if unconsciously, by the dissenting, evangelical Protestantism of his British forebears. He was nominally an adherent of one of the distinctive southern churches (Baptist, Methodist, Campbellite, or Holiness), but was not necessarily a churchgoer or church member. His outlook on life, or world view, was strongly shaped by the God-centered fatalism of his religious conditioning, and his music was influenced crucially by that of the camp meeting, all-day singings, and shape-note schools. Intellectually and emotionally, he was torn by the conflicting impulses of Puritanism and hedonism. His was a rowdy but God-fearing existence.

Our hypothetical folk/hillbilly musician was also rural. His ruralism, however, did not necessarily connote an agricultural existence. He may have been a timber cutter, a sawmill worker, a coal miner, a textile worker, a railroad man, a farmer, or some other kind of worker. If he was a farmer he was no doubt conscious of the declining status of his work and of the economic penury from which so many of his fellow southern agriculturalists suffered in the years after World War I. The impulse or deep-seated anxieties that perhaps lured him away from farming and into such areas as railroading and coal mining may also have made music all the more attractive to him.

He was also folk. His folkness, though, was not a conscious posture (the folk are never aware that they are folk until someone tells them so). He was strongly marked by the culture of his ancestors and by the social conservatism of his society, but was not consciously committed to their preservation. Neither he nor his society had ever been totally isolated from the world outside. He very likely had served in the recent Great War or perhaps even earlier in the Spanish-American War. He had also roamed around considerably, as many southern men had done, and a little bit of that larger world had rubbed off on him. He still sang traditional songs (they after all represented the world of his parents even if they did not quite represent his own), but he and his society had changed them, lyrically, structurally and melodically, to the point that his Old World forebears could scarcely recognize them.

Finally, he was southern. The soon-to-emerge hillbilly music world would have its quota of midwesterners, westerners, New Englanders, and even Canadians, but the genre would be dominated by southerners such as our hypothetical character. Whether they came from East Texas, North Georgia, Kentucky, or any number of other southern locales, they would share a musical culture that each could readily understand. Our composite character's southernism was strongly displayed in his speech, values, and attitudes, and in the presumptions which colored the lyrics of his songs. The presumed southernness of his music would also affect public attitudes toward it for years to come. Both the negative and the positive images which clung to southern rural life would always affect public perceptions of country music. Nevertheless, much of his music came from nonsouthern sources, a very large percentage, in fact, from the North (from black-face minstrelsy and Tin Pan Alley). Very soon, that same northern society, represented by recording company talent scouts and broadcasting executives, would contribute powerfully to the exploitation and national dissemination of southern rural music, simultaneously shaping and transforming its character forever.

The Carter Family: *left to right*, Maybelle, Sara, and A. P. Carter. Courtesy of Bob Pinson.

2. The Early Period of Commercial Hillbilly Music

At the opening of the twentieth century, American music was urban-oriented. Both the fine-art and commercially directed groups neglected the rural population (or else tried to "urbanize" their tastes) and instead catered to the interests of people in the cities. The record companies in fact appear to have become aware of the potential of city ethnic sub-cultures more quickly than they did the native rural cultures of the nation. The recognition of an ethnic buying population, of course, may have made record industry people cognizant that a similar market existed out in the hinterlands.

Before World War I, the music industry—then represented chiefly by vaudeville, the sheet music business, and the phonograph interests—concentrated on urban America because of its population density and easy accessibility. The rural market was not totally neglected, but it received the same entertainment material that was directed to the cities. Rustic types were staples of American entertainment, but these were usually so-phisticated entertainers, such as Josh Denman and Cal Stewart, who merely acted the parts of hayseeds or rubes. Folk or rural songs likewise were not absent from either the stage or phonograph records, but they were generally done by urbane song-and-dance men like Billy Golden or the Edison Male Quartet. Genuine rural performers were rejected because they sounded strange and primitive to urban music executives, who be-lieved that the urban buyer would be repelled by the raw country sound. The commercial people, of course, were not displeased when country people bought their products, but the product was usually urban produced and urban performed.

The music industry's antirural attitude might have persisted had it not been for the emergence of one medium of communication and the temporary submergence of another. In general, the discovery of southern grass-roots music was only one result of a general communications revolution which has gradually broken down southern rural isolation and narrowed the distance between city and farm. Along with the automobile, the phenomenon that has exerted perhaps the most profound urbanizing influence upon rural areas is the radio, a device that in the 1920's temporarily stifled the growth of the phonograph industry and brought a welcome measure of entertainment and information to the rural population.

Only in the research stage during World War I, and chiefly a diversion for amateur operators, radio became a craze in the twenties and experienced a phenomenal growth in sales and popularity. In only a few years radio was transformed from an expensive plaything to a widely popular and inexpensive pastime for millions of Americans. Social observers recognized immediately that radio would revolutionize rural existence. It did that, while transforming American popular tastes as a whole.

The financial figures on radio sales during the 1920's are little short of astounding. From a relatively modest figure of $60,000,000 in 1922, sales rose to a total of $842,548,000 in 1929, and some observers estimated that radio had penetrated every third home in the country. According to the federal census of 1930, 12,078,345 families owned radio sets. Of this number, the smallest percentage of ownership was in the South, a fact attributable in part to the existence of a large low-income black population which could not afford the purchase of radio sets.[1] One report maintained that "the ownership ratios among the white populations of southern states would doubtless be much higher than general state ratios indicate."[2] Broadcasting stations, the majority of them small and low-powered, made early appearances in the South. Of 510 active broadcasting stations operating on 360 meters at the end of 1922, 89 were in the South. The numbers ranged from Texas' 25 to Mississippi's 1.

The development of southern radio broadcasting was important in the discovery, refinement, modification, and eventual standardization of southern country music. Southern folk musicians found radio to be an irresistible attraction and an indispensable outlet for their entertainment energies. Rural musicians saw in radio the first real opportunity ever to build a broad and ever-widening audience outside their home locales. Radio promoters, on the other hand, quickly recognized the utility of this cheap and abundant source of entertainment.

Many southern broadcasting stations, therefore, featured live country entertainment almost from the day they opened their doors. In the years following 1920, radio remained the most important means of country mu-

1. Frederick Lewis Allen, *Only Yesterday* (New York: Harper and Brothers, 1931), pp. 147–148.
2. President's Research Committee on Social Trends, *Recent Social Trends in the United States* (New York: McGraw-Hill Book Company, 1933), pp. 211–212.

sic dissemination, eventually in the form of disc-jockey programs. The first high-powered radio station in the South, and possibly the first to feature country music, was WSB in Atlanta. It was only fitting that Atlanta should play this role. Breathing an aura of Old South romance and charm, the city simultaneously suggested the spirit of urbanity and industrial growth that would soon overshadow the old image. Country music, after all, was a fusion of these conflicting impulses. The WSB officials surely also knew of the large rural and working-class audience that lay within the station's range, and that in fact many of these people lived within Atlanta itself.

Owned by the *Atlanta Journal*, WSB went on the air on March 16, 1922, with a 100-watt transmitter, which was subsequently increased to 500 watts on June 13. Less than three months later, on September 9, 1922, Fiddlin' John Carson, well known because of his musical performances in fiddle contests and in political campaigns, appeared on a station broadcast. He was soon followed by a wide variety of other folk performers. For approximately one year before the first recording expedition went to Atlanta searching for folk talent, singers and string bands had been appearing on WSB, providing a reservoir of talent for any recording scout who might venture into the city.

With WSB probably leading the way, radio stations all over the South and Midwest began featuring country talent in the early 1920's. Although exhaustive research on the relationship between broadcasting and early country music has not yet been completed, collector and folklorist Guthrie T. Meade, who is the most knowledgeable authority on this particular subject, has pointed to the very significant role played by WBAP in Fort Worth.[3] WBAP can justly lay claim to having produced one of the first, if not the first, radio barn dances in the United States—about a year and a half before the WLS (Chicago) *National Barn Dance*, and about three years before the WSM (Nashville) *Grand Ole Opry*.

In the first several months of its existence WBAP—as was true of almost all early radio stations—programmed nothing but popular, jazz, sacred, and semiclassical music. But on the night of January 4, 1923, WBAP featured an hour-and-a-half program of square-dance music directed by an old-time fiddler and Confederate veteran Captain M. J. Bonner. The music was performed by a string band which normally played only Hawaiian music (Fred Wagner's Hilo Five Hawaiian Orchestra), and Captain Bonner's was the only fiddle music provided. The program provoked the largest audience response—in the form of telegrams and telephone calls— that the station had experienced in its short history. Touching an unexploited but eager audience, WBAP thus inaugurated the hillbilly radio

3. Letter to the author from Guthrie T. Meade, College Park, Maryland, February 21, 1967.

barn dance. In those early unregulated days of American broadcasting, WBAP programs were picked up by listeners as far away as New York, Canada, Hawaii, and Haiti, and the square-dance shows which followed periodically—featuring such groups as the Peacock Fiddle Band from Cleburne, Texas—may have triggered the entire wave of hillbilly barn dances that began appearing on radio stations throughout the United States. After the striking success of the first program, WBAP presented the country-music shows on a rather unplanned, periodic basis, usually two or three times a month, but by 1927 a regularly scheduled Friday night program was broadcast. Broadcasting executives at stations like WBAP, WSB, WLS, and WSM were the first members of the commercial fraternity to devote any consideration to the musical interests of America's rural and working-class population.

In the commercial exploitation of southern folk music the phonograph industry was only a step behind the broadcasting business. This thrust came at the precise moment when recording as a whole was experiencing a sharp downturn in volume of sales, due largely to the competition of radio, which lured listeners away and gave them a greater variety of entertainment. Business dropped off tremendously in 1923 and 1924 as radio became an established facet of American entertainment. People preferred to sit in comfort and listen to an entire program of music without having to change records every few minutes. The public discovered, too, that the better-grade radio sets were superior in tone and quality to the then-existent phonographs. The peak in record sales had been reached in 1922, when the figure neared 100 million; the market diminished during the next ten years under the combined assaults of radio and the national Depression. In the period between 1927 and 1932, record sales declined to one-fortieth of what they previously had been.

Although radio competition forced the phonograph industry to search for new marketing outlets, it had already moved in this direction before radio made such terrific inroads. At least a few of the recording executives had recognized earlier that a market might exist among America's rural population. This recognition came first as a result of the new-found buying habits of American blacks in the post–World War I period. Lured by wartime prosperity and fleeing a century or more of racial oppression, blacks by the thousands migrated to northern urban centers in pursuit of employment in shipyards and mills.

In the spring of 1920, a young black vaudeville singer, Mamie Smith, recorded for two Okeh recording scouts, Fred Hagar and his assistant, Ralph Peer. Miss Smith was neither a blues singer nor a southerner (she was from Ohio), but her recording of Perry Bradford's "Crazy Blues" set off a boom for blues music and launched the General Phonograph Corporation (owner of the Okeh label) into a ranking position as a record company. A market for black music was found to exist among blacks themselves.

This was music produced in the cities and by city people, however. As yet, the record companies had not seen fit to concentrate on the rural or "country blues" performers, and when the recording executives learned that rural southern blacks, whether back home or in Chicago, desired to purchase recordings by members of their own race, such enterprising recording men as Ralph Peer resolved to venture into the South to find native singers in their own habitats. Through this kind of scouting activity the white hillbilly recording industry came into being.

The recording of early hillbilly talent was, in part, accidental and unexpected; it was also partly a byproduct of the recording of black talent. The identity of country music's "earliest" recording performer is still being debated. Nevertheless, no one seems to have a stronger claim than Eck Robertson, champion old-time fiddler from Amarillo, Texas, and Henry Gilliland, another active contestant in fiddle matches from Altus, Oklahoma. Alexander Campbell "Eck" Robertson, born in Arkansas on November 20, 1887, and named for a famous Disciples of Christ minister, was a legendary fiddler in the Southwest long before he made any phonograph recordings. He sometimes played in silent movie houses for early western films but was best known for his constant and winning performances in fiddle contests. In June 1922, he and Gilliland traveled to Virginia to play for a civil war veterans' reunion. Apparently on the spur of the moment, both fiddlers decided to go to New York to make some records. The Victor recording people, who up to this point had shown no interest in rural talent, must have been taken aback when Gilliland and Robertson, dressed in Confederate uniform and cowboy suit respectively, marched into the Victor offices and asked for auditions. We do not know what went on in the minds of the Victor directors—they may very well have been charmed by the music they heard (or by the romantic symbols of the Old South and Old West being displayed before them)—but they did permit the tests, and several selections were subsequently released. Robertson recorded a few tunes with Gilliland, but his solo version of "Sallie Gooden" is one of the most justly famous renditions in country music; after sixty-plus years of history, Robertson's virtuosity still dramatically commands the attention of the listener.

Although Victor released a publicity blurb describing the records, and although sales were reasonably good, the company did not immediately follow through in its exploitation of the untapped folk reservoir. In fact, Robertson himself was not recorded again until 1930, when Ralph Peer (by then a Victor talent scout) arranged another session for the Texas fiddler and his family. On March 29, 1923, about a year after his unsolicited New York recording session, Robertson performed on WBAP the two numbers that he had earlier recorded, "Sallie Gooden" and "Arkansas Traveler." These radio performances may have been the first by a folk musician who had earlier recorded for commercial records. In doing these numbers, in fact, Robertson—termed a "Victor artist" by the *Fort Worth Star Tele-gram*—may have been the first country performer to "plug" his recordings on a radio broadcast. This important Texas folk musician thus played significant roles in two important commercial media whose dual exploitation of folk talent coincidentally converged in the early twenties to produce that brand of music which we now call country music.

Almost a year after Robertson's first trip to New York, a similar incident occurred: Henry Whitter, a textile worker, singer, and multi-instrumentalist from near Fries, Virginia, traveled uninvited to New York in March 1923 and made some test recordings for the General Phonograph Corporation. The recordings were shelved away and remained unevaluated until Fiddlin' John Carson's successful recording in June 1923. Whitter was invited back to New York in December 1923, when he recorded nine numbers including "Lonesome Road Blues" and a famous song for which he claimed partial authorship: "The Wreck of the Southern Old 97." Whitter was a good harmonica player (he was one of the first country musicians to use a harmonica rack around his head), a passable guitarist, but a mediocre singer at best. Probably his greatest claim to fame, apart from his association with "Wreck of the Old 97," lay in his recordings with the blind fiddler and singer Gilliam Banmon Grayson. Several of Grayson's and Whitter's songs, such as "Lee Highway Blues," "Handsome Molly," "Little Maggie," and "Little Omie Wise," were destined to become standards in country music. By the time Whitter's own solo records were released in January 1924, Ralph Peer's field trips were reaping a rich harvest of old-time performers.

Ralph Peer played a crucial role in the recording of much early country talent (including Jimmie Rodgers and the Carter Family), but strangely was not elected to the Country Music Hall of Fame until 1984. His involvement in the record business began as a teenager with Columbia, but by the early 1920's he had joined the General Phonograph Corporation as an assistant to Fred Hagar. Born in Kansas City, Missouri, Peer had no intimate association with either rural people or rural music. He was, though, a brilliant businessman and, like many Americans, had preconceptions about the South's alleged richness in music. His most significant innovation in recording, perhaps, was the field trip which went directly to where the talent resided. Peer generally traveled by automobile, with two engineers, to such cities as Asheville, North Carolina; Bristol and Johnson City, Tennessee; St. Louis; Dallas; and, most important, because of its strategic location, Atlanta. Peer rarely advertised his visits, but instead sometimes managed to get himself interviewed by area newspapers, or, more often, collaborated with someone who had an intimate knowledge of local talent.

Although Peer was the agent who first presented country music to the American public and thereby inaugurated its development as a commercial force, Polk Brockman was the catalyst. As director of the phonograph department of his grandfather's furniture store, James K. Polk, Inc., in Atlanta, Brockman had, by 1921, built up a flourishing business selling race records and had made his firm the largest regional distributor of Okeh records in the country. A business trip to New York in June 1923 kindled in Brockman an idea which led directly to Ralph Peer's historic 1923 trip to Atlanta and the subsequent birth of the hillbilly industry. During Brockman's stay in New York he visited the Palace Theatre on Times Square, where he saw a newsreel of a Virginia fiddlers' contest. The astute Brockman, who was well acquainted with the country talent of his own Georgia area and particularly with those who had been performing on WSB for the preceding year, immediately recognized the commercial possibilities of recorded hillbilly music. He instantly thought of one person, Fiddlin' John Carson, who had built up a wide popularity performing over Station WSB. As he thought of Carson, Brockman picked up a memorandum pad and wrote the following words: "Let's record."

Brockman could scarcely have avoided some kind of contact with Carson. Fiddlin' John (born March 23, 1868, on a hill country farm in Fannin County, Georgia) had been a vital presence in North Georgia folk music for nearly forty years before his first recordings, playing his fiddle in political campaigns, at a multitude of social functions, and at the annual Georgia Old-Time Fiddlers' Association convention held in Atlanta after 1913. Between 1913 and 1922 he won the Old-Time Fiddlers' championship at least seven times. And since 1922 he had been winning an even larger audience through his performances on WSB.

When Peer came to Atlanta in mid-June 1923, he was searching for black talent, but Brockman persuaded him to listen to Fiddlin' John also. Brockman rented an empty lot on Nassau Street where Okeh engineers Charles Hibbard and Peter Decker installed their acoustical equipment. Peer listened to and recorded several performers, mostly in the blues and popular categories: Warner's Seven Aces; Eddy Heywood, a black pianist; Bob White's syncopating band, and others. But with the recording of Fiddlin' John Carson on June 13 or 14, Peer made his initial venture into the unexploited field of country music. When Peer listened to the two songs which Carson chose to record—"The Little Old Log Cabin in the Lane" and "The Old Hen Cackled and the Rooster's Going to Crow"—he responded with disbelief. He thought the singing was awful and insisted that only Carson's fiddle tunes be recorded. Brockman, however, understood the Georgia entertainment market and realized that the small farmers and mill workers enjoyed Fiddlin' John's vocalizing as much as his instrumental virtuosity. Brockman offered to buy five hundred copies of Carson's unpressed numbers immediately. Unable to conceive of a regional or national market for such items, Peer issued the record uncatalogued, unadvertised, unlabeled, and for circulation solely in the Atlanta area. By late July, when the first shipment of five hundred records had been sold and after Brockman had ordered another shipment, Peer acknowledged his early mistake and gave the recording the label number 4890, a move which placed the songs in Okeh's popular catalogue and gave them national publicity. In November, as sales continued to mount, Carson was asked to come to New York, where he recorded twelve more songs and signed an exclusive Okeh contract. Needless to say, while Ralph Peer's esthetic appreciation of country music may not have been improved by the incident, Fiddlin' John nonetheless made him a believer in the commercial value of the medium.

With the recording of Fiddlin' John, the first southern white folk musician to have his songs recorded and marketed on a commercial basis, the hillbilly music industry began its real existence. Peer now remembered the recorded but unreleased tunes of Henry Whitter, and, after Brockman gave these a favorable review, Whitter was invited back to New York for further recordings. The popularity shown by Carson's, Robertson's, and Whitter's records encouraged other record companies to enter the virgin hillbilly territory in order to bolster their lagging sales capacities. In the years up to the Great Depression such companies as Brunswick, Gennett, Paramount, Victor (hesitantly), and Columbia began emulating the successful tactics used earlier by Ralph Peer and Okeh. Recording directors and engineers took their portable equipment all over the South and Southwest, converting available building space into temporary recording studios and implanting the music they heard on wax discs which were then shipped in dry ice back to company headquarters. It is difficult to generalize about the talent scouts (now called artists-and-repertoire, or A&R men), because they went about their work with a variety of conflicting motivations. Essentially, such men as Frank Walker and Dan Hornsby (both with Columbia), James O'Keefe (Brunswick), Eli Oberstein (Victor), Arthur Satherley (American Record Company), and, of course, Ralph Peer were businessmen who had little knowledge of music. They were, on the other hand, unwitting folklorists who collected (and therefore preserved) an immense and valuable body of musical, social, and cultural materials dealing with the rural South. As Charles Wolfe has observed, the old 78 rpm records of the 1920's document more than just the folk music of southern whites; they also tell us much about the dialects, folkways, customs, and lifestyles of the plain people.[4]

The talent scouts used a variety of methods to find folk talent (including newspaper advertisements), but they all relied on local agents to supply them with names. The scouts varied in the kind of control which they tried to exercise over the talent which came before them. Ralph Peer, for example, encouraged the use of traditional or old-timey material, while

---

4. Charles Wolfe, "Toward a Contextual Approach to Old-Time Music," *Journal of Country Music* 5, no. 2 (Summer 1974): 65–75.

others left the choice of songs to the performers. Some recording sessions were conducted with meticulous care; others were done haphazardly, almost as if the ignorant rubes who presumably bought the records wouldn't know the difference anyway.

As the number of rural bands and musicians proliferated in the mid-twenties, observers, friendly and otherwise, were hard-pressed to find a name which correctly described the kind of music they performed. Record company release sheets and catalogues camouflaged the songs under a variety of headings, most of them evoking a romanticized conception of southern rural music. Interestingly, no one ever described the music as "country," although a term like "hill country tunes" might sometimes be used. The presumed "southernness" of the music was often evoked in accompanying illustrations showing happy "darkeys," doleful or feuding mountaineers, or cotton fields, and early Brunswick catalogues described their recordings as "songs from Dixie." The folkness of the music was dimly recognized in such labels as "old familiar tunes" (used by Columbia to advertise its 15000-D series) or "old-time music" (favored by the Okeh label and by many fans and musicians).

The word, though, which was destined to crowd most of the romantic terms aside, and which has persisted to our own day, was "hillbilly." "Hillbilly," as Archie Green has noted in a discerning *Journal of American Folklore* article, has been used in print since at least 1900 as a catch-all designation for the southern backwoods inhabitants. Not until 1925, however, was the term used in association with the music of the rural South.[5] Employment of "hillbilly" as a generic term for the commercial country music of the South may be traced to a January 15, 1925, recording session in the Okeh studios in New York City. A string band composed of members from the mountain counties of Watauga, North Carolina, and Grayson and Carroll, Virginia, had journeyed to the Okeh studies after an earlier unsuccessful attempt with Victor. The group—originally composed of Al and Joe Hopkins, Tony Alderman, and John Rector—was destined to compile a number of "firsts" in country music: they were the first hillbilly musicians to make their base in Washington, D.C. (broadcasting over WRC for sev-

5. Archie Green explored the origin of the term "hillbilly" and its identification with rural music (as popularized by Al Hopkins' string band), in "Hillbilly Music: Source and Symbol," *Journal of American Folklore (JAF)* 78, no. 309 (July–September 1965): 204–228. Joe Wilson contributed most of what is known about Hopkins and the Hill Billies in his notes to *The Hillbillies*, County 405 (I am grateful to Mrs. Dot Wilson Moss, of Charlotte, North Carolina, for reminding me about this album and about the role played by her father, Frank Wilson, in the band). Wayne W. Daniel, the leading historian of Atlanta country music, has put forward another candidate for the band that did most to popularize "hillbilly": George Daniell's Hill Billies, who performed on powerful WSB as early as February 18, 1925. See his "George Daniell's Hill Billies: The Band That Named the Music?" *John Edwards Memorial Foundation Quarterly (JEMFQ)* 19, no. 70 (Summer 1983): 81–84.

eral years after 1925); they were among the earliest to perform in New York City (1927); they were the first to perform before a president (at a press reception for Calvin Coolidge); they were the first to appear in a movie (a fifteen-minute short subject for Warner Brothers); they were the first to use a piano (played by Al), and one of the first bands to include a Hawaiian steel guitar (played by Frank Wilson from North Carolina). Most crucially, they were also the first to be described on a record label as "Hill Billies." After recording six songs for Ralph Peer at the January 1925 session, Al Hopkins suggested that Peer find a suitable name for the group. Hopkins said, "Call the band anything you want. We are nothing but a bunch of hillbillies from North Carolina and Virginia anyway." Peer then instructed his secretary to list the six selections on company ledger sheets as performed by the "Hill Billies" (it was also spelled occasionally with a hyphen, but then finally as only one word).

Despite considerable misgivings on the part of some of the band members about the seemingly disreputable name, the group was advertised as such on personal appearances and in Okeh catalogues. Hopkins and his associates became more confident about the use of the title after an old friend and highly respected Virginia musician, Ernest Stoneman, told them he approved of the term. They lived to see "hillbilly" applied widely to the entire field of country music.

The term "hillbilly" has had a curious history within country music. It was seldom used by recording companies or radio stations to describe the down-home musical culture they were so busily disseminating. But it was commonly used by country musicians and by their fans and detractors alike, although no one can document the precise moment when the label began to attain such currency. Country musicians and fans have always reacted ambivalently to the term, sometimes resenting it as a presumed denigration of their music and the way of life it supposedly represents, but often proclaiming it proudly as an accurate description of their musical and cultural tastes. Many country entertainers, such as Waylon Jennings, Loretta Lynn, and Tammy Wynette, still privately describe themselves as hillbillies, but respond bitterly if someone else calls them that. Archie Green suggests that the ambivalence Americans have shown toward country music and the terms used to describe it arises largely out of a similar love-hate relationship with rural life: "Out of the long process of American urbanization-industrialization there has evolved a joint pattern of rejection as well as sentimentalization of rural mores. We flee the eroded land with its rotting cabin; at the same time we cover it in rose vines of memory. This national dualism created the need for a handle of laughter and ridicule to unite under one rubric the songs and culture of the yeoman and the varmint, the pioneer and the poor white."[6]

6. Green, "Hillbilly Music: Source and Symbol," p. 223.

Al Hopkins and the Hill Billies: *left to right,* Tony Alderman, John Hopkins, Charlie Bowman, Al Hopkins. Courtesy of Archie Green.

The tension described by Green tells only part of the story. Hillbilly music was not simply rural; it also came before the American public as a southern art form. Like the South itself, hillbilly music suffered and profited from a conflicting set of images held by Americans that ranged from stability and enchantment to decadence and cultural degeneracy. The music took shape as a commercial entity during a decade when the South's reputation seemed at a particularly low ebb. To many people hillbilly music was just one more example, along with Ku Kluxism, Prohibition, sharecropping, racial violence, and religious bigotry, of the South's retarded and degenerate culture. On the other hand, many people no doubt responded positively to the South as a bastion of traditional values and orthodox religion in a nation given over to rapid and bewildering change. The role that hillbilly, or old-time, music played in the revitalization campaigns of the 1920's may never be realized conclusively. We simply do not know who the audience was, or why it was attracted to the music. Recording companies and promoters seemed to assume that the passion for "old familiar" music was strongest among conservative southerners. Consequently, it has been assumed that hillbilly music was little more than a vigorous expression of a regional culture, and that such songs as "Why Do You Bob Your Hair Girls" appealed only to fundamentalist citizens south of the Mason-Dixon line. But how widely did hillbilly records circulate among northerners, and what impulses motivated those Americans, North and South, who bought the records and listened to the radio barn dances?

The most famous example of the political uses to which old-time music could be put was Henry Ford's highly publicized campaign to revive old-time fiddling and the dances of his youth. Ford's mixture of technological curiosity and commitment to tradition was not at all odd; it was in the American grain, and if the efforts made by this technologically innovative industrialist to recover an imagined "American innocence" seem strange, they nonetheless reflected an illusion which many of his compatriots shared. Ford was appalled at the ragtime and jazz rhythms which had engulfed American music since the turn of the century, feeling that a similar decline in morals was somehow related. His concern for "pure," white, Christian America spilled over into the nativist feelings expressed by his magazine, the *Dearborn Independent*, and yet this same impulse had its more positive manifestations. He sponsored the publication of a book describing old-time dance steps, invited traditional musicians to Dearborn, Michigan, and sponsored fiddle contests throughout the United States. In 1926 Ford encouraged his dealers, principally in the East and Midwest, to hold a series of local, state, and regional contests to determine the final entries who would compete for the national championship in Detroit. Uncle Bunt Stephens, representing the South, won the championship playing "The Old Hen Cackled." Uncle Bunt won a new car, $1,000 in cash, and a new suit; Henry Ford received wonderful publicity as the champion of common men and common values; and old-time fiddling gained wide coverage in the national press.

If we do not really know the makeup of the hillbilly audience, we are only a little more knowledgeable about the hillbilly entertainers. The early hillbilly musicians, for the most part, were folk performers who stood in transition between the traditional milieu that had nourished them and the larger popular arena which beckoned. They performed in the only way they knew, according to the dictates of the culture that had shaped their values and musical tastes. And they performed a body of music that was similarly drawn from family or community resources. These musicians absorbed songs and styles from people like themselves, but they had no success models in their own communities on whom to draw. The only known symbols of musical success at the beginning of the 1920's were vaudeville or light-comedy people like Harry Lauder, George M. Cohan, or Al Jolson. Folk musicians did not cease to be folk merely because they stepped in front of a recording or radio microphone, nor did the original audience change instantaneously. But once a career began to blossom and the audience began to expand through radio coverage, record sales, and the like, the temptation to alter a style or freshen one's repertory might become irresistible. Most of the early hillbillies, though, could be nothing more than what they were. Riley Puckett or Charlie Poole might experiment with pop songs of recent vintage, and even Uncle Dave Macon might try his hand at a modern sentimental ditty, but the marks of their southern folk cultural origins clung resolutely to them.

The early commercial performers were, by and large, working people who played music in their leisure hours. A rare person like Vernon Dalhart was in full-time show business (but he adopted hillbilly music after a long career as a pop and light-opera singer); most, though, worked as textile mill workers, coal miners, farmers, railroad men, cowboys, carpenters, wagoners, painters, common laborers, barbers, and even an occasional lawyer, doctor, or preacher. Generally, they were people who had established only local reputations as entertainers, although a few of them, such as Dick Burnett and Charlie Oaks, had traveled widely beyond their homes playing music and selling song sheets, and a few—like Uncle Dave Macon and Charlie Poole—had appeared regularly in medicine shows or on the vaudeville circuit. Instrumentally, these pioneers encompassed a wide range of approaches. Kelly Harrell, for example, played no instrument and refused to learn one. A few singers, like Blind Alfred Reed and Fiddlin' John Carson, sang to their own fiddle accompaniment, while others sang to their own guitar or banjo backup. String instrumentation predominated on the early records, with the fiddle, five-string banjo, and guitar being the favored instruments. Actually, an extraordinarily wide range of instruments can be heard on the old records, including kazoos, whistles, French harps, Jew's harps, zithers, organs, pianos, mandolins, autoharps, Hawaiian steel guitars, ukeleles, accordions, tenor guitars, cellos, trumpets, clarinets, etc.

Generalizations concerning vocal styles and types of voices are just as difficult to make. Voices were as diverse as instrumental styles, echoing the singer's place of birth and rearing, age, extent of vocal training, religious beliefs, and other related factors. Southernism and ruralism were the two main constants affecting vocal style, but some musicians, such as Carson Robison and Frank Luther, possessed neither conditioning trait. Some singers sang in a high, strained register, or with the pinched-throat style of the "classic" folk singer. Riley Puckett, on the other hand, sang with a relaxed baritone, while Bradley Kincaid sang with a soft, sweet tenor voice. Uncle Dave Macon was anything but relaxed and soft, projecting instead a vital, energetic sound made doubly distinctive by his southern-country-gentleman style of enunciation. Some singers sang with noticeable nasal twangs, as in the case of Dock Boggs and Charlie Poole; drifted off into a falsetto, as did Gid Tanner; or yodeled like Jimmie Rodgers. Fiddlin' John Carson sang with a style suggestive of rural hymn singing, while a few singers, such as Lester McFarland and Robert Gardner (Mac and Bob), showed evidence of formal musical instruction. Vernon Dalhart sang with the studied affectation of a trained concert singer.

The song choices favored by early hillbilly performers also resist easy categorization. The music was "traditional," for the most part, but very little of it came over "on the boats" in the forms in which it was presented in the 1920's. Song origin is an admittedly speculative topic, and little hard research has been done on the subject. Anne and Norm Cohen, though, have made some interesting but tentative judgments.[7] In their sampling of 280 recordings made by eighteen different performers between 1922 and 1924, they conclude that surprisingly little material (2 percent) was of British origin. Twenty-six percent came from pre-1900 Tin Pan Alley and 6 percent from post-1900 TPA sources. Fifty-nine percent had pre-1900 "folk" origins (presumably from anonymous grass-roots composers). Impressionistic surveys of titles listed in record and mail-order catalogues from the period would seem to bear out the Cohens' conclusions. Such a study as theirs, however, does not sufficiently measure the wealth of material which circulated in fragmentary form, that is, the maverick lines, phrases, and stanzas which survived from earlier British songs.

Virtually all of the material performed in the early period was "anonymous" to the hillbilly musicians, whether it was a sixteenth-century ballad like "Barbara Allen," a play-party song like "Fly Around My Pretty Little Miss," a minstrel tune like Dan Emmett's "Jordan Is a Hard Road to Travel," or a recent parlor song such as Charles Harris' "Hello Central Give

    7. Anne and Norm Cohen, "Folk and Hillbilly Music: Further Thoughts on Their Relation," *JEMFQ* 13, no. 46 (Summer 1977): 50–57.

Me Heaven." These were indeed a body of "old familiar tunes" remembered by many Americans, northern as well as southern, and cherished perhaps as artifacts of an older and simpler society than the one taking shape in the 1920's. Most hillbilly repertories contained little original material, but nearly all musicians made changes, unconscious or otherwise, in the songs they performed. Lyrics were often only half-remembered; melodies were often forgotten; and titles were altered. In a sense, virtually every hillbilly musician was an "arranger," but few bothered to copyright their arrangements until A. P. Carter began producing his prolific "compositions" after 1927. Of course, original composers began to appear very early among the hillbillies, and people outside the country tradition soon emerged to supply material for the burgeoning field. As the infant country music industry expanded, the inherited storehouse of songs began to diminish, and fledgling performers began to search for fresh material. One consequence was the emergence of individuals who were as well known for their writing as for their performances, or who were known for their writing alone. Carson Robison, for instance, became involved in hillbilly music through his association with Vernon Dalhart. Born in Chetapa, Kansas, in 1890, Robison had a background similar to Dalhart's, in that he began his career as a popular, vaudeville-style entertainer. He became a professional musician in the Midwest at the age of fifteen, and in the early 1920's he worked briefly in Chicago with Wendell Hall, "the Red-Headed Music Maker." In 1924 he went to New York, where he recorded for Victor, chiefly as a whistler. In the same year he became associated with Vernon Dalhart, in a rather stormy relationship that lasted for three years. His association with hillbilly music, however, was a colorful and influential one which lasted until his death in 1957.

Robison was one of several individuals who successfully wrote songs which appealed to the hillbilly public. Beginning with his first popular hillbilly composition, "Way Out West in Kansas," Robison wrote many of the favorite songs of the twenties (such as "Blue Ridge Mountain Blues," "Wreck of the Number Nine," "Little Green Valley," and "Carry Me Back to the Lone Prairie"), many of which were recorded by Vernon Dalhart. Along with writers like Blind Andy Jenkins, Charlie Oaks, and Bob Miller, Robison specialized in a type of song—the "event" song—that was a throwback to the British broadside and a characteristic genre of hillbilly music in the twenties. The event-song writers concentrated on the leading news topics of the day, and especially on violent or sensational incidents such as train or plane wrecks, murders, kidnappings, robberies, mine explosions, and related material. Southern folk music had long been filled with such ballads, but Robison developed the practice almost to a science. He supposedly read all the newspaper accounts of an event, then wrote the song according to a formula which began with a happy mood that degenerated into tragedy. The last stanza usually pointed out the moral to be learned.

It is now difficult to know whether Robison's lyrics represented his own feelings, or whether they merely represented what he believed his audiences wanted to hear. Consequently, we do not know whether he wrote with tongue in cheek when he concluded his song about the famous Monkey Trial of 1925, "The John T. Scopes Trial," by saying that "Mr. Scopes will know wherever he may go, that the old religion's better after all." If Robison's songwriting motives are less than clear, those of some of his balladeer contemporaries seem much more certain.

Richard (Dick) Burnett, Charlie Oaks, Alfred Reed, and Andrew Jenkins, to cite examples of a few of the hillbilly bards who happen to be known, were all genuine folk musicians who wrote from within the culture of their birth. They also all happened to be blind, and were therefore forced into a life of music through economic and social necessity. Each of them, of course, had an audience which helped to shape his musical perspectives, and Jenkins was particularly affected by commercial considerations. Nevertheless, there seems to be little or no gap between the men and the messages conveyed by their lyrics. Burnett was a banjoist, guitarist, and singer from near Monticello, Kentucky, who made several important recordings with fiddler Leonard Rutherford between 1926 and 1930. He was a valuable link to country music's folk past and was a repository of material which he had both preserved and rewritten: "Pearl Bryan," "Short Life of Trouble," "Weeping Willow Tree," "Little Stream of Whiskey," and a ballad known to all folk revivalists through its inclusion in the famous Folkways anthology, "Willie Moore." Burnett's most famous song, though, documented the tragedy which accompanied much of his early life. He was orphaned by the time he was twelve and blinded in 1907 at the age of twenty-four after being shot in the face during a robbery attempt. Soon thereafter he began his life as a wandering musician, singing and selling his song "ballets" on sheets about the size of a postcard. One of these broadside pamphlets in about 1913 contained his mournful "Farewell Song," known today in altered form as "Man of Constant Sorrow."

Dick Burnett and Charlie Oaks were living reminders to hillbilly audiences in the 1920's of the folk roots from which country music grew, and both easily made the transition from printed broadsheets to phonograph recordings as a means of disseminating their compositions. Oaks came from Richmond, Kentucky, and was well known in the Upper South before World War I for his performances at public gatherings and for the song sheets he sold (two of his compositions even showed up in an issue of the *Journal of American Folklore* in 1909). When Oaks' songs appeared on recordings in the 1920's, he was merely continuing a tradition, albeit in a new media setting, that had characterized his life for several decades. His 1925 tribute to the great Democratic leader William Jennings Bryan not only exemplified the survival of the centuries-old broadside tradition; it also reflected the lingering populist impulse that made Bryan a hero among millions of rural southerners.

Carson Robison. Courtesy of Bob Pinson.

Alfred Reed and Andy Jenkins wrote from much the same perspective as Burnett and Oaks, but their songs were also permeated with a moralism that probably came from religious conviction. Both men were preachers, and both seemed much influenced by the Holiness impulse that swept across the South at the turn of the century. Reed was born in Virginia but spent much of his life in West Virginia. The twenty-one songs he recorded for Victor, all presumably original, included secular material which, however, was laced with a fundamentalist and moral view of life. He wrote excellent "event songs" such as "The Wreck of the Virginian," but his most interesting compositions dealt with social commentary. "Why Do You Bob Your Hair Girls" took jibes at one of the social fashions of the 1920's, with Reed seeing the practice as unscriptural as well as unsettling. "How Can a Poor Man Stand Such Times and Live" commented on the inflation of the decade, while "There'll Be No Distinction There" projected a kind of social and racial liberalism that was rare among the hillbilly songs of the era. The song was conventional in its depiction of relief beyond the grave, but it went a step beyond this traditional religious fare when it posited a future condition of equality in Heaven among Gentiles, Jews, blacks, and whites.

A real folk bard of the 1920's, and a producer of some of the most popular hillbilly songs, was Andrew "Blind Andy" Jenkins. Born in Jenkinsburg, Georgia, in 1885, Jenkins, who became totally blind in middle age, developed a proficiency for several instruments, including the French harp, banjo, guitar, and mandolin. In 1910 he became a Holiness preacher, and except for occasional odd jobs—such as selling newspapers on the streets of Atlanta—he remained a revivalist until his death in 1956.

His second marriage, in 1919, brought him into a musical family. When Station WSB opened its doors in 1922 the Jenkins Family—Andy and two stepdaughters, Irene Spain and Mary Lee Eskew—were well prepared to move into studio entertainment. Their radio debut of August 14, 1922, was followed by recordings about two years later (August 29, 1924). With songs like "If I Could Hear My Mother Pray Again," the Jenkins family became probably the first country music family to be recorded, and one of the first groups to do both country and gospel music.

Although Jenkins was an accomplished musician and entertainer, he achieved his greatest fame as a songwriter. He composed well over eight hundred songs, the majority of them sacred. His repertory of compositions includes the murder ballad "Little Marian Parker," "God Put a Rainbow in the Clouds" (much performed by radio quartets), "Ben Dewberry's Final Run" (recorded by Jimmie Rodgers), "Kinnie Wagner" (about an Alabama badman), and his two most famous songs, "Billy the Kid" and "The Death of Floyd Collins." The last two songs were written at the urging of Polk Brockman who, once again, demonstrated an understanding of the needs and tastes of the country music audience just as he had done in his earlier promotion of Fiddlin' John Carson. "Billy the Kid" sounds like a traditional cowboy ballad, but it was written by Jenkins in 1928 after Walter Noble Burns' biography of the boy outlaw (*The Saga of Billy the Kid*) appeared. "The Death of Floyd Collins," recorded by Vernon Dalhart and others, chronicled the sad story of a young spelunker who became trapped in a sandstone cave near the Mammoth Cave in 1925. The incident won national attention because of radio coverage, and Polk Brockman, who at that time was in Jacksonville, Florida, communicated with Jenkins and asked him to write a ballad. Jenkins' composition, arranged by his stepdaughter, Mrs. Irene Spain, was mailed to Brockman, who paid twenty-five dollars for it. Brockman in turn sold it to Frank Walker of Columbia Records, who gave it to Dalhart for recording purposes. Both songs were typical of the event ballads of the period in that they were highly moralistic in tone and informed the listener of the dire fate that awaited young men who chose a life of crime or who, like Floyd Collins, disregarded their fathers' warnings.

Country music's expanding popularity inevitably lured writers who had no direct experience with the tradition. Some of the music's greatest writers, such as Fred Rose, have come to it after earlier careers in popular music or jazz. Bob Miller provides the first great example. Miller was born in 1895 in Memphis, where he was introduced to some of the great forms of southern music, if not to country music. In the early twenties Miller played the piano for a dance band called the Idlewild Orchestra, which performed on the steamer *Idlewild* on the Mississippi River. In 1928 he moved to New York, where he worked as an arranger for the Irving Berlin Company before establishing his own music concern, the Bob Miller Publishing Company. Although he composed numerous blues and popular tunes, the most important items in his repertory of over seven thousand songs were the hillbilly compositions. In the decades following the 1920's, Miller produced scores of lucrative and lastingly popular numbers, including the well-known "Eleven Cent Cotton and Forty Cent Meat"; the prison song which has inspired countless others, "Twenty-one Years"; the sentimental favorites "When the White Azaleas Start Blooming" and "Rocking Alone in an Old Rocking Chair"; and the World War II hit "There's a Star Spangled Banner Waving Somewhere." As the event composer par excellence, Miller was always alive to the possibility of exploiting any incident that struck the fancy of the people. In fact, he was sometimes ahead of a story. He supposedly prepared an obituary song for Huey Long two years before his assassination, and even went so far as to predict accurately that the killing would occur in the state capitol.

Regardless of the origins of the songs circulated by the hillbillies in the 1920's, whether taken from "tradition," written by the musicians themselves, or penned by professional composers like Bob Miller, the music quickly began to move into the possession of the "folk." Eventually, when later generations of folklorists moved into the byways and backwaters of the South, promoted by academia or subsidized by the Library of Congress, they collected such songs as "The Death of Floyd Collins" as authentic specimens of the folk-produced songs of the region. Only rarely were the hillbilly origins of such songs either known or recognized, but, as D. K. Wilgus has noted, "a commercialized tradition was being established."[8]

When we turn from the writers to the performers themselves, we find in the early period that singing is incidental to instrumentation. On recordings and on the radio barn dances, the fiddle and its accompanying string instruments predominated. The hillbilly string bands of the early commercial era were the direct descendants of (and in many cases were the same as) the folk entertainers who played for house parties, barn dances, church socials, tent shows, and political gatherings in the decades before 1920. Although the term "string band" did not appear on a record label until about 1925, string musicians had grouped themselves into bands since the nineteenth century. As is often the case, the term evolved long after the music had been formed. The identity of the first recorded string band is a bit shadowy, but if such a band can be considered as consisting of as few as two members, then the early fiddle-and-banjo duos would hold the distinction. Gid Tanner and Riley Puckett recorded with fiddle and banjo on March 7–8, 1924, as did Samantha Bumgarner and Eva Davis on April 22–23, 1924. That same April, Fiddlin' John Carson combined his eccentric, undisciplined solo style of fiddling with a trio of other musicians to create a band called the Virginia Reelers. Among the members the Reelers sometimes included were Fiddlin' John's daughter, Moonshine Kate, who sang and played the guitar and banjo, and (after 1927) one of the great North Georgia fiddlers, Earl Johnson. Fiddlin' John never permitted other band members to interfere with his style; he stuck resolutely to his own rhythm, time, and meter. Before the end of the year 1924, other bands with two or more members began swelling the ranks of those who had made records. Henry Whitter recorded in late July 1924 with a group named the Virginia Breakdowners, and in late August, Fiddling Powers and his family recorded a few breakdown instrumentals for Victor. In November 1924, Chenoweth's Cornfield Symphony Orchestra became perhaps the first Texas string band to record. Ernest Stoneman, performing with a group called the Dixie Mountaineers, made his first recording for Okeh on September 1, 1924. In the course of a long and distinguished career, which took him from Edison cylinder recordings to television, Stoneman introduced some of the most durable, and even legendary, country songs—such as "We Parted by the Riverside" and "The Titanic" (his first recording). He made the autoharp a solo instrument capable of playing melodies, and he sired a large group of children who became outstanding

8. Donald Knight Wilgus, *Anglo-American Folksong Scholarship since 1898* (New Brunswick, N.J.: Rutgers University Press, 1959), p. 73.

musicians in their own right. Until his death in June 1968, Stoneman, now universally described as Pop Stoneman, continued to appear in concerts with his children in one of the most sensational bluegrass bands of the modern period.

The radio and recording entrepreneurs definitely contributed to the shape and tone of the hillbilly bands by suggesting band names (as in the case of Ralph Peer and Al Hopkins' Hill Billies), style of costumes, and repertory. The businessmen sensed the public fascination with rustic types during the twenties and consequently urged such images upon the musicians. Often the images projected by the promoters coincided with the desires and self-conceptions of the musicians; there were hillbillies who were pleased to have the opportunity to perform and who had no pretensions of being anything other than hillbillies. But there were others who resisted the rube stereotype and who chafed at the limitations placed on their art. Above all, the hillbilly musicians were ambivalent about their status, and would become increasingly so as the decades passed. Therefore, we find within the string bands, and among hillbilly musicians in general, a confusion about who they were and what they wanted to be.

The careers of two of the finest bands of the period, Charlie Poole and his North Carolina Ramblers, and the Skillet Lickers, illustrate the conflicting impulses that worked upon hillbilly musicians. The two groups were highly dissimilar in repertory and style, but both had wide and enthusiastic followings. Poole was one of the earliest examples in country music of the hard-living, hard-drinking young man who burns his life away, a type which has appeared periodically and which seems endlessly appealing to country music fans. Before his death from a heart attack at the age of thirty-nine, Poole and the North Carolina Ramblers made some of the most irresistibly infectious sounds heard in early hillbilly music. The Alamance County native did a lot of rambling and worked as a doffer at the Haw River Mills before turning to a career of full-time music. As a singer, Poole bore the marks of his southern country origins in his dialect and tight nasal sound and in the traditional songs which he and his group often performed. His musical interests, though, ranged far beyond the rural material of his youth. His singing idol was Al Jolson, and one can hear traces of the great vaudeville singer in Poole's style. Poole and his group also favored songs from the vaudeville and ragtime traditions: tunes like "Goodbye Sweet Liza Jane," "Leaving Home," and "Milwaukee Blues."

Poole and the other two original Ramblers—fiddler Posey Rorer and guitarist Norman Woodlieff—began entertaining at dances and fiddlers' conventions in the area around Spray and Leaksville, North Carolina, in about 1917. It was not until 1925, however, when they made their first records for Columbia in New York, that they gained enough financial security to free them from the textile employment at which they had periodically worked during their earlier musical career. After the success of their first recording, "Don't Let Your Deal Go Down" (always their most popular song), the Ramblers became much sought after for personal appearances, mostly in the Upper South and in Ohio. In the years before Poole died, the Ramblers' personnel changed, first in 1926 with the addition of an outstanding guitarist and one-time railroad engineer named Roy Harvey, and then in 1928 when fiddler Lonnie Austin replaced Posey Rorer. The group sometimes included a piano and second fiddle, but the trio format was their most popular combination and the sound with which they are always identified. The Rambler sound was predictable: a bluesy fiddle lead, backed up by long, flowing, melodic guitar runs, and the finger-style banjo playing of Poole. Predictable though it might be, it was nonetheless outstanding. No other string band in early country music equaled the Ramblers' controlled, clean, and well-patterned ensemble sound.

The Skillet Lickers, on the other hand, were anything but orderly and well disciplined. They were one of several North Georgia bands who were famous for their rough, hard-driving sound (Earl Johnson and His Dixie Entertainers, Bill Helms Upson County Band, Fiddlin' John's Virginia Reelers, Lowe Stokes' Georgia Potlickers, and, on occasion, the Georgia Yellow Hammers). The original Skillet Lickers had performed extensively in various combinations around Atlanta before 1924, but it was not until March 7 of that year that any of them appeared on recordings. James Gideon (Gid) Tanner, a chicken farmer and old-time fiddler from Dacula, Georgia, combined with George Riley Puckett, a blind guitarist from Alpharetta, Georgia, to become the Columbia label's first hillbilly talent. They, in turn, were joined in Columbia recording sessions in 1926 by two other popular WSB performers and Georgians, fiddler Clayton McMichen and five-string banjoist Fate Norris. McMichen and Norris had been members of a group called the Home Town Boys, but McMichen suggested that the new organization be called the Skillet Lickers—after an earlier group that had played at Atlanta conventions, the Lick the Skillet Band. In their Columbia recording period from 1926 to 1931, the Skillet Lickers recorded, in a wild, raucous, but highly infectious style, everything from traditional ballads, breakdowns, and rural "dramas" (humorous skits) to the latest popular hits from Tin Pan Alley. Much of the band's popularity can be attributed to the energetic personality and showmanship of Tanner, who whooped, sang in falsetto, and in general played the part of a rustic fool. His hoedown fiddle style was just as unrestrained and, according to some observers (including Clayton McMichen), tended to detract from the overall quality of the band.

Several musicians played with the Skillet Lickers from time to time, including Lowe Stokes, one of the outstanding fiddlers of the period who was equally adept at breakdowns or pop tunes. The mainstays of the group were Puckett, as popular for his singing as for his multiple guitar runs, and McMichen, a wonderfully inventive fiddler who resisted being con-

Charlie Poole (seated) and the North Carolina Ramblers. Courtesy of David Freeman. *Left to right:* Posey Rurer, Charlie Poole, Roy Harvey.

fined to any one style of music. McMichen's career well illustrates the contrasting impulses that tugged at the hearts of some old-time musicians. McMichen grew up in a household of Scotch-Irish fiddlers in Dallas, Georgia, and many of the tunes he knew, such as "Boil Them Cabbage Down," "Nancy Rollin," and "Billy in the Lowground," came directly from his father. No one ever doubted his ability to play breakdowns or other forms of old-time music. He was a frequent participant at the Atlanta Old-Time Fiddlers Contest and, in fact, continued to stage contests, many of them on the radio, long after he left the Skillet Lickers. McMichen, though, always resented the narrow hillbilly focus to which he thought the Skillet Lickers were being limited. He participated in the "rural skits" (humorous rural dialogue interspersed with short musical phrases) and even wrote much of the material contained within them. He also submitted to the stereotyping of the group as a wild bunch of young country boys who made and drank whiskey and played a little music on the side. But McMichen was also drawn to jazz and popular music, and with his own groups, such as the Georgia Wildcats, he tried to create a mixture of sounds that sounded much like the "hot dance" style featured by Bob Wills and similar musicians in the Southwest. The hillbilly image, however, remained with him for the rest of his life. It was always a point of some bitterness to him that later generations of listeners who discovered his music were more interested in what he called "swamp opera" than in his attempted pop fusions.

Much of the vocal music of early country music was merely tangential to the string band emphasis. String band members took turns at doing vocals, but only rarely did someone forge an identity apart from the band of which he was a member. Charlie Poole, of course, was as well known individually as his band was collectively, and a few others, like Fiddlin' John and Ernest Stoneman, attained some reputations as singers. Of all the early musicians, Riley Puckett was the one who came closest to achieving both popular and commercial recognition as a singer and instrumentalist. Born in about 1890 in Alpharetta, Georgia, Puckett was accidentally blinded at the age of three months when a lead acetate solution was used to treat a minor eye irritation. He attended the School for the Blind at Macon, Georgia, and turned to a life of music soon after his graduation. Puckett was one of the few pioneer hillbillies who tried to make music a full-time profession, and he was an active participant on WSB well before he made his first records. His recording career began in 1924 with "Little Log Cabin in the Lane" and "Rock All Our Babies to Sleep" (Columbia 107-D). On the second song he yodeled, becoming probably the first hillbilly singer to do so and preceding Jimmie Rodgers, of "blue yodel" fame, by about three years. Puckett's smooth, clearly articulated baritone singing was a major source of the Skillet Lickers' popularity; Clayton McMichen said, in fact, that Puckett's singing "sold" the group. Puckett remained with the Columbia label until the 1930's, and then moved to Decca and Bluebird. Many of his songs came from rural or traditional sources but, like McMichen, he ranged far and wide for his repertory and showed no reluctance to record any song that caught his fancy. He could dip back into the rustic song bag to do a song like "I'm Going to Georgia," or into the vaudeville tradition to something like "Ragged but Right" (one of his finest numbers done with mandolin player Ted Hawkins), or he could draw from turn-of-the-century Tin Pan Alley with a song like "Let Me Call You Sweetheart." Puckett was a rural musician, but like most rural singers, before and since, he took songs wherever he found them.

Early country singers exhibited an ambivalence toward their profession similar to that which we have observed among instrumentalists. The hillbilly image and label were troublesome to some, while repertory and style of performance were problems to others (whether to perform old-time songs or not, and whether to adhere to a "rural" sound or to blunt it in favor of smoother and presumably more salable sound). Riley Puckett demonstrated a wide-ranging eclecticism and opted for a smooth, well-rounded sound. Bradley Kincaid's sound was even smoother, but he resisted the urge to do modern pop songs. Born in Garrard County, Kentucky, in 1895, Kincaid grew up hearing old-time songs and strumming his own accompaniment on the "hound dog guitar" his father had given him (his dad had traded a fox hound for the instrument). Kincaid harbored no thoughts about a professional career until he moved to Chicago in 1924 to begin training as a YMCA worker. While attending George Williams College, Kincaid began singing occasionally with the college quartet. A fellow classmate and member of the quartet informed Don Malin, the WLS music director, that Kincaid also knew a lot of folksongs. Malin contacted Kincaid about doing a fifteen-minute show on WLS, and Kincaid, who had not sung folksongs for years, borrowed a guitar and began brushing up on the old songs from back home. His initial show evoked a tremendous audience response, and by the fall of 1926 he had become a regular on the *National Barn Dance*, where he remained for about four years. Kincaid received more than 100,000 letters a year on WLS, but he did not fully understand the impact he made on his radio listeners until he offered a songbook for sale. His first songbook sold over 100,000 copies in six printings, and he had to prepare additional folios (by the time he left WLS about 400,000 copies had been sold).

No phenomenon of the 1920's provides better evidence of the tremendous appeal of old-time music to Americans in that decade than does Kincaid's popularity. Performing only to the sometimes-unsure accompaniment of his own guitar, and singing wtih a clear, sweet, uncomplicated tenor, Kincaid won a devoted following in the Midwest and Upper South. The powerful WLS provided him his first audience; several other stations, including WLW in Cincinnati, KDKA in Pittsburgh, WBZ in Boston, WGY in Schenectady, WEAF in New York, and eventually WSM in Nashville, introduced him to additional millions. Kincaid also toured widely, giving concerts throughout the Midwest and in New England. One member of his entourage was a young man named Louis Marshall Jones who joined him in 1935. While traveling with Kincaid, Jones began playing the role of an old man and singing songs which he picked up from his mentor. Kincaid gave him the title of "Grandpa" which has ever since clung to him.

From the very beginning of his long career Kincaid bitterly resented being called a "hillbilly," a term which he associated with bums, prisoners, and other disreputable elements. Kincaid seemed to identify his old-fashioned songs with old-fashioned morality, and he appears to have picked up some of his attitudes about music and about mountain culture from his settlement-school teachers at Berea College. He often spoke of the pure "Anglo-Saxon" blood of the mountains and seemed to equate that with a similar purity in morality and music. Actually, Kincaid's repertory was much wider than that usually favored by the settlement teachers (who generally preferred the older British or British-derived material). He preferred to call himself a "singer of mountain songs," but, as his repertory demonstrates, a large concentration of nineteenth-century parlor songs, gospel songs, and modern-composed country songs had made their way back into the mountains. His tastes ran toward sad, beautiful ballads such as "Barbara Allen" and "Fatal Derby Day," sentimental songs from the late nineteenth century such as "Letter Edged in Black" and "I'll Be All Smiles Tonight," and religious ballads such as "The Legend of the Robin Red Breast." Through his recordings (first made for the Starr Piano Company's Gennett label in 1927), personal appearances, and radio broadcasts, Kincaid probably did more to popularize old-time songs and ballads among Americans than any other individual.

Kentucky contributed to country music some of its finest traditional singers. Kincaid, Dick Burnett, and Charlie Oaks, as we have seen, made enduring contributions to the country music repertory. Their careers should also tell us, though, that there have been not one but many folk traditions in southern music. The choices of songs favored by these men were not radically dissimilar (although one can hardly envision Kincaid doing Burnett's "Little Stream of Whiskey"!). The style of presentation, however, was indeed different. Another Kentuckian, Buell Kazee, reveals still another approach to traditional music and suggests further ambivalence in the performance of America's new-found rural music. Like Kincaid, Kazee was a genuine mountain boy, from Magoffin County, Kentucky, who grew up in a family of traditional singers. He began fooling with the banjo when he was five years old and at an early age became a popular performer at neighborhood social functions. At the age of seventeen he became a Missionary Baptist minister. He then attended college at Georgetown, Kentucky, where he studied voice and music and majored in

English. His study of Elizabethan literature revealed to him the importance of the ballads he had known all his life. As a result, his concerts, usually performed in a college setting, were marked by an erudition rare among
country performers. From 1927 to 1929 he recorded fifty-two selections
for Brunswick, only forty-six of which were issued. When the Brunswick
Company collapsed in 1930 at the onset of the Depression, Kazee terminated his recording career. Like cowboy singer Carl Sprague, Kazee was
never a full-fledged commercial performer, largely because he had committed himself early in life to the Baptist ministry. Kazee alleged that he
had two voices, a hillbilly one which his recording promoters encouraged
him to use (the voice, that is, of his mountain youth), and a more cultivated one that came out of his academic training. He had a genuine respect for the old-time songs of his mountain inheritance, but he seemed
to harbor a bit of bitterness for having been expected to perform them in
a certain way. Probably the finest ballad singer found on early commercial records, Kazee recorded such songs as "The Lady Gay" (an American
variant of "The Wife of Usher's Well"), "The Butcher's Boy," "Faded Coat
of Blue," and "The Wagoner's Lad." Under the prodding of his Brunswick
directors, Kazee also recorded "Election Day in Kentucky" and "A Mountain Boy Makes His First Record," attempts by his company to rival the
Skillet Lickers' popular rural dramas. Rediscovered by modern folk enthusiasts on the Folkways *Anthology of American Folk Music*, Kazee won
another, and probably larger, audience late in life. Before he died on August 31, 1976, a new generation of listeners thrilled to his haunting, lop-
ing banjo style and learned that time had not diminished the power of his
affecting voice.

Kentucky was not alone in the spawning of traditional ballad singers,
but some of the singers from other states, such as Peg Moreland, Texas'
"King of the Ditty Singers," may never be properly documented. Other
singers, such as Bascom Lamar Lunsford, had only a fleeting relationship
with commercial hillbilly music but were prolific singers of folk-songs and
ballads. Lunsford, a product of Asheville, North Carolina, and a lawyer by
trade, made a handful of commercial recordings, but was exhaustively
recorded by the Library of Congress and by academic folklorists. He was
an indefatigable collector and sponsor of folk festivals, which were generally more receptive to hillbilly acts than were other festivals. His life often crossed paths with country music in positive ways. For example, he
was a friend and sponsor of Scott Wiseman, one half of the team of Lulu
Belle and Scotty, and a longtime member of the *National Barn Dance*.
Lunsford also wrote the original verses of "Good Old Mountain Dew," a
song which is now one of the standards of country music.

Tennessee made contributions to the performance of old-time music in
a number of important instances. Knoxville's strategic location in the Ten-
nesee hills made it a focal point for old-time musicians who congregated

there to sing on its street corners, in its railroad depots, and on its radio stations. G. A. Nennstiel, the record manager for Sterchi Brothers in Knoxville, a furniture company which was also the chief southern distributor for Vocalion Records, astutely recognized the folk talent which gathered in the city and set out to attach it to the Vocalion label. Charlie Oaks, Mac and Bob, and George Reneau, all blind musicians who often frequented Knoxville, became Vocalion recording talent because of Nennstiel's sponsorship. Of the group, Reneau had the most unusual career in that he did not sing on the early records on which he alone was listed! Vocalion seems originally to have been interested only in Reneau's harmonica and guitar playing. Consequently, when he made his first records in 1924, the singing was done by popular crooner Gene Austin, who was then about three years away from the smashing success of "My Blue Heaven." Austin's boyhood in Texas and Louisiana may have given him an acquaintanceship with southern rural music that enabled him to do a convincing imitation, or he may merely have been a skillful mimic. At any rate, few people seemed to discern that a Tennessee mountain boy was not in fact singing "You Will Never Miss Your Mother Till She's Gone" and "Life's Railway to Heaven."

In 1925 Reneau was finally permitted to do his own singing. For the most part his songs were little different from those done by other hillbilly singers, and several were in fact "covers" of earlier recordings. But he did record the first version of "Old Rattler," the comic dog song that Grandpa Jones later made famous, as well as a humorous complaint about female assertiveness called "Woman's Suffrage." Reneau made no records after 1927 and, in a sense, it is remarkable that his recording career lasted as long as it did into the Jazz Age. His rough-edged, singular style did not conform well with the search for smooth vocalists that characterized both pop and country music in those years. As Charles Wolfe notes, Reneau was "one of the relatively few traditional musicians to make the transition from the wandering street corner minstrel to recording artist."[9] Unfortunately, his life as a musician ended as it had begun. He contracted pneumonia while working the streets of Knoxville and died in a local hospital a few days later. He was only thirty-two years old.

Clarence "Tom" Ashley's life had a much happier ending. This East Tennessee musician lived long enough to experience, as did Buell Kazee and a few other early hillbilly performers, a second career in music. Born in Bristol, Tennessee, in 1895, as Clarence Earl McCurry, he legally adopted the name of his grandfather, Enoch Ashley, who reared him. He had become an accomplished banjoist and guitarist by the time he reached his early

    9. Charles Wolfe, "George Reneau: A Biographical Sketch," *JEMFQ* 15, no. 56 (Winter 1979): 205.

teens and had absorbed an extensive repertory of traditional material from friends and relatives in the Mountain City area of northeastern Tennessee, where his family had moved in 1899. As yet another example of country music's commercial history prior to the coming of radio and recording, Ashley had been a commercial performer for several years before he made records. At the age of sixteen he joined a medicine show in Mountain City as a featured singer and remained on the medicine circuit, with some exceptions, until World War II. He gained invaluable experience in this type of format and met other performers—including Roy Acuff, the future great star of the 1940's.

Ashley's recording career began in the mid-twenties when he joined with fiddler Clarence Greene, harmonica player Gwen Foster, autoharpist Will Abernathy, and lead guitarist Walter Davis to form the Blue Ridge Mountain Entertainers. In this and other organizations, such as the Carolina Tar Heels (originally composed of Gwen Foster and Dock Walsh, and named by Ralph Peer) and Byrd Moore and His Hotshots, Ashley played the guitar. To folk revivalists of the 1960's Ashley was best known as a five-string banjoist, and his renditions of such songs as "The Coo Coo Bird" and "The House Carpenter" were highly valued by young folk musicians who heard them for the first time on the Folkways *Anthology*. These were his "lassy-makin'" tunes, so called because they were learned at molasses-making time back home, and were among the oldest songs he knew.

Virginia also figured prominently in the shaping of early commercial country music. As we have seen, Virginians like Henry Whitter and Ernest Stoneman did much to inaugurate country music's history, and as we shall be reminded in a later portion of this chapter, Virginia's Carter Family gave the music one of its dominant styles. But there were many others: fiddlers, banjoists, string bands, and vocalists. Kelly Harrell, for example, was born in Drapers Valley, Wythe County, Virginia, in 1899. He never learned an instrument, but as a singer with a large storehouse of traditional songs, he was never long without an accompanist. He rambled around the country for several years as a young man, but settled down in about 1927 in Fieldale, Virginia, where he went to work for the Fieldcrest Mill as a loom fixer. He was still employed by the mill when he died from asthma in 1942. Even before he took up a permanent life as a mill worker, Harrell had ventured into commercial music, and he continued to combine it with textile work until the Great Depression ended his singing career. He recorded a few songs for Victor in January 1925 (after having traveled to New York for an audition) and several later in the year for Okeh with his friend Henry Whitter. His greatest performances came in 1927, when he returned to the Victor label with an outstanding band composed of Posey Rorer on fiddle, R. D. Hundley on banjo, and Alfred Steagall on guitar. On songs like "I'm Nobody's Darling on Earth," "Charles Guiteau," "Henry Clay Beattie," and "In the Shadow of the Pines," the group created a sound very much like that of the North Carolina Ramblers, a well-patterned sound featuring a fiddle lead, melodious guitar runs, and a three-finger-style banjo backup. Harrell even sounded a bit like Poole, with his backcountry dialect and nasal timbre. But his voice had a resonance and full-bodied quality that Poole's did not always possess, and his enunciation was considerably clearer than that of the North Carolinian. Harrell's recordings made his name a popular one in the southeastern region where he made his home, but they brought him only moderate commercial success. His greatest claim to fame came through the composition of "Away Out on the Mountain," a wonderful hobo song about a mythical land of abundance somewhere in "the land of the sky." Ralph Peer persuaded him to let Jimmie Rodgers have the song, and, coupled with "Blue Yodel No. 1," it brought Harrell $985 in writer's royalties for the first three months of sale. The Great Depression made it difficult for tradition-oriented performers to survive, and Harrell made no serious attempts at professional music after 1929, even though his last recordings show him to be at the peak of his vocal powers.

Another Virginian, Moran Lee "Dock" Boggs, took traditional music in a direction radically different from that followed by Harrell. Boggs' repertory was filled with traditional songs too, but, like his contemporaries in West Virginia, Frank Hutchison and Dick Justice, Boggs also successfully adapted black material to traditional white rural performing styles. All three were coal miners who either worked with black people or heard them play at dances or as street musicians. But unlike Hutchison and Justice, who became skillful blues guitarists, Boggs concentrated on the five-string banjo and was one of the few old-time banjoists who seemed drawn to the blues idiom. Boggs began playing the five-string banjo as a teenager, not long after he began working as a coal miner. Music was never more than a sideline to him, and he remained a miner until he retired in 1952. Boggs began recording more or less by chance in 1927, when he wandered into a hotel in Norton, Virginia, where two Brunswick scouts were holding auditions. With a borrowed banjo, he won his opportunity to record by playing two of the songs that would later appear in his recorded repertory: "Country Blues" and "Mistreated Mama Blues." Old-time ballads and love songs predominated in Boggs's music, but blues songs such as "Down South Blues" (which he learned from a phonograph recording) have been most interesting to collectors and to fans who rediscovered his music in the 1960's. Boggs' banjo style has been as intriguing to listeners as his song choices. His style was unlike that of any other performer; he did not strum or frail but instead picked out the melodies note for note as he sang.

As the fledgling country music industry grew, it was inevitable that it would attract musicians with minimal rural influence who were either drawn to it through a genuine love or through opportunism. One such individual, and probably the most important, was Vernon Dalhart (Marion Try Slaughter). Although Dalhart was an urban man with urbane musical tastes, his biographer Walter Haden argues that his subject was intimately familiar with southern rural life and singing. Dalhart was born in Jefferson, Texas, a once-thriving port city on Big Cypress Creek in northeastern Texas, and was the son of a prominent rancher whose fortunes, however, were on the skids by the time Dalhart reached young manhood. Dalhart worked as a cowboy in the region between Vernon and Dalhart, Texas, the towns which he drew upon for his stage name. Dalhart, then, was not unfamiliar with cowboy songs and other types of folk material when he enrolled at the Dallas Conservatory of Music. Fired with the ambition to be a grand opera singer, he moved to New York after his graduation and became part of that city's active music scene. He gained employment as a popular and light-opera singer, spent several years with the Century Opera Company, and later appeared at the New York Hippodrome in Gilbert and Sullivan's *H.M.S. Pinafore* in 1913–1914.

Dalhart began recording for Edison in 1916 and later free-lanced for practically every recording company in the United States. He recorded under his stage name and also under innumerable other pseudonyms (Haden has counted at least 110). Prior to 1924, he was listed in the record catalogues as a "tenor." Few of his songs were even remotely close to the hillbilly category, but he did do many songs with southern themes, including some, like "Can't Yo' Heah Me Callin', Caroline," done in a heavy black dialect. As a popular singer, Dalhart was only moderately successful. In fact, by 1924 his popularity on the Victor label was waning, and he desperately needed something to reinvigorate his career. He recognized the growing popularity of hillbilly songs and asked the directors of the Victor company to permit him to record a hillbilly number. Although Dalhart's financial woes were shared by the company, they were hesitant to allow one of their popular artists to record a song of questionable artistic quality. Their eventual affirmative decision, however, gave hillbilly music a national boost, bolstered the sagging Victor sales capacity, and made Vernon Dalhart one of the best-known recording stars of the 1920's.

Two songs served to convert Dalhart to the status of "hillbilly singer" and catapulted him to national attention. These were the "The Wreck of the Old 97" and "The Prisoner's Song." "The Wreck of the Old 97," probably the most seminal hillbilly event song, tells of the fatal crash of the Fast Mail of the Southern Railway on its run between Monroe and Spencer, Virginia, on September 27, 1903. Engineer Joseph A. (Steve) Broady and twelve others died in the tragedy. Several ballads, including one by Fred Lewey and another by Charlie Noell, were composed about the wreck. In 1927 a Virginia farmer named David Graves George, seeing the great commercial success that the song enjoyed, filed a claim for compensation asserting that he was the real author of the song that Dalhart and others had recorded. Although the Circuit Court of Appeals concluded in 1934 that Graves was not the composer and had, in fact, copied his version from the Dalhart recording, the song's legitimate authorship has never been conclusively ascertained.

"The Wreck on the Southern Old 97" had been subjected to the molding influence of oral tradition for over twenty years before it was recorded in 1923; the "finished" product, therefore, was probably the work of several people, including Lewey and Noell. One individual who contributed to the song's structure and popularity was the well-known Virginia hillbilly musician Henry Whitter, who had kept the ballad alive through local performances in the Fries, Virginia, area. Using a melody inspired by "The Ship That Never Returned," he recorded the great railroad ballad in 1923 on Okeh 40015. Not only was his recording one of the very earliest in the commercial hillbilly field, but its popularity also directly inspired the entrance of Vernon Dalhart (and others) into hillbilly music.

Whatever Dalhart's motives may have been, he persuaded the Victor people to allow him to record the number, which he had already recorded on Edison Diamond disc no. 51361. He used the lyrics from the Whitter recording and sang them in an exaggerated rural dialect similar to Whitter's (he even repeated Whitter's mistakes). The Victor directors asked Dalhart to find something to go on the other side of the record, and he produced the manuscript of a song supposedly written by a cousin, Guy Massey. Nathaniel Shilkret, Victor's staff accompanist, added a few words to the song and thought up a melody. This song, actually based on fragments that had floated around for many years, was "The Prisoner's Song": best known to Americans by the lines "If I had the wings of an angel, over these prison walls I would fly." The biggest-selling record in Victor's pre-electric recording history (selling a little over one million copies), it also appeared on eighteen masters and over sixty labels. While the exact number of total record sales is unknown, both songs made their way into the repertory of all country singers and into the consciousness of most Americans. After the smashing success of these two numbers, Dalhart remained firmly in the hillbilly field forever, thereafter recording only rural and folk-flavored melodies.

Vernon Dalhart therefore became the first recording artist "to attain an international following for himself and commercial country music."[10] At a time when popular record sales in general were declining, hillbilly records, because of the low budget required to produce them and because of the small but reliable audience for them, were considered to be a profitable investment. Although coming out of a light-opera background, Dalhart knew how to perform rural songs in a sincere, plaintive style that hillbilly

    10. Walter Darrell Haden, "Vernon Dalhart," in *Stars of Country Music*, ed. Bill C. Malone and Judith McCulloh (Urbana: University of Illinois Press, 1976), p. 69.

Bradley Kincaid. Courtesy of JEMF.

Vernon Dalhart. Courtesy of JEMF.

fans loved. In his first Edison hillbilly recording, he was accompanied by his own French harp and the Hawaiian guitar of Frank Ferera. Ferera was a Hawaiian of Portuguese descent who came to the United States in 1914 as an entertainer at the Panama Pacific Exhibition; he claimed to have introduced the Hawaiian guitar to Americans.

From 1925 to 1931 Dalhart became one of the most commercially successful hillbilly singers, recording under many different pseudonyms. "The Prisoner's Song," which he recorded for a dozen or more companies, is said to have brought him well over a million dollars in royalty. "The Death of Floyd Collins" was also a big-selling record for Dalhart. His repertory, recorded by practically every recording company of even the slightest importance in the United States, was found on literally thousands of records and included both traditional numbers and newly written ones. The Dalhart collection includes nearly every type of song with which rural southerners were familiar. There were comical songs that evoked the Gaslight Era like "The Little Black Mustache," pathetic songs like Gussie Davis' "The Fatal Wedding," badman ballads like "Sydney Allen," train songs like "The Wreck of the Old 97," sentimental-religious tunes like "The Dying Girl's Message," and, of course, unrequited love ballads like "I'll Be All Smiles Tonight."

Dalhart enjoyed a commercial dominance in the new hillbilly field for a few years, and even influenced the sound of some of its performers. (Carson Robison and Frank Luther, for example, were vaudeville-style entertainers who moved into country music and who often recorded with Dalhart. But even some pure country types, like cowboy singer Carl Sprague, sometimes used a kind of stilted studio sound reminiscent of that of Dalhart.) However, Dalhart bequeathed no permanent style to country music, although he did contribute to the popularity of singing. String bands continued to flourish on into the 1940's, but the outlines of the singer's future dominance in country music began to become clear by the end of the 1920's.

In one of the great coincidences of country music history, two of its most influential acts made their first records for the same company in the first four days of August 1927. Jimmie Rodgers and the Carter Family took to Bristol, Tennessee, two of country music's most imitated styles and two of its most appealing impulses. Rodgers brought into clear focus the tradition of the rambling man which had been so attractive to country music's folk ancestors and which has ever since fascinated much of the country music audience. This ex–railroad man conveyed the impression that he had been everywhere and had experienced life to the fullest. His music suggested a similar openness of spirit, a willingness to experiment, and a receptivity to alternative styles. The Carter Family, in contrast, represented the impulse toward home and stability, a theme as perennially attractive as that of the rambler. When the Carters sang, they evoked images of the old country church, Mama and Daddy, the family fireside, and "the green fields of Virginia far away." Theirs was a music that might borrow from other forms, but would move away from its roots only reluctantly.

The recording of Rodgers and the Carter Family was the work of the indefatigable commercialist-folklorist Ralph Peer. In late July 1927, Peer and his two hardy engineers set out for a tour of the South with Atlanta, Savannah, Memphis, and Bristol, Tennessee, scheduled as their main stops. Bristol, which lay on the Tennessee-Virginia border, was destined to be the site of Peer's most successful talent excursion and the scene of one of country music's most seminal events. On about July 21 or 22, Peer began recording a few musicians who had previously recorded, such as Ernest and Hattie Stoneman, and Ernest Phipps (a Holiness preacher and singer of religious songs). Peer persuaded the editor of the *Bristol News Bulletin* to run a short story about the sessions on the front page of the July 27 issue. This was the "advertisement" which lured Rodgers, the Carters, and a host of other old-time musicians to Bristol.

In the following days some of early country music's most interesting and powerful acts made their first recordings: Alfred Karnes, a preacher and gospel singer from Corbin, Kentucky; the Tenneva Ramblers, who had earlier performed in and around Asheville, North Carolina, as the Jimmie Rodgers Entertainers; Blind Alfred Reed; B. F. Shelton, a Kentuckian whose haunting renditions of such ballads as "Pretty Polly" and "Darling Cory" are among the finest on early country records; and several others. Of the several groups recorded, however, only two, Rodgers and the Carters, were to experience any kind of long-range commercial success. They recorded within two days of each other (the Carter Family on August 1 and 2, and Rodgers on August 4).

The Carter Family endured as significant country performers until the early 1940's. Although the original group ceased to make commercial records in 1941, they did not actually retire from radio work until 1943. Coming as it did at the beginning of World War II, their retirement assumed symbolic significance to many people; the war seemed to be a great watershed, marking the end of country music's golden age. The Carter Family, which in many respects dominated the so-called golden age, was composed of A. P. Carter, his wife, Sara, and his sister-in-law, Maybelle Addington Carter.

Alvin Pleasant Carter was born at Maces Spring, Scott County, Virginia, in 1891. Reared in a strict Christian environment, A. P. learned to love religious songs but was nonetheless attracted also by the sound of the fiddle. His religious parents rejected the fiddle as the devil's instrument, and so A. P. had to wait until he had earned enough money as a fruit-tree salesman to acquire one. While visiting relatives on Copper Creek in Scott County, he met Sara Dougherty (born in 1898 in Wise County, Virginia), who was an accomplished young singer and instrumentalist. After their marriage on June 18, 1915, they settled at Maces Spring, where their home became a neighborhood attraction because of A. P.'s and Sara's singing. Maybelle Addington, born in 1909 at Nickelsville, Virginia, married A. P.'s brother Ezra in 1926. She brought to the Carter Family an exceptional talent for the autoharp, banjo, and guitar. When Ralph Peer arrived in Bristol, the Carter Family was well prepared to record.

According to statements made by Sara Carter, the Family recorded over three hundred sides for several companies: Victor (1927–1934); American Record Company (1935); Decca (1936–1938); Columbia (1940); Victor (1941). At the first Bristol session the Family led off with "Bury Me under the Weeping Willow" and then followed that with five more songs, all of which were released. The sound established on these initial recordings never varied substantially in the sixteen years that followed. The Carters did not change; they merely got better. Ralph Peer was most impressed with Sara's singing, and though he did not interfere with their choice of songs, he insisted that she be the centerpiece of the Carters' records. Sara almost always led the singing with her clear, strong soprano voice; Maybelle countered with a gentler alto harmony; and A. P., always an idiosyncratic singer, sang bass or baritone when he felt like it. Sara often sang solos, and even reluctantly attempted a bit of yodeling at Peer's urging. A. P. sang an occasional solo with a rather tentative, tremulous voice, which was peculiarly affecting in its gentle shyness. The highpoint of the Carter vocal sound, however, was the duet singing of Sara and Maybelle, most strongly displayed in their Decca recordings of 1936–1938.

The Carters' instrumental sound was as distinctive and recognizable as their vocal approach. Maybelle played a much-copied guitar lead on all of their records, while Sara seconded with autoharp chords or a second guitar. Maybelle sometimes picked finger-style blues guitar licks, and on occasion even played a steel guitar. The style which attracted generations of guitar pickers, though, was her thumb-brush technique (in which the thumb picks the melody on the bass strings while the fingers provide rhythm with a downward stroke of the treble strings). Featured on her big Gibson L-5 cello model guitar, which she played from 1928 on, Maybelle produced an infectiously rhythmic and melodic sound which captured the interests of guitar players everywhere. In the decades after 1927 it became the height of accomplishment for southern country guitarists to learn the Maybelle Carter guitar style; her rendition of "Wildwood Flower," for example, was the model used by most subsequent fledgling guitarists when they did their first solo guitar piece.

The Carter Family never made extensive tours; most of their appearances were arranged personally by A. P. and confined largely to schoolhouses, churches, and little movie houses in the Upper South. Their popularity was garnered mostly through phonograph recordings and through radio broadcasts made over the powerful Mexican border stations after

1938. They sang both traditional songs and their own compositions, although it is extremely difficult to tell the difference between the two. Most of their songs were arranged or written ("worked up," as A. P. called it) by A. P., who was one of the first individuals in country music to protect his repertory by securing copyrights on the music—even on that very large percentage which was in the public domain. This practice was insisted upon by Ralph Peer (who followed the same procedure with Jimmie Rodgers). Peer then published the songs through his own Southern Music Company and shared the profits fifty-fifty. Carter readily admitted that he took many of his songs from traditional sources, but, as Archie Green has said, "every time A. P. Carter recorded a song or published it in a folio, he 'collected' a variant as does any folklorist in the field with his notebook, acetate disc, or tape."[11] The Carters, of course, absorbed a lot of songs as they were growing up, but after their commercial career began, A. P. periodically went on song hunting trips, collecting sheet music or gospel hymnals, or writing down lyrics as his informants sang to him. One known Carter informant was Leslie Riddles from Kingsport, Tennessee, a black guitarist and singer, who taught the family "Cannon Ball Blues" and sometimes accompanied A. P. on collecting trips.

Given his song-collecting habits, it should not be surprising to find A. P. Carter listed as author of songs that he could not possibly have written, such as "I'll Be All Smiles Tonight," "Wildwood Flower," and "The Wabash Cannon Ball." Nevertheless, modern country and folk music enthusiasts owe A. P. and the Carter Family a great debt because they preserved and disseminated such a large body of old-time material that might otherwise have been lost forever. Carter Family records were never million-sellers, and no single record of theirs seems to have experienced any great commercial success, but "Carter Family songs" (as they are generally described) have circulated widely and have become the staples of the repertories of a multitude of country, bluegrass, and urban folk singers. And there is no way to count the number of plain folk who faithfully listened to their broadcasts and transcriptions over XERF in Del Rio, Texas, after 1938, or who bought their records and then bequeathed their songs to children and grandchildren. "I'm Thinking Tonight of My Blue Eyes," "Little Darling, Pal of Mine," "Jimmie Brown the Newsboy," "Keep on the Sunny Side" (their radio theme), "Engine 143," "Worried Man Blues," and "Will the Circle Be Unbroken," are only a few of the Carter songs that yet endure.

The Carter Family sang of an America that was gradually disappearing, an America whose values had seemed inextricably interrelated with rural or small-town life. That America had been fading since even before the

11. Archie Green, "The Carter Family's 'Coal Miner's Blues,'" *Southern Folklore Quarterly* 25, no. 4 (December 1961): 231.

Carters were children, though its vision may have burned brighter in the rural South or Midwest than anywhere else in the nation. Songs about wandering boys, abandoned mothers, dying orphans, and forsaken lovers had a special poignancy for people who saw the stable world of their parents disintegrating around them. The paeans to the "Homestead on the Farm," the "Little Village Church Yard," or "The Little Poplar Log House" became increasingly meaningful as such nostalgic symbols of rural innocence and security receded farther and farther into memory. The Carters themselves surely knew the pangs of parting and family dissolution; A. P. and Sara separated in 1932 and divorced in 1933. They sang together for ten years after they parted as husband and wife.

The emphasis on home and mother and old-fashioned morality lived in country music long after the Carter Family dissolved their commercial partnership. It is a self-image that the country-music industry has carefully cultivated, and to which it has resolutely clung (albeit with increasing difficulty). The radio barn dances, to cite one example, were designed to recreate the atmosphere of wholesome family fun and entertainment associated with village or rural life. Radio, as a matter of fact, reached more Americans than did phonograph recording, and hillbilly entertainers therefore won a much wider public through the broadcasting medium than through any other forum. Rural-flavored variety shows seemed peculiarly appropriate for those radio stations located in farm states, or which reached out to far-flung rural areas: WSB, which covered a large portion of the deep rural South; WBAP, which could be heard far outside its home base in Fort Worth; and various farm-town stations like WNAX in Yankton, South Dakota, and KMA in Shenandoah, Iowa, both owned by seed companies which recognized the commercial potential of homespun music.

The barn dance name, if not the explicit format, was introduced to radio by WBAP as early as 1923. The first barn dance show to experience any kind of longevity or national recognition, however, was the one broadcast by WLS in Chicago. WLS inaugurated a hillbilly show on about April 19, 1924, only one week after the station went on the air. WLS (World's Largest Store) was a Sears-Roebuck station from its beginning until September 1928, when it was purchased by the *Prairie Farmer* newspaper. From the very first it aimed many of its broadcasting features at rural and small-town listeners in the Midwest. The first WLS barn-dance show got off to a rather inauspicious beginning on the small mezzanine of the Sherman Hotel in Chicago where a group of country-style fiddlers alternated with the popular Isham Jones dance band from the College Inn. The identities of the country musicians are not recalled, although it is believed that fiddler Tommy Dandurand from Kankakee, Illinois, was accompanied by banjoist Jesse Doolittle. The music, which was made doubly realistic by the square dance calls of Tom Owen, elicited hundreds of requests for fiddle tunes over the course of the next few days. This humble beginning on April 19 ultimately led to the development of the popular *National Barn Dance*.

Throughout its long history (it did not really come to an end until 1968, after having been broadcast on WGN in Chicago for about seven years), the *National Barn Dance* had a broader musical perspective than most country shows. From the time of its inception in 1924 the *Barn Dance* featured a high proportion of sentimental pop tunes and "heart songs" along with country and folk music. Although criticized by some observers, the inclusion of old-fashioned pop music was natural in that, to most midwesterners, such songs as "Down by the Old Mill Stream" were the closest approximations of folk music that they knew. These songs were the songs of their youth, and they remained basic ingredients of the *Barn Dance* long after performers from the South and West brought their mountain and cowboy tunes to the Chicago radio show. Fiddle bands and balladeers appeared from the very beginning, but often in conjunction with performers of old-time pop and standard melodies. Organist Ralph Waldo Emerson played such songs as "Silver Threads among the Gold" while Ford and Glenn (Ford Rush and Glenn Rowell), the Maple City Four Quartet, and Bill O'Connor (the Irish Tenor) sang sentimental melodies and novelty tunes from earlier years. The two most famous singers of "heart songs" ever to appear on the *Barn Dance* were Henry Burr and Grace Wilson. Burr did not join the *Barn Dance* until 1934, but he came with a well-established reputation as a tenor who had performed extensively on the theater and concert circuits since World War I.

Grace Wilson, a popular contralto, was born in Owesso, Michigan, on April 10, 1890. She became a professional singer in 1906 in musical comedy and vaudeville. Between this time and her radio debut in 1922 on WTAS in Elgin, Illinois, she introduced such songs as "In the Shade of the Old Apple Tree" and "I'd Love to Live in Loveland with You." She already had a wide following, therefore, when she joined the *Barn Dance* in 1924. From then until her retirement in 1960, Grace Wilson remained one of the best-loved *Barn Dance* stars with her most popular rendition being "Bringing Home the Bacon."

Hillbilly entertainers gradually moved on to the show after 1925, although the noncountry performers—as evidenced by Grace Wilson's career—never left the program. Tommy Dandurand and his Barn Dance Fiddlers were there from the very beginning, and southern performers began to appear in 1925, when Chubby Parker, a singer and banjoist from Kentucky, brought such songs as "Stern Old Bachelor" and "Little Old Sod Shanty" to the show. Bradley Kincaid brought his hound-dog guitar and storehouse of old-time songs to the *Barn Dance* in 1926. Missouri-born Luther Ossenbrink, who billed himself as Arkie the Woodchopper, came up from KMBC in Kansas City in 1929; he was still on the *National Barn Dance*, singing his mountain, country, and cowboy ballads, when the show was dropped from WLS in 1960. His tenure on the show was second only to that of Grace Wilson.

The modern-day giant among country-music radio shows, the *Grand Ole Opry*, had a slightly later beginning than the WLS program and, for a number of years, had a lesser influence and popularity. The *Grand Ole Opry* was the brainchild of George D. Hay, a native of Attica, Indiana. Hay became involved in radio in Memphis in 1923, after having been a popular columnist for the *Memphis Commercial-Appeal*. Within a year he had moved to WLS in Chicago, where he became one of the most popular announcers in America (according to a *Radio Digest* poll). Calling himself the "Solemn Old Judge," and blowing blasts from a steamboat whistle, Hay helped to give the new *Barn Dance* show an authentic, homey atmosphere. By November 9, 1925, he had moved once more, this time to the brand-new station in Nashville, Tennessee, WSM, which was owned by the National Life and Accident Insurance Company. As its new station director, Hay soon began trying to steer WSM toward the successful rural format he had witnessed earlier in Chicago. Although there was a rather strong bias against rural music among the Nashville upper crust (who gloried in the city's reputation as "the Athens of the South") and a similar distaste among WSM's directors, Hay was permitted to make his experiments. The National Life and Accident Insurance Company sold weekly policies to working-class people, and its managers eventually recognized the commercial possibilities of old-time music even if they could not always see its artistic qualities.

On November 28, 1925, Hay launched a hillbilly radio show, the *WSM Barn Dance*, with only two entertainers, a seventy-seven-year-old fiddler named Uncle Jimmy Thompson and his niece, Eva Thompson Jones, who accompanied him on piano. Uncle Jimmy was a hard-living, hard-drinking man from LaGuardo, Tennessee, whose repertory of tunes extended back to the antebellum era. He had spent some time in vaudeville and had participated in fiddle contests all over the South, particularly in Texas, where he had lived for ten years and had picked up the long-bow style associated with that state. At his WSM debut, Uncle Jimmy was seated in a comfortable chair in front of an old carbon microphone. At the end of an hour, Hay asked the old fiddler if he was tired of playing, and Uncle Jimmy replied: "Why, shucks, a man don't get warmed up in an hour. I just won an eight-day fiddling contest down in Dallas, Texas, and here's my blue ribbon to prove it."[12] Uncle Jimmy claimed to know a thousand tunes, and he evidently wanted to be given a chance to play all of them.

The fiddle playing brought an immediately favorable response, and telegrams and letters requesting tunes poured into the station. As a result,

12. George D. Hay, *A Story of the Grand Ole Opry* (Nashville: privately published, 1953), p. 1.

Uncle Jimmy, his niece, and Hay carried on for an hour each Saturday night for several weeks. This small group did not long remain the total personnel of the *Barn Dance* show. As George Hay later recalled, "after three or four weeks of this fiddle solo business, we were besieged with other fiddlers, banjo pickers, guitar players, and a lady who played an old zither."[13] Most anyone who could perform was accepted; the entertainers (mostly from the Middle Tennessee region) performed without pay, and the performances were given without commercials. The musicians for the most part were amateurs who worked as farmers and laborers during the week and then performed at WSM on Saturday night. Hay zealously worked to preserve the informal, down-home atmosphere of the shows, and he constantly admonished the musicians to keep things "down to earth," while he also gave the string bands names that seemed appropriate to the rustic image: Possum Hunters, Clod Hoppers, Fruit Jar Drinkers, etc.

As was common on nearly all early radio stations, the early WSM shows emphasized instrumental music. The first old-time string band to be featured was Dr. Humphrey Bate and the Possum Hunters. Dr. Bate, a well-educated physician, surgeon, and harmonica player from Sumner County, Tennessee, led a group which included his thirteen-year-old daughter, Alcyone, who played the piano. Dr. Bate was no stranger to radio when he joined WSM on October 24, 1925; he had appeared on WDAD in Nashville over a year previously.

Shortly after the arrival of Bate's group, three similar string bands joined the regular Saturday night broadcast. These were the Crook Brothers, the Gully Jumpers, and the Fruit Jar Drinkers. Following not far behind these groups was a brother team from the rural area around Franklin, Tennessee, Kirk and Sam McGee. Sam was one of the finest finger-style guitarists of the early period, known especially for his renditions of songs like "Railroad Blues" and "Buck Dancer's Choice." Although the McGee boys were raised in a family that often played string music (their father was an old-time fiddler), Sam did not become interested in the guitar until shortly before World War I, when he heard it being played by black street musicians in Perry, Tennessee. From that time forward, although he also played the five-string banjo competently, McGee's chief instrument was the guitar, which he put to proficient use in 1923 when he began touring with Uncle Dave Macon. By 1925 the two McGees were playing on *Grand Ole Opry* broadcasts and touring along with Dr. Bate and the Possum Hunters on *Opry*-sponsored shows on the RKO vaudeville circuit in the Midwest and Upper South.

Although the early *Grand Ole Opry* string bands did vocal numbers as well as instrumentals, none of them had a featured vocalist. Obed "Dad" Pickard came as close as anyone to being a star singer. Pickard was a mas-

13. Ibid.

ter of many instruments who eventually became the leader of the Pickard Family, a group which played on radio stations all over the United States (including WJR in Detroit, 1928). On WSM he specialized in such sentimental parlor tunes as "Kitty Wells" and "Bury Me Not on the Lone Prairie." The chief singing star of the *Grand Ole Opry*, before the coming of Roy Acuff, was a colorful five-string banjoist named Uncle Dave Macon. David Harrison Macon, a superbly gifted musician and comedian, was born between McMinville and Smartt, Warren County, Tennessee, on October 7, 1870. The musical education that would one day make him such a versatile performer began when his parents moved to Nashville in 1873 and opened a boarding house that catered to theatrical people. At an early age he learned songs, stories, and instrumental techniques from the colorful vaudeville and circus personalities who passed through the city. One performer to whom he paid special tribute was Joel Davidson, a circus comedian and banjoist who fired young Dave's resolve to become an entertainer. After Macon's marriage to Mathilda Richardson, he moved to a small farm in Kittrell, not far from Readyville, Tennessee, where, in 1900, he established the Macon Midway Mule and Wagon Transportation Company, which hauled material from Woodbury to Murfreesboro for the next twenty years. Uncle Dave frequently sang as he and his team slowly plodded toward their destinations. (The company is immortalized in Uncle Dave's recording of "From Earth to Heaven.")

Before 1918, music was no more than an amusing, but constant, diversion for Uncle Dave. He was known for miles around as a first-rate comic, an extraordinary finger-style banjoist, and a thorough professional in his approach to audiences and musical skills, but he had never performed for money. His performances at picnics and social functions had been strictly for fun. The commercial world of show business beckoned, however, in 1918, when he demanded fifteen dollars to play at a large party given by a farmer whom he believed to be a bit pompous. To Uncle Dave's great surprise, the farmer accepted. A talent scout for Loew's Theatre Circuit, who happened to be present at the party, approached Macon after the performance and booked him for a concert at a leading theater in Birmingham. From there he went on to bookings all over the South.

When Uncle Dave Macon joined the *Grand Ole Opry* in 1926, he was fifty-six years old; he had been a professional entertainer for eight years and a semiprofessional for much longer. He brought to the *Grand Ole Opry* both the versatile skills of a seasoned vaudeville and minstrel entertainer and a storehouse of folk material garnered from a host of southern sources. He also knew a wide variety of complex picking and frailing styles (some of minstrel origin) which modern banjoists might well envy. In his commitment to traditional styles he certainly deserves the praise given to him by Ralph Rinzler: "With the exception of the Carter Family, Uncle Dave preserved more valuable American folklore through his recordings

Uncle Dave Macon and his son Dorris. Courtesy of Ralph Rinzler.

than any other folk or country music performer."[14] Many of his songs also
came from minstrel, vaudeville, and nineteenth-century Tin Pan Alley
sources, or from the vast reservoir of southern gospel music. Others had
been picked up through the years from friends, relatives, or other folksingers, both black and white. Uncle Dave's recordings are important repositories of social commentary about politics, fashions, and the industrial
revolution that steadily moved across the South in the decades following
the Civil War: there are songs about life on a Georgia chain gang ("Way
down the Old Plank Road"); bitter labor upheavals in Tennessee in the
1880's occasioned by the use of convict labor in the coal mines ("Buddy,

14. Ralph Rinzler, notes to *Uncle Dave Macon*, Decca DL4760.

Won't You Roll down the Line"); Henry Ford's car and the Muscle Shoals project ("On the Dixie Bee Line"); political corruption in Tennessee ("Tennessee Gravy Train"); presidential politics ("Governor Al Smith"); evolution ("The Bible's True"); agricultural distress ("Farm Relief"); the Great Depression ("All In Down and Out Blues").

Uncle Dave's recording career began in 1924, when he and fiddler Sid Harkreader (his vaudeville companion for the previous two years) recorded fourteen sides for the Vocalion label in New York. His first session included some of his most popular songs, such as "Keep My Skillet Good and Greasy," as well as the first song to carry "hillbilly" in its title: "Hillbillie Blues." In later sessions beginning in 1926, he was generally supported by those talented brothers from Tennessee, Sam and Kirk McGee, and by old-time fiddler Mazy Todd. Their 1927 sessions resulted in some of the most exciting string band sounds heard on records; Uncle Dave's delight is clearly evident in his whoops, hollers, and shouted words of encouragement.

Until his death at the age of eighty-three, Uncle Dave Macon played with a zest and enthusiasm which few, if any, modern country entertainers can equal. He continued to record off and on up through 1938, being accompanied by the McGees, the Delmore Brothers, Smoky Mountain Glenn, and his son Dorris. His radio work and his appearances in tent shows and the like continued almost to his death in 1952. Although thoroughly professional in his approach to show business and in his musical skills, Macon was totally unaffected and unpretentious, and he loved to perform for the pure personal enjoyment of it. When the *Grand Ole Opry* began sending out tours in the late twenties and early thirties, Uncle Dave was a source of considerable consternation to the show's directors. Harry Stone, former manager of the *Grand Ole Opry*, said that Macon sometimes had to be restrained from giving the whole show away through his willingness to perform in hotel lobbies, free of charge, before the main program got underway. He cut a striking figure in his double-breasted waistcoat, high wing collar, bright red tie, and broad-brimmed hat of black felt. He looked the part of a merry country gentleman of the 1890's, and with his old-time songs, homey sayings, shouted enthusiasms, and boundless vitality, he captivated his audiences and recaptured the spirit of rural, small-town America that was about to be submerged by the sophistication and glamor of urban twentieth-century America.

The popularity of the WSM show necessitated its gradual enlargement. The program's cast had grown to about twenty-five when Uncle Dave Macon joined it, so WSM decided to build a much larger studio, Studio B, with a large plate-glass window through which spectators could watch. Soon the WSM executives decided to allow about fifty or sixty people to listen from within the studio. From this small beginning WSM gradually expanded the facilities for the show, first building an auditorium studio with a seating capacity of five hundred, and later renting the Hillsboro Theatre, which also proved to be too small for the program's fans. The show moved next to a large tabernacle in East Nashville, then on to the War Memorial Auditorium before finding a suitable location. In 1941 the show relocated to a converted tabernacle replete with church pews and a balcony dedicated as a Confederate memorial, the historic Ryman Auditorium. This "mother church of country music," originally built by Captain Thomas Ryman, a riverboat man, as a memorial to his religious conversion by the great evangelist Sam Jones, remained the home of the *Grand Ole Opry* until 1974, when the show moved to its present location at Opryland Park.

In 1927 announcer George D. Hay gave the *WSM Barn Dance* its present title of *Grand Ole Opry*. The program, then three hours long, followed NBC's *Musical Appreciation Hour*, conducted by Dr. Walter Damrosch. While introducing a number on one of his evening programs, Damrosch remarked that "while most artists realize that there is no place in the classics for realism, I am going to break one of my rules and present a composition by a young composer from Iowa. This young man has sent us his latest number, which depicts the onrush of a locomotive . . ." When the WSM country music show came on the air, Hay announced that while there was no room for realism in the classics, the following three hours would be devoted to nothing but realism. Then in an obvious, good-natured jibe at Damrosch, Hay introduced one of the show's most popular performers, Deford Bailey, a black harmonica player, who played a train song, "Pan American Blues," which had been inspired by the famous southern train that ran near Bailey's home. When the performance was over, Hay said, "For the past hour we have been listening to music taken largely from grand opera, but from now on we will present 'The Grand Ole Opry.'"[15] The name proved to be popular with the listeners and came to be the official title of the show.

In the years that followed, Hay introduced the show each Saturday night with his steamboat whistle and his warm command, "Let her go, boys." Deford Bailey did his country harmonica blues; Uncle Dave regaled the audiences with his wit and zestful songs; and Dr. Bate and the other old-time string bands kept the mood close to that of the hoedowns of rural America. But the mood of spontaneous simplicity could not last, because the barn dances had demonstrated that country music could sell. Judge Hay lived long enough to see his "down-to-earth" show become a national institution and the longest-lasting program on American radio. The popularity of the *Grand Ole Opry* and other barn dance shows presaged country music's coming commercial success—and its incorporation into the American popular culture mainstream.

15. Hay, *A Story of the Grand Ole Opry*, pp. 9–10.

The Singing Brakeman.

Jimmie Rodgers. Courtesy of JEMF.

3. The First Country Singing Star: Jimmie Rodgers

Country music's evolution as a star-oriented phenomenon, with traits increasingly national rather than local in scope, is largely the legacy of Jimmie Rodgers. One of the top Victor record sellers of the 1920's and the "father of modern country music," Rodgers introduced new techniques and styles to the music and inspired a legion of followers who sought to emulate their master. In his repertory of 111 recorded songs, Jimmie Rodgers exhibited his debt to the diverse strains that made up the South's musical culture. He recorded almost every type of song with which the rural southerner was familiar, but strangely only one religious piece. He may be most famous for the novel fusion which he introduced to country music, the "blue yodel," but neither the blues nor yodeling constituted the whole of his musical approach. To concentrate primarily upon his debt to black music, as is often done, would create a highly incomplete picture of Rodgers.

Jimmie Rodgers was a small-town southern boy who wanted very much to be a popular singer. As he reached manhood in the World War I years, the only show-business models available were entertainers associated with vaudeville and Tin Pan Alley. As recordings became available to him, they certainly included black performers, and like most young people of the time he could not have been unaffected by the jazz rhythms and blues music which flowed into the public consciousness. But as a singer he probably made few distinctions between musical forms, and he gravitated toward whatever types of songs Al Jolson, Harry Lauder, and other stage singers favored. When Rodgers ventured into music, the enthusiasm for hillbilly music had begun, and he was fated—because of his background and deep southern dialect—to be drawn into the new rural music business. It was a route that he could follow easily, and probably with no reluctance, because the vast panoply of American popular music on which he drew included the sentimental, blues, and bum songs which appealed to the hillbilly audience.

James Charles Rodgers was born in the rural Pine Springs Community just north of Meridian, Mississippi, on September 8, 1897. He was the son of Eliza Bozeman Rodgers and Aaron W. Rodgers, an extra gang foreman on the Mobile and Ohio Railroad. His mother died when he was about five or six years old, and his father was left with the prime responsibility of rearing him to manhood. Jimmie's debt to his father is verbalized in his great sentimental song "Daddy and Home." The young Rodgers had only an occasional encounter with formal schooling and learned what he knew in the "school of hard knocks," while following his father from place to place as he pursued his railroad duties. Aaron Rodgers' work as an extra gang foreman took him for extended periods to different cities in the South, including New Orleans, because it was the duty of the extra gang to travel by railroad car to those sections of the line that needed repairing. This kind of life, plus the experience of growing up in a succession of relatives' homes, introduced to Jimmie Rodgers a broader knowledge of life's varieties—both the exciting and the sordid—than most small-town southern boys had known.

Rodgers also grew up faster than the average youth. He went off on his own occasionally, but always writing scrawled postcards to let his relatives know where he was. He joined a medicine show at the age of thirteen and at fourteen began working with his dad's railroad crews. He stumbled into an early, unfortunate marriage on May 1, 1917, but was separated by fall. The marriage, though, resulted in a child and, eventually, an embarrassing and costly lawsuit over child-support payments. He knew very well the world of ramblers and rounders of which he sang.

Rodgers' association with railroading has always lent an air of romance to his life, and it contributed greatly to his later commercial success as a singer. The image of "the singing brakeman" was irresistibly appealing, particularly during the Great Depression, to millions of Americans, who could identify with an allegedly liberated and rambling life that they personally could not enjoy. Railroad work, however, is something that Rodgers did only by necessity, and not by choice. Even before tuberculosis robbed him of much of the strength necessary to do outside work, Rodgers sought the means—preferably through music—to escape the "romantic" profession. From the time he joined his father's extra gang until he retired from railroad work in 1925, Rodgers worked sporadically as a railroadman, often unemployed, living a hardscrabble life with his second wife, Carrie (whom he married in 1920), and often roaming throughout much of the United States looking for work. During his career he worked on lines all over the Southwest, usually as a flagman or brakeman, but the line he worked most was the New Orleans and Northeastern on the run between

Meridian and New Orleans. Rodgers became thoroughly conversant with the vocabulary and music of the railroad workers, a hardy breed of men that he was later to commemorate so well in his best-selling Victor records. As a wandering railroad man, he had the opportunity to sample many kinds of music, including the fragments of songs shouted out by black workers who traveled on the extra gang. We do not know where the song originated, but a line from his well-known "Muleskinner Blues"—"Hey, little water boy, bring that water 'round"—may very well have been inspired by the times when, as a teenager, he carried water to the black workers.

Through all his years as a railroad worker, Rodgers' thoughts were never far away from music. Among the many contributions made by biographer Nolan Porterfield is his demonstration that Rodgers tried hard to be a professional entertainer long before he made his first Victor records. He learned to play the banjo and guitar at a very early age and often entertained his fellow workers during lunch and rest breaks. In his off hours he occasionally played with black musicians down around Tenth Street in Meridian or for his favorite southern belles, who would gather in their well-chaperoned parlors to hear him play. During his teenage fling with the medicine show, he may have performed music, but there is no record of it. In 1923 he spent a few weeks with a tent-repertory show, Terrell's Comedians, playing the small towns between Hattiesburg, Mississippi, and New Orleans. His most sustained activity as a professional musician, before he left the railroad permanently in 1925, was with a trio composed of Slim Rozell (violin), Rodgers' sister-in-law, Elsie McWilliams (piano), and Rodgers on banjo, guitar, or mandolin. The trio played dance music and pop standards at fairs, picnics, and political rallies, and at a resort area north of Meridian called Lauderdale Springs. Rodgers apparently did not sing at all at these functions, but he obtained a touch of the show-business experience that would later prove to be invaluable; the experience also introduced him to a repertory of pop music that would one day appear with great frequency in his "hillbilly-oriented" recordings.

Rodgers embarked upon a full-fledged professional career in 1925 when he signed on as a blackface entertainer with a medicine show that toured the mountain and hill-country districts of the Upper South as well as southern Ohio and Indiana. This type of show-business experience—shared by so many other big-time country stars—helped to give him ease and confidence in front of audiences and further kindled his desire for stardom as he heard the people applaud and saw their delighted faces. After spending a brief period on the medicine-show circuit, he and Carrie went back to Geiger, Alabama, where they briefly operated a roadside café. He tried one last fling at railroading and then moved to the mountain resort city of Asheville, North Carolina, in search of a more healthful climate and of outlets for his entertainment ambitions. In Asheville, in about April

1927, he met a group of string musicians who called themselves the Ten-neva Ramblers (Jack Pierce and the Grant Brothers, Jack and Claude). Jimmie was already appearing occasionally on WWNC in Asheville, and he won the boys over with the visions of a radio career. They reconstituted themselves as the Jimmie Rodgers Entertainers and began making scattered personal appearances, as well as singing occasionally on WWNC. The connection with WWNC did not last long, and by June 1927 Rodgers had gone to work as a city detective, working at that job and performing locally until Ralph Peer came south on one of his recording ventures in late July.

Peer had gone into business for himself as a music publisher, but had worked out a relationship with Victor in which he selected artists and supervised hillbilly recordings for the company. In return, his publishing firm owned the copyrights, and Peer was compensated by the royalties resulting from the compositions he had selected for recording (the basis for the Peer-Southern complex). Under this new arrangement he made a survey of various southern cities and decided to make initial recordings for Victor in Atlanta, Savannah, Memphis, and Bristol. As noted in the previous chapter, newspaper publicity generated extensive excitement about Peer's visit to Bristol. In Peer's words, "This worked like dynamite and the very next day I was deluged with long-distance calls from the surrounding mountain regions. Groups of singers who had not visited Bristol during their entire lifetime arrived by bus, horse and buggy, trains, or on foot."[1]

One of those singers who made a hopeful long-distance call was Jimmie Rodgers, who came down from Asheville with the little string band which he called his "hillbilly ork." After reaching Bristol, Rodgers was disappointed to learn that the Jimmie Rodgers Entertainers had decided to try their luck at recording without him. Disagreeing over proper billing, and probably chafing at the loss of identity caused by the association with Rodgers, the group resurrected their old name, the Tenneva Ramblers, and made a number of important recordings, including an interesting variant of "In the Pines" called "The Longest Train."

When Rodgers appeared before Peer, it was "just him and his guitar," and he nervously sang a couple of old songs that he had earlier tried out on his WWNC audiences. In most of his Asheville performances, Rodgers' song choices had usually been the current hits, the compositions of New York publishers. But in his first recording session he chose two deeply sentimental old-time tunes for his first renditions: "The Soldier's Sweetheart" and an old lullaby, recorded earlier by Riley Puckett, called "Sleep, Baby, Sleep." He yodeled on "Sleep, Baby, Sleep," thus inaugurating a fashion that was to endure in country music for at least a decade.

1. Ralph Peer, "Discovery of the First Hillbilly Great," *Billboard* 65, no. 20 (May 16, 1953): 20.

Rodgers' first quarterly royalty check reached the discouraging total of twenty-seven dollars, and the fame he had long sought still seemed to be very far away. By the end of 1927, however, his popularity had begun to mount, and the Victor people realized that they had signed a potential star. Rodgers was soon permitted another recording session, this time at the Victor studios in Camden, New Jersey. At this second session he recorded the first of his twelve blue yodels (popularly known as "T for Texas," but listed by Victor as simply "Blue Yodel"). Backed with Kelly Harrell's composition "Away Out on the Mountain," it became the hillbilly hit of the year, and at last fame and success were at hand. In its structure the song resembled the typical blues form, but at the conclusion of the third line, Rodgers lifted his voice to a higher octave and uttered the blue yodel that made him the most famous hillbilly star in history.

Between 1927 and 1933, Jimmie Rodgers became a household name in thousands of rural and small-town American homes, particularly in his native Southland. His recording popularity was augmented by vaudeville and tent-show appearances and by radio performances throughout the southern region. Rodgers' barnstorming potential was greatly hindered by his affliction with tuberculosis, the grim disease which drained his strength and forced him to seek a permanent home in the drier regions of Central Texas.

He made no tours in the northern United States, although schedules for such appearances were sometimes planned. Concerts in Washington, D.C., in August 1928—at the Earle Theatre, on WTFF, and at local social functions—were about as close as he ever got to the Mason-Dixon line. WTFF announcer Ray McCreath became Rodgers' manager for a short time but was never able to secure the national bookings that he sometimes talked about.

By the time he began his first southern vaudeville tour on November 5, 1928, Rodgers was sporting at least two images, that of the Singing Brakeman and that of the Blue Yodeler. He no doubt thought of himself as a vaudevillian, or as a popular singer in the broadest sense of the term (an eclectic musician who was wedded to no one style), but his song material was closest to the hearts of working-class people and not to the urban middle class who set the standards of pop music. His vaudeville tour carried him into Norfolk, Atlanta, Memphis, New Orleans, and Houston, where he generally received top billing and appeared to favorable reviews. When he completed his tour of the circuit in December, he joined a tent-repertory show, the Paul English Players, working out of Mobile, Alabama. The employment of a "name attraction" for limited engagements was said to be something new in the tent-rep line, and Rodgers' appearances doubled the company's business. Rodgers remained with the English Players until March 1929 and traveled with them from Mobile to Texas. Working only as a concert feature, about fifteen to twenty minutes a night, he earned $600 a week. His performances greatly increased the company's receipts and stimulated the sale of Victor records, since the show had tieups with Victor dealers in all of the towns visited.

Rodgers made still another vaudeville tour, for RKO Interstate, from May to July 1929 in theatres extending from Atlanta to Oklahoma. In the years that followed he made occasional solo performances, usually in lodge halls, schoolhouses, or auditoriums, and occasionally on radio, and traveled with assorted tent-show groups similar to the Paul English organization. He appeared regularly with such groups unless his health interfered, or until Ralph Peer called him away for another recording session. With each show Rodgers was usually the major attraction. During the spring and summer of 1930 he traveled with the W. I. Swain show, Hollywood Follies, through Louisiana and Texas. The show carried a number of acts, including an Irish comedian, a Hawaiian group, and a blues singer, but, according to *Billboard*, Jimmie Rodgers was the "outstanding hit of the show." The Swain show drew capacity crowds during its one-night stands in Texas, but attendance declined sharply in Kansas and Oklahoma. By this time, though, Rodgers had become ill and had left the show in mid-May.

During the last few years of his life Rodgers made most of his appearances in Texas. At Kerrville, in the heart of the Texas hill country, he built in May 1929 a $25,000 home, "Blue Yodeler's Paradise." He lived there with his wife, Carrie, and daughter, Anita, until mounting medical costs and luxurious living necessitated the sale of the house. Thereafter, until his death in 1933, he and his family lived in a much more modest cottage in San Antonio.

In the spring of 1931 he and Will Rogers conducted a benefit tour in Northeast Texas for the victims of a recent Red River flood. The pair also gave a number of charity performances throughout the Southwest for the unemployed. In March of that year he journeyed to Austin, where he was appointed an honorary Texas Ranger; he took great pride in this honor and eventually composed a song called "The Yodeling Ranger." When the Texas Rotary Club held its statewide meeting in Austin in March 1931, Rodgers appeared as the featured attraction. Upon receiving an invitation from the chairman of the program committee, Adjutant General William W. Sterling, Rodgers responded with these words "I am ready and happy to obey any order from my superior officer."[2] The audience gave his performance an enthusiastic reception, and at the conclusion he presented Ranger chief Sterling with one of his fabulous Weyman guitars, worth an estimated $1,500.

The last year and a half of Rodgers' life was filled with recording dates, radio shows, tent theatre appearances, costly medical treatments, a law-

2. William W. Sterling, *Trails and Trials of a Texas Ranger* (privately published, 1959), pp. 189–191.

suit with his first wife, and never-realized plans for nationwide tours. During the winter of 1931–1932 he appeared with Leslie E. Kell's tent theatre company in an extended engagement in Houston and a shorter one in San Antonio. The Kell Company was a variety show which featured, in addition to Rodgers, a fan dancer named Holly Desmond.

Rodgers and Kell made elaborate plans for an extensive tour which would carry them through the Northwest, British Columbia, eastward through Canada to New York, and finally back to Texas. The plan was never completed, however, because Rodgers left Kell in March 1932 to join the J. Doug Morgan show for its spring and summer tent tour in East Texas. During his off-months Rodgers remained in San Antonio, where he became a twice-weekly feature on station KMAC. Here he remained until an intensification of his disease necessitated his entry into the Baptist Hospital in Houston in January 1933. He remained in the Houston hospital for about a month, charming the nurses and keeping Mickey, his Boston terrier, beside his bed despite the hospital restrictions banning dogs. He returned to San Antonio in February 1933, partially recuperated and with orders to remain in the Alamo City for at least a six-month rest. But, despite the doctors' orders and despite a prediction made two years earlier by Dr. I. W. Cooper that he could not live longer than two years, Rodgers decided to make a recording trip to New York in May 1933, probably knowing that it would be his last.

His last recording session is one of the most heart-rending episodes in show-business history. He had become so weak that the Victor company provided him a special cot in a room near the studio. At the conclusion of each recorded take, he lay down until he regained adequate strength for another performance. He recorded almost to the very end; his last session was on May 24, two days before he succumbed in the Taft Hotel. On the day of his death he went to Coney Island on a sight-seeing tour with his private nurse, Cora Bedell, and while there suffered an attack of spasms. He died that night in his hotel room, far from his native home and family. When his death train pulled into Meridian, Mississippi, late at night, the engineer, Homer Jenkins, blew the whistle in a long moaning wail that grew in intensity as the train rolled toward the terminal station. This was the train crew's tribute to the "Singing Brakeman" who now lay in a coffin in one of the baggage cars.

In assessing Jimmie Rodgers' influence on American folk music and on a later generation of commercial performers, one can safely use the adjective "phenomenal." Indeed, one would be hard pressed to find a performer in the whole broad field of pop music—whether it be Al Jolson, Bing Crosby, or Frank Sinatra—who has exerted a more profound and recognizable influence on later generations of entertainers. No one as yet has made a full-scale attempt to determine how many of his songs have gone into popular or folk tradition, and there is no way to measure the number of people, amateur and professional, who have been inspired by him to take up the guitar or try their luck at singing. With the emergence of Jimmie Rodgers, country folk finally had one of their own to use as a model—a personification of the success that might be possible in the world of music, and the possessor of a magnetic style and personality that might be used to attain that success. Rodgers singlehandedly originated a new tradition in country music and inspired a host of followers—most of whom heard him only on records—to become country musicians. The center of country-music activity shifted more heavily toward the Southwest, and a new generation of hillbilly entertainers, captivated by Rodgers' blue yodels, his unorthodox guitar style, and his intriguing songs, began to dominate the country-music scene. The new group of performers arising in the late twenties and early thirties would have repertories significantly different from those of the earlier hillbillies and would perform them in styles that were often direct imitations of Jimmie Rodgers. The record companies, of course, searched for Rodgers sound-alikes who could be competitive with him, and Victor immediately looked for successors when Rodgers died. Ernest Tubb estimated that perhaps 75 percent of modern country-music performers were directly or indirectly influenced to become entertainers either through hearing Rodgers in person or through his recordings. Rodgers' popularity and influence, moreover, were not confined to this country. His records sold widely in various parts of the British Empire, where they were introduced and favorably reviewed as early as 1928, and John Greenway found that in Australia "all contemporary country singing is clearly attributable to Rodgers' compositions, themes and styles." Greenway found, too, that Rodgers' popularity reached beyond the confines of the English-speaking world—one of his correspondents reported seeing a large collection of the "Blue Yodeler's" records in an Eskimo's hut near Point Barrow.[3]

No other hillbilly star of the twenties rivaled Rodgers in popularity. He was one of the few country performers to receive any notice in the major trade publications, and his records, which sold more widely than those of any other hillbilly, exceeded the sales of most pop performers in the Victor catalogue. The actual sales figures of Rodgers' records are unknown, and as a result "guesses" have ranged as high as twenty million. Writing in 1979, Nolan Porterfield estimated that the figure (from the issuance of Rodgers' first record to then) was closer to twelve million. He further asserted that the Blue Yodeler had only one million-seller, "Blue Yodel No. 1," and that the second-highest seller, "Waiting for a Train," sold in the neighborhood of 365,000 copies. Most crucially, Porterfield pointed out that total record sales are irrelevant and are an imprecise measure of Rodgers' popu-

3. John Greenway, "Folk Song Discography," *Western Folklore* 21, no. 1 (January 1962): pp. 71–72.

larity. Rodgers' records were played repeatedly until their labels were bare and scratchiness obscured their sound, and they were lent to neighbors and friends and made the center of neighborhood gatherings.

Rodgers' lifestyle, or public perceptions of it, was almost as important to his success as was his music. He spent money freely, before his career ever began and after his record sales declined during the Depression. Big cars, jewelry, guitars, expensive clothes, and the "mansion" in Kerrville were all lavishly consumed even as his medical expenses mounted. His extravagant tastes made him all the more alluring to his fans; such behavior, after all, was expected of a "star," and especially condoned when one was deemed to be as free-hearted as Jimmie with friends and down-and-outers. The light-hearted demeanor he displayed in the face of what was then terminal illness brought only admiration. Rodgers sang "TB Blues" and "Whipping That Old TB" even as he succumbed to its effects. His fans marveled at his ability to hit those high-yodeling notes despite his affliction, or they theorized that, somehow, his lung-crippling disease contributed to the making of his yodels. Jimmie's liking for good whiskey was also magnified by his fans, and many people still have favorite stories about the time he visited the local bootlegger. It was not always understood that alcohol helped to numb the pain that was constantly with him, or that he could not possibly have consumed the amounts attributed to him. Jimmie did not have the health or stamina to be the kind of rounder that his personal image suggested or that public myth would have him be. Nor did his songs necessarily mirror the reality of his life, even though he liked to give the impression that they did—an affectation that his fans heartily endorsed. If he sang "I've Ranged, I've Roamed, and I've Travelled," his listeners were sure he had done just that. When he sang "Lullaby Yodel," many people were convinced that he was singing to an estranged wife who had taken their child with her (even though his wife's sister wrote the song!). "High Powered Mama," of course, just had to be about that same wife who "just wouldn't leave other daddies alone." Rodgers would not be the last country singer whose public image and personal music style were strongly intermeshed.

Any discussion of Jimmie Rodgers' remarkable popularity would be incomplete without at least some attempt to analyze his distinctive performing style. Although he recorded with a diverse assortment of instrumental accompaniment—violins, banjoes, ukeleles, Hawaiian steel guitars, and jazz bands—his personal appearances were almost always made in solo fashion, just Jimmie and his guitar. For his stage appearances he generally dressed in a white or tan lightweight suit and sported a jauntily cocked straw sailor hat (he often posed for publicity pictures in a cowboy costume or railroad brakeman's attire but seldom dressed this way during a performance). He looked and acted the part of a young man-about-town out for an evening of pleasure. He would put his foot on a chair, cradle his guitar across his knee, and captivate his audiences with a selection of both rakish and sentimental tunes that generally consumed no more than twenty minutes. In a voice unmistakably southern, he kidded his audiences in a whimsical fashion and beguiled them with songs that seemed to catalogue the varied memories, yearnings, and experiences of small-town and rural Americans: nostalgia for the departed mother or "the old southern town" of childhood; pathos for the homeless hobo dying in a boxcar or trying to bum a southbound freight; unrequited love; laughter for the rakes and rogues who "loved and left them" in every town; and a variety of other emotions with which most people could identify.

As he sang and recorded, he teased both himself and his accompanying musicians with a running patter of commentary. As an accompanist took an instrumental break, Rodgers would occasionally say something like "Play that thing, boy," or he would say to himself or no one in particular, "Sing them blues, boy," "Hey, hey, it won't be long now," or "Hey, sweet mama." The total effect of his performances was an air of effortless informality, marked by a very personal approach which insinuated its way into the hearts of listeners, making them feel that the song was meant just for them. His voice—a nasal tenor distinguished by the lazy drawl of the Mississippi Black Belt—was capable of adjusting itself to almost any kind of song—a spirited railroad piece, a rollicking blues number, or a tender, plaintive lullaby. He sang them all with sincerity and in the particular spirit in which they were written. When his audiences of railroad workers, truck drivers, laborers, farmers, and small-town people heard his songs, they recognized him as one of their own, and the deadening, bleak years of the Depression were thereby made more endurable.

Jimmie's records popularized a number of sounds and styles, both ephemeral and permanent, that made their way into country music. He did not introduce the steel guitar to country music, but his records certainly popularized the instrument. Ellsworth T. Cozzens played what was then called a Hawaiian steel guitar on Rodgers' second session of February 1928, and it appeared periodically in other sessions, played by such men as Cliff Carlisle, John Westbrook, and Joe Kaipo (Kaipo was an authentic Hawaiian). Jazz sounds appeared in his recording sessions as early as October 1928, and he was joined in a historic session in Hollywood in July 1930 by Louis Armstrong on trumpet and Lillian Armstrong on piano. The jazz style did not immediately win the day in country music, but such sounds heard on Rodgers' records may very well have influenced the styles of young musicians who idolized the Blue Yodeler.

Rodgers himself influenced the style and content of country music through his singing and choice of songs. His unique contribution to American folksong, the blue yodel, had the most immediate impact on country music. Blues singers and yodelers had preceded Rodgers in American entertainment, but nothing corresponding exactly to the blue-yodel song had been collected in American folklore. As a Mississippian, Rodgers could not have avoided contact with the blues in some form. He worked as a railroadman during the years when the blues form was originating, and, as a waterboy for black construction groups, he accumulated maverick blues fragments and work-song stanzas which he eventually incorporated into his own songs. As an inveterate record buyer, the young Rodgers would have had ample opportunities to sample the blues records that began to appear in great profusion after 1920. We do not know how much Rodgers borrowed, or how much he created (song fragments introduced by him may very well have moved into the repertories of black musicians). But one thing is certain, he did much to inspire an interest in the blues in at least a generation of country musicians.

If Rodgers' introduction to the blues can be readily understood, the antecedents of his yodeling cannot so easily be discerned. One can posit the existence of a number of possible folk ancestors of the yodel, any one of which might have influenced him. Hollering, for example, has a venerable history in the South as an accompaniment of work, as a means of communication, and as an emotional release. Street cries would have been familiar to Rodgers through his residence in New Orleans, and even the Mexican *grito* and the lonesome cowboy wail might have wafted into his consciousness during his wanderings in the Southwest. As a railroadman he might have been inspired to recreate vocally the distinctive locomotive whistles that reverberated across America in those pre-diesel days. Yodeling, though, had been quite common in American entertainment before Rodgers combined the practice with the blues. Black-face minstrels experimented with yodeling from at least 1847, when Tom Christian introduced the technique into a minstrel routine. The minstrels may have borrowed the yodel from folk sources or, as appears more likely, they may have picked it up from Tyrolese minstrels who toured widely in the United States during the mid-nineteenth century. Yodelers began to appear on recordings in the 1890's and were fairly common in vaudeville before World War I. Rodgers was even preceded as a yodeler in country music by Riley Puckett, who recorded, complete with yodel, "Rock All Our Babies to Sleep" (Columbia 107-D), in 1924.

Regardless of its origin, Jimmie Rodgers fashioned the blue yodel into a distinct form which captivated his listeners and stimulated a new generation of hillbilly performers. As Alan Lomax has said, "Jimmie's yodeling songs sounded as if they might have been composed by a lonesome Texas cowboy or a hobo kicked off a freight in Tucson or Albuquerque."[4] Rodgers' yodels expressed a variety of emotions, ranging from the nostalgic moan of "Daddy and Home" to the blue lament of "Never No Mo' Blues" and the spritely yodel of "My Little Lady."

4. Alan Lomax, *Folk Songs of North America* (New York: Doubleday and Company, 1960), p. 281.

The popularity of the Rodgers yodel and of his blues renditions should not obscure his multifaceted repertory. He recorded almost every conceivable type of song—serious, humorous, maudlin, religious, risqué, and rowdy. There were railroad songs like "The Southern Cannonball" and "Waiting for a Train," "rounder" tunes like "Frankie and Johnny" and "My Rough and Rowdy Ways," risqué numbers like "Pistol Packin' Papa," lullabies like "Sleep, Baby, Sleep," cowboy songs like "When the Cactus Is in Bloom," hobo melodies like "Hobo Bill's Last Ride," and a large number of sentimental songs depicting semireligious, nostalgic, and romantic themes. Sentimental love tunes were quite popular in the twenties, and in his recording of such songs as "My Carolina Sunshine Girl" and "Old Pal of My Heart" Rodgers performed the same type of item that his friend Gene Austin was recording for the popular-music audience. In fact, Jimmie Rodgers was the first person to record and publicly perform "The One Rose," a song which has gained its most lasting fame in popular music. Rodgers' own tastes seemed to run toward such sentimental and melancholy tunes as "Daddy and Home," which evoked memories of "an old southern town" and the only parent he had ever known. His sentimental songs have had a more lasting effect on country entertainers than have his other offerings. Blue yodels, or songs similar to them, were performed for a few years after his death but are a rarity in country music today. Many of his other songs, however, have made an enduring impression. Love songs are now predominant in country music, and even the very sentimental and seemingly dated "Miss the Mississippi and You" was a major hit for country-pop singer Crystal Gayle in 1981.

Like many of the country performers who followed him, Rodgers wrote or arranged—usually in conjunction with his sister-in-law, Elsie McWilliams—a substantial number of the songs he recorded (his name, at least, appears on them). After he completed his third recording session in February 1928, Rodgers felt the need for fresh material. He contacted Elsie, his wife Carrie's oldest sister, who was then teaching in a Meridian business college. Elsie played the piano and had had musical training, and she already had acquired the reputation of local poet and songwriter with her writings for church and club periodicals. She contributed several songs to his June session that year and, according to her own memory, she wrote or helped to write altogether thirty-eight songs recorded by her brother-in-law (some of which do not bear her name on the composer credits). These include the beautiful sentimental ballads "Sailor's Plea," "I'm Lonely and Blue," and "Mississippi Moon," and novelty tunes like "My Little Lady" and "Everybody Does It in Hawaii." Elsie McWillams, however, was only one of several individuals who either wrote songs for Rodgers or collaborated on songs with him. The list includes Kelly Harrell ("Away Out on the Mountain"), Clayton McMichen ("Peach Picking Time in Georgia"), Shelly Lee Alley ("Traveling Blues"), Waldo O'Neal ("Hobo

Bill's Last Ride"), Carey D. Harvey ("Down the Old Road to Home"), and Andrew Jenkins, of "Floyd Collins" fame, who wrote such songs as "The Drunkard's Child" and "Ben Dewberry's Final Run." The most interesting of the writers, if not the best known, was Raymond Hall, a convict serving a life sentence in the Huntsville, Texas, state prison in 1929, when he sent Rodgers his first song, "Moonlight and Skies." Hall eventually contributed such songs as "Ninety-Nine Year Blues," "Gambling Polka Dot Blues," "TB Blues," and "The Southern Cannonball."

During his lifetime, Rodgers' popularity was greatest in the Southwest, particularly in his adopted state of Texas. His popularity there can be attributed in part to his residence and to his tours and radio broadcasts in that state. He became so closely identified with Texas that many people believed him to be a native, and even Alan Lomax has referred to him as a Texas brakeman. Rodgers took great pride in the Texas heritage, especially its romantic cowboy past. He must be given much of the credit for starting the trend toward the "singing cowboy" and the association of country music with the romantic "western" image. In the lyrics of his Texas songs Rodgers projected a conception of the West typical of that held by many easterners; that is, the depiction of the cowboy as a self-reliant, unselfish individual, free from the shackles and restraints of society, who whiled away the lonely hours with song. This attitude was expressed in "The Yodeling Cowboy" which asserts that "My cowboy life is so happy and free, out where the law don't bother me." And again in "The Yodeling Ranger," which describes "that old ranger band" singing carefree songs as it rides into dangerous situations. The Rangers were no doubt a courageous group, but it is doubtful that any of them went into a critical confrontation in as lighthearted a manner as that described in the song. Indeed, if Rodgers' philosophy had been the accepted one of the Texas lawmen, "that old ranger band" might well have vanished.

Rodgers' reverential and romantic concept of the West colored a variety of songs—such as "When the Cactus Is in Bloom"—which were the progenitors of a spate of Hollywood and Tin Pan Alley cowboy songs that flourished in the United States during the 1930's. It is significant that the man who did most to inaugurate the era of romantic cowboy songs in the coming years was Billy Hill, who wrote "Prairie Lullaby" for Rodgers in 1932 under the name of George Brown.

Whatever the source of his popularity, Rodgers made a profound impression on most of the young country boys and girls who heard him. Some of them went on to found country-music traditions of their own. Bill Bruner, a seventeen-year-old Western Union messenger boy in Meridian, Mississippi, substituted for Rodgers one night when the Blue Yodeler became too ill to fill an engagement with the Paul English Players. After this appearance in February 1929, Bruner began touring with tent shows as "The Singing Messenger Boy" and singing Jimmie Rodgers' songs in a yodeling style that was almost a carbon copy of Rodgers'. Until the mid-thirties, scores of other country singers, partly through their own inclinations and partly through the prodding of record producers, made records that bore strongly the imprint of the Rodgers style. Frankie Marvin appears to have been the first to "cover" a Rodgers song, but he was soon followed by Gene Autry, Jimmie Davis, Cliff Carlisle, Billy Cox, Rex Griffin, Jerry Behrens (who was called the "Dixie Blue Yodeler"), Dwight Butcher, Leon Huff, Tex Morton (in Australia), and a host of others. These singers used a style that not only employed the Rodgers repertory and yodel technique but borrowed his "hey hey hey" style of spoken commentary as well.

The Rodgers' influence was so pervasive in the period running roughly from 1928 to 1935 that not even the Carter Family was immune to it. Encouraged by Ralph Peer, Sara Carter yodeled on a few songs, and the entire Carter Family joined in at least two recording sessions with Rodgers. Gene Autry, known to most Americans today as a corporate executive and baseball magnate, got his initial start as a singer of Jimmie Rodgers songs. Equally important, because of his longevity within the country-music field, was Ernest Tubb, who idolized Rodgers and in his early performing years tried to recreate the identical sound of the Blue Yodeler. Although Tubb never met Rodgers personally, he can almost be considered his protégé because of the personal encouragement he received from Carrie Rodgers.

The Rodgers appeal was felt in far-off Canada. Motivated by reports of Rodgers' commercial success, the RCA Victor offices in Montreal decided to branch off into country music. The Canadian country-music industry dates, therefore, from the signing by Victor in 1932 of a young yodeler named Wilf Carter, a native of Nova Scotia, who gained his first musical inspiration from hearing a vaudeville yodeler who was an "added attraction" at a performance of *Uncle Tom's Cabin.*

The Rodgers influence was exerted more directly in the case of a young Nova Scotia farm boy who became so enthralled with Rodgers' recording of "Moonlight and Skies" that he resolved to become a country entertainer. He taught himself the guitar and sat by the phonograph for hours trying to master the Rodgers technique. His recording career began with Victor in 1936 when he recorded two of his own compositions, "Lonesome Blue Yodel" and "Prisoned Cowboy." Calling himself the "Yodeling Ranger," by the end of the 1930's he rivaled Wilf Carter for the title of Canada's most popular country performer. After his voice deepened, his yodeling facility began to vanish. He thereupon changed his performing title to "The Singing Ranger" and went on to become one of the greatest stars in the United States. This was Clarence E. "Hank" Snow, one of the few country singers who have continued the train-song tradition of Jimmie Rodgers.

Although the continuing careers of people like Hank Snow and Ernest Tubb are lasting memorials to the greatness of Jimmie Rodgers, the more immediate memorials were the songs of tribute that were recorded at the time of his death by such singers as Gene Autry, Bradley Kincaid, Dwight Butcher, and Leon Huff of the W. Lee O'Daniel and Light Crust Dough-boys' organization. Even more important, perhaps, as testimonies of his popularity are his recordings, which have continued to enjoy a wide sale in the many years since his death. Tribute lp's have periodically reintroduced his name and music to younger generations of fans. One of the greatest of these tributes was by Lefty Frizzell, a Texas singer who knew of Rodgers only through the old 78's that his parents had saved through the years.

The bulk of Jimmie Rodgers' career came during the bleak years of the greatest depression the United States has experienced. And his perfor-mances were concentrated in the area of greatest regional poverty, the South. Nevertheless, farmers and workers attended his concerts and bought his records when they became available. The notes to one of his memorial albums relate a legend concerning his popularity among hard-pressed Depression-era folk: "Legend has it that in his heyday, general-store customers would approach the counter and say: 'Let me have a pound of butter, a dozen eggs, and the latest Jimmie Rodgers record.'"[5] His records, of course, did not sell quite that universally, but his songs were widely known and cherished. When he died in 1933, he was un-known to the great majority of the American people, but in the South, where hillbilly music has always gained its most devoted following, Rodgers had become a hero to millions.

5. Roy Horton, notes to *Country Music Hall of Fame*, RCA Victor LPM-2531.

The Coon Creek Girls: *left to right*, Rosie Ledford, Violet Koehler, Lily May Ledford, Daisy Lange. Courtesy of Bob Pinson.

4. Country Music during the Depression

When Jimmie Rodgers died in 1933, one decade had elapsed since Fiddlin' John Carson made his first Okeh record and inaugurated country music's commercial history. The music had become a secure part of American entertainment and gave every indication of expanding both in popularity and in personnel.

In this one decade of commercial life, however, country music had already changed significantly in content and style. Traditional songs still appeared in great numbers in the radio and recording repertories of people like the Carter Family, and would continue to do so in the performances of newer musicians such as Mainer's Mountaineers, the Monroe Brothers, and the Blue Sky Boys. Increasingly, though, the old-time songs were learned from earlier commercial hillbilly performances, not from folk sources. A singer might learn a song like "The Fatal Wedding" from Mama, but Mama probably learned it from a Bradley Kincaid recording. Newly written compositions or arrangements of older songs gradually edged the traditional ballads aside. In a quest for fresh material, or the means to supplement the meager royalties awarded to recording artists, performers began writing many of their own songs. Led by Ralph Peer, the founder of Peer-International and Southern Music Company, and soon joined by other organizations such as M. M. Cole of Chicago, publishers appeared who concentrated heavily on the hillbilly market. Hillbillies in the 1930's routinely advertised their picture-songbooks on radio broadcasts and sold them by mail or at personal appearances. Some performers made a fairly good living just from the sale of their books.

Perhaps the most remarkable fact of country music's history during the Great Depression is that the music not only survived but expanded. The once-modest hillbilly business began to take shape as an industry with booking agents, promoters, advertising firms, publishers, music-licensing agencies, and motion picture representatives recognizing the gold that might be mined from this new territory. The music also took great strides toward national dissemination and eventual national homogenization during the Depression years: Sears-Roebuck catalogues advertised the same records in all sections of the country; powerful radio stations boomed the music out to city and farm alike; advertising agencies linked the music with such brand names as Alka-Seltzer and won new consumers for each; radio transcriptions permitted musicians to popularize themselves on stations far beyond their own geographical areas; touring units took the music to all sections of the country; and Hollywood films made many of the performers visible, while also introducing their music to millions of Americans who would not have heard it in any other format.

The record industry did not succumb to hard times, but it was forced into a massive reorganization. Only 6 million records were sold in 1932, a striking contrast to the 104 million that had been sold in 1927. Some of the pioneer hillbilly performers who had exhibited little commercial appeal were not permitted to record again. Some record companies followed the precedent of Victor, which established a cheaper subsidiary line, Bluebird, for its race and white country artists. The Okeh label (originally owned by the General Phonograph Corporation but bought by Columbia in 1926) was re-established in 1940 (after a six-year submergence) as Columbia's country and race subsidiary. Brunswick, one of the traditional leaders of the record business, had been taken over by the American Record Company, a producer of cheap discs sold by chain stores (under such labels as Melotone, Perfect, Banner, Oriole, and Romeo). Gennett, another old-time label owned by the Starr Piano Company, went out of business and sold its catalogues and labels to the newly formed American Decca Company. Sears-Roebuck and Montgomery Ward continued to issue their low-priced records (dubbed from the big companies' masters) aimed at the rural population.

American Decca was organized in 1934 and, with its thirty-five-cent records, immediately became one of the dominant phonograph companies. The issuance of Decca's inexpensive records encouraged other companies, which had generally charged seventy-five cents, to lower their prices, and a "platter war" began. Decca made a successful "raid" on the major companies and emerged with some of their leading performers; its most important acquisition was Bing Crosby.

Led by talent scout David Kapp, who traveled through America with a portable recording crew, Decca sought energetically to build a hillbilly catalogue. Although his travels ranged far and wide, Kapp's most productive efforts came in the Southwest: Louisiana, Oklahoma, Texas, and California. The thirties definitely saw a shift in the recording of hillbilly personnel from the Southeast to the Southwest, with a corresponding shift in the character of the music. The newer performers were more influenced by "western" styles, that is, by cowboy songs, ersatz and real, and by the eclectic, "hot dance" music that evolved in southwestern dance halls. The fiddle was as central to the music of the Southwest as it was to that of country music elsewhere, but some southeastern-based instruments, such as the five-string banjo, did not thrive among musicians in the West.

One of the significant aspects of recording in the thirties was that the utilization of hillbilly talent continued despite the economic woes of the phonograph industry. Throughout the Depression new hillbilly singers were continually discovered and placed on records. Statistics on record sales in the thirties are rare, but it is generally agreed that, compared with popular music figures, hillbilly sales were low. Paul Cohen, former director of Decca's country music division, estimated that a "hillbilly hit" during the Depression was one which sold a total of ten thousand copies. Nevertheless, hillbilly music was still considered to be a profitable venture for the companies because of the low expense of recording.

Whatever the appeal of recording—and hillbillies probably enjoyed the prestige of being "recording artists" even if they made no money from the venture—radio was probably more important to the budding country music industry. The 1930's marked the heyday of live radio entertainment in the United States. The typical hillbilly musician of that decade was an itinerant entertainer, moving from station to station, seeking sponsors and working a territory until it provided no further dividends. No region of the United States was alien to the country musician, but the greatest concentration of such performers could be found in the South, in the Midwest, and on the West Coast. Musicians played on the smallest stations imaginable, and at hours presumed to be "farmers' hours"—usually early in the morning or at noon—but the prize plums were the fifty-thousand-watt stations which blanketed many states with their coverage. The hillbillies performed their music, put on comic skits, read religious recitations, hawked their sponsors' wares, and sold their picture-songbooks or records. Personal appearances were generally made within the area covered by the broadcast and were negotiated through listener contacts. The hillbillies were sincere when they asked their audience to "Keep them cards and letters coming in." Furthermore, when the hillbilly musician signed off his program by saying, "That old clock on the wall says it's time to be getting out of here," he probably meant that literally, too. Quite often, he and his musicians had to pack up their instruments hastily, tie the bass fiddle on top of their car, and drive immediately to their next personal appearance.

Musicians played wherever they could get a hearing, but the Saturday-night barn dances broadcast on the high-powered stations provided the most security and exposure. The *Grand Ole Opry* expanded beyond its Middle Tennessee base during the Depression years and became an institution of South-wide significance. Indeed, the acquisition of a thirty-minute time slot on NBC in 1939 put the *Opry* well on the way to becoming a national phenomenon. The first step in the *Opry*'s elevation came in 1932, when WSM became a fifty-thousand-watt clear-channel station. The show could be heard distinctly all over the southeastern United States and, on most nights, at least as far west as Texas. Then in 1934 Harry Stone, who had become station manager four years earlier, established an Artists' Service Bureau designed to promote bookings for *Opry* performers, a decision which advertised WSM and the *Opry* while also furthering the professionalization of the musicians. Along with Vito Pellettieri, WSM's music librarian, who dealt with the problems of publishing and performance rights, Stone actively campaigned to increase the number of sponsors supporting the country show. As the *Grand Ole Opry* became more commercially attractive to musicians, performers began to join the show from areas outside the Middle Tennessee region. The Delmore Brothers (Alton and Rabon) did not have far to travel when they left their North Alabama home to join the *Opry* in 1933, but the Vagabonds, who came in 1931, relocated from Chicago, where they had performed both pop and country music. This smooth-singing trio (Herald Goodman, Curt Poulton, and Dean Upson) were probably the first true "professionals" (entertainers who did nothing but perform music) to join the *Grand Ole Opry*. Their arrival on the show, along with that of the Delmores, Roy Acuff (1938), and Bill Monroe (1939), greatly broadened the horizons of the *Opry* and put it well on the road toward being a haven for "stars."

As the *Grand Ole Opry* solidified its popularity in the South, the *National Barn Dance* was building a similar reputation in the Midwest. By the late thirties hillbilly music had become one of the staples of midwestern small-town entertainment, and WLS entertainers were making personal appearances all over the region. In a later discussion of the phenomenon, Lewis Atherton argued that hillbilly music was "surpassing even the minstrel show in popularity" and had become "the favorite of Main Street."[1] The *Barn Dance* experienced its greatest development in the seven or eight years immediately following 1930. In that period the show's cast expanded and the program's listening range increased to take in a major section of the United States. Some of the entertainers—like Gene Autry—stayed for only a couple of years; but others—like Lulu Belle and Scotty (Myrtle Cooper and Scott Wiseman)—remained for twenty years and more. One of the most important of the early groups was the Cumberland Ridge Runners, an assemblage of singers and musicians who came to the *Barn Dance* in 1930 from the areas around Mount Vernon and Berea, Kentucky. The creator and leader of the Ridge Runners was John

1. Lewis Atherton, *Main Street on the Middle Border* (Bloomington: Indiana University Press, 1954), p. 296.

Lair, an authority on and collector of old-time music, who eventually founded, at his home in Kentucky, the popular *Renfro Valley Barn Dance*. Several fine musicians, including Clyde "Red" Foley and Hugh Cross, appeared periodically with the Ridge Runners. The most tradition-oriented members, perhaps, were Slim Miller, an old-time fiddler and comedian; Doc Hopkins, who sang traditional ballads; Kentucky-born Linda Parker, an alumna of the Chicago pop music scene who nonetheless sang old sentimental favorites like "I'll Be All Smiles Tonight"; and Karl Davis and Harty Taylor, a mandolin and guitar duo, who introduced such well-known favorites as "I'm Just Here to Get My Baby Out of Jail."

Spurred by the *Barn Dance*'s popularity, WLS became the first radio station to construct a studio theatre. By 1932, with reservations being made seven months in advance for the show, WLS began looking for larger audience accommodations and, as a result, took over the Eighth Street Theatre, broadcast the program in two complete shows, and charged admission. The Eighth Street Theatre remained the home of the *National Barn Dance* for the next twenty-five years. Only one year after moving into the theatre, the *Barn Dance* moved well beyond its midwestern scope when Alka-Seltzer, in 1933, began the sponsorship of a one-hour Saturday night segment on NBC. This coast-to-coast radio coverage, augmented by the road-show units that left WLS in an ever widening arc after 1932, made the *National Barn Dance* the nation's leading country-music show in the years before the *Grand Ole Opry* became predominant.

The *Opry* and the *National Barn Dance* may have been the most important hillbilly radio shows, but they were far from being the only ones. Some were clearly spinoffs from the *National Barn Dance* and featured the same kind of variety entertainment heard on the Chicago show. The *Iowa Barn Dance Frolic*, for example, heard after 1932 on WHO in Des Moines, was a highly eclectic mixture of old-fashioned pop music, barbershop singing, novelty tunes, and folk music. Like the WLS show, the *Iowa Barn Dance Frolic* had a high percentage of non-southern performers, but it also included in the thirties occasional southern country musicians such as Texas Ruby and Zeke Clements.

Other barn dances were obviously inspired by the success enjoyed by the *Opry* and the *National Barn Dance* or were organized by men who had been affiliated with these shows. The *Boone County Jamboree*, broadcast on WLW in Cincinnati after 1938, was the brainchild of George Biggar, a former Farm and Market editor at WLS and producer-announcer for Sears-Roebuck Farm, Home, and Musical Programs on several stations. The famous *Renfro Valley* show was conceived by John Lair while he was working at WLS with the Cumberland Ridge Runners. The show went on the air in Cincinnati in 1937, but by November 4, 1939, had moved to Renfro Valley itself, a little village near Mount Vernon, Kentucky, where its cast played to an audience of five thousand or more each Saturday night.

The Crazy Barn Dance in Charlotte, North Carolina, was an example of a radio variety show organized by a business for merchandising purposes. Making its debut on WBT in Charlotte in 1934, the show was created and named by J. W Fincher, the southeastern representative of the Crazy Water Crystals Company of Mineral Wells, Texas. All of these barn dances played important roles in presenting country music to an ever-widening audience; none, however, was more instrumental in introducing the music to the Northeast than the *Wheeling Jamboree* in Wheeling, West Virginia. Inaugurated on WWVA on January 7, 1933, the show became a forum for the talents of some of country music's major entertainers during the following decades: Harry Auliffe (Big Slim, the Lone Cowboy), Jimmy Dickens, Wilma Lee and Stoney Cooper, Hank Snow, Hawkshaw Hawkins, and a balladeer from Pennsylvania, Doc Williams, who joined the show in 1937 and remained there for over forty years. WWVA's powerful directional signal beams north and east, easily blanketing much of Pennsylvania, New York, rural New England, and eastern Canada. Many northeasterners who later tried their hands at country music first became attracted to the music through the broadcasts of the *Wheeling Jamboree*.

In the dissemination of country music throughout the United States, no stations were more important than those along the Mexican border. These powerful X-stations (so-called because of their call letters) operated just across the border in Mexico, and could be heard quite clearly throughout much of the United States and even occasionally in Canada. The border stations operated on wattage that was as much as two or three times in excess of the maximum limit in the United States. This practice was condoned by the Mexican authorities presumably because of a prior snubbing of Mexico by its northern neighbors. The American and Canadian governments had divided between themselves the entire AM broadcast band, leaving neither Cuba nor Mexico any clear channels at all. Therefore, for many years Mexico rejected American protests about the border stations.

These stations, generally leased to American entrepreneurs, aimed their transmitters toward the United States and, operating on 100,000–150,000 watts, cut in on wavelengths used by U.S. and Canadian stations. With this powerful means of transmission, American advertisers were able to exploit their products throughout much of the United States. The border station era was inaugurated in October 1931, when Dr. John R. Brinkley's XER (changed to XERA in 1935) began operations with about 100,000 watts at Villa Acuña, Mexico. Born in North Carolina about 1885, Brinkley moved to Kansas in 1916 armed with a shrewd business wit and what many people considered to be a bogus medical license. He opened radio station KFKB in 1923 in Milford, Kansas, and made himself a political power in the state while also making the station one of the most popular in the nation. Brinkley's ticket to fame and wealth was his goat-gland opera-

The Cumberland Ridge Runners: *standing, left to right,* Slim Miller, Karl Davis, Red Foley, Harty Taylor; *seated,* John Lair, Linda Parker. Courtesy of George Biggar.

tion, designed to restore sexual potency to men, which was advertised on his station and performed in his hospital. In Kansas Brinkley had employed the services of hillbilly performers such as fiddler Uncle Bob Larkin. Brinkley's use of a hillbilly band in his races for governor of Kansas in 1930 and 1932 made him the predecessor of such famous hillbilly politicians as Texas' W. Lee O'Daniel and Louisiana's Jimmie Davis.

When the Federal Radio Commission refused renewal of his license, Brinkley moved to Del Rio, Texas, and became the first of the X-station entrepreneurs. Not only did he advertise his own medical remedies and the hospital which he built in Del Rio, he also pushed products of other United States businesses. In addition to the almost incessant advertising, the radio listener was given a steady diet of religious evangelists, hillbilly singers (mostly by transcription), and, on many occasions, right-wing politicians. Brinkley, on XERA and later acquisitions XEPN and XEAW, set a pattern that was closely followed by later border entrepreneurs (there were eleven border stations by 1938, several of which had more than fifty-thousand watts). His success inspired numerous other individuals in the following decades—some of them, like Brinkley or Norman Baker, of a not-too-savory reputation. Baker plugged his cancer-cure over XENT, across from Laredo, before he was convicted of using the mails to defraud. Brinkley sold XEAW, his station at Reynosa, to Carr Collins, who made himself a millionaire through the selling of Crazy Water Crystals. XEAW, like most of the other border stations, sold commercial time to a motley assortment of patent-medicine proprietors, evangelists, and small business establishments, such as chick farms. Collins felt that in his programming he was giving listeners the unsophisticated material that the big networks neglected. The merchandising habits of the border stations have become part of the nation's folklore. Long-winded announcers talked incessantly about such products as Resurrection Plants, portraits of Jesus that glowed in the dark, autographed pictures of Jesus Christ (they didn't always explain whose autograph it was), prayer cloths, baby chicks, "genuine simulated" diamonds, and, of course, hillbilly and gospel songbooks.

If one could endure the seemingly never-ending advertising, one might occasionally hear a hillbilly song of the best quality. Eventually phonograph recordings dominated border programming, but in the mid-and-late thirties hillbilly music was disseminated through live performances and transcriptions. Several singers who did not have nationally established reputations nevertheless built loyal followings through border broadcasts. Cowboy singers thrived on border radio, just as they did elsewhere in the America of the 1930's. Jesse Rodgers (Jimmie's cousin from Waynesboro, Mississippi), Nolan "Cowboy Slim" Rinehart (from Brady, Texas), and J. R. Hall (the "Utah Cowboy," who actually hailed from Crowley, Texas) were just a few of the cowboy balladeers who popularized their songs on the border stations. The cowboy singers were joined by close-harmony duet singers, string bands, gospel quartets, yodelers, folk balladeers, and family groups. The most famous of the latter were the Pickard Family, who came to San Antonio in 1936, and the Carter Family, who moved to the same city in 1938. Both groups came to Texas through the sponsorship of the Royal Chemical Corporation of Chicago, maker of such products as Kolorbak hair dye and Peruna tonic, and an early and major advertiser on border radio stations. The Pickards and Carters made live broadcasts, as all early hillbillies did, but they also made numerous transcriptions so that their performances could continue when they were unable to do them in person. Studio broadcasts were often transcribed and re-broadcast at a later time, but, increasingly, transcriptions were made through an independent service, such as Don Baxter's in San Antonio, and then sold to radio stations. Transcriptions obviously made it easier for hillbilly musicians to popularize their songs and talents on more than a regional basis, and, disseminated on Mexican border broadcasts, the music actually made its way throughout North America.

As country music circulated around the nation, it demonstrated its power to sell, whether the product was politics, religion, or commerce. In the realm of commerce, products identified with hillbilly music ranged from work clothes and farm implements to flour (to make those good biscuits that every farmer and worker ate) to patent medicines. The percentage of drugs and medicinal products ranged so high among hillbilly advertisers that it almost seemed as if the format of the old-time medicine show had been transferred to the hillbilly radio show. Advertising concerns, such as the William Wade Agency of Chicago, evidently perceived the country audience to be made up of rural and small-town Americans who clung to a folk fear of doctors or who had no money to invest in proper medical care. Alka-Seltzer, for example, was a new and unknown product until it was advertised on the *National Barn Dance* in 1933. Wine of Cardui, designed to ease the discomforts of "women's complaints," and Black Draught, a laxative, were well known in southern rural homes in the late nineteenth century (chiefly because of the famous wall calendars distributed by their manufacturer, the Chattanooga Medicine Company). But their commercial lives were no doubt extended through their association with hillbilly music after the 1920's.

Black Draught was only one of several laxatives aimed at the rural public and popularized by hillbilly advertising. The most ubiquitous of the laxatives, though, and the one most identified with country music, was Crazy Water Crystals. This product was a white concentrate of mineral water taken from the Crazy Well in Mineral Wells, Texas. Although the well was discovered in 1885, the company did not embark on a national campaign of radio exploitation until 1930. Originally claiming grandiose curative qualities for their product, the company's directors eventually settled on the claim that it would facilitate proper elimination (which was probably true). The Crazy Water Company sponsored various types of entertainment on radio stations all over the United States, in Canada, and on the Mexican border stations. Country music, however, was the medium most often favored by the Crazy Water people. The company's general manager in the region of the two Carolinas and Georgia, J. W. Fincher, began utilizing hillbilly talent soon after he was transferred to the territory in 1933. Capitalizing on the local availability and popularity of hillbilly music, Fincher soon established Crazy Water sponsorship on fourteen stations in the three-state area. The capstone of the coverage was the establishment of the *Crazy Barn Dance* on WBT in Charlotte, March 17, 1934. Several of the bands who worked under Crazy Water sponsorship carried "crazy" in their performing titles (Crazy Hickory Nuts, Crazy Mountaineers, etc.). Country musicians profited from the relationship with the Crazy Water Company (if only through radio exposure), but probably not nearly as much as the company gained from the association. At the peak of Crazy Water Crystals radio involvement in the Southeast, the company sold an estimated refrigerator carload of crystals per day.

One of the most pervasive methods used by radio stations to link advertising and country music in the 1930's was the P.I. account—a system in which royalties were paid to a station "per inquiry" for an advertised product. The fifty-thousand-watt, clear-channel stations, with their broad rural coverage, made particularly effective use of this system because it brought them revenue with only a minimal outlay for talent. Even the powerful station in New Orleans, WWL—owned by the Jesuit-run Loyola University—specialized in P.I. accounts for several years after 1932. Though located in the heart of a city that had few discernible leanings toward country music, WWL catered to the tastes of the rural population that lived in northern Louisiana and in surrounding southern states. Therefore, for several years during the 1930's such musicians as the Pickard Family, Hank Penny, the Shelton Brothers, Curly Fox, and, above all, Lew Childre performed live on WWL, hawking their sponsors' products and disseminating the best in hillbilly music. Many entertainers, or their announcers, were famous for the warm, convincing manner in which they gave commercials. Of course, an entertainer who sold the music effectively would have little trouble in selling the merchandise described on the show; hillbilly audiences were acutely loyal to their favorite musicians' sponsors. The spectacle of a Catholic-owned station disseminating music to a rural, Protestant audience was surely lost on few people, but the Jesuit fathers were more embarrassed by the nickname their station acquired: "the ache and pill station of the South." It was hard to quarrel with the increasing royalties that flowed into the station, though, and so the hillbillies remained at WWL through much of the 1930's.

With a few exceptions, the hillbilly musician of the 1930's was a radio performer. Some performers were permanent members of barn dance casts, and a few, like Bob Wills at KVOO in Tulsa, remained at the same radio station for several years. Others, though, moved from station to station and from state to state, always looking for a better financial deal. A large percentage of them never made phonograph recordings; instead they depended upon the sale of songbooks or upon personal appearances for economic sustenance. But once these generalizations are made, we find that these musicians had little else in common. Their choice of songs and styles of performance were so radically dissimilar that it is difficult to discuss them in any systematic way. Some singers accompanied themselves on guitar and sang ballads in styles reminiscent of Bradley Kincaid or Doc Hopkins. Many musicians were eclectic in their absorption of songs and styles, but few were the complete "entertainers" that Lew Childre was (a singer, instrumentalist, comedian, dancer). Some singers were carbon copies of Jimmie Rodgers, imitating his guitar runs, his yodel, and every vocal nuance. Others specialized in the blues, drawing their style from black singers rather than Rodgers. Many paraded before the public as cowboy singers, an affectation favored by easterners and westerners alike; still others sang only gospel or "moral" material. Duets and family groups abounded, but with harmony styles that differed greatly, and instrumental styles and combinations that varied just as strongly. Some string bands sounded little different from the bands of the twenties, reflecting the hoedown tradition from which the music evolved while other bands borrowed substantially from pop and jazz music. Fiddlers abounded as always, but they too differed both in style and in approach to tradition; mandolin-and-guitar groups arose in profusion, and the steel guitar made its way into more and more bands. By the end of the thirties musicians were learning how to electrify the steel guitar and other instruments as well, an innovation that radically changed the nature of country music. While these traits were discernible throughout the South, there were nevertheless measurable differences between musical styles in the Southeast and Southwest. The discussion that follows will concentrate, primarily, on musicians from east of the Mississippi River. ("Western" musicians will be discussed in Chapter 5.)

For much of the decade of the thirties Jimmie Rodgers' influence could be heard everywhere, from Daddy John Love in North Carolina to Jerry Behrens in New Orleans. Not every yodel, of course, sounded like Rodgers'; some were very primitive, and some were in the sophisticated, Swiss style favored by Montana Slim (Wilf Carter) and Patsy Montana. Singers also went a step beyond Rodgers when they fashioned duet yodeling (or even multiple yodeling as in the case of the Sons of the Pioneers). Reese Fleming and Respers Townsend of Memphis are said to have been the first to introduce duet yodeling, in their recordings of the early thirties, but Alton and Rabon Delmore, the Callahan Brothers, and the Girls of the Golden West (Millie and Dolly Good) took the art to greater harmonic heights.

Blues singing remained popular among country singers, but only part of it came from the Rodgers tradition; much of the feel for the blues style came directly from black singers (either in the flesh or on records). The fascination with the blues had been exhibited by country singers ever since the country industry began. Out of ten songs recorded by Henry Whitter at his December 1923 session for Okeh, five had "blues" in the title. Excellent blues performances by men like Frank Hutchison, Dick Justice, Jimmie Tarlton, and the Allen Brothers had been recorded in the late 1920's; Tarlton and the Allens were still recording blues songs, along with other types of traditional material, well into the 1930's.

Johnny James Rimbert Tarlton, who came out of a South Carolina family of textile workers and folksingers, is one of the most interesting figures in the rich history of country music. He possessed a penetratingly clear tenor voice and an individualistic instrumental and vocal style which placed him in the front rank of country singers of that or any other era. Beginning with the banjo but capable of playing almost all the stringed instruments, he eventually settled upon the steel guitar, which he played bottleneck style until he learned the steel technique from Hawaiians whom he met in California at about the time of World War I. By the time of his first recording session in 1927, he had already hoboed around the country, working in everything from cotton mills to oil fields and singing his way as far north as New York and as far west as California. He met Tom Darby, a singer and guitar player, in Columbus, Georgia, sometime in 1927. The two made their first records in April of that year, but they did not make history until their second session on November 10, 1927. They recorded two songs arranged by Tarlton: "Columbus Stockade Blues" and "Birmingham Jail" (both released on Columbia 15212). These two songs, which are known by country music fans around the world, earned Darby and Tarlton seventy-five dollars, the only remuneration they ever received for the songs. Darby and Tarlton knew and recorded all kinds of songs, including old standards like "Where the River Shannon Flows" and British ballads like "Lowe Bonnie," but they were both much influenced by black music. The guitar style of each suggests a black influence, Tarlton's a modification of bottleneck playing, and Darby's an adaptation of finger-picking. It is in Tarlton's singing, however—especially in a song like "Slow Wicked Blues"—that we find the greatest infusion of the "soul" usually attributed to black people. There is no greater example of the "white blues."

None of the "hillbilly blues" singers of the 1930's sang blues exclusively; scattered through their repertories one can hear ballads, love songs, religious pieces, and virtually every other kind of song favored by hillbilly singers. One duo, however, the Allen Brothers, was so competent at performing the blues that their recordings were sometimes erroneously catalogued as "race" performances. The Allens reportedly left the Columbia label (for whom they first recorded in April 1927) because of this mixup.

Whatever their racial views may have been, Austin and Lee Allen undoubtedly listened to a lot of black music. The Sewanee, Tennessee, natives recorded a body of songs for Columbia, Victor, and Vocalion, between 1927 and 1934, that has no analogue in the recorded repertory of any other white musician. Their songs were, for the most part, original compositions or adaptations of older blues tunes such as "A New Salty Dog." Although their vocals were strong (with Austin doing most of the singing and Lee sometimes joining in on tenor harmony), the Allens' instrumentation was the most interesting facet of their performances. There was nothing extraordinary about their banjo and guitar work, but Lee's kazoo playing was little short of sensational. He took this child's toy of presumed limited range and converted it to a lead instrument of exceptional flexibility. On Allen Brothers recordings the kazoo is used like a trumpet; the result is a sound not unlike that heard on Charlie Poole's string-band recordings, a syncopated but structured swing.

The singers who experimented with the blues idiom also, as a matter of course, ventured into the rowdy underworld of sex, sin, and bawdiness that was absent from much of the standard hillbilly fare. The Elizabethan penchant for bawdy and earthy song material had not been entirely eliminated from southern folk culture by a puritanical Protestantism, but the blues genre, as the product of an allegedly uninhibited people, did seem to give license to sample rowdy and risqué songs. Many of the hillbilly songs dealing with drink and drugs, masculine boastfulness, and sexual hijinks, were couched in the blues form. Jimmie Rodgers was not alone among southern singers in growing up with the blues; everywhere, in mountains and flatlands alike, white people heard black singers either in person or on records. Some of this material made its way on to hillbilly records in relatively unaltered form, but much of it provided the inspiration for original compositions by hillbilly writers.

Prohibition, of course, evoked ambivalent responses among hillbilly singers (reflecting a similar ambivalence in the culture that produced them), but blues tunes generally commented negatively on the phenomenon and welcomed its demise when repeal came in 1933. Singers often mentioned the unfortunate personal consequences of drinking (headaches, hangovers, fights, love complications, etc.), but only rarely did they denounce the habit in general terms. The Allen Brothers endorsed the art of moonshining in "Fruit Jar Blues," and David McCarn commented on one of the cheapest substitutes for whiskey in "Bay Rum Blues" (Bay Rum was a hair tonic with a high alcoholic content). The Allens, however, responded cynically to one of the most tragic consequences of illicit drinking when they recorded "Jake Walk Blues," one of at least seven hillbilly songs recorded between 1928 and 1934 that dealt with the affliction that came from drinking Jamaica Ginger ("Jake").

The only addiction to which hillbillies readily admitted was that of alcohol; nevertheless, mention of drugs was not totally absent from recordings. The few overt references to hard drugs seem to have come from black sources. One of the greatest early "hillbilly blues" performances, in fact—Dick Justice's "Cocaine"—was a 1928 "cover" of Luke Jordan's "Cocaine Blues," recorded the previous year. Another cocaine song, "Take a Whiff on Me," also moved into hillbilly music, but in a modified form which more readily reflected the habits of southern country folk. Charlie Poole and the North Carolina Ramblers did it as "Take a Drink on Me." Many southern people would neither knowingly take hard drugs nor imbibe alcohol, but they did consume both in the form of patent medicines, which were staples in southern homes and in hillbilly radio commercials.

Much more common than drinking and drug references in the hillbilly blues were the assertions of male ego and sexual prowess, preoccupations that were important to many men who were otherwise socially and economically emasculated during the Depression era. The blues provided yet another mode of expression for the omnipresent macho impulse that lay deeply imbedded in southern rural culture. Of course, black blues singers in the previous decade had proven that "naughty" lyrics were commercial also, and Jimmie Rodgers had demonstrated that a white market existed for such material. Rodgers' rounder songs and risqué tunes (such as "Ground Hog Rootin' in My Back Yard") were actually rather mild compared to the songs which came in the early thirties. The young Gene Autry recorded a body of songs that were populated with "high stepping mamas," "low down mamas," "bear cat papas," and "do right daddies." "Do Right Daddy Blues," one of his most affecting songs, was filled with assertions of boasting and some of the sexiest lines in hillbilly music: "You can feel of my legs, you can feel of my thighs," etc.

The three greatest "imitators" of Jimmie Rodgers—Gene Autry, Cliff Carlisle, and Jimmie Davis—all had racy repertories which were considerably spicier than that of the Blue Yodeler. Clifford Raymond Carlisle was born at Mount Eden, Kentucky, in 1904. Although he grew up in a family where traditional music was prominent, he was drawn to a career in music through an early fascination with the Hawaiian guitar and black blues styles, both of which he heard as a teenager. Both influences remained with him until he retired as an entertainer in 1947. He was one of the first country musicians to play a dobro steel guitar, and his yodeling blues were unsurpassed in the hillbilly field. Jimmie Rodgers' partisans would no doubt find such an assertion sacrilegious, but there are those who think that Carlisle, while less original than Rodgers, was a better singer and yodeler. Carlisle sang with unusual clarity of tone and featured an effortless yodel that combined both a Jimmie Rodgers sound and Swiss techniques. Carlisle began his recording career with Gennett in 1930, and during the next seventeen years he recorded sometimes alone, but most often with a partner such as guitarist Wilbur Ball, Fred Kirby, or his brother Bill (as the Carlisle Brothers). His repertory was diverse, but his prison, hobo, and "rowdy" songs are probably the most interesting items he recorded. "Pan American Man," one of his finest songs, asserts two themes: the movement of a famous train across the southern landscape and the prowess of a free-born man who equates his own freedom with that of the train he rides. The theme of masculine boasting is more aggressively asserted in songs like "Shanghai Rooster Yodel," "Tom Cat Blues," and "Black Jack David," the hillbilly version of "The Gypsy Laddie" (Child 200).

James Houston "Jimmie" Davis was born in a sharecropper's cabin at Beech Springs, Louisiana, in 1902. His has been not only the longest career in country music (commencing as a radio entertainer in Shreveport in 1928), but also one of the most richly diverse. A number of factors have unfortunately obscured his importance for modern country music fans. His association with "You Are My Sunshine," the theme of his Louisiana gubernatorial campaigns and one of the most-performed songs in country music, has made him seem as hackneyed as the song. His current absorption with gospel music has tended to make people forget that he ever did any other kind of music, while his notoriety as a segregationist governor in the early 1960's has inhibited the appreciation that should be due him as a performer. Davis himself, of course, has been largely responsible for the limited view of his career. In speaking to interviewers, he invariably talks only of his association with Decca after 1934, and neglects the very important records made for Victor from 1929 to 1933. By the time he signed his Decca contract, he had already lived a very full and active life, and one much unlike that of the typical hillbilly. He earned a bachelor's degree from Louisiana College (Pineville) and a master's degree from Louisiana State University, taught history at Dodd College, and somehow found time to sing regularly on Shreveport's KWKH, make records, and give occasional concerts. His popularity as an entertainer, along with his interest in public affairs, combined to give him an exposure that proved invaluable in politics. His election as Public Service Commissioner was merely the first step in a career that would ultimately lead him to the Louisiana governorship in 1944 and again in 1960.

Davis' stylistic diversity and his long association with such Texas performers as Moon Mullican, Cliff Bruner, and the Shelton Brothers make it difficult to place him in any category. His early stylistic preferences drew him firmly toward the country blues camp, a genre in which he excelled. Davis was an excellent Jimmie Rodgers–style yodeler, with a repertory strongly reminiscent of his Mississippi mentor. In "Where the Old Red River Flows," for example, Davis wrote a sentimental evocation of his Northwest Louisiana home, redolent of plantation imagery and singing "darkeys." Black musicians were indeed important in his career. He was one of the few hillbilly performers to be accompanied on records by black musicians, having been joined on his 1932 Victor recordings by guitarists

Oscar Woods and Ed Schaffer, two bluesmen who came from the area around Shreveport. Many of his songs from this period likewise show a strong black influence, and, like the music of Autry and Carlisle, they are much more openly sexual than those of Rodgers. "Down at the Old Country Church" is a heavy-handed monologue/song, done in Negro dialect, and suggestive of a black-face minstrel routine. But in songs like "Tom Cat and Pussy Blues," "High Behind Blues," "Red Nightgown Blues," and "Do-do-daddling Thing," Davis recorded some of the most risqué numbers found in the country repertory.

Blues of the type fashioned by Carlisle, Davis, and others did not endure past the mid-thirties, but fascination with the style, and with other black-derived forms, survived into the following decades. It even surfaced frequently in duet singing, a style usually associated with gentle parlor or gospel songs. The duet teams, like most country singers of the period, performed a mixed bag of songs, and some of them sought a commercial formula that would permit the performance of both traditional and innovative material. Several duets, such as North Carolina's Callahan Brothers, Texas' Shelton Brothers, and Alabama's Delmore Brothers, were especially versatile, with rowdy blues, old-time ballads, and sentimental parlor songs.

Of all the eclectic duet groups, none exerted a stronger or more lasting impact than the Delmore Brothers. Alton and Rabon Delmore were born in Elkmont, Alabama, in the hilly Tennessee River region that has produced such great country musicians as Rex Griffin, the Anglin Brothers, and the Louvin Brothers. The Delmores began performing for community gatherings at an extremely early age (when Rabon was ten and Alton eighteen), but their boldest step toward a commercial career came when they won first prize in 1930 at the old-time fiddlers' contest in Athens, Alabama. In 1931 they recorded two songs for Columbia (the only ones they would ever make for that label), and in 1932 they successfully auditioned for the *Grand Ole Opry*. Their first session for Victor's Bluebird label in December 1933 yielded two of their most famous songs, the slightly-risqué "Brown's Ferry Blues" and "Big River Blues" (now widely known as "Deep River Blues" because of Doc Watson's performances), both inspired by the Tennessee River. Blues tunes, thus, figured prominently in the Delmore Brothers' repertory from the very beginning of their career (their first recording for Columbia in 1931 had been "I've Got the Kansas City Blues"). As might be expected, they were much impressed by Jimmie Rodgers, and even wrote a song especially for him, "Blue Railroad Train." Rodgers was far from being the only blues influence in their lives, for they learned from black musicians who worked in the fields in the Tennessee Valley bottoms or who recorded during the brothers' formative years. The Delmores picked up a fondness for ragtime and eight-to-the-bar rhythms which surfaced repeatedly in their music, although the boogie beat did not figure prominently until they recorded "Hillbilly Boogie" for King in 1945. Both men were excellent guitarists, but Rabon did most of the lead instrumental work on his tenor guitar, an instrument that rarely appears in country music.

While blues music was always attractive to the brothers, they did not by any means confine themselves to that form. Their vocal harmony was dramatically different from their instrumentation, but was just as influential. They sang in a soft, gentle style, with clearly enunciated diction and a carefully worked-out harmony. Placid love songs (such as Alton's own compositions "Southern Moon" and "When It's Time for the Whippoorwill to Sing"), gospel songs, and nineteenth-century parlor pieces figured just as prominently in their repertory as did blues tunes. Still, the Delmore Brothers did not sound like other "brother duets" (though they influenced them all); their unusual blending of lively, syncopated guitar work and soft, close harmony set them apart from most other musicians and made them a much-admired act. Perhaps the greatest tribute to their work is the large number of "Delmore Brothers songs" still found in the repertories of modern country singers.

The brother duets of the pre–World War II era favored a diverse assortment of songs and performed them with a variety of instrumental combinations. Of course, they also differed greatly in vocal sound and quality and in their ability to harmonize. Howard and Dorsey Dixon, from Darlington, South Carolina, featured Howard's steel guitar and Dorsey's finger-picking style of rhythm guitar. Vocally, their rough and sometimes-strident harmony was far removed from that of the smooth Delmores.

The Dixon Brothers came from the same type of textile-mill environment that spawned a long line of important country musicians, from Henry Whitter, Kelly Harrell, and Jimmie Tarlton to Lester Flatt. Although music was always an integral part of their lives, the Dixon Brothers were never permanently away from the mills. Howard went to work there as a child of ten and died on the job at the age of fifty-eight; Dorsey went to work at twelve and remained there until he retired in 1951.

The two brothers played music as children but made no serious attempt at a professional career until the early thirties. In 1931, Jimmie Tarlton, in one of his frequent forays through the country, stopped in East Rockingham, North Carolina, where he worked temporarily at the same mill where the Dixons were employed. Because of this chance encounter, Dorsey was inspired to develop a finger-picking style on the guitar and Howard began playing the steel guitar. In 1934 the Dixon Brothers inaugurated their professional career with a performance on J. W. Fincher's *Crazy Barn Dance*. Although their recorded repertory of over sixty songs recorded for Victor over a two-year period never-earned them enough money to free them from textile employment, they introduced several songs (most of them written or arranged by Dorsey) which have endured in country music: "Intoxicated Rat," the widely circulated "Weave Room Blues," and Roy

Acuff's great hit "Wreck on the Highway," which the Dixons entitled "I Didn't Hear Nobody Pray." Dorsey Dixon continued to write long after his professional music career ended. One of his most compelling songs, "Babies in the Mill"—a recollection of the textile child labor that he and his brother had known—was written in the sixties after his music experienced a temporary resurgence because of the folk revival.

Unlike the Dixon Brothers, the Callahan Brothers made music their full-time career. Many of the brother groups had little name recognition outside of the southeastern states. Homer and Walter Callahan, on the other hand, roamed from radio station to radio station in the South and Midwest before finally settling down in Dallas, where they built a large territorial following. Radio transcriptions broadcast over the Mexican border stations contributed further to their wide appeal. They also maintained a commercial viability in the years after the 1930's because they successfully adapted their style to the electric-based country and western fusion that became ascendant in the 1940's.

They came from Madison County, North Carolina, one of the richest storehouses of traditional music in the United States. They learned gospel songs and such old ballads as "Katie Dear" and "Banks of the Ohio" from their mother but were swept away by the music of Jimmie Rodgers in the late twenties. They experimented with duet yodeling for the first time at the Rhododendron Festival in Asheville, North Carolina, in 1933. The delighted audience response was enough to kindle the young men's dreams of a professional entertainment career. Soon thereafter they landed their first radio job in Knoxville for the JFG Coffee company, and in 1934 they recorded fourteen songs for the American Record Company in New York. The boys demonstrated their penchant for the blues at this first session by doing songs like "Corn Licker Rag," "Gonna Quit My Rowdy Ways," and "St. Louis Blues." In the following years they would continue to do songs like "Rounders Luck" (better known today as "House of the Rising Sun"), "Step It Up and Go," and "Rattlesnake Daddy" (a hillbilly blues much unlike the black song of the same title). Gospel songs, traditional ballads, and modern-composed country songs always competed with the blues tunes, however, and a song called "She's My Curly Headed Baby," made up of old fragments, appeared in their first recording session of 1934. It always remained the song most identified with them.

The Callahans' career as hillbilly singers took them as far east as Wheeling, West Virginia, as far north as Cincinnati, as far west as Springfield, Missouri, and Tulsa, Oklahoma, before reaching Texas. During those years (1935–1941), they worked with the famous vaudeville hillbillies, the Weaver Brothers and Elviry, and with Red Foley. In 1941 they were associated with hillbilly promoter and announcer Gus Foster ("who could sell anything") and had radio shows on KRLD in Dallas and KWFT in Wichita

Jimmie Tarlton. Courtesy of Norman Carlson.

The Callahan Brothers.

Falls. In Texas they acquired the radio names of "Bill and Joe," and became one of the most popular bands of the Southwest.

In Texas the Callahans ceased to be just a simple mountain duet. They progressively absorbed modern country songs into their repertory; added a growing retinue of musicians, including a much-admired fiddler named Georgia Slim Rutland and the superb mandolin player Paul Buskirk, who was one of the first "modern" exponents of that instrument (that is, jazz-influenced) in country music; adopted electric instruments; and devised a variety stage show built around the brothers' harmony and Bill's (Homer's) zany comedy. By the time of their last recording session in 1951, there was little to distinguish their music from the dominant honky-tonk sound of that era.

One of the most common instrumental combinations supporting the duet vocal sound was the mandolin and guitar. The mandolin had been a popular middle-class instrument before World War I, much favored by chamber musicians and college students. Precisely how and when it moved into rural music is unknown, but it was widely advertised in the mail-order catalogues during the 1920's. It has become one of the most versatile instruments in country music, capable of supporting anything from a mournful dirge to a progressive jazz tune. In the 1930's it was sometimes heard as a ragtime instrument—as played by Ted Hawkins on Riley Puckett's 1934 recording of "Ragged but Right"—but its proper domain seemed to be the music of the brother duets.

Interestingly, the duet which may have done most to popularize the instrument was not composed of brothers. Lester McFarland and Robert A. Gardner came from Gray, Kentucky, and Oliver Springs, Tennessee, respectively; they first joined their musical interests in 1915 at the Kentucky School for the Blind, where both were enrolled as students. McFarland usually sang tenor on their duet performances and picked the instrumental leads on his mandolin. His mandolin playing on their Brunswick recordings after 1927, and on *National Barn Dance* broadcasts after 1931, did much to stimulate the general popularity of the instrument among country musicians. Along with Gardner, who played guitar and sang lead, McFarland began entertaining in schoolhouses, county fairs, and on the Keith vaudeville circuit in 1922. From 1925 to 1931 they performed over WNOX in Knoxville, and in 1931 they moved to Chicago, where they became part of the *National Barn Dance* cast (here they were generally advertised only as "Mac and Bob"). On radio shows and recordings made for Brunswick and the American Record Company after 1927, the duet introduced some of the classics of country music: for example, "When the Roses Bloom Again" (their first recording), "'Tis Sweet to Be Remembered" (later done by bluegrass musicians in a much-modified form), "Twenty-one Years" (the great prison song written by Bob Miller), and "That Little Boy of Mine." Mac and Bob actually had one of the most wide-ranging repertories in country music, including everything from "I'm Forever Blowing Bubbles" to "Midnight on the Stormy Deep" and "The East Bound Train." Their sound was not necessarily rural but instead had an old-fashioned, cultivated flavor, suggestive of the music hall or barbershop singing. It was a rather formal style, much like that sometimes used by Buell Kazee, the McCravy Brothers, and a Texas duo, Sloan and Threadgill—but it was a charming, if sometimes stilted, sound.

Still another non-brother duet which profoundly influenced the sound of those who were brothers was Karl and Harty. Karl Davis and Hartford Connecticut Taylor came to the *National Barn Dance* in 1931 as part of John Lair's Cumberland Ridge Runners. Both men came from the vicinity of Mount Vernon, Kentucky, and received part of their grade-school instruction from Lair, the man who would eventually accompany them to the WLS country show and back in the late thirties to the *Renfro Valley* show in Kentucky. Although they often performed as part of a larger group, Karl and Harty made their most distinctive mark on country music through their duet harmonies, mandolin and guitar instrumentation, and influential songs. Karl learned to play the mandolin at the age of twelve after hearing the instrument played by Doc Hopkins, the well-known mountain balladeer and later member of the Ridge Runners. Along with Harty, who had taught himself to play the guitar, Karl began playing for local parties in Mount Vernon. In their later recording and performing career the duo featured a somewhat-formal style of singing probably much influenced by Mac and Bob, who were their contemporaries on the *Barn Dance*. More important than their performance style was the body of songs they introduced to country music. Beginning with "I'm Just Here to Get My Baby Out of Jail," a song which Davis set to the melody of "Old Reuben," and continuing with others like "Prisoner's Dream," "The House Where We Were Wed," "They're All Going Home but One," and "Kentucky" (Davis' most beautiful composition), Karl and Harty bequeathed a large number of songs which have moved into the repertories of entertainers as diverse as the Blue Sky Boys and the Everly Brothers.

Among the bona fide brother acts which performed with mandolin and guitar, two stand out because of the lasting contributions which they made to country music: the Bolick Brothers and the Monroe Brothers. Popularly known as the Blue Sky Boys, Bill and Earl Bolick uncompromisingly adhered to traditional patterns in their style of singing and instrumentation, and in their selection of old-time songs. The student of American folksong could begin in no better place than the Blue Sky Boys' repertory, for there one can find a myriad of examples of the song types that found their way into the hearts and homes of southern country people. However, one will find few examples of the raw, rowdy, or sexy side of human experience, for, like Bradley Kincaid before them, the Bolicks believed that music should serve a moral purpose.

As Bill and Earl grew up on a small farm near Hickory, North Carolina, on the edge of the mountain region known as the "Land of the Sky," they were exposed to a set of moral values and a variety of song sources that would one day affect both their performing style and their choice of songs. They learned from friends and relatives in the mountains, from Church of God hymnals (Anderson, Indiana, branch), and from the recordings of such singers as Bradley Kincaid, Riley Puckett, and Karl and Harty. Both young men had a passionate commitment to traditional songs and styles, and Bill Bolick, in particular, viewed his songmaking role as a folkloristic one of collecting and preserving the ballads and gospel songs of earlier years.

Bill Bolick sang briefly in 1935 for a group called the East Hickory String Band (renamed the Crazy Hickory Nuts after they gained sponsorship by the Crazy Water Crystals Company), and in that same year he and Earl teamed up with fiddler Homer Sherrill as the Good Coffee Boys (JFG Coffee) on WWNC in Asheville. The Bolicks were immediately popular there, and on WGST, Atlanta, where they performed for a few months in early 1936 as the Blue Ridge Entertainers. Their recording career began in June 1936, for Victor's Bluebird label; at this time, it is said that Eli Oberstein, the Victor talent scout, gave them their permanent performing title, the Blue Sky Boys, which was a composite of "Land of the Sky" and "Blue Ridge."

From the date of their first recording until they retired in 1951, the Blue Sky Boys made little substantial change in either material or style of performance. Their harmony got higher; newly composed songs moved into their repertory; and, after 1946, a string bass and fiddle were added to the original mandolin and guitar. But their sound remained distinctive and predictable and much like that with which they began in 1936. Their harmony, probably the closest and certainly the sweetest in country music history, was carefully contrived and was produced by the skillful blending of Earl's resonant baritone voice with Bill's smooth tenor. Their instrumentation was just as unique. Bill Bolick never chorded the mandolin, but instead played tremolo passages, and even a third harmony to his own tenor harmony. Set against the background of deep, rhythmic guitar tones supplied by Earl Bolick, the instrumentation created a mood similar to that evoked by their singing.

And it was mood which really set the Blue Sky Boys apart from other singers during the Depression years. When one recalls that "hot dance" rhythms were winning the day at that precise moment in the Southwest, the Bolicks' commitment to a serious and moralistic body of songs assumes an even more singular significance. Comedy was not absent from their performances; they occasionally sang a novelty song like "Cindy," or a high-stepping vaudeville tune like "Are You from Dixie?" (their radio theme), and Earl created a character, replete with whiskers and old-man's gait, called Uncle Josh. Nevertheless, the dominant theme of their music was the "tragic side of life." In plaintive, close harmony they sang tales of death, sorrow, and unrequited love, and they approached each number with a compassion and tenderness that has seldom been equaled in country music.

In choosing selections for recording, the Bolicks sometimes chose numbers that had already demonstrated popularity when recorded by earlier performers. In other cases, they merely recorded those songs that were often requested by their large and loyal radio audience. The Blue Sky Boys' inclination toward somber and sentimental melodies was evidently shared by their listeners. The bulk of their recorded numbers were traditional songs like the American murder ballad "Banks of the Ohio" and the British broadside "The Butcher's Boy," sentimental Tin Pan Alley melodies like "There'll Come a Time" and "I Believe It For My Mother Told Me So," unrequited-love songs like "Why Not Confess," and religious songs like "Only One Step More."

The Blue Sky Boys' harmony has been often imitated by modern country singers (one even hears a touch of it in the Everly Brothers), and their songs have been widely preserved, particularly in bluegrass music.[2] Still, their influence has not been as profound as that of the Monroe Brothers. Originally composed of brothers Birch, Charlie, and Bill (and finally only Charlie and Bill), the Monroes contributed a style and repertory of songs that have inspired thousands of country and city musicians. As a duo, Charlie and Bill touched the lives of many young musicians, such as Lester Flatt, Ira and Charlie Louvin, Ralph and Carter Stanley, and Everett and Mitchell Lilly, igniting within them the flames of musical ambition. As separate acts, Charlie and Bill provided employment for scores of musicians who later went on to forge important careers of their own.

The Monroe Brothers, in existence only from 1934 to 1938, featured Bill's inventive mandolin style and high harmony singing and Charlie's lead singing and dynamic, run-filled guitar playing. Through his independent work after the forties, Bill Monroe became famous as a solo singer of great power and range; but with the Monroe Brothers he never sang anything but tenor harmony. He and Charlie became a full-time duet in 1934, working on a series of radio stations in Gary, Indiana, Shenandoah, Iowa, Omaha, Nebraska, and finally, in 1935, in Greenville, South Carolina, and

2. Although such songs are still performed today, particularly by bluegrass musicians in high-powered and often strident fashion, almost no one does such material in the gentle and subdued style favored by the Blue Sky Boys. The best remaining link to the Bolicks, and to the mandolin-and-guitar tradition of the thirties, is a wonderful husband and wife team, Ray and Ina Patterson. Ray and Ina are Texans who now live in Colorado. They are rarely heard in live performances, but their recordings are well worth having: *Old Time Ballads and Hymns*, County 708; *Old Time Songs*, vol. 2, County 715; *Songs of Home and Childhood*, vol. 3, County 737.

Charlotte, North Carolina, all under the sponsorship of Texas Crystals (not to be confused with the Crazy Water Company). In February 1936, they recorded the first of what would eventually be sixty songs for Bluebird; the first session included their best-selling song, "What Would You Give in Exchange for Your Soul?" From 1936 to 1938 they and their popular announcer, the Old Hired Hand, Byron Parker (a native of Hastings, Iowa), worked the Carolinas under the sponsorship of Crazy Water Crystals, becoming probably the most popular hillbilly act in the southeastern United States. Superficially similar in style and repertory to other mandolin-and-guitar duets, they were nonetheless crucially different. In songs like "Nine Pound Hammer," "Feast Here Tonight," "Roll in My Sweet Baby's Arms," and "My Long Journey Home," all of which have become country standards, they impressed listeners with the high vocal pitch of their singing, the aggressiveness of their instrumentation, and the break-neck speed of their tempos.

When we leave the blues singers and the duets, we find an almost-bewildering array of entertainers who tried to make country music their profession during the thirties. The broadening coverage of radio encouraged what Bob Coltman has called a cross-fertilization of styles as well as a softening of sound among country musicians.[3] Once-local styles moved across the country and became intermeshed with those found elsewhere to the point that it becomes dangerous indeed to speak precisely of "southeastern" or "southwestern" traits. Furthermore, as Coltman argues, country music became smoother and more polished, with much of its wild, tangy backwoods flavor removed, as broadcasting executives discovered that women and children comprised the bulk of the audience that daily listened to the radio sets. This same perception of woman's gentleness and refinement may have encouraged the search for and greater cultivation of women entertainers.

Women had played important, if often unseen, roles since the beginning of country music; their visibility became much more pronounced, and their influence stronger, in the decade of the thirties. Myrtle Eleanor Cooper, popularly known as Lulu Belle, made one of the most important breakthroughs for women entertainers. She joined the *National Barn Dance* in 1932 as a comedienne and singer, working first with Red Foley, and then with Skyland Scotty Wiseman, a versatile singer, writer, and banjoist from North Carolina, whom she married in 1934. As Lulu Belle and Scotty, they became one of the most popular acts on the *Barn Dance*, known for their comic repartee, novelty songs, and sentimental numbers

3. Bob Coltman, "Across the Chasm: How the Depression Changed Country Music," *Old Time Music*, no. 23 (Winter 1976–1977): 9–11.

The Blue Sky Boys: Bill (*right*) and Earl Bolick, 1964. Courtesy of Norman Carlson.

The Monroe Brothers: *left to right,* Charlie Monroe, J. W. Fincher, Bill Monroe. Courtesy of Pat Ahrens.

(such as "Remember Me When the Candle Lights Are Gleaming" and "Have I Told You Lately That I Love You," both written by Scotty). Both entertainers were immensely talented, but Lulu Belle won an enormous audience for them with her vivacious personality, attractive looks, and saucy singing style; she won a *Radio Digest* poll in 1936 as the most popular radio entertainer in America.

Women also began to create identities apart from their husbands, families, or supportive instrumental groups. Cynthia May Carver, a Kentucky girl discovered by John Lair, broke into show business at the end of the thirties as a madcap but versatile entertainer called Cousin Emmy. She sang, played the banjo (she claimed to be the master of fifteen instruments), danced, acted the fool, but also found the time to do hymns. She was seldom recorded, but she left as part of her legacy a rollicking tune called "Ruby Are You Mad at Your Man?", a song now deeply ensconced in the repertory of bluegrass music.

Kentucky was also the birthplace of Lily May Ledford, another five-string banjoist and balladeer, who became the founder of the first all-female string band, the Coon Creek Girls. Lily May joined the *National Barn Dance* in 1936 at the age of nineteen but spent only one year in Chicago before journeying on to Cincinnati to become part of John Lair's new *Renfro Valley Barn Dance*. Lair, who played a leading role in the encouragement of women entertainers, organized and named the Coon Creek Girls, a band built around Lily May (banjo), her sister Rosie (guitar), Esther "Violet" Koehler (mandolin), and Evelyn "Daisy" Lange (fiddle and bass). The Girls became a trio in 1939 when Susie Ledford joined her sisters after Daisy and Violet departed to become members of the Callahan Brothers' Blue Ridge Mountain Folk in Dallas. The Coon Creek Girls excelled as both singers and instrumentalists and were known both for their gospel and sentimental pieces and for hard-driving mountain songs such as "Pretty Polly" and "How Many Biscuits Can You Eat?"

Although women made important breakthroughs in the thirties, they still had very far to go. Negative images still clung to women who would forsake their "traditional" roles and venture into an area formerly reserved for men. It may be significant that though many of the leading women entertainers were of southern origin, most of them made their mark outside the Deep South—in the border states, on the *National Barn Dance*, and as western cowgirls. Women still found it difficult to go before the public without at least giving the impression that they were related, by blood or marriage, to the musicians with whom they played. The story has often been told of how Rachel Veach, comedienne and banjo player for Roy Acuff after April 1939, was depicted as dobro player Beecher Kirby's sister in order to discourage censure of an unmarried woman traveling with a group of male musicians. Even the pioneering sister acts of the thirties, such as Millie and Dolly Good (the Girls of the Golden West) and Maryjane and Caroline Dezurik (known as the Cackle Sisters because of the "cluck-ing" style of harmony they developed), had the advantage of traveling to-gether, so that each sister could be considered a chaperone for the other. The real "liberation" of women country singers would not come until de-cades later.

Innovation reared its head repeatedly in the country music of the thir-ties, but singers still appeared everywhere who adhered to traditional forms of music, or who promoted a down-home or family ambience. When-ever hillbilly singers who lived during the thirties reminisce about those days, talk will invariably turn at some point to a father-and-son team called Asher Sizemore and Little Jimmie. Few radio entertainers from that era seem to have been more popular. Sizemore was born in Manchester, Ken-tucky, and began his radio career on WSAZ in Huntington, West Virginia, in 1931. By 1932 he was joined on WSM by four-year-old Jimmie in a "home and hearth" type show that lasted until 1942 (they were on other stations after this date). Audiences were sufficiently impressed with the Sizemores to send in an enormous amount of fan mail, up to forty thou-sand pieces in a single week.

Many entertainers of the period were like the Sizemores in that their reputations were built almost exclusively on radio or by personal appear-ances. Grandpa Jones, one of the major talents of country music history, made no records until 1943, although he had been a radio entertainer since 1929. Another extraordinarily versatile entertainer, Lew Childre, did make some obscure recordings in the thirties (for Gennett and the Ameri-can Record Company), but his public name recognition came principally as an itinerant radio performer. The Opp, Alabama, native was basically a country vaudeville performer whose skills as a buck dancer, steel guitarist, comedian, and singer had been perfected on the tent-rep circuit in the twenties and thirties. Regrettably, neither a phonograph recording nor a radio broadcast could effectively communicate the exuberant personality or performing genius of the man. Childre was meant to be seen as well as heard.

Some singers had only regional radio followings. Two WWVA perform-ers, Big Slim, the Lone Cowboy, and Doc Williams, were immensely popu-lar in the Northeast because of the powerful signal transmitted by the sta-tion. Big Slim (Harry Auliffe) did make some recordings in the thirties, and one of his compositions—"Sunny Side of the Mountain"—eventually became one of the classics of country music. Slim's reputation, however, was made principally through his thirty-plus years of performance on the big West Virginia station. His colleague Doc Williams (an ex-coal miner from Pennsylvania named Andrew J. Smik) did not record until 1947, but had been a popular MC and balladeer since he joined the station in 1937 (he was still there in the 1970's).

Buddy Starcher, on the other hand, worked on not one but many stations. He made no records either until 1946, but had a following in the 1930's that was surpassed by few country entertainers. This Ripley, West Virginia, native began his radio career on WFBR in Baltimore in 1928 (he was only eighteen), but he moved to a succession of stations, mostly in Virginia and West Virginia, during the next several years. Starcher was a true radio personality, with a warm, reassuring voice that easily won the confidence of his listeners, selling them songbooks, commercial products, and himself. He sang songs to his own Carter-style guitar accompaniment and saw several of them (such as "Those Brown Eyes," "I'll Still Write Your Name in the Sand," and "Sweet Thing") become standards in the repertories of country singers everywhere.

The instrumental music of the thirties was subjected to the same type of "cross-fertilization" observable in singing. Musicians learned at home or from local community resources, but also absorbed new techniques as they traveled from one region to another or as they listened to radio broadcasts and phonograph recordings. The sounds of pop music, jazz, and even the Hot Club of France (Django Reinhardt, Stéphane Grapelli) made their way into the consciousness of "traditional" musicians. Music in the Southeast tended to be more conservative than that of the Southwest, preserving much of the tangy flavor, and repertory, of the hoedown bands. Nevertheless, musicians there had always exhibited a fascination with pop sounds too, and many of them filtered into the performances of the most traditional entertainers. Clayton McMichen, as we have seen, had leaned toward "modern" material even when playing with the Skillet Lickers. In 1931 he organized the kind of band he had always wanted, the Georgia Wildcats, which had an ultra-eclectic repertory ranging from "Farewell Blues" (from the Benny Goodman collection) to hoedowns like "Boil Them Cabbage Down." The band left Atlanta and relocated for several years in Louisville, where it included some of the most progressive musicians in country music: Hoyt "Slim" Bryant, who began playing single-string solos and "sock" rhythm (a percussive, closed-chord style) long before most guitarists; Carl Cotner, a "hot" violinist who later became Gene Autry's musical director; and the young Merle Travis, who joined the band in 1937 with his seminal "thumb style" of guitar playing. McMichen, however, made little money from his new sound, and he had to resort to promoting fiddling contests, or to participating in the contests staged by Larry Sunbrock. The Sunbrock contests usually involved McMichen and Natchee the Indian (backed by Cowboy Copas), and were resolved by audience vote.

McMichen, then, was experimenting with hot and swinging rhythms well before Bob Wills made them popular out in the Southwest. However, McMichen's innovations never caught fire as he envisioned them, and when the hot sounds caught on among southeastern musicians, they usually came through the influence of the Texas and Oklahoma musicians. The Kentucky Ramblers, the Tennessee Ramblers, and Hank Penny's Radio Cowboys were among the earliest of the southeastern bands to adopt songs and styles from their southwestern contemporaries. The Kentucky Ramblers, organized in 1932, were composed of Charles Hurt, Jack Taylor, Shelby "Tex" Atchison, and Floyd "Salty" Holmes. By 1934 the western image had exerted its irresistible attraction, and the boys changed their title to Prairie Ramblers. In their long tenure on the *National Barn Dance*, from 1933 to 1948, the Ramblers performed a repertory that reflected the appeal of both the cowboys and the southwestern swing bands. The Tennessee Ramblers (led by Dick Hartman and later by Cecil Campbell) popularized themselves on the *Crazy Barn Dance* in Charlotte, and by 1937 were recording their swing sounds on the Bluebird label. Herbert Clayton "Hank" Penny, of Birmingham, Alabama, was the musician most directly influenced by what he called "Texas fiddle music." Penny had never cared for hoedown music, and though virtually living at its back door, he was contemptuous of the music he heard on the *Grand Ole Opry*. The Texas sounds, therefore, swept him away when he heard them for the first time in New Orleans where he was playing on WWL. He returned to Birmingham with hot fiddler Sheldon Bennett and banjoist Louis Dumont and organized a band closely modeled on Milton Brown's Musical Brownies: the Radio Cowboys. Performing on WSB's *Crossroad Follies* in Atlanta, and recording for Arthur Satherley and Okeh records after 1938, Hank Penny popularized "western swing" throughout the South. Many innovative musicians played for Penny during the following decades, including violinist Boudleaux Bryant (who would become one of country music's greatest songwriters) and pioneering steel guitarists Noel Boggs and Eddie Duncan, both of whom borrowed freely from jazz trombonists and saxophonists.

While Penny and the Radio Cowboys were doing their country-jazz versions of "Hesitation Blues," "Hot Time Mama," and their signature song, "Won't You Ride in My Little Red Wagon," most other southeastern bands were clinging to a more traditional repertory of hoedowns and country tunes. The most influential of the old-time string bands was a group from Buncombe County, North Carolina, Mainer's Mountaineers. Headed by fiddler Joseph Emmett (J. E.) Mainer and his banjo-playing brother Wade, the Mainers were an important transitional organization in that they preserved much of the heritage of traditional country material—breakdowns, reels, ballads, folksongs—while at the same time anticipating many of the stylistic features of modern bluegrass music. The Mainers experimented with harmony sounds that later showed up among bluegrass singers, popularized a large body of songs that appeared in the repertories of many later singers, and featured the full retinue of instruments now associated with bluegrass music: fiddle, five-string banjo, mandolin, guitar, and string bass.

Most of the original musicians in the Mainer group came out of a cotton mill background, with J. E. himself going to work in such an environment at age twelve. Music was never more than an amateur diversion for J. E., except for the fiddle conventions which he often entered, until 1932 when he began playing on a station in Gastonia. In 1934, J. E., Wade, an old friend and guitarist called Daddy John Love, and Claud "Zeke" Morris began performing over WBT in Charlotte, North Carolina, as J. E. Mainer's Crazy Mountaineers, a name inspired by their first sponsor, the Crazy Water Crystals Company. The Mainers eventually played on radio stations as far west and south as New Orleans and the Mexican border, but their longest tenure was at stations in the Upper South. The group's personnel changed many times before J. E.'s death in 1972, but it included many of the most important musicians of the Southeast, such as Homer Sherrill, Steve Ledford, Dewitt "Snuffy" Jenkins, and two of Zeke Morris' brothers, Wiley and George.

The Mainer repertory, first recorded on Bluebird in August 1935, was filled with traditional songs, including many fiddle pieces such as "Run Mountain" and J. E.'s wonderful version of "Johnson's Old Grey Mule," religious songs such as the very popular "Take Me in the Lifeboat," sentimental parlor duets like "Maple on the Hill" (sung by Wade and Zeke), ballads such as "John Henry," and yodeling blues songs (done by Daddy John Love). Performing with great verve and abandon, the Mainers created a tangy backwoods atmosphere, reminiscent of the Skillet Lickers, that lay a vast cultural distance from the music of the Georgia Wildcats and Radio Cowboys.

Mainer's Mountaineers influenced the styles of other musicians, while also spawning other bands which flourished in the Upper South in the late thirties and early forties. By 1937 Wade Mainer had organized his own band, the Sons of the Mountaineers, which included such musicians as Jay Hugh Hall, Steve Ledford, and Clyde Moody. Hall and Moody in turn later worked as a duet called the Happy-Go-Lucky Boys. Fiddler Homer Sherrill and banjoist Snuffy Jenkins began one of the longest partnerships in country music in 1937 when they joined with announcer Byron Parker at WIS in Columbia, South Carolina, to form the WIS Hillbillies. Through this medium Snuffy Jenkins became the first five-string banjoist to popularize the three-finger roll before a large audience. Many young musicians listened in awe to Jenkins' syncopated sound; two of them, Don Reno and Earl Scruggs, would later introduce it to the world. Musicianship was a major factor in building the Hillbillies' audience, but announcer Byron Parker, the self-styled "Old Hired Hand"—who had earlier been associated with the Monroe Brothers—contributed mightily to their success. Widely recognized as a super-salesman, Parker was as well known as the musicians with whom he worked, and many people all over the Southeast can still recall his closing lines: "Goodbye, good luck, and may God bless you, everyone."

Band personnel shifted constantly among hillbilly musicians in the thirties. Homer Sherrill, for example, found time to play with other groups while serving as a member of the WIS Hillbillies. He appeared on Wiley and Zeke Morris' first recording session for Bluebird in January 1938. Wiley and Zeke performed in typical brothers' fashion with guitar and mandolin, and at their second session in September 1938 recorded their famous and influential version of "Let Me Be Your Salty Dog" (later recorded as "Salty Dog Blues"). Not only did they introduce one of the great warhorses of bluegrass music, they also were the first employers of the seminal bluegrass banjoists, Earl Scruggs and Don Reno.

Among the several southeastern bands which shared the radio audience at the end of the thirties, few were as popular as Roy Hall and his Blue Ridge Entertainers. Hall was a textile worker from Waynesville, North Carolina, who inaugurated his career as a professional musician in February 1937 with a dozen recordings along with his brother Jay Hugh. The Hall Brothers had two more sessions in 1938, before Roy formed the larger band—the Blue Ridge Entertainers—which became one of the most popular regional bands in the years down to Roy Hall's death in an automobile accident on May 16, 1943. Hall and his musicians were undistinguished as singers, but they popularized songs, such as "Come Back Little Pal," "Can You Forgive," and "Don't Let Your Sweet Love Die," which have endured in country music, and they introduced to southeastern audiences some songs identified with western musicians, such as Bob Wills' "New San Antonio Rose" and Johnny Bond's "I Wonder Where You Are Tonight." Working out of their base at WDBJ in Roanoke, Virginia, the Blue Ridge Entertainers functioned as a transitional band, performing both old-time and modern material, providing a bridge between the mountain hoedown bands and the country and western bands of the forties.

By the end of the thirties both individual singers, like Roy Acuff, and individual musicians had begun to achieve identities apart from specific bands. With an occasional exception, such as Charlie Poole or Clayton McMichen, the old-time string bands had generally had neither "stars" nor individual soloists who stood apart from the other band members. But by the beginning of World War II, specific musicians were recruited by various bands, and some instrumentalists traveled widely across the country, either giving shows of their own or finding employment in one band or another. There were a number of southeastern fiddlers in the thirties who were prized for their individual contributions. Roy Hall's fiddler, Tommy Magness, was an old-time fiddler in the J. E. Mainer mold, but he had a smoothness and individual verve that few hoedown fiddlers possessed. Magness was sufficiently prized to be lured away by other prominent band leaders, first by Bill Monroe (with whom he became one of the first blue-grass fiddlers), and later by Roy Acuff.

Magness seems to have been one of the few prominent fiddlers who never traveled outside his native region to find employment. Some southeastern fiddlers, such as Clifford Gross and Carl Cotner, left permanently to be closer to the kind of jazzy or popular-based country music that they really preferred. Others, like Georgia Slim Rutland, Howard "Howdy" Forrester, Arnim Leroy "Curly" Fox, and Arthur Smith, left their homes to become barnstorming entertainers. Georgia Slim and Howdy Forrester went to Tulsa as part of Herald Goodman's Tennessee Valley Boys, and then on down to Dallas, where they were associated for several years with the Callahan Brothers and other local entertainers. Curly Fox, from Graysville, Tennessee, was probably the greatest showman of all the fiddlers. He led his own band on WSB in 1932, but spent most of the decade winning fiddle contests throughout the South, and playing on various radio stations with his wife, Texas Ruby Owens, and with other entertainers such as the Shelton Brothers. He was an outstanding hoedown fiddler, and he excelled at trick tunes on which he could assert his personality and showmanship: "Listen to the Mockingbird" (replete with bird imitations and woodpecker rappings), "Orange Blossom Special," and "Johnson's Old Grey Mule" (in which the voice and scraped fiddle strings combine to simulate the braying of a mule).

Of all the southeastern fiddlers, Arthur Smith was generally acknowledged to be the best. Born in Humphreys County, Tennessee, Smith worked as a railroadman for several years on the North Carolina and St. Louis Railroad; this was the Dixie Line, the inspiration for his first band, the Dixieliners. He appeared on the *WSM Barn Dance* as early as December 1927 but did not become a regular until 1932, when he teamed with Sam and Kirk McGee. Smith was often associated with outstanding musicians, including the Delmore Brothers, with whom he toured and recorded in 1935 and 1936; the Shelton Brothers, with whom he played at KWKH in 1940; and cowboy singer Jimmy Wakely, whom he accompanied and made movies with from 1945 to 1947. He was also a singer and songwriter, having written or arranged such well-known songs as "Beautiful Brown Eyes" and "There's More Pretty Girls than One." But it was as a fiddler that he touched the lives of musicians everywhere. With his rapid fingering and cleanly-noted style of playing, Smith moved fiddling dramatically away from the shuffling hoedown style, and he left a host of songs, such as "Red Apple Rag," "Blackberry Blossom," and "Dickson County Blues," that have forever attracted fiddlers.

The fiddle preserved its dominance in country bands in the thirties, but other instruments rapidly challenged its hegemony, and in so doing radically changed the nature of the country sound. The mandolin, as we have seen, flourished during the decade, but its gentle, parlor sound did not survive the wholesale introduction of electrical amplification into country music. Instead, in the hands of men like Bill Monroe and Red Rector, it became an aggressive, and even percussive, instrument capable of holding its own in a large ensemble and in a high-powered strident style such as bluegrass. In Knoxville at the end of the thirties a teenage musician named Kenneth Burns was already beginning to make the mandolin a jazz instrument; in later years he would be best known as Jethro (of Homer and Jethro). In the Southwest such musicians as Joe Shelton, Leo Raley (probably the first person to electrify the instrument), and, preeminently, Paul Buskirk (a North Carolinian who relocated in Texas), demonstrated that the mandolin could not be confined to any one type of music.

The five-string banjo had declined as the mandolin-and-guitar combos proliferated. Uncle Dave Macon, of course, remained active during the decade, and a few musicians, such as Lily May Ledford, Cousin Emmy, and David "Stringbean" Akeman, used it to accompany old ballads and mountain breakdowns. The instrument came to be perceived as old-fashioned or comic and was presumed to have little value in a band other than as a rhythm instrument. Nevertheless, men like Wade Mainer, with his distinctive two-finger style, kept the instrument alive, and Snuffy Jenkins popularized the syncopated, three-finger technique that was common in his part of western North Carolina. As the thirties ended, the five-string banjo was only a few years away from a sensational resurgence that only a few instruments have enjoyed.

Guitars were common in all country bands, as were string basses. Only the expense involved in purchasing the instrument and the inconvenience of finding space in a touring car to transport it had deterred the acquisition of string basses (also known as bass fiddles, bull fiddles, or stand-up basses). But country musicians had long desired some kind of "bottom" for the sounds of the fiddle bands (which may be one reason why accompanying guitarists often favored bass runs), and bowed cellos were sometimes used to achieve a bass sound. String basses were easily observable in jazz or popular dance bands, but when country bands adopted them, there seemed so little for the bass player to do that he was often given the extra duty of being a rube comic dressed in hillbilly clown clothing.

Most guitar players played a simple open-chord, back-up style, marked by occasional bass runs between chords. Although guitarists bought expensive, finely crafted Martin or Gibson guitars as soon as they could afford them, most beginning instrumentalists had to be content with cheap, low-volumed, hard-to-play brands. Thumb picks, rather than flat picks or finger picks, were favored because they required less exertion and fit readily into the kind of "claw-hammer" style of strumming favored by many players. A few guitarists, such as Sam McGee, Maybelle Carter, Roy Harvey, Dave McCarn, and Dick Justice, had earlier excelled as solo musicians, but it was not until the mid- and late thirties that major breakthroughs were made in the art of guitar playing. Most of the advances in guitar picking came in the West, largely under the influence of such blues and jazz men as Charlie Christian, Eddie Durham, and Aaron "T-Bone" Walker, and with the help of electrical amplification which came after 1934. Still, the portent of the guitar's distinctive future could be heard in the playing of such southeastern musicians as Slim Bryant and Merle Travis, through whose innovations the guitar began to move out of the shadow of the fiddle and banjo to become an instrument of melodic and improvisatory capabilities.

Even more prophetic of country music's future was the sound heard at the end of the thirties in bands like Roy Hall's Blue Ridge Entertainers and Roy Acuff's Smoky Mountain Boys, that of the steel guitar. This was the instrument which did most to set such groups apart from earlier string bands and which in the 1940's would come to be virtually the defining feature of country music. The steel guitar, or its equivalent, appeared early in country music. Frank Hutchison used a knife-style on his October 1926 recording of "Worried Blues," and the Johnson Brothers (Paul and Charles) and Jimmie Tarlton made similar steel recordings by the end of 1927. Such early steel guitarists as Hutchison and Tarlton seem to have been more influenced by black bottleneck styles than they were by Hawaiian influences, although Tarlton picked up some of the latter in his travels too. The steel guitarists who popularized the instrument on Jimmie Rodgers' recordings were either real Hawaiians like Joe Kaipo or men like Ellsworth Cozzens, John Westbrook, and Cliff Carlisle, who learned directly from Hawaiian musicians either on the chautauqua, vaudeville, and tent-rep circuits before World War I or in special courses on the style.

In the days before electrical amplification, the American enthusiast either converted a conventional guitar by elevating the strings or bought one of the specially constructed amplified guitars which the manufacturers began placing on the market. Two brand names predominated among these manufactured guitars: National, which appears to have been the first, and Dobro, which was the most popular. Both were equipped with metal vibrating discs (the National had three and the Dobro one) which amplified them without benefit of electrification. The Dobro was the creation of the Dopera Brothers (Ed, Robert, and Rudy) of California. The brothers had been partners in the National Musical Instrument Company, the manufacturer of a metal-bodied tri-cone resonator guitar, but in 1928 they formed a new organization which introduced the Dobro, a single-resonator instrument whose wooden body permitted a much more melodious sound than the tinny quality conveyed by the Nationals. Cliff Carlisle was one of the first musicians to play a Dobro, but its real popularization in American life came through the recordings of Roy Acuff in the late thirties and early forties. Acuff's rise to fame as a *Grand Ole Opry* artist permitted the Dobro, played in his band first by Clell "Cousin Jody"

Summey and later by Beecher "Oswald" Kirby, to receive a similar recognition. Acuff had many great musicians, but the Dobro was the distinctive feature of his instrumentation.

Although the dobro (the name became a generic term) appeared periodically in country bands throughout the nation, it was fated to carry an old-time and southeastern identification (and after its temporary eclipse after World War II, it was reintroduced to country music as a bluegrass instrument). The real wave of the future in steel guitar playing came in its electrification and in its emergence as a flexible instrument capable of playing either country music or jazz. Most of the innovative developments in steel guitar style came from musicians west of the Mississippi River, but southeasterners sometimes played crucial roles, as in the case of Noel Boggs, who was applying jazz-derived techniques to the instrument as early as 1939. Above all, in the playing of Jerry Byrd one could hear the sound of country music's future.

Byrd grew up in Lima, Ohio, where as a boy he developed an enthusiasm for Hawaiian music that has never left him (as of 1984 he resides in Hawaii and is a member of the Hawaiian Music Foundation). As a fledgling musician he played songs of the Islands, but he gravitated toward country music in the late thirties, a time when the music was receptive to the melodious and full-chorded sound of the steel guitar. He began playing on WLW in Cincinnati in 1939 and became a regular member of the *Renfro Valley Barn Dance* in the early forties. He later became a member of Red Foley's band and was one of the first sessions musicians in Nashville. Probably more than any other musician, he made the electric steel guitar the dominant and defining instrument of the mainstream country music that began to concentrate in Nashville in the forties.

Before ending our discussion of the thirties and the transformations affecting the traditional music of the Southeast during that period, it would seem appropriate to explore further the economic context in which those changes occurred: the Great Depression. The Depression promoted the rediscovery and consequent romanticization of "the folk." Southern farmers and workers, "ill clad, ill housed, and ill nourished," commanded the attention of social workers, politicians, artists and intellectuals, reformers, radicals, and folklorists. In this new age of the "common man," the southern folk, once dismissed as cultural degenerates and snakehandlers—H. L. Mencken's "booboisie"—now emerged as a people whose folkways deserved commemoration, if not preservation. The photographic division of the Farm Security Administration, the WPA's cultural projects (for writers, artists, actors, and musicians), and the Library of Congress' Archive of American Folk-Song all contributed to the documentation of southern folk culture. Under the leadership of Robert Winslow Gordon, from 1928 to 1933, and John and Alan Lomax after 1933, the Archive of American Folk-

Song embarked on a massive campaign to collect, on field recordings, folk material from all over the United States.

In the meantime, the plain folk were making themselves dramatically visible as never before. Unemployed people haunted the relief offices; and hobo jungles appeared on the edges of every American city, luring the homeless and jobless who rode the rails or merely wandered across the country. The hoboes were generally individuals who acted alone; the Okies, on the other hand, migrated as families. Dispossessed southwestern farmers, made homeless by automation, hard times, and dust storms, trekked westward toward the fabled land of California, seeking the illusory promise of jobs and material abundance which the Golden State supposedly possessed. Most people, however, did not migrate but instead remained at home to deal with hard times as best they could. Tenant farmers and sharecroppers in the Arkansas and Tennessee delta region roused themselves briefly against their landlords and organized the Southern Tenant Farmers Union. Their brothers and sisters in the Appalachian coal fields and Piedmont textile mills marched into the national headlines with a series of strikes that gave the lie to the image of fatalism and docility that surrounded southern workers.

The labor uprisings that spread across the South between 1929 and 1933 were largely spontaneous affairs, generated by declining wages, the uncertainty of labor, and harsh working conditions (the most notorious being the textile industry's "stretch-out system"). Indigenous protest, though, soon attracted the support of northern labor organizers, reformers, radicals, and the liberal intelligentsia. The northerners who came south to promote the cause of social justice, whether at Marion or Gastonia, North Carolina, among the "lintheads" (a term that "polite" southerners had affixed to the cotton mill workers), or in "Bloody Harlan County," Kentucky, among the coal miners, found themselves among a people who sang and made ballads. Archie Green has described well the musical phenomenon that resulted from the mating of radical and intellectual ideas from the North with the conservative and rural tradition of ballad-making in the South: "From this setting came a group of topical songs using old melodies to set off intensely stark and militant texts. In a sense, Piedmont mill villages and Cumberland mine camps became meeting grounds for the ideologies of Andrew Jackson and Karl Marx, Abraham Lincoln and Mikhail Bakunin."[4]

Every struggling social group had its balladeers: Aunt Molly Jackson, Sarah Ogan, Jim Garland, and Florence Reece, in the Kentucky coal fields; Ella May Wiggins, who was shot to death near Gastonia because of

---

4. Archie Green, notes to Sarah Ogan Gunning, *Girl of Constant Sorrow*, Folk-Legacy Records FSA-26.

her activism; John Handcox, the song poet of the Arkansas sharecroppers; and, most famous of all, Woody Guthrie, the bard of the Okies. When the northern liberal/radical coterie went back home, they took a body of songs, such as Florence Reece's great labor hymn "Which Side Are You On?" and John Handcox's "Roll the Union On," which have ever since served the cause of human justice in the United States. Northern social activists soon saw people like Aunt Molly and Jim Garland in the flesh, because these mountain balladeers moved north when the movement for which they fought was defeated. But when Woody Guthrie took his Okie songs to New York in 1940, the radical community felt they had discovered a "new Joe Hill," a proletarian who sang protest material. Thus, the seeds of what would later be called "the urban folk revival" were planted. Young people like Pete Seeger and Cisco Houston passionately attached themselves to Guthrie, sang his songs, and passed them on to a later generation of "folk singers." The urban folk movement's radical origins have always affected public perceptions of it, and the linking of "protest" and "folksong" has contributed to false impressions about the nature of the folk and the music they have made. Furthermore, a regrettable distinction between "folk" and "hillbilly" music developed in the popular mind. "Folk" music, which had become largely the province of intellectuals and reformers, became increasingly removed from the folk, while "hillbilly" music, the creation of the folk, developed in its own independent fashion.

Hillbilly music's response to the Great Depression reflected the varied, and often conflicting, impulses of the society which gave it birth. Despite the efforts made by its friends and foes alike, there has been no clear-cut, consistent ideology in country music, just as there has been none in southern rural culture. Rural southerners have been socially conservative in their personal habits, but, historically, they have veered radically in their patriotism (the 250,000 deaths in the Civil War should suggest that national allegiance has not always been a cardinal virtue among southerners), and they have sometimes responded explosively to public injustice, as in the wave of strikes that dotted the southern landscape in the early thirties. Furthermore, neither the strong strain of populism that erupted in the 1890's nor the religious-bred suspicion of materialism has ever totally vanished from southern rural life. Woody Guthrie, whose stylistic debt to hillbilly music was profound, represented one political posture. Merle Haggard today, with his "conservative" songs, represents another. But neither man represents the whole of country music's history nor of its sociopolitical. perspective.

If country music has had no clear-cut political stance, it has nonetheless been a music of social commentary, and scarcely any phenomenon in American life has escaped being brought into its purview. The reaction to hard times of hillbilly musicians and their audiences ranged from outright indifference to passionate activism. The 1930's, after all, were marked by a popular culture of escapism; many Americans sought relief from the Depression through detective movies and Busby Berkeley musicals, marathon dancing and big band swing. Country music audiences sought similar escape or cathartic release through western swing dance music, cowboy songs, gospel music, and parlor songs of old-fashioned love and morality. In commenting directly on the Depression, some songs adopted the Hoover view that economic decline was basically a product of public doubt and that prosperity would accompany a revival of confidence. The Light Crust Doughboys, for example, took the idea to an extreme when they talked of putting Depression on the run with "My Million Dollar Smile." In "No Hard Times Blues" Jimmie Rodgers exuded the confidence of a man who had "corn in my crib and chickens in my back door"; Jimmie, though, spoke from a position of economic security that few of his listeners shared.

Religion, as always, colored the responses of some singers to economic distress. In "No Depression in Heaven," the Carter Family saw the disaster as merely one more trial that humanity had to suffer, and opined that the only true relief lay beyond the grave. Most religious songs, of course, made no references to public events, but instead brought their traditional messages of private hope and salvation to millions of poor people who found little solace this side of Heaven. Such songs as "Farther Along," which consoled troubled hearts by saying that someday "we'll know all about it," and Charles Tindley's "We'll Understand It Better By and By" did not explain the world's problems, but they did promise eventual release from them. Tindley, the great black gospel composer from earlier in the century, contributed several songs such as "Stand By Me" and "Leave It There" which seemed peculiarly suited to the needs of poor or oppressed people. They entered the white gospel hymnals in the 1930's, along with those of the younger black writer Thomas Dorsey, whose 1932 composition "Precious Lord, Take My Hand" was destined to become the cherished possession of whites and blacks alike. Oklahoma-born Albert E. Brumley, the most popular of the white gospel composers, found his first receptive audiences among rural southerners in the 1930's. His visions of a caring, personal Savior and of an abundant, pastoral Heaven where old acquaintances would be renewed were images especially satisfying in a world of deprivation. Brumley's 1931 composition "I'll Fly Away"—one of the most performed gospel songs in the world—entered the repertories of country and gospel singers alike, and his nostalgic songs, such as "Dreaming of a Little Cabin" and "Did You Ever Go Sailin'? (Down the River of Memories)" poignantly evoke recurrent longings universal to his audience.

Some country songs expressed compassion for the victims of suffering but drew no social lesson and made no political statement about them. Grady and Hazel Cole's "Tramp on the Street," first recorded by them in 1936 but based on a much older poem, is one of the great pleas for Christian compassion found in country music. The song's compelling lyrics make an analogy between "the angel unaware" and the tramp on the street. Hobo songs, of course, had appeared in country music since the 1920's, but usually as a facet of the romantic idealization of rambling men. Jimmie Rodgers, on the other hand, recorded two songs which identify with the misfortunes of hoboes: "Hobo Bill's Last Ride," recorded in November 1929, and "Hobo's Meditation," recorded in 1932. Both of them were very much in the tradition of sentimental songs, but they probably profited, as did "Tramp on the Street," from the heightened public awareness of homeless, wandering men during the depression. "Hobo's Meditation" refers to "tough cops and brakemen," but, like "Hobo Bill," places no blame on society and instead sees its subjects as part of the natural flotsam and jetsam of life. To find statements of overt political import dealing with hoboes or migratory workers, one has to turn to the music of the Wobblies (who are outside the scope of this book), or to the songs of Woody Guthrie.

Woodrow Wilson "Woody" Guthrie occupies an unusual position in American country and folk music and is admittedly difficult to categorize. He began as a hillbilly singer with strong traditional roots and advanced to the position of America's most revered urban folksinger and writer. Born in Okemah, Oklahoma, in 1912, Woody absorbed a wide variety of folksongs and ballads from his parents and from the commercial hillbillies. Plagued by a restlessness that may have been accentuated by the family disease of Huntington's Chorea, Guthrie went out on his own rather early in life and traveled over much of the Southwest doing odd jobs. In Pampa, Texas, where he experienced the dust storms for the first time, he learned a few basic guitar chords from his uncle Jeff, one of the local deputy sheriffs. The two of them formed a hillbilly band and began entertaining at local functions in the Pampa area.

Guthrie's wanderlust led him in 1937 to California, where he became part of the horde of Okies who had already been thronging into the state. On July 19, he and his cousin Jack Guthrie began singing on KFVD in Los Angeles; they were joined soon thereafter by a woman called "Lefty Lou" (Maxine Crissman) who often sang duets with Woody. At the beginning of his radio career, Guthrie was very much in the mold of the hillbilly singer. His guitar playing was a modification of that of Maybelle Carter, and his songs came from the Carter Family, Jimmie Rodgers, and other hillbilly singers. And when he wrote his own songs, they were invariably set to older melodies of commercial and noncommercial origin (for example, "Oklahoma Hills" follows the melody of "The Girl I Loved in Sunny Tennessee"; "The Philadelphia Lawyer" is set to the melody of "The Jealous Lover"; "This Land Is Your Land" is to the melody of "Little Darling, Pal of Mine"). Guthrie's hillbilly emphasis, however, was accompanied by a flowering of radicalism. Guthrie felt a strong emotional kinship with the homeless and often persecuted migratory workers, especially his fellow

Okies, and he began to compose songs which expressed his sympathies as well as his anger at the system which caused their misfortunes. By the end of the thirties he had accumulated an extensive collection of original compositions dealing with the dust bowl refugees and other victims of social and economic persecution: "Talking Dust Bowl Blues," "I Ain't Got No Home in This World Anymore," "Pastures of Plenty," "Vigilante Man," and "Do-Re-Mi," a wonderfully sardonic song warning poor people about the perils of migrating to California. When Guthrie moved to New York in 1940, he was no longer simply a singer of hillbilly songs and would never again be identified as such (even though some of his songs, such as "Oklahoma Hills" and "Philadelphia Lawyer," remained permanent and beloved elements of the country repertory). The post-1940 Guthrie would always be known as a protest singer.

Migrant workers were not the only economically oppressed people chronicled in hillbilly songs. One of the richest, but as yet incompletely documented, bodies of industrial and protest songs on hillbilly records consists of those from the textile-mill villages of the southeastern piedmont region. The existence of the textile factories—with their regimentation, long hours, low pay, and child labor—provides a grim refutation of the idea that the South has had no industrial tradition. The textile mills were brick-and-stone testimonials to those "New South" propagandists who sought to bring progress to the South by ending its economic colonial dependence on the North. They sought to "bring the factory to the field." The textile mills did bring progress to the South, and prosperity to some, but they also brought misery to many. Thousands of mountain and hill-country people willingly left their farms to seek the promise of a better life, only to find that they had merely traded rural deprivation for an industrial poverty which robbed them even of their independence. Kept close to economic penury, depressed by a burdensome regimentation, and ostracized by middle-class southerners who called them "lintheads" and "factory trash," the textile operatives found solace in old-time religion, protection through the trade-union movement, and comfort in their age-old tradition of ballad-making.

The textile mills not only produced an important body of folksongs; they also spawned a high percentage of commercial country singers (a phenomenon that needs to be explored). While many of the textile songs of the period were performed by comparatively well-known entertainers such as the Dixon Brothers (of "Weave Room Blues" fame), some important songs were recorded by individuals who regrettably have had a much more obscure place in country music history. Two interesting protest items, "The Marion Massacre" (about the killing of unarmed strikers in North Carolina) and "The North Carolina Textile Strike," were recorded in October 1929 on the Paramount label by Frank Welling and John McGhee under the name of the Martin Brothers. Welling and McGhee were prolific recording entertainers from West Virginia who usually recorded sentimental and religious material. Although both songs clearly expressed sympathy for the strikers, Ivan Tribe asserts that "the ultimate message is of the next world and the joys of Heaven."[5] Wilmer Watts' recording of "Cotton Mill Blues," on the other hand, contains no mixed messages; it is overtly class-conscious when it notes that "uptown people call us trash." David McCarn, from Gaston County, North Carolina, similarly did not permit sentimental or religious trappings to cloud his picture of mill work. McCarn went to work in the mills when he was twelve years old, and while working in a series of factories (and somehow also finding enough time to roam around much of the United States) he developed one of the "hottest" guitar styles heard on early country records as well as a flair for writing topical songs. In 1930 and 1931 he recorded twelve songs for Victor, six of which deal directly with cotton mill conditions. These include "Poor Man, Rich Man," "Cotton Mill Colic," and the sardonic "Serves 'Em Fine," which poked fun at the mountaineers foolish enough to leave their placid homes for the material allure of the textile mills.

There were also a rather extensive body of songs which commented directly upon the Depression or upon the government's response to it. Uncle Dave Macon, always a perceptive and witty critic of the social scene, recorded a few songs that at least touched the borders of protest. Uncle Dave would no doubt have said "I told you so" when news of the stock market crash appeared. He had campaigned for Hoover's opponent in "Governor Al Smith," which significantly also called for the repeal of Prohibition. "All I've Got's Gone" described what had happened to people who lived beyond their means during the twenties, and "All In Down and Out Blues" argues that for millions of Americans "Wall Street's propositions were not all roses."

Hoover's handling of the Bonus Bill for World War I veterans also received scathing criticism from hillbilly singers. Buddy Starcher, for example, went to Washington at the time of the 1932 Bonus March; he sang for the marchers and passed out broadsides containing two of his compositions, "Bonus Blues" and "Hoover Blues." Starcher's songs did not enjoy wide circulation, but another song inspired by the suffering of the marchers—"The Forgotten Soldier Boy"—was later recorded by the Monroe Brothers in 1937, and then reintroduced to a new generation of country fans by the Lilly Brothers in the 1960's.

Support for Franklin D. Roosevelt was hardly radical or surprising given the state of the economy in 1932; therefore, the appearance of pro-FDR and pro–New Deal sentiments on hillbilly records is not at all remarkable.

5. Ivan Tribe, "John McGhee and Frank Welling: West Virginia's Most Recorded Old-Time Artists," *John Edwards Memorial Foundation Quarterly* 17, no. 62 (Summer 1981): 61.

Slim Smith's "Breadline Blues" was partisanly political, castigating the "big-legged elephant" and advising listeners to "vote away those blues" in 1932. Fiddlin' John Carson probably spoke for most southern farmers when he sang "Hurrah for Roosevelt" who was doing all within his power to "bring the farmers through." Much of the political commentary of the period was personal in its preoccupation with Roosevelt, but songs also commented occasionally on New Deal legislation or agencies. Billy Cox, a West Virginia yodeling disciple of Jimmie Rodgers, was also acutely partisan in his Democratic sympathies. This composer of "Sparkling Brown Eyes" and "Filipino Baby," two of country music's great perennials, also wrote "NRA Blues," which extolled the effort of one of the major New Deal agencies to alleviate unemployment and to improve working conditions. The Allen Brothers' "New Deal Blues" was ardently supportive of the whole range of relief legislation, including the NRA. Although one hears no overtly anti-Roosevelt sentiments expressed on hillbilly recordings, one does encounter an occasional doubt concerning some of the social movements of the time. Roy Acuff's "Old Age Pension Check," for example, poked good-natured fun at the Townsend Movement, the California crusade which lobbied for a monthly $200 pension for Americans above the age of sixty. The song described how "poor old grandma" would suddenly become like a frivolous sixteen-year-old when the monthly payments started rolling in. In the final analysis, Billy Cox probably summed up the feelings of most working-class southerners when, on November 28, 1936, only a few weeks after FDR's stunning re-election, he gleefully recorded "The Democratic Donkey Is in His Stall Again" and "Franklin Roosevelt's Back Again."

By the end of the thirties, country music, in its myriad forms and impulses, had not only survived the ravages of hard times but had broadened its horizons and moved well beyond the boundaries of its original regional identity. The music, though, had changed substantially since it first took shape as an industry in the early twenties. Even in the Southeast, where tradition was presumed to be most strongly cherished, novel styles and sounds had moved in alongside the older forms. And while the musicians of the Southeast and Deep South were perpetuating certain styles and modifying others, musical winds were blowing in from the Southwest— particularly from Texas—which would have far-reaching and dynamic effects upon the future course of the music.

Floyd Tillman. Courtesy of Floyd Tillman.

5. The Cowboy Image and the Growth of Western Music

The emergence of the western image in country music was probably inevitable; throughout the twentieth century the cowboy has been the object of unparalleled romantic adulation and interest. Given the pejorative connotations that clung to farming and rural life, the adoption of cowboy clothing and western themes was a logical step for the country singer.

The increased emphasis on western themes and attitudes came unsurprisingly in the westernmost southern states—Louisiana, Oklahoma, Texas—and in California. In these areas country music assumed forms differing from those in the more easterly southern states. Oklahoma, Louisiana, and Texas were part of the southern tradition yet also significantly different. All three were touched by the oil boom of the early twentieth century, and each possessed population groups that stood apart culturally, while also influencing the dominant "Anglo" element of the state. Oklahoma and Texas were settled, for the most part, by former residents of the older southern states, who had brought with them their values, traditions, and institutions. Louisiana, on the other hand, was a land of two great cultures: a Roman Catholic, "Latin" culture in the South, and an "Anglo," Protestant culture in the north. Immigrants brought slaves and the cotton culture to all parts of the Southwest, making Texas and Louisiana parts of the southern economic and political orbit. They also transported their evangelical Protestantism to southwestern soil and brought many features of their folk heritage. Some of the old British ballads survived the westward migration, although they had lost many of their former characteristics. In some Texas communities, particularly in remote East Texas areas such as the Big Thicket, the old ballads and old styles of singing endured well into the twentieth century. Many of the East Texas communities were, and are, replicas of the older southern environment. And, in many of them, folk traditions died slowly.

Texas folk music, then, was basically southern-derived. Texas rural musicians used instruments common in the rest of the South, sang in styles similar to those of other rural southerners, frequently attended house parties where old-time fiddlers held sway, and learned to read music at the shape-note singing schools. But despite its close cultural affiliation with the South, Texas had a culture all its own—a culture produced by the mingling of diverse ethnic strains: southern "Anglo," black, German and Central European (in the south-central region of the state), Mexican, and Louisiana Cajun (in the area extending from Beaumont to Houston). A passion for dancing was common among all these groups, and in this heterogeneous society musical styles and songs flowed freely from one group to another, modifying the old southern rural style. Rural music was prevalent and pervasive, but it was substantially different from that produced in the Southeast or in the Deep South.

The discovery of oil at Spindletop, near Beaumont, in 1901 was the first of a series of finds in southeastern Texas, southwestern Louisiana, Oklahoma, and Arkansas, in the years extending up through World War I. The discovery of the great East Texas oil field in the early 1930's, along with the rapid industrialization that began during World War II, further set Texas apart from the other southern states. While these factors contributed to Texas' uniqueness, they are probably less important than the fact that it was also part of the West. In fact, to most Americans Texas was and is the West. And this West was a glorious land peopled by cowboys.

The romantic concept of the West, shared by most Americans, has a history virtually as old as the nation itself. James Fenimore Cooper's early novels describing the restorative qualities of the frontier were not substantially different, nor less romantic, than the themes emphasized later in Bret Harte's stories, in the western "dime novels," or in such books as Owen Wister's *The Virginian*. The cowboy and the West had been subjected to the romanticizing process long before Hollywood and the television industry began their exploitations of the theme. And, too, the American people had long demonstrated a general interest in the songs of the cowboy (beginning with Nathan Howard Thorp's *Songs of the Cowboys*, 1908, John A. Lomax's *Cowboy Songs and Other Frontier Ballads*, 1910). Although concert-musician Oscar Fox (from Burnet, Texas) adapted some of the cowboy songs for high-art purposes, the western theme did not make any significant impact on American music until the thirties. But when it did, even Tin Pan Alley reverberated with the melodies of the range. The farther Americans became removed from the cowboy past, the more intense became their interest in cowboy songs and lore. Hillbilly singers and musicians did much to implant the romantic cowboy image in the minds of their American audiences.

Before the thirties a few musicians recorded songs which genuinely reflected the cowboy heritage. Concert singer Bentley Ball (who did many programs of patriotic and traditional songs—many of them in colleges—recorded "The Dying Cowboy" and "Jesse James" for Columbia in 1919,[1] and Charles Nabell in November 1924 recorded some cowboy songs for Okeh, along with other types of traditional material. Several of the early cowboy singers came from Texas, and their songs, for the most part, came out of genuine cowboy experience. Among the Texans, Carl Sprague may have done most to generate an immediate interest in the recorded songs of the cowboy. He grew up on a South Texas ranch near Alvin, where he learned many of the songs (most of them from his cowboy uncle) that he later recorded for Victor. His 1925 recordings of cowboy songs—topped off by the immensely popular "When the Work's All Done This Fall"—mark him as one of America's first singing cowboys. While attending Texas A&M he became convinced, through Vernon Dalhart's success as a singer of mountain songs, that a similar market for cowboy singers might exist. He traveled to New York and had a successful audition with Victor Records; his earliest recordings had a sound very similar to that of Dalhart (guitar and studio violin). Singing, however, was never more than a hobby with Sprague, and aside from his recordings he made few commercial appearances. For many years he was on the coaching staff at Texas A&M, and, in addition, he attained the rank of major in the United States Army.

Another Texan, Jules Verne Allen, had been an actual working cowboy and had therefore experienced the rugged life he sang about. Born in Waxahachie, Texas, Allen began working cattle in Jack County at the age of ten. From 1893 to 1907 he worked as a rough string rider and bronco buster from the Rio Grande to the Montana line. Unlike Sprague, he used cowboy music as the basis for a professional career. During the twenties and thirties Allen sang over numerous radio station, including WOAI in San Antonio, where he performed as "Longhorn Luke." Neither he nor Sprague was a drugstore cowboy, and, like most of the pioneer recording performers of the twenties, they drew most of their material from turn-of-the-century cowboy life (although some of their songs were learned directly from the Lomax collection).

Other cowboy singers of the early commercial period varied widely in the amount of actual range experience they possessed. The Cartwright Brothers (Bernard and Jack) grew up in Boerne, Texas, directly on the route of "the long drive" that proceeded on to Kansas. Essentially a fiddle band, the Cartwrights performed a variety of songs; their version of "The

---

1. Ball acknowledged that he learned the two songs from the Lomax book, and Columbia paid Lomax copyright fees of two cents per side for each record manufactured (John Lomax Family Papers, Eugene C. Barker Texas History Center, University of Texas at Austin).

Texas Ranger," however—marked by Bernard's haunting fiddle—is one of the greatest performances of a cowboy song heard on early commercial records. Curley Fletcher, from California, was a rodeo performer and itinerant hawker of songs long before he made any commercial recordings. His greatest claim to fame came through his writing in 1915 of the poem "The Strawberry Roan," which he sold on broadside sheets. At least a couple of the pioneer cowboy singers, Goebel Reeves and Harry McClintock, worked at a wide variety of occupations in the West; both also spent some time in the famous Industrial Workers of the World (IWW, or Wobblies). Both men were southerners whose wanderlust drew them west.

Goebel Reeves ("the Texas Drifter") was born in Sherman, Texas, in 1899, and before his death in California in 1959 he had enjoyed a varied career which led him across the United States and around the world. Although he came from a respectable middle-class family (his father served in the Texas legislature), Reeves deliberately chose the life of a hobo. During the course of his wanderings, he enlisted in the army, saw front-line service in World War I, worked as a merchant seaman, became active in the IWW, toured the vaudeville circuit, performed on radio, and recorded under several names for such companies as Okeh and Brunswick. In his recording career as a singer and yodeler—he claimed to have taught Jimmie Rodgers the yodeling style in about 1920 while living in New Orleans—Reeves introduced some of the most interesting examples of both cowboy and hobo songs found in American music. These included the well-known "Hobo's Lullaby," "The Hobo and the Cop," "Railroad Boomer," and the cowboy songs "Bright Sherman Valley" and "The Cowboy's Prayer."

Harry McClintock was as well-traveled as Reeves, having also been a merchant seaman, a soldier, and a hobo. Born in Knoxville, Tennessee, he traveled widely throughout the United States and became a member of the IWW in the early twentieth century. Because of his musical talents, McClintock was a welcome addition to the Wobblies, who had a well-known fondness for singing and whose *Little Red Songbook* became virtually the bible for labor/protest singers in America. McClintock's claim that he wrote "Hallelujah, Bum Again" and "Big Rock Candy Mountain," two of the world's most famous hobo songs, has never been seriously challenged. Once he settled down from his wanderings, McClintock began a career as a radio cowboy singer as early as 1925 on KFRC in San Francisco. "Haywire Mac," as he was often called, also recorded for Victor from 1927 to 1931. Along with his superbly performed cowboy songs such as "Sam Bass," "Jesse James," and "Texas Rangers," McClintock's labor songs make him one of the important progenitors of western music.

John White and Otto Gray contributed to the shaping of western music by presenting it widely to a national audience. White was an unlikely "westerner," hailing from Washington, D.C. However, he was the first person to introduce cowboy songs on radio to a New York audience (on NBC from 1927 to 1936). He also recorded cowboy songs, as well as hillbilly material, from 1929 to 1931, under several pseudonyms including "the Lonesome Cowboy." White specialized in the history of cowboy songs, and over the years he did more than any other person to describe the origins of the ballads, while also dispelling much of the romantic claptrap that had gathered around them.

Otto Gray, a prosperous rancher from near Stillwater, Oklahoma, pioneered in the commercialization of cowboy music. In about 1923 Gray assumed the leadership of a string band that earlier had been composed of real cowboys—the McGinty Cowboys (named for Billy McGinty, an Oklahoma rodeo performer). Gray's group had the distinction of being one of the few country groups publicized in *Billboard*, although Gray paid for most of the advertising. From 1928 to 1932, Gray and the Cowboys made a tour of radio stations throughout the country and performed on the northeastern RKO vaudeville circuit. Momie Gray (Otto's wife) was the featured singer of the organization, specializing in sentimental songs. The Cowboys were a highly professional group that possessed most of the characteristics of slick show-business organizations. A special publicity man traveled in advance of the group, and appearances on radio stations provided further exposure. Two agencies, the Weber-Simon Agency in New York and the William Jacobs Agency in Chicago, handled the group's RKO bookings. The Gray performers, dressed in plain, western-style clothing, traveled in Gray's $20,000 custom-built automobile, which was wired for sound reproduction and had a radio receiver and transmitter.

If Otto Gray contributed significantly to the commercialization of "western" music, Jimmie Rodgers played an equally important role in fusing it with country music. As discussed earlier, Rodgers spent the last few years of his life in Texas and conducted many of his most successful tours there. He took great pride in the Texas heritage and the romantic cowboy past. The modern concept of the "singing cowboy" and of "western" music may very well date back directly to Rodgers.

Scores of singers who modeled themselves after Jimmie Rodgers emerged in the thirties, and it is significant that many of them gave themselves "cowboy" titles and dressed in western attire. Young Hank Snow, for example, in far-off Nova Scotia, dressed in cowboy regalia and called himself "the Yodeling Ranger." In even more remote Australia, Tex Morton described himself as "the Boundary Rider" and sang cowboy songs with a bizarre, trilling yodel about both the Australian bush and the Texas Plains. Others, like Ernest Tubb, included few cowboy songs in their repertories but wore cowboy boots and ten-gallon hats. The western attraction was very strong, and even young hillbilly singers from the Deep South or from the southeastern mountains, whose associations with cowboys were through story and song, became involved in the western image and imagined themselves "way out west in Texas for the roundup in the spring."

Perhaps because of Rodgers' close association with Texas, many of the successful Texas hillbilly performers—Ernest Tubb, Lefty Frizzell, Floyd Tillman, Bob Wills, Tommy Duncan—credited Jimmie Rodgers as their inspiration. One of the most important of these individuals, and the one who completed the "romantic westernizing" process began by Rodgers, was Orvon Gene Autry. Autry owed most of his initial success to the fact that he could perform Rodgers' repertory in Rodgers' yodeling style. Autry was born on a horse farm near Tioga, Texas, on September 29, 1907, but moved to Oklahoma with his parents while in his teens. Although his father was a horse trader, there was little of the cattle ranch experience that Autry's promotional material later stressed. At any rate, he left the "ranching" life as quickly as he could, working as a railroad telegrapher and singing at every opportunity.

According to a much repeated story, confirmed by Autry himself, his decision to become a professional musician was inspired by Will Rogers. One day in 1927 the great humorist came to Chelsea, Oklahoma, where Autry was working as a telegrapher for the St. Louis and Frisco Railroad, heard the young man singing and strumming his guitar, and encouraged him to go to New York and become a professional. Autry's first trip to the big city in 1927 was unsuccessful, but he returned to Tulsa and got a job on KVOO as "the Oklahoma Yodeling Cowboy." He went back to New York in 1929 and made his first records for Victor, accompanied by the Marvin Brothers, Johnny and Frankie. In December of the same year he began a crucial association with Arthur Satherley, who recorded him for the American Record Company (ARC), producer of records for chain stores and for Sears. It was through the association with Sears' Conqueror label that Autry made it to WLS and the *National Barn Dance*.

In Chicago after 1931, Autry was an immediate success. His appearances on the *Barn Dance* and on his own radio program, *Conqueror Record Time*, made him one of the most popular performers in WLS history. His records, released on Sears labels, were those most prominently displayed in the Sears-Roebuck catalogue. As a result of his growing popularity, a number of Gene Autry songbooks and guitar instruction books began to appear in the early thirties. An ad for a Gene Autry "Roundup" Guitar, priced at $9.95, reminded the reader that Autry had become a famous performer "simply because he learned to play a guitar while on the ranch."[2] Autry's promotional mentors, Art Satherley and Ann Williams of the WLS production staff, capitalized on the "western" motif and made him a singing cowboy long before the bulk of his recorded repertory came to include western numbers.

In his early years as a professional singer, and on through the WLS period from 1931 to 1934, Autry was a hillbilly singer. Only rarely did he sing

2. *Sears-Roebuck Catalogue*, Fall and Winter, 1933–1934, p. 535.

anything of a western variety. In song selection and in style of performance he was strictly in the southern rural tradition. His Jimmie Rodgers
imitations were among the best in country music, and his own "compositions" included such songs as "A Gangster's Warning," "A Hillbilly Wedding in June," "My Old Pal of Yesterday," and, in 1931, one of the biggest-
selling records in hillbilly music's then-short history, "Silver Haired Daddy
of Mine," recorded as a duet with the song's co-composer, Jimmie Long.
Autry's recorded selections, which were many and varied, even included
at least one labor song. This was "The Death of Mother Jones," recorded
on at least seven labels, which applauded the life of a famous and radical
labor leader. This song was rather far away from the type one would expect
from a cowboy singer.

His success on the Chicago radio stations and on record labels gained
for Autry in 1934 the position that was to make him the best-known cowboy
in the United States and one of the most famous hillbilly singers. In that
year he went to Hollywood and began his career as the "Nation's Number
One Singing Cowboy." Beginning with a small part in Ken Maynard's *In
Old Santa Fe*, he then starred for thirteen episodes in a strange cowboy/
science-fiction serial called *The Phantom Empire*. He went on to a featured role in 1935 in *Tumbling Tumbleweeds*, a film that also included his
old sidekick from Chicago days, Smiley Burnette. In the following decades
Autry made more than ninety movies for Republic, Columbia, and Mascot,
eighty-one of which included the multi-talented Burnette, who usually
played a bumbling character called Frog Millhouse. While becoming one
of the most popular and wealthy actors in Hollywood, Autry also created
the stereotype of the heroic cowboy who was equally adept with a gun and
guitar. Autry was not the first individual to sing in a western movie—Ken
Maynard had done so as early as 1930—but he was the first to institu-
tionalize the phenomenon. With Autry ensconced as a singing movie cowboy, hillbilly music now had a new medium through which to popularize
itself. The Silver Screen further romanticized the cowboy and helped to
shape the public idea of western music. After signing his Hollywood contract, Autry made a radical shift in his repertory from "country" themes to
"western" motifs. Instead of singing songs about the mountains, he came
increasingly to perform songs with such titles as "Riding down the Canyon" and "Empty Cot in the Bunkhouse." Both in Autry's singing and in
the instrumentation which accompanied him, one hears a distinctly measurable change in the records he made from 1929 to 1939. There was a
definite smoothing out of presentation—a lower vocal pitch, well-rounded
tones, honey-coated articulation—as the one-time hillbilly singer reached
out to a larger audience. Instrumentally, Autry's sound exhibited a similar
evolution, particularly after violinist Carl Cotner became his musical director. Soft guitars, muted violins, a melodious but unobtrusive steel guitar, an accordion, and occasionally even horns moved into Autry's instru-

mentation, as he and his directors sought a sound that would give no offense to America's broad urban middle class. Whatever vocal sound was featured, though, Autry demonstrated a mastery of it. No country singer has ever shown more versatility.

Autry's popularity inspired other movie companies to present their own versions of the singing cowboy. In searching for likely candidates, the companies usually delved into the ranks of country music, acquiring acts that had already established themselves on hillbilly radio shows or on record labels. Following Smiley Burnette, the Light Crust Doughboys were the first country group to join Autry in a movie (*Oh, Susanna*). Some Autry sidemen went on to become important entertainment personalities in their own right. Johnny Bond, Jimmy Wakely, and Dick Reinhart, for example, came to Hollywood in 1940 (as the Jimmy Wakely Trio) and joined Autry's *Melody Ranch Show* in September of that year. Reinhart became one of the early exponents of the honky-tonk style, with songs like "Fort Worth Jail" and "Truck Driver's Coffee Stop." Wakely eventually starred in many movies of his own, became one of country music's smoothest singers, and made several seminal recordings such as "One Has My Name, the Other Has My Heart" (one of the first successful "cheating" songs in country music). Bond remained on the *Melody Ranch* program until it ended in 1956, playing the role of a comic sidekick and opening the show each Sunday with the bass guitar run introduction to "Back in the Saddle Again." Bond also became one of country music's greatest songwriters, writing such songs as "Cimarron" (performed by all western groups), "I'll Step Aside," and "I Wonder Where You Are Tonight" (now a standard in both bluegrass and mainstream country music).

A long line of hillbilly singers made only occasional appearances in western movies, usually as supporting actors for such leading cowboy stars as Charles Starrett and Johnny Mack Brown. The Sons of the Pioneers were in numerous movies, while Bob Wills and his Texas Playboys appeared in about eight. A few singers, such as Ernest Tubb, Jimmie Davis, and Bill Callahan made only rare appearances.

Other singers, however, became leading men and posed at least modest challenges to Autry's dominance. Alabama-born Ray Whitley became a movie star in 1936 after an earlier successful career in New York as a cowboy singer. Tex Ritter also began his movie career in 1936, and, in the fifty-six movies which he eventually made, he became the most believable of all the singing cowboys. The most successful challenge to Autry came from Roy Rogers, who signed with Republic in 1937; his visibility in American public life would last, because of television, well into the 1960's. The singing cowboy genre persisted in American movies on into the fifties, with Arizona-born Rex Allen being its chief exponent after 1949. In many ways this last singing cowboy was the best singer of them all; Allen's rich voice ranged from a deep bass to a sweeping tenor—a sound that almost no other country singer could equal.

Largely as a result of Hollywood exploitation, the concept of "western music" became fixed in the public mind. After the heyday of Gene Autry the term "western" came to be applied even to southern rural music by an increasing number of people, especially by those who were ashamed to use the pejorative term "hillbilly." Not only did the public accept the projection—most hillbilly singers became fascinated with the western image and eventually came to believe their own symbols. Autry was the first of a long line of country singers who clothed themselves in tailored cowboy attire; in the following decades, the costuming became more elaborate and gaudy, with the brightly colored, bespangled and sequined uniforms made by Nudie the Tailor in Los Angeles being the most favored fare. Eventually, most country performers, whether they came from Virginia or Mississippi, adopted cowboy regalia—usually of the gaudy, dude cowboy variety.

Along with the clothing, country bands and singers—particularly in the Southwest and on the West Coast—adopted cowboy titles. Singers with names like Tex, Slim, Hank, Red River Dave, the Utah Cowboy, and Patsy Montana, and groups with such titles as the Cowboy Ramblers, Riders of the Purple Sage, Radio Cowboys, Swift Jewel Cowboys, Lone Star Cowboys, and Girls of the Golden West (Dolly and Millie Good) abounded on radio stations (and record labels) all over the nation. Radio and record promoters, of course, were very much alive to the appeal of the western myth, and they often encouraged musicians to adopt appropriate western monikers. Millie and Dolly Good, for example, were farm girls from Illinois who sang and yodeled in sweet, close harmony. Their agent advised them to dress like cowgirls, gave them the romantic title Girls of the Golden West and then, after scanning the map of western Texas, attached to their promotional literature the statement that they were born in Muleshoe, Texas. The Girls very carefully preserved this fiction to the end of their performing career.

Patsy Montana's career was similarly shaped by romantic conceptions of the West. She was a singer and fiddler from Arkansas named Rubye Blevins, but on the West Coast in the early thirties Stuart Hamblen renamed her Patsy Montana, and she thereafter cultivated carefully the performing image of the cowgirl. Although much of her career saw her appearing as a "girl singer" with such groups as the Prairie Ramblers, Patsy made dramatic history in 1935 when "I Want to Be a Cowboy's Sweetheart" became the first big hit by a woman country singer, and a virtuoso yodeling piece that still influences the style of women singers (Austin country-rock singer Marcia Ball, for example, made the song and yodel standard parts of her repertory in the late 1970's).

Gene Autry, about 1930. Courtesy of
Bob Pinson.

Carl T. Sprague.
Courtesy of Carl T. Sprague.

The Girls of the Golden West: Dolly (*left*) and Millie Good. Courtesy of Bob Pinson.

The Prairie Ramblers: *left to right*, "Happy" Jack Taylor, Charles "Chuck" Hurt, Shelby "Tex" Atchison, Floyd "Salty" Holmes—and Patsy Montana (*center*). Courtesy of George Biggar.

Many of the "western" entertainers performed cowboy songs, usually highly romanticized, but more often their titles and attire were the only ties they had with the "West." Several groups, however, stayed rather close to the cowboy repertory. Some of them had been in existence long before Gene Autry achieved Hollywood fame, and many of them, such as "Haywire Mac" McClintock and the Crockett Family (John H. "Dad" Crockett and his five sons, originally from West Virginia), had performed on California radio stations since at least 1925. Other early California groups included Len Nash and his Original Country Boys, broadcasting from KFWB, Hollywood, as early as March 1926; Sheriff Loyal Underwood's Arizona Wranglers; Charlie Marshall and his Mavericks; and perhaps the most important (and certainly the most interesting), the Beverly Hillbillies.

The Beverly Hillbillies were the brainchild of Glen Rice, station manager at KMPC in Los Angeles. Reversing the trend toward adoption of western names during the thirties, Rice used the eastern moniker Hillbillies for the group of western musicians that he built around accordion player Leo Mannes (renamed Zeke Manners) and conducted a ballyhoo campaign which alleged that a group of strange and primitive musicians had been unearthed in the hills of Beverly. The band made its debut on KMPC on April 6, 1930, and remained a popular feature throughout the decade. The Hillbillies attracted several fine musicians, such as Manners, who had no background in country music but had been attracted to California because of the lure of Hollywood. Other Hillbillies included genuine country types, such as sky-high yodeler Elton Britt (James Britt Baker), who came from Arkansas in 1930, and Stuart Hamblen, who came from Texas in the same year. Britt went on to become one of country music's most gifted yodelers (virtually the last of that once-hardy breed) and a leading soloist during the forties. Hamblen, the son of a Methodist minister in Abilene, Texas, was a fixture on West Coast radio from 1930 to the 1950's. He hosted his own shows in Hollywood after 1931, boosted the careers of other performers, wrote many of the most successful songs of the decade (including "My Mary," "The Texas Plains," and "My Brown-eyed Texas Rose"), was the first country performer signed by Decca in 1934, and became sufficiently known to become a candidate for Congress in 1938.

The western group that ultimately was to become the most famous, and the most frequently emulated, was the Sons of the Pioneers. They sang every type of country song and even ventured into popular music, but the majority of their melodies dealt with western themes. Perhaps more than any other group, they preserved a western repertory and exploited the romantic cowboy image. More "western" stylistically than any other group, they were among the least western in terms of origin. Bob Nolan (Robert Clarence Nobles) was born in New Brunswick, Canada, but he moved with his parents to Tucson at the age of fourteen. In Tucson he developed a fascination with the desert which never left him, and which eventually inspired some of country music's greatest songs, such as "Cool Water," "Tumbling Tumbleweeds," and "At the Rainbow's End." Tim Spencer was born in Missouri, but grew up in Oklahoma, Texas, and New Mexico. Roy Rogers came from southern Ohio.

The three musicians came to California in the early thirties and soon fell into a pattern common to most country singers during the decade, moving from group to group before they formed their own organization. Roy Rogers, the prime organizer of the trio, was born Leonard Slye in Cincinnati, on November 5, 1911, but grew up on a small farm near Portsmouth, in southern Ohio. Here he garnered his earliest musical training from his Kentucky-born mother and his mandolin-and-guitar-playing father. In 1931 he and his father moved to Tulare, California, and worked as migratory fruit pickers. In the following three years, beginning with a duo called the Slye Brothers (Leonard and a cousin), he worked with several western-style groups until the Pioneer Trio was formed in 1933. Renamed the Sons of the Pioneers in 1934, the trio soon became famous for their smooth and inventive harmonies and for the finely crafted songs that Nolan and Spencer created. They became so famous for their harmony that their instrumental accompaniment is often forgotten. They were joined in 1934 and 1935 by two extraordinarily talented brothers from Llano, Texas, Hugh and Karl Farr. The Farrs were jazz-influenced country musicians whose progressive styles were sometimes obscured by the vocal emphasis of the Pioneers. Hugh Farr, who also sang a low-down bass with the group, was one of the hottest fiddlers of the period, and his brother Karl was a master of both the rhythm and single-string approaches to the guitar.

Performing on an early-morning radio program over KFWB in Hollywood, the Pioneers had gained enough recognition by 1936 to be invited to appear with Will Rogers and at the Texas Centennial. Leonard Slye left the group in 1937 after signing a movie contract with Republic Studios. At this point his name was changed, first to Dick Weston and later to Roy Rogers. Thereafter, his performances were made on an individual basis, and he eventually rivaled Gene Autry as America's most popular singing cowboy. He was replaced in the Sons of the Pioneers by Lloyd Perryman from Ruth, Arkansas, whose natural tenor was the first the group had ever had, and who gave them an even closer harmony than they had earlier possessed. The Sons of the Pioneers underwent numerous personnel changes after 1937, but have never disbanded. Their songs moved into the repertories of country singers everywhere, and their style of harmony was widely copied (most effectively by Foy Willing [originally Willingham] and the Riders of the Purple Sage, who appeared with Monte Hale and Roy Rogers in Republic Pictures from 1942 to 1952).

The flourishing singing cowboy industry inspired the emergence of songwriters. Two of country music's greatest songwriters, for example—

Fred Rose and Cindy Walker—made their debuts as country composers in the 1940's when they wrote songs for movies (Rose for Autry, Walker for Bob Wills). The interest in western music in the 1930's, however, was not confined to country performers and their supporters. Writers from Tin Pan Alley also reacted to the western craze, and soon the whole nation was humming western-style tunes such as "Gold Mine in the Sky," "Home in Wyoming," and "I'm an Old Cowhand." Some of these tunes were written by easterners who had never been near a cow, but the Happy Chappies at least lived in California in the midst of the Hollywood industry. The Chappies were a pop-singing duo named Nat Vincent and Fred Howard who wrote or arranged such songs as "When the Bloom Is on the Sage," "Mellow Mountain Moon" "My Pretty Quadroon," and "Strawberry Roan" (the last a musical adaptation of Curley Fletcher's earlier poem). The most successful of the western-oriented popular songwriters was a Bostonian, William J. (Billy) Hill. Hill's birth and musical training gave no indication of his future success as a western songwriter. Born in Boston in 1899, he studied violin at the New England Conservatory of Music and performed for a short time with the Boston Symphony Orchestra. In 1916 he traveled west, riding the rails and working at odd jobs until he had seen most of the western states. He returned to New York in the late twenties after becoming thoroughly acquainted with western life—everything from camp cooking to cowpunching. In New York he worked as a doorman at a fashionable hotel and composed songs occasionally. Over the years his compositions ranged from popular melodies like "The Glory of Love" to hillbilly songs like "They Cut Down the Old Pine Tree" and "The Old Spinning Wheel." His chief success, however, came with western-style songs like "Call of the Canyon," which were distinguished for their beautiful melodies and for their rhythms which suggested the gait of a horse. He experienced his most spectacular success in 1933 with "The Last Roundup." This song really awakened the general public to the romantic West, and it became the most popular tune in the country. Performed by both hillbilly and popular groups, its appeal perhaps stimulated a greater interest in the more "authentic" country and western material and ensured a greater national following for country music.

Billy Hill's New York songwriting ventures were directed primarily to big-city popular-music audiences, although most of the western bands in California and the Southwest used his material. In general, country music has always encountered its coolest reception in the Northeast, particularly in the city of New York. In New York, when country music has been performed it has usually been under the more acceptable and "respectable" name of "folk" music. In the thirties, however, and even in the pioneer days of the twenties, a few groups were able to win some success in that area.

Ethel Park Richardson did much to educate New Yorkers about the beauties of folk culture between 1933 and 1935 with her weekly dramatizations on WOR and the NBC Network. Each week she was assisted by such singers as Frank Luther, Carson Robison, and Tex Ritter as she dramatized a famous folk song. Luther and Robison had been in New York since the twenties, but Ritter was one of several cowboy singers who kept New Yorkers range-conscious during the mid-thirties. Others included Texas Jim Robertson, a deep-bass singer from Batesville, Texas; Zeke Manners and Elton Britt, who had moved from California; Dwight Butcher, a Jimmie Rodgers disciple from Tennessee; Ray Whitley from Alabama, who sang regularly at the Stork Club and on WMCA; and Wilf Carter, the Nova Scotia yodeler who performed over CBS as Montana Slim.

The most singular of all the cowboy singers in New York, however, was Woodward Maurice "Tex" Ritter. Born in Murvaul, in deep East Texas, January 12, 1905, Ritter was far removed from the scene of any cowboy activity. He attended the University of Texas for five years (singing in the university glee club under the direction of Oscar Fox) and then went to Northwestern Law School for one year. Throughout his youth he had collected western and mountain songs, so he had a storehouse of interesting songs when he began singing on KPRC in Houston in 1929. In 1930 he joined a musical troupe on a series of one-night stands through the South and Midwest. By 1931 he had gone to New York, where he joined the Theatre Guild and began his acting career with a featured role in *Green Grow the Lilacs* (which eventually became the basis for the musical *Oklahoma*). With his thick Texas accent and storehouse of cowboy lore, Ritter was a New York sensation. He became greatly in demand for lecture recitals in eastern colleges on the cowboy and his song. During the fall of 1932 he was the featured singer with the Madison Square Garden Rodeo and from there went on to a recording contract with ARC and a program slot on WOR entitled *The Lone Star Rangers*, one of the first western radio shows ever featured in New York City. From 1932 to 1936 he appeared on other New York stations, including a *Barn Dance* on WHN where he acted as co-host with Ray Whitley. Then, inevitably, in 1936, he made the first of several movies, *Song of the Gringo*. Ritter was not a cowboy, but was instead a very believable interpreter of cowboy songs. Impressionable easterners were easily convinced that he came, not from a small East Texas community and a college background, but from a working cattle ranch. And Tex very skillfully lived up to the part.

Tex Ritter's exploitation of the western theme was typical of what was happening all over the United States in the mid-thirties. From New York to California, individuals responded to the western myth and "cowboy" singers and groups sprang up in all sorts of unusual places. "Western" became a rival and often preferred term to "hillbilly" as a proper appellation for country music. It is easy to understand, of course, why "western" would be preferred to the seemingly disreputable backwoods term. "Western," specifically, suggested a music that had been developed by cowboys out on the Texas Plains; more generally, it suggested a context that was open, free, and expansive. In short, the term fit the American self-concept.

In reality, except for the fabric of usable symbols which surrounded him, the cowboy contributed nothing to American music. The "western" music which became fashionable in the mid-thirties came from other sources. A modification of the older southern rural music, it was a product both of the southwestern cultural heritage and of the new social and economic forces that were developing in the region. In the Southwest the country musician could borrow from an abundance of musical influences. Some, of course, were also available to musicians in the Southeast: southern traditional and gospel music, popular music, commercial recordings of all kinds (including blues and jazz), and, crucially, black music. Southwesterners could draw additionally on Mexican, Cajun, German, and what generally was described as "Bohemian" music (that is, the polka-derived styles of people who emigrated to South-Central Texas from what is now Czechoslovakia). Young people who grew up in any of the several ethnic communities that extended from Southwest Louisiana to the Texas hill country were torn between strong competing loyalties: the Old Country music of their parents (from France, Mexico, Germany, Poland, Bohemia), and the fashionable music that drifted in from the outside world. Consequently, musical styles became strongly intermeshed, and often in wonderfully exciting ways. Cajun musicians, therefore, freely mixed their traditional forms with country, blues, and jazz, while over in South Texas it was not at all uncommon to find "western" bands composed of musicians with names like Fojtacek or Wolenski who played polkas, schottisches, hoedowns, and the latest country hits. Musicians who hoped to prosper playing for dances in the broad territory extending south, east, and west from Austin, Texas, learned quickly that they must be prepared to play anything from "Allá en el Rancho Grande" and "Herr Schmidt" to "Jole Blon" and "Cotton-Eyed Joe."

The career of Texas country-band leader Adolph Hofner vividly illustrates the cross-cultural matrix that characterized the music of Texas. Hofner's paternal and maternal grandparents came from what is now Czechoslovakia to the area near Praha, Texas (one of the oldest Czech communities in the United States). He could not speak English when he first went to school, and at home he had heard only "Bohemian" music, usually waltzes and polkas, played by his mother on the accordion and experienced also at the big community dances. Hofner still knows and plays much of this music today, but as a teenager he was also attracted to Hawaiian music, and then later to the music of the western swing bands. Since he became a professional musician in the early thirties—he still tours actively in the eighties with a band called the Pearl Wranglers (sponsored by Pearl Beer)—Hofner's music has reflected the richly eclectic culture in which he matured. His band still typically plays songs like

"Dreamland Waltz" (a Bohemian tune learned from his mother), as well as "Maria Elena," "San Antonio Rose," "Cotton-Eyed Joe," (which he helped to make famous in South-Central Texas), and any other songs his dance-conscious audiences desire. Of course, when he goes back home to play in one of the few surviving Czech community halls, his repertory becomes centered more strongly on the music of his youth.

While competing styles of music had filtered into Hofner's little home community, such forms did not become irresistible until his family moved to San Antonio in 1928. Soon after the repeal of Prohibition, he and his brother Emil began playing in local beer joints—a decisive act that was being performed by thousands of other musicians throughout the South and West. The factors which contributed to the emergence of new forms and styles in country music were in evidence in much of America. It was in Texas, however, that conditions proved to be most fertile for new developments. Since the thirties Texas has contributed many of the most spectacular stars to country music, and most of them received their basic musical training in a common school. This was a social institution, springing up in the chaotic ferment of the Depression, and acutely attuned to the needs of rural dwellers: the honky-tonk. Saloons and taverns, of course, were not new to the American scene, nor was the relationship between drinking and music a recent thing. But they assumed a new significance in the thirties. The Texas oil boom had put money in the pockets of a large number of people who otherwise would have been destitute during the Depression years. Country musicians found receptive audiences in the oil communities, sometimes playing for nickels and dimes at root beer stands or in the wide-open taverns and dance halls where illegal liquor was consumed by oil workers. With the repeal of Prohibition in 1933, the taverns were given a confirmed status. These establishments usually were built on the outskirts of town for a variety of reasons. In such locations tax rates were lower, police supervision was apt to be more lax, and they were easily reached by both city and rural dwellers. In Texas, with some counties "dry" and others "wet," the county-line tavern developed (as did state-line taverns). This convenient location could attract customers from both wet and dry areas. These out-of-the-way clubs were sometimes only small, dingy bars, but many contained dance floors. A few were large and elaborate dance halls which described themselves as "ballrooms" or "night clubs." All were emblazoned with neon lights. Whatever the size, they were generically described as "honky-tonks" by the plain people who frequented them. People went to the honky-tonks for the widest variety of reasons, and as both occasional and habitual drinkers, but many working-class folk looked forward to the weekend when they might move from club to club, drinking, dancing, and socializing (this is still described as "honky-tonking").

Music was indispensable to the honky-tonk's business. Musicians were sometimes hired, or permitted to play for tips, but the jukebox was more reliable. Led by the Wurlitzer Company, which introduced its ornate, gaudily painted model in 1928, the automatic coin-operated phonograph experienced heavy sales after 1934 when Prohibition repeal opened up thousands of beer halls and taverns that needed some kind of musical entertainment. The jukebox, so called because of its popularity in southern roadhouses called "juke joints," could be purchased for about $250 and originally played twelve records. Its popularity was further enhanced by the end of the thirties when remote control devices permitted song choices without leaving one's booth or stool. By 1940 more than 300,000 jukeboxes were in operation.

When country music entered the honky-honk, it had to change, both in lyrics and in style. The older pastoral or down-home emphasis of the music could not survive in such an atmosphere. Songs about "poor old Mother at home" and "The Old Country Church" seemed somewhat out of place in the honky-tonk environment. Instead, songs reflecting the problems and changing social status of the ex–rural dweller became paramount. Songs seldom commented on work, but they spoke often of family fragility, the insecurities of love, marriage dissolution, drinking, and having a good time. Many songs, beginning with Al Dexter's "Honky Tonk Blues" in 1937, commented on this new milieu in which country music thrived. "Stompin' at the Honky Tonk," "I Ain't Goin' Honky Tonkin' Anymore," "Honky Tonk Mama," "Driving Nails in My Coffin" ("every time I drink a bottle of booze"), and "Headin' down the Wrong Highway" were just a few of the songs that commented on both the joyful and the depressing side of honky-tonk life. The songs inspired by the honky-tonk world were topical in that they spoke of experiences that were becoming increasingly common, but they were often far from realistic. Country musicians and fans generally sought escape from reality, and even the songs about "honky-tonk mamas" avoided the realities of women's lives. Fundamentalist Protestant culture still gripped the lives of the honky-tonk musicians, coloring the lyrics of even their drinking and cheating songs. Guilt and self-pity lay at the core of such early classic honky-tonk songs as "The Last Letter," "Born to Lose," "Driving Nails in My Coffin," and "It Makes No Difference Now."

Country instrumentation changed significantly within the honky-tonk atmosphere. In the honky-tonk, with its laughter and merriment, clinking of glasses, and shuffling of dancing feet, instrumentation changed to accommodate the environment. Amidst the din and revelry there had to be, for both the dancer and the passive listener, a steady and insistent beat which could be felt even if the lyrics could not be understood. The music became louder: "sock rhythm"—the playing of closed chords, or the striking of all six strings in unison in order to achieve a percussive effect—

became characteristic of honky-tonk rhythm playing; the string bass became a fixture in bands; pianos became more common; and in rare cases drums were used. By the end of the thirties, hillbilly bands were steadily adopting that bane of traditionalists, the electric guitar.

Honky-tonks of one variety or another became the "schools" in which hundreds of country musicians gained invaluable experience. The honky-tonk was a hard, but instructive, school. The entertainer who worked there, and in the early days that might mean working with only a fiddle and a guitar, had to contend with competing noise, fights, and low income. The most violent phase of honky-tonk history probably came during the 1940's, when servicemen and defense workers began thronging into these good-time arenas, but even in the thirties the honky-tonks had already become what Glen Campbell would call "the fightin' and dancin' clubs." In these clubs musicians quite often had to be just as tough and brawling as the customer, and a smashed guitar might be the least that a physically endangered musician had to worry about.

Most honky-tonk musicians lived obscure lives, working hard at day jobs and then spending much of the night playing music. A few were fortunate enough to receive a fixed salary; most received a percentage of the beer sales, or whatever patrons were willing to drop into the tip box ("the kitty"). Very few musicians ever moved far outside the honky-tonk's perimeter. One man who did was a singer who ultimately became one of the most influential performers in modern country music: Ernest Tubb. Tubb was born on a farm near Crisp, in Ellis County, Texas, in 1914, but lived in a succession of relatives' homes in various parts of Texas after his parents separated in 1926. He was inspired at the age of fourteen to become a country singer when he heard one of his sisters singing Jimmie Rodgers' "In the Jailhouse Now." He bought every Rodgers record that became available and tried to model his style completely after that of the Singing Brakeman; he practiced diligently for months trying to perfect a yodeling style. It was always Tubb's greatest regret that he did not meet his hero, though they lived in the same state (and even in the same city, San Antonio, in 1932). After a short stay with another sister in West Texas, Tubb returned to San Antonio in 1933 (after Rodgers' death) and began making the rounds of the radio stations, willing to do shows free in order to gain the exposure. Eventually, KONO gave him fifteen minutes twice a week at 5:30 in the morning. He was singing and yodeling at this station and working full-time for the WPA and any other useful job he could find, when he met Carrie (Mrs. Jimmie) Rodgers. Mrs. Rodgers did not think that Tubb sounded like her deceased husband, but she was strongly impressed with the young man's sincerity and devotion. She took Tubb under her tutelage, lent him one of Jimmie's valuable guitars, helped him arrange a tour through South Texas, and used whatever influence she had to get him a recording contract with Victor. Two sessions with that company in 1936 and 1937 yielded eight releases (including two tribute songs to Rodgers), but no hits.

For almost five years, from 1936 until he recorded his first great Decca hit, "Walking the Floor over You," in 1941, Tubb struggled to make a breakthrough into the world of professional country music. The removal of his tonsils in 1939 destroyed his ability to yodel. Though Tubb was bitterly disappointed, the incident was probably a boon to his career; it forced him to abandon imitation in favor of his own unique style. During these years Tubb roamed from San Antonio to Midland, Texas, and from there to Beaumont, San Angelo (twice), Corpus Christi, and Fort Worth. He sang on radio stations, at root beer and hamburger drive-ins, and in innumerable clubs. He even operated his own honky-tonk in San Angelo, the E and E Tavern, for several months in 1940. Tubb never managed to make music his full-time profession until the fall of 1940, when he moved to Fort Worth and commenced a six-day-a-week, fifteen-minute program on KGKO. He received a modest weekly salary for about a year, but had no sponsor until "Walking the Floor" demonstrated his popular appeal.

Tubb's recording career with Decca began on April 3, 1940, under the direction of veteran talent scout Dave Kapp; it did not end until 1975, when MCA (the new owner of the Decca label) began emphasizing its newer talent to the exclusion of the old-timers.[3] "Walking the Floor over You," released in the fall of 1941, won him his first sponsor: Universal Mills, the maker of Gold Chain Flour. As the Gold Chain Troubadour, Tubb made numerous personal appearances for his sponsor, singing from a stage built on the top of a white Plymouth automobile. After years of frustration, Tubb made a rather rapid ascent to stardom and by the end of 1942 was appearing on the *Grand Ole Opry*, where he became the inspiration for thousands of young country singers all over the United States.

The evolution of Ernest Tubb's instrumental accompaniment is suggestive of what happened in country music as a whole during the late thirties and early forties. In his earliest appearances he accompanied himself, à la Jimmie Rodgers, on the guitar. Later, another musician joined him as lead guitarist, playing single-string passages while Tubb supplied a background rhythm. His earliest Decca recording session in 1940 featured a sound that always endured in his music, despite the gradual enlargement and electrification of his band in the following years. Jimmie Short, whom Tubb had first heard in San Angelo as part of the Short Brothers (Jimmie and Leon), played a melody lead on an acoustic guitar. All subsequent Tubb guitarists (even the most jazz-influenced) played a similar style, al-

---

3. Tubb made at least two lp's in the late seventies for Pete Drake's First Generation label. One, called *The Legend and the Legacy*, was made up of duets with such singers as Willie Nelson, George Jones, and Loretta Lynn.

though it was a later musician, Billy Byrd (a Tubb accompanist for thirteen years), who popularized the ascending four-note run that became virtually the defining feature of Tubb's instrumental sound.

The next phase in Tubb's instrumental evolution—the adoption of electrical amplification—came as a result of country music's entry into the honky-tonks. Not long after Tubb's first Decca recordings began to circulate, a Forth Worth jukebox operator complained to him that it was difficult to hear the acoustic sound of Tubb's recordings once business picked up during the night. At his next recording session, in April 1941, Tubb added an electric guitar in order to increase the volume of his sound. Jimmie Short could not be present at the session, so Tubb was accompanied by Fay "Smitty" Smith, the staff guitarist at KGKO. In order to preserve the sound heard on his recordings, Tubb instructed his regular guitarist, Jimmie Short, to attach an electric pick-up to his conventional Martin guitar. Ernest Tubb was not the first country musician to feature an electric guitar, but as a *Grand Ole Opry* star with national exposure, he lent the instrument a legitimacy which contributed to its rapid dissemination.

Guitar electrification had long been a dream of musicians, and experiments with the process had been made since at least the early twenties. Pop guitarist Alvino Rey (Albert McBurney) began his own experimentation in 1921, when he was only twelve years old. By 1924 he had invented an electrical amplifier for the guitar which, however, was not patented. Lloyd Loar, of the Gibson Company in Kalamazoo, Michigan, was conducting similar experiments as early as 1924. While other experiments, both amateur and commercial, were no doubt made during the following decade, the electric guitar did not appear in a country band until 1934, when Bob Dunn began playing the instrument with the Musical Brownies. Dunn grew up amidst traditional hoedown music at his home near Braggs, Oklahoma, but he did not become interested in the steel guitar until he heard it used by a group of Hawaiians who played a stage show in the World War I boom town of Kusa, Oklahoma, in 1917. During the next several years Dunn obtained a steel guitar, took lessons through correspondence with a native Hawaiian, Walter Kolomoku, and finally in 1927 became a professional by joining an Oklahoma group called the Panhandle Cowboys and Indians. For seven years (1927–1934) Dunn played with several groups on vaudeville tours and on radio stations in the Midwest and on XEPN on the Mexican border. His real involvement with country music, however, came in late 1934 when he joined the extremely popular Milton Brown and his Musical Brownies in Fort Worth. Dunn converted a standard round-hole Martin guitar into an electric instrument by magnetizing the strings and raising them high off the box. He then attached an electric pickup to the guitar, which in turn was connected to a Vol-U-Tone amplifier that Milton Brown had purchased in Mineral Wells, Texas. In January 1935, when Dunn used the electrical amplifier in a recording session in Chicago, he was probably the first country musician to do so. Within the next two or three years other electric instruments appeared on country recordings and in other performances: Leo Raley, for example, was playing an electric mandolin with Cliff Bruner's Texas Wanderers by 1936; Bobby Simons played an electric standard guitar on recordings with Al Dexter in 1937; and Muryel "Zeke" Campbell was playing his influential, single-string style of electric guitar with the Light Crust Doughboys by 1938. Bob Dunn's innovations on the steel guitar prompted other masters of that instrument—such as Ted Daffan, Leon McAuliffe, Lefty Perkins (who replaced Dunn in the Musical Brownies), Noel Boggs, and Kermit Whalen—to make similar electrical adaptations. Leon McAuliffe's recording of "Steel Guitar Rag" in September 1936 probably did most to popularize the electric guitar among a national audience and was a portent of that instrument's coming dominance in country music. By 1936 such guitar manufacturers as Gibson had begun to introduce their own electric models, and the mail-order catalogues were advertising guitars that included built-in pickup devices and volume controls.

It is no accident that electrification made its first inroads among the southwestern string bands which played in honky-tonks and in large dance-halls and ballrooms. Many of these musicians played a style of music which, after the war, would be described as "western swing." By the end of the thirties Americans were becoming well aware of the "hot dance music" or the "Okie jazz" coming out of the Southwest (particularly after Bing Crosby's recording of "San Antonio Rose" took the country by storm in 1941), but few were cognizant of the roots of the music. Western swing was, in part, a stage in the development of the southern string-band tradition and was performed by rural musicians whose ancestors had emigrated from the southeastern cotton states bearing a legacy of fiddling and hoedown music. But western swing also reflected the diverse mingling of musical cultures (Cajun, Tex-Mex, German, Bohemian, black, cowboy, Anglo) that prevailed in the Southwest. Southwestern musicians had eclectic repertories, and they honed their skills at the dances which were common to all of the cultural groups. Fiddlers played at innumerable house parties and at scores of fiddle contests where they learned to improvise.

Despite the obvious cultural divergence demonstrated by southwestern music, one can easily make too much of the remote historical rootedness of western swing. The current preoccupation with hot fiddling and country-jazz fusions unfortunately obscures the fact that southwesterners also heard and loved more traditional forms of rural music: cowboy music, ballads, sentimental and gospel songs, and breakdown fiddling. There is no "swing" at all in the cowboy ballads of Carl Sprague or the Cartwright Brothers, nor in the old-time material favored by balladeer Peg Moreland in his many years of performances on Texas radio stations, nor in the

Bradley Kincaid style of singing and repertory featured by Cecil Gill, who maintained a large radio audience for decades with only his guitar and sweet-tenor style of singing. Western swing musicians did borrow frequently from older and diverse folk resources; but they more often drew upon commercial music forms popular in their own day. Immersed in the popular culture of their time, such powerful music personalities as Milton Brown and Bob Wills forged a highly successful fusion of contemporary popular music and the rural music of their forebears and inspired a host of other musicians to follow their example.

Brown and Wills received their earliest musical schooling in the most important seedbed of western swing, the fiddle-and-guitar band. A host of such instrumental combinations, playing at barn dances, house parties, and fiddlers' contests, had performed all over the Southwest before and during the twenties, and several of them made their way on to phonograph recordings after 1922. Some of the groups were famous in their own time and milieu, but left only a few recordings by which modern enthusiasts can judge their abilities. At least three units came from the musically rich area around Terrell, about forty miles southeast of Dallas: Oscar and Doc Harper, Ervin Solomon and Jay Hughes, and Prince Albert Hunt, who sometimes played with the Harpers and sometimes with his own group, the Texas Ramblers. While Hunt's fiddling anticipated the melodic variations of western swing, he was no more accomplished as a fiddler than Oscar Harper and Ervin Solomon, both of whom are less well known. Hunt, though, was assured of a kind of immortality when he was shot to death outside a Dallas tavern by a jealous husband on March 21, 1931. Hunt was the subject of a public television documentary in the 1970's, a project inspired as much by his star-crossed, bad-boy image as by his fiddling skills.

Farther south and west in the region around Burnet, Texas, the Humphries Brothers (Jess and Cecil) won a large local following playing for civic functions, at fiddlers' contests, at the annual Old Settlers' Reunion in Round Rock, and on Central Texas radio stations (such as KUT, Austin's first radio station, which was located at the University of Texas). They made only eight recordings for the Okeh label in 1930 (presumably not enough to warrant a modern reissue) and were not widely known outside Central Texas. Their repertory was characterized by the eclecticism generally found among southwestern fiddle bands. Not surprisingly, "Listen to the Mockingbird" was their most-requested tune (it was almost mandatory for fiddlers everywhere to play it), but Jess also knew such tunes as "Beaumont Rag," "Ragtime Annie," "Black and White Rag," and "St. Louis Tickle." Jess Humphries was an unusual old-time fiddler indeed; he played trombone in an army band during World War I, was the organizer and "violinist" of one of Central Texas' first Dixieland bands, and was a popular musician at weddings and similar social occasions with his pianist wife, Cynthia.

Even more anticipatory of western swing were the East Texas Serenaders of Lindale, a little community near Tyler. The Serenaders received their name from their practice of going from farmhouse to farmhouse and standing out in the yard entertaining the people. (The custom may have been widespread; the Taylor-Griggs Louisiana Melody Makers, another early recording band, got their start the same way in Bienville Parish, Louisiana.) The center of the band was fiddler Daniel Huggins Williams, a left-handed musician who absorbed both style and repertory from his Tennessee-born father, but who also learned formal technique from a Lindale music teacher named Ellen Cannon. Williams was backed by a strong rhythm section dominated by the guitar of Cloet Hamman, the tenor banjo of John Munnerlyn, and the truly unique cello playing (sometimes plucked, but most often bowed) of Henry Bogan. The Serenaders played at house parties and civic functions throughout East Texas from the Oklahoma line to Houston, but never really made music their full-time profession (although Williams played with country and western groups in the forties). The twenty-four songs which they recorded for Columbia (1927), Brunswick (1928–1930), and Decca (1936) show a preference for syncopated dance tunes, and especially rags from the early twentieth century. Their choice of songs suggested the stylistic directions that the western swing bands would later follow. Fiddler Huggins Williams had a more direct influence on western swing musicians; at least two of the great modern fiddlers, Buddy Brady and Johnny Gimble, often came over from Tyler to learn directly from the Lindale master.

A crucial step in the development of western swing came in the late twenties, when Bob Wills and Herman Arnspiger began playing house parties in the Fort Worth area as Wills' Fiddle Band. When Wills, the fiddler, and Arnspiger, the guitarist, were joined by vocalist Milton Brown in 1930, they became known as the Aladdin Laddies (because of their sponsorship on Fort Worth station WBAP by the Aladdin Mantle Lamp Company). By 1931 the trio had obtained jobs with Burrus Mills advertising Light Crust Flour over KFJZ in Fort Worth at 7 A.M. and at noon. During the rest of the day they worked for the flour company in other capacities, Brown as a salesman, Arnspiger and Wills as dock loaders and truck drivers. They also played many nights at the Crystal Springs Ballroom in Fort Worth. By early 1932, Arnspiger had left the group and had been replaced by the multi-talented Sleepy Johnson, who could play the guitar, fiddle, tenor guitar, and tenor banjo. This group, joined by Brown's younger brother Durwood, recorded two songs for Victor on February 9, 1932. Known first as the Fort Worth Doughboys and later as the Light Crust Doughboys, the organization became one of the important parent groups of western swing. Their 12:30 P.M. show on WBAP after 1933 (also carried by WOAI in San Antonio and KPRC in Houston) made their music known all over the Southwest.

Wilbert Lee "Pappy" O'Daniel, the Burrus Mills general manager who hired them and served as their master of ceremonies, rode to fame and political success through his association with the popular musicians. O'Daniel had little association with country music before he cast his fortunes with the Doughboys. He was born in Malta, Ohio, in 1890, but grew up in Kansas, where he became a flour mill owner. He came to Fort Worth in 1925 to be the sales manager of the Burrus Mill and Elevator Company; by June 1935, when he left to organize his own business, he had served as general manager and president. O'Daniel was indifferent toward the Doughboys until he found out how popular they were, but he then took a very personal interest in their careers, affixing his name to theirs on record labels, serving as their announcer, and writing approximately 150 poems and songs (including the very popular "Put Me in Your Pocket" and "Beautiful Texas"). O'Daniel had a warm, folksy, and appealing radio voice, at a time when radio was the most potent political image-maker in the nation. By the time he made his first successful race for the governorship in 1938, O'Daniel was known in thousands of Texas homes, where he was perceived as an almost fatherly presence and a quasi-populist champion of common people.

The family aura projected by O'Daniel, however, masked the fact of dissension within the Doughboy ranks, and its founding members, Milton Brown and Bob Wills, had left the band by the time it made its next recordings in October 1933. Brown organized a rival band called the Musical Brownies in September 1932 and began performing on another Fort Worth station, KTAT. Bob Wills left in 1933 over a wage dispute and soon began forming the group that would one day be called the Texas Playboys. O'Daniel himself severed his connections with Burrus Mills and the Doughboys in midsummer of 1935 when he formed his own flour company and began promoting a product called Hillbilly Flour. He also organized a band, the Hillbilly Boys, who helped him sell flour and campaign for political office. The group included a cowgirl singer named Kitty Williamson whom O'Daniel dubbed Texas Rose (he gave nicknames to all of his musicians), Kermit Whalen, O'Daniel's sons, Pat and Mike, and one of the finest singers and yodelers of the thirties, Leon Huff (the Texas Songbird), who remained until 1940. After the Hillbilly Boys warmed up his audiences, O'Daniel attacked the "professional politicians" and promised the old folks a modest monthly pension. Hillbilly music and folksy rhetoric proved to be an unbeatable combination, and O'Daniel swept into office with landslide votes in both 1938 and 1940; he also won a special election to the United States Senate, over Lyndon B. Johnson, in 1941, and a full Senate term in 1942. O'Daniel's success was most certainly noted by entertainers elsewhere, and Jimmie Davis would ultimately win two elections to the Louisiana governorship by emulating the Texas politician's campaign tactics (once in office he would project a plain folk image while pursuing an essentially ultraconservative political course).

In the meantime, the Light Crust Doughboys endured as a popular radio and recording group, while changing personnel frequently. Tommy Duncan brought his warm, fluid vocal style to the group for a brief period in late 1933. Clifford Gross, a hot fiddler from Kentucky, joined the Doughboys in the same year as a replacement for Bob Wills; Gross took the string band more firmly into the parameters of jazz. Sixteen-year-old Leon Mc-Auliffe also joined the group in 1933, but by 1934 had taken his steel guitar into Bob Wills' new and popular band. Muryel "Zeke" Campbell came in 1935, and by 1938 was playing his electric standard guitar on recordings with the organization. By the end of the decade, the Doughboys, who had always been eclectic in their song selections, had become even more oriented toward hot dance music, and an array of talented musicians, who were as comfortable with jazz as they were with country music, had become members of the group. Pianist John W. "Knocky" Parker and tenor banjoist Marvin Montgomery, for example, were educated musicians who had considerable experience playing in pop and jazz bands.

The organization created by Milton Brown was equally committed to "country jazz." The original members of the band included Jesse Ashlock on fiddle, Ocie Stockard on tenor banjo, Wanna Coffman on bass, Durwood Brown on guitar, and Milton Brown as vocalist. When fiddler Cecil Brower and pianist Fred "Papa" Calhoun joined the group, the Musical Brownies gained musicians who were comfortable in any musical idiom. Calhoun was a veteran of jazz bands in the Fort Worth area, and Brower had studied music and violin at Texas Christian University and had also played briefly with the Dallas Symphony Orchestra and with Ted Fio Rito's Orchestra. Brower was one of the most jazz-influenced fiddlers of the era, and he sharpened the jazz perceptions of other fiddlers (such as Jesse Ashlock and Cliff Bruner) who played with him in the Brownie organization. The Brownies' jazz emphasis was further accentuated in late 1934 when steel guitarist Bob Dunn joined the band. Dunn's style was virtually unique in steel-guitar circles. He played the steel guitar like a horn, with his short, staccato notes resembling the bursts of a trumpet. Dunn, who had played in jazz bands earlier, was involved throughout his life in a personal campaign to make the steel guitar a jazz instrument, or what he termed a "modern instrument."[4]

The Brownies' recorded repertory, found on Bluebird and Decca, only rarely touched conventional country music (as in "Little Betty Brown," "Get Along, Cindy," and "My Mary," beautifully sung by Milton Brown). More often, the Brownies' recordings were direct copies of current "popu-

4. Interview with Bob Dunn, Houston, July 17, 1966.

lar" hits. The musicians would often gather at Will Ed Kemble's, a Fort Worth furniture store, to hear the latest records as they came in. They would then adapt them to the string band style. In addition to their radio shows on KTAT, the Brownies played regularly at the Crystal Springs Ballroom and frequently at dances throughout North Texas and Oklahoma. Consequently, they played what their dance audiences wanted to hear: pop standards such as "Girl of My Dreams," "The Object of My Affection," and "The Waltz You Saved for Me"; jazz chestnuts such as "Joe Turner Blues," "Hesitation Blues," "Black and White Rag," and "St. Louis Blues"; and a few "foreign" tunes such as "Cielito Lindo" and "El Rancho Grande."

The Brownies were far from being exclusively an instrumental organization. With his husky, virile voice, Milton Brown set a standard which other western swing vocalists found difficult to equal. His version of "St. Louis Blues" is the finest done by any country entertainer. Brown's tragic death on April 18, 1936, as the result of an automobile accident a few days earlier, came at the peak of the Brownies' popularity and was a demoralizing blow from which the band never recovered. Milton's brother Durwood tried to keep the band intact and even arranged one more Decca recording session in March 1937. Musicians, however, had begun to drift away soon after Milton died, either forming their own bands or joining other organizations.

The Brownies permanently shaped the course of country music history, and they did so without ever abandoning the string band format. Milton Brown's singing was greatly admired and widely copied; fiddlers Cecil Brower and Cliff Bruner featured improvisational styles which still appear in the work of modern instrumentalists; Fred "Papa" Calhoun introduced jazz piano playing to country music; and Bob Dunn pioneered in the electrification of the steel guitar while also moving that instrument dramatically away from the chorded, Hawaiian style. More immediately, the Brownies inspired the creation of bands all over the Southwest—even in Cajun country, and as far away as Birmingham, where Hank Penny organized the Radio Cowboys. Several of the bands, of course, were led by erstwhile Brownies: Cliff Bruner, Bob Dunn, and Ocie Stockard each had a band by 1937. Bruner and Dunn both moved to Houston in 1936 and played with musicians who were often interchangeable; therefore, Bruner's Texas Wanderers and Dunn's Vagabonds, for recording purposes at least, were virtually the same band. From 1936 on up into the years of World War II, Bruner's band became the most successful musical organization on the Texas Gulf Coast, or in the region from Houston through the Cajun territory of Southwest Louisiana. Bruner's dazzling fiddle style defined his band's sound, but he was joined from time to time by other versatile musicians, such as Leo Raley, who fashioned an electric mandolin out of a homemade pickup device built in Ted Daffan's radio repair shop; J. R. Chatwell, a hard-driving, jazz-style fiddler, who however played piano with Bruner; and Aubrey "Moon" Mullican, a country boogie pianist and singer who joined Bruner in 1937. Musicians moved from band to band frequently in the mid- and late thirties, and in a fashion often bewildering to the researcher. Bands, furthermore, periodically experienced secessions, and new groups came into existence; for example, the Modern Mountaineers and the Village Boys (headed by Bruner vocalist Dickie McBride) were spinoffs from Bruner who performed in the Houston area in the late thirties.

Houston was, in fact, a very fertile region for hot country dance bands in the thirties. The Swift Jewel Cowboys (sponsored by Jewel Oil and Shortening) were organized in 1933, but remained in the city for only about a year before relocating in Memphis. The Blue Ridge Playboys, the Bar-X Cowboys, and Shelly Lee Alley's Alley Cats, on the other hand, remained fixtures in the musical life of the city for several years. The Playboys and the Cowboys evolved out of a traditional country string-band background, while Shelly Lee Alley began his career as a violinist in a pop dance orchestra; all three groups, however, were irresistibly drawn to the hot dance styles pioneered by Milton Brown and Bob Wills. Alley appeared on radio as early as January 1923, when he played on WFAA in Dallas in a pop dance orchestra called the Dixie Serenaders. Although he appeared on a Jimmie Rodgers recording in 1931 and wrote a couple of songs for Jimmie ("Traveling Blues" and "Gambling Barroom Blues"), he remained a pop musician and vocalist until the mid-thirties, when he met fiddler Leon Selph in Houston and began turning toward western swing. Along with his brother, Alvin Alley, he organized the Alley Cats and began recording for ARC in November 1937. The Alley Cats stayed close to the mold cast by the Musical Brownies (even employing Cliff Bruner for recording purposes), but they also used horns on occasion. The Bar-X Cowboys (led by brothers Ben and Elmer Christian) did not confine themselves to swing material but also did cowboy songs and country tunes. They performed on such stations as KTRH in Houston and in local clubs, and found a particularly receptive audience at the family-oriented dance halls in the German communities near Houston. The Blue Ridge Playboys were also eclectic in style and repertory, as most Texas bands had to be, and they were a seedbed of honky-tonk talent that would dominate country music for years to come. The Playboys were named by Jesse Jones, a Houston oil millionaire and radio station owner (KXYZ), who affixed upon them the name of one of his properties, the Blue Ridge oil patch located between Houston and Stafford. The group was led by Leon "Pappy" Selph, a fine fiddler in his own right, and, drawing upon the floating circle of musicians that populated the western swing bands of the era, the band also enlisted the services of tenor banjoist Chuck Keeshan, bass player Lou Frisby, and a remarkable trio of innovative musicians, Ted Daffan, Floyd Tillman, and

The Light Crust Doughboys, 1933: *left to right*, W. Lee "Pappy" O'Daniel, Henry Steinbarth (the driver), Sleepy Johnson, Raymond DeArman, Leon McAuliffe, Leon Huff, Clifford Gross, Herman Arnspiger. Courtesy of Bob Pinson.

Milton Brown and His Musical Brownies, 1935: *left to right*, Ocie Stockard, Fred Calhoun, Wanna Coffman, Milton Brown, Cecil Brower, Bob Dunn, Durwood Brown. Courtesy of Bob Pinson.

Moon Mullican, who remained as giants of country music on through the forties.

Theron Eugene "Ted" Daffan was born in 1912 in Beauregard Parish, Louisiana, but grew up in Houston, where he developed an early and undying fascination with the Hawaiian guitar and electronics. He was drawn to country music through the recordings and broadcasts of the Musical Brownies and played in a succession of Houston bands (including the Blue Ridge Playboys, the Alley Cats, and the Bar-X Cowboys), before forming his own influential Texans in 1940. Daffan pioneered in the electrification of instruments—his radio repair shop was the center of much of the experimentation with homemade pickups and amps that went on in the Houston area—but he made his most enduring contributions to country music through his songwriting. Striving to augment the pitifully low royalties that musicians received from recordings, in the late thirties Daffan began writing songs that would ultimately make him one of the charter members of the Nashville Song Writers Association Hall of Fame. They included the first truck-driving song, "Truck Driver's Blues" (1939) and three of the classics of honky-tonk music: "Worried Mind" (1940), "Born to Lose" (1943), and "Headin' down the Wrong Highway" (1945).

Floyd Tillman made significant contributions in three areas of country music—guitar playing, songwriting, and singing—although only the first two were sufficiently exploited during the thirties. Tillman was born in 1914 in Ryan, Oklahoma, but was brought to Post, Texas, by his parents when he was less than a year old. He began honing his skills as a guitarist by backing up fiddlers at innumerable ranch parties in West Texas, but his introduction to the honky-tonk world came in 1933, when he joined Adolph and Emil Hofner at Gus's Palm Garden in San Antonio. At this point in his career Tillman was playing a single-string style of guitar on an instrument amplified by a metal disc; three years later he would be playing an electric guitar with a Vol-U-Tone amplifier and homemade pickup supplied by Ted Daffan. Like Daffan, Tillman became one of the most respected songwriters in country music, contributing "I'll Keep on Loving You," "They Took the Stars Out of Heaven," "Each Night at Nine," and the perennial favorite "It Makes No Difference Now." He sang regularly with the Blue Ridge Playboys, but was fated to see his biggest song of the prewar era, "It Makes No Difference Now," recorded first by Dickie McBride, who sang with Cliff Bruner's Texas Wanderers. Tillman did not really come into his own as a vocalist until after World War II when he recorded his superhits "Slipping Around" and "I Love You So Much It Hurts." He was named to the Country Music Hall of Fame in 1984.

Aubrey "Moon" Mullican, the third member of this stellar Houston fraternity, brought a new style of piano playing to country music, the barrelhouse style pioneered by itinerant black juke joint musicians. Mullican was born in 1909 in Corrigan, Polk County, in the heart of the East Texas piney woods. While there is no hard evidence that he ever listened directly to the piano players who entertained the black lumber workers, he did hear black guitar players in Corrigan, and he picked up elements of style from one of them in particular, Joe Jones, who sometimes worked on the Mullicans' sharecrop farm. At about the same time (when he was eight years old), Mullican began applying these blues licks to the little pump organ that his father had bought to encourage his daughters to learn church songs. At the age of sixteen he hopped a train to Houston, where he began receiving a hard indoctrination in the world of honky-tonk entertainment. He later acknowledged that "the only place a piano playing kid like me could get work in those days wasn't exactly high class. The ladies of the evening, who worked there, would come and set on the piano bench and fan me while I played."[5] Mullican did not introduce the piano to country music, but his earthy, rollicking style was significantly different from that of Fred Calhoun or Al Stricklin (Bob Wills' famous pianist), who played with a more jazz-derived, New Orleans style. With the Blue Ridge Playboys and the Texas Wanderers, Mullican featured a melodic-based, boogie style of playing which was designed, in his own words, "to make the bottles bounce on the tables." Mullican's piano playing, combined with his zestful singing, made him one of the most colorful personalities of southwestern country music.

San Antonio did not experience quite as much musical activity in the thirties as did Houston or the Dallas–Fort Worth area, but important musicians thrived there nonetheless. In 1936 Jimmie Revard created a band which was obviously inspired stylistically and commercially by Bob Wills' glittering success. Revard even named his band the Oklahoma Playboys. The Hofner Brothers (Adolph and Emil) constituted the heart of the band, but they went out on their own by the end of the thirties to form Adolph Hofner's Texans. Just as popular as the Oklahoma Playboys was another group, the Tune Wranglers, which was organized in 1935 by singer and guitarist Buster Coward. The group's repertory and instrumentation was similar to that of other western swing bands and was marked by the hot fiddling of Tom Dickey (who left to form the Show Boys in 1938), the jazzy piano of Eddie Whitley, and the similarly sophisticated steel guitar stylings of Eddie Duncan. The Tune Wranglers played in a freewheeling, exuberant style, replete with spoken asides and shouted commentary that were no doubt borrowed from Bob Wills. None of the San Antonio groups were known very far outside their home area, but the Tune Wranglers did record two songs, "Hawaiian Honeymoon" and "Texas Sand," which moved among a wider audience. "Texas Sand," written by Buster Coward, won a

5. Quoted by Gordon Baxter, "Pop Never Wanted Me to Be a Musician," *Music City News* 4, no. 8 (February 1967): 27.

renewed life in the 1950's, when Webb Pierce reintroduced it to country music on a Decca recording.

The Dallas territory was dominated by the bands of Roy Newman and Bill Boyd, whose membership often overlapped, and by a string band headed by the Shelton Brothers (Bob and Joe). Neither Newman nor Boyd spent much time as a touring musician; instead, both were associated for many years with Dallas radio stations—Newman as a studio musician with WRR and WFAA, and Boyd as a long-time announcer and disc jockey on WRR. The two men drew upon a common pool of talent, yet were markedly dissimilar in their overall approach to musical style. Newman had been a radio staff pianist since the early twenties, but in the bands which he began to organize after 1931 he seldom played a lead or solo passage and was instead content to provide a rather unobtrusive, rhythmic background. Newman demonstrated a remarkable talent for finding superb musicians, and performing as Roy Newman and His Boys on WRR's *Noontime Varieties* after 1933, they produced an infectious dance music which revealed little indebtedness to country music and much to blues and New Orleans jazz. Although Newman did not consider his music to be country, some of the greatest country performers of the era saw service in his band from 1933 to 1939. Bob Dunn and Cecil Brower sat in on at least one recording session soon after they left the Musical Brownies; Art Davis, Walter Kirkes, and Jim Boyd sometimes came over from Bill Boyd's band to help Newman out (it was in these sessions that Jim Boyd first tried out his electric guitar phrases); and a lengthy retinue of hot fiddlers (such as Art Davis, Thurman Neal, Brower, Jesse Ashlock, and Carroll Hubbard) played with Newman at one time or another. These talented string musicians, along with Holly Horton, a veteran ragtime clarinet player, contributed toward making Newman's band the most genuine country jazz band of the era.

Bill Boyd's Cowboy Ramblers, on the other hand, remained basically a country string band even as they moved progressively toward the performance of jazz and dance music. Bill and Jim Boyd were born on a cattle and cotton farm in Fannin County, Texas, in 1910 and 1914 respectively. The brothers performed country music on radio in Greenville as early as 1926 but were always identified with the music scene in Dallas, where they moved in 1929. Bill became active immediately as a local musician, and even appeared in Jimmie Rodgers' Dallas recording session in 1932. Bill and Jim organized the Cowboy Ramblers in that same year and in 1934 made the first of their recordings for Victor (an association that lasted until 1951). The Cowboy Ramblers were built around a nucleus of Bill and Jim Boyd (guitar and bass), Art Davis (fiddle), and Walter Kirkes (banjo), all of whom were studio musicians at WRR. This was the group that made the first recordings in 1934, although their number was augmented by other musicians from time to time, such as fiddler Jesse Ashlock and steel guitarist Lefty Perkins, and, on recordings, by such Light Crust Dough-boys members as Knocky Parker, Kenneth Pitts, and Marvin Montgomery. The Cowboy Ramblers were essentially a recording band, for the members often played with other groups, and Bill Boyd remained associated with WRR as a musician and announcer for many years. As recording musicians the Cowboy Ramblers were very influential, and some of their tunes remained country standards long after the thirties. "Under the Double Eagle," for example—featuring Bill Boyd's guitar lead and Art Davis' bluesy fiddle—was one of the most popular instrumentals in country music and was probably second only to "Wildwood Flower" as the favorite number in the country guitarist's repertory.

As important as Newman's and Boyd's bands may have been, they did not enjoy the popularity of another Dallas-based group, the Shelton Brothers. The music of the Shelton Brothers is difficult to categorize. It was not western swing, although they shared some of the repertory of the hot fiddle bands. The Sheltons were a brother duet who often performed with mandolin and guitar and who performed songs similar to those of their duet contemporaries in the Southeast. Nevertheless, their repertory also contained a blues component that most of the mandolin-and-guitar teams did not possess, and Joe Shelton's mandolin style was characterized by a syncopation and blues feeling that was rare among other players of the instrument. The Sheltons thought of themselves as hillbillies—and many of their songs did reflect a rural impulse—but they ranged far and wide for their material, demonstrating that none of the southwestern groups could totally resist the swing and honky-tonk trends of the period.

Bob and Joe Attlesey, who performed under the name of Shelton, were born on a cotton farm in Rylie Springs, Hopkins County, Texas. The poverty of tenantry and the need to help take care of their eight younger brothers and sisters contributed to their decision to become professional entertainers. They began singing in Longview, an East Texas oil boom town, in 1929, for tips at root-beer and near-beer stands, and at Clint Aycock's café, where twenty-five cents would buy "all you could eat." In late 1929 they moved to Tyler, where they played with Leon Chappalear, as the Lone Star Cowboys, on KGKB. During the thirties they spent much of their time in Louisiana, playing on powerful KWKH in Shreveport (the personal mouthpiece of W. K. Henderson, who promoted his iron works and Hello World Coffee and castigated the chain stores), and on WWL in New Orleans, where they were teamed with Lew Childre and Curly Fox. In 1934 they became one of the earliest groups to sign with the new Decca Company (they had made one previous recording with Victor as the Lone Star Cowboys), an arrangement that resulted in the issuance the following year of their two most popular songs: "Just Because" and "Deep Elem Blues."

In the late thirties the Shelton Brothers alternated between KWKH (where they were also billed as the Sunshine Boys) and WFAA in Dallas, where they became securely ensconced after 1941. They also maintained a close relationship with Jimmie Davis, both musically and politically; Joe Shelton, for example, fronted Davis' band from 1943 to 1949 and was prominently involved in his successful race for the Louisiana governorship in 1944. During their performing career the Sheltons maintained a hillbilly image that was unusual in the Texas musical scene of the thirties, and Bob Shelton, in fact, continued to play the role of a rube hillbilly comic (complete with overalls and brown flop hat) on into the seventies. Their repertory always included "rustic" songs like "Stay in the Wagon Yard" (learned from their hero, the Texas radio singer Peg Moreland) and "Who Wouldn't Be Lonely" (a sentimental parlor-style song written by Leon Chappalear), but blues and hokum jazz tunes also occasionally intruded into their music: "Match Box Blues," "Sittin' on Top of the World," "Four or Five Times," "Knot Hole Blues," and similar songs. Instrumentally, the Sheltons tried to resist some of the swing emphasis of the period, even to the point of forbidding their brother Merle, who often played with them after 1935, to play bar chords on his rhythm guitar. The newer sounds, though, could not long be excluded, and by the time they retired from full-time entertainment in the late forties, electrification and hot instrumental licks had all but submerged their original acoustic and hillbilly-based identity.

The man who did most to make the newer sounds irresistible to country musicians was James Robert (Bob) Wills (born in Kosse, Limestone County, Texas, in 1905). Wills did not invent western swing—men like Milton Brown and Cecil Brower should certainly share much of the credit—but he did the most to popularize it around the United States in a long career that extended from the late twenties to 1969. Wills could scarcely escape being a fiddler, inheriting the art from his father and from relatives on both sides of the family (the Wills and the Foleys). From about 1915 and on through the twenties, Wills and his father, John, became locally famous in the area around Memphis, Texas (where the family had moved in 1913), playing in contests and at innumerable house parties. Wills served a musical apprenticeship with a medicine show in 1929 and then, as previously noted, played with Herman Arnspiger as Wills' Fiddle Band and with Arnspiger and Milton Brown as the Aladdin Laddies and the Light Crust Doughboys. When he left the Doughboys in 1933, he moved first to Waco, where the Texas Playboys were born, and then, in 1934, to Oklahoma, where he was to experience his most glittering success. From 1934 to 1942, Wills and the Texas Playboys performed daily on KVOO in Tulsa, almost every night at a large ballroom called Cain's Academy, and occasionally at dances in Oklahoma, Arkansas, Kansas, and Texas. These live performances, combined with his popular Okeh recordings after 1935, made Wills the most famous southwestern musician and an influence for change that has seldom been equaled in country music history.

Bob Wills and the Texas Playboys, at KVOO (Tulsa), 1937: *left to right*, Everett Stover, Zeb McNally, Leon McAuliffe, Al Franklin (announcer), Herman Arnspiger, Al Stricklin, Joe Ferguson, Smokey Dacus, Tiny Mott, Bob Wills, Tommy Duncan, Son Lansford, Sleepy Johnson. Courtesy of Bob Pinson.

Although the Texas Playboys used horns and reeds after 1935 and had become a large, versatile organization that could play big band jazz with skill by the end of the thirties, they always remained essentially a fiddle band. Wills himself was a hoedown fiddler, and while he had an undoubted affinity for the blues (Bessie Smith and white bluesmen Emmett Miller and Jimmie Rodgers were some of his favorite musicians), he could not play the hot, swinging style that became so characteristic of western swing. Wills' genius lay in his ability to attract musicians who could play jazz and other forms of music, and in his skill to extract from them every ounce of musicianship they possessed. When Wills pointed at musicians or called on them by name to take an instrumental break, he expected them to play something original and innovative. Wills employed a long string of fiddlers, such as Jesse Ashlock, Louis Tierney, Joe Holley, and Johnny Gimble, who were adept at jazz, blues, and breakdowns, and who possessed technical skills which their employer admired but could not duplicate.

The Texas Playboys' jazz experiments have seldom been re-created by modern country bands, and horns and reeds only rarely appear in country performances. Other traits pioneered or popularized by Wills, however, have endured in country music. Al Stricklin, described by Wills as "the old piano pounder," further popularized the improvisational style pioneered by Fred Calhoun. Smokey Dacus apparently introduced drums to country music when he joined the Playboys in 1935. Eldon Shamblin, formerly with the Alabama Boys, came to the Playboys in 1937 with his electric standard guitar; he and such contemporaries as Muryel Campbell, Junior Barnard, Jim Boyd, and Floyd Tillman popularized the single-note jazz style that probably came to them from the playing of such black musicians as Charlie Christian and Aaron "T-Bone" Walker. Leon McAuliffe, who electrified his steel guitar not long after Bob Dunn made the innovation, did more than any other musician to make his instrument one of the dominant stylistic forces in country music. His 1936 recording of "Steel Guitar Rag" made that tune a standard in the country repertory and was a vivid forecast of the prominence the instrument would enjoy in the coming decades. As these great musicians demonstrated their instrumental prowess, vocalist Tommy Duncan (from Whitney, Texas) caressed his audiences with a smooth, liquid, and extraordinarily supple baritone that moved easily from slow, romantic ballads to yodeling blues tunes. This disciple of Jimmie Rodgers and Emmett Miller was singing for tips at a Fort Worth root-beer stand in 1932 when Wills hired him to replace Milton Brown in the Light Crust Doughboys. He remained with Wills until the early fifties; he was universally admired, frequently emulated, but never surpassed as a singer. And not the least of his accomplishments was his ability to maintain his composure as Wills kept up a running fire of silly patter even during the most serious of songs.

Wills' repertory was wide and varied and reflected the broad range of influences that affected the music of southwesterners. Many of his popular tunes came from his southern rural forebears: fiddle pieces such as "Beaumont Rag," "Lone Star Rag," "Prosperity Special," or tunes that featured both lyrics and breakdown instrumentation such as "Cotton-Eyed Joe," "Ida Red," and "Take Me Back to Tulsa." Wills' extensive debt to traditional country music has not yet been fully measured, and it is somewhat camouflaged by the fact that he and his musicians often gave new names to old melodies.

Traditional rural music, however, was only one source that contributed to the Bob Wills catalogue. His very first recordings, made with Herman Arnspiger in November 1929—two unissued selections for Brunswick— illustrate the two major impulses that would always dominate his performances: "Wills Breakdown" and Bessie Smith's "Gulf Coast Blues." Wills had been fascinated with the blues since his youth, but there is no hard evidence that he picked up the style through direct contact with black people. Rather, his songs came from the performances of professional musicians, and especially from the recordings which he and other young western swing partisans avidly listened to. Even some of his spoken patter came from the performances of earlier minstrel entertainers such as Al Bernard (e.g., "You're a man after my own heart, with a razor"). Like a host of country musicians who came before him—beginning at least as early as Dock Boggs, Sam McGee, and Frank Hutchison—Wills borrowed heavily from black musicians, an indebtedness that would extend on through the days of Big Band jazz. "Sittin' on Top of the World," "Corrine, Corrina," "Basin Street Blues," "St. Louis Blues," "Trouble in Mind," and "Big Beaver" were only a few of the songs that came to Wills, at least indirectly, from the performances of black artists. Other tunes, such as Emmett Miller's "Right or Wrong" and "I Don't Love Nobody" (sung impeccably by Duncan), and Jimmie Rodgers' "Gambling Polka Dot Blues," "Mississippi Delta Blues," and "Blue Yodel No. 1," came from the repertories of white blues singers.

Along with this extensive catalogue of older borrowed material, Wills and the Playboys also utilized modern compositions written either by themselves or by other songwriters. Their most profitable association with a songwriter came during the forties, when Cindy Walker began contributing songs to the several movies that Wills made. Such Walker compositions as "Cherokee Maiden" and "Dusty Skies" (inspired by memories of the great dust storms of the late thirties) and songs that came from the pens of other writers, such as "My Confession," "Whose Heart Are You Breaking Now," "Roly Poly," "Time Changes Everything," "Rose of Old Pawnee," and, most popular of all, "Faded Love," are still known by most country singers and will endure long after Wills' jazz imitations have been forgotten. The majority of Wills' national hits did not come until the war years, but early in 1941 one composition forecast the future popularity that both Wills and country music would attain. This was "San Antonio Rose." It was first recorded as a country instrumental on November 28, 1938, and on April 16, 1940, was recorded with the addition of lyrics performed by Tommy Duncan. The Duncan recording achieved wide popularity, but in 1941 the song as recorded by Bing Crosby sold over eighty-four thousand copies in the month of January alone. The Bob Wills style, if not the Bob Wills name, was now being given national distribution.

Bob Wills left his brand on country music in an uncountable variety of ways. His irresistible personality dominated every performance, and dancers and spectators could scarcely keep their eyes off him as he strutted across the stage, dressed in the attire of a rancher, chomping on a cigar, and pointing toward musicians as they took their instrumental breaks. Certainly, no one could ignore his shouts and hollers which punctuated the performance of virtually every song: "Ahh haa," "Take it away, Leon," "Brother Al Stricklin," "Aw, come in, Tommy," and on and on. While musicians marveled at Wills' energy, they also borrowed permanently the songs and instrumental licks which he and his musicians had introduced. Long after the large western swing band had declined in popularity, the Bob Wills "beat" and style of fiddling continued to attract the attention of country musicians. All through the southwestern states, particularly, in literally hundreds of taverns, dance halls, and country night clubs, countless groups—such as Hoyle Nix and his West Texas Cowboys, who have worked a three-hundred-mile radius around Big Spring, Texas, since 1946—are living testaments to the Bob Wills influence. And a phenomenon which folklorists should begin to ponder—because it provides clues to the future directions that folk music will follow—is the influence exerted by Bob Wills upon participants at the old fiddlers' contests. In these contests, long acknowledged as arenas for authentic old-time music, many of the performers (usually the younger ones) practically duplicate old Bob Wills recordings.

By the end of the thirties such southwestern performers as Bob Wills, Gene Autry, Ernest Tubb, Al Dexter, Cliff Bruner, Jimmie Davis, Floyd Tillman, Ted Daffan, and the Shelton Brothers were beginning to dominate the jukeboxes. The eclectic and infectiously improvisatory sounds heard in their performances were appealing to country musicians everywhere. By the end of the forties the honky-tonk and dance-hall inspired styles of the Southwest had found receptive audiences all over the nation. Traditional "rural" acts still abounded in country music—such as Roy Acuff, the Blue Sky Boys, and Mainer's Mountaineers—but few performers could resist the temptation to experiment with the dynamic and increasingly electrified sounds then being popularized by the musicians of the Southwest. Although World War II contributed most toward its nationalization, hillbilly music had already made giant strides toward national acceptance by the end of the thirties. Some songs became so widely popular, and were performed in such an extensive variety of stylistic formats, that they virtually lost their country identities. *Billboard* in 1941 described "You Are My Sunshine" as the "tavern and taproom classic" of the year,[6] but it was destined to be much more than that. First recorded by the Rice Brothers (Paul and Hoke) in 1939, but given its widest hearing through the performances of Gene Autry, Bing Crosby, and Jimmie Davis (who used it as his theme song in his successful race for the Louisiana governorship in 1944), the song eventually became one of the most commercially programmed numbers in American popular music. Sung to death at innumerable parties, hayrides, fraternity bashes, and assorted social functions, it became one of the few country songs that everyone knows. "You Are My Sunshine" represented both the national flowering of country music and its eventual absorption into the maintream of American popular culture.

6. *Billboard* 53, no. 34 (August 23, 1941): 13.

Ernest Tubb.

6. The War Years: The National Expansion of Country Music

The Japanese attack on Pearl Harbor abruptly ended American isolation. The war that followed brought full employment and heightened prosperity, but it also quickened the tempo of American life and accentuated social tensions that would eventually give rise to the racial, sexual, and generational conflicts of the late fifties and early sixties. The war also encouraged mass population shifts as young men marched off to training camps and civilians moved into defense occupation centers. In a very real sense, America's rural population was liberated by the war, especially in the South, where poor white and black tenant farmers, sharecroppers, and mill workers left their meager farms and jobs and trekked to the urban areas in quest of better economic and social conditions. In the 1930's there had been relatively little out-migration from the South, except for the significant movement of the Okies. But during the war years southerners moved often and in great numbers to contiguous cities in their own region (from the Georgia countryside to Atlanta, from rural Alabama to Mobile or Birmingham, from East Texas into Houston, Dallas, or the industrial Gulf Coast, etc.), and to industrial-defense centers all over the United States (Baltimore, Washington, D.C., Cincinnati, Chicago, Detroit, Los Angeles).

The population movements of World War II brought Americans into closer contact with each other, intermingled differing cultures, and contributed to the breaking down of regional differences. World War II, and the prosperity it generated, accentuated the inherent American tendencies toward mobility and dynamism. Rural and small-town Americans found themselves subjected to increasingly irresistible pressures to conform with the new society that was taking shape.

Just as the war enlarged the scope and magnitude of American life, so did it affect the character and popularity of country music. The music had taken great strides toward national acceptance during the thirties but was still basically regional at the end of the decade; it would become a national phenomenon during the war. Expanded popularity brought increased commercial attention—from recording companies, promotional and booking agencies, and associated endeavors—whereas augmented incomes, particularly in the years immediately following the war, encouraged increased activity among the performers themselves. Together, these influences exerted terrific pressure upon country musicians to modify their styles and performing images in order to attract a potentially new and larger audience, but they also promised greater material benefits and public gratification than previous country entertainers had possessed.

Jukebox expansion, heightened road-show activity, movie exposure, and radio coverage (particularly on the fifty-thousand-watt channels and Mexican border stations) suggest that country music was achieving a national footing before the war. But events during the forties, some of them independent of the military conflict, further served to strengthen the music's public and commercial positions. A major conflict between ASCAP (American Society of Composers, Authors and Publishers) and the nation's broadcasters over music licensing rights helped to open the door to greater protection for country composers. A five-year contract between ASCAP and the radio networks expired on December 31, 1940. In negotiations for a new contract ASCAP demanded about $9 million a year, or twice what it had been receiving. The National Association of Broadcasters resisted the increased rates and had, in anticipation of the difficulty, established a rival licensing concern on October 14, 1939. The new organization, Broadcast Music, Inc. (BMI), was at a great disadvantage in its competitive struggle with ASCAP, which controlled most of the music written and published in the United States after 1884. The only exceptions were songs in the public domain and a small number held by a noncompetitive performance-rights society, SESAC (Selected Editions of Standard American Catalogues). On January 1, 1941, the broadcasters imposed a ban on all material controlled by ASCAP and determined to use only those songs protected by other licensing organizations. BMI, however, originally had few songs in its musical reservoir. Most music publishers were hesitant about joining the fledgling organization because they believed that it would ultimately collapse. BMI, therefore, had to rely upon new and inexperienced songwriters. The fortunes of BMI had begun to rise in July 1940, when the established publishing firm of Edward B. Marks, with its extensive catalogues of popular and Latin material, became a member. The Marks acquisition established a precedent which other publishing firms followed. Important in the furthering of hillbilly music were Ralph Peer's Southern Music and M. M. Cole of Chicago, both of which had extensive country music catalogues.

During the first ten months of 1941, BMI steadily expanded its catalogue until it included over thirty-six thousand copyrights from fifty-two publishers. As the sole source of music for broadcast purposes during that period, BMI attracted a number of composers who had been thrown out of work because of the ban. Hillbilly music owes much of its success in the forties to the protection granted it by BMI (ASCAP traditionally had been reluctant to admit hillbilly composers, and those who did gain admittance often complained about the delays involved in obtaining compensation). During the ten-month ban, hillbilly songs gained increased airplay because of the new catalogue acquisitions and because of the increased reliance upon public-domain melodies. When ASCAP and the radio networks resolved their differences in October 1941, BMI had secured a firm footing in the entertainment world and was well on the way to success. It provided a measure of competition for ASCAP and contributed to the economic security of fledgling songwriters. BMI was instrumental, therefore, in breaking New York's, or Tin Pan Alley's, monopoly on song writing. The American music industry consequently became more decentralized. Songwriters were encouraged all over the United States, and producers of the so-called grassroots material (country and race music) were given a decided boost.

Less than a year after the settling of the ASCAP-broadcasters feud, a new controversy erupted in the music industry. This was the strike called by James C. Petrillo and his American Federation of Musicians, a phenomenon that gave a further impetus to the development of country music. Petrillo argued that jukeboxes, which now numbered over 400,000, and broadcasting stations which used phonograph records were driving musicians out of work. Asking for the establishment of a fund for unemployed musicians, payable by the recording companies, the American Federation of Musicians went on strike on August 1, 1942, declaring that there would be no more recording. Having been warned on July 25 that such an event was imminent, the record companies had built up a heavy backlog of records by operating their studies on a round-the-clock schedule. By the fall of 1943, however, the companies began to feel the pinch, and they noticed too that their reservoir was inadequate in one important respect: it did not contain the new songs that caught the public's fancy in musicals and movies. When these songs were asked for at a record store, they were not available.

Decca was the record company most adversely affected by the strike, because its revenue came almost entirely from popular music. In September 1943, faced with possible bankruptcy, Decca signed a contract with the American Federation of Musicians. Columbia and Victor followed suit in November 1944, when they concluded similar agreements with the musicians' union.

The musicians' strike was a great boon to numerous small and independent record firms. Most of these signed contracts with Petrillo immediately, and the others followed when Decca came to terms. Of the newer firms, Capitol Records, a Los Angeles company headed by Johnny Mercer, proved to be the most durable. Organized shortly before the strike went into effect, Capitol achieved a strong position which might not have been won so quickly had the strike not been in progress. Capitol profited from the great pool of talent associated with the movie industry, and its country music roster drew upon the large number of entertainers who flocked to the West Coast during and right after the war to become part of the region's booming club business. Tex Ritter was the first country artist to sign with the label, and his 1942 hit "I've Got Spurs That Jingle, Jangle, Jingle" was the first of many successes for the popular cowboy singer.

The recording strike was important in furthering hillbilly music because many of the small record companies specialized in hillbilly and race music. This fact, along with the shortage of "popular" tunes, created a demand for specialized types of recordings, which the record companies were quick to supply. Hillbilly records began to circulate in areas where they formerly had been rare, and their success inspired the major companies to capitalize on the music's success. Decca's first release after the resumption of recording in September 1943 was Bing Crosby and the Andrews Sisters' version of "Pistol Packin' Mama," a hillbilly song first written and recorded by Al Dexter. Crosby, in fact, recorded many of the country and western favorites of the period (a phenomenon that some student of country music ought to explore).

While the strike was in progress, BMI suffered because of the lack of depth in its catalogue. Most of the older recordings were songs listed in the ASCAP catalogue. In 1942, however, at the height of the strike, songwriter Fred Rose withdrew from ASCAP and signed with BMI. He and country singer Roy Acuff organized the publishing firm of Acuff-Rose, with headquarters in Nashville. This event strengthened BMI and heralded the beginning of Nashville's preeminence as a country music center. The most important publishing house developing out of the increased interest in hillbilly music was Hill and Range, organized in 1945 when Julian Aberbach, a naturalized American of German birth, returned to the United States after his army duty determined to capitalize on the widespread popularity of country music. He had heard the music often during his army duty and decided that the country was ripe for a hillbilly music boom. Along with his brother Gene he organized two country music firms, Hill Music and Range Music, which were eventually merged into one organization. It became one of the largest BMI firms.

The phonograph industry, which suffered from the ASCAP-BMI controversy and the recording strike, languished also because of the pressures of the war effort. At the outset of the war, shellac, important in the manufacture of records, was frozen by government order. Although the restrictions were later relaxed, record issues did not regain their prewar levels until after the war's end. Recording studios could not operate at full capacity, because new machinery was unobtainable and trained personnel was scarce. Under these pressures only about 50 percent of previous record quotas could be filled, but the entertainment-hungry public was eager to obtain anything that could be produced.

Because of the pressures of shellac rationing, hillbilly record releases were limited. Some hillbilly entertainers temporarily stopped recording either because of the shellac scarcity or because gas and tire shortages curtailed their abilities to tour and advertise their new recordings. Many musicians, of course, were inducted into the armed forces. Companies released an average of only three hillbilly records a week, and at one critical point only one a week.

But even at the most critical points of shellac rationing, the companies continued without interruption to release some hillbilly records—an illustration of the importance attached to country music by the recording companies. And the public bought the records or played them on jukeboxes. Although few songs were released, jukebox operators and record-retailing firms found that the tunes experienced a strong and enduring popularity. Long after a popular song had declined in popularity, melodies like Ted Daffan's "Born to Lose" or Roy Acuff's "The Great Speckled Bird" continued to attract the nickels of jukebox patrons.

By 1942 there was a general awareness of country music's growing national popularity. *Billboard,* the leading trade music magazine, after decades of neglect, began to devote some attention to country performers. At first this was done with considerable hesitation, for no one was quite certain how permanent the popularity would be. *Billboard*'s first accounts dealt primarily with the astonishing expansion of country music, and it was some time before the periodical devoted an entire column to the music. *Billboard* did not quite know what to do with the music, or what to call it. In its first cautious ventures into the exploitation of hillbilly music, the periodical lumped the country tunes in a category along with foreign numbers. In January 1942 *Billboad* inaugurated a column entitled "Western and Race," which featured current releases of everything from Tex Ritter to Louis Armstrong. Then in February 1942 the designation was changed to "American Folk Records," and that title remained throughout the war years. In 1944 *Billboard* began a brief listing of the most popular hillbilly songs found on jukeboxes and included them along with popular race recordings. It was not uncommon to see a song like Floyd Tillman's "They Took the Stars Out of Heaven" included with Ella Fitzgerald's "When My Sugar Walks down the Street."

Country music flourished in some northern urban areas simply because southern rural people had moved there during the late thirties and early forties in search of defense work. Such cities as Baltimore, Washington, D.C., Detroit, Cincinnati, and Chicago reported heightened country music activity as southern migrants—particularly from such border states as Kentucky, West Virginia, Virginia, and Tennessee—poured into the areas and demanded a music for their own tastes. The migrants sought out their own kind and frequented the churches, community centers, and taverns that most reflected their socioeconomic backgrounds. The proprietors of the "hillbilly" bars and taverns, as well as the jukebox operators, found it advantageous to feature songs by Jimmie Davis, Ernest Tubb, and other country singers. Hillbilly tunes were said to be especially popular at places patronized by former West Virginians and North and South Carolinians. The demand for country music in Baltimore became so enormous that the jukeboxes were inundated with hillbilly selections. The migration from contiguous rural areas into Baltimore and nearby Washington, D.C., and the consequent burgeoning there of country music interest helped to lay the basis for the future flourishing of the bluegrass style in the region. Detroit jukebox operators reported in 1943 that hillbilly recordings were the most popular single class of music present on their machines. Hillbillies had been migrating to Detroit at least as early as World War I, when Henry Ford and his marvelous machine began attracting the marginal laborers of the South. The second great war inspired an even greater influx of southern workers seeking defense work. The West Coast, which had experienced the Okie migration in the mid-thirties, reported a tremendous growth in country music popularity as southerners and midwesterners—both civilians and military personnel—poured into the area. Working-class cities like Bakersfield began to experience a rapid growth of clubs and dancehalls which catered to the needs of the new arrivals. In Los Angeles, as many as five to ten hillbilly songs were appearing on coin machines that formerly had no more than one. Country musicians began to relocate themselves in great numbers in California, and Bob Wills himself had moved to a San Fernando Valley ranch by November 1943. Popular bands in California that normally featured only swing and jazz music began adding country tunes to their repertories in response to demands from their audiences. Crowds in Southern California particularly insisted that the popular swing bands perform in the Bob Wills style.

The intermingling of people from different backgrounds in the armed services was an important factor in the spread of country music. Military personnel sought the cheapest possible forms of entertainment and were the main source of the jukebox boom in the early forties. Young southerners, many of whom had scarcely been more than a few miles from the place where they were born, marched off to training centers carrying their musical tastes with them. Barrack rooms reverberated with the sounds of guitars, lonesome rural voices, and the current hillbilly songs. Quite often, these same rooms echoed with arguments as to who was the better singer, Roy Acuff or Frank Sinatra. Country music was transported all over the United States by servicemen and women who listened to the professional singers and by those who formed their own amateur bands. And, ultimately, the music was carried around the world. By 1943 the Special Services Division of the European Theatre of Operations included at least twenty-five hillbilly bands. Once the war was over, the Armed Forces Network would broadcast country music to an even larger audience of people in Europe and Asia.

In order to satisfy the musical hunger of soldiers and sailors, the R. J. Reynolds Tobacco Company and the *Grand Ole Opry* organized in August 1941 a traveling unit of twenty entertainers called the Camel Caravan. The Nashville-based country group (one of three sponsored by the Reynolds company—two popular, and one country) was composed of comedienne Minnie Pearl, Pee Wee King and his Golden West Cowboys, and the young Eddy Arnold, who was just a few years away from superstardom. Typically giving a concert climaxed by a public square dance, the Caravan by late 1942 had traveled more than fifty thousand miles in nineteen states (and had appeared in Panama) and had presented 175 shows in sixty-eight army camps, hospitals, air fields, and naval and marine bases.

The popularity of the Camel Caravan was only one example of the striking success exhibited by traveling hillbilly units during the war. Throughout the United States, country entertainers were drawing larger crowds and larger box-office receipts than ever before. The personal-appearance field, now becoming highly developed, was based primarily on the established radio barn dances such as the *Grand Ole Opry*, the *National Barn Dance*, Cincinnati's *WLW Barn Dance*, the *Wheeling Jamboree* in West Virginia, and the *Renfro Valley Barn Dance* in Kentucky. These programs sent their touring units on an ever-widening arc depending on the appeal and range of the radio show.

Chicago's WLS *National Barn Dance* continued to be an important source of the personal appearances made in the midwestern and southern border states. Featuring such musicians as Kentucky-born Bob Atcher, whose comic, "crying" version of "I'm Thinking Tonight of My Blue Eyes" was a huge hit in 1939, the WLS road shows, which had played more than six thousand personal appearances since 1932, grossed over $500,000 in the period from 1939 to 1942. These performances, as was true of the other hillbilly shows of the period, were conducted with a minimum of initial investment. Profits, thus, tended to be rather substantial. The Hoosier Hot Shots, a small instrumental group featuring homemade and off-beat instruments and singing comic songs, frequently grossed between $3,000 and $5,000 on one-day stands. Lulu Belle and Scotty, who performed periodically over WLS in Chicago and WLW in Cincinnati, were in constant demand for public appearances, for which they commanded $500 a day and transportation.

Other barn dances experienced similar financial successes. The WLW *Boone County Jamboree* on occasion grossed as much as $12,000 on one-day stands. The *Renfro Valley Barn Dance*, conducted by folk-music authority John Lair, maintained two tent roadshows which averaged about $5,000 a week. Biggest one-day grosses for the *Renfro Valley* organization were a $5,500 matinee and night show in Indianapolis and a $4,000 gross in Dayton, Ohio. These road shows, plus radio performances, won an extensive popularity for the *Renfro Valley* show. The show began its existence in Cincinnati in October 1937 and moved from there to Dayton in the fall of 1938, before moving on to Renfro Valley itself in November 1939. Renfro Valley (near Mount Vernon, Kentucky) is a small village sixty miles from Lexington and two and a half miles from any railroad station, but the paid attendance at the regular Saturday night show averaged about five thousand and was sometimes as high as ten thousand. The *Renfro Valley* show satisfied a hunger for down-home security that was particularly felt in the chaotic and lonely years of World War II. Audiences that could not attend the live concerts heard the Saturday night broadcasts or the *Sunday Morning Gathering*, the latter broadcast nationally. Listeners were alternately left weeping or somber by the old-time ballads and hymns of the Coon Creek Girls or hysterically amused by the antics of Aunt Idy (Margaret Lillie) and her overgrown brat, Little Clifford (played by Harry Mullins). The *Sunday Morning Gathering* gave listeners a heavy dose of nostalgia. The show was heavily scripted and narrated by Lair, and based each morning around a common theme (songs of the Civil War, the songs of Stephen Foster, and the like).

Despite the success experienced by the barn dances and their roadshow units, it became increasingly evident during the war years that Nashville's *Grand Ole Opry* was becoming the most important country music show. The program, which boomed out all over the South over the clear-channel, fifty-thousand-watt WSM, became nationally known when it gained network status in 1939. For thirty minutes each Saturday night the National Broadcasting Company carried a segment sponsored by Prince Albert Tobacco. The thirty-minute program, representative of the larger four-and-a-half hour show, was hosted by Roy Acuff and featured a variety of "guest" acts, including such comedians as Lazy Jim Day (known for his "Singing News" routines) and Minnie Pearl. Minnie Pearl, created by Sarah Ophelia Colley, was as responsible for the *Opry*'s popularity as any of the musicians. Colley's background and culture suggested little of the hayseed naïveté that surrounded Minnie Pearl. Although she came from a rural background in Centerville, Tennessee, her parents were sufficiently prosperous (Mr. Colley was a lumber man) to send her to the fashionable Ward-Belmont School in Nashville. Colley worked from 1934 to 1940 for the Sewell Production Company, a dramatic troupe that staged plays all over the South by training and using local talent. One night in January 1936 she stayed with a humble rural family in northern Alabama who kindled the idea for Minnie Pearl and her brother. Representatives of the

National Life and Accident Insurance Company, the owner of WSM and the *Grand Ole Opry*, heard her at a convention where she played the part of Minnie Pearl and invited her to appear on the Saturday night show. She became a regular member of the NBC segment in early 1942, and audiences thereafter responded enthusiastically to the guileless country girl who wore a straw hat with the price tag hanging prominently from it, who greeted each audience with a "How-dee, I'm so proud to be here," and who told jokes about Brother, her boyfriend Hezzie, and Uncle Nabob, that were perversely appealing in their utter corniness.

As Minnie Pearl's career suggests, the *Grand Ole Opry* was well on the way to becoming a haven for "stars." During the forties the show became famous for its vocalists and featured comedians: Roy Acuff, Bill Monroe, Ernest Tubb, Lloyd "Cowboy" Copas, Eddy Arnold, Minnie Pearl, Lazy Jim Day, the Duke of Paducah (played by Benny Ford, and famous for his closing line: "I'm going to the wagon, boys, these shoes are killing me"), and Rod Brasfield. Even before America's entry into the war in 1941, the *Opry* had begun sending its troupes far beyond the bounds of Middle Tennessee. Some *Opry* units performed in huge tents which attracted thousands of fans all over the South. A black-face team, Jamup and Honey, headed one such unit; Bill Monroe traveled with another; and the great fiddler, Curly Fox, headed another, which included his wife, Texas Ruby, as well as Lazy Jim Day and Uncle Dave Macon.

The *Grand Ole Opry*'s upsurge in popularity was attended, as was true in the case of other country music shows, by the rise of independent promoters who were quick to recognize the financial possibilities of the country music business. At the beginning of the war the most important promoters were individuals like Earl Kurtze, George Ferguson, and Dick Bergen, who gained success through their associations with the WLS Artists' Bureau. By 1943 they were being rivaled by independent promoters such as Larry Sunbrock and, in the South, Oscar Davis, "Happy" Hal Burns, Tom Parker (the famous "Colonel" who later gained international notoriety through his association with Elvis Presley), and J. L. Frank, who capitalized on the wealth of southern hillbilly talent, particularly that found on the *Grand Ole Opry*. Frank, the father-in-law of Pee Wee King, was instrumental in the careers of Gene Autry, Roy Acuff, and Ernest Tubb (whose first southern tours he arranged), and, because of his pioneering efforts on behalf of expanded country road shows, he was called the "Flo Ziegfeld of country music show business." In October 1967 Frank was named, as a deceased nonperformer, to the Country Music Hall of Fame.

In promoting hillbilly performances, all of the promoters used similar methods. Heavy emphasis was placed on radio saturation instead of billing or newspaper advertising, although many groups continued to tack their placards and posters on posts, windows, and walls. Scores of hillbilly acts still played in schoolhouses or gymnasiums, or between films at movies, but an increasing number took their performances into city auditoriums or other public arenas. "Folk music parks" also attracted touring country units. These resort areas were concentrated primarily in New England (where they seem to have originated in the early thirties), New York, Pennsylvania, the Midwest, and such border states as Maryland and Delaware. They were distinguished from regular parks in that they contained large outdoor stages with seating areas where weekly country music performances were given. Such parks as Buck Lake Ranch, at Angola, Indiana, and Ravine Park, at Blairsville, Pennsyvlania, attracted southeastern migrant musicians long before the professional acts began frequenting them.

Country acts booked by such promoters as Oscar Davis and Hal Burns played to large audiences all over the United States. Other entrepreneurs, though, concentrated on more limited areas. Foreman Phillips, for example, a country disc jockey in Los Angeles, made California his sphere of operation. In June 1942 Phillips converted the ballroom on Venice Pier into a country-music haven when he opened the *Los Angeles County Barn Dance*. He could draw upon a large storehouse of local talent for the *Barn Dance*, and for the dance halls which he established throughout Southern California, but he also brought big-name country performers in from other parts of the country. The two most successful appearances were those of Bob Wills, who attracted 8,600 customers to the pier, and Roy Acuff, who set an attendance record of 11,130.

Foreman Phillips was only one of many individuals who contributed to country music's great wartime surge. By 1944 more than six hundred hillbilly radio programs could be heard on stations ranging from the tiny one-hundred-watt WAGM, at Presque Isle, Maine, to a score or more of powerful fifty-thousand-watt stations such as WSM. The number of recording performers was also extensive. In a list prepared by *Billboard* in 1943, a total of 608 recording artists was led by hillbillies, with a total of 198. The entire aggregate of hillbilly performers, ranging from the professionals to the amateurs who struggled for success in the honky-tonks or on obscure radio barn dances, must have been enormous. Of the total, only a small percentage did well enough financially to warrant independent professional careers; most could not "give up their day jobs." It is impossible to determine and hazardous to guess who the most successful country entertainers of the period were. Certainly, no one has a stronger claim to the distinction—at least at the beginning of the war—than Gene Autry. Autry's movie appearances kept him in the public eye, and shrewd business activities made him a wealthy man. His phonograph records were among the nation's top sellers, and he commanded a greater popularity in northern areas than any other country performer. Autry would have gained even greater success had he not volunteered for military service, at the age of thirty-five, in 1942. He was part of a Special Services unit at first but soon became a flight officer in the Air Transport Command in Burma and India. At the time of his induction he commanded $1,000 a performance and was said to be a profitable investment at that figure. Autry's popularity suffered a gradual decline after his induction, and he was never able to regain his leadership as a recording star (even though the phenomenal success of "Rudolph the Red Nosed Reindeer" was yet to come). He even lost to Roy Rogers his title of "America's Number One Singing Cowboy."

Texas musicians, in general, won extensive recognition during the war years. Bob Wills was well known far beyond the range of KVOO when he too enlisted in the army in December 1942. Upon receiving a medical discharge about a year later, Wills moved to California, reorganized the Texas Playboys, and began playing to turnaway crowds all over the West Coast. Wills never really tried to gain much exposure outside the Southwest and West, but his one guest appearance on the *Grand Ole Opry* in December 1944, when he shocked traditionalists by his use of drums, evoked an enthusiastic response. Wills, Ted Daffan, Al Dexter, Floyd Tillman, Tex Ritter, and Ernest Tubb all produced records which, according to BMI estimates, dominated the jukeboxes during the first half of the forties. Tubb was destined to have the greatest longevity and, in many respects, the most widespread influence.

Tubb took his Texas style to the *Grand Ole Opry* in January 1943, and there he popularized such songs as "Walking the Floor over You," "Blue Eyed Elaine," "Our Baby's Book" (inspired by the death of his infant son, Rodger Dale), "Time after Time," and "When the World Has Turned You Down" (all of which were written by Tubb himself). By this time Tubb had gone beyond the rather simple accompaniment that characterized his first Decca releases (just two guitars), and had begun devising the full-blown electric honky-tonk sound, complete with steel guitar and takeoff guitar, that would remain an integral part of his style. Tubb's move to Nashville was more than symbolic of the "West's" growing influence in country music and of the mixing of regional styles that occurred in the forties; through his popular broadcasts and recordings he became the direct inspiration of many of country music's future stars, several of whom came from states far removed from Texas (Loretta Lynn from Kentucky, Harold "Hawkshaw" Hawkins from West Virginia, Jack Greene from Tennessee, Hank Williams from Alabama).

Southwestern singers may have dominated the jukeboxes during the war, but they did not monopolize the country field. Southeastern musicians remained active and popular, and one of them, Roy Acuff (who will be discussed later), won unprecedented success as a singer. War-time rationing and restrictions made it difficult for some acts, such as the Delmore Brothers, to remain active, while others, such as the Blue Sky Boys, were called to military service. Some old-time groups, such as Mainer's

Mountaineers, were fixtures on the radio barn dances but rarely made records of hit proportions. Roy Hall and the Blue Ridge Entertainers had a few moderately successful records, such as "Don't Let Your Sweet Love Die," but were best known in Virginia and the Carolinas through their radio shows. Before Hall's death in an automobile accident in 1943, few groups surpassed them in popularity in the Upper South. The duet tradition ebbed significantly during the war. Martha and James Carson, however—a husband-and-wife team from Kentucky—performed regularly on the *WSB Barn Dance* in Atlanta; Bill and Joe Callahan from North Carolina had settled down in Dallas, where they performed daily on KRLD; and Wiley and Zeke Morris, another North Carolina duo, amassed a large following through their mandolin-and-guitar-backed renditions of such songs as "Salty Dog Blues." Another stellar duet from the thirties, the Monroe brothers, had gone their separate ways well before the war started, but each had organized bands that achieved prominence during the forties. Charlie Monroe's Kentucky Pardners were one of the most popular North Carolina hillbilly bands, and although they stayed close to the older string band format, several musicians who later became identified with the bluegrass style—Lester Flatt, Red Rector, and Curly Sechler—got their start with the group. Bill Monroe's Blue Grass Boys had been a leading act on the *Grand Ole Opry* since 1939, but their collective talents had been subsumed by the sky-high tenor voice of their leader, heard to great advantage on such songs as "Muleskinner Blues" and "Footprints in the Snow." With the addition of guitarist Lester Flatt and banjoist Earl Scruggs in 1944 and 1945 respectively—musicians who could command attention equal to that accorded Monroe—the Blue Grass Boys began making the crucial transition from old-time string band music to bluegrass.

Many musicians achieved recognition during the turbulent war years, but none so dominated and symbolized country music as did that mountain boy from East Tennessee, Roy Acuff. With his showmanship and relaxed stage presence, an utterly sincere and believable vocal style, and skill at choosing appropriate songs, Acuff won an immense audience that is all the more remarkable in that it came at a time of growing "western" dominance in country music. Neither Acuff's singing nor his instrumental accompaniment echoed any of the honky-tonk or "hot dance" traits of the Southwest.

Roy Claxton Acuff was born September 15, 1903, in Maynardville, Tennessee, the son of Neill Acuff, a Missionary Baptist minister and lawyer. A country preacher's income proved insufficient to support the family, so Roy spent his early life in a succession of homes in the foothills of the Smoky Mountains while his father sought additional means of livelihood. When Roy was sixteen, the family moved to a Knoxville suburb, Fountain City. During his attendance at Central High School in Knoxville, Acuff became a star athlete and won a total of thirteen athletic letters. His dream of a professional baseball career did not materialize, even though the New York Yankees invited him to a summer training camp. An almost fatal sunstroke in July 1929 (during a Florida fishing trip), ended his hopes for athletic stardom and, in the long period of recuperation which followed, his interests turned toward music.

Acuff had always shown an aptitude for music and probably received his greatest inspiration from his father, who played the fiddle in the wee hours of the morning before doing the chores. A recurrence of his illness kept Acuff in Knoxville for two years, a period in which he practiced both the fiddle and his singing style. His boyhood experience of singing in Missionary Baptist church services did much to shape the lusty and emotional vocal style for which he became famous, but he also learned from a sister who had taken voice lessons and from the hillbilly records (Fiddlin' John, Gid Tanner, the Carter Family, etc.) to which he often listened. Acuff ventured into the world of show business in the spring of 1932 when he joined Doc Hauer's medicine show which toured eastern Tennessee hawking Moc-A-Tan Compound. Performing in blackface, or playing the part of "Toby," the red-haired rube character well known to traveling rural entertainment, Acuff developed the ease and showmanship that have remained with him throughout his career.

In 1933 Acuff began performing with a group of friends at dances and private parties, but soon obtained a spot on WROL in Knoxville. Calling themselves the Tennessee Crackerjacks, the boys had moved by 1934 to rival station WNOX, where they were among the earliest performers on Lowell Blanchard's *Mid-Day Merry-Go-Round*, a show which became a Knoxville institution and a forum for the music of such entertainers as Chet Atkins, Bill Carlisle, Pee Wee King, and Kitty Wells. In 1935 Roy and the Crackerjacks returned to WROL to inaugurate a rival noontime show. Renamed the Crazy Tennesseans by an announcer who was impressed by their rather casual approach to formal radio entertaining, they remained on the station until Roy joined the *Grand Ole Opry* in 1938.

Acuff began his recording career in 1936, when William R. Calaway of the American Record Corporation heard him singing "The Great Speckled Bird" (the original record labels, however, spelled it "Speckle," and to many people it will always bear that title). Set to a melody reminiscent of "I'm Thinking Tonight of My Blue Eyes," the song came to Acuff through the performances of another Knoxville radio group, Charlie Swain and the Black Shirts. The authorship of this famous song will probably always remain unknown, although it has been attributed to a Rev. Gant and to Rev. Guy Smith (Acuff also wrote four additional verses which became "The Great Speckled Bird No. 2.") The song, which pictures the church as a group of persecuted individuals who ultimately will gain eternal salvation as a reward for their earthly travail, is based upon the ninth verse of the twelfth chapter of Jeremiah: "Mine heritage is unto me as a speckled bird, the birds round about are against her." The song was popular not only as a recording hit but as a favorite in some of the Pentecostal Holiness churches as well. Vance Randolph, for example, heard it sung in Pawhuska, Oklahoma, as an official Assembly of God hymn, and W. J. Cash claimed that it was "the official hymn of the Church of God."[1]

After repeated tries, Acuff moved to the *Grand Ole Opry* on February 19, 1938, largely through the influence of J. L. Frank, who urged the show to take the gamble, and as a possible replacement for fiddler Arthur Smith, who had left the show. Acuff's fiddle debut tunes did not particularly impress either the audience or the *Opry* staff, but his heartfelt performance of "The Great Speckled Bird," done as his third number, elicited a large response of cards and letters. The move to the *Opry* eventually made Acuff one of the most well-known country performers in the nation, and the *Opry* the most famous radio barn dance in the United States. Accompanied by his string band, now called the Smoky Mountain Boys, he became the first real singing star of the *Grand Ole Opry*. When NBC began its thirty-minute coverage in 1939, no one but Acuff seems to have been considered for the host position. In the years that followed, "Roy Acuff" and "*Grand Ole Opry*" became almost synonymous.

As the leading star of the *Opry*, Roy Acuff performed a repertory heavily weighted with sacred and traditional-style songs, all rendered in an emotionally earnest and plaintive manner. Like all great country singers, Acuff felt strongly the sentiments he expressed and was able to communicate his feelings to his listeners. On some of his most serious numbers he became so emotionally involved with the lyrics that he wept openly. His intense delivery and graceful stage presence made him a crowd-pleaser and a great drawing card.

Oddly enough, two songs from his first recording session have always remained most strongly identified with him: "The Great Speckled Bird" and "The Wabash Cannon Ball." "The Wabash Cannon Ball" is usually attributed to A. P. Carter, but it is actually of traditional derivation, telling of a mythical train that would carry the hobo to the land of fantasy. Acuff's version seems more inspired by a 1929 recording made by fellow East Tennessean, Hugh Cross, than by that of the Carter Family. Ironically, Acuff did not sing on the first recording of the song—harmonica player Dynamite Hatcher did—but Roy supplied an imitation train whistle (inspired by his days as a callboy for the L&N Railroad) which contributed to the song's great success. He did not record the song with his own vocal until 1947. But in the meantime he had been singing it constantly on the *Opry*

---

1. Vance Randolph, *Ozark Folksongs*, vol. 4 (Columbia: State Historical Society of Missouri, 1950), p. 59; W. J. Cash, *The Mind of the South* (New York: Alfred A. Knopf, 1941), p. 297.

and on his many road shows. He is still singing it and "The Great Speckled Bird" in the 1980's.

Acuff resisted electrical amplification long after it had become the norm in most country bands and instead adhered to the style and format of the older acoustic string bands. Lacking confidence in his ability to play the fiddle (which he actually played rather well), he left the bulk of the instrumentation to other band members. Acuff always employed outstanding fiddlers, such as Tommy Magness and Howard "Howdy" Forrester, but the center of his instrumentation, and a defining feature of the Roy Acuff sound, was the dobro steel guitar. On his earliest recordings the instrument was played by James Clell Summey, who later became a popular baggy-pants comedian known for his toothless grin, Cousin Jody. After 1938 Acuff's dobro player was Beecher Kirby (best known as "Bashful Brother Oswald"), who sang one of the highest and most easily recognized harmonies in country music, frailed the five-string banjo, and did comedy routines, often with Rachel Veach, who was advertised as his sister. Kirby, who is still with the Acuff organization as of 1984, made the unelectrified dobro the most prominent feature of the Smoky Mountain Boys' instrumentation at the very time when electric instruments were becoming the rage in other country music groups.

Instrumentation was only one aspect of Acuff's effort to keep his music as traditional as possible. His singing style and choice of songs suggested the mountain country churches. When his entire group joined him on gospel numbers, no attempt was made to achieve close harmony, for Acuff wanted to keep the style similar to that heard in his boyhood church. The Smoky Mountain Boys were unaffected by the western image. Acuff wore sport clothes during his stage appearances, while his band members dressed in overalls or other casual attire. Acuff's repertory was largely of his own choosing, but it also reflected (at least during the Columbia years) the inclinations of his artists and repertory (A&R) man, Arthur Satherley. The British-born Satherley, who came to the United States as a young man filled with visions of cowboys and romantic isolated mountaineers, tried to keep country music moored to its traditional roots, and he found Acuff to be much more committed to old-time songs than his other two famous "discoveries," Bob Wills and Gene Autry. There is not a single "cowboy" or western-style song in Roy Acuff's repertory, and very little that suggests a western swing influence. Acuff's song catalogue is heavily weighted with sacred numbers like "The Great Judgment Morning," sentimental songs of unrequited love like "Come Back Little Pal" (learned from Roy Hall) and "All the World Is Lonely Now," old-time novelty numbers like "Ida Red," and tragic numbers such as "Unloved and Unclaimed" (about the suicide drowning of an anonymous woman in Nashville).

Acuff seems to have written some of his most popular songs, such as

"The Precious Jewel"—a song about the death of a young prospective bride set to the melody of a mournful mountain ballad, "The Hills of Roane County." But most of his repertory came from other composers. Some of them, like Fred Rose, were very well known. Much of his material, though, came from obscure or anonymous writers. Jim Anglin, for example—a one-time member of the Anglin Brothers singing team in the late thirties—wrote many of Acuff's finest songs: "Lonely Mound of Clay," "Branded Wherever I Go," "Stuck Up Blues," "They Can Only Fill One Grave," "As Long As I Live," "Just a Friend," and "Unloved and Unclaimed."

Acuff gained success as a "mountain" singer when the majority of country performers seemed to be discarding traditional rural numbers and accepting "western" styles and techniques. His great success came partly because he presented a musical alternative to the country music fans who were being deluged with the newer musical styles and partly (and this probably helps to explain country music's overall popularity) because the war "caused people to turn to simpler and more fundamental things."[2] When Roy Acuff raised his voice in his mournful, mountain style, he seemed to suggest all the verities for which Americans were fighting: home, mother, and God.

Regardless of the source of his appeal, Americans packed any place in which Roy Acuff appeared, whether it was Nashville's Ryman Auditorium for the Saturday night *Grand Ole Opry*, or the site of one of his numerous touring appearances. A capacity crowd at Constitution Hall in Washington paid as much as $6.60 each to see him; at Cincinnati's Music Hall a country music show starring Acuff and Ernest Tubb attracted 13,000 people for two performances; and at Venice Pier, California, Acuff drew the largest crowd that had ever gone to a Foreman Phillips promotion. The 11,130 paid admissions gave rise to fears that the pier would fall from the weight.

Acuff's income, which over the years has been among the highest in the country music business, was estimated at well over $200,000 in 1942. Largely through the business acumen of his wife, Mildred, Acuff built an immense personal fortune through adroit financial dealings, through his co-ownership of Dunbar Cave Resort near Clarksville, Tennessee (after 1947), and through his co-ownership of Hickory Records.

His popularity was not confined to American audiences. A two-week popularity contest held on the Armed Forces Network's *Munich Morning Report* gave Acuff, out of 3,700 votes cast, a lead of 600 votes over popular crooner Frank Sinatra. As a result, the AFN instituted a new show, *Hillbilly Jamboree*, directed from Munich at American occupation forces in Europe.

---

2. This quote has been attributed to popular songwriter Frank Loesser: *Billboard* 55, no. 43 (October 23, 1943): 66.

An incident that reveals the world-wide significance of Roy Acuff's name, and is probably the greatest tribute he ever received, occurred on the remote island of Okinawa. Upon attacking a Marine position, a Japanese banzai charge used a battle cry which it thought would be the ultimate in insults: "To hell with Roosevelt; to hell with Babe Ruth; to hell with Roy Acuff!"

An important figure in Acuff's career, and one of the major forces behind country music's commercial evolution, was Fred Rose, who grew up outside the country music world and spent his early career as a popular music entertainer. Despite his "nonrustic" origins, he became one of the most successful country songwriters of all time, and a major discoverer and promoter of young country talent. He was one of the first three individuals elected to the Country Music Hall of Fame. Rose was born in Evansville, Indiana, on August 24, 1897, but grew up in St. Louis. Before the forties, he had little association with country music, but had pursued a career as a pianist and popular songwriter in Chicago. Elected to ASCAP in 1938, Rose had gained considerable success as the writer of such songs as Sophie Tucker's "Red Hot Mama," "'Deed I Do," and "Honest and Truly."

His first venture into the writing of country-style songs came on the West Coast in 1940, when he wrote sixteen songs for Gene Autry, including the very popular "Be Honest with Me." In the next decade Rose wrote hundreds of songs that were recorded or otherwise performed by most country performers. When Rose moved to Nashville and became the staff pianist for Station WSM, he became acquainted with Roy Acuff—an association that proved mutually profitable and beneficial. Rose commented that he never truly understood the real meaning of country music until he stood backstage one night at the *Grand Ole Opry* and watched Acuff, with tears streaming from his eyes, sing a song about a dying child, "Don't Make Me Go to Bed, and I'll Be Good."[3] Writing often under assumed names, such as Floyd Jenkins and Bart Dawson, Rose composed many of the most popular and enduring songs of the forties and fifties. Like Cindy Walker and Boudleaux and Felice Bryant, Rose could easily adapt to any style of country music, from gospel to secular. Songs like "Be Honest with Me," "Pins and Needles (in My Heart)," and "No One Will Ever Know" are known by all country fans. His biggest hit came posthumously: "Blue Eyes Crying in the Rain," though recorded by earlier singers, was a massive success for Willie Nelson in 1975.

In 1942 Rose and Roy Acuff organized the first exclusive country music publishing house in the United States, Acuff-Rose Publications. This firm provided the nucleus for Nashville's later rise to eminence in the music industry and brought further financial success to each of its founders. In December 1945 Fred Rose turned the operation of the business over to his

3. Interview with Wesley Rose, Nashville, August 28, 1961.

son Wesley and began devoting most of his time to the aid and encouragement of prospective young songwriters, the most famous being Hank Williams.

Country songwriters explored a variety of themes during the forties, but nothing attracted their attention more than the war itself. Continuing a tradition set by their ballad-making ancestors centuries earlier, the country singers and writers chronicled the war as they talked of the experiences, sufferings, and death of the departed soldiers, and of the anxieties and sadness of their loved ones. Patriotic songs and related war songs were among the most popular numbers in the hillbilly repertory from 1941 to 1946. Carson Robison's "1942 Turkey in the Straw" was, according to *Billboard*, the most popular hillbilly song during the first year of the war. No song, however, surpassed in popularity Elton Britt's version of "There's a Star Spangled Banner Waving Somewhere." Written by the prolific songwriter Bob Miller, the song was first released in May 1942 as the "B" side of a Bluebird record. Recounting the story of a crippled mountain boy who yearned to do his part in the war effort, the record gained astounding success because it attracted not only hillbilly enthusiasts but popular music fans as well. Britt's recorded version sold over a million and a half copies, while almost as many copies of sheet music were sold. Remaining popular well into 1943, the song was eventually recorded by many acts, popular and hillbilly. In his recorded version, however, Elton Britt, billed as "the highest yodeler in the world," became the first hillbilly singer since Vernon Dalhart to record a song of national hit proportions which transcended the bounds of most musical categories.

Some of the songs, like Roy Acuff's "Cowards over Pearl Harbor," expressed Americans' shock and anger at their sudden and undesired entry into the war. "Smoke on the Water," recorded by its writer, Zeke Clements, and also by such singers as Red Foley, breathed a defiant tone as it described what would happen "when our army and navy overtake the enemy." Few songs responded to the war as naïvely as did "I'll Be Back in a Year Little Darling," but several expressed similar promises of faithfulness: "Each Night at Nine," "We'll Meet Again, Sweetheart," "I'll Be True While You're Gone," "When My Blue Moon Turns to Gold Again," "I'll Wait for You," "Silver Dew on the Blue Grass Tonight," "Mother, I Thank You for the Bible You Gave." Some songs, of course—such as "Are You Waiting Just for Me," "At Mail Call Today" (about a "Dear John" letter), and "Have I Stayed Away Too Long" (written by pop composer Frank Loesser, who admitted a liking for hillbilly music)—discussed unfaithful love or the anxieties felt by servicemen about their loved ones back home.

The most poignant wartime songs dealt with the tragedy of war. Tex Ritter's "Gold Star in the Window" told of "the price a mother paid to keep us free." Songs like "Stars and Stripes on Iwo Jima" and "White Cross on Okinawa," both recorded by Bob Wills, told of American sacrifices for the cause of freedom. "The Soldier's Last Letter," written by Ernest Tubb and Sergeant Henry "Redd" Stewart (Pee Wee King's long-time vocalist and partner), told of a mother's sorrow upon receiving word that her son had been killed in action. Red River Dave McEnery's "The Blind Boy's Dog" was more ludicrous than pathetic, and it probably provoked more laughs than its composer intended, but it no doubt touched a few hearts with its tale of a blind boy who patriotically sent his lead dog off to die in the war. The two most affecting songs about war's tragedies were "Teardrops Falling in the Snow" (written by Mac McCarty and beautifully sung by Molly O'Day) and "Searching for a Soldier's Grave" (written by Jim Anglin and recorded by the Bailes Brothers). "Teardrops Falling in the Snow" tells of a mother's trip to a the railroad station to receive the casket "wrapped in red, white, and blue" that bears her son. "Searching for a Soldier's Grave" tells of a person who travels abroad to find the final resting place of a loved one, and it universalizes the individual tragedies produced by the war when it remarks that beneath the white crosses lie buried the hearts of thousands of Americans back home across the ocean.

Apart from the patriotic songs, wartime country music continued to mine the same veins that had attracted earlier writers. Except for the songs composed for motion pictures, however, "cowboy" melodies declined significantly as a part of the hillbilly repertory. The western myth nevertheless remained in the wearing of gaudy cowboy paraphernalia. The honky-tonk had definitely come to exert a powerful and dominating role in country music. Among songs of the honky-tonk variety, those of Texas origin generally predominated: Ernest Tubb's "Walking the Floor Over You," Ted Daffan's "Worried Mind," "Headin' Down the Wrong Highway," and "Born to Lose," Jerry Irby's "Driving Nails in My Coffin," and Floyd Tillman's "They Took the Stars Out of Heaven" and "It Makes No Difference Now." The composers of "The Last Letter" and "When My Blue Moon Turns to Gold Again" were not born in the Lone Star State, but they were strongly identified with Texas because of long residence there, and their songs competed for the nickels of beer hall patrons all over the state. Neither Rex Griffin ("The Last Letter") nor Gene Sullivan ("When My Blue Moon Turns to Gold Again") were honky-tonk musicians; they were instead radio performers who merely happened to write and record songs that made their way into honky-tonks all over the country. Griffin was a Gadsden, Alabama, native who wandered into radio stations all over the South before winding up in Dallas in the early forties. His great song of forsaken love, "The Last Letter," has traveled much farther than its creator; it has entered the repertory of almost every country singer. Gene Sullivan and his long-time singing partner Wiley Walker were Alabama boys, too, who traveled separate routes as entertainers before organizing their duet in Texas in 1939. Walker was a fiddler and singer who traveled with Lew Childre for several years and who had been a dancer, singer, musician, and actor with Harley Sadler's West Texas tent show in the late thirties. Sullivan belonged to several bands, including those headed by Happy Hal Burns in Birmingham, the Shelton Brothers in Shreveport, and Roy Newman in Dallas, before finally teaming up with Walker in Dallas. They made radio transcriptions, performed in Fort Worth and Lubbock, and then moved to Oklahoma City, where they became ensconced on local radio (WKY) for many years. They had settled down in Oklahoma City when their two most famous songs, "When My Blue Moon Turns to Gold Again" and "Live and Let Live," appeared as opposite sides of the same Okeh record. The melancholy lyrics, combined with Walker's and Sullivan's gentle, low-pitched harmony, made the songs extremely popular with country fans everywhere. They captured the mood of loneliness and separation that so many people felt during the war years, and they have never since lost their appeal to people.

Many songs demonstrated popular appeal in the early forties, but few were as commercially successful as "Pistol Packin' Mama." Although it was released by Okeh in March 1943, the song was inspired by the violence and turbulence of East Texas oilfield days. Its performer and writer, Al Dexter (Albert Poindexter, born in Jacksonville, Texas, in 1905), had been the proprietor of a honky-tonk near Longview, Texas, in about 1933. The idea for the song came to him one day when a gun-toting woman chased her husband's girlfriend (and one of Al's waitresses) through a barbed-wire fence. Some years later he attached the words to a melody borrowed from Bob Wills' "Take Me Back to Tulsa," and ultimately saw his song become one of the smash hits of American country and popular music. The rollicking novelty tune, which offended some people because of its open reference to drinking beer, succeeded "There's a Star Spangled Banner Waving Somewhere" as the country's most popular hillbilly song and reached even greater commercial heights when that remarkable urban bucolic, Bing Crosby, and the Andrews Sisters performed it as their first post-strike recording in September 1943. Within six months of its issuance, over a million copies of the record had been sold; the song itself ranks as one of the two or three most popular hits of the war years. The song, however, did not appear on CBS' *Lucky Strike Hit Parade*, then the chief means of denoting America's most popular melodies, until October 1943. The reasons it was rejected earlier were unknown, but *Life* magazine suspected that it might be because of the sponsor's dislike or because Frank Sinatra, the show's star vocalist, could not sing the little ditty.[4] The song sold more than three million records in less than two years, and Dexter was still receiving royalties on it up into the 1960's.

Country music came out of the war years, therefore, exhibiting a strength that was remarkable given the context of scarcity and restrictiveness in

4. *Life* 15, no. 11 (October 11, 1943): 55.

which it operated. The process of nationalization that had begun in the thirties accelerated during the war when servicemen and women and migrating civilians introduced their musical tastes to new people in distant climes. The names of such entertainers as Jimmie Davis, Ernest Tubb, Gene Autry, Ted Daffan, Bob Wills, and Roy Acuff had become known, in varying degrees, all over the United States. Throughout the late thirties and the war years, songs had occasionally transcended the bounds of country music to become national favorites. The music industry as a whole certainly took note of country music's great gains during the early forties. *Billboard* noted prophetically that the music had "shown by its work against adverse conditions that when the war is over and normalcy returns it will be the field to watch."[5]

5. *Billboard* 55, no. 9 (February 27, 1943): 94.

Hank Williams. Courtesy of Bob Pinson.

7. The Boom Period: The Emergence of a Big Business, 1946–1953

The uncertain peace that followed World War II ushered in a period of unparalleled prosperity. Freed from wartime restraints, anxious Americans now sought the stability and material abundance that had been denied them in earlier eras. The pursuit of pleasure and amusement proceeded apace, and country music profited as a result. In many respects the dawning period was to be the real "golden age" of country music. Later decades would bring greater material rewards to country musicians, but no period would experience a happier fusion of "traditional" sounds and commercial burgeoning than did the immediate postwar era.

As the nation converted successfully to a civilian, domestic economy, the music industry, unhampered by wartime restrictions, geared itself for a highly prosperous period. Records could now be produced in quantities above their prewar levels, and an entertainment-hungry public was ready to buy them. Country music, which had prospered despite (or perhaps because of) defense regulations, was already giving signs of increased national recognition. Songs like "Oklahoma Hills," performed by Jack Guthrie (soon to die in a veteran's hospital), Spade Cooley's "Shame on You," Wesley Tuttle's "Detour," Arthur Smith's "Guitar Boogie," and Merle Travis' "Divorce Me C.O.D." were jukebox favorites all over the nation in 1946. Bing Crosby, moreover, crossed once more into the country field and recorded the biggest song of all, "Sioux City Sue" (done the previous year by Dick Thomas).

At the conclusion of the war at least sixty-five recording companies, fifteen of them on the West Coast, were releasing country records. Radio continued to be an indispensable means of exploiting hillbilly talent. By 1949 at least 650 radio stations used live country performers. In the early commercial years most of the hillbilly shows had been broadcast at noon or during the early morning hours, since program directors felt that only early-rising farmers listened to the programs. But with their newly discovered popularity, country entertainers were scheduled at more advantageous hours and were produced with the same care given to other musical offerings. In addition to established shows like the *Grand Ole Opry*, the period saw the emergence of regional barn dances like Atlanta's *WSB Barn Dance*, Bristol, Virginia's *Farm and Fun Time* (heard each day at noon over a five-state area), Dallas' *Big D Jamboree*, Los Angeles' *Town Hall Party* and *Dinner Bell Roundup* (later called the *Hometown Jamboree*), and, most important of all, Shreveport's *Louisiana Hayride*. In addition to providing local entertainment, these shows started many successful country musicians on the road to wider fame.

Country music, therefore, was in the midst of a burgeoning commercial success that was most evidenced, perhaps, by the growth and development of the personal-appearance field. *Billboard* claimed that country performers were major box-office attractions almost anywhere in the United States, even in "sedate New England."[1] The South, as usual, was a lucrative area for hillbilly entertainers, but Pennsylvania, Ohio, and Michigan were recognized as important markets for country music. Country music even ventured into historic Carnegie Hall in October 1947, when a *Grand Old Opry* unit headed by Ernest Tubb played two nights for a gross of over $9,000.

The most vigorous region for live country performances may very well have been California, where major emphasis was devoted to ballroom performances and the big radio barn dances which began in the mid-forties. When Bob Wills relocated in California in September 1943, the dance hall business had already begun to thrive, but he soon became a major musical force in the state, breaking attendance records everywhere he went, operating a club in Sacramento called Wills Point, and occasionally making cross-country tours. His Texas Playboys had moved away from their earlier emphasis on horns and had once again become basically a fiddle band. Wills himself was devoting more attention to fiddle hoedowns, and he acquired two new fiddlers, Johnny Gimble (from Texas) and Keith Coleman (from Oklahoma), who were at home in any style. Wills had also added another twist to his band by adding a female vocalist, Laura Lee McBride, the first featured woman singer in the western swing genre. McBride was well-connected in the country field; she was the daughter of radio cowboy singer Tex Owens, the niece of Texas Ruby Owens, and the wife of bandleader Dickie McBride.

The era of country ballrooms had begun in 1942 when Foreman Phillips opened the Venice Pier Ballroom, catering to transplanted Okies, defense workers, and servicemen. Before his retirement in 1952, Phillips had

1. *Billboard* 59, no. 52 (December 27, 1947): 18.

opened three other thriving ballrooms in Culver City, Baldwin Park, and Compton, and had begun to hire such musicians as Ray Whitley, Hank Penny, Ted Daffan, Curley Williams, T. Texas Tyler, and Red Murrell to head his house bands. Phillips also was instrumental in the creation of the band that did most to give western swing its name, Spade Cooley and His Orchestra.

Donnell Clyde "Spade" Cooley's story is one of success and tragedy. Cooley came to Modesto, California, with his family from Grande, Oklahoma, in the 1930's and soon became a fiddler with various bands in the area around Los Angeles. Foreman Phillips hired him away from the Jimmy Wakely Trio in about 1942 to head a band at Venice Pier. He was joined late that same year by a singer and bass player from Illinois, Sollie Paul "Tex" Williams, who was to have a profitable relationship with Cooley until 1946. In 1943 Cooley took his band to the Riverside Rancho Ballroom, where they played nightly to overflow crowds until 1946. During these busy and prosperous years, and at the Santa Monica Ballroom after 1946, Cooley became known as the "King of Western Swing," apparently the first use of the term to describe the music which Bob Wills and Milton Brown had pioneered. Cooley's music was more heavily orchestrated than that of Wills (whose musicians generally improvised what they felt), but his large band included some remarkably innovative musicians, such as jazz-style steel guitarist Joaquin Murphy, and an instrument or two, such as a harp, that almost never appeared in other country bands. Cooley maintained his popularity until one sad night in 1961 when, in a fit of drunken rage, he beat and stomped his wife to death. Tragedy remained with Cooley for the last few short years of his life. He was in prison for eight years and died of a heart attack in 1969 while on a temporary parole to attend a concert in his honor.

Cooley's former vocalist, Tex Williams, formed his own band, the Western Caravan, in 1946 and went on to become one of the most-admired singers of the period. His smooth, ultra-deep voice was first heard on "Shame on You," a big Columbia hit for Spade Cooley in 1945–1946, but Williams had a successful string of recordings on his own for the Capitol label after 1946. One of them not only was financially satisfying to Williams but also was well ahead of its time in the message it conveyed. This was his 1947 hit, "Smoke! Smoke! Smoke!" a half-sung, half-recited complaint about the inconveniences caused by chronic smokers.

"Smoke! Smoke! Smoke!" was the brainchild of Merle Travis, one of country music's most brilliant and multi-talented entertainers. When Travis left the Marines and moved to California in 1944, he became part of a rather large migration of musicians, such as Speedy West, Ted Daffan, Adolph Hofner, Hank Thompson, and Lefty Frizzell, who wandered to the West Coast in the late forties and early fifties. Travis had already made a name for himself back east, and had made a few records with his old friend Grandpa Jones. He had developed his much-admired guitar style by building on tips picked up from such guitarists as Kennedy Jones and Mose Rager in his home county of Muhlenberg in the coal-mining district of western Kentucky. Guitarists everywhere now describe the style as "Travis picking," but Merle himself calls it "thumb style" (the use of the thumb to maintain a bass rhythm while the forefinger plays a syncopated melody on the treble strings). When Chet Atkins was growing up in East Tennessee, he heard Travis on the radio and was later amazed to discover that so much music could be made with only two fingers.

In California, Travis was quickly swept into a busy whirl of music as both a soloist and a sideman. He made records of his own for Capitol after 1946, and some of them—such as "Divorce Me C.O.D." and "So Round, So Firm, So Fully Packed"—are excellent examples of the West Coast honky-tonk sound. He appeared on hundreds of recordings as a supporting musician for other acts; he performed on the *Town Hall Party* and *Dinner Bell Roundup*; he kept friends and audiences amused with his wit and storehouse of tales; he drew cartoons and wrote stories; and he wrote some of country music's greatest songs. Travis generally wrote rather happy-go-lucky songs, such as "So Round, So Firm," and "Sweet Temptation," but he also demonstrated a flair for writing religious numbers and songs of social commentary. When asked in 1947 to record some folksongs from "back home," he responded by writing some of his own. They included the now well-known religious piece "I Am a Pilgrim" and two famous documents of coal-mining life, "Dark as a Dungeon" and "Sixteen Tons."

Country musicians who flocked to California also found outlets for their talents on the local radio stations, and particularly on the barn dances which flourished after the mid-forties. Along with Foreman Phillips, Cliffie Stone probably did more to popularize country music in the region than any other person. Stone had a daily variety show, the *Dinner Bell Roundup*, on KXLA in Pasadena. Many country entertainers appeared on the program, one of the most notable being the swing fiddler and bandleader Red Murrell, who had one of the most popular bands in California. Other important members included Herman the Hermit (Cliffie Stone's father and a popular banjo player); ace fiddler Harold Hensley; Tennessee Ernie Ford; and the Armstrong Twins (Lloyd and Floyd), a mandolin and guitar duo who brought a touch of their native Arkansas countryside to the West Coast. In 1949 the show moved to the Legion Stadium in El Monte, California, where it became known as the *Hometown Jamboree*. Another show which endured up to the sixties as a haven for country entertainers was the Saturday night *Town Hall Party* in Compton, broadcast on KFI Radio and KTTV-TV. The show featured a nucleus of established performers such as Tex Ritter, Johnny Bond, Tex Williams, Joe and Rose Maphis, Eddie Kirk, Eddie Dean, Lefty Frizzell, Skeets McDonald, Wesley Tuttle, and

Merle Travis, and it also served as a launching ground for such future stars as Freddie Hart. The young Buck Owens, for example, appeared as a sideman on the show playing his electric guitar for most of the featured acts.

California's vigorous country music scene inspired innovations that eventually affected musicians elsewhere. Country entertainers had long shown a preference for western attire, but the passion for gaudy, be-spangled, and sequined uniforms began in California when Nudie the Tailor started supplying his unique creations to local musicians. Nudie Cohen (whose complete name is seldom printed) came to the West Coast from Brooklyn shortly after World War I and, after a brief career as a boxer, began sewing costumes for Warner Brothers. Before Tex Williams hired him to make costumes for his band in the late forties, Nudie had also had some experience as a brassiere and G-string manufacturer for the strip-tease industry back in New York City. The western suits supplied to the Tex Williams organization were tasteful and restrained, but the costumes commissioned thereafter became progressively more outlandish with their bright colors, ornate decorations, and fringe. Success for country musicians became almost defined by the number of Nudie suits in their wardrobe.

California also provided a context for the flourishing and maturation of electrical amplification. A trio of manufacturers—Rickenbacker, Bigsby, and Fender—supplied electric standard guitars, steel guitars, and basses to the scores of musicians who played in the club bands in the Greater Los Angeles area and in Southern California. The specific origins of solid-body guitars, vibrators, and pedal steel instruments are unknown, but they were coming into general use by the end of the forties. Some special brands were made on demand for certain musicians; Paul Bigsby, for example, made a guitar to Merle Travis' specifications which was of solid wood body, had all the keys on one side of the headstock, and was cut deep into the body so that the fingers could move far down the neck. In the meantime, Leo Fender was supplying from his home in Anaheim a steady stream of solid body electric guitars to such musicians as Jimmy Bryant (one of the most respected of the jazz-country guitarists in California) and Arthur Smith, a country guitar wizard in Charlotte, North Carolina (not to be confused with the fiddler) whose hit recording of "Guitar Boogie" in 1947 ironically had been made with an acoustic guitar. Fender introduced his Broadcaster model in 1948, and this popular instrument, whose name was soon changed to Telecaster, became the most favored guitar among country musicians. The name Fender almost became synonymous with "electric guitar," and in the hands of such musicians as James Burton, Roy Buchanan, Buck Owens, and Roy Nichols (who was just beginning his career in the mid-forties as a teenage guitarist with the Maddox Brothers and Rose), the Fender guitar contributed crucially to the making of the "California sound." The sharp, staccato bursts of the Fender guitar, combined with the high-pitched, strident, wailing sound of the pedal steel guitar, gave California country music a distinctive flavor. Leo Fender's bass guitar, introduced in 1951, contributed further to the thoroughgoing electrification of country music; it also freed the bass player to be a more mobile and flexible member of a band. Musicians no longer had to drag the big stand-up, acoustic bass across the stage in order to get close to the microphone to sing, and they found that they could easily transport the electric instrument and amplifier on roadshow engagements. When hillbilly bands no longer roamed across the country with the "bass fiddle" tied to the top of their touring car, an era of American music had truly come to an end.

In the postwar years country music was characterized not only by commercial success and stylistic innovation, but also by the entertainers' growing sophistication about the world of show business. Many country performers, like Gene Autry, owned radio stations. A few, like Roy Acuff, owned publishing houses, an activity that would increase tremendously in the following decades. Universally, country musicians were learning to manage their own promotional and contractual affairs or were employing skilled managers to do it for them. No longer, as was often true before 1940, was the hillbilly easy prey for the crafty promoter who ventured into an area laden with portable recording apparatus, made some quick recordings, paid a small sum, and then dashed off again. Hopeful country entertainers everywhere evidenced a growing understanding of contract stipulations. By 1946, performers were demanding from $150 to $200 for each record side, asking for advances against royalties, and exhibiting familiarity with copyright laws and American Federation of Musicians regulations. With the rise of BMI, hillbilly songwriters had begun to receive greater protection and profits in the performance rights of their songs. ASCAP had come to recognize the legitimacy of country music and was becoming more favorably disposed to the admission of hillbilly songwriters. Conceding that hillbilly songs had been inadequately covered in previous surveys, ASCAP in 1947 promised to improve its logging surveys of independent radio stations, where the majority of hillbilly songs were played.

As the number of professional country musicians increased, and the number of entertainment outlets with them, a new group of personal managers and bookers emerged. Until the end of the war, most country-talent promotions were handled by radio-station talent bureaus, such as those of WSM and WLS. Under this arrangement the scheduling of personal appearances was often limited to the immediate territory blanketed by the station's transmitter. After the war a number of major talent offices concerned with cross-country touring became interested in country music. Such booking agencies as Jolly Joyce in Philadelphia, Stan Zucker in New York, American Corporation in Hollywood, and Gene Johnson in Wheeling, West Virginia, by 1949 had expanded their touring operations to the forty-eight states. In addition, such personal managers as Oscar Davis, J. L. Frank, and Colonel Tom Parker made huge sums of money through their superintendence of talent, and their ranks were gradually being joined by such native southern entrepreneurs as Hubert Long, Jim Denny, and Jim Halsey.

If some doubts had existed in previous years, there was now no question that the *Grand Ole Opry* had become "king" of barn-dance radio shows and that Nashville had become the leading country music center. The *Opry*, with its wide radio coverage on WSM augmented by the thirty-minute NBC segment, had become universally known as the "hillbilly heaven." Roy Acuff's immense popularity had transformed the *Opry* from a localized barn dance to a national program featuring "star" talent. Regardless of their commercial origins—honky-tonk or small radio show—most hillbilly performers dreamed of someday being invited to become members of the *Opry* cast. The *Opry* paid only the most minimal of fees, but membership on its roster lent prestige to an individual and indispensable aid in obtaining bookings everywhere. Most performers were willing to appear on the *Opry* for a modest fee on Saturday night and then tour with an *Opry* unit during the week in the belief that their overall income would be increased.

By the late forties many country fans had come to look upon the *Grand Ole Opry*, perhaps unfortunately, as synonymous with country music. All rabid country enthusiasts felt that before they died they must make at least one trip to the mecca of country music. As a result, every Saturday night people from all over the United States, and from Canada and other foreign countries, gathered in Nashville to view the program. Those without reserved seats gladly stood in line outside the Ryman Auditorium for hours and then sat inside for hours more to view their favorites. The schedule has since changed radically, but the *Grand Ole Opry* in the late forties was carried over WSM from 7:30 P.M. until midnight.

As the *Grand Ole Opry* grew in size and popularity, it lost both its original geograpical identity (that of a Middle Tennessee barn dance) and much of its down-home ambience. George D. Hay's dream of an uncommercialized "folk" format had long before been obliterated under an avalanche of commercial advertising, and "stars" had proliferated in the show's firmament ever since Roy Acuff joined its cast. Nevertheless, "good old boys and girls" from the South still predominated overwhelmingly on its roster, and they and the *Opry* management strove mightily to preserve the sense of family and informality for which the show was famous. Friends and relatives still sat on benches at the back of the stage, and performers walked in and out while their colleagues performed before the microphones. The whole effect was one of organized confusion or controlled chaos, and was held together largely through the patience and planning of Vito Pellettieri, the *Opry*'s long-time stage manager.

By 1950 the *Grand Ole Opry* had a cast of about 120 individuals, including singers, instrumentalists, and comedians. The program was divided into fifteen- and thirty-minute segments each of which featured a leading performer supported by other acts. Millions of Americans heard the show on the lengthy WSM broadcasts, but many heard only the thirty-minute NBC segment. The NBC "Prince Albert" show was hosted for about eight years after 1946 by Clyde Julian "Red" Foley. Foley was, arguably, the most versatile singer of the 1950's, and none has surpassed him since. He came from Blue Lick, Kentucky (not far from Berea), where he was born in 1910. He went to the *National Barn Dance* in 1930 as part of John Lair's Cumberland Ridge Runners, and while in Chicago, in 1933, he married Eva Overstake, one of the Three Little Maids and a sister of Jenny Lou Carson, a talented country music songwriter. Foley was one of the Chicago show's most popular entertainers, beloved for his comedy, his duets with Lulu Belle Cooper, and his solo singing. He was a founder and charter member of the *Renfro Valley Barn Dance* and was a regular on that show for about three years. Foley was recognized very early as a person who was at home with any kind of song material, and he is said to have been asked on occasion to forsake country music for a career as a pop singer.

As a *Grand Ole Opry* host, Foley acted as a genial master-of-ceremonies, served as a straight man for the antics of comedians Minnie Pearl and Rod Brasfield, introduced guest acts, gave serious recitations, hawked his sponsor's products, and sang a wide variety of songs. Foley could give convincing interpretations of the most sentimental material. His version of "That Little Boy of Mine" was a much-requested song, while "Old Shep"—a song about an aged, dying dog—evoked tears from an array of listeners (including Elvis Presley, according to his own testimony). He was just as believable on boogie, blues, and jump tunes. "Chattanoogie Shoe Shine Boy" was a giant hit for him, while "Birmingham Bounce," "Tennessee Saturday Night," "Hearts of Stone," and "Pinball Boogie" demonstrated his thorough knowledge of and liking for black-derived tunes. It is a testimony to his skill that he could so readily move from a slightly raunchy song like "Pinball Boogie" ("you rattle and you shake it 'til it gets in the hole") to his soulful versions of the spiritual/recitation "Steal Away" and such gospel songs as "Just a Closer Walk with Thee" and "Peace in the Valley." Recorded in March 1951, "Peace in the Valley" (written by the great black gospel composer Thomas A. Dorsey) became one of the first religious songs to receive wide commercial exposure.

Although Foley did much to make the *Grand Ole Opry* the most famous country radio show in the nation, the program certainly had no monopoly on country broadcasting. Throughout the United States, in small towns and cities alike, scores of shindigs, hoedowns, jamborees, and barn dances commanded the attention of radio listeners on Saturday nights or, as in the cases of Knoxville's *Mid-Day Merry-Go-Round* or Bristol's *Farm and Fun Time*, at lunch time. Each of the bigger shows, such as the *Wheeling* (West Virginia) *Jamboree* or Dallas' *Big D Jamboree*, had its quota of well-known stars, but few could equal Shreveport's *Louisiana Hayride* as a forum for musical exposure, nor as a launching ground for future stardom. The *Hayride* appears to have been the joint creation of three men associated with powerful KWKH: station manager Henry Clay, announcer and program director Horace Logan, and commercial manager Dean Upson, who had once been a member of the smooth-singing trio, the Vagabonds. The show which played for three hours on Saturday night, April 3, 1948, built on an earlier tradition of country music on KWKH dating back to the early thirties which had included at least a couple of variety shows—a Sunday afternoon talent show conducted by the Shelton Brothers in 1936 and a *Saturday Night Roundup* featuring the Rice Brothers Gang and other groups after 1940. The April 3 show included some musicians who had been present at the station for several years (such as West Virginian Harmie Smith and western swing bandleader Pappy Covington), but it also featured some acts, such as the Bailes Brothers (Walter, Johnnie, and Kyle) and Johnny and Jack (along with Johnny's then-unknown wife, Kitty Wells), who had come to Shreveport only a few months previously. Broadcasting each Saturday from the Memorial Auditorium, the show found a large and receptive audience in the three-state area (Louisiana, Texas, Arkansas) contiguous to Shreveport which, according to *Hayride* historian Stephen Ray Tucker, "was experiencing an economic upsurge that was tied to the area's expanding oil and gas industry."[2] Fifty-thousand-watt KWKH, of course, was heard over a much broader swath of territory, but *Hayride* performers typically gave concerts during the week in towns whose proximity would permit them to get back to Shreveport on Saturday night.

On August 7, 1948, only four months after the show got underway, Hank Williams joined its cast and soon became its, and country music's, dominant star. Largely on the strength of his sensational recording of "Lovesick Blues," Williams moved to the *Grand Ole Opry* in November 1949, a pattern that would be repeated by many performers in the following ten or eleven years. Despite the *Hayride*'s considerable popularity, it never really threatened the *Grand Old Opry*'s leadership because as soon as *Hayride* performers gained wider exposure (usually with a hit record or two) they left to join the Nashville barn dance. This happened with such frequency—as in the cases of Webb Pierce, Faron Young, Johnny Cash, George Jones, Johnny and Jack, the Wilburn Brothers, and Jim Reeves—

2. Stephen Ray Tucker, "The Louisiana Hayride, 1948–1954," *North Louisiana Historical Association Journal* 8, no. 5 (Fall 1977): 188.

that the *Hayride* gained the sobriquet of "the Cradle of the Stars." The *Hayride*'s most famous member, Elvis Presley, who joined in 1954, brought a new audience to the show, but when he left for bigger and better things, much of that audience went with him. The *Hayride* endured into the 1960's, but its glory days had come earlier, in the years from 1948 to 1955.

Even though live radio performances preserved their potency up into the fifties, the trend toward the playing of phonograph recordings proved irresistible. Disc jockeys proliferated during the fifties, and many of them proved to be as popular as the musicians whose records they played (many of them, of course, were musicians). They were men and women with distinctive voices, engaging personalities, and high-powered but homey patter that appealed to country music's working-class audience. Country music had not yet become so concerned with respectability, nor so removed from its rural roots, that it was embarrassed by the hayseed imagery and parlance which some DJ's conveyed. And country music had not yet become so prosperous that it attracted people into its midst who had little knowledge of its traditions. Consequently, most of the disc jockeys were people who had a genuine love for the music they played and who had grown up with it or had tried to make a living from it. A few of the announcers, such as Lee Moore at WWVA, Nelson King at WCKY (Cincinnati), Randy Blake at WJJD (Chicago), Rosalie Allen at WOV (New York), Eddie Hill at WSM, Hugh Cherry at WKDA (Nashville), Biff Collie at KLEE (Houston), and Squeakin' Deacon Moore at KXLA (Pasadena), had national reputations. They and the hundreds of disc jockeys who appeared on smaller stations, and who were seldom known outside of a rather limited geographical area, all contributed to country music's popularization in the postwar years, and each played a part in preserving much of the music's down-home distinctiveness while also extending its commercial appeal.

The long-range trend in the recording business, of course, was toward merger and consolidation. But in the fifties, scores of small companies specialized in the recording of country, blues, ethnic, and gospel performers. Gold Star in Houston, Four Star and Imperial in Los Angeles, Bullet in Nashville, Starday in Beaumont, Rich-R-Tone in Johnson City, Tennessee, Dot in Gallatin, Tennessee, Sun in Memphis, and King in Cincinnati were only a few of the labels that circulated country music in the postwar years. The most important of these record companies, King, was owned by Sydney Nathan in Cincinnati. Nathan began his career in the music business in the thirties as a record retailer, and during World War II he began buying used records which he then resold. His experience as a used record dealer introduced Nathan to the large population of southern migrants who lived in Cincinnati and its immediate environs. A recognition of their musical tastes led him, in August 1944, to the recording of both black and white talent. Grandpa Jones and Merle Travis, performing as the Sheppard

Brothers, made the first recording for King in 1944 in Dayton, Ohio. After that date a large number of important musicians, such as Lloyd "Cowboy" Copas, Moon Mullican, Harold "Hawkshaw" Hawkins, Clyde Moody, the York Brothers (George and Leslie), Jimmie Osborne, the Bailes Brothers, Wayne Raney, and the Delmore Brothers, recorded for the King label in its Cincinnati studios. Sydney Nathan took a personal interest in each recording and was therefore responsible for much of the distinctive sound heard on the King records. The King sound represented a fusion of southeastern and southwestern traits and was therefore indicative of the larger process of stylistic borrowing and blending then going on in country music. Even the most tradition-based entertainers, such as Grandpa Jones and the Bailes Brothers, typically combined electric guitars with the older, acoustic instruments on King records. Steel guitars probably would have been used in any case, but Syd Nathan loved to hear a tremolo sound on them, so he often implored his steel guitarists to "put more jelly"[3] into their playing. Nathan also encouraged his black and white performers to use each other's material; consequently, King artists sometimes "covered" each other's records. The impulse toward the performance of blues and boogie material had always been strong among white musicians, but Nathan's encouragement was no doubt instrumental in the decision made by such King artists as the Delmore Brothers and Moon Mullican to record their classic boogie tunes in the early fifties.

The kind of field recording pioneered by such men as Ralph Peer and Frank Walker in the 1920's was gradually coming to an end in the 1950's. Nevertheless, the recording industry remained decentralized, and musicians were able to put their songs on wax or tape in a wide variety of cities from Cincinnati to Los Angeles. Many of Columbia's country recordings in the early fifties, for example, were made in the studios of Jim Beck in Dallas. Such singers as Marty Robbins, Ray Price, and Lefty Frizzell sang to the accompaniment of some of the large group of talented sidemen who lived in the Dallas–Fort Worth area. The most significant development in recording, however, was the emergence of Nashville as a music center.

Much of Nashville's evolution toward musical preeminence is directly attributable to Paul Cohen. Cohen, who had been associated with Decca since the thirties, became that company's country artists-and-repertory director in the mid-forties. Cohen and the Decca company inaugurated the modern era of recording in Nashville in the spring of 1945 when Red Foley recorded in WSM's Studio B. In late 1945 or early 1946 two WSM engineers, Aaron Shelton and Carl Jenkins, organized a commercial recording enterprise called the Castle Recording Company with a studio in the Tulane Hotel. Cohen was the first A&R man to use the Castle facilities exten-

---

3. The Nathan quote came from Homer Bailes (interview, Jennings, Louisiana, August 16, 1974).

sively, and the recordings of such Decca artists as Red Foley, Ernest Tubb, and Kitty Wells were important milestones in Nashville's eventual emergence as one of the four or five music capitals of America.[4] The Castle studios were used by virtually every recording company that utilized country talent, at least until Owen Bradley opened his barnlike studio in 1953 and until such companies as RCA began operating their own independent studios toward the end of the fifties.

The growing concentration of recording in Nashville led also to the appearance there of sessions musicians, that talented group of men, musically uneducated for the most part, who could improvise in any style. For all practical purposes, the first members of this fraternity were Red Foley's band—Zeke Turner, electric guitar; Jerry Byrd, steel guitar; Louis Innis, rhythm guitar; and Tommy Jackson, fiddle—who played on their leader's sessions and on numerous others, including those of the early Hank Williams, as well. This group, in effect, also became the house band for King records in Cincinnati in late 1948 when they sat in on the first of their many sessions there. By the early fifties other musicians had stationed themselves permanently in Nashville and were beginning to appear on most of the recordings made in the city: electric guitarists Hank Garland and Grady Martin, bass players Ernie Newton, Willie Thall, Hal Smith, and Junior Huskey, rhythm guitarist Ray Edenton, drummers Farris Coursey and Buddy Harman, and pianists Marvin Hughes, Gordon Stoker, and Owen Bradley. When Chet Atkins arrived in the city in 1950, as a guitarist for Mother Maybelle and the Carter Sisters, he immediately began to shape and direct the style of music heard in Nashville sessions. Atkins' smooth, finger-and-thumb style of playing was admired by every musician in Nashville, and he was soon employed by recording directors to gather appropriate pickers for various recording sessions. Most important of all, in 1952 he became assistant to Steve Sholes, RCA's chief recording man in Nashville, a step that would eventually put Atkins at the center of country music's revolutionary stylistic changes in the sixties.

Nashville's burgeoning as a leading music center, evidenced first by the assembling there of top-ranking country talent, was accentuated also by the arrival of the music entrepreneurs—the booking agents, the A&R men, the promoters, and the publishers. Sheet music had ceased to be the most important product of the music industry; instead, the typical music publishing house came to depend on phonograph recordings for its existence. After a song was copyrighted and published, the publishing house,

---

4. At least one scholar has challenged the conventionally held ideas about early Nashville recording. Cary Ginell claims to have uncovered evidence in the Decca files at MCA in Los Angeles showing that Red Foley's records of 1945–1947 were actually made in Chicago and given New York matrix numbers. Ginell has promised an article which will explore the subject further (letter from Cary Ginell, Reseda, California, April 24, 1984).

if it expected a financial return, had to get the song recorded by some performer. In effect, the publishing house became a vehicle for the recording of a written composition. Scores of publishing firms, many of them owned by country performers, eventually appeared in Nashville, but the giant among them was Acuff-Rose.

Acuff-Rose's ticket to commercial supremacy, and a vivid example of country music's great postwar expansion, was "The Tennessee Waltz." Now an international pop standard and one of Tennessee's state songs, "The Tennessee Waltz" was first released in 1948 as a hillbilly song (via Pee Wee King's and Cowboy Copas' recordings) which gained considerable immediate popularity and then was seemingly forgotten. Resurrected in November 1950 by popular vocalist Patti Page and considered, strangely enough, as the "B" side of her record, the song had become the nation's favorite by December of that year. "The Tennessee Waltz" was written by band leader and accordionist Pee Wee King and his vocalist Redd Stewart, who received the inspiration for the song after noting the popularity of Bill Monroe's "Kentucky Waltz" in 1948. "The Tennessee Waltz" was a typical country song in its depiction of a broken romance, but its simplicity and haunting melody made it a national favorite.

"The Tennessee Waltz" alone must be given much of the credit for country music's commercial surge and the future integration of America's popular music forms. By May 1951, 4,800,000 records of the song had been sold, and it had earned its writers and Acuff-Rose a gross of $330,000. These totals did not include foreign-language recordings or rhythm-and-blues and minor country recordings. It was generally believed that "The Tennessee Waltz" was the biggest hit in modern popular music history, and it was certainly the top song ever licensed by BMI. The song brought extensive financial profit to its composers and launched Acuff-Rose on the road to publishing success. Acuff-Rose actually had been surprised by the song's popularity and had neglected, or had been unable, to exploit it nationally. The Nashville publishing firm had no contact people or business representation in the three traditionally accepted centers, New York, Los Angeles, and Chicago.

Country music's prosperity also stimulated the further growth of a songwriting industry. Country singers continued to write much of their own material, but the ranks of the professional composers grew enlarged as the music demonstrated its permanence and viability. As country music edged closer to pop, the distinctiveness of country songs began to fade somewhat, and some country songwriters, such as Felice and Boudleaux Bryant, even denied that there was a basic difference in the lyrics of the two musical forms. Nevertheless, country songs tended to concentrate on the concerns and preoccupations of working people and to have melodies that the average person could hum or sing. The music was "realistic" in that it sang less and less of mountain cabins, village churchyards, and sunbonnet mothers, and more and more about the everyday concerns of urban-industrial existence. Country songs, however, seldom protested against larger political and social problems, but instead voiced a preoccupation with private sins and worries. Some songs responded joyously and affirmatively to life; some exhibited a healthy willingness to combat the world's problems and adversities; while others succumbed to guilt and self-pity or otherwise sought escape through nostalgia or fantasy.

The question of song authorship is often a cloudy and troublesome one. Song credits often reveal only the owner of a piece and not its composer or arranger. Rumors abound in country music that such-and-such individuals did not actually write the songs attributed to them, and the experience of songs sold outright by their writers for twenty-five dollars or so is more than just folklore. It is common knowledge among country musicians, for example, that Arthur Q. Smith of Knoxville wrote some of the hits of the fifties, and that his name appears on only a few of them. Jim Anglin has fared somewhat better. His authorship of such songs as "What about You" and "Ashes of Love" (recorded by Johnny and Jack) is properly recognized, but a much larger body of material, dating back to the early forties and appearing on scores of recordings (such as "Branded Wherever I Go" and "Stuck Up Blues"), has gone unacknowledged. Mac Odell, on the other hand, popularized his own song creations by performing them on radio stations throughout the South. Odell (whose real name is Odell McLeod) was one of several country-gospel performers in the fifties who kept alive the spirit of folk simplicity and down-home fundamentalism that had once been characteristic of country music. Such songs as "From the Manger to the Cross," "Purple Robe," "Thirty Pieces of Silver," and "The Stone Was Rolled Away," recorded in the fifties by such singers as Cowboy Copas and Wilma Lee Cooper, and since preserved by bluegrass musicians, demonstrated that some country music was indeed different from pop music.

Writers like Anglin and Odell preserved the folksiness of country music but regrettably received little commercial advantage from it. Closer to the commercial mainstream, and consequently better known, were such writers as Johnny Bond, Floyd Tillman, Jenny Lou Carson, Vaughn Horton, Cy Coben, Cindy Walker, and Felice and Boudleaux Bryant. Of all the writers of the fifties, Walker and the Bryants have exhibited the greatest endurance while also showing a remarkable ability to weather, and in fact to prosper from, successive stylistic changes in country music.

Walker's success has been a product of luck, pluck, and talent. While on a trip to Los Angeles with her parents in 1942 (her father was a Texas cotton merchant), she impulsively dropped in at Bing Crosby's office and persuaded Bing's manager to accept one of her songs, "The Lone Star Trail," for an upcoming Crosby film. Her very profitable association with Bob Wills began also in 1942 when she saw Wills' bus driving down a Los Angeles street on the way to a recording session. She was actually on the way to a post office to mail a sheath of songs to Wills in Tulsa. A subsequent meeting with Wills and his manager, O. W. Mayo, at their hotel resulted in the successful auditioning of several of her songs. She wrote all of the songs used in Wills' movies, including the great standards "Dusty Skies" and "Cherokee Maiden." Since the mid-forties, beginning with the songs which she wrote for Al Dexter and Ernest Tubb, Walker has skillfully tailored her songs to fit the styles of specific singers. Few writers have equaled her ability to write country-pop love songs such as "Thank You for Calling" and "You Don't Know Me," honky-tonk numbers like "Bubbles in My Beer" and "Warm Red Wine," bluegrass songs like "Flying South to Dixie," cowboy songs such as "Dusty Skies," and teenie-bopper songs like Roy Orbison's "Dream Baby."

If anyone has demonstrated a similar versatility, it would surely be Felice and Boudleaux Bryant. From the time Jimmy Dickens recorded a composition of theirs called "Country Boy" in 1947, the Bryants have experienced over thirty-five years of commercial writing success. Their songs have always exhibited more of a "rural feel" than those of Cindy Walker, even though neither of the Bryants grew up with much exposure to country music: Felice was from Milwaukee, and Boudleaux studied violin at his home in Shellman, Georgia, with hopes of becoming a classical violinist. He played with Hank Penny's western swing band in Atlanta, however, and had received a thorough grounding in country music by the time he and Felice married in 1945. They have since written about 7,000 songs, and about 1,500 of them have been recorded. Such Bryant-composed songs as "We Could," "Take Me As I Am," and "Hey Joe" are known by all country singers, and their "Rocky Top" is the most famous bluegrass song in the world.

The writers wrote for a wide array of stylists in the late forties and early fifties, the last such display of stylistic diversity that the homogenizing country field would experience. "Traditional" is a relative term, and even the most "old-time" entertainers of the period, such as the Blue Sky Boys, Grandpa Jones, and Molly O'Day, exhibited certain stylistic traits which set them apart from the performers of earlier years. The Blue Sky Boys returned from military service with a style of harmony that was even more precise and clear than that of the prewar years. Their recordings now featured a bass and fiddle in addition to the mandolin and guitar, and their repertory included a greater percentage of modern-composed songs than in the thirties. Their beautiful performance of "Kentucky" in 1947 was probably the most commercially successful of their career. Their retirement in 1951, a product of conflicting career choices made by the brothers, came at the peak of their vocal powers.

The duet tradition persisted into the fifties, but only a few performers clung to the mandolin-and-guitar format. Martha and James Carson, known as the Barn Dance Sweethearts at WSB, used such instrumentation to back up their wonderful duets on such songs as "Budded on Earth," "Man of Galilee," and "The Sweetest Gift" (one of the first country recordings of this gospel/mother song). But by 1950 the two had separated as husband and wife, and Martha went on to become one of the most popular solo performers of the decade. Other mandolin-and-guitar teams tended, like Charlie and Danny Bailey or Jim and Jesse McReynolds, to adapt to the bluegrass style or, like the Bailes Brothers and the Louvin Brothers, to augment their acoustic sound with an electric standard or steel guitar. The Bailes Brothers included, in varying combinations, the brothers Johnnie, Walter, Homer, and Kyle, from Charleston, West Virginia. The brothers performed during the war in Huntington, West Virginia, and at Nashville's WSM, where they were *Grand Ole Opry* regulars and hosts of an early morning show sponsored by Martha White Flour. In December 1946, they moved with Dean Upson to KWKH in Shreveport, where they became charter members of the *Louisiana Hayride*. Performing first as a duet composed of Johnnie and Walter, and later of Johnnie and Homer, the Bailes Brothers became immensely popular in the Arkansas-Louisiana-Texas region, appearing frequently in churches and schoolhouses and making daily broadcasts marked by an informal, down-home atmosphere. Their repertory was strongly reminiscent of that of the Blue Sky Boys—exclusively sentimental and gospel in nature except for an occasional fiddle or steel guitar instrumental—but their vocal style was radically different from that of the Bolicks. The Bailes Brothers sang in a lusty and emotionally heartfelt style, and with an evangelical zeal that suggested the singing and preaching heard in Pentecostal Holiness churches (Walter, in fact, has since become an itinerant Pentecostal minister, and Homer is a United Methodist preacher with Pentecostal leanings). Many of their songs were certainly didactic in nature, such as "Whiskey Is the Devil," "Building on the Sand," and "When Heaven Comes Down," but their most commercial and enduring songs were "Dust on the Bible," "Oh, So Many Years," "I Want to Be Loved," and "Give Mother My Crown." Instrumentally, the Bailes Brothers always featured a mandolin (played at various times by either Ernest Ferguson or Clyde Baum), but the distinctiveness of their sound came from the dobro and electric steel guitar work of Shot Jackson, the most respected of the old-time steel guitar players.

With the emergence of the Louvin Brothers, country music found its greatest duet. Ira and Charles Loudermilk came from Henagar, Alabama, in the hill country area that had also spawned the Delmore Brothers. The Loudermilks grew up listening to folk and gospel music at home, and to the records and broadcasts of the Monroe Brothers, Delmore Brothers, and Blue Sky Boys. The boys had some radio experience before they went into military service, but their first real attempts at a full-time professional career came in 1946. They adopted the stage name Louvin and set out on a grueling schedule that would take them to several radio stations in the Upper South before they finally found a position with the *Grand Ole Opry* in 1955 (but they did not become securely ensconced on the show until after 1957). The Louvins always had ambitions of being mainstream country singers, but their first big commercial breakthrough came in 1952 with the success of a gospel song, "The Family Who Prays." They became typecast as gospel singers for a few years, and they had no trouble in playing the role. Such songs as "Preach the Gospel," "Satan and the Saint," "Satan Lied to Me," and "Don't Let Them Take the Bible Out of Our Schoolrooms" breathed with the biblical fundamentalism that they grew up with in northeastern Alabama. Shortly after joining the *Grand Ole Opry*, they recorded for Capitol a "secular" song called "When I Stop Dreaming," their most popular number and one of the finest performances of pure country music heard on recordings. In 1956 they recorded an album of old-time country and folk songs called *Tragic Songs of Life*, a beautiful reminder of their (and country music's) roots. One song from the album, "The Knoxville Girl" (an American variant of a British murder ballad dating from 1744), received extensive airplay and has since become a standard in the bluegrass genre.

The Louvins' use of duet harmony and mandolin-and-guitar instrumentation suggested their old-time origins, but their additional employment of an electric guitar (played on their first Capitol recordings by Chet Atkins, and later by Paul Yandell) pushed them closer to mainstream country music. Although several of their songs have become part of the bluegrass repertory—"Are You Missing Me?" "Childish Love," "I'm Changing the Words to My Love Song," "I Don't Believe You've Met My Baby," "The Family Who Prays"—the Louvins always vehemently resisted the categorization of their music as bluegrass. The Louvins actually were in a class by themselves. No one in country music before or since achieved the kind of crisp, precise, and yet sky-high style of harmony heard in their music. Before they dissolved their partnership in 1963, the Louvin Brothers had built a body of songs and a style of performance that have ever since influenced the music of American entertainers, some of them as far afield from traditional country music as Gram Parsons and Emmylou Harris.

Johnny and Jack (Johnny Wright and Jack Anglin) provide one of the best examples of the fusion of old-time and modern elements heard in the music of the fifties. Both men started out on the kerosene circuit in the thirties, playing in schoolhouses, small-town theaters, and country churches, and arriving bleary-eyed at some radio station at 5:30 in the morning to do a broadcast of sentimental and gospel songs. They possessed genuine rural voices which reflected their East Tennessee and North Alabama origins. Along with Ira Louvin and Bill Monroe, Jack had one of the highest and most penetrating tenor voices in country music.

Soon after leaving the Anglin Brothers group, Jack teamed with his brother-in-law Johnny Wright in 1940 at WBIG in Greensboro, North Carolina. Through the war years and on into the postwar period their repertory remained close to that of the earlier brother duets and to that of Roy Acuff: old-time gospel songs like "The Eastern Gate," sentimental weepers such as "The Little Paper Boy," and some wonderful songs like "This World Can't Stand Long" and "Jesus Hits like an Atom Bomb," which reflected the political preoccupations of the day. Their tenure on the *Louisiana Hayride*, from 1948 to 1950, witnessed a significant shift in style and repertory and their first breakthrough into mainstream country music. Performing as Johnny and Jack and the Tennessee Mountain Boys, with Miss Kitty Wells (Johnny's soon-to-be-famous wife), they began turning out a long string of hits such as "What about You," "Ashes of Love," and "Poison Love." On the *Grand Ole Opry* after 1950 Johnny and Jack broke new ground for country duets with their Latin-beat country songs (such as "Down South in New Orleans" and "Poison Love") and with their mixture of traditional acoustic and electric instrumentation. An all-star lineup of supporting musicians, including fiddler Paul Warren, mandolin player Clyde Baum, and steel guitarist Shot Jackson, helped to give them a peculiar, but commercially appealing, blend of church-style and honky-tonk music.

The Maddox Brothers and Rose represented the most eclectic mix of all and were a graphic example of a musical form that still showed its rural roots even as it reached out toward modern stylistic innovations. Few groups could perform so many styles as ably as did the Maddoxes: gospel, honky-tonk, sentimental parlor, blues, and incipient rockabilly. They could sound like a mandolin-and-guitar band from the thirties, or they could sound like a raucous rock-and-roll band of the late fifties. The family's migration from Boaz, Alabama, to Modesto, California, in 1933 is part of the folklore of country music. Mama and Papa Maddox and five of their children hitchhiked to Meridian, Mississippi, and then hopped a freight train to the San Joaquin Valley, befriended by sympathetic railroad men and fed by Salvation Army workers. They became migratory fruit pickers for a few years, but then drifted into radio work in Modesto in 1937. Their early career as hillbilly performers was as migratory as fruit picking had been; they played at rodeos and in honky-tonks all the way up to Oregon. Twelve-year-old Rose sang in honky-tonks where no patron below the age of eighteen was admitted. It was during one of these rambles that she heard Woody and Jack Guthrie singing "Reno Blues." Later, under the title of "The Philadelphia Lawyer," it became her most famous hit.

When her brothers returned from military service in 1946, the family regrouped as the Maddox Brothers and Rose and gradually began to take their music outside of California. In California they played for enthusiastic audiences of servicemen, defense workers, and Okies, and they learned to put on a show that their listeners would enjoy. Dressed in bright and gaudy costumes (which earned them the title of "the most colorful hillbilly band in America"), the Maddoxes presented high-energy performances characterized by hollers, spoken asides, and Cal's maniacal laughter. Only a religious song such as "I'd Rather Have Jesus" or "Gathering Flowers for the Master's Bouquet" could dampen their boundless exuberance. On such songs as "Step It Up and Go" and "Hangover Blues," which featured Fred's slapped bass and the hot electric guitar work of men like Roy Nichols (who got his start with the Maddox Brothers), they even foreshadowed the sound of rockabilly music. Although Rose Maddox's career soon surpassed that of her brothers and extended well past their retirement, her deserved success should not obscure for us the considerable achievements made by this family of musicians. They conveyed a spontaneity and zest for life and music that is rarely displayed among country musicians today.

One country musician, however, who has never lost that enthusiasm is Grandpa Jones. Of all the tradition-based performers of the fifties, none had a career that began earlier nor lasted longer. When Grandpa went into the army in 1945, his career already reached back for about sixteen years, including a valuable apprenticeship with Bradley Kincaid in the mid-thirties. While in service he organized the Munich Mountaineers and did much to popularize American country music in Europe through his broadcasts on the Armed Forces Network. During the years from 1946 to 1952 he spent time on several radio stations before finally settling down at WSM and the *Grand Ole Opry*. (Jones actually had three stints on the *Opry* before finally settling down to permanent residence there in 1959.) Jones has always been a performer of great versatility and irrepressible energy, and is the kind of entertainer who needs to be seen as well as heard. He is first and foremost a showman, and a living reminder of what minstrelsy and country vaudeville must have been like. His contemporary prominence on the *Hee Haw* show, where audiences hear and view his droll humor, has reinforced public perceptions of him as a comedian. He is indeed a comic—one of the greatest natural wits in country music—but he is also a singer and yodeler of considerable ability, and the possessor of one of the largest and most varied repertories in the country field. He is best known for his hard-driving, banjo-backed renditions of "Old Rattler," "Mountain Dew," and "Eight More Miles to Louisville," but he also yodels Jimmie Rodgers songs (one of them, "T for Texas," was a hit in 1963), and has written and recorded some of the finest sentimental songs in the country genre, such as "The Tragic Romance" and "Fallen Leaves." Between 1945 and 1947, and periodically thereafter, he also recorded gospel songs as part of a quartet called the Brown's Ferry Four, an all-star group which included from time to time such singers as the Delmore Brothers,

Merle Travis, Wayne Raney, and Red Foley. While remaining a versatile musician, Jones has also been a faithful partisan of old-time country music, and his only real concession to modern tastes has been his use of an electric lead guitar (played by Merle Travis on Grandpa's early recordings). Since the fifties Jones has become even more traditional in approach, and he performs often with his daughters and talented wife, Ramona Riggins Jones, in a program that re-creates the family-and-home atmosphere of pre–World War II country music.

Ramona Jones was one of several women who began to gain some recognition in a musical form long dominated by men. Virtually all of the women in the immediate postwar years—Martha Carson, Kitty Wells, Molly O'Day, Texas Ruby, Wilma Lee Cooper, Anita Carter, Rose Maddox—worked with their husbands or family groups, but each eventually began to carve an independent identity. Some of the women, such as Rose Maddox, Molly O'Day, and Wilma Lee Cooper, always overshadowed the groups with which they worked, but they generally assumed no leadership roles within their respective units. Of the performers named, only Anita Carter anticipated the modulated, pop-country sounds of the sixties. As Mother Maybelle's youngest daughter, she usually sang as part of the family group with her mother and two sisters, Helen and June. (After the original Carter Family disbanded in 1943, Maybelle went on the road with her three daughters as "Mother Maybelle and the Carter Sisters.") But possessing what was often described as an "achingly pure" soprano voice— one of the finest natural voices in country music—Anita soon stood apart from her sisters as a popular solo act.

All of the others possessed rural and almost rough-hewn voices, and, except for Texas Ruby, who sang in a deep vocal register, and Kitty Wells, who performed with a marked physical restraint, they sang in lusty, freewheeling styles. Martha Carson (who was born Irene Amburgey in Neon, Kentucky) made the charts in 1951 with a hand-clapping, Holiness-style song called "Satisfied," a tune she wrote during the emotionally low period following her divorce from James Carson. She eventually took her gospel act on to the night club circuit, arguing that Jesus meant for his message to be taken out of the churches and directly into the midst of sinners.[5] Rose Maddox, of course, had never been a stranger to night clubs or honkytonks. She did not aggressively pursue an independent solo career until the late fifties, but her performances with her brothers made her one of the most beloved and highly regarded singers of the fifties. Her energetically emotional, open-throated style strangely suggested the influence of both the honky-tonk and the country church. However, if any religious touches crept into her singing, they probably came from home or some source other than the church. She admits to no religious influence and

5. Interview with Martha Carson, Nashville, August 16, 1973.

says that, while she admires Pentecostal/Holiness singing, the theology of the movement leaves her cold.[6]

On the other hand, religious influence permeated the styles and repertory of Wilma Lee Cooper, Molly O'Day, and Kitty Wells. Cooper and O'Day can scarcely be discussed apart, for their vocal styles were similar—they have been called the female equivalents of Roy Acuff—and their repertories often overlapped. One significant difference lies in Cooper's longevity. She was still performing actively in the 1980's, while ill health and religious convictions contributed to O'Day's retirement from professional music in the mid-fifties. Molly O'Day was the stage name of LaVerne Williamson from Pike County, Kentucky. When she began singing in the late thirties, she was much influenced by the leading female singers of the day: Texas Ruby, Patsy Montana, and Lulu Belle Wiseman. She called herself Dixie Lee at this stage of her career and clothed herself like a cowgirl, one of the two or three appropriate performing images for a woman singer. In 1942, after her marriage to Lynn Davis, she adopted the name of Molly O'Day and moved more logically toward the mountain style of gospel and ballad singing for which she became famous. O'Day was a good five-string banjo player, but her chief forte lay in the singing of ballads with moral messages, such as "Don't Sell Daddy Anymore Whiskey," "Drunken Driver," and "Matthew 24," or tender story songs such as "Teardrops Falling in the Snow" and "Tramp on the Street." The last song, which proved crucial to her career, came from Hank Williams, whom she heard singing it in Montgomery, Alabama, in about 1942. Williams in turn had learned it from its authors, Hazel and Grady Cole, who recorded the song, with a substantially different melody, on the Bluebird label in 1939. One of the great songs of compassion in country music, "Tramp on the Street" soon moved into the repertories of country singers everywhere (first through the performances of Wilma Lee Cooper, who heard Molly singing it on the radio). O'Day had a fateful association with Hank Williams. She learned her most famous song from him and, through the encouragement of Fred Rose, she recorded some of his first important compositions in 1946: "Six More Miles to the Graveyard," "The Singing Waterfall," "When God Comes and Gathers His Jewels," and "I Don't Care If Tomorrow Never Comes." No woman country singer enjoyed a greater popularity in the southeastern United States in the late forties, and no one sang with a greater emotional urgency or heartfelt sincerity. Many people could easily agree with veteran Columbia talent scouts Arthur Satherley and Don Law who described Molly O'Day as the greatest woman country singer of all time.[7]

6. Interview with Rose Maddox, Ashland, Oregon, January 23, 1982.
7. Quoted in *The World of Country Music* (New York: Billboard, 1963), p. 61.

The Bailes Brothers: Homer (*left*) and Johnnie Bailes.

Merle Travis, 1977. Courtesy of Bobbie Malone.

Left to right, Ernest Tubb,
Hank Snow, Mrs. Carrie
Rodgers, George D. Hay.
Courtesy of Bob Pinson.

Molly O'Day (*right*) and Lynn Davis, 1950.
Courtesy of Ivan Tribe.

Left to right, Johnny Wright, Kitty Wells, Jack Anglin. Photograph courtesy of the Country Music Foundation Library and Media Center, Nashville, Tennessee.

Wilma Lee Cooper began as part of the Leary Family Singers from Valley Head, West Virginia: Mom and Dad Leary and four daughters. The Learys represented West Virginia at the National Folk Festival in Washington, D.C., in 1938, and managed to record a few songs for the Library of Congress while in the city. They toured widely after that, wandering as far north and west as Chicago and Nebraska. Stoney Cooper joined them as a fiddler in the early forties, and by the end of the war he and Wilma Lee had married and organized their own music act. Fred Rose, who had a keen ear for talent, heard them in 1947 while they were recording for Rich-R-Tone, the little company in Johnson City, Tennessee. Rose helped them to get a contract with Columbia which lasted from 1948 to 1955, and then signed them to his own label, Hickory, after that date. Wilma Lee and Stoney were regulars on WWVA's *Wheeling Jamboree* from 1947 to 1957. During this period they and their band, the Clinch Mountain Clan, kept old-time country music alive and were one of the few groups in country music to preserve the sound of the dobro steel guitar, played by Bill Carver and Buck Graves. Wilma Lee and Stoney often sang duets—as on the song which became their theme, "The West Virginia Polka," written for them by Ira and Charlie Louvin—but the real strength of the group lay in Wilma Lee's soulful solo singing. She sang a few songs also identified with Molly O'Day, such as "Tramp on the Street" and "Matthew 24," but she also introduced a number of story songs and recitations, such as "Thirty Pieces of Silver," "Legend of the Dogwood Tree," and "Walking My Lord up Calvary's Hill," which are still staples in the country repertory. Since Stoney's death on March 22, 1977, Wilma Lee has continued to perform as a touring entertainer and has become even more traditional than before; she continues to dip into the bag of old-time songs and has even begun to play the five-string banjo, an instrument that she earlier ignored in deference to the guitar.

The first bona fide female country superstar proved to be the modest and unassuming Kitty Wells. No "Queen of Country Music" ever wore her crown more lightly. Born Muriel Deason in, of all places, Nashville, Tennessee, she was given the stage name "Kitty Wells" by her husband, Johnny Wright, who remembered an old parlor song of the same name that had once been popular on the *Grand Ole Opry*. Kitty appeared regularly with Johnny and Jack and the Tennessee Mountain Boys, sometimes singing solos and often joining in on the choruses of songs. She made a few records for RCA in the late forties, but her own career did not catch fire until she signed with Paul Cohen and Decca in 1952. In that year she crossed the threshold to stardom with a song called "It Wasn't God Who Made Honky Tonk Angels," an answer to Hank Thompson's smash success of a few months earlier, "The Wild Side of Life" (known generally by its first line, "I didn't know God made honky tonk angels"). Kitty's recording was number one on *Billboard*'s country chart for six weeks and was, in fact, the first song by a woman to attain the top position since *Billboard* had begun compiling such listings in 1948. Kitty did not have another number one record until 1961—"Heartbreak U.S.A."—but during the period from 1952 to 1963 she recorded nineteen songs which appeared in the top ten. She competed with the men on more-than-even terms, and such songs as "Paying for That Back Street Affair," "A Wedding Ring Ago," and "Whose Shoulder Will You Cry On" moved on to jukeboxes everywhere.

Although she took her songs into the honky-tonks and often sang songs which reflected that seamy environment, Kitty Wells preserved an image of wholesomeness and domesticity that was far removed from the world she often sang about. Kitty was not a "honky-tonk angel," nor was she particularly liberated even though her commercial success helped to make it possible for other women performers to thrive. She always preserved an aura of gentle dignity and conveyed the impression that she was a country housewife who had gotten dressed up to sing at the church social or community pie supper. The aggressively competitive country music world, of course, was much harsher than any church social, but Kitty seems to have been protected from much of its reality by her husband, who handled the details of her career and who generally spoke for her. Revolutions come slowly in country music and, although her first big hit—"It Wasn't God Who Made Honky Tonk Angels"—is often interpreted as a breakthrough for woman's liberation in country music, it would be another ten years or so before women would really begin to stand alone as performers.

The more country music changed, the more it remained the same. Although the music stood on the brink of the rock-and-roll deluge that would sweep away many of the older concepts of popular music, country musicians in the early fifties still held to preoccupations that had attracted their predecessors. Religious music remained a staple in the country repertory; in fact, no period since that time has seen so many singers committed to the gospel genre nor so many religious songs making their way into the popularity charts. Although all country singers included such numbers in their performances, some entertainers, such as the Masters Family (Johnny and Lucille) from Florida, the Johnson Family from North Carolina, the Chuck Wagon Gang from Texas, and Mac Odell, performed gospel music exclusively. Other performers, such as the Bailes Brothers, the Louvin Brothers, and Martha Carson, either started out as gospel singers or made such songs a basic part of their repertory. The Brown's Ferry Four did as much as any group of entertainers to keep the songs from the old shape-note hymnals alive, but they were a shifting group of musicians (Grandpa Jones, Alton and Rabon Delmore, Wayne Raney, Merle Travis, Red Foley) who got together only for recording purposes. Foley also sang religious material on his own and was one of several singers, such as Cowboy Copas, Johnny Masters, Jimmie Davis, Martha Carson, and Stuart Hamblen, who experienced commercial success with the genre. Foley demonstrated his remarkable versatility as a singer when he moved into the popularity charts with such songs as "Just a Closer Walk with Thee," "Peace in the Valley," and "Steal Away" (the last song also featured an old recitation about a Negro funeral, done in dialect). Stuart Hamblen, a veteran of country music since the thirties, probably had the greatest success of all the country-religious singers because he both wrote and recorded his material. Hamblen began writing sacred songs soon after his well-publicized conversion in one of Billy Graham's Los Angeles crusades. His "It Is No Secret" became a standard in country music, while "This Old House" went on to become a pop sensation after being recorded by Rosemary Clooney.

Comic songs also figured prominently in country music, and some singers specialized exclusively with such material, or made it the most prominent part of their repertory. Little Jimmy Dickens, for example, did all kinds of songs very effectively but was generally typecast as a novelty singer because of such songs as "Country Boy," "Out behind the Barn," "Bessie the Heifer," "Sleeping at the Foot of the Bed," and "Take an Old Cold Tater and Wait"—all bittersweet recollections of growing up poor and rural. Dickens was a genuine country boy from Bolt, West Virginia, who acquired the title of "Little Jimmy" because of his diminutive size: 4 feet, 11 inches. A dynamo of energy on stage, Dickens began his career in the late thirties at a radio station in Beckley, West Virginia, where he opened Johnnie Bailes' morning show by crowing like a rooster. Another performer who was almost as energetic as Little Jimmy was Bill Carlisle, a Kentucky entertainer who had been involved in country music since the thirties. Carlisle had been rhythm guitarist and singing partner with his brother Cliff in the thirties and early forties, but toured in the fifties with his own band. Known as Jumping Bill Carlisle because of his stage antics, he introduced some of the most popular comic tunes of the period, such as "Too Old to Cut the Mustard" and "No Help Wanted." The most consistent, and probably most popular, performers of comic music were two duets, Lonzo and Oscar and Homer and Jethro. Of the two groups Lonzo and Oscar always maintained the strongest rustic identification, while Homer and Jethro gradually evolved into a sophisticated night club act. The Lonzo and Oscar team began in the late thirties when Ken Marvin (Lonzo) and Rollin Sullivan (Oscar) organized a comedy routine on WTJS in Jackson, Tennessee. Another alumnus of WTJS, Eddy Arnold, later gave them their stage names while they were touring with him. Marvin retired in about 1945, and John Sullivan (Rollin's brother) became Lonzo until his death in 1967; David Hooten has played the role since that time. Throughout most of their career Lonzo and Oscar affected a cornball image, wearing rube costumes, engaging in silly repartee, and singing novelty songs in hillbilly harmony style. Two of their earlier songs, "I'm My Own Grandpa" and "Hole in the Bottom of the Sea," always remained the ones with which they were most closely identified. Homer and Jethro (Henry Haynes and Kenneth Burns in real life) also started out as "stage hillbillies," replete with ill-fitting hayseed costumes and droll, backwoods humor, but by the 1950's they had abandoned rube attire in favor of business suits or casual street dress. They featured deadpan humor as opposed to the rather strident, freewheeling style employed by Lonzo and Oscar, and they specialized in song parodies. "How Much Is That Doggie in the Window" became "How Much Is That Hound Dog in the Winder" (replete with the memorable line: "You know what a basketball nose is, it dribbles all over the floor"), and "Let Me Go Lover" became "Let Me Go Blubber." They gradually took their act off the barn dance stage and into supper clubs and night clubs around the country. Their dialogue tended to be considerably more sophisticated than their song lyrics, and their musicianship won support from many people who were normally not attracted to country music. Homer and Jethro performed often on recordings and in concert with their old friend Chet Atkins (all were from Knoxville). When they departed from their song burlesques, they played some of the finest string band jazz heard in country music. Homer was an incomparable rhythm guitarist, and Jethro's mandolin playing made him a much-admired "musician's musician."

Boogie tunes also enjoyed great popularity during country music's postwar commercial surge. Country musicians had long demonstrated an affinity for the blues and for other black-derived forms, but the term "boogie" did not appear on a country record until Johnny Barfield recorded "Boogie Woogie" in 1939. Other songs appeared periodically which embodied the essence of boogie woogie, even if they did not bear the label, but the postwar preoccupation with the style began with the Delmore Brothers' recording of "Hillbilly Boogie" for the King company in 1945. Before they ceased recording in 1952, the Delmores did at least eleven songs with "boogie" in the title, including "Freight Train Boogie" (in 1946), which has had the longest life of any of these songs. Between 1945 and the early fifties a wide variety of country musicians recorded boogie material, including the Maddox Brothers and Rose, Hardrock Gunter, Jack Guthrie, Wayne Raney, Arthur Smith, Moon Mullican, Tennessee Ernie Ford, and Red Foley. Some of their songs were among the most popular in the entire country field: Arthur Smith's big hit of 1946–1947, "Guitar Boogie"; Moon Mullican's "Cherokee Boogie"; Tennessee Ernie's "Shotgun Boogie"; and Red Foley's "Chattanoogie Shoe Shine Boy." The fascination with the boogie form reached its zenith (although some would say "depths") in 1948, when a white gospel group, the Homeland Harmony Quartet, recorded "Gospel Boogie." The gospel field has seldom seen such a major hit.

Despite the popularity of various kinds of country music, the sounds which predominated during the booming postwar years were those which reflected the honky-tonk and dance hall scene of the Southwest. The fiddle was universally used, but the electric steel guitar reigned supreme in almost every band; it and the electric standard guitar (sometimes called a "takeoff" guitar) provided most of the melodic or improvisatory passages heard on country performances. The large western swing bands had declined in national popularity and were now confined largely to the West Coast, Las Vegas, and Oklahoma. Many of their styles and innovations, however, had become standard features of the smaller bands. A few musicians prospered through their ability to combine honky-tonk vocal and lyric approaches with the instrumental sound of western swing. Leon Rausch, for example, had been one of Bob Wills' best vocalists (surpassed only, perhaps, by Tommy Duncan), but after the mid-fifties he generally fronted his own smaller bands in the Dallas–Fort Worth area and specialized in songs similar to those of his honky-tonk contemporaries. Similarly, down in the sprawling territory between Waco and Austin, Jimmy Heap led a group called the Melody Masters which played regularly for dances in such well-known night spots as the Skyline Club and Dessau Hall. Like most dance hall bands, the Melody Masters possessed a big repertory of Bob Wills-style songs, but they also featured beer-drinking tunes, which were becoming paramount in country music. The Melody Masters, as a matter of fact, introduced to country music two of its classic honky-tonk songs: "Release Me" and "The Wild Side of Life" (both sung by Perk Williams).

No one achieved a more commercial fusion of honky-tonk and western swing than Waco-born Hank Thompson. Before the war Thompson sang as "the Hired Hand" on local Waco radio stations, but he did not really hit his stride as a professional performer until he returned from military service in 1946. He was encouraged and promoted by a Dallas radio personality, Hal Horton, who featured Thompson on his noontime show, *Corn-bread Matinee* (Thompson was even married on the show), and by Tex Ritter, who persuaded the Capitol record company to add Thompson to its roster. Thompson immediately showed a facility for writing clever and engaging lyrics, both of which appeared in two of his hits of 1947, "Humpty Dumpty Heart" (a pleasant little honky-tonk number) and "Whoa Sailor" (a delightful song, inspired by his recent Navy tenure, about a sailor who was repeatedly rebuffed by a bar girl until he flashed his six months' pay). Thompson became noted for his beer-drinking honky-tonk songs—particularly after his super hit of 1951, "The Wild Side of Life"—but his vocal style never embodied the plaintive or emotionally heart-wrenching sounds featured by most honky-tonk singers. His was a clean and crisply articulated sound which eschewed emotional involvement in favor of a precise narration. While Thompson recorded his hit vocals (mostly for the Capitol label), his band, the Brazos Valley Boys, won poll after poll as the nation's best western swing group.

Several singers of the period often projected a honky-tonk sound or flavor but were not exclusively wedded to the genre. Cowboy Copas, T. Texas Tyler, Carl Smith, and Little Jimmy Dickens, for example, sometimes sang in front of electric instrumental accompaniment that suggested the noisy environs of a Texas beer joint, and they frequently did songs which resembled or came from the western swing and honky-tonk repertories. Copas and Tyler, however (from Ohio and Arkansas respectively), came out of the 1930's and carried the marks of the tent-show–schoolhouse–and–church circuit with them. Copas was best known for "Filipino Baby," an 1890's song about an American sailor and his South Seas sweetheart which was updated to fit the context of World War II. He also specialized in waltz tunes and old-style sentimental songs such as Grandpa Jones' great composition "The Tragic Romance." But with a song like "Signed, Sealed, and Delivered," he set tears to flowing in a thousand beer glasses around America. T. Texas Tyler, who was born David Myrick near Mena, Arkansas, had also been a barnstorming hillbilly entertainer in the thirties and was a storehouse of traditional material which he reshaped for modern tastes. One of the big hits of 1948 was his version of a very old British folk tale which Tyler renamed "Deck of Cards." Tyler reshaped the tale into a story about an American soldier in the North African campaign who used his deck of cards as an almanac, prayer book, and Bible (the Ace representing the One God; the Deuce representing the two divisions of the Bible, the Old and New Testaments; the Trey representing the Holy Trinity; and so on). The recitation has since been recorded many times and has been periodically recast to suggest America's subsequent wars. Al- though Tyler performed a large number of old-fashioned songs such as "Deck of Cards," "Black Jack David," and "Remember Me When the Candle Lights Are Gleaming" (which he spiced with a bizarre and virtually inimitable growl), he sang to the beat and blare of honky-tonk in- strumentation, and he was a fixture on the California western ballroom circuit in the mid- and late forties.

Carl Smith came from Roy Acuff's hometown of Maynardville, Tennessee, but little in his style suggested the traditional mountain influence that one hears in the singing of Acuff, Wilma Lee Cooper, or Molly O'Day. Smith did have a large repertory of gospel music, and he eventually recorded an album of bluegrass songs; nevertheless, his personal tastes were inclined heavily toward "western" styles. He dressed in western attire; he built a horse farm near Nashville (where he now lives in semi-retirement); and he borrowed extensively from the areas of honky-tonk and western swing music. Vocally, his sound veered close to that of the crooner, although there was little sweetness in his lusty and heartfelt style. Smith rose to prominence in country music in 1952 when two of his songs, "Let Old Mother Nature Have Her Way" and "Don't Just Stand There," became successive number one songs on *Billboard's* country chart. Few of his songs gained such a distinction in the following years—other than "Hey Joe" in 1953 and "Loose Talk" in 1955—but several of his recordings appeared in the top ten, and a few, like "I Overlooked an Orchid," "Let's Live a Little," and "Hey Joe," are still known to country fans today through the recordings of other people. It is regrettable that Smith is so seldom remembered today, because few singers enjoyed the commercial prominence that he had, in this country and in Canada, during the first half of the fifties.

As noted earlier, Jimmy Dickens became famous for his novelty songs. His skill at comic songs, however, should not be permitted to obscure his excellence as a singer of more serious material. Dickens' voice conveyed great emotional strength (a trait displayed by many West Virginia singers) and he possessed probably the most pronounced vibrato in country music. No one has ever been a better performer of "heart" songs (love songs) or of honky-tonk weepers. Dickens' soulful intensity—displayed on such songs as "Take Me As I Am," "We Could," "Just When I Needed You," and "What about You"—made him a much-admired entertainer among his singing contemporaries and contributed to his success on jukeboxes all over the nation.[8]

Among the pure-and-simple honky-tonk singers of the early fifties, Texas names still predominated, some of which had been around since the first stirrings of the style in the mid-thirties. Three of the Grand Old Masters of the genre were very active and commercially successful in the postwar years: Ernest Tubb, Floyd Tillman, and Moon Mullican. Tubb had become sufficiently institutionalized in country music that he not only exerted great influence on younger singers but also did much to shape the style and tone of the country music industry. He, Kitty Wells, and Red Foley launched the modern era of recording in Nashville with their performances for Decca in the years right after the war; he became one of the first country singers to make records with other established stars, including the pop-singing Andrews Sisters; and he and Red Foley were instrumental in persuading the music industry to replace the word "hillbilly" with the seemingly more respectable "country." Above all, Tubb remained true to the honky-tonk style that he had done so much to create and perfect, and he took it into dance halls and Carnegie Hall alike.

After toiling obscurely for years as a sideman in southwestern bands, Floyd Tillman gradually began to create a solo identity during the war with such songs as "They Took the Stars out of Heaven." In 1948 and 1949

8. In the aftermath of Dickens' 1983 induction into the Country Music Hall of Fame, Columbia issued a welcomed anthology of his music, concentrating on the years 1949–1960: *Little Jimmy Dickens*, Columbia Historic Edition, FC 38905. Unfortunately, nine of the eleven songs are uptempoed novelties, and modern listeners will receive a mistaken impression of Dickens' range and stylistic versatility. None of his great heart songs are included in the collection.

he recorded his greatest hits, "I Love You So Much It Hurts" and "Slipping Around," both of which were covered and made into even greater successes by Jimmy Wakely. As a singer, Tillman featured a lazy, drawling baritone style replete with peculiar swoops and note bendings that was too irresistibly appealing to avoid imitation. As a writer he was equally respected, and his songs moved into the repertories of country singers everywhere. "Slipping Around" was one of the first, and probably the best, of a spate of "cheating songs" that began to circulate in country music, evidence perhaps of the social realism that gradually crept into the music as its audience became increasingly urban and working class. However, while country singers and writers might comment upon illicit behavior, few could openly condone it. Tillman, for example, soon followed his song with "I'll Never Slip Around Again" (opining that the one he had slipped around with was now slipping around on him).

Tillman's long-time friend and colleague Moon Mullican also rose to prominence as a singer during the fifties. Mullican, of course, has been singing since he entered professional music in the thirties, but his identity, if not his voice, had generally been subsumed by the groups with whom he played. But, recording for the King label in the late forties and early fifties, Mullican revealed a vocal versatility that had scarcely been suspected in the bluesy and swing material in which he had earlier specialized. His piano playing remained his most distinguishing trait, ranging from a rather sedate style appropriate for romantic ballads to the aggressive, barrelhouse style which he had perfected in the honky-tonks and sporting houses of Houston and the Gulf Coast. Mullican could still "make the bottles bounce" with an array of blues and boogie tunes which anticipated rock-and-roll, but he could also sing honky-tonk and sentimental tunes as convincingly as any singer of the period. His husky tenor voice showed the effects of a thousand noisy, smoke-filled dance halls, but it was peculiarly effective on such poignant heart songs as "I Was Sorta Wondering" and "I'll Sail My Ship Alone" and even on "Sweeter than the Flowers" (a rather uncharacteristic song for a honky-tonk singer about a family's remembrances of a deceased mother). Mullican also dabbled with Cajun music, a form that he certainly would have been aware of through his long tenure as a musician in the region between Lafayette, Louisiana, and Houston, Texas. In 1946 Harry Choates recorded on the Gold Star label an old Cajun song called "Jole Blon" and saw it become a hit in the Houston area. Mullican played around with the tune in the King studios in Cincinnati but, not understanding the French lyrics, he substituted his own nonsense words, a potpourri of Louisiana clichés about dirty rice, filé gumbo, and the like, and also of rural metaphors such as "possum up a gum stump" and "turning plow." The resulting fusion was one of the most commercially successful songs of the era.

Harry Choates was one of the younger breed of honky-tonk musicians and the man most responsible for bringing Cajun sounds and rhythms into country music. Choates was born in Rayne, Louisiana, but grew up in Port Arthur, Texas, and had been a guitarist in a band led by Leo Soileau, a fiddler and singer and one of the pioneer recording performers of Cajun music. Choates probably picked up some of his fiddle style from Soileau and may have even learned "Jole Blon" from him because Soileau had recorded a version of the song in 1935, "Le Valse de Gueydan," which was punctuated by the same shouts and high-pitched wail later heard in Choates' version. After "Jole Blon" popularized his name, Choates became a regular on the Texas honky-tonk circuit. He might have gained some national support had his life not ended tragically at a relatively young age. The wild and hard-living young Cajun was arrested in Austin in 1951 for nonpayment of child support. He died in the Austin city jail under clouded circumstances, a victim of delirium tremens or, as many of his friends insisted, of police brutality.

Choates performed in a social milieu shared by many hopeful young entertainers, the honky-tonk and dance hall world of eastern and southeastern Texas. This hard but busy environment molded the styles and careers of many of country music's greatest modern entertainers. George Jones and Ray Price, for example, were just inaugurating their famous careers in the early fifties but were listening to and learning from men like Mullican, Tillman, Choates, and Tubb. Jones had not yet found his own style, but was instead a composite of all he had heard. Price too was searching for a commercial sound, but he gained much encouragement as a protégé of Hank Williams. The two best young honky-tonk singers— with the exception of Williams, who spilled across several categories— were Lefty Frizzell and Webb Pierce.

William Orville "Lefty" Frizzell's stature has steadily risen in the years since his death in 1975. He is today recognized as one of the great stylists of country music history, and his influence is clearly detected in the styles of such modern performers as Stoney Edwards, John Anderson, and Merle Haggard. Frizzell was born in Corsicana, Texas, in 1928. As a youngster he lived in a succession of homes in Texas, Oklahoma, and Arkansas, moving frequently as part of the family of an itinerant oil driller. He discovered his parents' Jimmie Rodgers records very early in life, and by the time he was sixteen he was singing frequently in and around Eldorado, Arkansas, where the family lived for several years, and as far away as Dallas. The specific origin of the nickname Lefty is unclear; popular legend attributes it to Frizzell's participation in Golden Gloves contests in Eldorado, but his widow, Alice Frizzell, denies that he was ever involved in that boxing program.[9] Whatever the source of the moniker, Frizzell probably needed a good left hook to survive in some of the places he played in Arkansas and

9. Interview with Alice Frizzell, Dallas, March 2, 1982.

Texas. A honky-tonk in Big Spring, Texas—the Ace of Clubs—inspired his most famous song, "If You Got the Money," while an overnight stay in a county jail in West Texas inspired his first recording, "I Love You a Thousand Ways." Lefty and Alice married when they were teenagers, and in "I Love You a Thousand Ways" he begged her to "please wait until I'm free." This would not be the last song inspired by this enduring but often turbulent relationship.

Lefty's rise in country music was meteoric. He made his first records for Columbia in 1950 when he was only twenty-two years old (his association with the company lasted until 1973), and by the time he was twenty-three he was one of the most successful acts in country music. A Merle Haggard recording, "The Way It Was in '51," asserts that Hank and Lefty ruled every jukebox in that year. At one point, for example, Frizzell had four songs in *Billboard*'s Top Ten chart (numbers one, two, six, and eight), an unprecedented accomplishment for a country singer. He also recorded the first of his Jimmie Rodgers songs in that year, and one of them, "Traveling Blues," became a popular hit. His Rodgers interpretations, eventually released in an lp called *Lefty Frizzell Sings the Songs of Jimmie Rodgers*, have been among the most highly valued of the performances made by the Blue Yodeler's disciples. Lefty did not try to imitate Rodgers (although he did yodel in a few of the songs recorded in 1953); he instead put his own individualistic stamp on the songs. At this stage of his career Lefty sang in a relatively high register (as opposed to the mellifluous baritone of his later years), but even then he was noted for his voice control (his ability to bend notes and stretch musical syllables) and for his habit of modulating from a high note to a low one and then back again.

Lefty worked out of Beaumont, Texas, for a year or two and then moved in 1953 to Los Angeles, where he became a member of the *Town Hall Party*. His hits became fewer after that year—a product of personal problems and of changing musical tastes in America—but he never lost the vocal artistry that he had so precociously displayed. If anything, his style became more intimate and more subtly nuanced as his public identity grew less pronounced. Already he was developing the personal mystique that has ever since clung to his memory.

Webb Pierce, on the other hand, has generated no personal mystique, and he was generally forgotten until 1982, when Willie Nelson recorded an lp with him. For several years previously Pierce had become largely content with drawing his royalties, overseeing his extensive business holdings, and exhibiting to tourists his mansion and guitar-shaped swimming pool in Nashville. Almost forgotten was the dominance he had enjoyed in country music during the fifties. No one, not even Hank Williams, monopolized the country popularity charts as did Webb Pierce during the first half of that decade. Pierce was born in West Monroe, Louisiana, in 1926, and he remained a rather obscure country singer, combining his

Lefty Frizzell. Courtesy of Bill Callahan.

music activities with his work as a Sears-Roebuck manager, until he joined the *Louisiana Hayride* in 1950. In 1952 he recorded his first big hit, "Wondering," which had been a Louisiana favorite since Joe Werner and the Riverside Ramblers introduced it in 1936. Pierce thereafter showed a great facility for resurrecting older songs, such as Buster Coward's "Texas Sand," Billy Cox's "Sparkling Brown Eyes," and Jimmie Rodgers' "In the Jailhouse Now," and converting them into commercial successes. He demonstrated an even greater skill at selecting modern-composed songs with popular appeal—such as "More and More," "I Don't Care," "Slowly," and "That Heart Belongs to Me"—although his performance of them contributed most to their success. Pierce's vocal and instrumental sounds were quintessentially honky-tonk. His wailing tenor voice easily cut through the din and babble of bars and dance halls, while his instrumental accompaniment set down a danceable beat that was hard to resist. Pierce's band was little different from other honky-tonk combos in its use of fiddle, electric lead guitar, and steel guitar, but it made history in the early fifties when Bud Isaacs popularized the pedal steel guitar on several of Pierce's recordings. Pioneered by West Coast musicians, but not widely heard until the mid-fifties, the pedal steel guitar became omnipresent in country music and eventually made its way into other kinds of music as well. Pierce's honky-tonk emphasis was also demonstrated in his use of lyrics. His "Back Street Affair" was one of the best of several "cheating" songs which appeared in the late forties and early fifties (it also inspired Kitty Wells' "Paying for That Back Street Affair"). "There Stands the Glass" (1953) became virtually the national anthem of beer drinkers. Its endorsement of drinking as an antidote to the pangs of unsuccessful love was both unique and controversial; some radio stations, in fact, refused to play the record.

The hard-edged and often rough sound of the honky-tonk singers was paralleled by the smooth, soft sound of another group of singers whose approach would eventually win the day in country music. The crooning, or country-pop, impulse goes back at least to the performances of Vernon Dalhart, who was never able to hide his music-hall and light-opera training. Gene Autry also anticipated the modern pop-country sound with his 1935 recording of "You're the Only Star in My Blue Heaven," an effort to reach out to that broader middle-class audience that was being attracted to his films. A few West Coast singers of the early fifties, such as Eddie Kirk, Wesley Tuttle, and Jimmy Wakely, featured styles that seemed more than a little indebted to Autry. Wakely, in fact, came to California from Oklahoma in 1936 and became part of a trio that backed up Autry on personal appearances. Wakely later became a singing cowboy in his own right and recorded several popular numbers such as his own composition, "Too Late," and Johnny Bond's "I Wonder Where You Are Tonight." In the late forties he recorded his greatest successes with pop vocalist Margaret Whiting—"Slipping Around" and "One Has My Name, the Other Has My Heart" (written and also recorded by another Hollywood cowboy crooner, Eddie Dean).

Texas-born Leon Payne also spent much of his time in California, but was also identified with the Nashville scene and with the honky-tonk music of his native state. Payne studied music at the Texas School for the Blind in Austin and began making an attempt at a professional career not long after graduating from the institution. Payne will always be best known for the songs that he wrote: "Lost Highway" and "They'll Never Take Her Love from Me" (both turned into hits by Hank Williams), "You'll Still Have a Place in My Heart," and "I Love You Because." But with his pleasant and smooth tenor voice, he was also one of the better singers of the period. Many singers, from Ernest Tubb to Elvis Presley, have recorded "I Love You Because," but no one has surpassed Payne himself in the vocal interpretation which he gave to the song which he wrote for his wife, Myrtie.

The southeastern United States also produced its quota of smooth country crooners: Pete Cassell, Zeke Clements, Hank Locklin, George Morgan, Red Foley, and Eddy Arnold. Cassell was another blind singer and a longtime performer on WSB in Atlanta. People who performed with him remember not only his easy and smooth vocal delivery but also his expertise in handling a microphone—a technical art that many country singers were slow in learning. Zeke Clements, from Warrior, Alabama, was a veteran of country music who had appeared on radio stations in the South and Midwest since the late twenties. He was one of the first singers to dress like a cowboy on the *Grand Ole Opry*, but his songs seldom commented on western themes (his most famous song was the militant anthem of World War II, "Smoke on the Water"). While his versatile style and repertory won him a big following among country fans, Clements won a measure of wider fame as the voice of Bashful in the movie *Snow White and the Seven Dwarfs*.

Hank Locklin, from McClellan, Florida, possessed a tenor voice that was sufficiently pure to make him the most popular country singer in Ireland, but with enough raw edge to also win him a honky-tonk audience in the United States. Locklin's first popular recording, "Same Sweet Girl," was a lovely tribute to faithful love—a rare genre in a music traditionally given over to broken, unrequited, or illicit love. "Let Me Be the One" and "Send Me the Pillow That You Dream on," both major hits for Locklin, were more in the mainstream of country music, and both anticipated the country-pop songs of the late fifties.

George Morgan, Red Foley (who was discussed earlier), and Eddy Arnold bore closer resemblance to the pop singers of the fifties than did any other country singers. Morgan, who was born in Waverly, Tennessee, but grew up among the large colony of southerners in Akron, Ohio, seems to have been groomed by the Columbia label as a successor to Eddy Arnold. Morgan, however, never abandoned country music for the sounds of pop

or pop-country, and he clung to the use of the Hawaiian-chorded steel guitar (the "ting-a-ling" sound, as he called it) throughout his career. His first
big hit, "Candy Kisses," was as saccharine and bland as its title, but most
of his other songs, such as "Almost," had greater emotional depth and
textual vigor. Although his vocal style was among the least rural in country
music, and was instead characterized by silken and softly modulated
tones, Morgan remained a missionary for the more traditional country
styles; he was president of ACE (Association of Country Entertainers)—
an organization devoted to the preservation of "real" country music—for a
brief period in the seventies.

Eddy Arnold has become virtually an institution in American life, with
an identity that is only peripherally related to country music. But in the
late forties he dominated the country charts with a sound that lay at
the center of mainstream country music. It was neither "mountain" nor
"honky-tonk," and it contained few traces of western swing. There was
certainly little backwoods flavor to his music, but yet it was not quite pop
either, although he would move persistently in that direction. His music
was somewhat suggestive of that of Gene Autry, but without the hard edge
of the early Autry nor the almost affected, pear-shaped phrasing of the
later cowboy singer. Arnold's sound was sweet, smooth, pleasant, and
plaintive—that of a down-home crooner. Arnold was every bit the "Tennessee Plowboy" he claimed to be. He was born in 1918 on a sharecropper's farm in Chester County near Madisonville and was educated in a
one-room school. He performed on WTJS in Jackson, Tennessee, and on
WMPS in Memphis, and spent some time in St. Louis with fiddler Speedy
McNatt before joining Pee Wee King and the Golden West Cowboys in the
early forties. The affiliation with the Golden West Cowboys was his ticket
to the *Grand Ole Opry* and to wider fame through appearances with such
troupes as the Camel Caravan. He made his first solo recording for Victor
in December 1944, "Mommy Please Stay Home with Me," a tender song
about a neglected, dying child which now seems greatly out of character
with the urbane and hip image which he projects. In his earliest recordings of such songs as "It's a Sin" and "Chained to a Memory," Arnold sang
in a simple, unaffected, and thoroughly appealing style. His 1945 recording of "Cattle Call," a somewhat altered version of Tex Owens' earlier
song, demonstrated that he was no stranger to yodeling either. It has since
remained his theme song, and is probably his most identifying number. Arnold's accompanying instrumentation brilliantly complemented his
singing. To many listeners the melodious, Hawaiian-chorded steel guitar
playing of Roy Wiggins was just as important as Arnold's singing in defining and popularizing the sound heard on his records.

Arnold's style, however, did not long remain down-home. By 1947, when
he recorded the very popular "Bouquet of Roses," his voice had become
fuller, his register lower-pitched, and his words more roundly articulated.

The country crooner was well on the way to becoming a mainstream pop singer. By the mid-fifties he could no longer be pictured as strictly a hillbilly singer, if indeed he had ever been one. Arnold has since claimed that he listened to and sang all kinds of music while growing up, and that he had been unaware that music was divided into categories. This catholicity of taste led him away from the old-time country repertory and toward an experimentation with sounds that would be more compatible with his pop-country blend. According to his own testimony, his 1954 recording of "I Really Don't Want to Know"—a soft, muted sound produced by two acoustical guitars and a bass guitar—came closest to achieving his stylistic ideal.[10]

Arnold left the *Grand Ole Opry* in September 1948, primarily because he had greatly outgrown that forum. He had already won a national exposure through a daily radio show for Purina Mills carried on at least three hundred Mutual stations. He also achieved a distinction that, until that time, had seldom been attained by country singers—a series of guest appearances on big-time radio shows. A half-page ad in *Billboard* in 1948[11] announced the following Arnold appearances: *RCA Victor Show*, *We the People*, *Spike Jones Show*, *Hayloft Hoedown*, *Luncheon at Sardi's*, *Paul Whiteman Club*, *Breakfast Club*, *Sunday Down South*, and *Western Theatre*. Later decades would see him also becoming a fixture on network television shows, first as the summer replacement for Perry Como on CBS in 1952. Arnold's growing visibility as a popular culture hero, however, should not obscure the overpowering role he played in country music. In the fifteen years after 1948, when *Billboard* began its Top Ten listings, he led all country performers with a total of fifty-three tunes, thirteen of which reached the number one position. His election to the Country Music Hall of Fame in 1966 may not have pleased country traditionalists, but it did indicate the almost-unparalleled impact that the Tennessee Plowboy had on the country field.

Eddy Arnold was one of several country singers in the fifties who defy precise categorization. Hank Snow and Slim Whitman were reminiscent of the cowboy singers of the thirties, but their repertories were broader than those of their predecessors. Clarence E. "Hank" Snow may very well have been the most versatile country entertainer of the mid-fifties. Red Foley, of course, also comes to mind, but Foley showed no particular strength as a guitarist. Snow, on the other hand, was a master of the flat-picking style of guitar-playing and could ably sing both slow and fast songs. A native of Nova Scotia, Snow as a youth was won to country music through the recordings of Vernon Dalhart and Jimmie Rodgers. When he began his radio

10. Eddy Arnold, *It's a Long Way from Chester County* (New York: Pyramid Books, 1969), pp. 85–86.
11. *Billboard* 60, no. 21 (May 22, 1948): 18.

career in the mid-thirties on CHNS in Halifax, Snow called himself the
Yodeling Ranger and projected a singing-yodeling style similar to that of
America's Blue Yodeler. Recording for Victor after 1936, an association that
would not end until the early eighties, Snow became one of Canada's favorite entertainers and was second in popularity only to Montana Slim.
Snow came to the United States in 1944 and began six rather frustrating
years trying to break into big-time country music. He spent some time in
Philadelphia, on WWVA in West Virginia, and in California, before finally
settling down in 1948 in Dallas, where his first big American hits began to
appear. Beginning with "Brand on My Heart," a well-written tale of unrequited love, and continuing with "Marriage Vow" in 1949 and "I'm Moving
On" in 1950, Snow became a big favorite in Texas and a popular act on the
Dallas *Big D Jamboree*. On the strength of "I'm Moving On," his first nationally charted number one song, and only one of several train songs
which he featured, Snow joined the *Grand Ole Opry* in 1950. With his
distinctive Canadian accent, nasally resonant voice, faultless articulation,
and formal stage manner, Snow—who now called himself the Singing
Ranger—created one of the most admired and distinctive styles in country
music.

Otis Dewey "Slim" Whitman, from Tampa, Florida, had a high, clear
tenor voice and a yodeling style that was virtually unique in the fifties.
Whitman was unusual in that he rarely recorded a novelty song or one of
the raw honky-tonk variety. His specialty was the sentimental or sad love
song, and he often delved into the popular field for material. Like many
country singers—from Roy Acuff to Charley Pride—Whitman's first love
was baseball, and he pitched one year for Plant City, Florida, where he
compiled an 11-1 record. He began singing in 1943 while serving in the
Navy on the *U.S.S. Chilton*, but did not record until 1949, when he joined
RCA. Several of his RCA recordings, such as "Tears Can Never Drown the
Flame," "I'll Never Pass This Way Again," and "Please Paint a Rose on the
Garden Wall," were lovely performances that were distinguished by the instrumental accompaniment of Jethro Burns' mandolin and Chet Atkins'
electric guitar. Lovely or not, Whitman's performances remained largely
unnoticed until the early fifties, when he joined the *Louisiana Hayride*
and began making records for the Imperial label. Whitman cut a striking
figure with his mustache, lean physical frame, and well-tailored cowboy
suits, and he enthralled audiences with his easy stage presence and
effortless yodeling and falsetto vocal breaks. He originally had a broad-
ranging repertory that included folk songs like "Birmingham Jail," old pop
tunes such as "When I Grow Too Old to Dream," modern-composed country songs like "Amateur in Love" and "Haunted Hungry Heart," and romantic cowboy songs such as "Casting My Lasso to the Sky." But after
"Indian Love Call" became the nation's number one country song in 1952,
Whitman moved more insistently into the field of popular material and re-

corded with great success such numbers as "Rose Marie" and "Secret Love." Traditionalists might prefer to hear him do such songs as "Bandera Waltz," a cowboy song about the famous Bandera Stampede in Texas, but Whitman has ever since adhered closely to the performance of pop or country-pop tunes, some of them of the most saccharine quality.

Not only was Whitman's style unusual; he was also unique in his own time for the kind of appeal he exerted abroad. After "Rose Marie" became the number one song in England for eleven consecutive weeks, Whitman began making periodic trips to the British Isles and was one of the first American country singers to appear in the London Palladium. British audiences were probably as intrigued by his cowboy persona as they were by his tenor vocalizing. He never lost his appeal in Great Britain. Even during the days of Beatles ascendancy—and at a time when neither his name nor his music was heard in the United States—Slim Whitman always found a loyal and receptive audience when he went to England.

Many stars illuminated the firmament of country music in the fifties, but none shown more brightly than that gifted but troubled boy from Alabama, Hank Williams. Williams, Jimmie Rodgers, and Fred Rose constituted the triumvirate first elected to country music's Hall of Fame. He was the most dramatic symbol of country music's postwar surge, and his sudden death at the beginning of 1953 signified the ending of the boom period. His early death solidified the legend that had already begun during his lifetime.

It is paradoxical that Hank Williams, whose compositions were more readily accepted by popular-music devotees than any other country writer's, was more firmly grounded in the rural tradition than most other hillbilly performers. King Hiram "Hank" Williams was born on September 17, 1923, in the little community of Mount Olive, Alabama, where he remained until the age of five, when his family moved to Georgiana, near Montgomery. Hank's dad, Lonnie, was a part-time farmer and log train engineer for the W. T. Smith Lumber Company until illness forced him into retirement and, eventually, into a veteran's hospital. Hank had little contact with his father, but he left an affectionate portrait of him in a song called "The Log Train," recorded on a home tape shortly before Hank died. Hank grew up in the care of his strong-willed and almost-smothering mother, Lilly, who tried to preserve a protective control over him well into his adulthood. It is hard to assess the influences, both good and ill, which came from this relationship, but Williams was at least introduced to religious music by his mother. He always loved and performed the hymns and gospel tunes which he heard in the fundamentalist Baptist churches of his childhood, and much of the style of gospel singing always remained in his own professional performances.

In many important respects, Williams grew up under no one's care but his own, and he was forced into a life of self-sufficiency much earlier than most children. As a small boy he helped to supplement the family income by selling peanuts and newspapers and by shining shoes. Most important of all, he was fronting his own hillbilly band by the time he was fourteen years old. Like most fledgling country singers of that era, Williams was part of all that he had heard. He absorbed much from the commercial singers of the day, and two of them—Roy Acuff and Ernest Tubb—directly affected his style. Williams' style and repertory were curious blends of country gospel and honky-tonk, a mixture that was rare in Hank's own day and is almost unknown now. As a product of the rural Deep South, however, Williams could scarcely avoid hearing the music of the blacks, and that too affected his style and song choices. When he was about twelve years old, Hank began listening to the music of a black street singer named Rufus Payne (known locally as Tee-Tot) who played for nickels and pennies on the streets of Georgiana and Greenville, Alabama, where the Williams family lived for a few years. Hank followed Tee-Tot around on many of his musical jaunts, sometimes sang with him, and Mrs. Williams occasionally fed the black musician from her kitchen. The extent of Tee-Tot's influence on Williams cannot be determined, but it is believed that he taught the little white boy a few guitar chords, gave him hints about how to please an audience, and bequeathed him at least one song, "My Bucket's Got a Hole in It."

During the same period of his life, Williams won an amateur-night contest at Montgomery's Empire Theatre, singing his own composition, "The WPA Blues." Encouraged by this recognition of his talents, he began performing at any affair that might be willing to listen to him. Reflecting the omnipresent western image, Hank in 1937 formed a band called the Drifting Cowboys and began sporting the cowboy attire which he wore for the rest of his career. He and the Drifting Cowboys began appearing on WSFA in Montgomery and in schoolhouses, private homes, medicine shows, or anywhere that an audience might gather. He also began paying his dues in the honky-tonks, particularly at Thigpen's Log Cabin, a rather primitive, barnlike building just a few miles north of Georgiana in Butler County. Butler County was dry, but patrons often brought bootleg whiskey into Thigpen's, where they bought ice and setups. Hank had a fatal weakness for alcohol, and he began developing the drinking problem that plagued him the rest of his life.

Williams' early years as a professional singer were fraught with struggle, disappointment, and economic penury, and he temporarily gave up music during the war years. He moved to Mobile in late 1942 and worked in the shipyards as a laborer and welder. Right at the end of the war he began playing regularly again, and did another stint in the honky-tonks, this time in the rough South Alabama clubs which were locally described as "blood buckets." His 1942 marriage to Audrey Sheppard began a tempestuous relationship which eventually ended in divorce and which inspired such famous songs as "Your Cheating Heart."

The series of events that made Hank Williams the most famous country singer in the world began in September 1946, when he and Audrey made an unsolicited call on Fred and Wesley Rose in Nashville. Williams auditioned a few of his songs for the Roses and, although this encounter did not immediately lead to the recording contract that he desired, he was signed on to the Acuff-Rose company as a writer. Several of his songs, such as "When God Comes and Gathers His Jewels," "Six More Miles to the Graveyard," and "I Don't Care If Tomorrow Never Comes," were subsequently recorded by Molly O'Day, whose career Fred Rose was busily promoting. In December 1946, Williams signed his first recording contract with a New York company, Sterling, which was just branching out into the country field. At this point in his career Williams still sang with a marked Roy Acuff influence, but he was backed by a trio called the Oklahoma Cowboys (Vic, Guy, and Skeeter Willis) whose music was more reminiscent of western swing. When *Billboard* reviewed "Wealth Won't Save Your Soul" and "When God Comes and Gathers His Jewels," it made the following revealing comments: "It's the backwoods gospel singing—way back in the woods—that Hank Williams sings out for both of these country songs taken at a slow waltz tempo. Both the singing and the songs entirely funereal." The journal added further that the songs were "not for music machines."[12] While the music magazine may not have been impressed with Williams' sound, Fred Rose was bowled over by both Hank's singing and his writing abilities. Rose helped Williams obtain a recording contract with a new company named MGM, where he came in contact with its owner and long-time talent scout, Frank Walker. Williams' first recordings for MGM, in 1947, were "Move It On Over" and "I Heard You Crying in Your Sleep."

Hank Williams' association with Acuff-Rose and MGM served to ensure the commercial success of those organizations. Hank also contributed directly to the fame of the *Louisiana Hayride*, which he joined on August 7, 1948, only four months after the Shreveport show began its existence. Hank became the headliner on the Saturday night show and on its personal appearances throughout the Southwest, and he reached still another audience as the guest host of the *Johnny Fair Syrup Hour* each weekday morning on KWKH. In the four-and-a-half-year period which followed, Hank Williams became the best known and most emulated country entertainer in the United States. Several of his early recordings were moderately successful, but the one which gave him his breakthrough to commercial fame was "Lovesick Blues," an old Tin Pan Alley tune that had been re-

12. *Billboard* 59, no. 14 (April 5, 1947): 123.

corded at least as early as the twenties by such singers as Jack Shea and Emmett Miller. Although Miller's recordings of the song in 1925 and 1928 (the second time with the accompaniment of Eddie Lang and the Dorsey Brothers) were similar to Hank's version, Hank seems to have shaped his performance after that of fellow Alabamian Rex Griffin, whose earlier yodeling version was almost identical to the one featured by Williams. When performed by Williams, the song won encore after encore and established him as the most popular country singer in America. It also earned him a position on the *Grand Ole Opry*, which he joined on June 11, 1949, against the misgivings of some of the *Opry*'s directors, who had been warned about the young singer's drinking problems.

After this date Hank Williams never again had financial problems. He earned an average of $200,000 a year from recordings and personal appearances down to his death in 1953; his estate has never since ceased earning money. In October 1951 he signed a five-year movie contract with MGM which, however, had not resulted in a motion picture before he died. Hank Williams' artistic worth, of course, cannot be measured in dollars, but his recording success was an indication of his ability to communicate with millions of listeners. And no one communicated as well as Hank Williams. He had a small, light voice capable of all sorts of peculiar twists and turns. He had a remarkably versatile vocal style and could perform equally well fast novelty tunes, blues numbers, religious melodies, and mournful love songs. And in the guise of Luke the Drifter, he also gave competent performances of recitations, a musical subgenre that was very popular with country audiences in the fifties. Williams sang with the quality that has characterized every great hillbilly singer: utter sincerity. He "lived" the songs he sang—he could communicate his feelings to the listener and make each person feel as if the song were being sung directly and only to him or her. On one occasion when asked to explain the success of country music, Williams replied: "It can be explained in just one word: sincerity. When a hillbilly sings a crazy song, he feels crazy. When he sings, 'I Laid My Mother Away,' he sees her a-laying right there in the coffin. He sings more sincere than most entertainers because the hillbilly was raised rougher than most entertainers. You got to know a lot about hard work. You got to have smelt a lot of mule manure before you can sing like a hillbilly. The people who has been raised something like the way the hillbilly has knows what he is singing about and appreciates it."[13]

When a heart attack brought a sudden and tragic end to Hank Williams' glittering career on New Year's Day, 1953, he had won a popular acclaim that no country singer had previously equaled. Neither popularity nor material success, however, had brought peace of mind to the twenty-

13. Quoted in Rufus Jarman, "Country Music Goes to Town," *Nation's Business* 41 (February 1953): 51.

nine-year-old entertainer. In fact, the last several months of his life were clouded by heartbreak and tragedy. Persistently troubled by a congenital birth defect of the lower spine that forced him to walk in a slightly stooped position and necessitated the periodic employment of drugs and medical attention, Williams lived a tortured physical existence. Physical sufferings, combined with mental anguish arising from marital problems, produced a lonely, unhappy individual who poured out his feelings in a steady stream of melancholy and tragic songs. The last few months of his life were materially rewarding, but emotionally draining. Fired from the *Grand Ole Opry* in August 1952 because of chronic drunkenness and instability, Williams returned to the scene of his earliest barn-dance triumph, the *Louisiana Hayride*. During this short period, while continuing to record such hit songs as "Jambalaya," he divorced his first wife, Audrey, and quickly married a beautiful model and singer named Billie Jones, the daughter of the Bossier City, Louisiana, police chief, in three ceremonies: once before a justice of the peace and twice before paid-admission audiences at New Orleans' Municipal Auditorium.

Death came to Williams in Oak Hill, West Virginia, while he was en route to a New Year's performance in Canton, Ohio. His funeral, held in Montgomery, Alabama, amid a background of gospel singing performed by Ernest Tubb, Carl Smith, Roy Acuff, Red Foley, and the Statesmen Quartet (a gospel quartet from Georgia), drew one of the largest gatherings in the city's history. An estimated crowd of twenty thousand people gathered in and outside the city auditorium to catch the last glimpse of the young singer. The event, termed the "greatest emotional orgy" in Montgomery's history,[14] provoked an outburst of weeping, wailing, and fainting spells.

On the day of Williams' death and periodically thereafter, country radio shows devoted major segments of their air time to songs that he made famous. (Many radio stations still typically broadcast tributes to Williams on each New Year's Day.) Almost immediately after his death, songs describing the event or commemorating his career made their appearances on jukeboxes and radio shows: Jack Cardwell's "The Death of Hank Williams," Jimmie Skinner's "Singing Teacher in Heaven," Johnny and Jack's "Hank Williams Will Live Forever," and, perhaps prophetically for the future of country music, Ernest Tubb's "Hank, It Will Never Be the Same without You."

14. Eli Waldron, "Country Music: The Death of Hank Williams," *The Reporter* 12, no. 10 (May 19, 1955): 35.

Chet Atkins. Photograph courtesy of the Country Music Foundation Library and Media Center, Nashville, Tennessee.

8. The Development of Country-Pop Music and the Nashville Sound

The years following Hank Williams' death witnessed a series of far-reaching developments which made country music a more secure commercial entity and yet threatened to dilute its unique identity. Country music would probably have followed the course that it did even had Williams lived, but, coming as it did at the beginning of a new era, his death symbolized the closing of country music's "high" period. It is ironic that Williams, whose style was so firmly grounded in rural tradition, did as much as any one individual to broaden the music's base of acceptance, thereby contributing to the dilution of its rural purity. Williams' success at song composition gained a wider acceptance for country music and, furthering the advances made by "The Tennessee Waltz," served to batter down the tenuous walls between popular and country music. With increasing regularity country songs made their appearances on the popular song charts. And as the number of songs accepted by popular vocalists increased, so did the desires of country performers to be recognized by the popular audience. Country singers hoped to place themselves as well as their songs on the popular music charts. "Crossing over," as it would ultimately be called, would be achieved with great frequency in the following years, but not without radical changes in the stylistic structure of both instrumentation and singing. Country musicians and singers adapted their sounds to fit the tastes of popular music devotees who refused to accept the traditional country styles. These changes, which brought grief to many supporters and joy to others, made country music a billion-dollar industry and completely "revolutionized" the popular music world.

For a year or two after Williams' death, country styles did not change materially. The songs played on radios and jukeboxes were still characterized by the honky-tonk beat and the sounds of the fiddle and steel guitar.

New singers continued to appear, many of whom would eventually become major stars in country music. Some of them, like Ray Price and George Jones (both from Texas), received their inspiration from Hank Williams. A few, like Marty Robbins of Arizona, Faron Young and Al Terry from Louisiana, and Jim Reeves from Texas, used crooning and quasi-pop styles somewhat suggestive of Eddy Arnold. Such veteran performers as Ernest Tubb, Red Foley, Kitty Wells, Carl Smith, and Webb Pierce more than held their own against the competition of new singers and new sounds well into the mid-fifties. Hank Snow, in fact, held down the number one position on *Billboard*'s country chart for twenty consecutive weeks beginning in June 1954. The song was a pure country weeper called "I Don't Hurt Anymore."

The year 1954, however, saw the emergence of a new musical force which completely engulfed the other musical forms, dominated American popular music for several years, and shattered the existing conceptions of what a popular song should be. The rock-and-roll phenomenon was, in part, a consequence of the heightened consciousness shown by American youth during World War II and in the immediate postwar years. A self-aware "youth culture" whose outlines had been only dimly perceived in earlier years became clearly visible during the fifties, and music became an identifying and rallying symbol for many young people who sought to set themselves apart from their elders. Young people searched for alternative role models on the Silver Screen, in the television medium which was becoming so ubiquitous in the mid-fifties, and among musical performers. Rock-and-roll was fueled largely by a revolution in the record-buying habits of America's teenage population. Postwar prosperity had placed more money in the hands of greater numbers of young people, who had expended an increasing proportion of it for amusement, particularly the buying of records. The teenage market had, in fact, accounted for much of the success of country music after the war. In the mid-fifties this market, taking in the ever-increasing youthful segment of the population, turned toward another product of grassroots America, and one that was scarcely known by their parents. This was a form of music that, in point of ultimate origin, was as old as country music and of an equally hybrid nature. One line of ancestry, of course, ran through black musical history. The country blues of the twenties, generally subsumed in record catalogues under the rubric of "race" music, had become metamorphosed by the early fifties into "rhythm-and-blues," an aggressive and highly electrified style that effectively mirrored the urbanization of American blacks.

Although rhythm-and-blues was a music produced for blacks by blacks, the walls dividing the musical genres had never been strong enough to keep individual songs and styles from crossing the boundaries. Throughout the late forties and early fifties, young white jukebox devotees became increasingly acquainted with such legendary rhythm-and-blues names as

Louis Jordan, Wynonie Harris, Big Joe Turner, Roy Brown, and Lloyd Price. Implanted on the multitude of small record labels that appeared after the war, such songs as "Good Rocking Tonight," "One Mint Julep," "Lawdy Miss Clawdy," and "I Got a Woman" appealed to teenagers as refreshing alternatives to the kinds of songs that then dominated mainstream popular music. It was inevitable that country music would be affected by the popularity of this music, because southern blacks and whites had promoted a vigorous musical interchange ever since the two races had been thrown together. When the two cultural traditions fused their musical chemistries in the mid-fifties, they created an explosion that still reverberates throughout the popular music world.

Rock-and-roll, a term coined by Cleveland disc jockey Alan Freed in 1951, was an intensely controversial musical phenomenon in its earliest years of development. To some listeners rock-and-roll was an example of musical barbarism or, worse, a reflection of a degenerate society. Sociologist Vance Packard, for example, asserted that the music had been foisted upon an unwilling public by BMI and was designed to "stir the animal instinct in modern teenagers." Other observers, however, welcomed the innovations introduced by the rock-and-rollers. Alan Lomax summed up the attitudes of many people when he termed rock-and-roll "the healthiest manifestation yet in native American music" and the furthest intrusion made by Negro styles into popular music.[1] It was this, and much more, however. Rock-and-roll was a conglomeration of musical forms. The music did draw much of its content and style from black sources, from both the juke joint and the church. Although black influence was obvious, rock-and-roll became essentially a music performed by white people for white audiences. Even the wide variety of black performers (such as Chuck Berry, Fats Domino, and the Platters) who worked with the rock-and-roll idiom generally presented smoothed-over or toned-down versions that would be palatable to white audiences. Unfortunately, few black musicians prospered from the rock-and-roll phenomenon.

Country music had long demonstrated its affinity for the stepped-up rhythms of black music, as evidenced in the performances of the Allen Brothers in the twenties, Jimmie Davis and the Delmore Brothers in the thirties, and Arthur "Guitar Boogie" Smith in the forties. The late forties and early fifties was an especially fruitful period of experimentation with black-derived forms. Black and white performers on the King label, largely

---

1. Vance Packard's comment came in his testimony before a U.S. Senate subcommittee: Hearings before the Subcommittee on Communications of the Committee on Interstate and Foreign Commerce, U.S. 85th Congress, 2d session, on S. 2834 (A Bill to provide that a license for a radio or television broadcasting station shall not be granted to, or held by, any person or corporation engaged directly or indirectly in the business of publishing music or of manufacturing or selling musical recordings), March 11–July 23, 1958. Lomax's statement is in *Esquire* 52, no. 4 (October 1959): 88.

through the prodding of owner Syd Nathan, sometimes recorded each other's songs and even sat in on each other's sessions. Beginning with the Delmore Brothers' "Hillbilly Boogie" in 1945, several country singers—including Red Foley, Tennessee Ernie Ford, Hardrock Gunter, Hank Penny, Moon Mullican, and the Maddox Brothers and Rose—recorded songs with "boogie" in their titles or songs that embodied that stylistic form. On songs such as "Hangover Blues," the Maddox Brothers and Rose foreshadowed the later rockabilly style with their interplay of electric guitar licks and slapped-bass techniques, as well as with the high energy content of their total performance. Much of this music, of course, remained confined to country audiences, but the musical deluge that had been foreshadowed by the independent work of black and white musicians came in 1954 when Bill Haley, who had directed a country organization with little success for several years, recorded the extremely popular "Rock around the Clock." Used as the musical background for a violent movie about inner-city youth—*Blackboard Jungle*—the song easily reinforced the popular attitude that rock-and-roll was identified with rebellious youth. To many observers, this was the real beginning of rock-and-roll. Bill Haley, with his band, the Comets, became the first country entertainer to anticipate the coming spectacular success of the new musical phenomenon. Many others, recognizing the financial possibilities, followed his example.

The performer who most ably illustrated the intermingling of country and rhythm-and-blues music, and the one who achieved the most fabulous success, was Elvis Presley. Presley was born in Tupelo, Mississippi, in January 1935, the son of poor, working-class parents. In September 1948, he and his family moved to Memphis, following a dream pursued by many rural southerners in the years following World War II. The family lived in a low-cost government housing project while Elvis attended Humes High School, worked at odd jobs, and quietly nourished his dreams of becoming a singer. On July 6, 1954, Elvis, who was then working as a truck driver for the Crown Electric Company, made some test records for Sam Phillips and his Sun Record Company. If Phillips was looking for "a white man who could sing like a Negro," as popular legend would have it, then he seems to have found him in the person of Presley. The details concerning Presley's first recording session have been discussed fully elsewhere[2] and will not be retold here, but his first release seemed to embody the two major influences that shaped the developing rock-and-roll genre. One side featured "That's All Right, Mama," an old rhythm-and-blues tune first recorded by Arthur Crudup, while the other consisted of a supercharged version of Bill Monroe's hillbilly waltz "Blue Moon of Kentucky." The record was immediately played with great success on a local radio show devoted to black music, and as this record and subsequent releases attracted atten-

2. See Greil Marcus, *Mystery Train: Images of America in Rock 'n' Roll* (New York: E. P. Dutton and Company, 1976; 2d rev. ed., 1982).

tion throughout the South, country disc jockeys realized that Elvis was a hybrid, and largely undefinable, phenomenon. Although his early tours were made with such country singers as Hank Snow, he was generally billed as "the Hillbilly Cat" (a name presumably coined by his first manager, Bob Neal), and his appeal was most intense among teenagers who were not normally drawn to country music.

Presley, in truth, belonged to no precise musical category, and the sources on which he drew were remarkably diverse and eclectic. Like many young people of his generation, Elvis Presley was largely a child of the media. His dress and demeanor were partially shaped by the movies and television, while his musical tastes were affected by the radio. He listened to the country music favored by his parents, but he also heard the gospel music, rhythm-and-blues, and mainstream pop music that boomed out over Memphis radio stations. Pop singer Dean Martin was just as appealing to Elvis as was country singer Red Foley or blues singer B. B. King. Much has been made of his Pentecostal church background (the Presley family were long-time members of the Assembly of God)—and Elvis may very well have picked up some of his theatrical stage presence from the dynamic preachers he had seen—but the most crucial religious ingredients in his style probably came from the white gospel singers who thrived in Memphis. Elvis loved the music of such groups as the Blackwood Brothers, who had their headquarters in the Tennessee city, and the Stamps Quartet, who could be heard in many of the all-night singing conventions which flourished in the 1950's. Elvis particularly resembled the quartet singers when he let his voice fall into the low registers, and he remained fond of religious music until the day he died.

The reasons for Presley's popularity are not difficult to gauge. To a certain degree he capitalized on the newly developing interest in rhythm-and-blues and with his extraordinary sense of rhythm could perform the music more ably than most of his white contemporaries. But Presley's appeal did not derive solely from his musical abilities; several of his competitors were also remarkably talented, and a few of them, such as Charlie Rich, Carl Perkins, and Jerry Lee Lewis, were probably more adept at re-creating black styles than was Elvis. Along with talent and energy, Elvis brought a sexual charisma into the music business that his colleagues did not possess. Certainly no country entertainer before him had exhibited such raw masculine appeal. Elvis' unusual combination of little-boy shyness and leering sensuality won him a legion of female followers of all ages. Nicknamed "Elvis the Pelvis" because of his peculiar dance gyrations, Presley awakened feelings among his young women listeners that not even they understood. Only nineteen years old when he made his first Sun recordings, Elvis was the first of a myriad of youthful entertainers who won large followings as much because of their youth and vitality as for their talent.

Rock-and-roll has gone far beyond the parameters originally established by Elvis and has traveled many stylistic roads, to England and back again. But it should never be forgotten that the music first vaulted onto the national scene with a southern accent and was performed by "good old boys" and even a few "good old girls" who were comfortable with both country and black music. Such male performers as Carl Perkins, Johnny Cash, Charlie Rich, Roy Orbison, Warren Smith, Bob Luman, Sleepy LaBeef, Gene Vincent, Jerry Lee Lewis, Buddy Holly, Conway Twitty, and the Everly Brothers and such women entertainers as Janis Martin (known as "the female Elvis"), Wanda Jackson (best remembered for "Fujiyama Mama," but now a born-again gospel·singer), and Brenda Lee (whose very successful career as a singer began in 1949 when she was only five years old) were generally described as "rockabillies" because of their successful fusion of "rocking" black music and "hillbilly" music. While their vocal and performing styles could be markedly dissimilar, on the whole they carried southern white traits farther into mainstream popular culture than any musicians before them, with their dialects, drawls, and vocal inflections setting them dramatically apart from other popular musicians of the day. Black music contributed to the "liberation" of southern rural youth, providing a vehicle for uninhibited expression, but the rockabillies actually gave vent to impulses that had long been imbedded, if often dormant, in southern culture—a hell-for-leather hedonism, a swaggering masculinity, or, in the case of the women, an uncharacteristic aggressiveness, and, strangely, a visceral emotionalism among both men and women that seemed as reflective of the church as of the beer joint.

Nowhere do these often-conflicting impulses find more vivid expression than in the music and persona of Jerry Lee Lewis, one of the most superbly talented individuals in country music history. Like Elvis, Lewis was reared in the Pentecostal faith (the Assembly of God), but, although he devoted much of his childhood energy to the music of that church, he was very early and irresistibly drawn also to the "music of the world." Born on September 29, 1935, in Ferriday, Louisiana, the precocious Lewis began playing the piano at the age of eight and was performing in a Natchez, Mississippi, night club (across the river from Ferriday) by the time he was a teenager. Lewis was a first cousin of Mickey Gilley and Jimmy Swaggart, and all three learned to play the piano in a similar style. Gilley eventually became a leading mainstream country and western performer, while Swaggart went on to become a successful radio-and-television Pentecostal evangelist. Lewis' parents also had ministerial designs for their son, and they sent him to the Assembly of God Bible college in Waxahachie, Texas, but according to legend he was dismissed after he played a boogie version of "My God Is Real" in chapel. The demands of the flesh and the spirit have always warred in Jerry. Although the religious indoctrination of his youth has always influenced him—he can still quote liberally from the Bible, and he periodically professes a sense of guilt—he has devoted most of his life to the flesh.

Back home in Ferriday he spent much time at Haney's Big House, a black night spot, and in other clubs there and in Mississippi. Inspired by Elvis' success, Jerry journeyed to Memphis and persuaded Sam Phillips to record him in 1956, his first song being a cover of Ray Price's "Crazy Arms." His first big hit was a song done earlier (in 1955) by pianist Roy Hall—"Whole Lot of Shaking Going On." His exuberant and hedonistic version was presented to a national audience on Steve Allen's television show, where Jerry kicked over the piano bench and otherwise bowled the audience over. In gratitude he later named one of his sons Steve Allen. This first hit, along with others such as "Great Balls of Fire" and "High School Confidential," made him one of the leading rock-and-rollers, in the United States and in Europe. A 1958 trip to England, however, proved to be ill-fated. His recent marriage to a thirteen-year-old cousin and his wild behavior drew harsh and hostile criticism. His career went into eclipse in the United States too, although he never stopped performing. In 1968 he re-entered the field of country music with a hit version of "Another Place Another Time," and soon followed that with another hit called "What Made Milwaukee Famous." Time revealed that he had lost little of the energy and abandon that had characterized his earlier career.

The impact made by Elvis, Jerry Lee, and the other rockabillies inspired an accent on youth in music generally and in country music specifically. The music business was now well aware of teenage power. Everywhere, teenagers were buying records in great quantities and were forming fan clubs, organizing sock hops and coke parties, and dancing the dirty bop. The record industry had made significant innovations that contributed to its massive expansion: introduction of 45 rpm singles and 33⅓ rpm long-play albums, all of which were made more appealing by the maturation of high fidelity and stereophonic sound reproduction. The 78 rpm record rapidly became a thing of the past. Radio stations everywhere responded to the teenage audience with shows oriented toward youth, while television shows such as Dick Clark's *American Bandstand* gave exposure to new performers and songs.

In the wake of Elvis Presley's astounding success, the country music industry began searching for new, youthful talent, while also encouraging older and established performers to record rock-and-roll material or peppy songs that would appeal to a young audience. Marty Robbins, for example, did a country version of "That's All Right, Mama" on December 7, 1954, and soon followed that experiment with covers of such rhythm-and-blues tunes as "Long Tall Sally" and "Maybelline." Robbins' versions of such up-tempoed country songs as "Singing the Blues" also reflected the desire to appeal to a young audience which liked to dance. Few country singers came out of the mid-fifties untouched by the rock-and-roll mania. George Jones, now known and revered for his dedication to hard country sounds, recorded several rock-androll songs, such as "Rock It," and even some bluegrass musicians succumbed to pressures to get on the rock bandwagon. The Stanley Brothers, who were famous for their traditional mountain sound, recorded a rock-spiced song called "So Blue" as well as a cover of a rhythm-and-blues song, "Finger Popping Time" (largely through the encouragement of King Records producer Syd Nathan). Even the king of bluegrass music, Bill Monroe, went so far as to speed up the tempo on later versions of "Blue Moon of Kentucky" after Elvis' rollicking adaptation came out. The most commercially successful spinoff from the rock-and-roll interest was Tennessee Ernie Ford's big hit, "Sixteen Tons." This song came from the pen of Merle Travis, who had included it in an excellent, but only moderately successful, album in 1947. Ernie's version was presented over a modest, rocking beat and was given immediate, national exposure on his television show. It attained the number one position on *Billboard's* charts in December 1955 and remained there through the spring of 1956.

A large number of musicians only dabbled with the rock-and-roll idiom and never really drifted very far from the country mainstream or from traditionally rooted styles. A few performers, on the other hand, were permanently affected by their rock-and-roll experiences, or by their flirtations with youthful audiences. Don and Phil Everly, whose beautiful and close harmony was to influence musicians around the world, were originally marketed as country singers. They began developing their singing style as children in a family group headed by their father, Ike Everly, a finger-style guitarist who was part of the circle of western Kentucky musicians from whom Merle Travis learned his famous style. The Everlys therefore were heirs to the brother duet tradition of country music, and though they are usually described as rockabillies, their sound and performance styles were very different from those of Sun's stable of musicians. Their traditional debts are strongly revealed in the superb, but regrettably out-of-print, album *Songs Our Daddy Taught Us*, where on such songs as "Barbara Allen," "Down in the Willow Garden," "Long Time Gone," and "Lightning Express," they employed a vocal approach that was strongly reminiscent of such earlier duos as Karl and Harty, the Blue Sky Boys, and the Bailes Brothers. Since they projected boyish innocence and vigor, and played guitars, the Everly Brothers were easily identified with other rock-and-rollers. During their peak years, from 1957 to 1959, the Everlys performed a repertory of songs that easily found favor among both country and rock fans. The Nashville songwriters Felice and Boudleaux Bryant supplied them with a steady stream of hits, including "Bye Bye, Love," "Wake Up, Little Susie," "All I Have to Do Is Dream," and "Bird Dog."

Sonny James also brought several years of experience as a country singer to the world of youth-oriented music. Like the Everlys, he came from a musical family, the Lodens from Hackleburg, Alabama. Performing as a regular on such regional country shows as the *Big D Jamboree*, the *Louisiana Hayride*, and the *Saturday Night Shindig* (Dallas), James revealed a versatile style as a singer, flat-top guitarist, and fiddler. Although he was well schooled in country music's rural traits, James easily made the transition to the rockabilly and country-pop genres in the late fifties. "Young Love" (1957), a quintessential teenie-bopper song, became one of the first giant crossovers in country music history, a number one song in both country and pop music, and one of the first examples of a country singer (rather than the song) moving on to the pop charts. This was the first of a long string of hits for James. He was never a rockabilly per se, but his songs often projected the kind of youth consciousness that was so strong in rock-and-roll. He has periodically resurrected songs from the fifties, and has succeeded commercially with them. He styles himself as the Southern Gentleman, and he performs generally with sparse instrumentation, often just his own cleanly played acoustic guitar and bass, but' almost always with background voices (an enduring legacy of fifties teen music).

Johnny Cash entered professional music in the mid-fifties as part of Memphis' Sun stable of rockabillies, and he has preserved some of those traits in his later performing years. Cash was born into a family of poor cotton farmers in Kingsland, Arkansas, but he moved with his family in 1936 to the New Deal–built community of Dyess (part of the government's program of resettling farmers on productive land which they had the option to buy). Cash's childhood experiences of growing up poor in the 1930's were strongly reflected in some of the songs he later wrote and recorded: "Pickin' Time," for example, which described the improved family fortunes that would hopefully accompany cotton harvest; and "Five Feet High and Rising" which recalled the devastating Mississippi River flood of 1937 that almost wiped out the Cash homestead.

The Cash family loved and sang music, but Johnny also enjoyed the songs he heard on his father's little battery radio. Fresh out of high school in 1950, Johnny joined the horde of hillbillies seeking employment in the mills and factories of the North. But after a brief stay at the Fisher Body Plant in Pontiac, Michigan, in 1950, the bored young man went back home and joined the Air Force. While stationed in Germany he began perfecting the musical skills he had exhibited since childhood, singing and playing the guitar and trying his hand at song lyrics. Back home in 1954 he began jamming with friends Luther Perkins (guitar) and Marshall Grant (bass). In 1955 they recorded two songs for Sam Phillips which reflected the contemporary interest in uptempoed and highly rhythmic music. One, "Hey Porter," an infectious, hard-driving train song, had been written during his military service. The other, "Cry Cry Cry," was written after Phillips asked for another song to accompany "Hey Porter." Luther Perkins' single-string electric guitar playing, Marshall Grant's slapped bass, and Cash's percussive rhythm accompaniment (enhanced by placing a piece of paper under the strings of the guitar), neatly complemented Cash's baritone-bass singing and established a sound from which the singer has never substantially deviated. His first major hit, "I Walk the Line," recorded in 1958, won him a considerable audience outside country music and was a good example of the country-rockabilly fusion. Although Cash experienced crippling personal problems throughout much of the sixties—marital strain, drug dependence—he was never absent very long from the center of country music action. He has always been a barometer of country music change and, while basically preserving his original performing style, he has often been in the vanguard of innovation and experimentation and has consistently lent encouragement to younger talent.

While Johnny Cash and certain other performers made their own individual adjustments to rock-and-roll, the country industry as a whole responded to the rock threat by trying to create a product that would appeal to the broadest possible audience. The industry also sought to expand on the crossover precedents set by "The Tennessee Waltz" and Hank Williams in the late forties and early fifties. Country songs had periodically made their way into pop repertories, but almost always as performed by musicians who were identified as "pop." In the new period the chief emphasis was to be on the marketing of the singer as well as the song. A country singer, it was believed, might win a new audience if the instrumental accompaniment was modified sufficiently (no fiddles or steel guitars, for example). The urban, pop audience must not be repelled by harsh or "corny" rural accoutrements. The mixing of pop and country sounds, of course, had never been absent from country music—one thinks of Gene Autry's "You're the Only Star in My Blue Heaven" (1935) or even of the violin accompaniment on the early Vernon Dalhart records (1924), for example— and country entertainers had never been resistant to popular recognition. Indeed, they had actively sought it. Nevertheless, never before had there been such an insistent quest for pop identification as that which came in the late fifties and early sixties.

Eddy Arnold, of course, had been making his own compromises since at least 1948, when he tried to shed both the title of "Tennessee Plowboy" and the image which went with it. According to Arnold's own testimony, however, his real breakthrough to pop acceptance—and the first real example of the kind of sound which he wanted to project—was "I Really Don't Want to Know" in 1954. Accompanied only by two acoustic guitars, a bass guitar, and background voices, the recording achieved a soft, muted, and romantic supper-club sound that has ever since marked Arnold's per-

Roy Acuff (*left*) and Johnny Cash at the *Grand Ole Opry*. Photograph courtesy of the Country Music Foundation Library and Media Center, Nashville, Tennessee.

formances. The peak period of country-pop fusion, however, came in 1957 and early 1958. Sonny James' "Young Love," Ferlin Husky's "Gone," George Hamilton IV's "A Rose and a Baby Ruth," Johnny Cash's "Ballad of a Teenage Queen," and, preeminently, Marty Robbins' "White Sport Coat" and "The Story of My Life" (written by Hal David and Burt Bacharach) were leading examples of the songs which were geared to teenage, sock-hop tastes. Recognizing the appeal of the country-pop fusion, merchandisers and chartmakers began advertising records without prefixes or labels. To cite one example, Nashville journalist Charles Lamb, who had been publishing the *Country Music Reporter*, dropped the word "country" from the title and began running the "one big chart" which lumped songs together according to popularity and regardless of style or identification.

Country traditionalists reacted bitterly to the pop trends, but the juggernaut of homogenization nevertheless rolled on. The fiddle and steel guitar seemed on the way to banishment from country recordings and could scarcely be heard on jukeboxes or country radio DJ shows in 1957. A major exception, however, was Bobby Helms' "Fraulein," written by Texas songwriter Lawton Williams, which was the number one country song in September and October 1957. The recording began with a rousing fiddle introduction by Tommy Jackson and was, in fact, the only song in the top ten during that period that featured a fiddle. Significantly, Helms' next big hit was "My Special Angel," a thoroughly poppish, teenage-oriented song which included no fiddle at all. An occasional honky-tonk-style song made its way through the tangle of country-pop offerings to become a hit— Charlie Walker's "Pick Me Up on Your Way Down," for example—but only Ray Price, a Texas-born protégé of Hank Williams, provided a consistent challenge to the pop fraternity. In August and September 1956 Price had warmed the hearts of traditionalists with "Crazy Arms," and he continued to perform such numbers down through the late fifties and into the early sixties: "City Lights," "My Shoes Keep Walking Back to You," and a host of others with no pop influence at all, each of them featuring heavily bowed fiddles and the pedal steel guitar.

Country-pop's emergence was paralleled by the burgeoning of Nashville as a music center. Together, this convergence gave rise to what was soon called the "Nashville sound." As described in Chapter 7, the *Grand Ole Opry* was a catalyst which after the war had attracted a pool of talent and an expanding network of promoters, booking agents, publishers, and the like to Nashville. The proliferation of recording studios and publishing houses, which fed off each other, encouraged the coming of musicians and songwriters who would be permanently based in the city. Sessions musicians, as they came to be called, rarely toured or acted as members of professional bands; instead, they were on constant call to back up any singer who happened to need them for recording purposes. They became thoroughly familiar, and at ease, with each other's styles, and they developed a "numbering system" which permitted them to adapt easily and transpose keys while learning new songs. The Nashville musicians became famous for their versatility and improvisational skills. Their expertise contributed to Nashville's growing reputation as "Music City, USA," and to the world-wide marketability of the musical product that emerged from there; unfortunately, their presence on record after record inspired a sameness of sound that inhibited creativity within the country music field.

Chester (Chet) Atkins had become the center, and driving force, of these musicians by the late fifties. He was as responsible as any person for the Nashville sound, or what would sometimes be called the Chet Atkins compromise. Atkins was born into a musical family in 1924 in Luttrell, Tennessee. His father was a a music teacher, and an older brother, Jim, was a guitarist who played professionally as a jazz and pop musician. As a fledgling guitarist Chet heard Merle Travis over a radio station from Cincinnati and was deeply impressed by what he heard. He did not realize that this unseen radio presence was playing with only his thumb and fore-finger, so Chet developed a three-finger style instead. Atkins' style, there-fore, though much influenced by Travis, was very much his own. In Nashville after 1950, while playing at the *Grand Ole Opry* and on numerous recording sessions, he came to know most of the musicians in the city. He also began making recordings on his own, and did much to make the electric guitar a distinctive solo instrument in country music. In 1952 Steven Sholes, the head of RCA's operations in Nashville, made Atkins his assistant. By 1957 Atkins had become chief of RCA's country division in Nashville. Some of the musicians who played on RCA's sessions, as well as on other labels' sessions in the city, were men who often played with Chet at the Carousel Club in Printer's Alley: Floyd Cramer, piano; Buddy Harman, drums; Bob Moore, bass; and Boots Randolph, saxophone. With the exception of Randolph, these musicians played on the majority of re-cording sessions in Nashville. Along with guitarists Grady Martin, Hank Garland (badly injured in a 1963 automobile accident that ended his play-ing career), pianist Hargus "Pig" Robbins, rhythm guitarist Ray Edenton, and a host of others, these men contributed mightily to the making of the Nashville sound. Their instrumental licks were complemented by vocal choruses contributed by a one-time gospel quartet, the Jordanaires, the Anita Kerr Singers and, a little later in the 1960's, the Glaser brothers.

Chet Atkins deliberately tried to create a middle-of-the-road sound (his "compromise") which would preserve the feel and ambience of "country" music while also being commercially appealing to a broader audience which had no experience with rural life and no liking for the harder sounds. RCA's leadership in the shaping of this sound came, first of all, through its association with Elvis Presley. Floyd Cramer, for example, played on many of Elvis' hits, including "Heartbreak Hotel," and quartets were often pres-ent on Elvis' records. Cramer's distinctive style, however—his slip-note technique (moving quickly from one note to another in order to bend notes a full tone rather than a half tone)—was borrowed from a demo tape made by West Coast pianist/songwriter Don Robertson. Robertson sent his composition "Please Help Me, I'm Falling" to RCA, where it was given to Hank Locklin, who recorded it with the accompaniment of Cramer, who copied Robertson's style. The commercial success of this record in 1960 encouraged Cramer to use the technique consistently thereafter, and he even recorded a big hit on his own called "Last Date."

The country-pop emphasis was tempting to many singers who recognized the commercial advantages of a larger audience. Only a few, however, were qualified to take advantage of the pop trends. One can scarcely imagine such deep-dyed rural singers as Ernest Tubb, Bill Monroe, and Roy Acuff enjoying much success as pop performers, even had they chosen to make the attempt. But those singers whose vocal equipment was palatable to pop fans, and whose stylistic preferences were sufficiently latitudinarian, were well positioned to prosper within the country-pop format. For example, when a brother and sister team from Sparkman, Arkansas, Jim Ed and Maxine Brown, began singing on the *Barnyard Frolics* over KLRA in Little Rock in 1953, their sweet and smooth harmony was warmly praised. They became a trio, known as the Browns, in 1954, when their sister Bonnie joined them. Their excellent three-part harmony was, in part, church-derived, but it also reflected the styles of contemporary pop groups such as the McGuire Sisters. Their repertory, however, was pure country, and ranged from such downright corny tunes as "Looking Back to See" and "Goo Goo Dada" to warmly romantic numbers like "I Take the Chance" (written by the Louvin Brothers) and "Here Today and Gone Tomorrow." Affiliated with RCA after 1956, the Browns gradually moved toward a repertory that was compatible with their sound. And under Chet Atkins' tutelage they recorded one of the premiere country-pop songs of 1959, "The Three Bells," an import from France which held down *Billboard's* number one slot from August to November.

RCA had at least three other performers who underwent a similar transformation under Atkins' leadership: Skeeter Davis, Don Gibson, and Jim Reeves. Davis, who was born Mary Frances Penick in Dry Ridge, Kentucky, began her music career singing with a schoolmate named Betty Jack Davis as a duo called the Davis Sisters. They sang throughout central Kentucky and southern Ohio and did a stint on the *Kentucky Barn Dance* in Lexington, where they were occasionally associated with the bluegrass team of Flatt and Scruggs. The Davises gave promise of becoming one of the major singing groups in country music after they signed with RCA in 1953. Their version of "I Forgot More Than You'll Ever Know" was one of the best-sellers of that year. Tragedy struck, though, in the midst of their newfound success. In August 1953, Betty Jack was killed in an automobile accident that also seriously injured Skeeter and left her physically and psychologically unable to continue her career. When Skeeter returned to professional music in 1959, she had little experience as a solo performer. Nevertheless, she achieved popularity in her new role and also began to carve out a niche in the developing country-pop genre. "Set Him Free," "Optimistic," and "The End of the World" were only a few of the Skeeter Davis songs which made it into the charts, and the latter, in 1962, became a crossover song of considerable popularity which introduced her to an audience far beyond that earlier enjoyed by the Davis Sisters.

Don Gibson was a highly commercial property for RCA as both a singer and a writer. His country credentials were very strong. He was born in Shelby, North Carolina, not far from where bluegrass banjo wizard Earl Scruggs grew up. Gibson even tried his hand at bluegrass music, and in fact generally adhered to hard country styles while performing on Knoxville's *Mid-Day Merry-Go-Round* before 1954. In that year he signed a writer's contract with Acuff-Rose, an event which contributed to the emergence of a new breed of writers in Nashville. As a writer Gibson made his most enduring impact on country music; such songs as "Oh Lonesome Me," "Legend in My Time," and "I Can't Stop Loving You" have become country standards while also representing the growing fusion of country and pop sounds. As a singer Gibson had a husky, soulful voice that was then unique among country singers, as well as an affinity for rockabilly rhythms that lent to his popularity outside the country field. The year 1958 was a big one for Gibson, with three of his recordings ("Oh Lonesome Me," "I Can't Stop Loving You," and "Blue Blue Day") reaching the number one position on the *Billboard* charts. An inability to cope with his commercial success and a growing addiction to pills seriously hampered the progress of his career, and he sought medical rehabilitation in 1961. Gibson has since resumed his professional career, but he has never regained the stature as a performer which he enjoyed earlier.

Of all the country-pop singers of the late fifties and early sixties, James Travis (Jim) Reeves had probably the greatest ability to appeal to popular audiences while maintaining a country identity. He was born August 20, 1923, in Galloway, Panola County, Texas, the same rural East Texas area that produced Tex Ritter. Since his father, Tom Reeves, died when Jim was only ten months old, his upbringing became the responsibility of his mother, Beulah Reeves, and his eight older brothers and sisters. Reeves discovered very early, as farmboys have always done, that farm life could be intolerable unless diversions were found. His diversions were baseball and country music.

Although Reeves had played the guitar since he was six and had often played in neighborhood sessions with Bill Price, a guitarist friend from Galloway, baseball initially seemed to hold the most promising future. After a successful athletic career at Carthage High School, he attended the University of Texas for about six weeks in 1942 but then dropped out and went to work in a Houston shipyard. He also began playing semi-professional baseball and was able to move from that into professional athletics as a pitcher in the St. Louis Cardinal system, playing for Marshall and later Henderson in the East Texas League. His baseball career ended, however, when he injured his leg in July 1947.

Despite his talents as a singer, it was Reeves' fine speaking voice that brought him into show business. He obtained a position as announcer and hillbilly disc jockey on a Henderson radio station, KGRI, which he later owned jointly with popular disc jockey Tom Perryman. Between 1947 and 1953 Reeves began singing in the Henderson area and in an ever-widening range of places throughout East Texas, including short stints as a sideman with Moon Mullican in Beaumont and as a singer/bandleader at one of Texas' most famous honky-tonks, the Reo Palm Isle in Longview. As a Henderson disc jockey, and program director at KGRI after 1952, Reeves occasionally picked up his guitar and charmed his listeners with a hymn or vintage sentimental song such as "Have I Told You Lately That I Love You." His earliest recordings were made in Houston in 1949 and were released on the Macy label. Real success, however, did not come until the early fifties when he signed a contract with Abbott Records (1952) and joined the *Louisiana Hayride* (1953). His first appearances on the *Hayride* were made, ironically, as an announcer, but his second Abbott release, also in 1953, "Mexican Joe," gave him an identity as a singer that no station or record label could resist. The song was only the beginning of a long string of successful recordings that took him to the *Grand Ole Opry* and earned him a contract with RCA (both in 1955).

When Reeves began his association with RCA, his performing sound was not far removed from the dominant honky-tonk style of the early fifties. Even as late as 1959 the sounds of the fiddle and steel guitar could be heard on his recordings. His voice, though, had begun to lower into its more natural and pleasing baritone registers and away from the high and rather strident sound heard on such early recordings as "Mexican Joe" and "Bimbo." He and Chet Atkins also began choosing songs that were appropriate for such a voice. "Billy Bayou," composed by Roger Miller and a number one song for Reeves in early 1959, had some echoes of his earlier hillbilly emphasis, but "Four Walls" later in that year and "He'll Have to Go" in early 1960 marked the real development of the style that would soon be described as "a touch of velvet."[3] Singing to the accompaniment of vibes and muted guitars, and backed by the mandatory chorus of voices, Reeves fashioned a mellow and caressing sound that somehow satisfied his original "hillbilly" listeners while winning him a legion of fans around the world. Reeves' popularity outside the United States may have sur-

3. Used as the title of a Jim Reeves album (RCA Victor LPM 2487), composed exclusively of pop songs.

passed that of any other country singer; a series of tours on the European continent, in Scandinavia, and in South Africa (where he made a movie called *Kimberly Jim*) in the late fifties and early sixties increased the following that had already been attracted to him through his recordings. Reeves' death in a plane crash on July 31, 1964, did not dim his popularity. RCA has skillfully marketed much of his unreleased material on a periodic basis, and some of these songs have become important hits. The record company still receives fan material addressed to Jim Reeves, an indication that for many people the singer has never died. Reeves' music does indeed live on. An appreciative public has demonstrated its loyalty through the records it has purchased and the Country Music Association made its tribute to Reeves by naming him to the Country Music Hall of Fame in 1967.

While Jim Reeves had an impact on country music that can still be measured twenty years after his death, Missouri-born Ferlin Husky probably won more immediate national exposure in the late fifties than any other country entertainer. He did so through a fortuitous combination of singing ability, comedy, and showmanship. He began his singing career on KXLW in St. Louis but spent most of his time in the late forties and early fifties performing in California, in the clubs around Bakersfield and on the *Hometown Jamboree* in Los Angeles. During this period of his life he styled himself "Terry Preston," and he began recording for the Capitol label under that name. His first big hit, recorded under the name of Ferlin Husky, came in 1953 when he and Jean Shepard did a song inspired by the Korean War separations called "A Dear John Letter." This hillbilly hit was far removed in tone and style from his super commercial recording of 1957, "Gone." This quintessential country-pop song, a slow romantic ballad punctuated by strings and vocal chorus, was the number one song in both country and pop music throughout the spring of 1957. However, he did not have another hit of such magnitude until November 1960, when he recorded the gospel-country-pop song "On the Wings of a Dove." Husky was a master stage entertainer, with a gift of gab and a cornball sense of humor. Much of his popularity was won through his mythical hayseed creation, Simon Crum, who told jokes, did imitations of other country singers, and sang comic songs. Husky managed to maneuver himself onto a wide variety of national television shows, such as *Kraft TV Theatre*, the *Ed Sullivan Show*, the *Steve Allen Show*, the *Rosemary Clooney Show*, the *Arthur Godfrey Show* (as guest host), and the *Tonight Show*. While Husky moved the music away from its rural moorings and into middle-class homes throughout America, his alter ego, the hayseed Simon Crum, told audiences in a song that "Good old country music's here to stay."

Another Capitol artist who flirted with the country-pop idiom, yet never really strayed very far from the mainstream, was Faron Young. Young, who was born on a dairy farm near Shreveport, Louisiana, joined KWKH's *Louisiana Hayride* in the early fifties, after a short stay at the local Centenary College. He was one of several country musicians, such as Floyd Cramer and Red Sovine, who profited from Webb Pierce's aid and encouragement. Young's first hit came in 1953, with "Going Steady," a tune that was sufficiently uptempoed and teenage-oriented to now warrant its inclusion in rockabilly anthologies. Young seems never to have consciously sought pop acceptance and has always shown a fondness for twin fiddle accompaniment; nevertheless, his big voice, precise articulation, and pop phrasing made him a likely candidate for country-pop stardom. With songs like "Country Girl" in 1959 and "Hello Walls" in 1961 (one of the first Willie Nelson compositions to be recorded by a major performer), Young became one of the dominant entertainers of country music. "The Young Sheriff," so-called because of his appearance in the movie *Hidden Guns*, became as well known for his outspoken, opinionated personality as for his musical talents.

Marty Robbins was one of the most diversely talented performers in country music, from the time he made his first Columbia recordings in 1951 to his death from massive heart failure in 1983. Born on September 26, 1925, in the desert outside Glendale, Arizona, Robbins drifted from job to job until he entered military service in World War II. Although he had had a childhood fondness for cowboy music, he did not begin to see the value of country music as such until he heard it performed by fellow soldiers from the South. After his return to civilian life, he began singing in local clubs and on radio in Mesa and Phoenix. On the strength of a recommendation from Jimmy Dickens, who heard him in one of these clubs, Robbins was signed to a Columbia recording contract in 1951. On his early recordings, 1951–1954, Robbins showed the influence of his childhood hero, Gene Autry, in his smooth tone and phrasing. There was also more than a little touch of the early Eddy Arnold, especially in the plaintive, ting-a-ling steel guitar accompaniment of James Farmer, who appeared on these original Columbia records. A penchant for sad and sentimental songs, such as "I Couldn't Keep from Crying" and "At the End of a Long Lonely Day," gained Robbins the sobriquet of "Mr. Teardrop."

Robbins soon demonstrated, however, that he was wedded to no single style, and that he was capable of enormous stylistic growth. He made the first country cover of Presley's "That's All Right, Mama," and he followed that with other rockabilly experiments. When the country-pop phase set in, Robbins was supremely qualified to prosper from the impulse; indeed, he often set the directions that the style would follow. After his successful performance of "White Sport Coat" and "The Story of My Life," Robbins never again strayed very far from the lucrative countrypolitan field. If his heart truly lay with any one area of performance, however, it was the songs of the West. Down deep, Robbins was a singing cowboy who had been born just a few years too late. He never forgot the open country of his birth, nor the singers like Autry and the Sons of the Pioneers who had fired his childhood imagination. He always made room in his concerts for cowboy songs, and his immensely popular recording of "El Paso" in 1960 did much to move country music back toward its roots.

With the emergence of Patsy Cline, the modern era of women country singers really began. Born in 1932, Cline (whose real name was Virginia Patterson Hensley) had sung since at least the age of fourteen on WINC in her hometown of Winchester, Virginia, but she made no significant break-through in commercial country music until the mid-fifties. She made her first records in 1954 for a California company, Four Star, which had also given Hank Locklin and Jimmy Dean their starts. Her career was only moderately successful until she joined the cast of *Town and Country Jam-boree*, which was broadcast each Saturday night from the Capitol Arena in Washington, D.C. This show, which featured such performers as Jimmy Dean, Roy Clark, George Hamilton IV, and Mary Klick, was merely one of many operations promoted by country music entrepreneur Connie B. Gay. In January 1957, Patsy appeared as a contestant on *Arthur Godfrey's Talent Scout Show* on CBS. She won first place with a torch song she had recorded for Decca the previous year, "Walking after Midnight." She appeared on Godfrey's morning show for about two weeks, and this national exposure contributed to the success of the song; it made both the pop and country charts. The year 1960 saw both her admission to the *Grand Old Opry* and her first giant recording: "I Fall to Pieces." Written by Hank Cochran and Harlan Howard, the recording remained on the charts for thirty-nine weeks and climbed as high as the number twelve position on *Billboard*'s pop music charts. The recording marked the beginning of Decca's all-out efforts to market Cline as a pop singer; she was backed by a full and lush retinue of strings and voices.

The ironic thing about Patsy Cline's country-pop orientation is that she did not seek such classification. She dressed in cowgirl attire until 1962; she always expressed a desire to yodel on her records; and she disliked the three songs which gave her national exposure: "Walking after Midnight," "I Fall to Pieces," and "Crazy" (another early songwriting venture by Willie Nelson after he moved to Nashville). Her strong and resilient voice, how-ever, was so well suited for the pop emphasis that was now selling millions of records that her managers could not resist such packaging. She had re-markable vocal control and commanded attention with a number of ap-pealing vocal mannerisms such as growls, sighs, and bent notes. By the time she died on March 6, 1963, in the plane crash that also killed Cowboy Copas and Hawkshaw Hawkins, she had reached out to an audience that had not earlier listened to country music and had taken older country fans into stylistic regions where they had not previously gone. Perhaps most important, she had moved female country singing closer to the pop main-stream and light years away from the sound projected by Molly O'Day, Rose Maddox, Jean Shepard, and Kitty Wells.

The broad commercial exposure enjoyed by Patsy Cline and other country singers at the beginning of the sixties was evidence that an industry that had faltered and acted indecisively during the rock-and-roll onslaught was now re-emerging with unparalleled economic strength. In part, this renewed vitality was a consequence of the work of men like Chet Atkins, Owen Bradley, and Jim Denny who reached out to win a new audience. The country-pop compromise may have attracted some rock-and-roll fans, but it was no doubt much more appealing to old-time pop fans who could no longer hear the kind of music to which they had been accustomed. Eddy Arnold, Marty Robbins, and Jim Reeves, to name only three members of a much larger fraternity, provided the kind of middle-of-the-road, easy-listening sound that many people were seeking. The Nashville sound, as a whole, soon lost definition and became identified with any kind of recording that came out of the city. The burgeoning music activity of Nashville gained the city the title of Music City, USA, an identity and reputation that must have embarrassed the high-culture partisans who lived there. The city officials began to pay great attention to the musical culture that was developing around them, particularly as the big bucks poured in. The almost ceaseless recording activity lured musicians who made the city their permanent home. These sessions musicians became famous far and wide, and all kinds of singers came to Nashville to take advantage of the ease and informality that characterized recording there (as pop singer John Sebastian said, "Nashville cats, been picking since they's babies"). The recording studios were joined by a vast, and generally interlocking, panoply of music business interests which made their headquarters in the city. Jim Denny, who had headed WSM's booking agency for several years, formed his own independent operation in 1954. Thereafter, virtually all country performers began signing contracts with Denny, Hubert Long, Hal Smith, and the growing retinue of booking and promotional organizations that congregated in Nashville. Recording, of course, spawned a vast network of songwriters and publishing houses. Acuff-Rose's leadership, made possible by the success of "The Tennessee Waltz" and by its ownership of the Hank Williams catalogue, was challenged in the mid-fifties by, first, Jim Denny's Cedarwood Publishing Company (which was lucky enough to control Webb Pierce's long string of hits) and, later, such companies as Pamper, Tree, and Sure-Fire. Publishing, now that sheet music had become relatively unimportant, had become inextricably interrelated with the recording business. A publishing house existed, in effect, to market a written composition to a recording company.

Reflective of country music's commercial growth, and largely responsible for it, was a new trade organization founded in 1958, the Country Music Association (CMA). This organization grew out of the Disc Jockeys Convention and was conceived as a device by which country music could attain respectability and achieve a wider popularity. It was, in other words, a facet of the music's counterattack against the threats posed by rock-and-roll in the late fifties. For several years the organization worked out of a small covey of offices in a nondescript building in downtown Nashville and was staffed totally by an executive secretary named Jo Walker (now Jo Walker-Meador). Walker, along with Frances Preston of BMI, was one of the few women to attain executive status in the country music business; she ran the fledgling CMA and did much to keep it afloat during its first tentative years. She is now its executive director. The CMA became an aggressive organization which frankly perceived its mission in economic and public relations terms. The organization was unconcerned with definition or stylistic integrity; instead, it saw country music as a product which needed to be marketed on the widest possible basis. It made no attempts to define what was or was not country music, and it argued that all forms of country music would prosper if the industry as a whole was healthy.

One of the most significant tasks undertaken by the CMA was the sponsorship of all-country-music radio stations. The identity of the first all-country station is still not conclusively known, but it has been argued that KXLA in Pasadena (1949) and KDAV in Lubbock, Texas, in the fifties were the first to program country music on a mass basis. By 1967 at least 328 stations broadcast country music on a full-time basis, while over 2,000 featured some country music during their broadcast days. Country music was undoubtedly presented to every sector of American life in this way, but critics argued that the music's identity was diluted and clouded through this mass exposure. Radio stations did not have enough personnel to staff their shows who were familiar with the music's traditions, and many of them frankly had little love for the music they were required to play, or, at best, they came from rock-and-roll backgrounds which forever colored their musical choices and selections. Even if they liked traditional forms of country music, they were given little opportunity to play them, because most stations moved rapidly toward the "tight playlist" concept which had been pioneered by rock stations. Only a handful of records, produced almost exclusively by the largest corporations, were played over and over again during the broadcast day. The old-time disc jockeys—the Eddie Hills, Nelson Kings, Paul Kallingers, and Wayne Raneys—were fading from the scene. These were men who had both known and loved the music they played (some of them, in fact, had served apprenticeships as country musicians). They were often corny, and even grotesquely hayseed in style, but they had individuality and warmth. They were often replaced by jive talkers, or ignoramuses who had no feeling at all for the music they spun.

The Country Music Association deserves much of the credit for country music's great commercial upsurge and worldwide expansion during the sixties. In its early years the CMA appeared to be wholly commercially oriented and to be little concerned with the traditions and historical importance of the music. As one CMA brochure noted, "the 'C' in country music means cash."[4] The annual conventions held in Nashville (along with the business meetings held in places like London and San Juan, Puerto Rico) demonstrate just how far removed from the rustic image country music has ventured and how much it has succumbed to the middle-class ethic of respectability and success. The yearly conventions remind one of a meeting of businessmen, replete with stockholders' reports, innovative merchandising ideas, fancy banquets, cocktail hours, and a final formal dance with music provided by one of the sophisticated, pop-style country bands such as that headed by Leroy Van Dyke. The organization's growth, in short, has paralleled that of the country music industry.

One of the most heartening contributions made by the CMA, and an indication that the organization was trying to at least combine history with promotion, was the establishment of the Country Music Hall of Fame and Museum. Largely through the devoted work of people such as Roy Horton and Steve Sholes, a massive fund-raising campaign resulted in the construction of a million-dollar structure, ultramodern in design, which in addition to museum facilities would also contain the offices of the Country Music Association, the plaques of Hall of Fame honorees, and a center for historical research. The dream, which had been conceived as early as 1961, came to fruition on March 31, 1967, when the doors of the Country Music Hall of Fame and Museum officially opened in Nashville. The gala opening ceremony began when CMA Board Chairman Roy Horton and President Paul Cohen cut the ribbons before NBC television cameras, and continued with speeches by Tennessee Governor Buford Ellington, Congressman Richard Fulton, and Nashville Mayor Beverly Briley.

In this beautiful building, which has become one of the major tourist attractions in the Music City, one can meander down the Walkway of the Stars, which is embedded with the names of those entertainers who have contributed at least $1,000 to the Hall of Fame, see the instruments, wearing apparel, and mementoes of the earlier stars, and top off the visit by watching a short film on the history of country music. Those with a scholarly interest can go downstairs to the Library and Media Center which houses an enormous collection of records, tapes, interviews, magazines, and other assorted material of usefulness to researchers.

The Hall of Fame itself was originally modeled on the one established by professional baseball at Cooperstown, New York, but the plan was modified when it was discovered that such rigid rules allowed admission of only a very few individuals. A special committee of the CMA in 1961 selected Jimmie Rodgers, Fred Rose, and Hank Williams as the first honorees. In November 1962, the CMA abandoned its initial intention to select only deceased entertainers and chose Roy Acuff as the first living member of the Hall of Fame. With the exception of 1963, when no one was chosen, the

4. *Behind the Record of the Country Music Association* (no date), p. 4.

CMA has yearly added new names to the Hall, and in 1967 a policy was adopted to name people from both performing and nonperforming categories. The Hall of Fame was criticized in its early years for its seeming bias toward Nashville and contemporary performers. With the exception of Jimmie Rodgers, every honoree up to the selection of Gene Autry in 1969 was a Nashville-based musician or businessman. Furthermore, some of the obvious giants of country music were not named until long after the Hall of Fame had been established.

At the end of the fifties, then, country music was beginning to be faced with the debate that has only intensified in the decades that have followed: would the music lose its identity, and its soul, as it gained the world? Had Chet Atkins' compromise saved the music and made it possible for all styles to thrive, or had he and other country-pop people headed it down the road to accommodation, homogenization, and ultimate extinction? Whatever the value of countrypolitan music, it and the urge to "cross over" into the lucrative pop field were here to stay. The pop urge, in fact, had been inherent in country music's development from the very beginning. In the years to come, reactions would sometimes come; alternatives would appear; and "back-to-the-roots" movements (such as bluegrass) would periodically manifest themselves; but the pop impulse would remain irresistible.

Dolly Parton. Photograph courtesy of the Country Music Foundation Library and Media Center, Nashville, Tennessee.

9. The Reinvigoration of Modern Country Music, 1960–1972

Although the rockabilly obsession and the subsequent country-pop emphasis were relatively short phases of country music history, they must have seemed like eternities to partisans of traditional country music. But as a matter of fact, the rockabilly craze introduced to music a large number of young people who later took their guitars and energy into the country field. In some cases, their styles of country music took on the manifestations of rock; in other cases (such as Conway Twitty and Jerry Lee Lewis), they revealed that they could perform hard-core or honky-tonk country as well as any of the old-timers. The country-pop urge, on the other hand, sometimes bred boredom, just as homogenization of any type often does, and the more tradition-based country styles steadily began to reappear.

Commercially, country music continued to burgeon. All-country radio stations proliferated. When WHN in New York City adopted the format, country music had indeed become chic. Perhaps more significant, though, than radio programming was the blossoming of country music on television. Country and cowboy singers had already appeared on early television experiments. Tex Owens, for example, claimed to have appeared on the tube as early as 1935; Bobby Gregory made an appearance on a New York demonstration sometime in the thirties; Red River Dave was on a show at the 1939 World's Fair in New York; and he and several other entertainers appeared on local country shows when television stations appeared in their cities (Red River Dave, for example, had a popular show in San Antonio in the late forties).

The barn dance format began to appear on television almost as soon as the medium became institutionalized after World War II. The *Midwestern Hayride* debuted on local television in Cincinnati in 1948 and secured an NBC affiliation in 1955. The *Grand Ole Opry* did not permit the televising of its regular programs (this was not done until the late seventies, when public television aired a couple of the shows in their entirety), but Al Gannaway did produce an extensive number of thirty-minute shows featuring Opry talent; they have been revised and newly syndicated in the 1980's. The king of the televised barn dances was the *Ozark Jubilee,* from Springfield, Missouri. The show itself had begun in 1946, but it assumed network status on ABC on January 22, 1956. It was hosted by Red Foley and featured at one time or another such performers as Brenda Lee (as a child star), Leroy Van Dyke, Sonny James, and Porter Wagoner, as well as the comedy team of Uncle Cyp and Aunt Sap Brasfield (tent vaudeville veterans who took their routines into country music).

Numerous television shows were syndicated and sold to a wide variety of markets around the nation. These shows were aimed at the hard-core country audience, but, of course, were sometimes watched by the casual or curious spectator (sometimes secretly). Among the more important were those of Ernest Tubb (often featuring a neatly dressed and clean-shaven Willie Nelson), Buck Owens, Flatt and Scruggs, the Wilburn Brothers, and Porter Wagoner. The two last-named programs were oases for "traditional" country music, humor, patter, and advertisements. Each show preserved much of the flavor of early stage and radio performances, and a large sampling of down-home traits that country music seemed to be in danger of forgetting. People who watched the *Wilburn Brothers Show* could hear the Wilburns (Teddy and Doyle) sing old-time gospel and country songs such as "Farther Along" and "My Little Home in Tennessee," as well as the modern hits. Born in Hardy, Arkansas, the Wilburn Brothers started out as child singers in their family's band but began to create an identity as a brother duet when they signed with Decca in 1954. Tours with Webb Pierce and Faron Young contributed immeasurably to their wider exposure. The Wilburns, in turn, furthered the careers of other entertainers who appeared on their television segments; Loretta Lynn, for example, began her rise to superstardom while singing on the *Wilburn Brothers Show* in the early sixties.

The *Porter Wagoner Show* became part of Americana, deeply beloved by those who cherished the rustic imagery it conveyed, and ridiculed by those who recoiled from its hayseed trappings. Wagoner's television program was the most widely syndicated country show in the nation and was the most important haven available for the older styles of country music. Wagoner grew up on a farm near West Plains, Missouri, and in 1951 began singing each morning from 5:30 to 6:00 A.M. on a local radio station that could be heard for only five or six miles. After a bus driver heard his program and passed the word on to the station manager, KWTO in nearby Springfield called Wagoner in for an audition. He gained additional exposure on the *Ozark Jubilee* and in 1955 signed a contract with RCA. His successful recording in 1956 of "Satisfied Mind," one of the most finely crafted songs in country music, was his main ticket to the *Grand Ole Opry*, which he joined in 1957. As a hillbilly in a time of stylistic cloudiness, Wagoner definitely did not fit into RCA's vision of a country-pop compromise. Nevertheless, the company recognized his commercial appeal and kept him on its roster. While resolutely remaining faithful to the hard country sounds and image, Wagoner more than repaid RCA's trust by recording some of the major hits of country music, including the classics "Green, Green Grass of Home" and "Carroll County Accident."

Wagoner's television show, introduced in 1960, was sponsored by a firm long familiar to rural southerners: the Chattanooga Medicine Company, the maker of Black Draught and Wine of Cardui (for "women's complaints") and the distributor of the famous wall calendars that were once found in nearly all rural homes. The thirty-minute television segment was a showcase for other talented performers besides Wagoner. Norma Jean Beasler (known simply as "Miss Norma Jean") was a sweet-voiced singer from Oklahoma who served as the show's "girl singer" until replaced by Dolly Parton in 1967. Parton, of course, rose to national fame on the strength of her appearances on the show and in concert with Wagoner up to 1975. Parton's and Wagoner's duet recordings for RCA were consistent award winners throughout the late sixties and early seventies. Comedian Speck Rhodes provided a light-hearted contrast with his baggy pants and burlesque style of humor, and Mack Magaha, who previously had been a member of Don Reno and Red Smiley's Tennessee Cutups, contributed some of the best old-time fiddling heard on any country show in the sixties. Buck Trent, a gifted instrumentalist who played both electric guitar and five-string banjo, probably made country music history when he successfully converted the banjo into an electric instrument—a development that could only bring dismay to tradition-minded enthusiasts. His innovation had the dubious distinction of making the banjo sound like an electric guitar.

Despite the presence of so many gifted individualists, the dominating presence of the show was Wagoner himself. Wagoner cut a striking figure, to say the least, in one of the many brightly colored, rhinestone-studded cowboy suits which Nudie Cohen had begun providing for him in 1953 (Wagoner's first suit cost $350; they now average about $5,000). Along with Hank Snow, Wagoner was one of the few country entertainers who persisted with such costuming at a time when everyone else was adopting business suits or modish attire. Making over two hundred concerts a year, appearing regularly on the *Grand Ole Opry*, and entering millions of homes via his syndicated television show, Porter Wagoner brought renewed strength and vitality to hard-core country music. Neither wealth nor success caused him to forget his rural origins and the people who had nurtured both him and his music.

While shows like Porter Wagoner's were important repositories for old-time country music, other shows did more to introduce the music to the masses, and particularly to the urban middle class who would have listened to it in no other guise. In 1957 CBS put the lanky and affable Jimmy Dean, from Plainview, Texas, opposite NBC's venerable Dave Garroway, and the country show more than held its own for several months. The program came on at 7 A.M. (Eastern Standard Time) out of WTOP in Washington, and was part of Connie B. Gay's country music empire, Gay was a promoter who had been born in Lizard Lick, North Carolina, and who had gotten into radio work through the government-sponsored *Farm Hour* in the 1940's. Dean had a remarkably winning personality and a better than average singing voice and piano style. His recitations, cornball humor, and country crooning were ably supported by Mary Klick's sweet ballads, Smitty Ervin's five-string banjo, and Buck Ryan's hot old-time fiddling. In short, the show did provide a format for real country music, while also helping to introduce newer entertainers, such as guitarist/singer Billy Grammer, to a wider public. However, when Dean returned to network television in 1964—this time in a prime night-time slot on ABC—the show was more fully in the country-pop camp and had about as many pop guests as country.

By and large, the network country shows that have followed in the wake of Jimmy Dean have been overproduced, slickly professional, and only marginally "country." The producers of such shows have generally been reluctant to give viewers a strong dose of the real thing. Above all, the proliferation of such shows indicates the "arrival" of country music and its growing respectability on the American scene. On the strength of his evident commercial appeal, Roger Miller was made host of a show on NBC for a few months in 1966. After spending several artistically successful, but economically unrewarding, years as a sideman, writer, and singer, Miller made the whole world of American show business sit up and take notice of his talents in 1964 and 1965. He won eleven Grammy awards during this two-year period (a feat that no other country entertainer has equaled), and he became an often-seen guest on such primetime national programs as the *Tonight Show*, starring Johnny Carson. Born and reared in Texas and Oklahoma, and a life-long disciple of Bob Wills' music, Miller emerged from a hard-core country background to become one of the most sophisticated lyricists in country music and a clever and witty singer and comedian. The diversely talented Miller, though, could not save his own show from the bland packaging that was imposed upon it. Country music received little emphasis on the show; therefore, many country fans did not mourn its rather abrupt departure from television programming.

In 1969 three country shows moved into network programming: *Glen Campbell's Goodtime Hour* (CBS), the *Johnny Cash Show* (ABC), and *Hee Haw* (CBS). Campbell, from Delight, Arkansas, finally moved from undeserved obscurity when he made his very popular recording in 1966 of

John Hartford's "Gentle on My Mind." Campbell had spent much of his life as a sessions musician in Los Angeles, where he contributed to the fame of other people. In the summer of 1968 he became the summer replacement for the Smothers Brothers, and he charmed his viewers with an easy, relaxed personality, a supple, tenor voice (sharply honed through a short stint with the Beach Boys), and his guitar virtuosity. Campbell's singing was pop-oriented, and he gravitated toward structurally sophisticated songs such as those written by Jim Webb ("By the Time I Get to Phoenix," "Wichita Lineman," "Galveston"), but he maintained a down-home atmosphere with his high-pitched country laugh and patter, and through the occasional guest appearances of his charming parents, who were indeed rural and folksy. Campbell's own show in 1969 was smooth, fast-paced, and countrypolitan in mood. Whatever the misgivings that some country fans might have had about the style of music heard on the Glen Campbell show, most were probably delighted at the success which one of their own had attained.

Country fans had much higher hopes for the *Johnny Cash Show* when it began in 1969. And Johnny tried his best to present a real country show: he performed his own dyed-in-the-wool country songs (such as "Folsom Prison Blues," which he had revived with even greater success than when first released in 1955); he sometimes featured his famous mother-in-law, Maybelle Carter; he gave much exposure to her daughter and his wife, June; and he ran a well-done segment, complete with movie and photo footage, called "Ride This Train," a combination of history and song. Cash was also receptive to young and innovative musicians, and to those who came from non-country backgrounds. Urban folk hero Bob Dylan, for example, appeared on the show to great fanfare, and Doug Kershaw, the frenetic Cajun/rock fiddler, began a major comeback in American music after a guest appearance on the Cash series. As time went by, though, the show's country flavor gradually became diluted under an avalanche of pop guests and over-stylized production numbers.

The third major television show of 1969, *Hee Haw*, was hillbilly to the point of grotesque parody; its commercial success was indeed strange. It presented an image of country music, and of rural life, that most musicians had been resisting for years: that of the hayseed buffoon. Nevertheless, the backwoodsy skits were produced and merchandised through the most sophisticated and urbane of techniques. The show's producer, Sam Lovullo, described it as a "fully computerized" production,[1] in that after enough scenes were shot to comprise as many as thirteen shows, the material was fed into a computer which selected the best and most effective groupings of skits. Inspired by the popular comedy series *Laugh-In*, *Hee*

1. John Fergus Ryan, "Press a Button and Out Comes 'Hee Haw'," *Country Music* 2, no. 1 (September 1973): 28–34.

Haw was an hour program that interspersed music with comic vignettes and shots of beautiful, scantily clad women. Most of the humor was freshly written by modern gag writers or by the performers themselves (as in the case of Grandpa Jones, who compiled his "country menus" from old cookbooks), but some of it was of hoary vintage: from jokebooks, from vaudeville, burlesque, and minstrel sources, and from the early country music tradition. The show's appeal suggested that the humor of country music was more traditional than its music. (There were many fine musical moments on the show, however. The best came each week when the Hee Haw Gospel Quartet [Kenny Price, Grandpa Jones, Roy Clark, and Buck Owens] sang old-time religious songs in Brown's Ferry Four fashion and to the sole accompaniment of Clark's guitar.) *Hee Haw* skits took place in barbershops, in cornfields, around pot-bellied stoves at the general store, in the front yards of rickety cabins, and in similar rustic settings. Buck Owens and Roy Clark, the hosts of the show, did a comic routine with guitar and banjo that was reminiscent of the venerable "Arkansas Traveler" skit, and Jack Pruitt and Jimmie Riddle did a takeoff on juba patting, keeping a highly-rhythmic pattern going by slapping their legs and chests, while also emitting wheezes and hiccough-like sounds which they called "eephing."

The *Hee Haw* cast constituted a "Who's Who" of country comedy. Old-time comedians such as Grandpa Jones, Stringbean (David Akeman), Minnie Pearl, and Archie Campbell gained access to newer and larger audiences through the popular show. Newer performers also won a national exposure through the show that most earlier country comedians had only dreamed of. Junior Samples, a natural, but semi-literate, rural comedian came to the show with virtually no professional experience. Sheb Wooley, a cowboy actor, singer, and songwriter from Oklahoma (who had attained notoriety and wealth as the writer of "Purple People Eater"), performed on the show as a drunken song parodist called Ben Colder. Kenny Price, a fine baritone singer whose rotundity garnered for him the title of "the round mound of sound," showed *Hee Haw* audiences that he was also a very funny man, and Jerry Clower, a former Mississippi fertilizer salesman, gave television audiences a sample of the humor that had been delighting clubs, service organizations, and seed conventions for years. Public visibility, however, carried dangers as well as delight. In November 1973, thugs went to Stringbean Akeman's secluded country home and killed the beloved comedian and his wife after ransacking their house in search of the large sum of money believed to be sheltered there.

Country music's expanding popularity was not confined to the United States. The music exhibited surprising strength and commercial viability in Europe, Asia, and South Africa. Country entertainers had never been totally unknown in other parts of the world. Even in the twenties and thirties American hillbilly records had been reissued rather extensively abroad, and Jimmie Rodgers, particularly, had built up at least a modest international following. Rodgers' reissued recordings contributed directly to the birth of the country music industry in Australia and New Zealand, a phenomenon fashioned primarily by the confluence of local folk music traditions (e.g., that of the Australian Bush) and the vision of American cowboys. The image of the cowboy and its identification with country music do much to explain why some country singers, such as Gene Autry and Slim Whitman, have experienced considerable success abroad. When Autry toured the British Isles in 1939, though, he was not the first American country entertainer to do so; Carson Robison had made earlier jaunts in 1932, 1936, and 1938 (and each time he projected the persona of a cowboy).

Despite the earlier manifestations of interest abroad, World War II was the force which really promoted the internationalization of country music. American military personnel carried all forms of their nation's popular music around the world, but it was the Armed Forces Network, which grew from a weak GI station using a borrowed transmitter into a mammoth system, which proved most instrumental in generating interest in American music among Europeans. By 1960 one report indicated that about fifty million Europeans listened to the AFN,[2] and the network received correspondence from interested listeners from every country in Western Europe, from North Africa, and even from Soviet bloc nations.

Country music experienced a remarkable popularity among American military personnel during the war, a preference that seemed only to deepen in the years that followed the conflict. Record purchases even seemed to suggest that country music had a wide lead in popularity over other brands of music on American military bases. Throughout 1960 and 1961, for example, country record sales in base PX's accounted for about 65 percent of the entire total, and even reached as high as 72 percent on one occasion. Obviously, the music appealed to many people who had neither southern nor rural backgrounds and was a morale builder that seemed to be a powerful reminder of home. An Army record buyer was quoted as saying: "Country and western strikes the troops as part of the American heritage, and the troops prefer it to sophisticated, schmalzy music."[3]

Servicemen formed string bands everywhere, and some of them were heard over the AFN. While fulfilling his military obligations in World War II, Grandpa Jones played with a group called the Munich Mountaineers, and in Japan the future recording star Charlie Walker introduced country music to that part of the world as the leader of a band that included the famous fiddler and songwriter Red Hayes ("Satisfied Mind") and other

---

2. Omer Anderson, "Fifty Million Europeans Can't Be Wrong," *Billboard* 72, no. 28 (July 11, 1960): 1.

3. *Billboard Music Week* 73, no. 33 (September 25, 1961): 3.

Eighth Army buddies. While live programming was important in the dissemination of country music, DJ shows—following the trend back home—ultimately reached a much larger audience of military personnel and European civilians. One of the more popular postwar programs carried by the AFN was a country record show called *Stickbuddy Jamboree*, conducted by Sergeant Tom Daniels from Texas. The *Jamboree* was said to have the biggest audience of any program on the air in Europe at that time (3:05 P.M.). Daniels also conducted another popular country show, *Hillbilly Reveille*, which was broadcast during the early morning hours. Other country DJ shows spiced up AFN programming, and at least one show was hosted by a future professional performer, Dick Curless, who broadcast in Korea during the early fifties as the Rice Paddy Ranger.

One of the most remarkable consequences of country music expansion was the emergence of people in other nations who became musicians, fans, collectors, or promoters. Kitty Prins, who conducted the *Melody Ranch Show* from Belgium, and Connie Tex Hat, who ran a similar show in Austria, were only two of a large number of foreigners who began promoting local country music in the late fifties. There are now country shows in nations around the world, although only a few are as ambitious as the Tokyo *Grand Ole Opry* or England's huge Wembley Festival (the last being an annual event which attracts dozens of American stars each year). Some non-Americans have pursued careers in the country music industry in the United States. It is not unheard-of to find a Japanese fiddler or steel guitarist in an American band, and occasional singers, such as Englishman Pete Sayers, who went to Nashville in the early sixties, have competed with American-born entertainers. Country music has also profited from the promotion of such people as Martin C. Haerle and Dixie Deen. Haerle was a former executive in the export department of a Stuttgart, Germany, refrigerator manufacturing company who became such an active producer of country shows on German radio and television that he was hired in July 1960 to head Starday Records' international sales and exploitation department. By 1961 Haerle had relocated to Starday's Nashville offices; he has since remained in the United States as an independent record producer. Dixie Deen was a trick rider for a Wild West show in her native England, but she did not receive an intensive introduction to country music until she came to the United States in 1960 at the urging of Starday Records' Don Pierce. After coming to the United States, she became an award-winning songwriter and an assistant editor and columnist of the *Music City News* (a country music publication that was then owned by Faron Young). Deen's association with country music was further cemented by her marriage to singer/songwriter Tom T. Hall.

Country musicians now routinely schedule performances in countries throughout the world, and a few, such as George Hamilton IV, Tennessee Ernie Ford, and Roy Clark, have performed in the Soviet Union. Hamilton, a North Carolinian who started his career in 1957 as a rockabilly, became one of country music's most zealous ambassadors abroad. He traveled extensively in the British Isles and on the European continent, giving performances and lecturing on the meaning and history of the music he had made his profession. Hamilton's dedication to the international acceptance of American country music was rivaled by that of Bill Clifton, a Maryland-born performer of bluegrass and old-time country music. After about eleven years of performance in the United States, Clifton moved to England in 1963 and became an entertainer in the folk clubs there. At first his audiences had little knowledge or appreciation of the music he performed, but he was such an avid missionary for old-time country music (as well as a competent performer) that by 1966 he was playing six nights a week in the clubs, appearing often on the continent, and hosting a weekly BBC radio show called *Cellar Full of Folk*. Clifton's schedule became so exhausting that he joined the Peace Corps in 1967 for a three-year stint. By October 1970, however, he had returned to England and was once again educating the folk club audiences about the beauties of American country music.

Clifton's success before foreign audiences was evidence that the older varieties of American country music were popular outside the United States. Smooth, country-pop style singers such as Jim Reeves and Don Williams have had large followings in various countries, but performers of older styles—bluegrass, honky-tonk, yodeling cowboy, and the like—have also exhibited remarkable appeal to foreigners. The Japanese have showed great facility in re-creating all kinds of American music, and many of them have become both avid fans and performers of bluegrass music. Bluegrass musicians who have toured in Japan, such as Jim and Jesse McReynolds, testify to the quiet attentiveness and knowledge of Japanese fans. The reasons for the appeal of older forms of music are no doubt many and varied, but visions of American cowboys, mountain individualism, and frontier simplicity probably do much to shape the perceptions of country music. Vernon Oxford, Boxcar Willie, and Slim Whitman, three examples of Americans who have achieved considerable popularity in the British Isles, have each profited from romantic fixations concerning America and its music. Oxford, from Rogers, Arkansas, proved to be "too country" for the tastes of most American top-forty DJ's, and he has consequently been little known in this country. In England, though, his hard country style of singing has been much appreciated. Boxcar Willie has also intrigued English fans with his hobo attire, railroad songs, and rambling man image. Born Lecil Travis Martin in Sterret, Texas, he came to traditional country music in the early seventies after a successful background in the Air Force and as a civilian flight engineer. Wearing overalls, a floppy hat, and a smudged face, and performing mostly older songs—from the Roy Acuff, Jimmie Rodgers, and Hank Williams song bags—Boxcar Willie demonstrated conclusively that there was a considerable hunger here and abroad for older country music and for the symbols that surrounded it. He went to England for the first time in 1977 and found a tremendous reception. Large record sales in that country only added to the luster of his growing popularity back home.

While Vernon Oxford's and Boxcar Willie's British popularity is fairly recent, that of Slim Whitman is considerably older, dating to the early fifties, when the Florida-born yodeler and tenor singer began giving his first concerts in England. The tall, mustachioed Whitman, who dressed in western-tailored costumes and yodeled an occasional cowboy song like "Cattle Call," was highly regarded in a country where fans often dressed in dude cowboy clothing to listen to country entertainers. When Whitman experienced his American resurgence in 1980–1981—a product of massive television advertising promoted by New York's Suffolk Marketing Company—he could point to almost twenty-five years of unbroken commercial popularity in Great Britain.

Slim Whitman's commercial strength in England, along with his eventual resurgence in the United States, indicates that the older styles of country music never lost the support of millions of people. Even during the peak period of rock-and-roll ascendancy, the more "traditional" forms of country music did not die, though they sometimes faded from public view or reappeared in modified forms. In 1957, when Elvis reigned supreme in American music, Wilma Lee and Stoney Cooper took their brand of mountain music to the stage of the *Grand Ole Opry*, and the Country Gentlemen, one of the most innovative and popular bluegrass bands, began their existence in Washington, D.C. And out in Texas, Ray Price and his Cherokee Cowboys were producing some of the most exciting honky-tonk music ever made. During the next few years, and especially after 1960, hard-core country performances became more frequent, and an increasing number of them began to make the popularity charts.

One powerful force which contributed to the revitalization of older musical traditions, while also inspiring a general urge to make music, was the "urban folk revival." The term "revival" is something of a misnomer, since the entire history of folk-music interest in the cities is a short one. Urban folk interest dates to the Depression years when Library of Congress field-recording units and WPA cultural researchers stimulated an interest in America's grass-roots music, and when social activists and labor sympathizers began using folk songs as political weapons. Beginning from this relatively narrow base, and centered primarily among the socially conscious intelligentsia, folk music gradually became more generally popularized as performers such as Burl Ives, Josh White, and Big Bill Broonzy took the music to college campuses, into the night clubs, and onto radio stations. The music's radical identification, however, was preserved by such entertainers as Woody Guthrie, Cisco Houston, Pete Seeger, and the

Almanac Singers who during World War II performed at anti-Fascist rallies and on behalf of "progressive" causes. Although its political bias remained left-of-center, urban folk music moved closer to the pop mainstream in the late forties when groups like the Weavers (an offspring of the Almanac Singers) began placing songs like "Goodnight Irene" and "Kisses Sweeter than Wine" on the popular music hit charts. Harry Belafonte continued the popularizing trend in the fifties by making the nation calypso-conscious.

The tremors of interest in folk music in the late forties became a groundswell in the late fifties and early sixties. In 1958 the Kingston Trio (Dave Guard, Bob Shane, and Nick Reynolds) recorded a song called "Tom Dooley," an old North Carolina murder ballad (about a man originally named Tom Dula), which vaulted to the top position in the nation's popular hit charts. Following up this ballad with other very popular songs (both traditional and modern), the Trio became one of the biggest concert attractions in the United States. More than any single recording, "Tom Dooley" set off the urban folk music boom. Almost immediately, a spate of Kingston Trio imitators bearing such names as the Brothers Four, the Cumberland Trio, the Chad Mitchell Trio, and the Wanderers Three appeared on record labels. The new groups, all quite young, directed their approach toward college and high-school age groups, but before long people all over the nation, old and young alike, were humming "folk" melodies and buying recordings. The college folk interest at the beginning of the sixties differed from that generated during the Depression and World War II years in that the modern folk movement was more inclusive and attracted a broad spectrum, including the fraternity and sorority groups, while the earlier movement had been identified with the more radical and intellectual segments of campus life. Although folksinging by the middle of the sixties had become deeply intertwined with the movements for peace and civil rights and had spawned an important body of protest material, such as that written by Malvina Reynolds, Phil Ochs, and Bob Dylan, the average folksong session (usually called a "hootenanny") attracted a wide assortment of Americans: the young and the old, the intellectual and the uneducated, the conservative and the liberal, and the poor and the prosperous.

Despite the name it bore, urban folk music was essentially a facet of pop music. Some people may have been drawn to it in reaction to rock-and-roll, and some may have seen in it a reflection of a simpler and more manageable society, but most probably gravitated to it because of its freshness or because it represented just one more phase of pop music's ever-changing contours. It gave young people an opportunity to pick and sing and to be creative. And many people, such as Janis Joplin and Gram Parsons, moved easily from rock-and-roll to folk and then to hard rock or other forms of music. American songwriting was greatly furthered by the folk interest. Led principally by such alumni of the folk movement as Bob Dylan and

Paul Simon, hundreds of people began writing songs, an urge that was also strongly displayed in country music.

Most would-be folksingers were content to perform in the styles of the Kingston Trio or Peter, Paul, and Mary, and were unconcerned with stylistic authenticity or with the sources of their songs. Many enthusiasts, however, found that pop-folk music merely whetted their appetites for something more real, and they ventured increasingly into the sampling of old-time music: country, blues, gospel, Cajun, Tex-Mex, and other "ethnic" forms. This search for "sources" inspired a recognition of the importance of early commercial hillbilly music, and as a result such names as Uncle Dave Macon, the Carter Family, and the Skillet Lickers began to assume great importance for many young "folkniks." A powerful catalyst that worked to stimulate an interest in hillbilly music among urban folk fans was a Folkways recording, *Anthology of American Folk Music*, originally issued in 1952 and widely available in public libraries as well as in record catalogues. Issued as six long-playing 33⅓ rpm discs, the *Anthology* included both white and black country selections recorded between 1927 and 1933, or from the advent of electrical recordings until the diminution of field recordings during the Depression. Taken from commercial recordings borrowed from the gigantic collection owned by Harry Smith, the *Anthology* was intended as an introduction to authentic country music of the days before the radio and phonograph had blurred regional distinctions. The *Anthology* introduced to urban folk fans such names as the Carter Family, Uncle Dave Macon, Buell Kazee, Dock Boggs, and Clarence "Tom" Ashley. Marketed as "folk music" and disseminated by the select Folkways Company, the *Anthology* reached the ears of countless individuals who would have ignored it had it been dispensed under the label of "country" or "hillbilly" music. Songs from the *Anthology* made their way into the repertories of such urban performers as Joan Baez and the New Lost City Ramblers, who, with their appetites whetted by this initial introduction, resolved to learn more about songs and performers from the early hillbilly era.

The urban folk discovery of early hillbilly music had several happy consequences. Not only did it promote the reissuance of early recordings, as well as the recreation of old styles, it also inspired the finding of still-living pioneer commercial performers. Dedicated researchers discovered that many of the original hillbilly, blues, and gospel musicians were still alive and, better yet, that some of them could still perform as well as they ever could. Bluesmen Mississippi John Hurt and Furry Lewis, and country musicians Buell Kazee, Tom Ashley, Jimmie Tarlton, and Dock Boggs were only a few of the individuals who were fortunate enough to have second careers performing at the festivals, clubs, and university concerts spawned by the folk revival.

The relationship between country music and the urban folk scene was often a reciprocal one. Urban musicians such as the New Lost City Ramblers (Mike Seeger, John Cohen, Tom Paley, and, later, Tracy Schwarz) and the Greenbriar Boys (Ralph Rinzler, Bob Yellin, Eric Weissberg, and John Herald) borrowed freely from the hillbilly repertory, with the Ramblers faithfully recreating early string band styles and the Greenbriar Boys playing in the more recent bluegrass fashion. Country musicians, on the other hand, sometimes borrowed from the urban folk fanciers (both pop and traditional), not always realizing that such material had originally been purloined from their country forebears. One of the most beneficial consequences of the country–urban folk interrelationship was the discovery of Arthel "Doc" Watson, one of country music's most superb entertainers. Watson was a blind musician and singer from Deep Gap, North Carolina, who had performed locally for years, as both an acoustic and electric guitarist, until 1960 when he was "discovered" by Ralph Rinzler as a by-product of the latter's interest in Clarence "Tom" Ashley. With Rinzler as his manager, Watson began appearing at folk concerts in the North, first with his Tennessee and North Carolina friends, Ashley, Fred Price, and Clint Howard, and after 1964 as a solo act. Watson amazed his new-found audiences with his storehouse of songs, his skill as a banjoist and French harp player, and, above all, his virtuosity as a flat-picking guitarist. Watson was not the first guitarist to play fiddle tunes on his instrument, or to otherwise play melodies with great rapidity (he freely admits his indebtedness to such musicians as Don Reno, Grady Martin, Merle Travis, and the Delmore Brothers), but he probably did most to revitalize the acoustic guitar and to encourage the flat-picking technique. His version of "Black Mountain Rag" is one of the classics of modern guitar picking. Such brilliant young guitarists as Dan Crary, Norman Blake, Tony Rice, and Clarence White, plus an untold number of bluegrass musicians, can be described as his musical children. Watson gained public exposure through his involvement in the urban folk movement and through his appearances at bluegrass festivals. Nevertheless, he is not a bluegrass musician (as he is quick to point out to interviewers),[4] nor is he exclusively an old-time performer, although he can perform both styles with great proficiency. Watson accumulated an immense repertory of traditional ballads, folk songs, and instrumental pieces as he grew up in the mountains, but he was never totally wedded to such material, and he supplemented it with songs learned from modern commercial sources. Launching his professional career in the midst of the urban folk revival and appearing at such events as the Newport Folk Festival in 1961, Watson tailored his repertory

4. In an interview for WWOZ-FM in New Orleans, Watson re-emphasized his independence from bluegrass (interview conducted by Svare Forsland and Bill C. Malone, 1982).

to fit the perceived needs of his folkie listeners. He did magnificent versions of traditional songs such as "Little Matty Groves" and "Omie Wise," but it was only in later years—particularly after his talented son, Merle, joined him as an accompanist in 1966—that audiences learned of his skills as a blues and modern country singer.

Watson was one of several country musicians who appeared at the Newport Folk Festival during the sixties. Earl Scruggs was the first to do so, in 1959, and he was followed by such performers as Mac Wiseman, Jim and Jesse McReynolds, Bill Monroe, Wiley and Zeke Morris, and Merle Travis. The first mainstream country and western singer to forge an alliance with the folk revival was Johnny Cash, who appeared at the Newport affair in 1964 and 1969. Cash had earlier affected a kind of Harry Belafonte style of stage behavior, dressing in black and projecting a dramatic and sensual presence that seemed reminiscent of method-school acting. His 1962 performance of "The Legend of John Henry's Hammer," for example, lasted more than eight minutes and was punctuated by grunts and the striking of two steel bars together at periodic intervals. Cash was fond of traditional material, such as Leadbelly's "The Rock Island Line," but he seemed much more in tune with the pop-folk fraternity and their modern-composed songs (his own writing increasingly showed their influence). He was the first country entertainer to cultivate a relationship with Bob Dylan, and he recorded some of the young poet's material, as well as songs written by such performers as Peter LaFarge.

Although no country singer was as thoroughly immersed in the urban folk waters as Johnny Cash, several of his colleagues flirted with the revival and, in so doing, began to win back some of that youthful audience that had moved away from country music in the mid-fifties. George Hamilton IV, for example, moved away from his earlier flirtations with rock-and-roll and country-pop to the performance of such folkish tunes as "Steel Rail Blues," "Abilene," "Break My Mind," and "Gentle on My Mind." Country-rock superstar Waylon Jennings began his career with RCA in 1965, just before the tremors of the urban folk movement faded away. The Littlefield, Texas, native had not yet found the highly commercial sound which now characterizes his performances, but even then he exhibited an eclecticism that has led him into all areas of popular music. Consequently, in this early stage of his career Jennings did such folk chestnuts as "The Real House of the Rising Sun" and "I'm a Man of Constant Sorrow," as well as such newer pop-folk offerings as "Kisses Sweeter than Wine" and "Four Strong Winds." Jennings' recordings were obviously shaped by the pop fashions of the day. Jimmy C. Newman, on the other hand, dipped back into his own cultural heritage to revitalize his performing career. Although Newman's first recordings in 1946 were performed in the French patois of his native Southwest Louisiana—he was a real Cajun boy from Big Mamou—his entry into country music in 1954, via a Dot recording of

"Cry, Cry Darling," was pure honky-tonk. In 1957 he made the transition to country-pop with "A Fallen Star," one of the most successful songs in that genre. Newman, however, was never very happy in the role of pop singer and, largely through the influence of the urban folk enthusiasm, he returned to the performance of Cajun-country songs in 1962. An album in that year, *Folk Songs of the Bayou*, featured the dobro steel guitar and the fiddling of Rufus Thibodeaux, one of the best-known Cajun fiddlers of the modern period. Since that time Newman has been a major participant in a full-scale Cajun music revival that has seen old-time Cajun bands, such as the Balfa Brothers, and country-Cajun fusionists, like Newman and Doug Kershaw, take their music to the Smithsonian Festival on the Mall and to concerts in Europe.

Of the various country performers who experimented with the urban folk genre in the early sixties, Bobby Bare was the most successful. With a compelling voice that could be alternately mournful or raucous, the Ironton, Ohio, native became one of the premier "song salesmen" in modern country music. His down-home demeanor and unalloyed rural voice have not deterred Bare from being on the cutting edge of country music. He has borrowed freely from other fields of music and has exhibited an uncanny ability to elicit highly commercial songs from a long string of outstanding songwriters such as Mel Tillis, Paul Craft, Shel Silverstein, Kris Kristofferson, Billy Joe Shaver, and Tom T. Hall. Above all, Bare has been a story-teller, a talent he has shown with great effectiveness in such songs as "Miller's Cave," "Detroit City," and "Marie Laveau." In recording songs like "500 Miles," a pop version of a traditional mountain song, and "Four Strong Winds," a lonesome love song dealing with Canadian migratory workers, he revealed his affinity for the urban folk style. Songs like these, while commercially advantageous to Bare, also reinvigorated the story-telling tradition in country music and moved the music a bit closer to its roots.

Another offshoot of the urban folk revival, and a phenomenon which contributed to the reinvigoration of country music, was the so-called saga song. Although similar in some ways to the event ballad of the twenties, the saga song was greatly different in its depiction of completely fictional episodes or remote historical events. Only rarely did the saga song describe events of contemporary significance. Such songs were clearly inspired by the success in 1958 of the Kingston Trio's "Tom Dooley." For several months the airwaves were filled with both pop and country songs about mythical and real heroes who gained fame or notoriety during America's pioneer period.

In the recording of the saga songs Columbia Records played a preeminent role. In late 1958 and early 1959 a variety of saga songs appeared, most of them in Columbia's 41300 Series, which suggests that someone in the Columbia offices was alive to the immediate commercial advantages of the pseudo-historical song. The series was inaugurated by Johnny Horton's "Springtime in Alaska," a ballad in the Robert Stewart Service tradition, which related the story of a prospector killed in a tavern brawl in the Klondike. To the delight of dyed-in-the-wool country fans, this ballad, performed with simple string accompaniment, attained the number one position on the country music charts and remained for several weeks against the competition of country-pop numbers.

"Springtime in Alaska" was followed soon after by the release of Johnny Cash's "Don't Take Your Guns to Town," an account of a young cowboy who disregarded his mother's warnings and was killed when he ventured into town. Cash followed this best-selling song with several songs about cowboys and Indians ("Old Apache Squaw," "The Ballad of Boot Hill," etc.), themes which he would return to again and again in the mid-sixties.

The most notable success won by a country saga song came in 1959 when Johnny Horton recorded "The Battle of New Orleans." The ballad first appeared in a 1958 album recorded by Jimmie Driftwood (James Morris), an Arkansas folklorist and schoolteacher who had written the song as a device to teach history to his students. Driftwood set the lyrics about Andrew Jackson's famous victory to an old hillbilly fiddle tune, "The Eighth of January," which had commemorated the event. Horton's version, considerably shorter than Driftwood's, first appeared on a Columbia record in April 1959 and by June of that year had vaulted to the position of number one song in the nation.

A native of Tyler, Texas, Horton was only a moderately successful honky-tonk singer and barn dance performer (the *Hometown Jamboree* and *Louisiana Hayride*) until he recorded "Honky-Tonk Man" in 1956. This dance-hall classic, with a modest rockabilly beat, gave Horton a national reputation, but it was only a dim suggestion of the diversity of his talents. Performing as "the Singing Fisherman" because of his highly acclaimed skill as a professional angler, Horton showed the ability to perform almost any kind of song, from a romantic tune like "All for the Love of a Girl" to a raucous novelty like "Ole Slewfoot." He was also the performer par excellence of the saga song. For a year and a half following the huge success of "The Battle of New Orleans," Horton recorded such songs as "Sink the Bismarck," "Johnny Reb," and "The Battle of Bull Run." Under the tutelage of his manager and bass player, Tillman Franks, who later had similar success with Claude King and David Houston, Horton seemed assured of a long and glittering career. But country music suffered a tragic loss on the night of November 5, 1960, when Horton was killed in an automobile collision near the small town of Milano, Texas. An ironic feature of the tragedy was that Horton's wife was left a widow for the second time; she had been the second wife of Hank Williams.

Several historical, or folkish, songs which had varying degrees of success were issued in 1959, but none approached "The Battle of New Orleans" in popularity. They included Carl Smith's "Ten Thousand Drums" and Hawkshaw Hawkins' "Soldier's Joy," both pseudo-revolutionary-war songs, although the latter was set to the melody of a famous old fiddle tune, and Eddy Arnold's "Tennessee Stud," another classic Jimmie Driftwood composition which has become a staple of Doc Watson's repertory. Of all the folkish ballads of the period, "The Long Black Veil," recorded by Lefty Frizzell, gave evidence of the strongest durability and most widespread appeal. Written by Marijohn Wilkin and Danny Dill, this ghostly song of death and mistaken identity was a vehicle for Frizzell's return to the popularity charts and was eventually recorded by a diverse group of performers ranging all the way from the Country Gentlemen, a bluegrass group, to Joan Baez, an urban-folk performer, and John Anderson, a modern honky-tonk revivalist.

In late 1959 the saga-song craze subsided somewhat, but the trend continued spasmodically in the following years with the appearance of albums and occasional singles devoted to fictional narratives or historical events. Some of these songs enjoyed extensive popularity. Marty Robbins, for example, in 1959 wrote and recorded a song which rivaled the success gained earlier that year by "The Battle of New Orleans." This was "El Paso," a meticulously crafted ballad with a Mexican flavor, which tells of a man who was killed fighting for the love of his border-tavern sweetheart. Impeccably sung by Robbins, it was one of many cowboy songs, both old and recently composed, which he recorded and included in his concerts. Television personality Jimmy Dean enjoyed similar success with a couple of songs in 1961 and 1962 which told dramatic stories. "Big John" told the story of a huge miner who gave his life to save his fellow workers, while "PT 109" chronicled the wartime exploits of John F. Kennedy. At least two other hit songs, Claude King's "Wolverton Mountain" in 1962 and Lefty Frizzell's "Saginaw, Michigan" in 1964, were humorous ballads which dealt with fictional characters and incidents. They were major commercial successes, and welcome signs that the narrative impulse had not vanished from country music.

Throughout the early sixties other songs and singers periodically appeared that suggested the healthy revitalization of older country music. In 1960 one of the veterans of country music, Lloyd "Cowboy" Copas, recorded for the Starday label an old ragtime-style song which he renamed "Alabam." This was essentially a reworking of Frank Hutchison's "Coney Isle," but it was made distinctive, and commercially appealing, by Copas' clean and crisp flat-picking, a talent that few fans knew he possessed. The song was number one on *Billboard*'s country charts for twelve consecutive weeks and marked the beginning of renewed popularity for Copas which lasted until his death on March 5, 1963. Fans of "hard country" music, as the older styles were now increasingly called, were also thrilled in early 1963 by Carl and Pearl Butler's "Don't Let Me Cross Over," a pure country song in lyrics and style of performance. Carl Butler's Tennessee mountain roots were strongly displayed in his full-throated, emotional singing, and his stylistic debts to Roy Acuff and the Bailes Brothers were apparent and proudly admitted. Carl and Pearl's duet singing sparked the revitalization of male-female harmonizing, a style that has since become common in country music (Porter Wagoner and Dolly Parton, Conway Twitty and Loretta Lynn, David Frizzell and Shelly West, and many others).

Nineteen sixty-three was a good year for hard country music. The popular television situation comedy *The Beverly Hillbillies* gave "The Ballad of Jed Clampett" the exposure it needed to become number one on *Billboard*'s country charts. This was a rare accomplishment for a bluegrass song, but its performers, Flatt and Scruggs, were richly deserving of the fame and profit they received. Hawkshaw Hawkins' untimely death in March 1963 certainly contributed to the commercial success of his "Lonesome 7-7203," which topped the charts in May and June of that year. But the reward was long overdue for the West Virginia–born Hawkins; his rich, smooth voice had long been one of the best in country music, but superstardom had generally eluded him. For Bobby Bare, on the other hand, 1963 marked the real beginning of his long and successful career. In that year he recorded one of the great standards of country music, "Detroit City," a song that effectively expresses the loneliness and homesickness felt by rural southerners in the industrial North. Although it contained a few faint echoes of urban folk music—particularly in its melody—the song made few concessions to the pop-country sound. Even less compromising in style was another recording of that year, "We Must Have Been Out of Our Minds." The song combined the talents of two of America's premier hard country singers, George Jones and Melba Montgomery, and featured the interplay of dobro and pedal steel guitar.

George Jones was at the center of a honky-tonk resurgence in the early sixties that stretched from his native Texas to California. These years marked the maturing of the vocal style that would make him one of the legendary singers of country music. Jones was born on September 12, 1931, in Saratoga, Texas, in the midst of a heavily forested area known as the Big Thicket, and very near the sites of some of Texas' earliest oilfields. His working-class parents represented the moral and social dichotomy that often surfaced in rural southern families: his hard-working father (a log truck driver, an oil worker, a shipyard worker) often sought solace from disappointment and poverty in music and the bottle; his mother, on the other hand, found her comfort in sobriety and fundamentalist religion. George absorbed traits from both parents, a love for music from both of them, but, unfortunately, a fatal weakness for whiskey from his father. He sang in his mother's church (the Full Gospel Tabernacle Church in Kountze, Texas), but the songs of the radio were much more appealing. He listened faithfully to the *Grand Ole Opry* and found his first heroes in

Bill Monroe and Roy Acuff. Acuff's influence was powerful in the singing of the early George Jones, and even today one can hear a trace of the Acuff sound, especially in Jones' phrasing on high notes.

The Jones family moved to Beaumont in 1942, following the lure of war-related jobs in that industrial sector of Southeast Texas. As thousands of rural Texas families poured into cities like Beaumont, Port Arthur, Texas City, and Houston in search of defense work, the country music–honky-tonk culture expanded to exploit their needs and satisfy their desires. Jones was not old enough to be a regular participant in this dance-hall culture, but he learned the songs that issued from it, and he developed an unquenchable desire to be a professional singer. In about 1943, when he was only twelve years old, Jones began singing on the streets of Beaumont, or anywhere that a crowd was willing to listen. A charming photograph from this period shows a serious, tow-headed youngster walking along a Beaumont street and strumming a guitar.[5] From this point on nothing but music could satisfy Jones, and by the time he was fourteen he was per-forming on radio stations in and near Beaumont. In 1948 he fell under the spell of Hank Williams, and that great singer became the kind of model and inspiration that Bill Monroe and Roy Acuff had earlier been. During a two-year stint in the Marines, from November 1951 to November 1953, Jones continued to sing as often as he could, particularly at a dance hall in Redwood City, California, near Camp Pendleton. When he returned to Beaumont, he was ready to begin his full-time professional career.

In January 1954, Jones made his first recordings for Starday, a company only recently organized in Beaumont by Jack Starnes and Harold W. "Pappy" Daily. The early Starday records were made at Starnes' residence in Beaumont, and they provided a wonderful means of exposure for the wealth of talent which played in the area from Louisiana through South-east Texas to Houston (the label's first big hit was "Y'all Come," written and recorded by former Texas schoolteacher and long-time radio person-ality Arlie [Arleigh] Duff). Jones' first recordings, "No Money in This Deal" and "You're in My Heart," were rollicking and slow respectively, an accu-rate prophecy of the alternating styles he would feature for the rest of his career. A 1955 release, "Why Baby Why," made the national popularity charts, but Red Sovine and Webb Pierce's duet version was more suc-cessful. Nevertheless, Jones became sufficiently known and appreciated to be named to the cast of the *Louisiana Hayride*, where he stayed for three months before moving on to the *Grand Ole Opry* in August 1956. By 1957 he had followed his producer and manager Pappy Daily to the larger Mer-cury label, and there he began carving out his own identity while making

5. The photograph appears on the cover of an lp, *The Best of George Jones*, Epic KE33352, and in Dolly Carlisle, *Ragged but Right: The Life and Times of George Jones* (Chicago: Contemporary Publications, 1984).

the first of his classic honky-tonk recordings. Under Daily's constant admonition to "sing like George Jones," he began casting off most of the vocal mannerisms borrowed from other singers. In turn, he developed the intense and unique style that has enthralled a generation of listeners. For the two or three minutes consumed by a song, Jones immerses himself so completely in its lyrics, and in the mood it conveys, that the listener can scarcely avoid becoming similarly involved.

Although Jones has excelled in the performance of uptempoed, novelty songs, such as "White Lightning" (his first number one *Billboard* hit), "Who Shot Sam," and "The Race Is On," his real strength is displayed in slower songs, particularly in the heart-wrenching complaints of unrequited or broken love. Some of his most powerful performances in this vein came in 1957 and 1958 when he recorded "Don't Stop the Music," "Just One More," and "Color of the Blues." Jones' searing emotional singing on these songs was almost undisciplined in its passion, but one could hear the stylistic traits that have made him famous: the alternating low moans and high wails, the bending and lengthening of notes to almost incredible lengths, and the enunciation of words either with rounded, open-throated precision or through clenched teeth.

Jones' first real dominance in country music came in the early sixties. He now sang typically in a lower and fuller register, and his managers began adding background voices and lusher instrumental accompaniment to his recordings. But no matter how full and engulfing these accoutrements might be, they could not blunt or hide his distinctiveness. He remained a hard country singer. Beginning with "The Window Up Above" in April 1960 and extending on through the sixties with an almost unending stream of hits such as "Tender Years," "She Thinks I Still Care," "A Girl I Used to Know," and "Walk through This World with Me," Jones strengthened his popular appeal and solidified his reputation as "a singer's singer," winning the admiration of singers as disparate as Waylon Jennings, Elvis Costello, Emmylou Harris, James Taylor, and Merle Haggard.

George Jones' great Texas contemporary, Ray Price, has not been quite so enduring in his faithfulness to hard country styles. Since the mid-sixties he has increasingly cast his lot with the country-pop fashion that he had earlier so resolutely resisted. Nevertheless, during the rockabilly and early country-pop years Price almost singlehandedly kept the hard country torch aflame and, in so doing, virtually created an industry of musicians who either wrote or played for him. He and his Cherokee Cowboys also created a form of music, a highly electrified and infectiously rhythmic honky-tonk style, that won them a legion of fans and was the envy of musicians everywhere.

Price was born near the East Texas community of Perryville in 1926, but he grew up in Dallas. His intentions of becoming a veterinarian were abandoned when he left North Texas Agricultural College (now the University of Texas at Arlington) in 1949 to pursue a career in music. He had already combined singing with student life, having sung in local clubs and on a radio barn dance in Abilene, Texas, in 1948. Like so many other American youth, Price was mesmerized by the music of Hank Williams, and his resolve to be a full-time professional was strengthened. From 1949 to 1950 he appeared regularly on the *Big D Jamboree* and made his first recordings for Bullet, a small label in Nashville. In 1951 he began his association with Columbia Records and became close friends with Hank Williams, a relationship that led to his being signed by the *Grand Ole Opry* in January 1952.

In these early professional years, and virtually up to 1956, Price's performing style was very close to that of his mentor, Williams, and he recorded at least one song, "Weary Blues," which the Alabama legend had written for him. Price toured briefly with Williams' band, the Drifting Cowboys, before organizing his own group, the Cherokee Cowboys. Although he was never merely a carbon copy of Williams, the first dramatic evidence of a truly original Ray Price sound came with his recording in 1956 of "Crazy Arms." Written by the inventive California steel guitarist Ralph Mooney, the song was a hit of major proportions for Price, a refreshing reassertion of hard-core country music at a time of rockabilly ascendancy, and a vehicle for the introduction of Price's shuffle-beat sound into country music.

In song after song—such as "City Lights," "My Shoes Keep Walking Back to You," "I've Got a New Heartache," "The Same Old Me," and "Invitation to the Blues"—Price adhered to an exciting and commercially winning formula. The pedal steel guitar and fiddles (played in the single-string rather than double-stop style) almost always took the lead passages, while a shuffling drum beat and an electric walking bass laid down a rhythm that no dancer could resist. The style drew some of its inspiration from Bob Wills, but it was made more distinctive through the thorough electrification of instruments, including the fiddles, in the Cherokee Cowboys' band. Vocally, the sound was dominated by Price's expressive singing and by the duet harmony that was almost always heard on the choruses of his songs (an innovation introduced to honky-tonk music by Price and George Jones). The style translated beautifully to phonograph recordings, but its proper milieu was the dance hall where would-be cowboys and cowgirls clung tightly to each other, following the electric, pulsating beat of the music, as Price's songs of hurt and disappointment insinuated themselves into their consciousness.

Price's music touched the lives of millions of plain people who knew the singer only through his songs. It also financially enriched the lives of many professionals who developed a working relationship with Price. Virtually every major songwriter from the mid-fifties up to the early seventies supplied songs to Price, and many of them, in fact, began building their reputations through the exposure that he gave their songs. Roger Miller, Bill Anderson, Harlan Howard, Hank Cochran, Mel Tillis, Willie Nelson, and Kris Kristofferson comprised only a portion of the roster of songwriters who profited from Price's great popularity. The roster of Cherokee Cowboys alumni also reads like a "Who's Who" of great country musicians. Price was once asked, after leaving the honky-tonk style for the more sedate field of country-pop, why he did not bring the Cherokee Cowboys back together. His reply that he could not afford them[6] becomes more understandable when it is recalled that at one time or another such musicians as Roger Miller, Willie Nelson, Johnny Paycheck (who was then known as Donnie Young), Johnny Bush, and Buddy Emmons were employees of Price. There is no way, of course, to document the number of musicians, unsung and otherwise, who were influenced by the Ray Price sound. On occasion, hit records appeared, such as the Wilburn Brothers' "Which One Is to Blame" (1959) and Mel Tillis' "Heart over Mind" (1970), which bore the obvious marks of Price's shuffle beat; and in dance halls throughout the country, especially in Price's native Texas, singers like Johnny Bush, Darrell McCall, and Tony Booth even yet perform in fashions reminiscent of the Cherokee Cowboy. The survival of the Ray Price honky-tonk sound among numerous disciples, great and small, is all the more remarkable given the fact that Price himself abandoned the style long ago. Price gradually lowered his singing voice to a more relaxed crooning register—one more appropriate to the supper club atmosphere he now favors. Most crucial, the pedal steel guitar and fiddles were replaced with the easy-listening sound of a string section and muted guitars. Price had experimented with the pop approach as early as 1957 in a religious album that featured the accompaniment of the Anita Kerr Singers and seventeen violins. "Burning Memories," in 1964, a good honky-tonk song written by Mel Tillis, aroused the ire of many traditionalists with its choral background and modest use of strings. Price's real transition to pop music, however, came in 1967 when he recorded "Danny Boy" with the backing of a forty-seven-piece orchestra. To the regret of many of his old-time fans, who felt disappointed if not betrayed, Price thereafter remained in the country-pop field. In 1970 he demonstrated his commercial mastery of that genre, too, when he recorded the first of several chart-making country-pop songs, "For the Good Times."

As Ray Price made his own personal and individualistic odyssey, the dynamic honky-tonk style that he had done so much to create and popularize continued to mature and evolve. Out on the West Coast important young musicians made crucial contributions that helped to fuel the hard country revival of the mid-sixties. The "California sound," as it came to be called,

6. Tom Ayres, "Ray Price Remembers Hank Williams," *Country Music* 5, no. 12 (September 1977): 56.

was the product of a coterie of musicians who often played together in the large number of clubs that dotted the landscape of the state. Ray Price influenced the musicians of California with his shuffle beat and high-duet choruses, but his style of fiddling had a lesser impact. Instead, California honky-tonk music was distinguished by the clarity and high-decibel sound of its electric and pedal steel guitarists. This was the sound, in fact, that guitarist Joe Maphis was thinking about when he wrote "Dim Lights, Thick Smoke, and Loud, Loud Music." Old-timers like Maphis, Jimmy Bryant, and Speedy West had originally set the standards to which the younger musicians aspired, but in the late fifties and early sixties such guitarists as James Burton, Roy Nichols, Buck Owens, Ralph Mooney, and Tom Brumley, who had grown up listening to both rock-and-roll and country music, set their own special brands upon the developing music. Turning the volume of their Fender Telecaster guitars to an almost ear-splitting pitch, the guitarists played a single-string style that often featured sharp, staccato phrases known as "chicken picking." The overall result was a crisp, sparkling, electronic sound with an infectious beat.

Although Los Angeles played the most important role in the formation of the California sound—because of its powerful radio stations, its active club scene, and the presence there of Capitol Records—its leadership was seriously challenged by Bakersfield. It was only fitting that Bakersfield should exert a strong influence. As an oil and cotton center in the San Joaquin Valley, it had attracted in the thirties a heavy migration of Okies who had transplanted their love for rural music to California soil. By the early fifties a rash of honky-tonks provided a steady supply of country music for the working folk of the city. Musicians like Ferlin Husky and Tommy Collins worked in and out of the city for short periods, while such bandleaders as Billy Mize and Bill Woods built more permanent bases as house musicians in various clubs during the fifties. Woods was an employer and father-figure for many of the young musicians who congregated in Bakersfield.

It was as a guitarist in the Bill Woods Band that Buck Owens made his entrance into the Bakersfield music scene. Alvis Edgar "Buck" Owens was born in Sherman, Texas, in 1929, but he grew up in Mesa, Arizona, where he had his first radio experience as a mandolin and guitar player. Owens moved to Bakersfield in 1951 and began working for Bill Woods and for other country musicians. He also became a busy sessions musician for Capitol Records, even though such work required frequent trips to Hollywood, about one hundred miles away. Owens was exclusively a sideman during the early fifties, and he was the lead guitarist on many of Tommy Collins' hit records during that period. Collins, whose real name was Leonard Raymond Sipes, wrote and recorded such successful songs as "You Better Not Do That," "You Gotta Have a License," and "High on a Hilltop."

Owens was not content to be a sideman, and he made his first solo recordings for a small label, Pep, in 1956. By 1958 he had joined the prestigious Capitol label and, beginning with "Above and Beyond," was soon one of the hottest commercial properties of the period. Owens sang with a pleading tenor voice and was joined on the choruses of songs by the even higher tenor sound of his fiddler-guitarist, Don Rich. Despite Owens' own background as a guitarist, he delegated most of the lead guitar work to Rich, who became one of the vital ingredients in the shaping of the Buck Owens sound. The steel guitar work on the early Buck Owens recordings was done by Ralph Mooney, an alumnus of Wynn Stewart's popular band and now a member of Waylon Jennings' group, the Waylors. During the peak years of Owens' popularity, however, his steel guitarist was Tom Brumley, a son of the famous gospel composer Albert E. Brumley, Owens and his band, the Buckaroos, created a sound that had the hard edge of honky-tonk and the bounce of rockabilly. It proved to be a remarkably winning composite. Few singers have had the consistent string of hit records that Owens produced in the sixties. During the decade, nineteen of his songs, including one instrumental, "Buckaroo," reached the number one position on the *Billboard* popularity charts. Although he recorded an occasional sad song, such as "Second Fiddle" or "Excuse Me, I Think I've Got a Heartache," his biggest successes were lively, upbeat numbers like "Act Naturally," novelties like "Who's Gonna Mow Your Grass," or slow songs expressing affirmative or successful love such as "Together Again."

Owens was highly visible during the sixties, first on his own syndicated television show, the *Buck Owens Ranch*, and then as co-host of *Hee Haw*, which was seen on over two hundred stations. He was such a dominating presence in American music that, in a euphoric moment in 1965, he took out a full-page ad in the leading music magazines expressing his undying loyalty to country music and pledging to perform no other style.[7] Like most pledges, it was eventually broken. But for several years during the sixties the music of Buck Owens and the Buckaroos blew like a breath of sparkling fresh air over the country music landscape, reinvigorating hard country enthusiasts with its sharp, clearly delineated string band sound, its high-hard harmony, and the absence of vocal choruses. Owens' musicianship was so profitable that he branched out into other areas, establishing a publishing house, acquiring radio and television stations and real estate, and assuming the promotion of other acts such as the Hager Twins, his son Buddy Alan, Doyle Holley, and an instrumental group called the Bakersfield Brass. His holdings and investments became so extensive that some people began referring to Bakersfield as "Buckersfield."

It is poetically appropriate that the biggest superstar of all to emerge from the California firmament should be a product of Bakersfield. Merle

7. Owens' pledge was first carried in *Music City News* 2, no. 9 (March 1965): 5.

Haggard was born near the city in 1937, only two years after his parents migrated from Checotah, Oklahoma. His parents had met at an Oklahoma country dance, but his devout Church of Christ mother soon put a damper on such worldly merriment and on the fiddling of which her husband was so fond. Haggard has always cherished fond memories of the father whose musical gifts he inherited, but, unfortunately, their ties were severed by his father's death in 1946. Haggard grew up in a converted boxcar, a restless, wandering child whose mother had neither the time nor the power to control him. He eventually documented these early experiences in "Hungry Eyes," a testimonial to his hard-working parents and their Okie contemporaries, and in "Mama Tried," a tribute to his mother's love and sacrifice.

Mama's efforts were indeed in vain, and Haggard drifted into a life of petty juvenile delinquency, and from there into detention homes and reform school. He eventually wound up in San Quentin Prison in 1956, only nineteen years old and seemingly with a permanently blighted life. Haggard, however, had not totally wasted his young years; he began perfecting his musical skills as a teenager, and he continued to pick and sing during his prison years. When he was released in 1960, he began trying to support a wife and growing family (one of several unsuccessful marriages) by working at odd jobs and playing at night and on weekends in the Bakersfield honky-tonks (the High Pockets, Blackboard, Lucky Spot, Barrel House). As with many fledgling singers, Haggard's early sound reflected the styles of older performers, particularly those of his hero Lefty Frizzell and of Wynn Stewart, who was one of the most popular club performers on the West Coast.

Wynn Stewart gave Haggard his first big break as a professional performer. A native of Morrisville, Missouri, Stewart had a very successful stint as singer and bandleader for three years at the Nashville Nevada Club in Las Vegas. An occasional hit record on the Capitol label—such as "Waltz of the Angels," "Keeper of the Key," and "Wishful Thinking"—also contributed to his commercial viability and to his reputation among musicians who sought positions in his very prosperous band. Haggard began playing bass for Stewart in 1962 and also began singing an occasional number when the bandleader took breaks. In January 1963, Haggard recorded on the Tally label a song written by Stewart called "Sing a Sad Song," and it became his first chart-making record (he had signed with the small California label in 1961, but had had only modest success). In April 1964 he had an even bigger hit with Liz Anderson's "All My Friends Are Gonna Be Strangers," a song which named his band—the Strangers—and led to his signing with Capitol Records.

Haggard's commercial progress to 1967 was steady but unspectacular, and his first real recognition came from his West Coast colleagues in the Academy of Country and Western Music who voted him most promising male vocalist in 1966 and best male vocalist in 1967. The California-based organization also voted Haggard and Bonnie Owens the best duet act in country music for three consecutive years, 1965–1967. The year 1967 proved to be the beginning of a period of rapid ascent for Haggard, largely because he discovered the commercial potential of his prison record. His convict experience was rarely mentioned in his early promotional litera-ture, but after 1967 it became a central theme in most stories dealing with Haggard, and it began to dominate the story line of many of his songs. The distorted stories dealing with Johnny Cash's alleged prison rec-ord—he had actually spent only two days in jail because of minor infrac-tions—may have reminded Haggard of the age-old public fascination with badmen. More likely, the success of one of Haggard's recordings, "I'm a Lonesome Fugitive," convinced him that a market existed for songs about outlaws, convicts, and prison life. The song was written by Liz Anderson and may have been inspired by a popular television series called *The Fugitive*. Whatever its source, it became Haggard's first number one re-cording. This song was followed in the next couple of years by "Branded Man," "Sing Me Back Home," "Legend of Bonnie and Clyde," and "Mama Tried" (the theme of a little-known movie named *Killers Three*), all dealing with prison/bad-guy themes, all number one songs, and all written by Haggard.

Another factor, then, in Haggard's vault toward stardom was the blossom-ing of his writing abilities. He has shown great sensitivity and skill in his treatment of a wide variety of topics, ranging from prisons and ex-convicts to disappointed lovers and truck drivers. His simple and direct language, homely metaphors, and preoccupation with the lives of plain, everyday folk evoke comparisons with Woody Guthrie and lead some observers to describe him as the "poet of the common man." Unlike Woody Guthrie's subjects, though, Haggard's common man is a middle-class worker who, while sometimes unemployed as in "If We Make It through December," works hard, drinks beer, rejects welfare, takes a dim view of reformers, and supports his country right or wrong. Haggard's compassion comes through most strongly in areas that touch upon his own life, or upon his family's history. Like Johnny Cash, who seems to have influenced him greatly, Haggard is fascinated with the thirties, and hoboes, railroad bums, and migratory workers frequently appear in his songs. "Hungry Eyes" presents Haggard at his most poetic and compassionate best; it will prob-ably stand the test of time as his greatest song. Unlike the modern workers he applauds, the characters described in "Hungry Eyes" work hard but do not succeed. In "Grandma Harp" and "The Roots of My Raising," Haggard lovingly discusses people and places that were central to his youth and to his parents' past, and in "They're Tearing the Labor Camps Down," he comments on the passing of an institution that made life bearable for many of California's Okies (about the closest he has ever come to endorsing government social legislation).

Although Haggard has been more preoccupied with social and historical topics than most writers, he has not ignored the other subjects that comprise the country music repertory. There has been no better statement of unrequited love than "Today I Started Loving You Again," while "Sing Me Back Home," ostensibly a prison song, is really a poignant evocation of the nostalgic power of music. The beer-drinking genre is well represented by such songs as "The Bottle Let Me Down" and "Swinging Doors," and alcoholism, the other side of the coin, is the subject matter of the beautiful "I Threw Away the Rose." And even in the often-hackneyed area of truck-driving music Haggard has risen well above the norm: "Movin' On" captures the aggressive excitement of long-distance trucking, while "White Line Fever" portrays its weariness. All in all, Haggard's songs typify country song writing at its best.

Any emphasis on Haggard's writing should not obscure the fact of his superb musicianship. As a singer he has few peers, and as an instrumentalist and band leader he has exhibited continual growth and inventiveness over a period of twenty years and more. Haggard moved away quickly from the early imitativeness that most young singers display, although a trace of Lefty Frizzell still lingers in his phrasing and in his nasally resonant vibrato. Haggard can sound sweet and smooth, as he did on "Sing a Sad Song" in 1963, but he can also, if the occasion calls for it, sound raucous, harsh, or strident. Few singers have had such suppleness of voice. Although he has forged his own unique style, Haggard remains loyal to his sources. Tribute albums and songs dedicated to Jimmie Rodgers, Bob Wills, and Lefty Frizzell attest to his respect for the giants of country music, while "Bill Woods of Bakersfield" and "Leonard" (about his old friend Tommy Collins) are loving recollections of two men who supported him in his early career. Haggard's admiration for Bob Wills sparked his interest in Emmett Miller, the minstrel-blues singer who influenced both Wills and Tommy Duncan. Most important of all, the interest in Wills has affected the total instrumental sound favored by Haggard and the Strangers. The Strangers once played classic California-style honky-tonk music, a style marked by the pedal steel work of Norman Hamlett and the searing, blues-tinged phrasing of electric guitarist Roy Nichols. The Strangers now include a retinue of horns along with the traditional string instruments, and they play what Haggard describes as "country jazz." Haggard himself has mastered the fiddle, a rare accomplishment for an adult musician, and he regularly includes Bob Wills songs in his concerts. Merle Haggard's emergence in the sixties was a development of major significance for country music in that he contributed to both its economic resurgence and its stylistic revitalization. His creativity as an artist and musician was well

Porter Wagoner and Dolly Parton (*front*) with the Wagonmasters: *left to right*, Spec Rhodes, Buck Trent, unknown, Mac Magaha, unknown, Don Warden. Photograph courtesy of the Country Music Foundation Library and Media Center, Nashville, Tennessee.

George Jones (*left*) and Merle Haggard. Photograph courtesy of the Country Music Foundation Library and Media Center, Nashville, Tennessee.

within the traditional framework he respected. He demonstrated that one could be simultaneously hard country and commercial.

Merle Haggard's career as a man who writes most of the songs he sings is not an unusual one. Country music has been blessed with an abundance of singer-songwriters. They, and the writers who have tried to parlay their craft into a full-time profession, have been responsible for much of the growth and general acceptance that country music has enjoyed since World War II. With some striking exceptions, the writers have been southern-born men and women from rural or working-class backgrounds who draw upon their own experiences and observations to paint musical portraits of popular and commercial appeal. Increasingly, however, these experiences have come to be much like those known by people elsewhere. Thrown into a common crucible of military service and war, provided with expanded educational opportunities, and exposed to television and other homogenizing aspects of industrial capitalism, Americans everywhere have exhibited a growing sameness of life. As musicians, country writers have heard and absorbed much from the other musical forms that have swelled around them, and such writers as Bob Dylan and Paul Simon have sometimes served as conscious models. Furthermore, the lure of the crossover record has often tantalized writers into seeking that which is broadly popular and commercial.

Nevertheless, the country songwriters have not been merely borrowers. They have had much to say that is fresh and original. Like their contemporaries, the southern novelists, they have retained a sense of place that is refreshing in an age of ceaseless change and dislocation. Although there is no evidence that William Faulkner ever recognized any kinship with the tunesmiths who proliferated around him, like the great Mississippi novelist, they have always shown skill at "teasing the universal out of the particular."[8] They may write about Carolina cottonfields or long, hot Texas roads, but they touch sensitive chords that run to the hearts of everyone, and the "Green, Green Grass of Home" and "Harper Valley PTA" could be anywhere in the United States.

The country writers have been part of the audience for whom they write. Although that audience has changed vastly in the recent past, it has been basically working class with middle-class aspirations. Country song lyrics have been realistic in that they concern themselves with the petty details of human existence; they can therefore be as inconsistent and contradictory as the people whose values they project. They describe life as it is, not as one might wish it would be.

Country songs, therefore, show little consciousness of history, but in-

---

8. The phrase was used by William C. Martin in his essay "Tom T. Hall," in *Stars of Country Music*, edited by Bill C. Malone and Judith McCulloh (Urbana: University of Illinois Press, 1975), p. 399.

stead tend to be intensely nostalgic. Private recollections of the past, often distorted by time and colored by romanticism or sentimentality (or put to the service of some present prejudice), appear frequently in country songs. Unpleasant remembrances of the past, as in Dallas Frazier's "California Cottonfields," Dolly Parton's "In the Good Old Days When Times Were Bad," or Johnny Cash's "Five Feet High and Rising," sometimes comprise the subject matter of country songs, but most writers cannot resist the temptation to cloak their songs with a veneer of romanticism that stresses the redemptive qualities of love that transcends suffering. In recalling her childhood as the daughter of a Kentucky coal miner, Loretta Lynn reminds her listeners that "We were poor but we had love." [9]

Familial love of this type lay at the center of the traditional scheme of values celebrated in country songs. While such precepts are often violated in both life and lyrics (home is abandoned, church is forsaken, laws are broken, husbands and wives separate, parents are neglected, etc.), the old-time code of conduct is nevertheless endorsed with great fervor. Familiar social relations, especially between men and women and adults and children, are reaffirmed. Male dominance is taken for granted in country songs, even though men often seem rendered helpless by love unfulfilled or gone wrong. Traditional morality and the belief in the certainty of punishments and rewards are stressed, and even the sins most often discussed in country lyrics—drinking and cheating—are "traditional" transgressions, although the latter did not become a major preoccupation of country lyrics until the late forties.

Country lyrics have remained profoundly topical. Event songs, as such, are not as common today as they were in the twenties, and writers are now more likely to concentrate on reactions to such phenomena as automation or war than on the concrete incidents themselves. Nevertheless, an occasional song such as "PT 109" or "Ballad of the Green Berets" climbs into the charts, and ballads commenting on current events, such as the Kennedy assassination and school integration, appear with great frequency on small record labels. The grand master of the modern event song, Red River Dave McEnery, who has written on such subjects as "Amelia Earhart's Last Flight" and the "Ballad of Emmett Till," still turns out reams of topical material dealing with everything from Watergate to the kidnapping of Patricia Hearst. Most writers, however, shun such explicit data and instead discuss general perceptions of the confusing world that forever seems to crowd around the "common man."

Although topicality is a major concern of country songs, the songwriters usually eschew explicit political identification. Like country musicians as a whole, they tend to be apolitical. Occasional songs complain about wel-

9. Loretta Lynn, "Coal Miner's Daughter," heard on the lp of the same name, MCA10.

fare programs or the Internal Revenue Service, and a few songs have circulated which criticize political corruption (as in the Watergate affair) or
Reaganomics. But both mainstream country and bluegrass writers endorse
establishment political positions, particularly in the realm of foreign affairs,
and take a dim view of organized dissent. While country music's identification with national establishment norms reflects the changing political
moods of the sixties and early seventies and is an indication of the conservatism of its audience and of the urge for "respectability" within the industry, this embracing of the status quo is a recent phenomenon. The 250,000
southerners who died in rebellion against the United States government
from 1861 to 1865 are dramatic reminders that political orthodoxy was not
always considered a virtue in southern culture.

Politics has actually been of minor concern to the country writers. Compassion, on the other hand, and even tolerance for many of the foibles of
humanity, have been motivating impulses behind a multitude of country
songs. Neglected old people, abandoned or mistreated children, and homeless hoboes and derelicts have always figured prominently in country
songs. Drunkards are often treated with humor or scorn, but they are also
made the objects of pity or sympathy. Some socially peripheral types have
received sympathetic treatment in country lyrics. The condemned prisoner
of "Sing Me Back Home," the prostitute in "The Son of Hickory Holler's
Tramp," the black river tramp of "Catfish John," and the emotionally dis-
turbed woman in "Delta Dawn" are recent examples of antisocial characters who have drawn the compassion of country writers. Clearly, there has
been virtually no political intent behind such concern. "Catfish John," for
example, is idealized, not because he is black, but because he is a worldly
wise old man who introduces a white boy to the joys of primitive river life.
Country songwriters recognize and exploit the poetic appeal of such characters; seldom do they suggest that they be made the objects of public or
legislative action.

Country songs, then, frequently exude compassion, but are rarely liberal in any conventionally defined sense. Johnny Cash in 1964 recorded an
album devoted to the plight of American Indians which contained both his
own compositions and those of other writers such as Peter LaFarge; but,
despite his reputation as "the Man in Black" (a sign of mourning for
the injustices of the world), Cash gave no meaningful support to any
of the other liberal crusades of the decade. Occasional country songs, such
as "Harper Valley, PTA," defend unconventional lifestyles (but not to the
point of homosexuality or, usually, free love), and for five weeks in early
1968 a didactic song called "Skip a Rope" held the number one position on
Billboard's country charts. This song was an indictment of parents who
set bad examples for their children by such acts as cheating on their income taxes and practicing racial discrimination. Country songs do sometimes protest—against job harassment or insecurity, hypocritical church-

goers, the high cost of living, declining moral standards, and a multitude of private ills and frustrations—but they generally remain skeptical of organized human solutions.

In country music individuals are usually left alone to confront life. The failures are many, and some people surrender to become "Driftwood on the River" or rolling stones on the "Lost Highway." In despair or frustration some turn to the bottle, often finding temporary relief, but occasionally becoming a "prisoner to drink" ("Warm Red Wine") or finding their lives "Out of Control." Some men are "Almost Persuaded" by the charms of honky-tonk temptresses; others succumb to the lure of "The Other Woman"; while most yearn for the security and permanence of "A Good Woman's Love." The rambling life and the open road continue to be attractive options for country song protagonists. Truck-driving song popularity can be understood, in part, as an identification with a group who are perceived as exercising power (if only over a machine) while also enjoying the freedom of mobility. The related machismo urge, of course, is also strongly displayed in country lyrics. The tough guy pose, or the image of a man who enjoys complete mastery over women (if nothing else), is presumably a motif that appeals to both men and women. Another venerable impulse which persists in country music is the desire to go back home—to a place that is comfortable because it is familiar—or to a mythical community like "Rocky Top, Tennessee," where life and cares are simpler and more manageable. In song lyrics, as well as in the real life they attempt to portray, individuals often discover that their strength and will are feeble weapons in the battle against loneliness and pain; they therefore seek the solace of religion and the fortitude to take "One Day at a Time."

Whatever the emotion or impulse, country lyrics address themselves to needs that all people have. But in a society where the open display of emotion is sublimated or considered to be in bad taste, country music is denigrated as "soap opera" or worse. The country writers show no reluctance to discuss the pain, disappointment, and insecurity that sometimes touch everyone's life. Un-self-conscious, rather than unsophisticated, country lyrics act as emotional cathartics, and remind the listener that his or her private pain has been felt by other people.

Few writers have shown such skill at converting the private pains and public preoccupations of average people into commercially successful formulas as the men and women who congregated in Nashville in the late fifties and early sixties. The modern era of country songwriting began in about 1958 when Bill Anderson and Harlan Howard began supplying songs to Ray Price and other singers who were resisting the rock-and-roll tide. Anderson always sought a successful singing career, and he achieved it in 1962 and 1963 when his recordings of "Mama Sang a Song" and "Still" became major hits. Now often known as "Whispering Bill" because of his soft singing style, he is well recognized because of his work as host of television game shows, and his writing has been all but forgotten. Few writers, though, have been so adept at exploiting homely sayings, metaphors, and clichés for commercial purposes (in "When Two Worlds Collide," co-written with Roger Miller, Anderson borrowed a phrase from science fiction and made it fit into the scheme of lovers' incompatibility), and few have had so many big songs recorded by other singers. Anderson was born in South Carolina, but grew up near Atlanta and was a graduate of the University of Georgia (a fact that he tried to hide from his early Nashville contemporaries). The first evidence of his ability came in 1958 when Ray Price recorded "City Lights," a song about urban loneliness and anonymity which was Billboard's number one country song for thirteen consecutive weeks. In the years that followed, songs like "The Tip of My Fingers" (for Roy Clark) and "Once a Day" (for Connie Smith) won him commercial acclaim and demonstrated his understanding of popular tastes.

Harlan Howard, reared in Detroit by Kentucky-born parents, was the acknowledged "king" of country songwriters, at least until the emergence of Kris Kristofferson in the early seventies. Although he had written songs since he was twelve years old, none were published until the late fifties, when he was living in Huntington Park, California, and working as a $90-a-week apprentice bookbinder. Johnny Bond published and recorded his first song, and soon thereafter he began writing songs for Wynn Stewart and Buck Owens. His first major hit, "Pick Me Up on Your Way Down," was written for Ray Price, who, however, passed it on to his friend Charlie Walker, a San Antonio singer and disc jockey, who recorded it and saw it become one of country music's honky-tonk classics. The song became popular almost simultaneously with two other Howard songs, "Heartaches by the Number," recorded by Ray Price, and "Mommy for a Day," recorded by Kitty Wells. Howard never seriously pursued a singing career, as did Anderson, but instead supplied a steady stream of songs for other singers such as Ernest Tubb (his boyhood idol), Ray Price, Patsy Cline, and Buck Owens. Owens, in fact, began his rise to fame singing songs written by Howard ("Above and Beyond," "Foolin' Around," and "Excuse Me, I Think I've Got a Heartache"). Howard's most successful song, "Heartaches by the Number," recorded in both popular and country music, grossed well over $50,000 for the writer's share alone. His songwriting earned him ten citations (awards of merit) from BMI in 1961 (a record) and well over $100,000 in that same year.

Howard moved to Nashville in 1960, at about the same time as did an old friend and songwriting buddy from California, Hank Cochran. Cochran was another southern boy, from Isola, Mississippi, who had drifted around from job to job before landing in Belle Gardens, California, in the mid-fifties, when he began writing songs for Pamper, a Nashville publishing house owned by Ray Price and Hal Smith. After his move to Nashville in January 1960, he began writing a series of very personal songs about hurting and loneliness such as Patsy Cline's huge hit "I Fall to Pieces" (cowritten with Howard), "Don't Touch Me," "Don't You Ever Get Tired of Hurting Me," and "A Little Bitty Tear" (recorded by the famous folk balladeer Burl Ives). Early in 1960 Cochran met a young musician fresh from Texas, Willie Nelson, who was almost starving while trying to pitch his songs to publishers. Cochran, Nelson, and other fledgling musicians such as Mel Tillis met often at Tootsie's Orchid Lounge on Broadway (just back of the Ryman Auditorium), where they drank, commiserated with each other, and tried out their songs on Tootsie and the bar patrons. Cochran secured a staff writer's job at Pamper for Nelson and arranged for the struggling writer/singer to receive royalty advances while waiting for his songs to be published and recorded.

Willie Nelson was born on April 30, 1933, in the little Central Texas town of Abbott. Like most Texas country musicians of his era, Nelson absorbed music from a wide variety of cultural and ethnic sources. He and his sister Bobbie, his long time pianist, grew up singing gospel songs in the Baptist Church, but he also played in honky-tonks all over the state. Before he was a teenager he began playing guitar in the German/Czech polka bands in the "Bohemian" communities of Central Texas; he listened to the country music of Bob Wills, Ernest Tubb, and Floyd Tillman, and kept his ear glued to the radio where he heard jazz and vintage pop music. All of these musical forms contributed to the shaping of the Willie Nelson style.

Despite his skills as a guitarist and unorthodox singer (with his blues inflections and off-the-beat phrasing), Nelson's ticket to Nashville came through his songwriting. While working the honky-tonks of Houston, Nelson wrote and sold outright two songs, "Family Bible" (recorded by Claude Gray) and "Night Life" (a big hit for Ray Price), which made him just enough spending money to finance the trip to Nashville. In Nashville his lean and struggling period came to an end when singers began to record his songs: Billy Walker, "Funny How Time Slips Away," 1960; Faron Young, "Hello Walls," 1961; and Patsy Cline, "Crazy," 1961. His days as a recognized singer and superstar were still far away, but, as a writer, he became valued by every singer in the country music business. The presence of Willie Nelson, Hank Cochran, and Harlan Howard on the Pamper roster made that company one of the most powerful in the country music industry (its catalogue now belongs to the giant Tree Publishing Company).

Nelson, Cochran, Howard, Roger Miller, Bill Anderson, and Mel Tillis all contributed to country music's economic resurgence and stylistic revitalization in the early sixties. By the middle of the decade a number of other writers, such as Dallas Frazier, Billy Edd Wheeler, Curley Putman, and Tom T. Hall, had moved country music even closer to its roots with their story songs and nostalgic, but often bittersweet, evocations of rural and small-town life. The recollections were sometimes disquieting, as in the case of Bobbie Gentry's superhit "Ode to Billy Joe," grim as in John D. Loudermilk's "Tobacco Road," tongue-in-cheek as in Wheeler's "Ode to the Little Brown Shack Out Back," ambivalent as in Putman's "As Long As the Wind Blows," but most often affectionate as in Putman's "Green, Green Grass of Home." Most of the talented new writers were intelligent young men who combined a cultivated sophistication, acquired in college or military experience, with an empathy and understanding of the plain people with whom they grew up and for whom they wrote.

Tom T. Hall is a tall-tale spinner whose mode of communication is music. Born in Olive Hill, Kentucky, Hall began his career as a teenage bluegrass musician and disc jockey. He began writing songs during his military tenure in Germany in the late fifties, and after he returned to the United States in 1961 he resumed his former life as a musician/radio announcer on a series of radio stations in Kentucky and West Virginia. In 1964 one of his compositions, "DJ for a Day," reached the ears of Jimmy Key of NewKeys Music in Nashville. After Jimmy C. Newman's recording of the song reached number one on the *Billboard* charts, Hall made plans to move to Nashville to pursue the writer's craft. He brought to the profession of songwriting a keen sensitivity to the problems and interests of plain people, a gift for story-telling, and an economical but direct style of writing influenced by his reading of Ernest Hemingway. He was at home in all realms of country expression, and he wrote two of the earliest songs about the Vietnam War ("Hello Vietnam" and "Mama, Tell Them What We're Fighting For"). His genius, though, lay in his almost conversational narratives of everyday life, somehow capturing "the subtlest nuances of the men in southern towns who sit around feed stores and filling stations swapping stories with the county agent and the butane man."[10] His first super hit came in 1968 when Jeannie C. Riley recorded her spunky version of "Harper Valley PTA," a song about small-town hypocrisy. Now freed to pursue his craft full time, he began turning out a steady stream of journalistic and highly commercial songs, mostly about his own experiences or observations—and mostly recorded by himself: "A Week in a Country Jail," "Ballad of Forty Dollars" (about a gravedigger's mixed feelings as he buries a man who owed him money), "Homecoming" (one of the best songs yet written about a musician's days on the road), "Trip to Hyden" (about the bleakness of life in a Kentucky coal community), "Old Dogs, Children, and Watermelon Wine" (about a wise old man he met in a lounge in Miami), "The Year That Clayton Delaney Died" (Hall's personal favorite, about a gifted Kentucky musician who had influenced him), and many others.

Hall captured a new audience for country music, and gave the music new economic strength, by restoring the old tradition of story-telling. That

10. Martin, "Tom T. Hall," in *Stars of Country Music*, p. 398.

impulse remained in country music, but it was accompanied increasingly in the late sixties and early seventies by a torrent of very personal songs (some in the vein of Hank Cochran's "Don't Touch Me" and some in an almost stream-of-consciousness mode like John Hartford's "Gentle on My Mind") which dealt with intimate relationships, individual soul-searching, and passionate quests for identity and self-fulfillment. Such writers as Mickey Newbury, Rodney Crowell, John Hartford, Shel Silverstein (a children's poet, cartoonist, and *Playboy* columnist), and Kris Kristofferson were poets whose perceptions were drawn from life and literature and from exposure to other forms of music. Hartford was a wondrous blend of old-time and contemporary influences, schooled in bluegrass music as a fiddler and five-string banjoist, inspired by Uncle Dave Macon, fascinated by the lure of the Mississippi riverboats, and a free spirit whose dress and lifestyle reflected the counterculture of the 1960's. Kristofferson was also a mixture of seemingly contradictory experiences, a military-trained person with liberal inclinations. As the son of a professional Air Force man—born in Brownsville, Texas, and reared in California—Kristofferson received an introduction to the world that made it difficult for him to identify strongly with any specific region or class. On the other hand, a childhood affection for the music of Hank Williams inspired an undying desire to write songs, while his liberal and worldly education contributed to a tolerance and compassion for plain, working people. There had never been a country songwriter quite like him. He was a Rhodes Scholar who prepared for a career as a professor of English literature, but who then changed direction and spent five years in the Army, working mainly as a helicopter pilot, with plans for settling down at West Point as an officer and teacher. Two weeks before his assignment to the military academy, in June 1965, he went to Nashville (largely through the encouragement of songwriter Marijohn Wilkin) and decided to try his hand at full-time writing.

Kristofferson went through the "starving years" that seem almost a prerequisite for country songwriters, but in 1969 his first big breakthrough came when Roger Miller recorded his "Me and Bobby McGee"—a song since recorded by many people. He began his own recording career with Monument Records and, in rapid fashion during the next couple of years, saw several of his songs recorded with great success by country singers: Johnny Cash, "Sunday Morning Coming Down"; Ray Price, "For the Good Times"; Bobby Bare, "Come Sundown"; Sammi Smith, "Help Me Make It through the Night." The high point of his career, and a kind of turning point for country music, was the selection of "Sunday Morning Coming Down" in 1970 as the CMA's Song of the Year. Wearing shoulder-length hair and bell-bottom suedes, and mumbling his acceptance of the award for a song that seemed clearly about a drug hangover, Kristofferson stunned many viewers and music-industry people, who swore he was stoned (Kristofferson later replied that he was merely tired and nervous when he walked to the stage). Kristofferson's lyrics spoke often of loneliness, aliena-tion, and pain, but they also celebrated freedom and honest relationships, and in intimate, sensuous language that had been rare in country music. The songs of Kristofferson, Hartford, and their contemporaries certainly represented a new departure for country music, but the jury is still out as to whether they were superior to the simple and direct lyrics written by Floyd Tillman, Rex Griffin, and other earlier writers. Sometimes self-consciously poetic, the new writers were probably more important for what they said, rather than for how they said it: they opened up new realms of expression for country singers and writers.

The emergence of a "new breed" of songwriters in country music has been paralleled by other significant departures from the traditional norms. The image, if not the outright fact, of a music dominated by adult male white Protestants has been severely shaken since the early sixties. As will be discussed in Chapter 11, young musicians have made major inroads into country music, bringing both innovative ideas and a commitment to older forms. Women have also emerged as superstars with independent identities, while at least one black, Charley Pride, has achieved immense fame and popularity as a country singer. Since Patsy Cline's trailblazing performances in the early sixties, women have increasingly built solo ca-reers apart from male companions or family groups; they have almost completely cast off the roles thought appropriate for women singers (cow-girls, Sunbonnet Sues, rustic comediennes); and they have begun to sing about subjects once deemed unsuitable for women. To a certain degree, the changes witnessed among women singers reflect similar transforma-tions in the lives of women in American and southern society. Women country singers now project, in some cases, a sexiness that their sisters (and brothers) of the past would have found scandalous, and they some-times sing about the experience, and even joy, of sex with unprecedented openness. Jeannie C. Riley was tough and spunky in her performances of such songs as "Harper Valley PTA" and "The Girl Most Likely," but she raised more eyebrows with the miniskirts and go-go boots which she then wore in her concerts. The honky-tonk angel, it seemed, had become a pub-lic performer. Fourteen-year-old Tanya Tucker, though, was even more se-ductive when she began her career in 1972 as a "country Lolita," combin-ing a childish innocence with a playful sexuality. Dressed in skin-tight pants suits, punctuating her songs with Elvis-like body movements, and singing in a style and voice far beyond her years, Tanya evoked audience responses that the young girl probably did not always understand. It was not until the end of the seventies, when an attempt was made to market her as a rock singer, that she and her managers began consciously to build the image of a brazen sex queen (posters showed her standing on six-inch spike heels and standing tightly enveloped in a red Spandex jumpsuit). The rock audience, however, remained unresponsive, and Tucker soon moved away from this sexually aggressive posture. The most open display of sexuality among women country singers appeared in the Las Vegas performances of Barbara Mandrell and Dolly Parton, which were marked by suggestive dance routines and revealing costumes, although Parton certainly moved into a bold territory never previously occupied by women singers when she played the role of a madam in *The Best Little Whorehouse in Texas*.

The lyrics sung by women also projected a greater boldness. Sammi Smith, for example, asked her lover to remain with her through the night (in Kristofferson's "Help Me Make It through the Night"), as did Linda Hargrove in "Just Get Up and Close the Door." Hargrove went farther than that in "Mexican Love Songs" when she spoke of waking up drunk with a big cowboy lying beside her. Tanya Tucker sang "Would You Lay with Me (in a Field of Stone)," and Barbara Mandrell moved into an even greater forbidden zone when, in "Burning the Midnight Oil," she spoke of cheating on her husband. Hargrove's songs were probably the boldest of those mentioned, because they were her own compositions; the others were written by men. Hargrove was nevertheless not alone as a female writer of songs which expressed a type of womanly independence. Both Loretta Lynn and Dolly Parton often spoke up for the right of women to be free and honestly expressive.

The examples of honesty displayed in some women's country performances should not obscure the fact that "revolutions" proceed slowly in country music. For the most part, the women still endorse traditional male-female relationships, and usually endorse the idea that man's frailties should be tolerated and his "good woman" should remain faithful to him. Woman's chief domain is still the home, and her basic roles are the preservation of its sanctity and the nurturing of her family. Women can and do admit their need for sexual satisfaction, but implicit in this new honesty is the idea that sexuality is a weapon that a woman should exploit in her relations with men (the presumption that woman is a sex object is not often challenged). Women country singers, of course, violate such precepts constantly—they do not "stand by their men" through thick and thin; they do not defer to the leadership of the "stronger sex"; and they certainly do not remain in their homes—but they publicly, and in their songs, adhere to the myth of domesticity.

The central fact about women country singers does not lie in the "rebellion" that their songs or performing images occasionally convey (Jeannie C. Riley, for example, has spent several years—particularly since she "found the Lord"—trying to shed the bad-girl image and memories of miniskirts that became attached to her during "Harper Valley PTA" days). Their singing is most strongly marked by the influences that come from other areas of American music; very few of them, frankly, sound country. Such singers as Dottie West (whose greatest success has come through her duet performances with Kenny Rogers), Crystal Gayle, Lynn Anderson, Donna Fargo, Barbara Fairchild, or Sylvia (her sole performing title) are virtually indistinguishable from contemporary pop singers. Such older, down-to-earth singers as Kitty Wells, Jean Shepard, and Melba Montgomery are heard infrequently (and almost never on the Top Forty programs), and even those bonafide rural/mountain girls, Loretta Lynn and Dolly Parton, have moved progressively toward the smooth countrypolitan sound. Down-home or hard country performances do sometimes appear in the repertories of such singers as Shelly West, Reba McEntire, Lacy J. Dalton, Margo Smith (who occasionally demonstrates that yodeling is not a totally lost art), and Jeanne Pruett (whose version of the pure country "Satin Sheets" topped the charts in 1973). Most young women singers, however, reflect the sounds and phrasing of soul, rock, and pop musicians (except for an occasional singer like Emmylou Harris who seems more in the mold of Joan Baez and the urban folk singers). No one is more instructive of the kind of influences that have worked on the young women than Loretta Lynn's talented sister, Brenda Gail Webb—better known as Crystal Gayle. Crystal grew up in Wabash, Indiana, after her family had left the coal country of Eastern Kentucky. She scarcely knew her country-singing sister until Loretta's first records were released in 1960. By that time Crystal had spent much time listening to the pop singers, such as Barbra Streisand and Lesley Gore, who were active in her own day. She had no real identification with the Kentucky mountains, and one can scarcely imagine her singing or writing a song like "Coal Miner's Daughter." Instead, Crystal Gayle has cast her lot with country-pop music (with such songs as "Don't It Make My Brown Eyes Blue" and "I'll Get Over You") and a style of clear, modulated, and slightly affected phrasing that bears absolutely no similarity to that of her famous sister.

While her singing may have lost some of its rough edges, Loretta Lynn still exhibits the traits of her mountain heritage. Along with two other authentic rural-bred girls, Tammy Wynette and Dolly Parton, she achieved a superstardom that no other woman—including her mentor, Patsy Cline, and country's first "queen," Kitty Wells—had ever enjoyed. Because of her best-selling autobiography, *Coal Miner's Daughter*, and the popularly acclaimed movie which came from it, Loretta's story is probably the best known of any country singer's: birth in a bleak coal community called Butcher Holler (near Paintsville, Kentucky); marriage at the age of fourteen; a move to the state of Washington in about 1951; her early days as a singer in the clubs and grange halls of her adopted state; her first recording of "Honky Tonk Girl" on the Zero label in 1960, and her and her husband Doolittle's barnstorming car trip from radio station to radio station pushing the song; the early struggling days in Nashville and appearances on the Wilburn Brothers' television show; and, finally, the zooming career that followed her first big Decca hit (the appropriately named "Success") in 1962. Starting out with a honky-tonk sound and a style that bore a strong resemblance to that of Kitty Wells, Loretta gradually developed her own unique style and began honing her talents as a writer. On the road to her selection as the CMA's Entertainer of the Year in 1972—she was the first woman to receive the award—she recorded a number of songs (mostly self-written) which spoke for working-class women in a way that no ardent feminist could ever do. With such "feisty" songs as "Don't Come Home a-Drinkin' with Lovin' on Your Mind," "You Ain't Woman Enough," "Fist City," "One's on the Way," and "The Pill" (an endorsement of birth control), she became "the spokeswoman for every woman who had gotten married too early, gotten pregnant too often, and felt trapped by the tedium and drudgery of her life."[11] Loretta also became a household word in American popular culture, highly visible because of her frequent appearances on television and in the pages of magazines and newspapers, and beloved because of her disarming honesty and simple country charm.

Tammy Wynette became extraordinarily popular with a message radically different from that of Loretta Lynn. One finds few of the spunky, talking-back-to-men songs in her repertory, other than "Your Good Girl's Gonna Go Bad" which was recorded soon after her career began. Instead, Tammy will always be identified with one powerfully commercial song, "Stand By Your Man," which feminists denounced as an outrageous display of female submission. Tammy always denied that the song counseled such abject surrender to masculine dominance, and, indeed, her three divorces and one annulment suggest that the philosophy exerted no real power over her own life. The title of another one of her hit songs, "D-I-V-O-R-C-E," best summed up the reality of her life, although as a true romanticist she clung to the philosophy of still another song, "I'll keep falling in love until I get it right."

Born Virginia Wynette Pugh in Itawamba County, Mississippi (near the Alabama line) in 1942, Tammy grew up on her grandparents' cotton farm, working in the fields and dreaming of a career as a singer. After the collapse of her first marriage, she decided to turn her fantasy into reality. She moved with three small children to Birmingham, enrolled in a beauty college, and began singing wherever she could gain a hearing—eventually at a local television station on a very early morning show. In 1966 she moved to Nashville and began making the rounds of the record companies before finally winning a successful audition with Billy Sherrill and Epic Records. Her first recording, "Apartment Number Nine," was moderately successful, but her second release, "Your Good Girl's Gonna Go Bad," climbed into the charts, and a duet recording with David Houston, "My Elusive Dreams," became her first number one song. Her commercial as-

11. Joan Dew, *Singers and Sweethearts: The Women of Country Music* (Garden City, N.Y.: Doubleday and Co., 1977), p. 8.

cent was spectacular, and "Stand By Your Man," recorded in August 1968, became the biggest-selling single ever recorded by a woman. Tammy gained immense public exposure when the song became part of the sound track of the movie *Five Easy Pieces*. Her marriage to George Jones in 1968 brought her even greater publicity, and as "Mr. and Mrs. Country Music," pursuing solo careers and singing duets together, the two singers profited greatly from the association with each other. Artistic compatibility, however, could not save the turbulent marriage, and Jones' acute alcoholism eventually drove a wedge between them which resulted in divorce in 1975. The soap opera qualities of Tammy's life—chronic illness and marital disappointment—seemed only to endear the singer even more to her many fans. Her clear, expressive, pleading voice tore at the emotions and pulled the listeners into her orbit of personal experience, making them feel that her songs of hurt and loneliness, which were somehow tempered by hope, mirrored their own and the singer's lives.

Dolly Parton's prominence in American popular culture, and indeed throughout the world, should not obscure the facts of her rural-mountain origins and of her thorough immersion in country music culture. She was one of twelve children born to a poor mountain couple in the hills near Sevierville, Tennessee. No ad writer or Hollywood script could create a story more appealing in its rags-to-riches qualities or in its depiction of her transition from folk simplicity to worldly sophistication. Dolly inherited an affinity for music from both sides of her family, and her mother was a singer of ballads and old-time songs. As a very small child, she made up songs which she then dictated to her mother; she sang in her Grandfather Owens' local Church of God congregation; and she was appearing on the Cas Walker television show in Knoxville by the time she was ten years old. Through the influence of an uncle who was then stationed in an Army camp in Louisiana, she even made a record in 1959, when she was only thirteen: a song called "Puppy Love" recorded on Eddie Schuler's Goldband label in Lake Charles, Louisiana. Dolly was already a seasoned performer, then, when she set out to Nashville by bus on the day after her high school graduation.

Within a few months after her arrival in 1964, Dolly had secured a recording contract with Fred Foster at Monument Records and had met her future husband, Carl Dean. Monument wasted a couple of years trying to market her as a pop-rock singer, but then in 1967 let her cut a country record called "Dumb Blonde" (its writer, Curley Putman, had also written Tammy Wynette's "My Elusive Dreams"). She joined Porter Wagoner in that same year as his "girl singer" but soon moved beyond that subordinate status to become a featured performer on his show and one of the most striking personalities in country music. Through Wagoner's influence she moved to the RCA label, and though her superhits—such as

"Joshua"—did not begin appearing until 1971, she did experience success as a soloist and as an award-winning duet singer with Wagoner.

Parton's appeal came through a fortuitous combination of physical attractiveness, singing talent, and a genius for song composition. Dressing extravagantly in blonde wigs, heavy makeup, and a profusion of jewelry, and wearing costumes that dramatically displayed her bountiful physical attributes, Parton not only caused people to look at her, she also fulfilled the fantasies of a childhood marked by material deprivation. As a singer she possessed a flexible soprano voice capable of soaring into the piercing, high-pitched yodel of "Muleskinner Blues" or of descending to the wistful, plaintive sound heard on "Coat of Many Colors." As a songwriter she has had few peers in country music, bearing a strong comparison with Merle Haggard in her wide range of interests and in her facility with a diverse array of idioms. Her compositions encompass virtually every major theme in country music, and at least three songs—"To Daddy," "Just Because I'm a Woman," and "Down from Dover"—grapple with the problems of contemporary women in sensitive and compelling ways. Her most interesting songs are those that draw upon her mountain folk beginnings— sometimes rhapsodically affectionate like "Tennessee Mountain Home," or rowdy like "Traveling Man," but more often bittersweet like "In the Good Old Days When Times Were Bad" or her masterpiece, "Coat of Many Colors." "Coat of Many Colors" is a tender recollection of a jacket made of rag patches, and of the love her "mother sewed in every stitch."

It is no wonder that Porter Wagoner was bitterly disappointed when Dolly left him in 1974 to pursue an independent career, but she had actually outgrown his show long before this. She won the CMA's Female Vocalist of the Year Award in 1975 and 1976, and in the spring of the latter year she became the first woman country singer to obtain her own syndicated television show (carried in 130 markets). The year 1976 also marked the beginning of her all-out campaign to achieve identity as a pop singer, a move that evoked great controversy within the country music industry and among her fans. Dolly has never abandoned the singing of country songs, but her arrangements and repertory have shifted heavily toward middle-of-the-road and pop material, and she seldom performs with other country entertainers or in country formats. Most important of all, her interests have expanded well beyond the performance of music and into the realms of television and movie-making, taking her into areas of public awareness where few country-derived entertainers have gone.

While women after 1960 were challenging the dominance once enjoyed by men in country music, other "new people" were beginning to trickle into the business as singers, songwriters, and musicians. The music's great commercial expansion lured talented newcomers who whittled away at country music's "Anglo-Protestant" consensus. Catholics, Jews, Mexicans, and other "ethnic" groups began to show up as sidemen and women in bluegrass and country bands, and particularly in country-rock groups, where a greater tolerance for beliefs and diverse lifestyles existed. At least one Jewish cowboy, Kinky Friedman, pursued a career in country music with an outrageous, irreverent style of humor and a band called the Texas Jewboys. Kinky profited from his involvement in the active Austin musical scene, but was particularly popular in New York City where he performed often at the progressive country bar, the Lone Star Café. Cajun musicians, of course, had never been absent from country music as both singers and instrumentalists, but the dynamic singer/fiddler Doug Kershaw, from Tiel Ridge, Louisiana, enjoyed greater national exposure than any of his French-American colleagues had ever won. Kershaw had experienced a first career in the late fifties with his brother Rusty (as the team of Rusty and Doug), a frenetic act which combined rockabilly and Cajun music. The duo introduced the song "Louisiana Man," written by Doug Kershaw, which was a richly evocative song about Cajun swamp life of Southwest Louisiana and a tribute to their deceased father. Doug Kershaw returned to music as a solo act in 1970, this time with long hair, a reputation as the "Cajun Hippie," and an exuberant style and repertory that reflected Cajun, rock, and country forms of music. Buoyed by the support of Johnny Cash, who featured him on his national television show, Kershaw began reaching a horde of young fans all over America.

Probably more significant than the emergence of Doug Kershaw as a quasi-country musician was the rise to commercial prominence of two Mexican-American country performers, Freddy Fender and Johnny Rodriguez. Chicano musicians, of course, had sometimes played in country bands ever since the thirties, but only rarely—and then usually in a local context—did a performer from such a background attempt a career as a solo country performer. Fender and Rodriguez emerged in the context of the increasingly tolerant racial atmosphere of the sixties, and in a region of the country—South Texas—where cultural forms had often intermixed. Obviously, they also profited from the precedent set by the black country star Charley Pride (discussed below). Freddy Fender was really Baldemar Huerta from Weslaco, Texas, and he, like Doug Kershaw, had had an earlier career in the fifties as a rock-and-roll singer, when his "Wasted Days and Wasted Nights" achieved moderate success. A Louisiana prison term for possession of marijuana destroyed his first career, but he returned to a successful professional career in 1975, this time as a country singer, with a bilingual version of "Before the Next Teardrop Falls."

Fender was preceded by Johnny Rodriguez from Sabinal, Texas, whose attachment to country music seemed much firmer and whose loyalty to the form has been more enduring. Rodriguez was a disciple of Merle Haggard, and his early records show a strong trace of the California singer's style. Rodriguez bore virtually no stylistic evidence of Tex-Mex or other Mexican-ethnic forms of music, but instead carried the influence of the cowboy-kicker culture of South Texas and of the honky-tonk and western swing bands which thrived in the region. Tom T. Hall heard him singing at Happy Shahan's Alamo Village in Brackettsville, Texas, and eventually hired him as guitarist for his band. Rodriguez' first hit record in 1972 was written by Tom T. Hall's brother, Hillman, and was a dyed-in-the-wool honky-tonk song called "Pass Me By." Rodriguez maintained this hard-edged beer-drinking style through several releases, while also mixing a few Spanish verses with the English lyrics, but by the mid-seventies he had moved toward a smoother, easy-listening sound. It is not hard to see why he and/or his managers made this decision. Rodriguez was strikingly good looking with a boyish Latin charm and was just about the first potential youth sex symbol that country music had ever had (he was only twenty when his first record was made, and he was often featured with Tanya Tucker in concerts). The promise of a major crossover into pop music was never realized, and Rodriguez survived a bout with drugs in the early eighties. By 1984 he had edged back somewhat toward the hard country, Texas style of music on which he was nurtured.

The man who did most to open the doors to new ethnic or nonwhite talent was the remarkable Charley Pride. The black contributions to country music are too well known to warrant repetition here, although we should be reminded that Charley Pride was not the first black "star" of the genre. Deford Bailey, a diminutive and partially crippled harmonica player, was on the *Grand Ole Opry* from 1925 to 1941 and was one of the most popular and frequently scheduled performers on the show. One of the pleasant byproducts of Charley Pride's ascendancy was the search for earlier black country musicians and the consequent rediscovery of Bailey.

When Pride made his first RCA recordings in 1965, the rhythm-and-blues legend Ray Charles had already made his groundbreaking lps, *Modern Sounds in Country and Western Music*, collections which introduced country music to a broader middle-class audience. According to their own testimonies, both men listened to the *Grand Ole Opry* when they were growing up, and both expressed an affection for country music. Charles' popular versions of such songs as "Born to Lose" and "I Can't Stop Loving You" were done in the singer's famous soul style. Charley Pride's singing, on the other hand, was so country that no one suspected he was black until they saw his photograph or saw him in concert.

Pride's country legitimacy is all the more remarkable given the place and context in which he was born. He was born on a sharecropper's farm on March 18, 1938, near Sledge, Mississippi, and in the heart of the Delta where "the blues was born." Unlike his contemporaries, and even his brothers and sisters, Pride listened to country music and began trying to pick and sing it when he was still a teenager. His two passions were baseball and music, and he hoped that one or the other would liberate him from "them old cotton fields back home." Between 1954 and 1964 he actively sought a baseball career, beginning with the Memphis Red Sox in the Negro American League, but a series of injuries at crucial moments kept him from fulfilling his desire to be a big-leaguer. While working at a zinc smelter in Helena, Montana, in 1963, playing semi-pro baseball, and singing in local clubs at night, he had a fortuitous encounter with Red Foley and Red Sovine. The two men gave a show in Great Falls, and after hearing Pride do a guest performance, Sovine encouraged him to come to Nashville.

Pride took his trip to Nashville in 1964, received the support of Jack Johnson and Jack Clement, who became his first co-managers, and somehow put his tapes into the possession of Chet Atkins. Pride's first RCA recordings, "Snakes Crawl at Night" and "Atlantic Coastal Line," were produced in the fall of 1965 and released in December. No photographs accompanied the first records, nor did the promotional literature mention that he was black. Disc jockeys played his records, and fans bought them for several weeks, without anyone knowing his racial identity. By the time Pride's face became known to people, his music had won them over for life.

Pride's acceptance by the country music public is attributable to many factors. His managers and record producers skillfully marketed him with a low-profile campaign during the crucial early months, and Pride carefully cultivated his audiences with a repertory of solid country songs (many of them standards taken from other singers such as Hank Williams) and with good-natured, self-effacing banter which put people at ease. He talked of his "permanent tan" and of being a person who "didn't sound like he was supposed to," and he built trust among his working-class listeners by talking about baseball and his days in the cottonfield. He was the right singer at the right time in history. His singing contained almost none of the vocal inflections identified with black singers, and his stage presence conveyed few of the body movements and postures identified with soul or rhythm-and-blues musicians. He was a handsome man but with little of the overt sexuality projected by many of the younger black singers, and he avoided any references to civil rights or political topics. He was therefore basically unthreatening to white masculinity, civil order, or the identity of country music.

Pride definitely profited from the heightened mood of racial tolerance promoted in the United States by the civil rights movement and from the desires of the country music industry to improve its image and broaden its audience. His appeal, though broad and knowing no regional bounds, was particularly intense in the South and among working-class whites. He was one of the first country singers to receive standing ovations at the end of his concerts, a tribute to his talent, one supposes, but also a means by

Tammy Wynette. Photograph
courtesy of the Country Music
Foundation Library and Media
Center, Nashville, Tennessee.

Charley Pride. Photograph courtesy of the
Country Music Foundation Library and
Media Center, Nashville, Tennessee.

which audiences rid themselves of racial guilt and announced to the world: "Look, we're not prejudiced after all." Above all, people responded to Charley Pride because he was such a good country singer, with a supple baritone voice that could easily accommodate itself to any style of music. His Grammy nomination in 1966 for "Just between You and Me" was merely the first of an unending stream of awards and accolades that have accompanied his rise to commercial music fame. By the time he received the CMA's Entertainer of the Year Award in 1971—a major milestone in country music history—he had already become an institution in American popular culture and had moved far beyond the country audience that originally gave him support.

Although Charley Pride broke down some racial barriers in country music, few black people have followed him across them. There is no way to document the number of black people who like and listen to country music, nor can one determine how many black musicians perform at the local level. Linda Martel from South Carolina, O. B. McClinton from Mississippi, and Big Al Downing and Stoney Edwards from Oklahoma have been among the handful of black singers who have recorded for major labels or who have otherwise gained some kind of national exposure. Of this group, only Stoney Edwards ever gave any indication of achieving major commercial acceptance. Born in Seminole, Oklahoma, of Black, Indian, and Irish extraction, Edwards received his first exposure listening on the radio to the music of Tommy Duncan and Bob Wills. He still has vivid memories of standing along the roadside with his seven brothers and sisters, watching the Bob Wills bus go by and picking up the candy which the Texas Playboys tossed to them. He sang country music all his life, but made no major efforts at a professional career until 1969, when an industrial accident took him out of circulation and when Charley Pride's success provided inspiration. Living in California at the time, Edwards made his first records for a major label, Capitol, which was no doubt delighted at the opportunity to compete with RCA and Charley Pride. From 1970 when his first records were made down to the mid-seventies, Edwards kept his name before the country music public with such songs as "Mississippi, You're on My Mind" (a poignant evocation of life in the rural Deep South) and "Hank and Lefty Raised My Country Soul" (an affectionate tribute to two of the giants of country music). Since that time, however, Edwards has slowly faded from the limelight, and Charley Pride has maintained his position as the only black on a major record label.

Although the entrance into its ranks of women, youth, divergent ethnic groups, and blacks and a more relaxed attitude toward sexual expression and alternative lifestyles suggest a broadening of vision within the country music industry, one should not interpret such changes to be a bold expression of liberalism. Commercialism, not ideology, has motivated many of country music's bold experiments. While much has been borrowed from urban folk and rock music—songs, instrumental licks, long hair, casual dress, and even relaxed attitudes toward drugs and sexual relations— country musicians have withdrawn from the encounters with a largely unaltered political consciousness. The politics of the urban folk revival, in other words, did not rub off on country music to any substantial degree, nor did the ideologies of such post-revival singers as Bob Dylan, Joan Baez, and Phil Ochs, who marshalled their protest songs to combat America's growing involvement in the Vietnam War.

Country music's identification with "the silent majority" in the mid-sixties was one consequence of at least twenty years of growing disquietude in the United States about the sweeping and bewildering social changes that occurred in the wake of the second world war. (The roots of these changes, of course, were much older and were products of the nation's rise to industrial power.) In a society swept successively by racial, youth, and sexual revolutions, torn by the tensions arising from long ideological conflict with the Soviet Union, and subjected increasingly to the alienation inherent in post-industrial technology, many Americans have sought reassurance that the older comfortable and predictable world they once knew is still intact. In the realm of popular culture, country music seemed a safe retreat to many because it suggested the "bedrock" American values of solidity, respect for authority, old-time religion, home-based virtues, and patriotism.

Some anticipations of a conservative political stance surface in the songs dealing with the Korean War and with atomic energy in the fifties. Most of these songs were merely topical items like Harry Choates' "Korea, Here We Come," Bill Monroe's "Rotation Blues" (written by Lieutenant Stewart Powell in Korea), the Louvin Brothers' "From Mother's Arms to Korea," and Fred Kirby's "When That Hell Bomb Falls," but a few made reference to the larger struggle with Communism, and some commented on the domestic consequences of that conflict: Lulu Belle and Scotty's "I'm No Communist," Elton Britt's "The Red That We Want Is the Red We've Got (in the Old Red, White, and Blue)," Roy Acuff's "Doug MacArthur," and Gene Autry's "Old Soldiers Never Die" (a defense of MacArthur after his dismissal by Truman). Nevertheless, such songs were few, and there was still room for an item like the Sons of the Pioneers "Ole Man Atom" which called for cooperation by world powers in the face of nuclear annihilation.

The civil rights revolution probably did most to politicize some country musicians. The struggles waged by black Americans to attain economic dignity and racial justice provoked one of the ugliest chapters in country music's history, an outpouring of racist records on small labels, mostly from Crowley, Louisiana, which lauded the Ku Klux Klan and attacked blacks (generally called niggers or coons) in the most vicious of stereotyped terms. George Wallace also forged an alliance with many country singers, such as Autry Inman, Hank Snow, and the Wilburn Brothers, who participated often in his campaigns for the Alabama governorship and for the presidency. Racism was certainly one factor which contributed to Wallace's popularity, but his southern rural/populist roots also made him appealing to many of the "good old boys and girls" who picked guitars and sang. Wallace identified with country music, but he also spoke the same language, ate the same food, and responded to the same cultural traditions (both good and bad) that most country musicians understood. He linked his southernness with their own, while also tapping vaguely understood, but often legitimate, feelings of alienation that many Americans everywhere felt.

The George Wallace–country music alliance was a major factor which contributed to the music's rediscovery by the media—the belief that at worst the music represented reactionary and racist politics, or that at best it spoke for alienated American working people. The appearance of a rash of songs after 1965 which defended American involvement in the Vietnam War and attacked those who protested against it gave renewed credence to the ideas that country music was either unthinkingly jingoistic or unabashedly patriotic in its sentiments. An indication that country music's response to the war was a bit more complicated than it might seem at first glance is the fact that two of the few writers in Nashville to be identified as political liberals (through their support of George McGovern and Jimmy Carter) wrote the first songs defending American activities in Vietnam: Kris Kristofferson with "Vietnam Blues" (for Dave Dudley) and Tom T. Hall with "Hello Vietnam" (for Johnny Wright) and "Mama, Tell Them What We're Fighting For" (Dave Dudley). Both writers claimed, perhaps unconvincingly, that they merely defended American soldiers and not American policy.

A number of songs appeared, mostly in 1966, that can be described as "protesting the protestors." These included the Hall song mentioned above (built around a soldier's letter to his mother); a recitation by Johnny Seay, "Day of Decision," which catalogued the alleged rending of the social fabric by dissent and radicalism; Stonewall Jackson's "The Minute Men Are Turning in Their Graves," which attacked the lack of patriotism shown by protestors; and at least three in 1970—Bobby Bare's "God Bless America Again," Bill Anderson's "Where Have All the Heroes Gone," and Merle Haggard's "The Fighting Side of Me"—which either complained about the polarization of American society or breathed threats against those who would "run down the country."

With songs like these, country music picked up support from Middle Americans everywhere and from grateful political administrations which appreciated such public displays of patriotism. The political realignments then taking place in the country—as people changed parties, joined George Wallace, or dropped out of politics altogether—were of course fed by much more than the debates over the war. Guy Drake's "Welfare Cadilac" [*sic*] in

1970 was clearly inspired by the Great Society's support of minority groups. The rise of the counterculture and the aggressive flaunting of alternative lifestyles alienated many people from their traditional political affiliations. Ernest Tubb, for example, a lifelong Democrat and ardent supporter of Adlai Stevenson, recorded a song called "Love It or Leave It." This attack upon hippies and Yippies was motivated by the same kind of suspicions that led to the most famous anti-protest song of the period: Merle Haggard's "Okie from Muskogee."

Recorded in 1969, and *Billboard*'s number one song for four consecutive weeks at the end of the year, "Okie From Muskogee" was about an allegedly typical small-town Middle American with conventional ways and ardent patriotism who was proud to be from a city where people didn't smoke marijuana, wear beads and sandals, burn their draft cards, or challenge authority. Written one day on the spur of the moment when Haggard's bus passed by the Muskogee city sign, and apparently intended as a joke, the song's giant success must have greatly surprised the singer. It led to his selection as the CMA's Entertainer of the Year in 1970; it won him standing ovations in such cities as Philadelphia and Duluth; and it gained for him and for country music the endorsement of President Richard Nixon. Although he may have stumbled into the commercial and popular success generated by "Okie," his next recording, "The Fighting Side of Me," was clearly calculated to capitalize on the "silent majority's" fear and disgust for hippies, peaceniks, and radicals. It deeply disappointed those fans who identified Haggard with the compassion and tenderness of "Hungry Eyes," but it was also his next big number one record.

When American involvement in the Vietnam War ended, and as the nation's polarization subsided, country songwriters began to lose their preoccupation with songs of anti-dissent. The obsession with politics had been out of character, just as had the unquestioning acceptance of national policies displayed in the war songs. Country music moved away from the endorsement of establishment values to a more comfortable, and traditional, absorption with the world of the working class. Country writers and singers became increasingly aware, however, that a message designed for plain, everyday people could also be appealing to suburban commuters and even to "hippies." While still trying to be all things to all people, country music nevertheless became more self-consciously working class in image and orientation at the end of the sixties. Both Merle Haggard and Tom T. Hall were described as "the poet of the working man," although Haggard's songs seemed more aggressively aimed at that constituency. Many of the "working men's songs," like Haggard's "Working Man's Blues" and Johnny Russell's "Rednecks, White Socks, and Blue Ribbon Beer," were more concerned with lifestyle than with work. Haggard's song describes a character who is hard-working, individualistic, patriotic, fatalistic, and opposed to welfare. Russell's song is a cliché-ridden paean to the working class and a not-so-subtle reminder of the social chasm that lies between workers and others. While worker loyalty and competency are often emphasized, work itself is seldom extolled, and problems inherent in the work process are frequently described. The main character of Haggard's "If We Make It through December" is laid off during the most critical season of the year, and "Oney," in a song written by Jerry Chesnut and recorded by Johnny Cash, patiently waits for his retirement day so that he can beat up his foreman. Johnny Paycheck's big hit, "Take This Job and Shove It" (written by David Allan Coe, and the basis for a movie), is self-explanatory.

Truck-driving songs constitute the single-largest category of modern work songs. The genre seems to have begun in 1939 when Ted Daffan wrote "Truck Driver's Blues," but it began to evolve into a full-fledged industry when Dave Dudley, from Spencer, Wisconsin, recorded "Six Days on the Road" in 1963. Dudley's confident, quasi-rockabilly performance effectively captured both the boredom and the excitement, as well as the swaggering masculinity, that often accompanied long-distance trucking. Since 1965 a massive number of songs have appeared which deal with every aspect of trucker culture: truck stops, waitresses, billboards, citizen band radios (CB's), highway patrolmen (Smokies), mountain roads, "lady" truck drivers, pills, logbooks, convoys, overloads, and trucking folklore (about such things as ghost truck drivers—as in "Phantom 309"—and tender-hearted truckers who help crippled children). The songs have multiplied in such profusion that their quality varies widely; nevertheless, a few will probably stand the test of time: "Truck Driving Man," "Give Me Forty Acres" (about an inept driver), "Tombstone Every Mile" (about a dangerous and icy stretch of road in the Maine woods), "Girl on the Billboard" (about a trucker's fantasy), and "White Line Fever" (Merle Haggard's lament about a trucker who watches his life slip away as he rolls his truck down the white line of a thousand highways). Most country singers have experimented with trucking songs at one time or another, but only a few, such as Dudley, Dick Curless, Red Simpson, and Red Sovine, have specialized in the material. Truck-driving songs remained largely confined to the country music world until the 1970's, when nationwide truckers' strikes and C. W. McCall's "Convoy," a major crossover hit and the inspiration for a movie of the same name, made Americans conscious of CB's, trucker lingo, and the whole culture that lay behind them. An indispensable ingredient of that culture was the late-night country music radio shows aimed at truckers and conducted by such eloquent personalities as Charlie Douglas on WWL in New Orleans and Bill Mack on WBAP in Fort Worth. These men's voices boomed out to thousands of truckers in virtually every state in the continental United States, and they played songs requested by their trucker buddies, advertised truck stops and trucking equipment, and gave valuable weather information. Douglas, who ran a popular show called the *Road Gang* before moving to Nashville in 1983, even served as a liaison to truckers during the crucial strike of independent owner-operators in 1972.

The popularity of truck-driving songs was merely one example of country music's renewed strength and vitality. Commercially, the music stood at the highest peak in its history, a tribute not only to Chet Atkins "compromise," but also to the work of such hard country performers as Merle Haggard and Loretta Lynn. Stylistically, the music stood at a crossroads. Some roads led toward pop music and the blurring of identity; others beckoned those musicians who could combine tradition and innovation in an effective and commercially winning manner. One of these roads led toward bluegrass.

Bill Monroe. Courtesy of the Bill Monroe Fan Club.

10. Bluegrass

Bluegrass music has had a curious history. Almost everyone has heard of it, but few people know what it is or where it came from. It is sometimes used as a catch-all term to describe any form of country music, usually acoustic in nature, that suggests pre–World War II styles. But in fact it is not an old-time style at all; it did not begin to take shape as a distinct entity until the mid-forties, and it was not named until a decade later, when fans, disc jockeys, and record merchandisers began using the term "bluegrass" to describe a sound associated with the music of Bill Monroe and his disciples. The music, of course, drew upon earlier string-band and vocal styles, as well as repertory (as most forms of country music did), but these inherited and borrowed styles were significantly modified. One need only compare the music of Bill Monroe, "the father of bluegrass music," with that of Charlie Poole, Grayson and Whitter, the Skillet Lickers, and other pioneer musicians from the twenties to discover how much Monroe and his bluegrass compadres have transformed the old-time styles. Much romanticism has grown up around bluegrass, as invariably happens when any musical form diverges from the commercial mainstream and gathers to it a host of true believers. Bluegrass, for example, is often equated with mountain music or seen as its natural outgrowth. Many of the major performers did indeed come from the southeastern hill country, but some seminal bluegrass musicians—including Bill Monroe—came from other areas. Stylistically, bluegrass is indebted to musicians and styles from a variety of nonmountain and mountain sources, and its songs come from no one region.

Although bluegrass is not an old-time style and is in fact a dynamic and ever-evolving form, it has nonetheless attracted a horde of fans and musicians with a traditional bent who have repaired to it as a refuge from the "progressive" and pop styles that have inundated mainstream country music. It is welcomed as one of the few areas of performance where acoustic instruments, high-lonesome singing, and down-to-earth songs can still be heard. As an increasingly popular phenomenon, however, and one that is marked by virtuoso styles of playing, bluegrass has also attracted many who have no commitment to tradition at all and who are instead charmed by the fresh and inventive musicianship which they find there. It has been the fate of bluegrass music to spawn the same kind of stylistic divergence, as well as debates concerning identity, that the larger country music field has experienced. "Traditional" bluegrass now competes with "progressive" bluegrass.

While the edifice of bluegrass was built by many hands, the chief architect was that master musician from Kentucky, Bill Monroe. William Smith Monroe was born on September 13, 1911, on a farm in western Kentucky, near Rosine and far from the aristocratic bluegrass district. Eight years younger than his nearest brother, Charlie, and plagued by poor eyesight, Monroe became a reclusive child whose most cherished retreat was music. Fortunately, he had several models and sources on whom he could draw. His mother, Malissa Vandiver Monroe, who died when he was ten, bequeathed a love for music to all of her eight children through her ballad singing and skill on the harmonica, accordion, and fiddle. Her talented son also received instruction in the shape-note singing schools which occasionally convened at the Baptist and Methodist churches in Rosine, but he seems to have absorbed more from the congregational singing of the churches, and especially from the Holiness people who occasionally held revivals in the little town.

The powerful vocal inspiration exerted by the religious groups was complemented by the instrumental training he received from a black musician, Arnold Shultz, and an uncle, Pendleton Vandiver (sometimes spelled Vanderver). At about the age of twelve, Monroe began playing guitar accompaniment for Shultz at dances in western Kentucky. Until his death on April 14, 1931, Shultz—a coal miner by day and a musician at night— gained fame as both a hoedown fiddler and a thumb-and-finger style guitarist. Shultz evidently played both "hillbilly" music and blues. The early indoctrination received from Shultz and other local black musicians, along with the sounds heard on the recordings of his favorite commercial performer, Jimmie Rodgers, gave Monroe a liking for the blues which has remained with him throughout his performing career.

The greatest noncommercial influence in Monroe's musical life came from his Uncle Pen Vandiver. He lived with his uncle for several years and as a teenager often accompanied the old fiddler with his guitar at country dances. Uncle Pen taught him timing and left him a large storehouse of tunes, such as "Jerusalem Ridge," which have endured in the bluegrass repertory. Monroe has memorialized his uncle in the songs he preserved, but also more directly in an original composition, now a bluegrass standard, called "Uncle Pen."

Monroe played the guitar frequently as a young man, but he eventually settled on the mandolin largely because his older brothers, Birch and Charlie, had chosen the fiddle and guitar respectively. Bill joined his brothers in Whiting, Indiana, in 1929, and began playing music with them shortly thereafter. The famous Monroe Brothers duet (Charlie and Bill) came into existence in 1934 when Birch decided to forsake a full-time professional career. As a duet team the Monroe Brothers set a standard of performing excellence that is still remembered by older country fans, particularly in the Carolinas, where they performed often from 1935 to 1938 (under the sponsorship of Texas Crystals and Crazy Water Crystals). The harmony of their musical performances, however, was not always matched by a similar consonance in their brotherly relations. They fought both physically and verbally, and their musical partnership was therefore terminated in 1938.

Charlie soon organized a new band called the Kentucky Pardners; they made their first recordings for the Bluebird label in September 1938. Charlie tried to preserve some of the Monroe Brothers sound and therefore sought tenor singers of Bill's caliber as well as musicians who could play the mandolin. Several well-known mandolinists, such as Curly Sechler, Ira Louvin, Red Rector, and Clyde Baum, eventually played for Charlie, and even the famed guitarist and lead singer Lester Flatt put in a stint as mandolin player and tenor singer for the Kentucky Pardners in the early forties. The Kentucky Pardners always had the sound and flair of an old-time band—their two most famous songs are "Down in the Willow Garden" ("Rose Conley") and "Bringing in the Georgia Mail"—and Charlie's ebullient, out-going personality always gave his performances an ambience far different from that of his serious and taciturn brother.

Bill had much to learn as he embarked upon an independent career. With the Monroe Brothers he had never sung lead or solo (only high tenor harmony), and he had never acted as a master of ceremonies. Although his mandolin playing had been rapid and dynamic, it had always been tied rather closely to the melodic line and was marked by the attempt to emulate the continuous flowing notes of the fiddle. There was little, then, of the jazz-like, improvisatory flair that later characterized his style. Monroe, however, was a man of rugged independence and intense, almost stubborn pride; his quiet resolve to be unique, coupled with brilliant musicianship, made him one of the most respected and influential performers in country music history.

Trying out his new independence, Monroe organized a band called the Kentuckians and played with them for three months on KARK in Little Rock, Arkansas. In that same year of 1938 he moved to the *Crossroad Follies* in Atlanta, where, in honor of his native state, he organized the Blue

Grass Boys (unaware that, like Al Hopkins with the Hill Billies, he had coined a title that would one day become a generic term for a style of country music). The original group included Cleo Davis on guitar, Art Wooten on fiddle, and Monroe on mandolin. A few months later John Miller joined them with his jug (one of several non-bluegrass instruments that Monroe used in the early years), but he was soon replaced by Amos Garin on the stand-up bass. In October 1939 the band auditioned successfully for a spot on the *Grand Ole Opry*, and Monroe delighted the show's founder, George D. Hay, with his high, clear tenor sound. Monroe has remained a pillar of the show for over forty years.

Until 1945 the Blue Grass Boys gave the surface appearance of being merely a string band in the mold of such groups as Mainer's Mountaineers and Roy Hall's Blue Ridge Entertainers. They were a string band, however, with a crucial difference: Bill Monroe. The listener was always aware that, despite the particular vocal or instrumental style conveyed, Monroe was the driving cog and all other musicians revolved around him. With his mandolin setting the beat and rhythm for the band, Monroe also did most of the singing, taking most of the solo parts and then generally sweeping up to a high tenor harmony on the choruses. Monroe's tenor singing—now often described as the "high, lonesome sound"—set a standard for which most bluegrass musicians have striven. "Why he can sing as high as Bill Monroe!" is one of the strongest compliments that a musician can receive.

On the strength of his Saturday night broadcasts on powerful WSM, along with the Victor records which he began making on October 7, 1940, Monroe's fame began to spread throughout much of the nation. Few people at this time bothered to distinguish between Monroe's style and other forms of country music, and his extraordinary musicianship attracted a wide range of followers such as the future honky-tonk ace George Jones and the rockabillies Sonny Curtis, Carl Perkins, and Elvis Presley. In his concerts Monroe remained a man of few words, letting his music stand as "the only communication of his complex creative philosophy."[1] His Victor recordings of 1940 and 1941 included the mixture of styles that has always characterized his performances: instrumental pieces (including the second known recording of "Orange Blossom Special"), solo songs by Monroe, traditional religious and secular numbers, contemporary songs both borrowed and original, and songs done by his lead singer (Clyde Moody, on the early sessions). Monroe began introducing such songs as "New Muleskinner Blues" (his debut song on the *Grand Ole Opry*) and "Footprints in the Snow" which have become standards in the bluegrass repertory.

1. Ralph Rinzler, "Bill Monroe," in *Stars of Country Music*, edited by Bill C. Malone and Judith McCulloh (Urbana: University of Illinois Press, 1975), p. 221.

By 1945 much of the drive, dynamism, and timing of bluegrass music, as well as much of its repertory, had been integrated fully into Monroe's music. The Blue Grass Boys were already becoming famous for their fiddlers, such as Art Wooten, Tommy Magness, Howdy Forrester, and Jim Shumate, and Bill Monroe's distinctive mandolin chop-rhythm gave the group an overall sound different from that of other country bands. But given the overriding importance assumed by the instrument in bluegrass music today, the most conspicuous omission from Monroe's band was the five-string banjo played in three-finger style.

Because of war-time restrictions, the Blue Grass Boys made no recordings between October 2, 1941, and February 13, 1945. When they resumed recording in 1945, this time on the Columbia label, their sound reflected the changes made in their performing style during the interim. Sally Forrester, wife of fiddler Howdy Forrester, played the accordion and, most significantly, David "Stringbean" Akeman, who had joined the band in 1942, played the five-string banjo. By the mid-forties the banjo was perceived as a solo instrument, most often used by comic performers such as Uncle Dave Macon, Grandpa Jones, and Bashful Brother Oswald, and when used in a band it generally played only rhythmic, backup passages. Stringbean was much admired as a droll comedian, but when he quit the band in 1945 to team up with Lew Childre, his departure was not greatly mourned by the other Blue Grass Boys. Stringbean had contributed little to the overall sound of the band and had, in fact, hindered their drive by his tendency to drag the melody. But when Earl Scruggs joined the Blue Grass Boys in 1945, he brought a sensational technique that rejuvenated the five-string banjo, made his own name preeminent among country and folk musicians, and established bluegrass music as a national phenomenon.

Earl Scruggs was born on January 6, 1924, on a farm near Flint Hill, North Carolina (outside Shelby), in a region where banjo pickers thrived. His father and older brothers played the banjo in a style peculiar to their section of North Carolina—a three-finger style (thumb and index and middle fingers) which permitted the instrument to be played in a melodic, syncopated fashion. Along with these models, Scruggs was also exposed to the style through the playing of other western North Carolinians such as Mack Woolbright, Rex Brooks, Smith Hammett (a distant relative of Scruggs'), and Snuffy Jenkins. Jenkins, a product of Harris, North Carolina, had taken the technique to the largest audience through his performances on WBT in Charlotte in 1934 and on WIS in Columbia, South Carolina, after 1937. Many banjoists, including Don Reno and Ralph Stanley, credit Jenkins with having given them their first exposure to three-finger picking.

Earl Scruggs, therefore, did not invent the style which now bears his name, but he perfected it and carried it to greater technical proficiency than anyone before him. Above all, as a member of the Blue Grass Boys and later as a partner with Lester Flatt, he did the most to introduce "Scruggs picking" to the world. When he joined Bill Monroe in 1945 as an instrumentalist, the twenty-year-old musician already had several years of professional experience, including a short stint with Wiley and Zeke Morris in 1939 over WSPA in Spartanburg, South Carolina. He was part of Lost John Miller's band in Nashville when Monroe hired him as a Blue Grass Boy in August 1945. Scruggs added a new and dynamic ingredient to the Blue Grass Boys sound, and audiences were bowled over by the boy who, with a shower of syncopated notes, had made the banjo a lead instrument capable of playing the fastest of songs. Here was something new under the sun—a banjo player who acted as a serious musician and not as a figure of comic relief. Even Uncle Dave Macon, watching from the wings of the *Grand Ole Opry*, supposedly said of the poker-faced young man, "He ain't one damned bit funny." [2]

Scruggs joined a band of superb musicians which, to many bluegrass partisans, will always rank as both the first and the best in the bluegrass genre. This was classic bluegrass at its zenith. In addition to Monroe and Scruggs, this seminal band included Lester Flatt on guitar, Robert "Chubby" Wise on fiddle, and Cedric Rainwater (Howard Watts) on bass. Between 1945 and 1948 the modern bluegrass sound came into being. According to bluegrass authority Pete Kuykendall, the first recorded numbers to bear all the elements of the new style were "Will You Be Loving Another Man," featuring the lead singing of its writer, Lester Flatt, and "Blue Yodel No. 4" (an old Jimmie Rodgers number), recorded for Columbia on September 16, 1946. [3] Well before the records came out, however, fans and musicians had ample time to be exposed to the exciting new sound through WSM broadcasts and the popular tent show tours sponsored by Monroe. The Blue Grass Boys traveled in a nine-passenger Packard limousine with a rack on top for the bass fiddle, and with a complement of five trucks which transported the tent, bleachers, and chairs. Periodically, Monroe and the boys also challenged communities to sandlot baseball games, an effective way of breaking the monotony of constant travel and of advertising the night concerts.

In the three-year period from 1945 to 1948 the banjo assumed a prominence in Monroe's music that it had never enjoyed in any previous band, and an ensemble style of music, much like jazz in the improvised solo work of the individual instruments, came into existence. Throughout the nation, largely unnoticed by the more commercial world of country music, a veritable "bluegrass revolution" got underway as both fans and musi-

2. Although this quote is used by Charles Wolfe in his essay on Uncle Dave in *Stars of Country Music* (p. 53), neither Wolfe or I know where it originated. It is just part of the large body of folklore that has circulated about Macon.

3. Pete Kuykendall, "Bill Monroe and His Bluegrass Boys," *Disc Collector*, no. 13 (no date): 19.

cians became attracted to the music. Young musicians began copying the sounds they heard on Bill Monroe records: the mandolin, banjo, and fiddle passages of Monroe, Scruggs, and Wise, the guitar runs of Lester Flatt, and the high, hard harmony singing of Flatt and Monroe or of the trios and quartets featured on gospel numbers. It is no wonder that Bill Monroe felt bitterly disappointed, and even betrayed, when Flatt and Scruggs left the group in 1948. His greatest band now seemed a thing of the past, and he perhaps did not realize that a host of great musicians were yearning to play for him.

The bluegrass "sound" did not become a "style" until other musical organizations began copying the instrumental and vocal traits first featured in Bill Monroe's performances. Neil Rosenberg believes that the Stanley Brothers' recording of "Molly and Tenbrooks," released in September 1948, is "the first direct evidence" that musicians were copying the sound of the "original" bluegrass band.[4] The Stanley Brothers learned their version from a live performance by Monroe and actually recorded the song before Monroe's 1949 recording of the exciting race-horse song was released. In their recording the Stanley Brothers featured the banjo played in Scruggs' style and, in an obvious copy of Monroe's vocal performance, entrusted the vocal duties to mandolin-playing, tenor-singing Pee Wee Lambert.

Ralph and Carter Stanley were part of a growing number of musicians in the mid- and late forties who either borrowed songs from Monroe or copied the style of the Blue Grass Boys note for note. Like the Stanley Brothers, some of them recorded for a small record company in Johnson City, Tennessee, called Rich-R-Tone. Records by such performers as Wilma Lee and Stoney Cooper, Carl Sauceman, the Bailey Brothers, Buffalo Johnson, and Jim Eanes circulated extensively in the southeastern hill country but received little exposure elsewhere. Some of the fledgling bluegrass performers were introduced to music through the performances of Monroe and the Blue Grass Boys; others, such as Jim and Jesse McReynolds, the Lonesome Pine Fiddlers, Jim Eanes, and Mac Wiseman (to name only a few), had already been pursuing musical careers before Monroe's exciting Columbia records were released. In many cases it was merely the addition of a Scruggs-style banjo player—such as Hoke Jenkins, who joined the McReynolds Brothers in 1949, or Allen Shelton, who teamed with Jim Eanes at about the same time—which marked the transition to bluegrass.

The Blue Grass Boys did more than inspire imitation; they also contributed musicians directly to the proliferating style. In the years since 1939 the personnel of the Blue Grass Boys has changed often, and the list of individuals who played with Monroe and then went on to found their own organizations or to play in other bands reads like a "Who's Who" of Blue-

4. Neil Rosenberg, "From Sound to Style: The Emergence of Bluegrass," *Journal of American Folklore* 80, no. 316 (April–June 1967): 146.

grass Music: Clyde Moody, Lester Flatt, Earl Scruggs, Don Reno, Gordon Terry, Carter Stanley, Mac Wiseman, Jimmy Martin, Vassar Clements, Peter Rowan, Roland White, Sonny Osborne, and James Monroe. The exodus began in 1948, when Flatt and Scruggs grew tired of the Blue Grass Boys' grinding road schedule and temporarily retired from the music business. Before the year was over, however, they had formed their own band, the Foggy Mountain Boys, named after a Carter Family song which they often performed. Joined by two other recent dropouts from the Blue Grass Boys, fiddler Jim Shumate and bass player Cedric Rainwater, along with another guitarist and featured singer, Mac Wiseman, Flatt and Scruggs began the independent professional career that would soon make them one of the most popular country acts in the nation.

After working for about three weeks in Hickory, North Carolina, Flatt and Scruggs moved in the spring of 1948 to WCYB in Bristol, Virginia, where they began receiving hundreds of cards and letters and requests for bookings too numerous to be filled. In that same busy year of 1948 they recorded the first of their songs for Mercury, a body of material that still stands as among the most exciting in the history of bluegrass music. Most bluegrass bands still include songs from Flatt and Scruggs' Mercury years (1948–1950) in their repertories: "My Little Girl in Tennessee," "Foggy Mountain Breakdown" (made doubly famous in 1967 as the theme for the movie *Bonnie and Clyde*), "My Cabin in Caroline," "We'll Meet Again, Sweetheart," "Old Salty Dog Blues," "Roll in My Sweet Baby's Arms." The popularity of the two last-named songs seems all the more remarkable in that they were recorded more or less as filler at the band's last Mercury recording session in October 1950, a session done in haste to fulfill a contractual obligation before moving to the Columbia label.

Flatt and Scruggs and the Foggy Mountain Boys also became one of the most active touring groups in country music, first in such "traditional" formats as store openings, drive-in movies, country schools, and county fairs, but eventually in the largest auditoriums in the nation, on college and university campuses, at folk festivals and clubs, at Carnegie Hall, and in Japan. A major breakthrough in their career came in 1953 when the Martha White Flour Mills hired them to do a fifteen-minute program on WSM each morning at 5:45. Fans came to know the Martha White jingle as well as they did other songs in the Flatt and Scruggs repertory, and the duo often received requests for the tune at their concerts. The association with Martha White Flour was mutually profitable for Flatt and Scruggs and the company. Their music was introduced to a steadily expanding public, even though the pace required to do personal appearances and then to return for the early morning radio show was a killing one (WSM eventually, and mercifully, permitted the shows to be taped). On the strength of their mounting popularity and best-selling Columbia records, WSM added them to the regular cast of the *Grand Ole Opry* in 1955. This coveted forum fur-

The Blue Grass Boys: *left to right*, Birch Monroe, Lester Flatt, Bill Monroe, Earl Scruggs, Chubby Wise. Courtesy of Ralph Rinzler.

The Blue Grass Boys: *left to right*, Art Wooten, Bill Monroe, Billy Borum, Jim Holmes. Courtesy of Ralph Rinzler.

ther contributed to their growing fame, a recognition that not even the impending rock-and-roll invasion could diminish. The Martha White Company was not hesitant about expressing its gratitude to the Foggy Mountain Boys. Cohen T. Williams, president of the firm that advertised Hot Rize (a self-rising ingredient in the flour and meal), stated unequivocally that "Flatt and Scruggs and the Grand Ole Opry built the Martha White Mills."[5]

Flatt and Scruggs' music communicated beautifully via the radio microphone and phonograph recording, but to be fully appreciated it needed to be seen as well as heard. The physical interaction between the musicians, the smoothness of their performances, and the diversity of their material made the Flatt and Scruggs show both an auditory and a visual delight. Lester Flatt was responsible for much of the easy-going ambience of the show. Ever since his birth in Overton County, Tennessee, in 1914, he had been consumed with making music; but until he joined Charlie Monroe's Kentucky Pardners in 1943 as a mandolin player and tenor singer, the demands of an early marriage had never permitted him much respite from long periods of employment in textile mills. From the Kentucky Pardners he went directly to the Blue Grass Boys, where he gained invaluable experience as a master of ceremonies and as a lead singer (the only Blue Grass Boy in history to be identified on record labels along with Bill Monroe). As co-leader of his own band, Flatt proved to be a genial and unassuming host, a singer with a relaxed and supple style, and a backup guitarist of considerable skill. When playing songs at breakneck speed with Bill Monroe, he devised a method of getting back on the beat before resuming singing after instrumental breaks. This was an ascending run which began on the bass E string and ended with a ringing note on the third or G string. Although this run was played most often in the key of G, the use of the capo permitted it to be used in other keys, such as A or B, which were popular in bluegrass. The Lester Flatt G-run, as it has come to be called, was widely copied by other guitarists. Bass runs of this type were among the most distinctive features of bluegrass music. Played on deep-toned acoustic guitars (usually Martin D28s), and coming at the end of fiddle, mandolin, or banjo sequences (and sometimes at the end of vocal phrases, as in Monroe's "Uncle Pen" or Jimmy Martin's "Sunny Side of the Mountain"), the runs added a dramatic note of emphasis or finality to the overall mood of intensity created by the supercharged music.

Many people, of course, came to hear the Foggy Mountain Boys solely because of Earl Scruggs. His dazzling banjo style was made to seem even more remarkable by the seeming ease with which he did it. He usually stood poker-faced on the stage, his body appearing almost motionless as

5. Don Walker, "Music Built Mills: Martha White Head," *CMA Close-Up*, February 1963, p. 3.

the three fingers of his right hand produced a torrent of notes. In October 1951 he introduced still another affecting technique which added further to his reputation as a master musician. On "Earl's Breakdown" he adjusted his tuning pegs at various intervals in the song to move from one chord to another and then back to the original. By the time he recorded "Flint Hill Special" in November 1952, he had devised a tuning mechanism which permitted quick retuning of the banjo's B and G strings. Scruggs was not content to be merely a banjo virtuoso; he occasionally picked up a guitar, especially on gospel numbers, and demonstrated a mastery of both finger-picking and Carter Family–style techniques.

Flatt and Scruggs were more than ably supported by the talented musicians who made up the Foggy Mountain Boys. Much of the verve and drive of the band came from its fiddlers, particularly Benny Martin (who also attempted a solo singing career in the fifties) and Paul Warren. Martin had played on the great Mercury recording sessions, but Warren, an alumnus of Johnny and Jack's Tennessee Mountain Boys, was with Flatt and Scruggs through all the important years after 1954. A high point of each Flatt and Scruggs concert was Warren's rendition of such hoedown tunes as "Sally Gooden" or his showpiece, "Black Eyed Susan." Probably in an attempt to build a sound different from Bill Monroe's, Flatt and Scruggs gave little prominence to the mandolin; instead, their mandolin players were best known for their harmony singing. Everett Lilly was a fine musician from Clear Creek, West Virginia, and he did take an occasional instrumental break. Nevertheless, his real value to the Foggy Mountain Boys came through his high, crisp tenor singing. Curly Sechler (also spelled Seckler) was even more important to the group because he remained with them for many years, during both the Mercury and Columbia periods, and after that was a mainstay of Lester Flatt's new group, the Nashville Grass. Sechler's mandolin was almost never heard—in his own words he just "held the mandolin"[6]—but his tenor harmony was unsurpassed in the whole field of bluegrass music. His powerful, ringing voice complemented Lester Flatt's perfectly, and on such songs as "Some Old Day" and "My Little Girl in Tennessee" they gave echoes of the brother-duet style of singing while also defining the essence of bluegrass harmony. Although the mandolin's relative unimportance was a factor in establishing a unique identity for Flatt and Scruggs, the addition of the dobro in 1955 was much more significant. Some bluegrass purists lamented the use of an instrument that had not been present in Bill Monroe's original band (forgetting that the master himself had once employed an accordionist), but the instrument immediately attracted the fancy of listeners and did much to give Flatt and Scruggs an entree into the broader country and western field.

6. Sechler said this to me during a taping of Flatt and Scruggs' WSM radio shows (Nashville, August 23, 1961).

The dobro player was Burkett "Buck" Graves (also known in his comedian's role as "Uncle Josh"). Graves may not have been the first dobro player in bluegrass music—Speedy Krise, for example, had played the instrument on a Carl Butler recording in December 1950—but he undoubtedly did most to revitalize it and to make it attractive to younger musicians. During earlier periods with such performers as Molly O'Day and Mac Wiseman, Graves had played the dobro in a style that was indebted to his hero, Cliff Carlisle, and to other musicians such as Bashful Brother Oswald. Graves, though, was captivated by Scruggs' rapid, multiple-noted banjo playing, and he became determined to adapt that style, or something similar to it, to the dobro. By the time he became a Foggy Mountain Boy, Graves had perfected a rolling, syncopated style that enabled him to play galloping breakdowns as well as slow love songs or ballads. With Graves leading the way, the dobro made a major comeback in country music, and some of the old-time masters of the instrument—most notably Shot Jackson, who appeared on scores of records during the sixties— began to re-emerge from undeserved obscurity. A growing number of young musicians, such as Mike Auldridge and Jerry Douglas, also began an experimentation with the instrument whose fruits would flower eloquently in the late sixties and early seventies.

The Foggy Mountain Boys did not merely play well; they also looked good while doing it. Since they used no electric instruments, they were heavily dependent on microphone amplification. Most of the places where they played had few microphones, so the musicians had to move in and out of the center stage in order to take their vocal and instrumental breaks, while also being careful not to bump into each other or to poke a fiddle bow into someone's eye. The Foggy Mountain Boys converted a technical necessity into an art, moving to and from the microphone with a smoothness and precision that seemed choreographed. The sight of Buck Graves weaving in and out of musicians in order to lift his dobro to the microphone was something that will not soon be forgotten. The dramatic stage presence exhibited by the group, along with the skillful blending of songs and instrumental pieces, sacred and secular numbers, and seriousness and comedy (usually performed by Graves and bassman Jake Tullock as "Uncle Josh" and "Cousin Jake"), all combined to make the Flatt and Scruggs show one of the legendary acts of country music history.

By the early fifties several major bands had emerged which exhibited a Monroe parentage or discipleship. Some of these groups, such as those headed by Don Reno and Red Smiley, Mac Wiseman, and the Osborne Brothers, often had songs which appeared on country DJ shows and on jukeboxes—a phenomenon that is now extremely rare. Country music had not yet fragmented decisively into "hard country" and "pop country" categories, and the "old-time" country styles had not yet become casualties in Nashville's campaign to recoup its losses after the rock-and-roll assault. Furthermore, the word "bluegrass" had not yet come into complete and systematic usage, although an increasing number of people were beginning to attach the term to the proliferating number of bands which seemed somehow to be in the Bill Monroe mold. Why and when this happened are questions that will probably never be conclusively answered. At some undetermined point, probably in the late forties or early fifties, fans, record sellers, and disc jockeys began using the term as an identifying description. Neil Rosenberg suggests that the first usage of the word may have come about when fans of Flatt and Scruggs, who were aware that a feud existed between them and Bill Monroe, requested the "old blue grass songs you used to do"[7] rather than mentioning their former boss by name. Sometime in the early fifties Jimmie Skinner's Music Center in Cincinnati, founded by a deep-voiced singer and writer from Blue Lick, Kentucky, began to advertise "bluegrass records" in its catalogues and newsletters. The music store had a large clientele of transplanted southern hillbillies who, like Skinner himself, still yearned for the music of home. The center also advertised on WCKY in Cincinnati, where such DJ's as Wayne Raney, Nelson King, Marty Roberts, and Jimmie Logsdon labored to give the developing bluegrass genre a wider circulation. Bluegrass attracted supporters for a wide variety of reasons, but one powerful source of its appeal lay in its down-home ambience and the belief that it was a refuge from both an overorganized, alienating society and an overstylized country music that was steadily forsaking its roots.

In those formative years before the urban folk revival introduced bluegrass to a new audience and a new repertory, at least six acts gave serious competition to Monroe and Flatt and Scruggs: Don Reno and Red Smiley, Mac Wiseman, the Osborne Brothers, Jimmy Martin, Jim and Jesse McReynolds, and the Stanley Brothers. Reno and Smiley headed a band called the Tennessee Cutups, even though neither of the two men hailed from that state. In a musical style where versatility seemed to be the norm, Don Reno, from Spartanburg, South Carolina, possessed a range of talents that almost staggers the imagination. He was a good songwriter, an excellent tenor harmony singer, a comedian, and a master of several instruments, including the mandolin, guitar, and banjo. His guitar work has often been overlooked in the flood of praise that surrounds his seminal banjo contributions, but he was one of the first men in bluegrass to play the guitar as a lead instrument in flat-picking fashion. The stellar Doc Watson credits Reno as an influence on his own style. As a banjoist Reno was surpassed by no one, not even Scruggs. He was a highly inventive banjo player, and was adept at both the three-finger and plectrum styles that were indebted to guitar and pedal steel playing. Reno learned the three-finger style from Snuffy Jenkins, and employed it with such groups

7. Neil Rosenberg, Notes, *Flatt and Scruggs* (Time-Life Collection), p. 12.

as the Morris Brothers in the forties. He played for Bill Monroe briefly in 1948, not long after Scruggs had resigned from the Blue Grass Boys, and then moved on to begin his own independent bluegrass career.

Reno organized the Tennessee Cutups in 1949, and was joined by Arthur Lee "Red" Smiley a few months later. The Asheville, North Carolina, native brought a warm and fluid baritone to the group which fit comfortably and closely with Reno's tenor. They performed on radio in Roanoke, Virginia, in 1949, and then moved on to the *Wheeling Jamboree*, broadcast on powerful WWVA in Wheeling, West Virginia. Although they made a few records for the Federal label, the real burgeoning of their career came in 1952 when they recorded the first of their songs for King. "I'm Using My Bible for a Roadmap," written by Reno, contained the basic elements for which they became famous: Reno's ringing banjo playing, which combined both a three-finger roll and plectrum-style chords; Smiley's dramatic, run-filled guitar backup; and the two men's close, smooth harmony. Reno's tenor harmony singing was modeled on that of two markedly dissimilar stylists, Bill Monroe and Bill Bolick, and he could move alternately and easily from a high, almost falsetto, sound to a low and plaintive tenor.

Their most productive years in the fifties and early sixties found them ensconced on the *Old Dominion Barn Dance* in Richmond, Virginia, and on a daily television program in Roanoke. Their stage shows rivaled those of Flatt and Scruggs for diversity. In addition to Reno and Smiley's fine musicianship, the shows also featured Mack Magaha's acrobatic old-time fiddling and zany comedy skits in which all the band members dressed in costume and drag and played the roles of ridiculous characters. Reno and Smiley did hard-driving bluegrass and gospel numbers, as all bluegrass groups did, but they also performed honky-tonk style songs and other types that were close to mainstream country. Some of these songs, such as "Let's Live for Tonight," were written by Reno himself, or by members of the band (such as Magaha's "I Know You're Married, but I Love You Still"), or by outsiders, as in the case of Buck Owens' "Sweethearts in Heaven." Beginning in about 1954, and partly through the requests of Syd Nathan at King Records, Reno began playing the guitar on many of their recorded numbers. Some of the group's most beautiful and compelling performances, such as "You Never Mentioned Him to Me," "East Bound Freight Train," and "Freight Train Boogie," were done with guitar accompaniment. In the midst of these busy years with the Tennessee Cutups, Reno made history in still another guise, as the banjoist on a recording of "Feuding Banjoes" with his old friend Arthur "Guitar Boogie" Smith. In this 1955 recording Reno traded licks with Smith, who played the tenor banjo. Several years later the song re-emerged in the soundtrack of the movie *Deliverance* as "Dueling Banjoes." A successful lawsuit by Reno and Smith established conclusively that their version had been the model on which the movie tune was based.

Although Reno and Smiley had outstanding individual identities, it is nevertheless difficult to think of them apart. Mac Wiseman, on the other hand, has hewed an independent course through most of his performing career, and in the process has become the best solo singer in bluegrass music. Wiseman is, in many ways, a man of paradox. He has never considered himself solely a bluegrass musician; yet it is in that field of music that he has established his reputation. No one knows more old songs than Wiseman, but no bluegrass singer has been more receptive to new songs from other genres. Tradition lives strongly in Wiseman—in his style of singing, and in his repertory of old songs—but he has never resisted innovation and has even been a staunch defender of country-pop music.

Wiseman was born in 1925 in Crimora, in the Shenandoah Valley of Virginia, and was a descendant of the sturdy, pietistic German stock that had settled the area from Pennsylvania. Growing up in an area where music was strongly valued and preserved, he gradually accumulated an immense repertory of songs that is among the largest known by anyone in country music. He had a particularly large storehouse of material from the turn of the century, including such songs as "Just Tell Them That You Saw Me," "Preacher and the Bear," and "Letter Edged in Black." Many of these songs, of course, were learned from professional entertainers, and Wiseman's recorded repertory reflects this influence in songs chosen from Buddy Starcher, the Carter Family, Molly O'Day, Bradley Kincaid, and others.

It was with Molly O'Day that Wiseman broke into full-time professional music. In 1946 he joined this great singer as a bass player, and worked with her in Knoxville and Atlanta. He also played on many of the recordings she made for Columbia and came away from the experience with an additional collection of songs, such as "Six More Miles to the Graveyard," which he still performs today. He organized his first band, the Country Boys, in 1947 and performed with them for about a year on personal appearances and on the popular *Farm and Fun Time* in Bristol, Virginia. Like other musicians of the time who had an old-time bent, Wiseman gravitated toward the bluegrass style that was then coalescing. He joined the first Flatt and Scruggs band as a guitarist and featured singer (a role he played in all bands of which he was a member), but then went with Bill Monroe to the *Grand Ole Opry* in 1949.

From 1950 to 1957, when he went out on his own with a new version of the Country Boys, Wiseman experienced a commercial success that was surpassed by no one in bluegrass music except Flatt and Scruggs (and possibly Bill Monroe). He and his band averaged three hundred personal appearances a year and recorded several songs that received extensive airplay throughout the United States. His band had an exciting, surging sound, marked by the use of twin fiddles and Wiseman's own inventive guitar runs, and Wiseman began building his reputation as "the voice with a heart." His voice was a husky tenor with excellent range and unusual expressiveness and, like Hank Snow's, his articulation was precise and somewhat mannered. He could sing lead or harmony and was equally adept at rousing, uptempoed tunes or slow, serious numbers. Whatever the style, Wiseman invested each song with a heart-felt sincerity that was hard to resist. On such songs as "I Still Write Your Name in the Sand," "Love Letters in the Sand," "I Wonder How the Old Folks Are at Home," "Little White Church," and "Dreaming of a Little Cabin," he demonstrated his knowledge of vintage material, both pop and country, while also bequeathing to country music some of its classic vocal performances.

Mac Wiseman always maintained close ties with mainstream country music, acting as Dot Records' country A&R man from 1957 to 1963 and recording an occasional song that employed standard country instrumentation. The Osborne Brothers, however, did more than any other group with bluegrass identification to fuse their music with country and western styles. Bobby and Sonny Osborne were born in the coal-mining town of Hyden, Kentucky, in 1931 and 1937 respectively, but they moved with their parents to Dayton, Ohio, in the early forties. The movement of country and incipient bluegrass musicians into and out of bands in the late forties and early fifties was almost labyrinthian, and the Osbornes' affiliations are no exceptions. The Osbornes were born into a musical family—their father sang, yodeled, and played the banjo, fiddle, and guitar—and this home experience was augmented by the broadcasts of the *Grand Ole Opry*. As a small boy Bobby was fascinated by Ernest Tubb, and he tried to emulate the sounds heard on the Texas Troubadour's records by singing in a low register and playing an electric guitar. By the time he was sixteen, though, his voice had changed to a high tenor, and he had heard the classic recordings of Monroe, Flatt, and Scruggs. He began performing locally in southern Ohio in 1949, and in July of that year he began the transition to bluegrass music in Middletown, Ohio, when he met Larry Richardson, a banjo player and tenor singer from Galax, Virginia. In November 1949 they joined a string band in Bluefield, West Virginia, called the Lonesome Pine Fiddlers. Richardson's three-finger banjo playing and Osborne's high tenor helped to pull that old-time group across the line into bluegrass music.

Between 1949 and 1951, or until Bobby was inducted into the Marines, he played for a shifting assemblage of musicians, but he began his fateful association with Jimmy Martin, with whom he made his first records for a major label (King), in August 1951. His younger brother Sonny began playing the banjo during this period, and Sonny, Bobby, their sister Louise, and Jimmy Martin made their first records for the small Kitty label in Miamisburg, Ohio, about 1951. By the summer of 1952, when he was barely fifteen, Sonny was appearing on the *Grand Ole Opry* with Bill Monroe and had made a series of recordings with the Blue Grass Boys. When Bobby returned to civilian life in 1953, he found that his brother was more than ready to join him in a professional music venture. They joined with Jimmy Martin again, played with him in Detroit for about a year, and in 1954 made a series of records in Nashville which are still highly prized by collectors of early bluegrass music. They spent much of 1955 at WWVA in Wheeling, West Virginia, working with Charlie Bailey (best known for his duet performances with his brother Danny), and then returned home to Dayton in 1956. In that year they began another fateful association, this time with Kentucky-born Red Allen. Together, they produced some major innovations in the style of bluegrass singing, and the Osborne Brothers began their march toward becoming the most commercially successful act in the bluegrass field.

By the time they joined with Allen, Sonny had begun to take a more active role in singing, so they began to devise a trio style (which in itself was rather rare for bluegrass music). Recording for MGM in 1956, they produced their first giant hit, "Ruby," which Bobby had been singing for years. Bobby had learned the song from his father, who in turn had picked it up from Cousin Emmy's 1947 recording. The song's instrumental backing was unusual—Bobby and Sonny both played banjoes—but it was Bobby's sky-high, piercing tenor singing that made the record so commercially appealing. Right at the end of the song the trio came in together and sang the last line with a slow, modulated, note-bending flourish that became one of their trademarks. In 1958 the trio made their most important innovations yet when they recorded a song called "Once More." Most bluegrass and country groups had typically put their harmony lines above the lead singer who sang the melody. In bluegrass trio singing, for example, someone usually sang a tenor just above the lead, and another voice either sang a baritone just below the lead or went up above the tenor into what was called a high baritone. The Osborne Brothers, on the other hand, put the two harmony voices below Bobby's high lead. They made this change in order to take advantage of Bobby's unusual tenor range and to make singing with him more comfortable for Sonny and Red Allen. Other bluegrass groups, though, were charmed by the style's uniqueness and found that it permitted a wider range of vocal arrangements and choice of keys. The style has been widely copied. For the Osbornes, this was only the beginning of a series of departures from the bluegrass norm. Compared to most bluegrass groups, they weathered the rock-and-roll storm very well, and when the country music resurgence came in the early sixties, the Osborne Brothers found themselves not only the most popular bluegrass band in America, but a highly competitive group in mainstream country as well.

The Osborne Brothers' occasional partner, Jimmy Martin, has clung steadfastly to the standards originally set by Bill Monroe. Through successive changes in bluegrass music, Martin has adhered faithfully to the acoustic, hard-driving instrumental sound and high-lonesome singing for which he became famous in the early fifties. James Henry "Jimmy" Martin was born on a farm near Sneedville, Tennessee, in 1927. Almost from the time he was born, music became the all-consuming passion of his life, and when he first heard Bill Monroe on WSM, the stylistic road he would follow became firmly fixed. Jimmy plowed corn one summer for his neighbors at fifty cents a day, and with the $7.50 accumulated, he bought his first Gene Autry guitar. He was working as a house painter and singing part time on radio in Morristown, Tennessee, in late 1949, when he went to Nashville and successfully auditioned for a place in the Blue Grass Boys. In the opinion of many, he became the best lead singer and guitarist Bill Monroe ever had.

Martin's high, reedy voice, and subtle intonations complemented Monroe's singing extremely well, and his strong rhythm guitar playing, punctuated frequently with dynamic bass runs, gave the Blue Grass Boys a surging, supercharged sound that not even the Lester Flatt years had witnessed. Martin's addition to the group coincided with Monroe's move to the Decca label, and during his two separate stints with the Blue Grass Boys, 1950–1951 and 1952–1954, he helped to produce a sound that was every bit as "classic" as that made by Flatt and Scruggs in the forties. On such secular songs as "Uncle Pen" (first recorded during these years), "On the Old Kentucky Shore," and "The Little Girl and the Dreadful Snake," and on such religious pieces as "River of Death," "Lord Protect My Soul," and "Voice from on High," Martin and Monroe evoked images of that lonesome, rural life that had originally been the context for bluegrass music's emergence. It was "white soul singing" at its best.

During his periods of absence from the Blue Grass Boys, Martin began forging professional relations with other musicians, including the crucial one with the Osborne Brothers. In 1951 he and Bobby Osborne formed the Sunny Mountain Boys, the name that he has ever since used for his band. As described earlier in the chapter, the Martin-Osborne association resulted in some memorable recordings—such as "20/20 Vision" for RCA— but they severed their partnership in August 1955, when the Osbornes left Detroit, where they had been working on WJR (they had also appeared on CKLW-TV in Windsor, Ontario). Martin remained in Detroit for a few months, but then moved to the *Louisiana Hayride* in about 1956. During this period, and on through his tenure on WWVA in the late fifties, Martin attracted several excellent young musicians to the Sunny Mountain Boys, including mandolinists Earl Taylor and Paul Williams and banjoists Sam Hutchins, J. D. Crowe, and Bill Emerson. In Williams and Crowe, who accompanied him to Shreveport, he found the musicians who came closest to matching him in timing, drive, and dynamism. Joined by Williams' high tenor singing and Crowe's crisp and powerful banjo playing, Martin produced songs such as "Sophronie" and "Ocean of Diamonds" that have become standards in bluegrass music.

Although Martin has often been a controversial entertainer, because of his outspokenness and his tendency to show his irritation with sidemen who cannot match his very high standards, he has nevertheless been a consistently loyal partisan of bluegrass music. And at his best (which is most of the time) he has given the music he loves some of its greatest moments both as a singer and as a guitarist.

Great moments also spiced the career of Carter and Ralph Stanley, from Stratton, Virginia. The Stanleys were probably the most tradition-based act in bluegrass music, with a repertory heavily laced with old songs and a style of performance that often suggested the mountain string bands of the twenties and thirties. Growing up in the mountains of southwestern Virginia, Carter and Ralph were born early enough (in 1925 and 1927 respectively) to hear the radio broadcasts and recordings of such people as the Carter Family, Grayson and Whitter, Mainer's Mountaineers, and Roy Hall's Blue Ridge Entertainers. They also learned directly from their musical parents and from neighbors in their boyhood Baptist church near McClure, Virginia. Their father was a sawmill operator who sang old songs like "Man of Constant Sorrow" and "Wild Bill Jones," while their mother, the most musical of the two parents, played claw-hammer banjo style (as all of her brothers and sisters did). The Stanleys often heard old hymns, such as "The Village Churchyard," lined out in the local church, usually by their father or an uncle, to a congregation that made no attempts to sing in parts. Much of the feeling, as well as a few of the songs, from that highly ornamented style insinuated itself into Carter and Ralph's music, although the boys' harmony obviously came from other sources.

When Carter and Ralph returned from military service in 1946, they began making attempts at a professional music career. By this time Carter had fallen under the spell of Bill Monroe, and his admiration for the bluegrass master was second to no one's, not even Jimmy Martin's. He joined a band which included another Monroe disciple, mandolinist Pee Wee Lambert, and guitarist Roy Sykes. When Ralph received his military discharge, he also joined the group, but by December 1946 he and Carter had formed their own independent band and were performing on WNVA in Norton, Virginia. Within about a month they moved to the king of bluegrass radio stations, WCYB in Bristol, Virginia, where the noontime *Farm and Fun Time* played host, at one time or another, to Flatt and Scruggs, Jim and Jesse, Mac Wiseman, Jimmy Martin, and Bobby Osborne. The sound of the early Stanleys is preserved in a small group of records which they made for Rich-R-Tone between September 1947 and June 1949. Their love for lonesome old songs is seen in their performance of items like "Little Glass of Wine," a murder-and-suicide ballad that was very popular with their hill country listeners. But even more discernible is the influence of Bill Monroe. Pee Wee Lambert, who played mandolin and sang tenor as Monroe did, sang the high harmony on most of their songs and performed the rousing "Molly and Tenbrooks" by himself. Ralph was a shy teenager when the Stanleys first organized, and his singing tended to be a bit hesitant. He usually sang a tenor just above Carter's lead, and Lambert sang a high baritone above him—a practice that endured on into their Columbia recording years. As a banjoist, though, Ralph was already excellent, possessing the ability to play the claw-hammer style learned from his mother, as well as the three-finger style picked up from Snuffy Jenkins.

The Columbia years, 1949–1953, are also distinguished by the maturing of Carter's songwriting abilities. He experimented with all the varieties of songs found in bluegrass, from gospel to secular, but he excelled in the writing of lonesome songs, full of pastoral imagery, that described personal loss or disappointment. Carter had a profound love for his mountain home and the beautiful rural landscape that defined its character. Like a true romanticist, he often wrote of the loss, or possible loss, of the people and places that he loved—parents, sweethearts, the old home place, the rural scenes of childhood. Bob Cantwell suggests that Carter was often singing about his own loneliness and private doubts, and about the growing distance between himself and his childhood home.[8] Like Will Hays and, above all, Albert Brumley, whose songs the Stanley Brothers eloquently performed ("Rank Stranger," "Nobody Answered Me," "If We Never Meet Again"), Carter often used nature or pastoral images as backdrops for his themes of parting, disappointment, and loneliness. In "The Lonesome River," one of the Stanleys' most haunting performances, "The lonesome wind blows and the water rolls high" as the narrator recalls his lover's betrayal. In "The Fields Have Turned Brown," nature seems to mirror the bleakness felt by a wayward son who returns to find his parents dead. And in "The White Dove," one of their most requested songs, the mourning dove, weeping willows, and deep rolling hills of old Virginia all combine to commiserate with the suffering child who recalls his departed parents and the peaceful mountain home they once shared.

By the time the Stanleys signed with Mercury in 1953, Ralph had overcome his early reticence and was using the assertive and penetrating tenor that had often been sublimated. His voice was unmistakably rural in phrasing and pronunciation, and he sang in the classic back-country pinched-throat style with a variety of affecting vocal turns and note embellishments. Over the years his harmony singing became so powerful that it became, in effect, a lead voice, dominating the other voices and pulling them along in its sway. The Mercury years found the Stanley Brothers at the height of their performing powers, and their recordings were characterized by a sharp, bright sound, full of verve and energy. Ralph's blossoming tenor was, of course, responsible for much of this sound, but their

8. Bob Cantwell, "The Lonesome Sound of Carter Stanley," *Bluegrass Unlimited* 10, no. 12 (June 1976).

Ralph (*left*) and Carter Stanley, 1966.
Courtesy of Norman Carlson.

Chubby Wise.
Courtesy of Bobbie Malone.

band, the Clinch Mountain Boys, was pushed along to greater rhythmic drive by the pulsating bass of George Shuffler, one of the first great bass players in bluegrass music. Well before the urban folk revival made Americans conscious of traditional songs and styles, the Stanley Brothers were fusing their mountain sound with the dynamic bluegrass style. The results were what Alan Lomax would soon describe as "folk music with overdrive."[9]

The Stanley Brothers' neighbors from southwestern Virginia, Jim and Jesse McReynolds, who would also play crucial roles in introducing bluegrass music to the world, were nonetheless significantly different from the Stanleys and the other entertainers thus far discussed. Unlike all the others, who either played for Bill Monroe or were directly influenced by him, the McReynolds Brothers drew little direct inspiration from the bluegrass patriarch. Their roots lay in the brother-duet tradition of such singers as the Blue Sky Boys and the Delmore Brothers. Their principal inspirations, above all, were Ira and Charlie Louvin, whose style they suggest and whose songs they often sing. Jim and Jesse were born in a coal mining region of Virginia in 1927 and 1929. Like the Stanley Brothers, they were heirs to a family musical tradition, and some forebears had even made a few records back in the late twenties. When they began their first regular radio stint in 1947 on WNVA in Norton, Virginia, the McReynolds Brothers were closer to the mold of prewar hillbillies than they were to bluegrass. They sang country and old-time gospel songs, and Jesse played both the mandolin and the fiddle (the latter learned from old-time fiddler Marion Sumner). Their career took them to several radio stations in the mountain area and into the Midwest. While working in Waterloo, Iowa, and Wichita, Kansas, they even tried their luck with western-style singing and affected a style similar to that of the Sons of the Pioneers.

When Jesse McReynolds heard the exciting banjo style of Earl Scruggs, he set out to create a similar syncopated sound on his mandolin. He devised a cross-picking technique, marked by the rapid alternating of a flat-pick from string to string, that gave the illusion of multiple picks; it permitted him to play fast songs with a profusion of syncopated notes. He debuted with the style in 1951 when he, Jim, and Larry Roll recorded an album of gospel songs (such as "I'll Fly Away" and "God Put a Rainbow in the Clouds") for the small, and now defunct, Kentucky record label under the name of the Virginia Trio. In 1952 Jim and Jesse moved to the prestigious Capitol label, where the style was introduced to a much larger audience, this time as the accompaniment of a Louvin Brothers song, "Are You Missing Me?"

The Capitol association also marked Jim and Jesse's transition to blue-

9. Alan Lomax, "Bluegrass Background: Folk Music with Overdrive," *Esquire* 52, no. 4 (October 1959): 103–109.

grass. They were joined on the recordings by the three-finger banjo play-ing of Hoke Jenkins, a nephew of Snuffy Jenkins who had first played with them back in 1949. The Capitol years were artistically rewarding but com-mercially disappointing for the McReynolds Brothers, and their tenure with the company was relatively brief. They worked with some of Nashville's out-standing studio musicians, such as fiddlers Tommy Jackson and Tommy Vaden and bassist Bob Moore, and they recorded some of the classics of the bluegrass repertory, including "Airmail Special," "My Little Honey-suckle Rose," and, of course, "Are You Missing Me?"

Although Jim and Jesse's band, the Virginia Boys, has always included great musicians—such as banjoist Allen Shelton and fiddler Vassar Clements—the group has always been most highly valued for its singing. Jesse McReynolds is the marvel of other mandolin players, admired for the remarkable dexterity and speed exhibited on songs like "Border Ride" and "El Cumbancero" and for his cross-picking innovations. Nevertheless, instrumentation was primarily a support for the precise, high harmony singing of the two brothers, and keys were chosen, for example, which highlighted singing rather than instrumental virtuosity. If Jesse was the instrumental mainstay of the duo, Jim was the key to their heralded vocal blend. His smooth and deceptively effortless tenor was sometimes remi-niscent of Ira Louvin, but without the latter's sharp edge. He was probably the least strident of bluegrass singers, and on some slow songs his voice assumed a plaintiveness that recalled the singing of Bill Bolick. Jim and Jesse brought a mellow, soft tone to bluegrass singing, and a receptivity to songs from other genres, that gave them an audience which extended well beyond the borders of their adopted musical field.

While bluegrass grew into a lush and fertile field, the man who had originally sown its seeds continued to evolve and improve as a musi-cian. And, for a time, he also remained unaware of the revolution he had wrought. Bill Monroe was clearly embittered when Flatt and Scruggs left his band, and his irritation only grew as his own contributions were ig-nored in the avalanche of publicity that accompanied bluegrass music's rising popularity in the late fifties. He did not speak to his two former col-leagues for many years. Imitation may be the highest form of flattery, but Monroe did not recognize the truth of the aphorism, at least in the case of the Stanley Brothers. When the Stanleys signed with Columbia in 1949, Monroe severed his relations with the company, complaining that this competitive group played music too similar to his own. The Blue Grass Boys, though, continued to attract outstanding talent, and Monroe's long tenure with Decca (now MCA) saw no break in the outpouring of distin-guished music that had long characterized the man.

As we have seen, the Decca years were inaugurated by Monroe's perfor-mances with Jimmy Martin, the man whose voice so superbly comple-mented his own. In Rudy Lyle, Monroe also found a five-string banjoist who was almost as good as Earl Scruggs. With Martin and Lyle he possessed a combination whose music more than held its own in competition with the sound of the Flatt and Scruggs era. Musicians have come and gone from the Blue Grass Boys with such great rapidity in the years since 1950 that it would be cumbersome, if not impossible, to discuss them all. It is significant that Monroe clung to the concept of the five-string banjo after Scruggs' departure, and such outstanding banjoists as Lyle, Don Stover, Sonny Osborne, Bill Keith, Bobby Thompson, and Vic Jordan spent some time as Blue Grass Boys. Of all instrumentalists, though, fiddlers were most highly prized by Monroe. Such men as Vassar Clements, Gordon Terry, Charlie Cline, Benny Martin, Bobby Hicks, and Benny Williams traveled and recorded with Monroe, but he did not find his consummate fiddler—the man he called "the best fiddler in bluegrass"—until Kenny Baker joined him in 1957. Baker was an ex–coal miner from eastern Kentucky who came to Monroe and bluegrass after earlier experience as a western swing and mainstream country performer. His smooth, flowing, jazz-inflected style made him popular with both fans and Monroe. Although his membership has not been continuous, Baker has been a Blue Grass Boy longer than any other person. Joe Stuart, on the other hand, spent fewer years with Monroe but in some respects has been the most remarkable musician ever employed as a Blue Grass Boy. Since 1955, when he came to the Blue Grass Boys as a banjo player, Stuart has played guitar, fiddle, bass, and banjo in the band. Only Monroe's monopolization of the mandolin has kept Stuart from playing that instrument too.

Over the years Bill Monroe mellowed significantly, becoming more open with interviewers and accepting his role as the patriarch of bluegrass. The urban folk revival contributed greatly to Monroe's personal resurgence. Young folklorists or folk music enthusiasts, such as Mike Seeger, Jim Rooney, and Ralph Rinzler, praised Monroe's achievements and helped to correct the critical imbalance that had arisen in the wake of the adulation given to Earl Scruggs. Ralph Rinzler also acted as Monroe's manager for a short period after 1962 and helped to get him bookings at colleges, folk clubs, and in other arenas of critical importance. Gradually, people began to understand that bluegrass was more than just a Scruggs-style banjo, and that Monroe had been the cog around which the bluegrass machine revolved. Monroe was particularly flattered, and humbled, by the response that young people made to him and his music. The interest evinced by some young northerners was both intriguing and gratifying to him, and a few of them became Blue Grass Boys: Richard Greene, Pete Rowan, Lamar Grier, Douglas B. Green, Roland White, and Bill Keith.

During the nine months he worked for Monroe in 1963, William Bradford Keith (born in Boston in 1939) introduced the first great departure from Scruggs-style banjo. Designed to enhance the playing of fast and complicated fiddle tunes on the banjo, Keith's "chromatic" style (also learned independently by Bobby Thompson in about 1958) stresses the "exact and complete"[10] melody of a tune. Scruggs style, on the other hand, features a shower of syncopated notes, but not all of them fall directly into the melody. Keith's rendition of such tunes as "Devil's Dream" was widely admired, and his style became an ingredient of the developing "progressive bluegrass" movement.

Keith was only one of many young musicians outside the South who were drawn to the bluegrass medium. Even before the urban folk boom began, the bluegrass sounds were beginning to circulate nationally. The powerful broadcasts of WWVA, in Wheeling, West Virginia, introduced the music of such people as the Lilly Brothers, Wilma Lee and Stoney Cooper, Tex Logan, the Osborne Brothers, and Jimmy Martin, to audiences in New England and the Northeast. Mac Martin, whose real name is William D. Colleran, grew up listening to WWVA at his home in Pittsburgh. He began his own music career in 1949 and after 1957 began a long tenure with his Dixie Travelers at Walsh's Lounge in Pittsburgh. His musical evolution is similar to that of Joe Valiante up in Boston. Valiante was won to bluegrass by the broadcasts of WWVA and other stations, and after hearing the in-person music of the Lilly Brothers at Boston's Hillbilly Ranch, he resolved to be a professional musician. Performing as Joe Val, with his New England Bluegrass Boys, he became famous for his high tenor singing and dynamic mandolin playing. Like Mac Martin and many of the northern converts to bluegrass, Val has adhered faithfully to the performance of traditional Monroe-style bluegrass.

Bluegrass bands played frequently at the country music parks which had flourished in the border areas contiguous to the Upper South since the mid-thirties. Southeastern Pennsylvania, Maryland, and Delaware have been a particularly fruitful area for bluegrass expansion, and both local bands and touring musicians have found enthusiastic audiences there. The New River Ranch at Oxford, Pennsylvania, which was one of the most active of these parks, was established by musicians Bud and Ola Belle Reed, who played bluegrass and old-time music to the large mixture of transplanted hillbillies who had migrated to the region and to native northerners who were attracted to the music. Such parks as the New River Ranch and Sunset Park (in West Grove, Pennsylvania) were crucially important cultural meeting grounds where tradition-based musicians, many of them southern-born, met northern fans who were just beginning to be awakened to the joys of folk music in the mid-fifties. The parks contributed to bluegrass music's national expansion and played a valuable role in the dawning urban folk revival.

Bluegrass musicians also found good receptions in many of the bars and

10. Thomas Adler, "Manual Formulaic Composition: Innovation in Bluegrass Banjo Styles," *Journal of Country Music* 5, no. 2 (Summer 1974): 55–64.

honky-tonks where southern migrants gathered in such cities as Baltimore, Washington, D.C., Cincinnati, Dayton, Middletown, Ohio, and Detroit. Not only did Detroit attract such professional musicians as Earl Taylor, Jimmy Martin, and the Osborne Brothers, it also spawned local bands among the large base of southern-born migrants there. Curly Dan and Wilma Ann (a husband-and-wife team) were fixtures on the local Detroit scene, as were Roy McGinnis and the Sunny-Siders, and George and Mary Williamson, who performed as the Old Kentucky String Band. These musicians tended to gravitate toward old-time country and gospel sounds as a binding reminder of those southern hills of home; Fay McGinnis, for example, the wife of musician Roy McGinnis, founded and led for many years the Stanley Brothers Fan Club, one of the most active country fan clubs in the nation.

One of the most fascinating cases of northern bluegrass interest is the phenomenon of Hillbilly Ranch. Located in a rough section of Boston, on the edge of the notorious center of bars and prostitution known as the "combat zone," the Hillbilly Ranch was home for several local and touring country music groups in the late forties and early fifties. Boston was not without its own native-grown country talent. One of country music's greatest yodelers and cowboy-style singers, Kenny Roberts, worked out of Boston and the New England area in the late forties and early fifties. Jerry and Sky (Jerry Howarth and Schuyler Snow), to cite still another example, were Portsmouth, New Hampshire, boys who generally performed over radio stations in Boston. They sang in brother-duet fashion and worked out a style of duet yodeling that was as good as anything done by southern hillbillies (their version of "Sparkling Brown Eyes," recorded for the Sonora label in about 1945, is still the model for most performances). The Lilly Brothers, therefore, did not introduce country music to Boston or to Hillbilly Ranch. Their music, however, had an impact on the local bluegrass scene that no other group had equaled.

Everett and Mitchell "Bea" Lilly were musicians from Clear Creek, West Virginia, who had grown up mesmerized by the music of the Monroe Brothers and the Blue Sky Boys. They began singing as teenagers and made appearances in the early forties on the *Old Farm Hour* at WCHS in Charleston, West Virginia. While playing on WWVA's *Wheeling Jamboree* in the late forties, they came to the attention of certain musicians who proved crucial to their later careers: fiddler Tex Logan and Flatt and Scruggs. Flatt and Scruggs hired Everett Lilly in 1951 and considered him to be one of the best tenor singers and mandolin players they had ever had. Tex Logan, the dapper and dynamic fiddler from Sweetwater, Texas, who had played with the Lillys and with Wilma Lee and Stoney Cooper in Wheeling, remembered the boys after he moved to Boston to attend graduate school at MIT. It was largely through Logan's encouragement that they moved to Boston in 1952.

Everett and Mitchell worked briefly at the Plaza Bar and Mohawk Ranch, and then settled down for their long stint at Hillbilly Ranch, playing seven nights a week for truck drivers, sailors, working folk, "combat zone" denizens, and college students who were brave enough to venture into the place. It seems incongruous that the clear, high Appalachian sound of the Lillys should thrive so long in the frigid, working-class atmosphere of a New England honky-tonk, but many people were charmed by the hard-driving musicianship and vocal purity of the Lilly Brothers. The Lillys, for their part, capitalized on the romance associated with the South, styling themselves the Confederate Mountaineers. Many besotted customers probably paid no attention at all to the Lillys (a fate suffered by most honky-tonk musicians), but to many of the local, budding musicians, the music of the Lilly Brothers and their great banjoist, Don Stover, was like manna from Heaven. Joe Val, Bill Keith, Jim Rooney, and the whole array of musicians who comprised the Charles River Boys—one of the first northern bluegrass bands to spring into existence—were all directly inspired by these transplanted West Virginia musicians.

Although bluegrass demonstrated its appeal in places like Detroit and Boston, it found no urban reception stronger than that in Washington, D.C. Country music had never been alien to the city; Eddie Nesbitt had performed his brand of old-time music there for many years; but bluegrass attracted a heavy following in this southern-flavored city and in nearby Baltimore. The music's core audience probably lay among the people from the surrounding small towns and rural areas in Virginia and Maryland who had ventured into the metropolitan area to work at government jobs or in defense-related industries. Ernest "Pop" Stoneman, for example—the pioneer hillbilly artist of the twenties—worked in a naval ordnance factory; his children organized one of the most sensational bluegrass bands of the sixties, and Pop, playing with them, found a new audience for his old-time singing and autoharp playing. Rural migrants, however, made up only part of the bluegrass audience. The full spectrum of Washington society, including U.S. representatives and senators, can usually be found in attendance at blue-grass concerts, and at least one senator—Robert Byrd of West Virginia, an old-time fiddler—has publicly performed the music. An abundance of outlets existed in the late fifties and early sixties for those who loved the music. Jimmy Dean's *Country Style* show on WTOP-TV included banjoist Smitty Ervin and fiddler Buck Ryan; Roy Clark, the son of Virginia migrants who had moved into the Washington area, played his banjo on Connie B. Gay's *Town and Country Time*; and a network of bars and clubs, such as the Shamrock in Georgetown and the Red Fox Inn in Bethesda, provided outlets for musicians in the greater Washington area. A profusion of musicians, such as Earl Taylor, Bill Harrell, Bill Clifton, Reno and Smiley, Benny and Vallie Cain, and Ola Belle and Bud Reed, played in clubs or parks in Baltimore, northwestern Maryland,

and northern Virginia. In Washington itself Buzz Busby served as a catalyst for bluegrass expansion. Born Bernarr Busbice in West Monroe, Louisiana, the fiery mandolinist and high tenor singer provided employment for budding bluegrass musicians in his Bayou Boys, while also contributing some of the finest examples of lonesome but hard-driving bluegrass songs: "Just Me and the Jukebox" and "I Stood on the Bridge at Midnight."

Bluegrass really began to flourish in the Washington area, though, when the Country Gentlemen came into existence in 1957. The personnel of this great band has changed radically through the years, but one of its founders, singer-guitarist Charlie Waller, has remained to give it an enduring distinctiveness. Born in Joinerville, Texas, but reared near Monroe, Louisiana, Waller came to Washington as a member of Busby's Bayou Boys. When an automobile accident temporarily halted Busby's ability to perform, Waller joined with another mandolin player and tenor singer named John Duffey, banjoist Bill Emerson, and bass player Tom Gray to form the original version of the Country Gentlemen. Eddie Adcock replaced Emerson in 1959, and the band assumed the complexion that it would preserve until Duffey retired in 1969. The Country Gentlemen are now remembered as founding fathers of the progressive bluegrass style, but they did not always seem so in the early days of their existence. Although their avoidance of the fiddle was probably a calculated attempt to resist the harder and more rural sound associated with Bill Monroe, they have nevertheless clung resolutely to the acoustic sound. In some ways, they and many of the other young musicians of the time were "hyper-bluegrass,"[11] in that they often exaggerated the stereotyped features of the music: Charlie Waller's guitar runs came often and imaginatively; John Duffey's tenor soared to rarefied heights; and songs were performed at breakneck speed. The acceleration of tempos sometimes resulted in dynamic performances and permitted the musicians to exhibit their instrumental virtuosity, but in some cases speed only robbed a song of its pathos or sensitivity (as when the Country Gentlemen galloped through their version of the old parlor song "They Say It Is Sinful to Flirt"). There was an energy, however, and an excitement of discovery among these young musicians that was refreshingly contagious; above all, they restored that sense of vitality that had accompanied bluegrass music's first stirrings back in the mid-forties.

The Country Gentlemen's support among both "classic" and "progressive" bluegrass fans was probably unmatched by any other group of musicians. While they clung to acoustic instrumentation and used instruments that were identifed with bluegrass music, the Country Gentlemen freely experimented with other musical forms. Duffey played jazz progressions

11. I picked up this term from a friend and bluegrass mandolin player, Edward Mellon.

on his mandolin, and Adcock was among the most versatile and inventive of banjoists, playing Scruggs-style, plectrum, and chromatic notes on his instrument. Like those of most bluegrass bands, their stage shows were spiced with comedy, but their humor tended to be more satirical and youth-oriented than that of most groups. Theirs was a style of comedy, sometimes zany in its manifestations, that was especially appealing to college students and urban folk enthusiasts. It was in their choice of songs, though, that the Country Gentlemen presaged the appearance of the progressive impulse in bluegrass music. They reached out for all kinds of music—folk, rock, pop, and vintage country—and converted them to bluegrass. Bob Dylan compositions such as "Baby Blue" and "Girl from the North Country," songs from Hollywood scores like "Theme from *Exodus*," Nashville tunes like Mel Tillis' "Matterhorn," pop standards like "Heartaches," hillbilly songs learned from old 78 rpm recordings such as Molly O'Day's "Poor Ellen Smith," all appeared alongside songs from the days of classic bluegrass. This search for an eclectic repertory, inspired partly by the diversity of their Washington audiences, was further motivated by the burgeoning of the folk revival after 1958.

When the urban folk craze came, bluegrass was quickly pulled into its orbit. Many fans who first became interested in folk or folk-like music by hearing the Kingston Trio or Pete Seeger later began searching for more authentic manifestations. Some people dug back into early hillbilly music and discovered the likes of Uncle Dave Macon, the Carter Family, or the Skillet Lickers, while others gravitated toward bluegrass, this dynamic sound which seemed to represent a vital updating and reinvigoration of traditional mountain string-band and vocal styles. The linking of folksong interest and bluegrass actually began as early as 1957, when folklorist D. K. Wilgus began reviewing bluegrass records in the *Kentucky Folklore Record* and when Folkways released *American Banjo Scruggs Style* (edited by Ralph Rinzler). The music really gained its first significant entree into the consciousness of America's literate, but nonacademic, urban middle class when Alan Lomax lent his support in 1959. In April 1959, Lomax sponsored a concert of folk music in New York at Carnegie Hall which included Earl Taylor and the Stoney Mountain Boys. In October of that year Lomax wrote a short article on bluegrass for *Esquire* magazine which called the form the "freshest sound" in American folk music. Journalist Robert Shelton probably reached a much larger readership when he began reviewing bluegrass as part of his folk music column in the *New York Times*; Shelton had nothing but enthusiastic praise for Earl Scruggs, calling him the Paganini of the five-string banjo.[12]

The participation of bluegrass musicians at folk-related affairs, which

12. Lomax, "Bluegrass Background," p. 108; Robert Shelton, *The Country Music Story* (New York: Bobbs-Merrill, 1966), p. 140.

was probably inaugurated by Earl Taylor's Carnegie Hall performance, increased dramatically in late 1959 and in the early sixties. Earl Scruggs' appearance at the Newport Folk Festival in 1959 (without Lester Flatt and the Foggy Mountain Boys) may have been the most prestigious of these events, but the Osborne Brothers' concert at Antioch College in February 1960 boded most favorably for the music's commercial expansion. Colleges were important forums for bluegrass exposure on up into the middle sixties. Several bluegrass bands became active on the college circuit, but Flatt and Scruggs and the Stanley Brothers seemed to be the most popular attractions. Bluegrass groups everywhere began increasing the percentage of traditional music in their repertories, or in some cases performed songs which had been learned from the urban folkies. The Stanley Brothers seemed to thrive artistically and commercially from their brush with the academic/folk community. When the first stirrings of the folk revival came, the Stanleys were living in Live Oak, Florida, appearing daily on television for the Jim Walter Corporation, but with their concert schedule greatly curtailed because of the rock-and-roll infestation of country music. Through the impetus of the folk revival, the Stanleys began resurrecting many of the old songs they had known since childhood (antiques or evergreens, as Carter Stanley called them), and Ralph began doing an occasional tune in the claw-hammer style learned from his mother. Recording now for the King label, and encouraged by Syd Nathan, who was forever seeking successors to the Delmore Brothers, the Stanley Brothers began featuring the sound of a lead guitar. Bill Napier, with his rapid notes and mandolin-style tremolo, was the first of their musicians to employ a flat-picking style, but George Shuffler did most to popularize the fashion while also introducing a major innovation in country guitar picking; Shuffler's cross-picking technique reproduced on the guitar a sound similar to what Jesse McReynolds achieved on the mandolin.

Flatt and Scruggs' association with the folk movement had more mixed results. The duo reached an immense audience through this relationship, and Earl Scruggs was lionized by urban folk enthusiasts. Flatt and Scruggs needed little encouragement to do old-time songs, for they had been performing such material all their lives. But they were also pressured—by their Columbia recording directors—to record contemporary material written by urban folk artists such as Bruce "Utah" Phillips and Bob Dylan, and with instrumental backing that sometimes smothered their fresh acoustic sound. This arrangement sometimes bore sweet melodic fruit, as in their popular performance of Phillips' "Rock Salt and Nails," but more often it resulted in listless, unimaginative renditions that seemed greatly out of character for the group. Earl Scruggs tolerated the material, partly through the influence of his musical sons, but Lester Flatt, who had to sing it, was uncomfortable with lyrics which he did not feel or, sometimes, understand. Differences concerning musical direction eventually contributed to the breakup of the famous team in 1969.

Most bluegrass musicians were affected in one way or another by the folk revival. For example, Frank "Hylo" Brown (so called because of his great vocal range) recorded an immense number of songs taken from or inspired by the urban folkies. Bill Clifton, though, was country music's most important link to the movement as well as being a bridge to the international community. Born William Marburg in Riverdale, Maryland, in 1931, Clifton was a most unlikely apostle of old-time music. The son of a wealthy investment banker, and himself the holder of a master's degree in business administration from the University of Virginia, Clifton was introduced to country music while visiting in the homes of the tenant farmers who lived on his father's estate. Listening to the hillbilly songs which came over his hosts' radios, Clifton equated the music with the values and lifestyles of the farmers; that is, the music was decent, unaffected, and down-to-earth. Not even his attendance at prestigious prep schools (St. Paul's and Adirondack) could shake his affection for old-time country music. He listened faithfully to the radio barn dances, collected records, and even made a pilgrimage to New York City to see Woody Guthrie. By the time he matriculated at the University of Virginia in 1949, he had learned the guitar and was ready to try his luck at radio singing. He performed on a local station in Charlottesville, Virginia, began a singing partnership with fellow student Paul Clayton (who eventually became one of the mainstays of the folk revival), and made his first records for the Stinson label in 1952. In 1954, performing with his Dixie Mountain Boys and recording for Blue Ridge, Clifton produced his first modest hit, "Flower Blooming in the Wildwood." This song came from the repertory of the Coon Creek Girls and was part of a large storehouse of songs he brought to bluegrass music. One hundred fifty of these songs were privately printed in a large-format paperback edition that has been indispensable for fledgling bluegrass singers for at least twenty-five years.[13] During the commercially bleak years of 1957 and 1958, when country music as a whole seemed in retreat from its traditional foundations, Clifton continued to record such melodic old-timers as "Little White Washed Chimney," "The Girl I Left in Sunny Tennessee," and "Mary Dear." Clifton, then, was already doing his part to preserve old-time music well before the folk revival exerted its influence. Furthermore, his contacts among both bluegrass people and urban folkies enabled him to work freely among both groups and to bring them together in common formats. He served as an adviser to the Newport Folk Festival and played a major role in the selection of country musicians for the affair.

Bluegrass definitely profited from the national preoccupation with folk

13. Bill Clifton, *150 Old-Time Folk and Gospel Songs* (privately printed, 1955).

music in the early sixties. Reviving from the doldrums of the rock-and-roll period, bluegrass musicians found new places to play and new audiences to appreciate them. But, strangely, when the country music industry as a whole revived in the early sixties, bluegrass found itself isolated from the country mainstream. Except when used as fillers, i.e., to introduce commercials or to go into newsbreaks, bluegrass tunes virtually disappeared from radio disc jockey shows—casualties of the industry's reassessment of itself after the rock-and-roll siege, and of the Top 40 format. Only rarely did a bluegrass song appear on a jukebox, and record buyers found it increasingly difficult to buy such items in retail outlets. Only those musicians who adopted country-and-western stylistic traits were able to achieve any kind of exposure in the country mainstream. Mac Wiseman, for example, received some airplay with songs like "Charlie's Pride and Johnny's Cash" which used country-style backing. Wiseman never complained about country music's drift toward pop, nor about the neglect from which bluegrass suffered; instead, he sought to succeed within the new formats that were coming into existence. Jim and Jesse McReynolds made a major attempt to thrive as country performers in the mid-sixties. Working from their base on the *Grand Ole Opry*, which they joined in 1964, Jim and Jesse built an act reminiscent of the Louvin Brothers, combining electric and acoustic instruments and singing songs that sounded much like those of their country-and-western contemporaries (e.g., "It's a Long Way to the Top of the World," "Stormy Horizons"). They traveled during this period with a group of musicians who could play drums and electric guitars as well as the conventional bluegrass instruments. Their biggest hit came in 1966 with a truck-driving song called "Diesel on My Tail," which was backed by electric guitar, pedal steel, drums, and piano. A 1965 album of Chuck Berry songs, called *Berry Pickin'*, was another departure from tradition and probably a greater irritant to classic bluegrass fans.

The most successful band to adjust to country-and-western dominance was unquestionably that of the Osborne Brothers. Always innovative, and never reluctant to experiment with musical forms, the Osborne Brothers enjoyed a wider exposure in American life than any other bluegrass group. They made a calculated attempt to overcome the resistance of country disc jockeys and promoters by using the modern material of Nashville songwriters (such as Felice and Boudleaux Bryant), by adopting drums, piano, and electric instruments, and, of course, by perfecting the unique, modulated style of harmony for which they were already famous. One of the biggest promoters of country music in the South, Carlton Haney, included the Osbornes in his big package shows along with such performers as Conway Twitty and Dottie West. The Osbornes more than held their own against such competition, but became even more resolved to use electric instrumentation in order to attract country-and-western fans who were conditioned to accept such a sound. Their performance of "Rocky Top" (written by the Bryants) became one of the most-programmed bluegrass songs in the world, and by the early seventies they had begun winning awards in CMA polls as the best vocal group in country music. Tours with Merle Haggard's country show, also in the early seventies, were icing on the cake. Experiments with electric sounds, of course, provoked heated controversy within the bluegrass ranks, and the Osbornes and Jim and Jesse were accused by purists of selling the music out. The Osborne Brothers, though, stuck to their successful format and responded to their critics with angry, and sometimes ill-chosen, words of their own. Speaking in the heady atmosphere of success, Sonny Osborne charged that there had been no new ideas in bluegrass since 1948, and, he asserted, "Truly I don't care all that much for bluegrass."[14]

As bluegrass faded from the country mainstream, it found itself in the unusual position of being, in one sense, highly prominent in American popular culture, while at the same time thriving as a musical subculture. Bluegrass-style instrumentation appeared often as backing for radio and television commercials, and bluegrass songs cropped up frequently as themes for movies or television shows. Flatt and Scruggs' "The Ballad of Jed Clampett" became the number one country song for several months in 1962 and 1963 after it was introduced as the theme of the popular *Beverly Hillbillies* television show on CBS. Their "Foggy Mountain Breakdown," first recorded in 1949, gained renewed popularity in 1967 as part of the exciting sound track of the movie *Bonnie and Clyde*. Bluegrass gained additional exposure in still another widely circulated movie, *Deliverance*. Eric Weissberg played Scruggs-style banjo on a tune called "Dueling Banjoes" (in this case, though, it was a "duel" between a guitar and banjo). After the movie came out, no banjoist could get through a concert without someone requesting this song, one of the few bluegrass tunes that most Americans know. (Incidentally, the movie also made Don Reno and Arthur Smith considerably richer as a result of their successful suit as the original "composers" of "Dueling Banjoes.")

Although such bluegrass musicians as Bill Monroe, Flatt and Scruggs, Jim and Jesse, and the Osborne Brothers did belong to the *Grand Ole Opry*, most other avenues of dissemination within country music were closed to the bluegrass folk. The major record labels showed little interest in bluegrass, and the genre therefore found its way to a host of smaller companies which often depended on mail-order or concert sales. Bluegrass musicians, thus, invariably hawk their records and tapes wherever a performance is given. In the early sixties Starday Records, the Texas-born company founded by Jack Starnes and Pappy Daily, became the most active bluegrass distributor in the nation. Under Don Pierce, who became the firm's principal owner after its move to Nashville, Starday strove to fill

14. "Sonny Tells It Like It Is," *Bluegrass Unlimited* 3, no. 12 (June 1969): 12.

the vacuum created by the major companies' preoccupations with modern and country-pop music. Starday not only concentrated on bluegrass performers, great and small, but also brought back to recording such old-time musicians as Sam and Kirk McGee, Lew Childre, and the Blue Sky Boys. When Starday declined, other labels such as County, Rebel, Rural Rhythm, Rounder, and Sugar Hill appeared to satisfy the needs of bluegrass and old-time music fans. Unfortunately, too many bluegrass fans are addicted to the taping of musical performances, whether at live concerts or festivals, or from someone else's records. To the great consternation of the musicians, and to the commercial detriment of the music as a whole, tape recorders abound at festivals or anywhere that bluegrass is played. Uncle Jim O'Neal, the proprietor of Rural Rhythm and an active mail-order distributor, complained that "You can't sell bluegrass records to bluegrass fans. Nine out of ten of 'em want the records free. Either that or they go to a bluegrass festival and sit there on the stage to where most of the audience can't even see with their cassette recorders."[15]

The festivals to which Uncle Jim referred have constituted the core and salvation of bluegrass music. While his criticism of bluegrass fans has some merit, it does not tell the full story of devotion and loyalty shown by the thousands of supporters who travel to festivals during the spring and summer months. Bill Clifton conceived the first festival, a one-day event held at Luray, Virginia, in 1961. Although the event was sparsely attended, it contained the germ of the idea that would characterize all later festivals—an outdoor meeting in which a wide variety of bands, amateur and professional, participate. The festivals got underway in earnest after Labor Day 1965, when Carlton Haney sponsored an affair at Cantrell's Horse Farm in Roanoke, Virginia. Haney was a North Carolina–born promoter who became involved in bluegrass when he began booking Bill Monroe and Reno and Smiley in the mid-fifties. Haney brought a sense of drama and history to bluegrass, and he began presenting little vignettes about the evolution of the music, tributes to individual musicians, and reunions in which former members of bands got back together on stage. Haney's own festival at Camp Springs, North Carolina, was long one of the most ambitious and best attended of these events, but it was certainly challenged by other festivals held at such places as Berryville, Virginia; McClure, Virginia (near Ralph Stanley's old home place); Cosby, Tennessee; Lavonia, Georgia; Kerrville, Texas; Hugo, Oklahoma; and Bean Blossom, Indiana. The Bean Blossom Festival is now the biggest of the three hundred or more similar gatherings held all over the United States. Held for several days each June on property owned by Bill Monroe in the beautiful rolling hills of southern Indiana, the Bean Blossom Festival attracts the

15. Unnamed article in *Music City News* 15, no. 8 (February 1978): 26.

best bands in bluegrass music and thousands of fans who journey there from all over the country.

The bluegrass festivals are reminiscent of the religious camp meetings held in rural America during the nineteenth century. As at the earlier camp meetings, the faithful attend in order to be revived, while the skeptics often go away converted. Many people camp out for days in tents or recreational vehicles (RV's), listen to the professional bands on stage, and participate in jam sessions that might last all night long. It is not uncommon to find such musicians as Kenny Baker and Joe Stuart playing into the wee hours of the morning alongside earnest amateur banjo pickers, fiddlers, and other instrumentalists. Nowhere else in country music can one find such camaraderie among fans and musicians. Bluegrass fans can actually meet and shake the hands of their heroes, or have their photos taken with people like Bill Monroe, Ralph Stanley, or the Osborne Brothers. The festivals have tapped a strong urge among Americans to return to the basics, to a simpler, more manageable, and allegedly more decent society. Most of the festivals ban drinking, drugs, and profanity, and attempt to create a wholesome, family atmosphere. Despite the best intentions, however, rowdy behavior and the free-wheeling ambience of the rock festivals have intruded into some of the bluegrass affairs, contributing to ugly confrontations among fans, musicians, and security guards.

On the whole, though, the bluegrass festivals have been remarkable manifestations of good will. Their chief flaw, as it is with most country music gatherings, is the absence of black people, but among the whites who attend the festivals there has been a broad diversity of age, economic, and philosophical groupings. Hippies and rednecks, college students and truck drivers, government workers and farmers, and liberals and conservatives share festival benches and often play in the same bands. During the 1972 presidential campaign, automobiles and campers at bluegrass festivals often sported either George Wallace or George McGovern bumper stickers, a suggestion that many disaffected people on both the left and right saw in bluegrass music an antidote to a complex, overorganized society. There is no evidence that political attitudes changed as a result of this shared musical experience, but for a brief moment generational, social, and ideological differences were narrowed, or forgotten, in the exhilaration of a bluegrass breakdown.

Those people who attend the festivals can hear music that is reminiscent of the "classic" period of the late forties and early fifties, or they can hear sounds that seem much influenced by rock, pop, or mainstream country stylings. Bluegrass, in short, has traveled many stylistic roads. While settling into his role as the bluegrass patriarch, Bill Monroe has continued to produce exciting and dynamic music. Musicians have come and gone from the Blue Grass Boys with great frequency, but Kenny Baker has remained as a bastion of tradition and excellence. Monroe's seminal work is now universally recognized, and he was named to the Country Music Hall of Fame in 1969. Perhaps most significant, Monroe now recognizes his own relationship to other musicians who bear the bluegrass label. Reconciliations with the Stanley Brothers and Flatt and Scruggs came long ago, and he has publicly performed with these and virtually every other bluegrass entertainer of stature. Monroe lends encouragement to all would-be bluegrass musicians, and one of the marvels of his Bean Blossom Festival is the giant jam session that includes literally scores of banjoists, fiddlers, guitarists, and mandolin players.

Other "old-timers" also endure in bluegrass, although their ranks have been thinned by death and retirement. The Flatt and Scruggs partnership dissolved in 1969, a victim of too many years together and of differences concerning future stylistic choices. Flatt returned to his real love—classic bluegrass—and he continued to produce good music with his new band, the Nashville Grass, until his death on May 11, 1979. Scruggs formed a band with his musical sons (Gary, Randy, and Steve) called the Earl Scruggs Revue. The Revue was only on the fringe of bluegrass, and Earl's banjo was generally smothered by the heavy cacophony of sound produced by his children's electric instruments. Earl, though, had the chance to exploit an opportunity presented to few fathers—the possibility of sharing his children's musical experiences—and in the person of Randy Scruggs country music was introduced to one of its greatest guitarists.

Carter Stanley's death on December 1, 1966, brought an end to the career of bluegrass music's most traditional act, the Stanley Brothers. Ralph Stanley remained in professional music, however, and as the leader of the Clinch Mountain Boys he became even more committed to old-time sounds and songs. While maintaining the high, hard-driving sound of classic bluegrass, Stanley has also added a broad sampling of a capella material to his performances—songs which reflect the congregational singing of the Primitive Baptist Church and of mountain quartet singing. In his search for a replacement for his brother Carter, Ralph brought some excellent young talent into bluegrass music—Larry Sparks, an Ohio-born guitarist and singer with a lonesome, rural sound; Roy Lee Centers, a Kentuckian whose voice bore an uncanny resemblance to that of Carter Stanley, but whose promising career was cut short by his murder on May 2, 1974; and Keith Whitley and Ricky Skaggs, also Kentuckians, who had emulated the sound of the Stanley Brothers since they were teenagers. Ralph Stanley's disappointment must have been as keen as that of Bill Monroe upon Flatt and Scruggs' departure when Whitley and Skaggs eventually departed to pursue their own brilliant careers.

Illness and death also caused the dissolution of the great team of Reno and Smiley. Because of complications arising from wounds suffered during World War II, Smiley temporarily retired from full-time musicianship in 1964 but occasionally rejoined Reno on recordings and in concerts before his death in January 1972. Reno formed a partnership for several years with Bill Harrell, the Virginia singer and guitarist who had been a mainstay of the Washington, D.C., bluegrass scene since the mid-fifties. Harrell now performs with his own band. Reno died in 1984.

The other major bluegrass performers from the classic period, Mac Wiseman, Jimmy Martin, Jim and Jesse, and the Osborne Brothers, are all active participants on the festival scene, and all have returned to the older styles which they originally performed. With his body trimmed down from its once-rotund shape, and sporting a graying beard, Wiseman lends dignity to any stage where he performs. Performing solely with pickup bands, he can generally be depended upon to perform his familiar numbers, such as "Love Letters in the Sand" and "I Wonder How the Old Folks Are at Home," as well as more "modern" numbers such as "Catfish John" and "Me and Bobby McGee." Jimmy Martin has clung tenaciously to hard-core bluegrass and has employed a profusion of musicians, including some of his children. Jim and Jesse and the Osborne Brothers have also utilized the services of family members, but, unlike Martin, they have sometimes strayed far afield from traditional bluegrass. By the early eighties, however, both of these groups had drawn back from their absorption with country and western and had moved closer to old-line bluegrass. Except for the electric bass, both groups abandoned the use of drums and electric guitars, and returned to the performance of old or old-style material (although neither group stopped playing modern-composed songs).

While many of the original bluegrass musicians still perform actively, they have been joined by a new generation of performers. Some of them hew closely to the sounds of the forties and fifties, while others have taken bluegrass far afield from the music originally heard on Monroe, Flatt and Scruggs, and Stanley recordings. There is no one label that accurately describes the new departures, because some groups, such as the White Family, play music that is reflective of country and western, while others employ styles that are clearly derived from folk, rock, blues, jazz, and popular forms of music. It is also difficult to define them in terms of instrumentation. Some of the most innovative musicians, such as the Country Gentlemen and Seldom Scene, have used only acoustic instruments, while others—including the traditional Jimmy Martin—have experimented with electrification. The changes that have come to bluegrass are the natural consequences of musicians' desires to be creative and experimental, and of the wishes of the performers—and their managers—to create a widely commercial product.

As we have seen, progressive bluegrass, or "newgrass," can be traced in part to experiments made by musicians within the "classic" bands. Don Reno, for example, always combined in his banjo playing innovative techniques borrowed from jazz and steel guitar playing with the more traditional mountain stylings. Bill Keith during his brief tenure with Bill Monroe in 1963 popularized the chromatic style that constituted the first real departure from Scruggs, and Frank Wakefield, a dazzling mandolin player from Tennessee (with whom Keith played before his Monroe period), was already experimenting with complex chord progressions and unorthodox tunings while playing with the traditionalist Red Allen in the early sixties. David Grisman, who was deeply impressed by Wakefield's inventiveness and flair, was only one of many "progressives" who were won over by the new sounds heard in bluegrass music in the early sixties.

Several bands, both obscure and prominent, popularized new approaches to material and style in the early sixties. A West Coast band, the Dillards (made up of Missouri transplants), introduced their Ozark humor and sophisticated musicianship to a national audience while performing on the Andy Griffith television show in the late fifties and early sixties. The Dillards and many of the other bluegrass bands of that period were influenced by the folk revival to perform songs that came not only from older sources but also from contemporary writers such as Bob Dylan, John Prine, Ian Tyson, and Gordon Lightfoot. Other California bands at the time, such as Clarence and Roland White and their Kentucky Colonels, and the Hillmen (which included Don Parmley, Chris Hillman, Rex Gosdin and Vern Gosdin), also dabbled with folkie material.

The band, though, that really did most to inspire the innovations eventually known as "newgrass" was the Country Gentlemen. Through the inspired musicianship of banjoist Eddie Adcock and mandolinist John Duffey, and through their eclectic choice of material, the Country Gentlemen attracted new musicians to their style of playing and brought a whole new audience to bluegrass music. Their boldness was not admired by everyone, and Duffey was convinced that they were omitted from the first major festival in 1965 because of their departures from the norm. The Gentlemen continued to be a force for change on in to the seventies, and when Duffey and Adcock left the band in 1969 and 1970, other experimental musicians (such as Jimmy Gaudreau, Doyle Lawson, and Ricky Skaggs) continued to contribute new ideas. In 1972 the Gentlemen's version of Crosby, Stills, and Nash's "Teach Your Children" was selected in a *Muleskinner News* poll as the Song of the Year.

As the above song's popularity would indicate, music continued to flow into the bluegrass repertory from other sources long after the folk revival subsided. Columbia record producers even persuaded Flatt and Scruggs to do such songs as Dylan's "Maggie's Farm" and "Wanted Man" (much to the disgust of Flatt, who disliked both the music and the liberal politics which surrounded it). Most younger musicians, however, probably had few reservations about performing non-bluegrass or non-country songs, and so the songs of the Beatles, the Byrds, the First Edition, Creedence Clearwater Revival, and other contemporary musicians appeared frequently in newgrass performances. One of the first musicians to dip into such material with regularity was Cliff Waldron, a Jolo, West Virginia, native who moved to Washington, D.C., in 1963. Beginning first with a band co-directed by banjoist Bill Emerson in 1967, and later with his own group, the New Shades of Grass, Waldron built a repertory composed of classic material and contemporary songs such as "Proud Mary," "I Just Gotta Get a Message to You," and "Fox on the Run" (Waldron and Emerson's version of the last-named song is still the definitive version).

By the beginning of the seventies a number of groups had become well known for their receptivity to contemporary song material. A few of the bands, such as J. D. Crowe and the New South (formerly the Kentucky Mountain Boys), the Second Generation (organized by Eddie Adcock in 1971), and the Seldom Scene (created by John Duffey in the same year), were composed of experienced musicians whose careers dated back to the late fifties. Other bands, such as Poor Richard's Almanac, the Bluegrass Alliance, Country Gazette, New Grass Revival, Spectrum (which included the remarkably versatile jazz-oriented banjoist Bela Fleck), and Hot Rize (a jazz-country-bluegrass fusion group led by scholar/musician Peter Wernick) were composed of younger performers whose musical sensibilities had been shaped by the post-Beatles rock revolution of the mid-sixties. Of the older groups, Adcock's Second Generation were the farthest removed from traditional bluegrass with their jazz-like experimentations and use of electric instrumentation. J. D. Crowe's New South never lost their identity as bluegrass musicians, nor their rapport with older fans, even though they roamed far and wide for material and pushed their instruments to limits generally not sought by other performers. Superb musicians, such as Larry Rice, Tony Rice, Doyle Lawson, and Ricky Skaggs, moved in and out of the New South, but all of them learned something from the timing, precision, and clarity exhibited by Crowe himself.

Seldom Scene not only was in the vanguard of the newgrass movement, but was also the most popular of all modern bluegrass bands. The band, for the most part, was composed of all-star musicians who had seen service in other groups in the Washington, D.C., area. In addition to Duffey, the group included banjoist Ben Eldridge and dobroist Mike Auldridge (formerly of Waldron's New Shades of Grass), bass player Tom Gray (an early Country Gentleman), and John Starling (an Army surgeon whose singing and guitar playing had been done mostly on an informal basis). Named Seldom Scene because of their infrequent concert appearances, the band settled down for a once-a-week gig at the Red Fox Inn in Bethesda, Maryland, and later for a weekly appearance at the Birchmere Restaurant in Alexandria, Virginia. Seldom Scene skillfully compiled a repertory of old and contemporary songs (some of them from country music's Top Forty) and performed them with mellow harmony and inventive instrumentation. A central, and almost defining, component of their sound has been the dobro playing of Mike Auldridge, one of the four or five great modern masters of the instrument. One of Auldridge's uncles, Ellsworth T. Cozzens, had played Hawaiian steel guitar on some of Jimmie Rodgers' records, but Mike seems not to have become impressed with the dobro until he heard Buck Graves playing one with Wilma Lee and Stoney Cooper in about 1950. Building on the styles earlier featured by Graves, Shot Jackson, and Brother Oswald, Auldridge developed his own unique bell-like and melodious style. The results have been some of the prettiest and most soulful sounds heard in modern country music.

Some of the younger musicians seemed more closely aligned with rock music than with country, and a few of them, in dress and hairstyles, suggested the counterculture of the sixties. The costuming and personal grooming habits of these musicians probably did more to alienate conservative bluegrass fans than did their music. Many people who heard the New Deal String Band (one of the first "hippie" bluegrass bands, from Chapel Hill, North Carolina), the Earl Scruggs Revue, or the New Grass Revival, could scarcely listen to their music without thinking "Why doesn't somebody cut their hair?" The Country Gazette were usually much more circumspect in appearance (although they have also, on occasion, sported long hair and beards), but they had direct ties with California rock musicians through their founder and fiddler, Byron Berline. After leaving the University of Oklahoma in 1967, Berline worked with Bill Monroe briefly, spent some time in the Army, and then went to California, where he worked as a sessions musician and played with the Dillard and Clark Expedition and Flying Burrito Brothers. In 1971 he founded the Country Gazette (to which he no longer belongs) along with guitarist Kenny Wertz, bass player Roger Bush, and Berline's old friend from Oklahoma, Alan Munde. Berline's proficiency at old-time, Texas, and bluegrass styles of fiddling, Munde's note-bending and precisely executed style of chromatic banjo, Bush's exuberant slapped-bass technique, and their intelligent use of both old-time and contemporary material made them one of the most appealing of the newgrass organizations. The Country Gazette, which now includes Roland White as guitarist and lead singer, has become one of the most widely traveled bands, appearing often on college campuses, where band members combine music with lectures and seminars.

Another group which made important contributions to the shaping and popularization of the progressive sounds was the Bluegrass Alliance of Louisville, Kentucky. Centered originally around the traditional fiddling of Lonnie Peerce and the sensational flat-picking guitar work of Dan Crary, the band moved farther and farther away from classic bluegrass as new members joined. Crary was followed by two other superb guitarists and singers, Tony Rice and Curtis Burch. The musician, though, who really moved the Alliance into new territories of experimentation was Sam Bush, a fiddler and mandolin player whose chief inspiration was Jethro Burns.

Bush came to the Alliance in 1970, along with banjo player Courtney Johnson, from another experimental group, Poor Richard's Almanac. By the time he and Johnson left the Alliance to form still another band, the New Grass Revival (in 1972), Bush had already become famous for his enthusiasm, his wild and extended improvisations, his perfectionism, and his tireless experimentations with other forms of music. For many people the New Grass Revival became the quintessential progressive bluegrass band, playing a style of music that "borrowed heavily from the realms of rock, jazz and blues" without losing "the drive and melancholy that characterizes bluegrass music."[16]

While the progressives went about their business experimenting with musical fusions and breaking new stylistic ground, other musicians hewed closely to styles which they perceived to be grounded in the music of the "classic period" (circa 1945–1955). Many musicians throughout America still cling to the old repertory, and many of them still adhere as closely as possible to the sounds first heard on Monroe, Stanley, or Flatt and Scruggs records. Among the "older" professional musicians, the Shenandoah Cut-ups (led by fiddler Clarence "Tater" Tate, mandolin player Hershel Sizemore, and banjoist Billy Edwards) and Vern Williams (an Arkansas-born mandolin player and tenor singer who led his own band in California) came closest to preserving the hard-driving energy and tangy, high-lonesome style of harmony that had once characterized bluegrass music.

In an obvious reply to Eddie Adcock and his Second Generation, three veteran musicians—Red Rector, Don Stover, and Bill Clifton—organized themselves into a group called the First Generation and set out in 1978 on a tour of festivals and concerts in the United States and in Europe. Gospel music continued to be a vital ingredient of bluegrass, and a force in the preservation of traditional styles. Some groups performed nothing but the old-time style of rural gospel: these included the veteran Carl Story from North Carolina, the Marshall Family from Ohio by way of West Virginia, the Sullivan Family from St. Stephens, Alabama, and the Lewis Family from Lincolnton, Georgia. The Sullivans represented the Pentecostal tradition of soulful, emotional singing, and strong traces of the Bailes Brothers and Louvin Brothers could be heard in their music. Margie Sullivan, an ordained minister (originally from Louisiana), reminded listeners of Molly O'Day with her rural phrasing and deep-felt, open-throated singing. The Lewis Family presented a joyous mixture of religion and tent-show comedy to their festival audiences. One heard little of the evangelism that sometimes surfaced in the Sullivans' concerts. Little Roy Lewis, the madcap banjoist of the group, was one of bluegrass music's finest natural entertainers.

16. Ronni Lundy, "The New Grass Revival," *Bluegrass Unlimited* 13, no. 5 (November 1978): 10.

Other musicians who have striven to preserve the feel, if not the exact form, of traditional bluegrass music include individuals old enough to have heard Monroe and his contemporaries in their heyday as well as those who were scarcely or not yet born when the "classic" style took shape. The discussion which follows is far from exhaustive, and it concentrates on those whose public performances, or whose entry into bluegrass, have come since the late fifties. Joe Wilson, from Eldorado, Arkansas, and the leader of a group called Bluegrass Kun-Tree, was one of the best singers in bluegrass music, with a soulful style that somehow suggested the phrasing and emotion of two great but dissimilar stylists: Ralph Stanley and George Jones. (Wilson died from a heart attack at his home in Eldorado, Arkansas, September 14, 1984.)

The Pinnacle Boys have been a force for revitalization in bluegrass through the twin fiddling of Randall Collins and Jerry Moore, and through their precise and smooth Louvin Brothers style of harmony. The Bluegrass Cardinals are a group founded in California by a Kentucky banjo player, Don Parmley, who had gone there in 1956 to work as a Trailways bus driver. Parmley founded one of the earliest bluegrass bands in California, the Golden State Boys, played with the Hillmen, and provided background banjo instrumentation for the *Beverly Hillbillies* television show for about nine years. Since making their first lp in 1975, the Bluegrass Cardinals— led by the singing of David Parmley, who was only fifteen when the group came into existence—have become widely admired for their inventive syncopated harmonies. The Boys from Indiana, led by guitarist and singer Aubrey Holt, have preserved the verve and drive of original bluegrass, while also becoming valued as one of the finest "show bands" in the music (presenting skits, history, impersonations). The late Charlie Moore was one of the greatest bluegrass singers to emerge in the postclassic era. His voice was smooth but soulful, and he had a sense of history and storehouse of old songs that he had been picking up since his boyhood in Piedmont, South Carolina. From 1962 to 1966 he performed with flat-picking guitar ace Bill Napier and recorded some popularly received lps with him for the King label. After 1966 Moore headed a band called the Dixie Partners, and in 1971 he introduced a song which has become one of the most popular standards of bluegrass music, "The Legend of the Rebel Soldier" (the tale of a Confederate soldier whose dying prayer was that his soul might return to the Southland).

The Oklahomans Bill Grant and Delia Bell began singing together in about 1960 on the *Little Dixie Hayride* in Hugo, Oklahoma, and they have since become fixtures on the festival circuit, and especially at Grant's big festival each August in Hugo (probably the biggest west of the Mississippi River). Both are important musicians, and Grant has become one of the few original writers in bluegrass (along with Jake Landers, Aubrey Holt, Tom Uhr, and a few others). Delia Bell, however, has become the rage of

New Grass Revival: *left to right*, Bela Fleck, Sam Bush, John Cowan, Pat Flynn. Copyright © 1984 by Scott Newton/Austin City Limits.

bluegrass, not only because she is about the only woman who has won acceptance in the genre, but also because of the patronage which she has received from Emmylou Harris. Harris was sufficiently impressed with Delia's singing, which she first heard on the lp *Bluer than Midnight* (County 768), to sponsor and produce a major album of her singing in 1983 on the Warner Brothers label. Unfortunately, the public response to it suggests that Delia's singing is too pure, mournful, and rural for today's tastes.

One of the most interesting phenomena related to the preservation of traditional bluegrass music—and one to which students of southern migration should pay more attention—is the role played by musicians who have either migrated to the North or who have been born there of southern migrants. Two of the finest traditional singers in modern bluegrass, Larry Sparks and Dave Evans, are northern-born children of southern migrants, while two other outstanding rural-tinged vocalists, Del McCoury and Dudley Connell, are southern-born boys who moved to northern states with their parents. All sing in the high-lonesome style with emotion-laden and rural-flavored phrasing, and each conveys a strong sense of fundamentalist Protestant morality which lends intensity and conviction to their performances. Larry Sparks, who was born in Lebanon, Ohio, of Kentucky parents, spent an apprenticeship with Ralph Stanley before going on to lead his own organization. Dave Evans, from Portsmouth, Ohio, in turn spent some time with Sparks (1973–1974) and with other groups such as the Boys from Indiana, with whom he played banjo and took an occasional turn as guest soloist. In 1978 he formed his own group, River Bend, recorded a couple of lps on the Vetco label, and immediately began impressing traditionalists with his emotional conviction and powerfully intense high tenor singing. Del McCoury moved to York, Pennsylvania, with his parents from Tennessee. Long-time residence in this northeastern state, and residence in other states such as California, has never diminished the flavor of his southern-born speech nor the soulful intensity of his singing. He played guitar and sang lead for Bill Monroe for about a year after 1963 (in the band that also included Bill Keith), and since that time he has remained close to the Monroe mold. Along with his brother Jerry he organized a band in 1969 called the Dixie Pals. While consistently using material of recent vintage (much of it from honky-tonk country sources), McCoury has nevertheless preserved the sound and style of traditional bluegrass. The youngest person among these hard-core bluegrass singers, Dudley Connell, heads a group which many people assume will be the saviors of the old-time bluegrass style, the Johnson Mountain Boys. Connell was born in West Virginia, but moved as a youngster with his family to Gaithersburg, Maryland. He and the other band members have resurrected old-time songs but supplemented them with numbers written by Connell. Known for their tight harmonies, brilliant musicianship, and commitment to tradition, this Washington, D.C.–based band is now being touted as the bluegrass band of the future, and is the hope of traditionalists everywhere.

It is clear that the choices made by bluegrass musicians in the eighties and the impulse to lean toward either tradition or innovation are not necessarily a matter of age. Young musicians like Connell and Evans have often demonstrated a preference for that which is old or historically rooted. Indeed, many musicians move easily back and forth between the classic and progressive, either making no distinctions between the two or being at home in both. Buck White and his talented daughters Sharon and Cheryl fill their concerts with the western swing that Buck grew up with in Wichita Falls, Texas, the mainstream country that the girls harmonize so beautifully, and bluegrass which spans the period from Bill Monroe to Seldom Scene. Doyle Lawson, the extraordinarily gifted musician from East Tennessee, has played every style of bluegrass music since he started his professional career as a banjoist with Jimmy Martin in 1963. A stranger to no string instrument, he played guitar with J. D. Crowe in 1966 and mandolin with the Country Gentlemen after 1971 (while also demonstrating his expertise as a tenor harmony singer). In 1979 he organized his own band, Quicksilver, which has become one of the prized progressive groups. Nevertheless, while the band is widely admired for its versatility and collective musicianship, Quicksilver's finest moments come when the musicians put down their instruments and do the a capella gospel songs which lie at the roots of country music's history. Lawson, J. D. Crowe, Tony Rice, Bobby Hicks, and Todd Phillips (each recognized as a premier progressive stylist) got together in 1982 to do an lp of material drawn from the forties-and-fifties repertories of Bill Monroe, Flatt and Scruggs, and other seminal musicians. The album was so well received that they subsequently recorded two other lps of such material, and then went on a short tour at the end of 1983 as the Bluegrass Album Band. Ricky Skaggs, of course, who has been associated with all of these musicians at one time or another, has played in bands that range from the old-timey, mountain sound of Ralph Stanley, to the jazz-related stylings of J. D. Crowe's New South (and for a short time he headed a band—Boone Creek—that tried to combine both impulses). Skaggs obviously has felt no incompatibility with any form of music.

No one can predict bluegrass music's future, but some of the most encouraging factors found today at the festivals, or anywhere that bluegrass is played, are the prevalence of family bands and of very young musicians, some as young as six or seven, who play fiddles, banjos, mandolins, and guitars. The McLain Family Band, for example, is a Berea, Kentucky–based organization which has taken its brand of traditional bluegrass music to over sixty foreign countries and to most of the states of the union; it includes father Raymond K. McLain, an ethnomusicologist at Berea College, and four of his sons and daughters (Raymond W., Ruth, Nancy Ann, and Michael). As young bluegrass musicians grow up, they certainly do not all cling to traditional styles. Mark O'Connor, for instance, won the Grand Masters Fiddling Championship in Nashville at the age of thirteen (in 1975), but soon moved beyond bluegrass and old-timey styles to membership in David Grisman's jazz-bluegrass fusion group and from there to the Dregs (a jazz-rock quintet). Marty Stuart, a Mississippi-born mandolinist and guitar player, has undergone a similar evolution since he began his professional career in 1972 as a thirteen-year-old musician with Lester Flatt's Nashville Grass. Some of the young musicians, though, will gravitate toward older, rural-based forms of music. Above all, they will continue to make some kind of music. The wellsprings of bluegrass will not soon dry up.

Conway Twitty and Loretta Lynn. Photograph courtesy of the Country Music Foundation Library and Media Center, Nashville, Tennessee.

11. Country Music, 1972–1984

Country music's history since the early seventies has been one of unqualified commercial success. The music's ascent in mainstream American culture, however, has been accompanied by internal debates concerning definition and future direction. Musicians, industry leaders, and fans have been confused about what the music is or where it should go. The country music industry has discovered that its best interests lie in the distribution of a package with clouded identity, possessing no regional traits. The industry has striven to present a music that is all things to all people: middle-of-the-road and "American," but also southern, working-class, and occasionally youth-oriented and even rebellious in tone.

The *Grand Ole Opry*'s move in 1974 from the Ryman Auditorium to the spacious and modern accommodations of the new Opry House on the outskirts of Nashville was an event which was more than symbolic of country music's ambivalence about its rural past. The Ryman had been the site of the *Opry* since 1941, and many people had come to look upon the historic old building—the "mother church of country music"—as almost sacrosanct. Reverence, however, was tempered by disquietude when one reflected upon the actual conditions of the building. Audiences dealt with excessive heat during the summer, draftiness during the winter, impaired vision much of the time because of the supportive columns that ran from the floor to the balcony, and limited parking facilities all of the time. While the acoustics were very good, performers had to contend with cramped and modestly furnished dressing rooms. The auditorium was located in a run-down section of downtown Nashville filled with souvenir shops, adult bookstores, and pornographic movie theaters. At the concluding show at the Ryman on March 16, 1974, Minnie Pearl cried unashamedly on stage as she reflected on the abandonment of the building where such hallowed figures as Uncle Dave Macon, Roy Acuff, Eddy Arnold, and Hank Williams had once held sway. Although the departure from the old auditorium inspired such songs as Tommy Howard's "Goodbye, Dear Ole Ryman," most fans and musicians applauded the move to the spacious, comfortable, air-conditioned Opry House, and millions of people have since gone there, and to the 110-acre Disneyland-like complex which surrounds it.[1]

Country music demonstrated its prominence in American life in a variety of ways. In 1973 Loretta Lynn appeared on the cover of *Newsweek* and was the central focus of the magazine's coverage of country music. One year later Merle Haggard enjoyed similar exposure in *Time*,[2] and the sympathetic treatment that he and the music received probably reflected the nation's shift toward conservatism and the music's identification with white working-class culture (an ironic development in that the similar "discovery" of white folk music in the thirties had been fueled by an awakening of liberal sentiment). In the proliferating published material that dealt with country music, the phenomenon was treated with a seriousness that had seldom before been witnessed. References to "corn," "hillbillies," "twang," and "nasal" that had dotted the usually condescending or hostile treatments of country music were missing and were replaced by attempts to understand the origins and contemporary meaning of the music.

Producer Robert Altman may have had little affection for country music as an artistic medium, but he was sufficiently impressed with its influence to make it the centerpiece of the movie *Nashville* in 1975. The Nashville music world was depicted as a metaphor for modern American culture, and the movie garnered great critical acclaim and public response. Many country fans perceived the movie not as a fable of a society that had lost direction and purpose but as a frontal attack on their music and the culture that embodies it. The movie, though, probably won a new audience to country music, and many people went away intrigued by the ingenuous expression of feeling conveyed by the songs.

While reactions to *Nashville* were mixed, few country fans had reservations about the movie depiction of Loretta Lynn's life, *Coal Miner's Daughter*, a critically acclaimed adaptation of her autobiography and a vehicle for Sissy Spacek's Academy Award–winning performance. The movie did not tell the full story of Loretta's life—it curiously omitted the crucial role

1. Much print was expended on the *Grand Ole Opry*'s move from the Ryman Auditorium, but the most sensitive account, as well as a discerning capsule history of the show, is Garrison Keillor, "Onward and Upward with the Arts at the Opry," *New Yorker* 50, no. 11 (May 6, 1974): 46–70. Keillor's trip to Nashville, which inspired the article, had a very positive consequence. The following month he went back home to St. Paul, Minnesota, and founded a delightful radio show, *A Prairie Home Companion*, designed to restore the flavor and ambience of old-time live broadcasting. The program is now carried for two hours every Saturday evening on 218 stations via American Public Radio (see Jon Bream, "A Prairie Home Companion," *Dallas Morning News*, July 1, 1984, p. 1C).

2. *Newsweek*, June 18, 1973; *Time*, May 5, 1974.

played by the Wilburn Brothers in the furtherance of her career—but it did present a vivid account of life in the mountains while also providing glimpses of both the euphoria and the frustrations of the music business.

Loretta Lynn enjoyed enormous public visibility in the wake of the movie's success. Movies, in fact, became major vehicles for the mass exposure of country entertainers, if not always for country music itself. Jerry Reed and Mel Tillis were among the most active of the entertainers who profited from the "good old boy" movies that began appearing in the seventies, and, of course, from their association with such superstars as Burt Reynolds and Clint Eastwood. The enormously popular *Smokey and the Bandit* was the prototype for shows both in theaters and on television which featured hedonistic, simple-minded young men and their sexy girlfriends riding in fast cars or trucks with a backdrop of country music. Most country entertainers who ventured into the movie business rarely got beyond the status of supporting actor, but Dolly Parton became a household name throughout the world and exhibited a natural comic flair in such popular movies as *Nine to Five* and *Best Little Whorehouse in Texas*. Dolly's prominence as a "personality" was a major factor in her success as an actress. While Willie Nelson profited from a similar aura, he also showed greater potentiality as a character actor than did Parton, first in a supporting role to Robert Redford in *The Electric Horseman*, and then in lead roles in *Honeysuckle Rose* and *Barbarosa*. *Honeysuckle Rose*'s thin storyline was merely a device to highlight Nelson's singing and the honky-tonk atmosphere of Texas, but *Barbarosa*, which had almost no music at all, permitted Nelson to demonstrate a natural flair for acting in the role of a legendary western outlaw.

Most of these movies had no real impact on American popular culture, but *Tender Mercies* in 1984, probably the finest movie ever made about country music, garnered several Academy Award nominations, including one for Robert Duvall as best actor. *Urban Cowboy* in 1981 (based on an *Esquire* article about alienated oil workers in the Houston area) generated a boom for ersatz cowboy material—designer jeans, hats, boots, mechanical bulls, and western dance steps. Gilley's Club in Pasadena, Texas, self-styled "the biggest honky-tonk in the world" and the principal site of the movie's action, became known to the world, as did its singing proprietor, Mickey Gilley, and the house-band leader, Johnny Lee. The soundtrack, however, carried very little that was really native to the Texas honky-tonk scene and instead featured country-pop and rock material. Johnny Lee's "Looking for Love," for example—a lilting little pop song—became the featured song of the movie, and a huge commercial hit, mainly because actor John Travolta expressed a liking for it.

Television continued to be a major vehicle for country music exposure, and country entertainers appeared in great profusion on commercial, public, and cable programming. The country awards shows, such as those produced by the CMA, the Academy of Country Music, and *Music City News*, elicited great audience response, as did occasional specials, such as HBO's *Dolly Parton Live from London*, or a popular series such as the *Barbara Mandrell Show*. Depictions of the lives of country musicians, fictional and real, sometimes appeared on commercial television, but with mixed results. *Boone*, a series built around the life of an aspiring young country singer in the early fifties, suffered from the romanticization of its subject and from a loose obeisance to historical fact (a not uncommon trait of television shows and movies devoted to country music). Occasionally a good biographical depiction of a country singer did appear on commercial television, as in the cases of Tammy Wynette (*Stand By Your Man*) and Hank Williams, Jr. (*Living Proof*), but the most accurate and sensitive documentation of country music tended to appear on public television. Public TV viewers, for example, were given the opportunity to see and hear excellent presentations of the life and music of such entertainers as Uncle Dave Macon, Prince Albert Hunt, Jimmie Rodgers, and Merle Haggard. Public TV also sponsored *Austin City Limits*, a marvelous showcase for all kinds of country music, along with impressive specials devoted to bluegrass, and the *Grand Ole Opry* carried live and in its entirety on at least two different occasions. Nowhere else on television did country music receive such an honest and serious treatment, although the independent Nashville Network, a cable enterprise that debuted in 1983, gave promise of providing the coverage that the music had always lacked.

The Nashville Network, however, began its existence with a mishmash of mediocre game shows, musical variety presentations, outdoor sports and hunting functions, old movies, and a thoroughly silly western dance program which seemed little more than a weak imitation of *Soul Train*. The network was saved from total mediocrity by a few shows of superior caliber: *Nashville Now*, a variety/talk show hosted by Ralph Emery; *The Tommy Hunter Show*, a fast-paced variety program from Canada; *Yesteryear in Nashville*, a series of interviews with older performers conducted by Archie Campbell; *Fire on the Mountain*, a presentation of bluegrass and old-time music; and, preeminently, *Bobby Bare and Friends*, a tribute to songwriters featuring interviews and live music.

Although television exposure dramatically signaled the ubiquity of country music in American popular culture, nowhere was the music's newfound respectability more strongly displayed than in its identification with presidential politics. Since Lyndon Johnson's administration, the appearance of country entertainers at White House or presidential-related functions has become almost routine, and musicians have sometimes been used to bolster administration positions. LBJ's famous Texas barbecues were often spiced with country music, and particularly with the antics of a comedy duo known as the Geezinslaw Brothers, a Texas act built around the mandolin playing and tenor singing of Sam Allred, a long-time Austin disc jockey. During the divisive period of the Vietnam War, Richard Nixon seized upon country music because a host of country songs criticized protestors and otherwise defended establishment values. Nixon consequently invited such singers as Merle Haggard and Johnny Cash to the White House. Cash's appearance sparked a minor controversy when the singer refused to do a couple of songs requested by Nixon's staff, "Okie from Muskogee" and "Welfare Cadilac" [*sic*]. His refusal, though, had nothing to do with political ideology; Cash did not know the songs, and he felt that they did not fit his style. It was not surprising that Nixon would journey to Nashville in 1974, in the midst of the Watergate crisis, to attend the official dedication of the new Grand Ole Opry House. The beleaguered president sought refuge in an institution that seemed solidly identified with Middle America. The Nixon–country music linkage seemed ominous to some liberal observers, and one writer was moved to describe the music as "the perfect musical extension of the Nixon adminstration."[3]

Jimmy Carter's well-known associations with country entertainers drew considerable inspiration from the political urge to cater to grass-roots Americans, but a stronger motivation lay in his and the music's mutual southernness. Carter was the only president who seemed genuinely to love and understand country music. He had listened to country music since he was a boy, and the music had figured prominently in his campaigns for the Georgia governorship and for the presidency. As president Carter often included country performers in government social functions, and he sometimes appeared on stage with them and even sang an occasional fragment of song. Singer James Talley, an Oklahoman who fused blues, country, and social comment in his songs, while eliciting some comparisons with Woody Guthrie, received extensive, though short-lived, publicity because First Lady Rosalynn Carter declared him to be her favorite singer. Such entertainers as Johnny Cash, Loretta Lynn, Tom T. Hall, Hank Snow, and Willie Nelson were prominent supporters of Carter and were active participants in presidential-related functions and in the 1980 campaign. Country musicians, of course, were grateful for the support which Carter lent to their profession, and they and he profited, at least for a time, from the resurgence of the South in American life.

The Ronald Reagan administration continued the practice of bringing country entertainers to White House functions. The CMA's twenty-fifth anniversary celebration, in fact, was held in Washington in 1983 before a large audience including President and Mrs. Reagan and other government dignitaries. A large parade of entertainers appeared in the lavish, flashily organized production, but the highest point, musically, came when Ricky Skaggs, Bill Monroe, Grandpa Jones, and Senator Robert Byrd, who

3. Richard Goldstein, "My Country Music Problem—and Yours," *Mademoiselle* 77, no. 2 (June 1973): 114–115, 185.

combined old-time fiddling with his Democratic leadership role, combined to do a version of "Lonesome Road Blues." Reagan's favorite country singer, though—judged by the frequency with which he appeared at presidentially sponsored affairs—was Merle Haggard. Haggard no doubt felt some loyalty to the man who had pardoned him during his earlier stint as governor of California, but his and Reagan's political presumptions did not seem incompatible. In the midst of the recession of 1982, Haggard endorsed Reagan's economic program,[4] but in songs like "Big City" he delivered a mixed message that commented on urban anonymity, wage inequities, and inadequate government support ("so-called social security"). Haggard's solution, though—a flight to the wilds of Montana—was a fantasy that working people may have shared but that only someone like a millionaire singer could realize.

Despite the identification of some country singers with political figures, country music's political stance remained difficult to categorize. Musicians voted both Democratic and Republican and stayed as free of ideological postures as did most Americans. Some performers leaned toward Reagan, but others supported the Democratic cause. Willie Nelson, Waylon Jennings, Jessi Colter, Dottie West, and Kris Kristofferson, among others, participated in the giant Democratic fund-raising telethon of May 1983.

Just as there was no monolithic country music stance toward politics, neither was there a fixed position on the music's definition or future direction. Increasingly in the mid-seventies voices were raised among fans and entertainers alike protesting country music's dilution and the fusion with pop sounds. Traditionalists bemoaned the Top Forty formats and tight playlists favored by most "country" radio stations, and they denounced the crossover mania that lured a proliferating number of singers into the commercially fertile pastures of pop music. Above all, many partisans wept because of the difficulties faced by hard country and older musicians in getting their music recorded and distributed.

The CMA received considerable criticism because of its apparent complicity in the blurring of country music's identity. The rivals that occasionally arose, however, did not necessarily differ from the Nashville organization in their approaches to style. The California-based Academy of Country Music, for example, challenged Nashville's dominance and strove to give West Coast musicians greater exposure; it did not trouble itself with controversies concerning stylistic direction, and its awards went to performers whose sounds were as pop-flavored as those favored by the CMA. The boldest challenge to the CMA came from the short-lived Association of Country Entertainers (ACE), an organization which gave voice to the legitimate complaints of many fans and musicians, but which suffered from

---

4. Bob Allen, "Haggard's a Working Man at Heart," *Music City News* 19, no. 12 (June 1982): 12.

undigested priorities as well as the powerful opposition of the deeply entrenched CMA. ACE came into existence in November 1974, after Olivia Newton-John, an Australian pop singer who was briefly packaged as a country artist, won the CMA's Female Singer of the Year award. About fifty people met at George Jones and Tammy Wynette's home to create an organization that would "preserve the identity of country music"[5] and would be confined solely to entertainers (as opposed to promoters, record merchandisers, and other industry people). In the few years of its existence, ACE insisted that country music awards should go only to those people who considered themselves country, asserting that some musicians were merely opportunists who had hopped on country music's burgeoning bandwagon and that many radio stations (such as New York City's WHN) adhered to a narrow selection of dubious country material. ACE encouraged radio stations everywhere to expand their playlists, and it sponsored concerts which were designed to give ignored performers opportunities to be heard.

Many people in the ACE leadership, such as Grandpa Jones and Vic Willis, were genuinely concerned about country music's growing fusion with pop. But the organization as a whole was timid about confronting the issue head on, partly because it was fearful of alienating the Nashville commercial establishment, but largely because it included performers who were strongly attracted by pop sounds. An organization that included Tammy Wynette as a charter member and Barbara Mandrell as one of its presidents could hardly be described as traditionalistic. It was easy for critics to argue, therefore, that ACE was primarily concerned with fostering a closed community among country musicians and that it was composed of jealous and parochial individuals who were trying to protect themselves from newcomers to the country field. Fans, of course, were excluded from membership in both CMA and ACE, and so the traditionalists among them stood by helplessly with no one to provide effective focus for their complaints.

Justin Tubb effectively summed up the feelings of many fans and musicians when he wrote and sang "What's Wrong with the Way That We're Doing It Now" (which, as one might expect, received very little airplay on the Top Forty stations). Tubb accurately described the difficulties that "hard country" musicians faced in getting their music recorded and played, but in discussing the "well-meaning people"[6] who were changing the nature of the music, he singled out only the "progressives" (a term usually associated with such people as Willie Nelson and Waylon Jennings). He made no reference to the country-pop stylists and the crossover phenome-

5. *Music City News* 12, no. 6 (December 1974): 3.
6. Justin Tubb, "What's Wrong with the Way That We're Doing it Now," on *Justin Tubb*, First Generation Records FGLP-GOOS-01.

non which were contributing most to the dilution and homogenization of country music. The crossover passion intensified in the late seventies and early eighties, and few singers, if their sound and style permitted it, could resist the temptation to go where the big money was.

Barbara Mandrell's career illustrated well the almost-irresistible allure of the pop sound. She won considerable commercial success with a song called "I Was Country When Country Wasn't Cool," but in a style that possessed no country flavor at all—and not even George Jones' cameo appearance on one verse of the song could save it from pop murkiness. Mandrell, then, was a good example of an entertainer who while identifying with both Nashville and country music was nevertheless drawn by pop sounds and styles. She was born in Houston in 1948, but grew up in California in a family that was associated with country music in both a business and a professional sense. Her father led a little family band while also working as West Coast representative for Standel Amplifiers. The precocious Barbara had learned how to play piano, bass, guitar, five-string banjo, saxophone, and triple-neck steel guitar by the time she was a teenager, but it was her proficiency with the steel guitar that led her into a professional performing career. Joe Maphis and Chet Atkins heard the twelve-year-old girl playing the steel guitar at the annual trade convention in Chicago in 1960. Largely through Maphis' recommendation, she began playing the instrument on the *Town Hall Party* in Los Angeles. By the time she arrived in Nashville in early 1969, her versatility as a musician was being subordinated to her ambition to become a leading vocalist. Recording for Columbia, and working under the direction of producer Billy Sherrill, Mandrell immediately began to create a middle-of-the-road sound that was closer to the Memphis and Motown soul singers than it was to country. Such songs as "Do Right Woman" and "If Loving You Is Wrong (Then I Don't Want to Be Right)" have continued to be the most prominent types of material in her repertory.

Whatever the sources of her style, Mandrell became one of the superstars of country music and was twice voted the CMA's Entertainer of the Year. Like Johnny Cash, she was an expert at self-promotion who showed an extraordinary skill at getting her name before the widest possible audience. A weekly television show in the early eighties presented Barbara and her two sisters to a huge public, and there was little on the slickly packaged show that could alienate even the most uncompromising country music hater. Like her occasional specials, the weekly show conveyed more of the essence of Las Vegas than of Nashville. An hour-long special made for HBO in 1983, *The Lady Is a Champ*, was a sophisticated, fast-paced, highly choreographed, and lavishly produced affair that permitted Mandrell to exhibit the full range of her talents. Alternately sexy, religious, and patriotic in her choice of songs, moving nimbly through highly synchronized dance routines; and jumping from one instrument to another, Mandrell dazzled her audience with a display of musical virtuosity, sincerity, and bubbling personality. Olivia Newton-John had never been so far removed from country music.

Barbara Mandrell was only one among dozens of performers who proved that there was a huge audience for country-pop music. No one knows exactly who that audience is, or how long it has been attracted to country sounds (ersatz or real). Many country-pop fans, of course, had been with country music all along, and either they changed as the music did, or they had always leaned toward the smoother sounds ever since Eddy Arnold made his first tentative experiments back in the late forties. A large segment of listeners make no distinction among country singers and will respond positively to anyone who is packaged as a country singer (whether a honky-tonk stylist like George Jones, a bluegrass-derived musician like Ricky Skaggs, or a pop-style vocalist like Larry Gatlin). An even larger number of fans probably make no distinctions among singers of any kind and do not trouble themselves with definition or categorization. They merely gravitate toward any singer, regardless of classification, who satisfies their musical cravings. Many people were first lured to music by the rockabillies and, above all, by Elvis in the late fifties. As the rockabilly fans grew older, they moved in a variety of musical directions, and some probably abandoned interest in any kind of rock-related music. Many men and women of this generation, though, never lost their fascination with performers who exuded energy, sexual appeal, charisma, and youthful good looks. Such fans continued to find in the seventies and eighties a large number of entertainers in the country field who fulfilled these requirements. Despite occasional experiments with other types of songs, Jerry Lee Lewis never strayed very far from his original rockabilly mold, and even the most conventional mainstream pop or country song received the special Lewis touch, a zestful, swaggering, and highly personal interpretation of the material. Among the younger performers, Billy Swan, Joe Stampley, and Gary Stewart seemed to hew most closely to the original rockabilly sound. With songs like "I Can Help," Swan re-created a fresh, gently rocking sound that suggested the early period of rock-and-roll music. Stampley and Stewart, on the other hand, wore several stylistic hats, and were competent performers in any genre they chose. Because of his rollicking, good-natured, good-old-boy duets with Moe Bandy in the early eighties (among the most commercially successful records that either had ever had), Stampley became temporarily miscast as a honky-tonk singer. Stampley was actually an all-purpose singer whose heart and musical preferences still lay close to the rock-and-roll on which he was weaned. Stewart was one of the finest young honky-tonk singers of the modern period, when he chose to do that kind of material, but his driving piano style and hedonistic singing made him seem more reminiscent of Jerry Lee

Lewis than of George Jones. Like many of the young singers of the South who came along during the seventies, Stewart also revealed a strong kinship with such Southern rock musicians as the Allman Brothers and the Marshall Tucker Band.

The rocking country singers were indeed influenced by a wide array of musicians who spanned the period from early Elvis right on up to their own time. And in the case of Presley, it was generally the later Elvis—the superstar of Las Vegas fame—who exerted the strongest influence. A host of performers, appearing in clubs all over America, and many of them nothing more than pale imitations of Elvis, provided enduring testimony of "the King's" pervasive legacy. Dressed usually in skin-tight sequined suits, and sporting open shirts and necklaces, these singers tried to evoke the aura of aggressive energy and playful sexuality that their hero had created. Ronnie McDowell made his first vault to fame with a song of tribute to Presley and then settled into a predictable groove of dynamic, macho song performances. The most bizarre manifestation of the Elvis cult in country music came in the career of a singer who called himself Orion. Dressed in a mask and cape, Orion sang in a deep, sensual baritone filled with an exaggerated, throaty vibrato. No other singer came so close to re-creating the sound of the mature Presley.

The singers who profited most from the revolution that Presley had wrought, either as disciples or as spinoffs, were entertainers who built independent identities. Razzy Bailey, for example, shared the preference for high-voltage, sensual performance that other neo-rockabillies had, but his style seemed closer to soul music than any other form; his was the "blackest" sound in modern country music. Billy "Crash" Craddock, T. G. Sheppard, Ray Griff, Narvel Felts, Eddie Rabbitt, Earl Thomas Conley, the Bellamy Brothers, and the Oak Ridge Boys were among those who exhibited obvious rock-and-roll traits while nonetheless creating distinctive styles which appealed to a broad spectrum of fans. Craddock bore the closest resemblance to hard-core rockabilly with such songs as "Knock Three Times" and the sexy "Rub It In," but by the beginning of the eighties, like most of his rock-and-roll contemporaries, he had opted for a softer and less rollicking beat.

Country-pop won much of its audience among people who sought a middle-of-the-road, easily understood form of music—and one that did not reek too strongly of rural or working-class life. In short, they sought a replacement for the pop music that had died or gone underground when rock-and-roll achieved its hegemony in the late fifties. If Perry Como and Doris Day were not available, then Glen Campbell and Crystal Gayle would have to do. As country singers crossed over to the lucrative area of pop music, they encountered a swarm of pop singers of all descriptions ("old-timers" like Dean Martin, Patti Page, and Teresa Brewer, and "newcomers" such as Anne Murray, John Denver, Kenny Rogers, and Olivia Newton-

John) who were trying to build or rebuild careers through an involvement in country music. Together, they plowed a common ground that increasingly defied definition, but one which in many respects constituted the new pop music of America. Glen Campbell, Roger Miller, and Eddy Arnold were already taking their music to Middle America when Olivia Newton-John made her fateful inroads into country music. In that same year, 1974, Charlie Rich recorded his giant hit "Behind Closed Doors," a dramatic departure from the blues and rockabilly tunes that had been the staples of his repertory ever since he began his career with Sun Records in the midfifties. The sensuous song was part of a growing list of such material, including Kristofferson's "Help Me Make It through the Night," Freddy Weller's "Sexy Lady," Conway Twitty's "You've Never Been This Far Before," and the Bellamy Brothers' "If I Said You Had a Beautiful Body (Would You Hold It against Me?)," that ventured into the area of eroticism with a greater suggestiveness and openness than at any previous time of country music history. Many people applauded what they considered to be a broader vision in country music, but others expressed dismay at the declining morality of the music. Grandpa Jones and Cindy Walker, for example, described such material as "skin songs,"[7] and such items were cited as evidence of the harm that had come from country music's flirtation with other musical cultures.

In the years after 1974 a profusion of singers moved into country music from a wide variety of performing backgrounds (this occurred with such frequency that some critics described country music as a refuge for musicians with failed or quiescent careers). "Moving into country" often meant nothing more than adding a pedal steel guitar to one's accompanying instrumentation, or it might mean merely the use of Nashville recording studios and musicians. The country-pop impulse did not necessarily preclude the use of down-home country instruments such as fiddles or dobros (or even the five-string banjo, which figured prominently in Nashville Brass performances), but being "country" was primarily a matter of being defined or packaged with that description. Pop-folk singer John Denver merely experimented with the idiom and seems never to have really sought full-scale country involvement; nevertheless, his ventures resulted in some major hits, such as "Back Home Again," "Thank God I'm a Country Boy," and the now classic "Country Roads," each of which was more rural than many of the songs then being recorded by mainstream country singers. Some singers, such as Olivia Newton-John, Charlie Rich, and Anne Murray, resisted country labeling even while prospering from the identification. None of them, of course, turned down either the rewards or the awards that emanated from the country music business, but they generally argued that their music was more broadly popular than a country cate-

7. Interview with Cindy Walker, Mexia, Texas, August 12, 1976.

gorization would suggest. The Canadian-born Anne Murray (from Spring Hill, Nova Scotia) grew up listening to every kind of music except country, which, according to her own admission, she hated: "I thought it was terrible, because at the time the only kind of thing I heard was Kitty Wells and to me it was more important that somebody could sing than what they were saying."[8] When she made her first tentative efforts at professional music in 1964, while pursuing a full-time job as a physical education teacher, she began to listen to country music seriously and to appreciate it. One of her first recordings in 1970 for Capitol's Canadian division was a folk-like song called "Snowbird," a crossover tune which received extensive airplay on both country and pop music radio stations in the United States and Canada. Murray has ever since maintained that kind of broad appeal, partly through an intelligent selection of material which cuts across musical categories (such as "You Needed Me," "Cotton Jenny," and "Could I Have This Dance"), but also because of her relaxed, direct, and clearly articulated style of singing. Her appeal has been much like that of Glen Campbell, who, in fact, contributed directly to her American acceptance by featuring her on his popular television show.

Murray's effective style of vocal communication and her preference for story songs were probably shaped by her involvement in the folk revival of the mid-sixties. Other singers, such as Don Williams and Kenny Rogers, who found a home in country music, also profited from that experience. Don Williams began his professional career as lead singer for the pop-folk trio the Pozo Seco Singers, but then found a comfortable niche in country music. Born in a working-class home in Portland, Texas (near Corpus Christi), Williams had no difficulty in relating to a type of music he had heard all his life. With his warm, rich, resonant baritone voice, projected over spare string instrumentation, he won a large following here and in England that spilled across most musical boundaries. Like Jim Reeves, with whom he was often compared, Williams preserved the allegiance of hard-core country fans while fashioning a smooth and almost-crooning style of delivery. His failure to cross over into the pop charts with the frequency of someone like Kenny Rogers is probably attributable to the down-home ambience and rustic simplicity that his music conveys. His version of "Amanda," about the disappointed dreams of an aging hillbilly singer, should have been satisfying to anyone; it is a classic performance which somehow combines the flavor of old-time country music with a middle-of-the-road approach.

Williams' fellow Texan Kenny Rogers (from Houston) followed several stylistic paths before becoming one of America's pop superstars. Although he has received an acclaim that few singers in American history have re-

8. John Gabree, "Anne Murray: The Girl Next Door Grows Up," *Country Music Beat* 1, no. 1 (January 1975): 43.

ceived, and has certainly acquired a wealth that few can equal, he can still refer to himself as "basically a country singer who's capable of doing other things."[9] Rogers began recording and performing actively while still in high school, and in the ensuing years he performed rock-and-roll, modern jazz, and pop-folk (with the New Christy Minstrels) before settling down for six years in a successful commercial format with the First Edition. The First Edition was an eclectic trio which did pop, folk, and soft-rock music, but the group also performed pop versions of country songs, such as "Reuben James" and the very popular "Ruby, Don't Take Your Love to Town," in which Rogers gave hints of the personal, sensual style that now characterizes his music. After the 1976 demise of the First Edition, Rogers cast his lot with country music and came up with a formula that gave him access to one of the largest audiences that any American singer has ever had. For three consecutive years in the late seventies he won the People's Choice Award as the top male singer (a survey conducted by the Gallup organization); from 1977 (when he recorded his first giant hit, "Lucille") to 1984, he sold an estimated $250 million worth of records; and he has branched out into television network specials and movies (one TV movie was based on his popular hit recording "The Gambler"). While his songs are often country in theme and mood, the production behind them (as well as his concerts) is thoroughly Las Vegas in tone. The sophisticated arrangements and lavish orchestration, however, do not explain Rogers' appeal. His handsome looks, combining boyish facial features with graying hair and beard, along with an equally intriguing mixture of machismo and classiness, certainly contribute to his popularity. But his singing style, above all, has been the chief source of his immense success. Rogers is a consummate story-teller, with an intimate and compelling style that almost demands the listener's concentration. When his husky tenor voice slips down into a raspy, gravelly register, as it sometimes does, Rogers pulls the listener even farther into his confidence.

Rogers' appeal to Middle America, though much stronger, is reminiscent of that of Conway Twitty. And like Rogers, Twitty has never been honored by the CMA with an award in any category, even though his attainment of number one songs (estimated to be forty-eight at the end of 1983) is unmatched by any other singer. Twitty was born Harold Jenkins in Friars Point, Mississippi, about seventy miles south of Memphis and only forty miles from Elvis Presley's home town of Tupelo. When he began his two-year army stint in 1953, he was still singing the country music that he grew up with. When he returned to the United states in 1955, he heard Presley's recorded version of "Mystery Train" and was caught up in the excitement that was affecting young people everywhere. He formed a rock-and-roll band, changed his name to Conway Twitty (taken from small

9. "Playboy Interview: Kenny Rogers" *Playboy* 30, no. 11 (November 1983): 69.

towns in Arkansas and Texas, respectively), and set out on a career that was to lead him to stardom in two different fields of music. His 1957 MGM recording of "It's Only Make Believe" became number one in country, pop, and blues; he still performs it in his concerts today.

Twitty returned in 1968 to country music, which he maintains he always preferred to rock-and-roll, and immediately established credibility with fans and disc jockeys. His first number one country song was a pure honky-tonk weeper called "The Image of Me," but since that time he has demonstrated a mastery over every kind of country material. His virtuosity is such that he has become virtually uncategorizable. He is mainstream country, with a tinge of pop, but, unlike Kenny Rogers, there is scarcely a hint of crossover in his approach. His best-selling duets with Loretta Lynn and his relationship with the powerful MCA corporation helped to give him access to a huge audience, but it would seem that many of his fans have been with him since "It's Only Make Believe" and have grown up with him and his music. An intense bond of loyalty exists between Twitty and his fans, many of whom are middle-aged women whose devotion to him began when he was a gyrating rock-and-roller. The sexuality of his lyrics is much more overt than that found in most other singers' material, and such songs as "You've Never Been This Far Before," "Slow Hand," "I'd Love to Lay You Down," and "Tight Fitting Jeans" have aroused controversy while also being major commercial hits for him. Twitty's performances, however, are physically restrained and contain none of the sensual body movements witnessed in the acts of many of the modern rockabillies. An affecting growl, similar to Kenny Rogers', is about the only peculiarity in his otherwise straight-ahead vocal style, but it is a highly effective communicator. Twitty's private life as a family man and successful businessman stand in striking contrast to the sexy world he often sings about. His musical success has enabled him to build one of country music's largest commercial empires. He owns a music promotion company, a minor league baseball team (the Nashville Sounds), much real estate, and a theme park, Twitty City, which contains his plantation-style home, homes for various relatives, a museum, gardens, and gift shops. In the first year after its opening in May 1982, Twitty City was host to a reported 200,000 tourists. The success garnered by Twitty City and other music-related theme parks, along with the profusion of mail-order programming on the Nashville Network, suggest that country music has still not traveled very far from the carnival and Mexican border atmosphere of its youth.

Larry Gatlin has not yet accumulated such an extensive portfolio of economic interests, but, like Twitty, he presents many faces to his listeners. He is, as one writer phrased it, "an arrogant young smartass to some, a prophetic truthseeker to others. A goodlooking, sexual fantasy to one, yet a fine young Christian man to another."[10] Gatlin has occasionally aroused anger by an aloofness to fans (such as a refusal to sign autographs) and by an air of supreme self-confidence. Interviews with him, however, as well as the evidence found in his song lyrics, suggest a man of considerable depth, sensitivity, intelligence, and compassion. His expressive tenor singing bears a strong resemblance to that of Glen Campbell, but is definitely closer to the country mainstream than that of the Arkansas superstar. His style and sound are of broad appeal, but he has never enjoyed a crossover success like many of his country contemporaries. The Odessa, Texas, native received his first musical experience singing in the Assembly of God church, but his entree to Nashville came as a songwriter when Dottie West heard some of his compositions and sponsored his move to the city. Gatlin has always sung only his own songs, first as a soloist, but later with the backing of his brothers, Rudy and Steve, in a group called Larry Gatlin and the Gatlin Brothers Band. Beginning with "Sweet Becky Walker" in 1973, Gatlin has recorded a succession of popular songs such as "Broken Lady," "I Just Wish You Were Someone I Loved," "Houston," and a controversial but compassionate song about derelicts in a rescue mission, "The Midnight Choir."

The Gatlin Brothers have been but one of several groups that have thrived in country music since the seventies. Country duets, of course, have always been common, but the modern period has seen a proliferation of major performers, such as Dolly Parton and Porter Wagoner, Conway Twitty and Loretta Lynn, and Merle Haggard and Willie Nelson, who have combined their talents in duet performances. At least one daughter and father team, the Kendalls, won some success with songs like "Heaven's Just a Sin Away" and "The Pittsburgh Stealers" (about love thieves and not the famous football team). Brother duets were rare outside of bluegrass music, but at least one act, the Bellamy Brothers (Howard and Dave) have prospered with a mixture of rock and country sounds and a repertory of sexy songs such as "Do You Love As Good As You Look" and "If I Said You Had a Beautiful Body (Would You Hold It against Me?)." Trios were even rarer, but an occasional group such as Dave and Sugar (composed of Dave Rowland and a shifting duo of beautiful female singers) competed favorably with other country entertainers. Much more crucial to country music's commercial burgeoning than the duets and trios, however, were the quartets that thrived at the end of the seventies.

Until the emergence of the Statler Brothers, the Oak Ridge Boys, and Alabama, quartets usually performed unobtrusively as backup voices for other singers. These singers, though, stepped out front to center stage and

10. Dolly Carlisle, "Larry Gatlin: Straight Ahead," *Country Music* 8, no. 7 (April 1980): 21.

became some of country music's brightest superstars. The Statler Brothers were boyhood friends who began singing gospel music while still in high school in Staunton, Virginia. Brothers Don and Harold Reid and their friends Lew DeWitt and Phil Balsley first called themselves the Kingsmen and sang in a style suggestive of such major gospel quartets as the Statesmen Quartet and Blackwood Brothers. Eventually selecting the name Statler as a performing title (from the brand name of a local tissue product), the quartet became active throughout the Upper South singing a mixture of country, pop, and gospel material. They joined Johnny Cash's touring organization on March 9, 1964, and remained with the Cash troupe for eight and a half years. Although described as a gospel quartet, the Statlers continued to perform a diverse repertory. Johnny Cash negotiated a Columbia recording contract for them, and their third release in 1965 was a massive hit and Grammy Award winner named "Flowers on the Wall." Despite this auspicious beginning, the Statlers felt ill served by Columbia, and they left the label in 1970. A new association with Mercury and producer Jerry Kennedy permitted them freedom of action as well as the promotion necessary to break through into a larger market. Beginning with "Bed of Rose's" in 1970, the Statlers built a popularity that led to their being named the CMA's Vocal Group of the Year for seven years in a row. Described by one journalist as "intelligent conservatives with a gift for communication and a respect for their conservative audience,"[11] the Statlers established a rapport with middle-class America that extended well beyond the borders of their native South. They reawakened memories of small-town radio for many Americans with their delightful spoof of amateur country bands, first heard in a 1973 recording called "The Saturday Morning Radio Show," and then followed up by an lp entitled *Live at Johnny Mack Brown High School.* Their mythical creations, Lester "Roadhog" Moran and the Cadillac Cowboys—sponsored by Burford's Barber Shop—were reminiscent of hundreds of similar earnest but plodding bands heard by Americans during radio's golden age. With their emphasis on traditional values, patriotism, and, above all, nostalgia, they struck responsive chords in 1970's America. Such songs as "The Class of '57" (about the failed dreams of a graduating class) and "Whatever Happened to Randolph Scott" (a tribute to the beloved cowboy movies of their youth) not only were commercially satisfying to the Statlers but also won the admiration of novelist Kurt Vonnegut, who praised the "shrewd innocence" found in these poems.[12]

The Oak Ridge Boys also came to country music from a gospel background. The current group of this name are heirs to a tradition that dates

11. Patrick Carr, "The Statler Brothers: How the Class of '57 Buys a Schoolhouse, Wins Eight CMA Awards in an Air of Complete Calm," *Country Music* 9, no. 7 (March 1981): 40.

12. From Kurt Vonnegut's autobiography, *Palm Sunday*, quoted in ibid., p. 45.

back to 1945, when the Oak Ridge Quartet (named in honor of the nearby atomic energy center) was founded by Wally Fowler in Knoxville, Tennessee. The Oak Ridge Quartet remained part of the evangelistic and all-night singing business (also pioneered by Wally Fowler), and underwent numerous personnel changes, down to the mid-sixties. Long before they converted to country music exclusively, they had already become quite controversial in the gospel field by letting their hair grow long, by wearing modish and flashy apparel, by mixing secular and religious material, and by employing sexy and highly choreographed movements on stage. They merely entertained; they did not preach. Oak Ridge apologists saw them acquiring a new audience for gospel music; their detractors saw them as blasphemers who used the gospel format for opportunistically commercial purposes. The quartet that made the leap to country, first by including a few country songs in their Las Vegas concerts in the mid-seventies, included lead singers Duane Allen and Bill Golden from Texas and Alabama, tenor Joe Bonsall from Philadelphia, and bass Richard Sterban from New Jersey. Their first country record in 1977, "Y'all Come Back Saloon," was a huge success. Their "crossover" into country music, followed by other hits such as "Leaving Louisiana in the Broad Daylight" and "Trying to Love Two Women," was merely the prelude to an even more lucrative intrusion into the broader area of pop music. That moment came in 1981 when they recorded "Elvira," a fifties-style rockabilly tune which vaulted to the top of the country music charts, moved on over into other fields of pop music, and won them a Grammy.

The Oak Ridge Boys talked openly of their desires to be the first group ever to win the CMA's Entertainer of the Year award. Despite their commercial viability and the dynamic showmanship for which they are known, this professed goal has never been attained. It must be a matter of some chagrin to the Oak Ridge Boys, then, that another vocal group with much less experience—Alabama—not only was the initial winner of this coveted award but has won it three years in succession (1982–1984). Alabama has cultivated an immense audience among both young and old listeners with a style that reflects the musical crosscurrents of the seventies—part country, part pop-rock (e.g., the Eagles, Jackson Browne), and with a tinge of southern rock. Unlike many of the entertainers who have thrived in country music's middle road, the musicians who comprise Alabama did not come from other musical backgrounds. They have succeeded commercially with the same sound and style with which they began as struggling teenagers playing in the clubs of Myrtle Beach, South Carolina, in the early seventies. Composed of three cousins, Jeff Cook, Teddy Gentry, and Randy Owen (all from Fort Payne, Alabama), and a drummer friend named Mark Herndon, the group stresses close harmony and the mellow lead singing of Owen. As a group they are also unique in that they provide their own instrumentation; Cook plays the lead guitar, as well as the fiddle on occasion, while Gentry and Owen play the bass and rhythm guitar. Alabama discovered a winning commercial formula by judiciously mixing romantic ballads such as "Feels So Right" and "An Old Flame Burning in Your Heart" with rousing uptempoed tunes like "Mountain Music" and "Tennessee River." The results have been a balanced and fruitful melange which has brought Alabama an enthusiastic and broad audience of both mainstream country listeners and youthful devotees. It is this youth audience which is an essential component for the success of any music.

It is one of the givens of cultural history that youth the world over have fueled the revolution in popular music, shattering traditional forms and contributing to the rise of innovative styles. The effect on country music, as we have seen, has been dramatic. Country music's recent history, then, has been all the more remarkable in that young people, both musicians and fans, have not only been in the vanguard of stylistic change but have also been forces for the preservation and revitalization of traditional elements. Admittedly, these have not been young adolescents but, instead, young adults who, for the most part, were originally won to music through rock-and-roll. The infusion of youthful styles and tastes into country music provided important and healthy alternatives to the "Nashville sound"; they were welcomed antidotes to the homogenization and mass production of country music.

The always-experimental Bob Dylan was a powerful catalyst in breaking down the resistance to country music among young fans. Dylan's lp *John Wesley Harding* was his first venture into the writing of country-style songs, and his 1969 album *Nashville Skyline* was recorded in the capital of country music with the assistance of some of Nashville's greatest sessions musicians. Dylan lent respectability to a musical form, and to a body of musicians, that had been perceived as "corny" or old-fashioned. Since the early seventies numerous young musicians identified with rock or pop-folk music have exhibited an interest in and facility for country music. John McEuen, of the Nitty Gritty Dirt Band, was one of the first musicians to play the five-string banjo in a folk-rock group. He and Jerry Garcia (the multi-talented instrumentalist of the San Francisco rock cult group the Grateful Dead), John Fogerty (the marvelous lead singer of Creedence Clearwater Revival), Leon Russell (who recorded a country album under the name of Hank Wilson), Linda Ronstadt, Gram Parsons, and Chris Hillman were only a few of the major performers who experimented with country music. These musicians, some of whom were identified with psychedelic and hard rock, showed an unexpected knowledge of country songs and harmonies and a talent for steel guitars, fiddles, mandolins, and five-string banjoes.

A high point in the merger of youth and country music came in 1972 when the Nitty Gritty Dirt Band (best known for their recording of "Mr.

Bojangles" in 1970) recorded a triple-disc album of country songs called *Will the Circle Be Unbroken*. The group had started out as a jug band in Orange County, California, in the mid-sixties, and, like many of the young musicians of that era, they were ultra-eclectic in repertory, playing everything from mountain music and bluegrass to hard rock. Largely through the inspiration of their manager and producer, William McEuen (the brother of banjo player John McEuen), the band did a marathon recording session with many of the great names of country music: Roy Acuff, Maybelle Carter, Merle Travis, Earl Scruggs, Doc Watson, Jimmy Martin, Vassar Clements, Norman Blake, Bashful Brother Oswald, and Junior Huskey. Intended as a tribute to some of the sources of contemporary music, the finished product was critically acclaimed and commercially successful. Many people bought the collection solely on the strength of the Dirt Band's name and reputation, but in so doing they were inadvertently introduced to some of the giants of country music.

Although many young musicians experimented with country forms, no one converted the enterprise into a mission until Gram Parsons appeared. Parsons was born Cecil Ingram Connors in Winter Haven, Florida, and was the inheritor of great wealth from his mother's family, the Snivelys of Florida, and from her second marriage to Robert Parsons of New Orleans. Despite his family connections and attendance at exclusive preparatory schools, Parsons developed a childhood affection for country music, although, as with most young people of his age, his first musical experience came through Elvis Presley. Parson's personal musical progression epitomizes that of many young people in the sixties. While still in high school, 1963–1965, he organized an urban folk group called the Shilos. During a brief stay at Harvard, in 1965, he moved toward the rock sound that the Beatles and other English groups had revitalized when he formed the International Submarine Band. This was a rock band, however, with a difference; it included the pedal steel guitar playing of J. D. Maness, one of the pioneers of the instrument in rock music, and it featured the performance of modern country songs. The band's 1967 recordings of such songs as "Miller's Cave" and "Satisfied Mind" were well in advance of similar experiments made by the Nitty Gritty Dirt Band and other rock-oriented musicians.

In 1968 Parsons joined the pioneering folk-rock band, the Byrds, and began urging that group to combine country with rock. The chief result was a 1969 lp called *Sweetheart of the Rodeo*, an extremely influential and thoroughly country collection which included such vintage country songs as "I Am a Pilgrim" and "Blue Canadian Rockies," a couple of Bob Dylan compositions, one Woody Guthrie song ("Pretty Boy Floyd"), and some original numbers, including Parsons' beautiful, and now classic, "Hickory Wind." Although the songs were not consistently country in origin, the

Byrds attempted, with erratic success, to render them in faithful country style, and once again the steel guitar work of J. D. Maness was given a prominent role.

After leaving the Byrds, Parsons and another alumnus of the group, Chris Hillman, along with steel guitarist Sneaky Pete Kleinow and bass player Chris Ethridge, founded a band which vividly illustrated the fusion of country music and youth-culture motifs. Choosing a self-mocking name, the Flying Burrito Brothers dressed in brightly arrayed and sequined Nudie suits which bore marijuana leaves instead of the traditional cactus plants and wagon wheels favored by country and western singers. Some of their songs, such as "Christine's Tune" and "Hot Burrito #1," were strongly rock-flavored, but they also borrowed songs from the Louvin Brothers, George Jones, Merle Haggard, and other hard-core country singers. Burrito instrumentation was similarly mixed, but the steel-guitar stylings of Sneaky Pete gave the group a distinctive honky-tonk flavor. The Burrito Brothers' most compelling songs were those written by Parsons and Hillman, especially the frequently performed "Sin City" and "Wheels," and they were rendered by these two singers in a sweet, clear duet harmony reminiscent of the Everly Brothers.

After he left the Burritos, Parsons continued to campaign for the fusion of country and rock audiences, but he won little success in his own lifetime. He made a few records on his own, including some excellent performances (such as "Hearts on Fire" and "Love Hurts") with Emmylou Harris, whom he met in Washington, D.C., in 1972. Parsons died of a drug overdose on September 19, 1973, and is buried near New Orleans in a modestly marked grave. Although Parsons' final resting place is obscure, his contributions to country music are much more strongly marked. His influence is still heard in the music of many young musicians, both unknown and professional (as in the cases of groups like the Eagles and the New Riders of the Purple Sage), but his chief legacy is displayed in the career of his protégé Emmylou Harris, whom he converted to hard country music.

Gram Parsons came to "traditional" country music from rock; Charlie Daniels and Hank Williams, Jr., moved in the other direction. And both found niches in a style generally described as "southern rock." Southern rock was essentially rock music performed by southern-born musicians, and hence little different from rock music elsewhere. These musicians nevertheless often demonstrated their southernness through their stylistic borrowings from blues and country music, but more often through an aggressive identification with the South, macho posturing, and good-old-boy imagery. The Marshall Tucker Band in South Carolina, the Allman Brothers in Georgia, ZZ Top in Texas, and Lynyrd Skynyrd in Alabama were a few of the groups that combined cowboy and hippie attire while also occasionally using country riffs and songs in a basically hard-rock context. Of

Willie Nelson. Photographs courtesy of the Country Music Foundation Library and Media Center, Nashville, Tennessee.

Alabama: *left to right*, Randy Owen, Teddy Gentry, Jeff Cook. Photograph courtesy of the Country Music Foundation Library and Media Center, Nashville, Tennessee.

Gram Parsons. Photograph courtesy of the Country Music Foundation Library and Media Center, Nashville, Tennessee.

Hank Williams, Jr. Photographs courtesy of the Country Music Foundation Library and Media Center, Nashville, Tennessee.

all these musicians, Charlie Daniels bore the closest relationship to country music. Born in Wilmington, North Carolina, Daniels parlayed a talent for the fiddle and electric guitar into a job as a sessions musician in Nashville (he was on Dylan's *Nashville Skyline* album, for instance). Daniels' own group, the Charlie Daniels Band, was very much in the mold of the Allmans and the Marshall Tucker Band, and he acknowledged his kinship with the southern rockers in "The South's Gonna Do It Again." His fiddling, on the other hand, was strongly indebted to western swing, and his singing was redolent with the flavor and accent of the rural South. This big, gruff, tobacco-chewing, outspoken musician embodied southern good-old-boy traits almost to the point of caricature. He was nationalistic, hedonistic, macho, . . . and lovable. He also made compelling music. His "Carolina, I Remember You" was an affectionate and poignant recollection of his state before the coming of the superhighways; "Still in Saigon" is one of the best songs yet written about the undying legacy of the Vietnam War; and his rousing "The Devil Went Down to Georgia" (a modern adaptation of the old theme of the Devil as a fiddler) was the CMA's choice as Single of the Year in 1980.

Hank Williams, Jr., of course, had one of the most famous pedigrees in country music. He grew up, as one of his songs phrased it, "standing in the shadows" of his revered father, and pushed into a mold by adoring fans and an overly ambitious mother. Hank, Jr., was an enormously talented child with an affinity for most of the country string instruments. He was on the concert trail at the age of fourteen, singing an occasional blues tune or rock-and-roll song, but most often performing his daddy's songs and in his daddy's style. Neither fans nor promoters would permit him to stray very far from the path originally blazed by Hank, Sr. Hank, Jr., was not unsuccessful during the early stages of his career, but his ascent to superstardom really did not come until he cast his lot with the southern rockers in the mid-seventies. With songs like "Dixie on My Mind," "Whiskey Bent and Hell Bound," and his high-powered, country-rock version of "Kaw-Liga," Hank built enormous followings in both country and rock music. In his banner year of 1982 he had nine lp's on the charts at the same time, a feat unequaled by any other country entertainer.

Despite his unparalleled commercial success, Hank, Jr., was not rewarded by the country music industry until 1987, when he was chosen as Entertainer of the Year. Some CMA voters may have questioned his authenticity as a country singer (although awards have been won often by performers less country than he), but his lifestyle and flaunting of the respectable conventions emphasized by the staid Nashville establishment have probably alienated a much larger number of people. His songs have consistently projected a mood of swaggering hedonism—a glorification of womanizing, hell raising, and drinking (with a preference for Jim Beam whiskey). In short, his music suggests a rowdiness that his father had only hinted at in his songs. Hank, Jr., was not chastened by his head-first plunge from a mountaintop in Montana on August 8, 1975. Recovering from the near-fatal accident required massive plastic surgery, including the complete rebuilding of his face. After his return to health, his songs became even more aggressively hedonistic and macho, suggesting among other things that the old fundamentalist strain that had inhibited free expression while encouraging guilt was losing its force among rural southerners. If God looked disapprovingly at his conduct, Hank, Jr., seemed not to care. He seemed similarly unconcerned about the responses made by northerners to his aggressive southern posture. "Dixie on My Mind" was one of several anti–New York City songs that appeared in country music in the seventies and eighties, and "A Country Boy Can Survive," while also taking potshots at that favorite scapegoat, was virtually a survivalist hymn with its emphasis on rural independence and its underlying hint of violence. With the appearance of such commercial songs, Hank, Jr., made himself a force to be reckoned with in the whole broad realm of popular music. Still, the ghost of his father would not disappear, and largely because Hank, Jr., seemed to feel a need to cling to the mystique, if not the reality, of Hank Williams. While complaining about having to live up to that myth, he nonetheless shamelessly exploited his famous family relationship by frequently alluding to his father in his songs, even up to the point of claiming Hank, Sr., as one of country music's original "outlaws," a self-serving designation designed to lend historical legitimacy to his own rebellion.

The mating of rock and country, so strongly displayed in the music of Hank, Jr., and Gram Parsons, was most strongly effected in Austin, Texas. The Austin musicians also came close to accomplishing Parsons' other dream, that of bringing youth and adult audiences together in a commonly shared musical environment. The vigorous and eclectic music scene found in Austin in the seventies was anticipated at Threadgill's Bar in the previous decade. Threadgill's was the scene of a meeting, if not mating, of cultures in which college students and "rednecks" enjoyed musical communion with each other. Kenneth Threadgill, the proprietor and bartender of a honky-tonk housed in an abandoned gas station in North Austin (allegedly the recipient of the first beer license granted in Travis County after Prohibition repeal), was a singer and yodeler in the Jimmie Rodgers tradition. He made his establishment available to anyone who wanted to sit around his big round tables and pick and sing, and when time permitted, Threadgill would also sing and yodel, still wearing his apron and invariably clutching a bottle of beer in his hand. In the late fifties Threadgill's became a refuge for, first, graduate students and, later, undergraduates from the University of Texas who were being won over to the emerging folk music revival. Janis Joplin was one of a small coterie of young musicians, many of them spillovers from the campus folk music club, who began frequenting Threadgill's in the early sixties, both to perform and to actually rub shoulders with the real "folk" who constituted much of the bar's regular clientele. The listeners who packed into the tiny establishment—an unlikely assortment of students and working folk—could hear everything from hoary hillbilly material (like that of the Carter Family) to bluegrass, blues, traditional ballads, and Woody Guthrie and Bob Dylan songs.

The cultural/musical mix witnessed at Threadgill's Bar was nevertheless an acoustic-dominated phenomenon, and one which drew upon grassroots musical material. Many of the musicians and fans who thronged to Threadgill's were soon won away by the supercharged and electronic sounds of the British and San Francisco rock groups. Janis Joplin was not the only local musician to journey to the West Coast, and in Austin itself a vigorous club scene emerged in the wake of the rock movement and the growth of the counterculture. The Armadillo World Headquarters, housed in a former national guard armory, was the center and symbol of this new musical culture. When it was established in August 1970, the club was intended as a forum for rock bands (such as the local Shiva's Headband) and as a refuge for. Austin's hippie, or "freak," community. The Armadillo, however, also featured an occasional country band, and so cowboys and rednecks began to rub shoulders with the long-haired counterculture community. Gradually a music culture emerged which enveloped them all, and one which reflected a curious combining of images and symbols: hippie, Texan, and, above all, cowboy (a usage which arose from the desire to find an indigenous and binding metaphor). The wearing of cowboy costumes, clubs with cowboy names (such as Split Rail, Broken Spoke, and Soap Creek Saloon), and the use of logos which suggested the Texas mystique (armadillos, Lone Star Beer, Longhorns), all became part of the rock/country music scene.

A colony of musicians emerged in Austin in the early seventies, most of whom gravitated toward country music after experiments with other forms of music. Bill and Bonnie Hearne demonstrated a thorough acquaintance with most forms of contemporary popular music, but their nice harmonies and Bonnie's piano-playing most readily exhibited their debts to country and gospel styles. Austin's best songwriter, Guy Clark, combined folkie, rock, and country motifs with an acute perception of Texas/cowboy images to produce such successful songs as "Texas Cookin'" and "Desperados Waiting for a Train." Steve Fromholz and Michael Murphey had begun their musical careers in the Denton/Dallas urban folk music circuit. Marcia Ball was a blues pianist/singer from Louisiana before she became the vocalist for the Austin country-rock group Frieda and the Firedogs. A young group of musicians from Berkeley, Asleep at the Wheel, had already begun combining rock-and-roll with western swing before they came to Austin, and Doug Sahm, who was in and out of the city, had long dabbled with Tex-Mex, country, and rhythm-and-blues forms before moving to hard rock in the mid-sixties (as the leader of the Sir Douglas Quintet, he was one of the first Americans to show the direct influence of the British rock groups). The best-known musician to relocate in Austin, before Willie Nelson, was Jerry Jeff Walker, a one-time folkie from New York whose perambulations around the country and a stint in a New Orleans jail had led to the writing of "Mr. Bojangles." Because of his loose, laid-back manner and free spirit, Walker seemed to epitomize, for many people, the atmosphere conveyed by Austin and the nearby Texas hill country. Austin was a good place to play music, but it was an even greater place to live.

Although Austin audiences were diverse, the large, and annually self-replenishing, student body of the University of Texas provided a crucial core of support for the clubs which flourished in the city. A trio of key supporters contributed mightily to the publicizing of the music. Rod Kennedy, a local promoter and folk music patron, provided exposure for the Austin musicians at his popular festivals in the hill country town of Kerrville. Townsend Miller, a stockbroker by profession and a country music fan by avocation, euphorically touted the local musicians in a weekly newspaper column, and Darrell Royal, the popular coach of the University of Texas Longhorns football team, lent the Austin scene further publicity by his appearances at local music functions and through his friendship with many of the musicians who came to the city (he was known as the biggest groupie in Austin).

Most of the musicians who congregated in the city were young, eclectic in musical taste, and relatively new to the country music scene. A few veteran performers, though, such as Floyd Tillman and fiddler Jesse Ashlock (a Texas Playboy alumnus) and, of course, Kenneth Threadgill, lived among them as patron saints. The Texas mystique clearly affected the imagery that Austin musicians used to describe themselves. The name and music of Bob Wills were often invoked because they supposedly embodied the spirit of liberation and innovation that Texas had contributed to music and on which the Austin musicians now drew. Folklorist Nicholas Spitzer referred to the Austin gestalt as "romantic regionalism,"[13] colorfully captured by Waylon Jennings' "Bob Wills Is Still the King,"[14] recorded live before an Austin audience which goes wild at certain catchwords such as "Red River," "Austin," and "Bob Wills." Even the listener gets caught up in the excitement.

Observers and musicians alike were hard pressed to find a label that sufficiently described the music coming out of Austin. Such terms as "country rock," "hip hillbilly," and "redneck rock" were occasionally used,

13. Nicholas Spitzer, "Bob Wills Is Still the King: Romantic Regionalism and Convergent Culture in Central Texas," *John Edwards Memorial Foundation Quarterly* 2, Part 4, no. 4 (Winter 1975): 191–197.
14. Heard on Waylon Jennings, *Dreaming My Dreams*, RCA APL1-1062.

but none of them gained much currency. Singer Michael Murphey coined a term that enjoyed a brief popularity when he sang "Cosmic Cowboy," a song that conjured up visions of hippies in cowboy costumes with free lifestyles and unbounded musical tastes. Radio station KOKE-FM in Austin also introduced a label that was widely used, although not exclusively as a description of Austin music, through its popularization of a format known as "progressive country" (1973–1977). KOKE's publicists argued that they were presenting an alternative to the Top Forty concept by playing a wide assortment of music which ranged from Roy Acuff to the Nitty Gritty Dirt Band. KOKE's claim, however, was more hype than reality, for the recordings played on the station tended to come most often from rock or rock-influenced musicians. "Progressive" seemed to suggest those musicians who borrowed from other styles or who tried to appeal to rock-bred youth by taking country music far afield from its traditional roots.

When Willie Nelson moved to Austin in 1972, a thriving music scene already existed there. And the way was already prepared there, and elsewhere, for a coming together of youth and country music. Contrary to the mythology that has grown up around Nelson, his departure from Nashville was not occasioned by his rejection by the music establishment. He had been quite successful as a songwriter, and he was highly respected by other musicians in the city. On the other hand, his dream of acceptance as a singer had not been realized. He felt that RCA did not properly promote his records and that the Nashville area possessed few places in which to perform. Nelson had always maintained his contacts in Texas, and he was a fixture on the honky-tonk circuit to which he periodically returned. The collapse of his second marriage and the destruction of his house by fire confirmed his resolve to leave Nashville. He moved back to an audience that had always been with him, to a climate and ambience that were appealing, and to an already growing music scene. Nelson could not have been unaware of Austin's youthful audience, but he became acutely conscious of its receptivity to him when he performed at the counterculture-oriented Armadillo World Headquarters. In the months following his return to Austin, Nelson began making a calculated attempt to appeal to young people, and particularly to those who had grown up with rock music and who had been touched by counterculture values. Nelson let his hair grow long, grew a beard, began wearing a headband, an earring, jeans, and jogging shoes—quite a contrast to the earlier Willie Nelson, who had worn short hair, a turtleneck sweater, and a Nehru jacket in Nashville television appearances in the 1960's. But Nelson claimed in an interview with Barbara Walters that the Nashville attire had been atypical, and that he had always favored jeans and informal dress.

The most highly publicized examples of Nelson's efforts to bring attention to himself and to bring disparate audiences together were his huge annual "picnics." The first of these outdoor festivals—a tentative experiment—was held at Dripping Springs, near Austin, in July 1971. The affair was an artistic success (it included old-timers like Roy Acuff, Tex Ritter, and Earl Scruggs, as well as a host of newer musicians like Tom T. Hall and Billy Joe Shaver) but a financial disaster attended by a relatively sparse audience. Subsequent festivals, held usually on the Fourth of July and in various Texas communities, were massively attended, all the more remarkable because they were held under the broiling Texas sun. Widely touted as events which would bridge the gaps between young and old, hippies and rednecks, and country and rock fans, Willie's picnics, in actuality, soon lost much appeal to older people or to traditional country fans. The swirling dust, unrelenting heat, boogieing fans, uninhibited youth in scanty or no clothing, marijuana fumes, and the proliferation of non-country performers such as Leon Russell combined to give the events the aura of country Woodstocks. Sociologist William C. Martin had such concerns in mind when he spoke of "growing old at Willie's picnic."[15]

Willie's picnics did attain the intended results: they made his name known far and wide (Nelson probably became better known than the Texas governor), and they cemented his relationship with the young, an association that brought him wealth and fame. After winning the youth, he then moved on to the conquering of Middle America and the adult market. In 1975 he and his wife, Connie, conceived an lp called *The Red Headed Stranger*, a concept album (one which is built around a central theme or story) which dealt with stolen love, retribution, and murder in the Old West. The album became the best-selling package he had ever put together, and one song from the lp, Fred Rose's gentle evocation of broken but undying love, "Blue Eyes Crying in the Rain," became the number one country song of the year. It is ironic that the first superhit recorded by this master songwriter was a song written by someone else. In the years following 1975 other songwriters continued to fuel his ascent to stardom.

As Nelson became more popular and commercial, this most "progressive" of artists moved increasingly toward the performance of older songs and toward a style that was ever more explicitly basic and uncomplicated. Nelson never abandoned his jazz style of phrasing, nor his propensity to sing behind the beat, but his arrangements were built around a rather spare and uncluttered scheme of instrumentation dominated by Nelson's own clean, inventive, single-string style of guitar playing. His audience was so loyal that it responded enthusiastically to everything he chose to do, whether it was country rock or the gospel songs that he and his sister Bobbie, his pianist, had been singing since they were children. His fans also stayed with him when he reached back to record an album of vintage pop songs. Such songs as "Stardust," "Georgia on My Mind," and "Blue

15. William C. Martin, "Growing Old at Willie Nelson's Picnic," *Texas Monthly* 2 (October 1974): 94–98, 116–124.

Skies" took him into another dimension of popular taste and won him another audience, that of the American middle class, which had little affinity for country music but had fond recollections of the pop songs that had largely disappeared.

Nelson's experimentations with songs, styles, and wearing apparel made him the hottest commercial property that country music had ever had, as well as one of the most visible figures in American popular culture. Awards and recognitions poured in upon him, and he branched out into allied areas of entertainment: record production, dance hall management, and movie making. His commercial viability was so proven that he became one of the few country entertainers who could produce his own records and who was permitted to take his road band into recording sessions. Nelson was voted the CMA's Entertainer of the Year in 1979, although many thought that the honor should have been his much earlier. He became a close friend of President Carter, and sang the "Star Spangled Banner" at the Democratic National Convention in 1980. He has also exhibited a natural flair for character acting, a penchant magnified by the weathered face and graying beard and hair that he sported in the mid-eighties. His movie roles may ultimately present him to a larger audience than his musical performances can ever provide.

Although Willie Nelson did much to revive interest in older songs and performers, while remaining stylistically close to the honky-tonk style that he grew up with in Texas, his ascent to national fame came through an identification with a group of musicians known as the Outlaws. The term "outlaw" is suggestive of lawless behavior, but if "rebellion" in any way marked the conduct of Waylon Jennings, Tompall Glaser, and their compadres, the rebellion was basically against the immobility and conservatism of the Nashville establishment. Like Willie Nelson, they were a group of musicians who sought artistic autonomy and the right to roam freely for material and style—objectives that ran counter to corporate Nashville's reluctance to experiment or to offend.

The Outlaws were not a discrete, cohesive group; they really lived only in the fertile minds of publicists and press agents, and in the fantasies of many listeners who wanted to believe that such a group existed. The Outlaws, of course, found it to be in their best commercial interests to promote such an image, and so they capitalized on the undying appeal of the cowboy (although in the guise of the desperado or badman) and of the rambler. They also profited, perhaps unconsciously, from a preoccupation with the antihero that had been manifested in American popular culture since World War II.

Standing at the center of the Outlaw group was a gifted singer from Littlefield, Texas, Waylon Jennings. Although his song preferences and performing image have sometimes roamed far afield from traditional country music, Jennings was an authentic son of the southern working class.

His mother was a devout member of the Church of Christ, and his father was a failed cotton farmer, truck driver, and moderately successful produce distributor. One of the few pleasant memories that Jennings had of growing up on the wrong side of town in Littlefield was the hours spent listening to his dad sing and play the guitar. Country music became an all-consuming passion for the young boy, and a means of escape from the cotton fields of West Texas. By the time he was thirteen Jennings was fronting a little band called the Texas Longhorns and was performing on a local station, KVOW, in Littlefield. During the next several years, while performing part time and working as a disc jockey in Littlefield and in nearby Lubbock, Jennings remained close to the traditional country music of his parents, and particularly to that of his first hero, Ernest Tubb. In 1958 he came in contact with what was perhaps the most pivotal influence in his life, the music of Buddy Holly. Holly took a special interest in Jennings, arranged for his first recording session ("Jole Blon," in Clovis, New Mexico, October 1958), and hired him as his bass player at the end of 1958. Holly's death in the plane crash of February 2, 1959, which also took the lives of the Big Bopper (J. P. Richardson) and Richie Valens, left Jennings demoralized for several months. It also left him permanently enveloped in the Holly mystique as the great rock-and-roll singer's protégé and as the man who had given up his plane seat to the Big Bopper before the fatal flight.

In the years following Buddy Holly's death, Jennings paid his musical dues playing in tough clubs throughout the Southwest and working as a disc jockey in Lubbock and in Phoenix, Arizona. The Phoenix years, 1961–1965, were crucial for the development of Jennings' career and for the shaping of his unique style. He signed his first major contract with Herb Alpert's A&M Records in 1963, and in the following year began singing six nights a week at a large country night club called J.D.'s. The audience at J.D.'s was a cultural mix which included businessmen, students from a nearby university, and cowboys—a prototype of the socially divergent audience found in Austin in the following decade. Jennings' already latitudinarian approach to music was accentuated further by the desire to please his heterogeneous listeners. He was singing at J.D.'s when Chet Atkins and RCA began showing an interest in him, a consequence of constant prodding by Jennings' friend, comedian Don Bowman, and Bobby Bare, who repeatedly reminded Atkins of how good this Phoenix singer was. His first RCA records were released in May 1965.

Waylon Jennings, the quintessential Outlaw of country music, has been associated with the great corporate giant, RCA, ever since 1965—and both the singer and the business have prospered greatly because of the relationship. The association, however, was often a stormy one, with Jennings struggling to gain control over the choice of material and the manner in which it was recorded. Chet Atkins first groomed Jennings to be a "folk-country" performer (with songs like "Man of Constant Sorrow" and "Scarlet Ribbons"), and he periodically supplied him with pop-country material such as "Love of the Common People" and "MacArthur Park." Jennings could perform any type of song, but he resisted all efforts to push him into any type of mold. His ascent to superstardom came when he was given free rein to record anything he desired, and in the rock-influenced country style that gave him access to listeners far beyond the normal country audience. Jennings' voice was a richly textured and well-balanced mixture of masculinity, sensuality, and mournfulness—there has been no better singer in country music.

Jennings' struggle for artistic independence has contributed to his reputation for rebellion, but his lifestyle and personality have done even more to fasten the label of Outlaw upon him. When he came to Nashville in 1965, his dress and grooming habits still reflected the fifties rockabilly culture from which he emerged. With his swept-back, unparted hair, high collars, and tight blue jeans, he looked like a hood hanging out on the corner or cruising around in his hotrod. His lead role in the Grade B movie *Nashville Rebel* (1966) only accentuated the image while also giving him a title. His dark good looks and natural shyness projected a kind of smoldering sexiness, and his experiments with drugs, drink, and high living (which were probably little different from those of many non-Outlaw musicians) did their part to evoke an aura of lawlessness.

Regardless of the personal mystique that surrounded Jennings, it is clear that the Outlaw phenomenon was largely a product of promotional hype, and most of it independent of Jennings himself. RCA nudged away from its conservative posture to endorse the concept of a bold highwayman who would ride away with the profits—for the corporation. In 1972 Jennings recorded a song called "Ladies Love Outlaws," and on the cover of a subsequent album of the same name he was shown dressed in badman attire, black clothing and six-gun, and facing an adoring young girl (posed for by his niece). From this point on the word "outlaw" began to replace "rebel" as a descriptive label for Jennings and his music, and he began to dress the part—beard, black hat, vest, black trousers. Music publicists of all descriptions lost no time in attaching "outlaw" to Jennings and other Nashville musicians who seemed at odds with the "establishment" and to the entire Austin community of musicians. Hazel Smith, the publicity chief at Glaser Music, for instance, recognized the commercial utility of outlawry and began using the word to describe the music produced by the Glaser Brothers and by the musicians who worked for them. The Glasers (Tompall, Jim, and Chuck) were a Nebraska-born trio who had long been admired for the smooth, soulful harmony which they developed as backup singers (most notably for Marty Robbins) and as an independent act. Tompall Glaser was also an excellent solo singer, writer, publisher, and free-thinking individualist whose establishment at 916 19th

Kenneth Threadgill.

Left to right, Kris Kristofferson, Johnny Cash, Waylon Jennings, Larry Gatlin. Photograph courtesy of the Country Music Foundation Library and Media Center, Nashville, Tennessee.

George Strait. Copyright © 1984 by Scott Newton/Austin City Limits.

John Anderson. Copyright © 1984 by Scott Newton/Austin City Limits.

Emmylou Harris. Photograph courtesy of the Country Music Foundation Library and Media Center, Nashville, Tennessee.

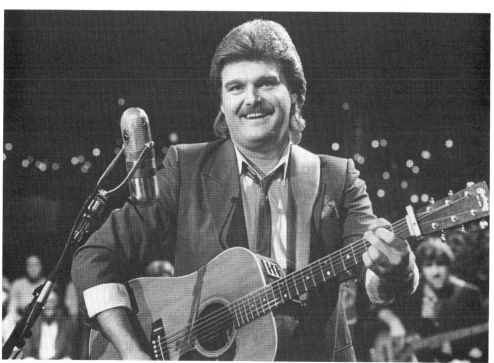

Ricky Skaggs. Copyright © 1984 by Scott Newton/Austin City Limits.

Avenue South was a kind of headquarters for other maverick musicians such as Bobby Bare, Billy Joe Shaver, and Waylon Jennings. Glaser and the people who congregated around him cultivated an air of laid-back informality, dressing generally in jeans, boots, and cowboy hats, and wearing long hair and beards. Their lifestyles were probably as scandalous to respectability-conscious Nashville as their music, but their "hedonism" was not at all unusual among country musicians (establishment figure Johnny Cash, for example, had earlier been known for his zaniness, pill habits, and rowdy practical jokes).

The only musician associated with the Glaser crowd who really seemed to go beyond fantasy to the borders of outlawry—the only one at least who seemed to delight in shocking audiences with antisocial behavior—was David Allan Coe. Originally billing himself as the Mysterious Rhinestone Cowboy, replete with mask and cape, Coe carried the Outlaw tag beyond the parameters of the Old West and suggested, instead, the lurid underworld of modern urban society. Coe was born in Akron, Ohio, and served several years in the Ohio State Prison. He claimed to have killed a fellow inmate, although researchers have failed to find corroborating evidence of the act. After abandoning his cowboy attire, Coe generally opted for biker, or motorcycle gang, costuming, and his entourage often included similarly clad bikers. He made X-rated recordings which were advertised in "adult" magazines, and in concerts he often conveyed a threatening mood. This kind of behavior undoubtedly got people's attention, but it is doubtful that he needed to do so. Coe is an excellent singer with a supple voice and a wonderful talent for mimicry, and a distinctive stylist in his own right. His "You Never Even Call Me by My Name"—written by Steve Goodman—is a delightfully outrageous spoof of country music, including all the clichés allegedly found in the music: trains, trucks, prisons, getting drunk, and mama.

Although some of the Nelson/Jennings/Glaser fraternity might sometimes flirt with errant forms of behavior—or at least give the impression of doing so—their rebellion was at base little more than an effort to assert their artistic independence within the confining context of a corporate musical structure. And, at least in the cases of Willie Nelson and Waylon Jennings, the maverick image was tremendously commercial. An album produced by RCA in 1976, composed of older material done by Nelson, Jennings, Jessi Colter, and Tompall Glaser, and entitled *Wanted: The Outlaws*, became country music's first documented platinum record (one which sold one million copies). Despite the hype surrounding the Outlaws, they did make a healthy challenge to Nashville's homogenization. And while they drew freely from other forms of music, such as rock, they also remained respectful of their own and country music's roots. In fact, if they used any term in private to describe themselves it was "hillbilly" and not "outlaw." The ultimate irony of the Outlaws may be that, while drawing upon a diverse array of musical sources and reaching out to new audiences, they did more to preserve a distinct identity for country music than most of their contemporaries who wore the "country" label.

If there is a real "conflict" in country music between traditionalists and country-pop or crossover advocates, it is seldom publicly aired. The country music fraternity tries to keep its problems private. Nevertheless, a growing concern about country music's clouded identity does manifest itself in the letter written to the trade journals, in the record reviews written by some critics, and in the comments made by occasional musicians on talk shows and in published articles (even Chet Atkins has expressed some reservations about country music's growing fusion with other forms).[16] The subject of country music's identity has been more openly discussed in the eighties than at any previous time, and frequent rediscoveries have been made that a market exists for the older sounds and styles. Television has provided some traditional acts, such as Grandpa Jones (on the *Hee Haw* show), Slim Whitman, and Boxcar Willie, with new formats in which to popularize themselves. The festivals, both here and in Europe, have lent further encouragement to individual musicians such as Doc Watson and to bluegrass music as a whole. Unfortunately, some of America's greatest hard-core singers, such as Hazel Dickens, receive very little public exposure. Dickens, for example, seldom appears before country audiences, but instead sings in folk clubs, at colleges, and at festivals such as that held in conjunction with the Knoxville World's Fair in 1982. Her voice, though, was heard with compelling clarity on the sound track of the great documentary film *Harlan County, USA.*

Hazel Dickens represented one of the oldest traditions of singing in country music, that of the mountain South. Other revivalists found their inspiration in the music of the Southwest and Far West. The 1970's saw a strong revival of western swing. A few bands, of course, had never stopped playing this kind of music: Hank Thompson and his Brazos Valley Boys, Leon Rausch and his group in Fort Worth, Hoyle Nix and the West Texas Cowboys, out of Big Spring, Texas. The patron saint of the style, Bob Wills, died on May 13, 1975, but was already becoming a cult figure long before that, especially in Austin. Two young bands, Asleep at the Wheel and Alvin Crow and the Pleasant Valley Boys, used Austin as their headquarters while combining western swing and rock-and-roll and otherwise projecting an ambience palatable to their youthful, rock-weaned audiences. These young musicians made Wills' name known to a new generation which had never actually heard Wills' music.

Western swing and the Bob Wills legacy were further preserved and popularized through the patronage of mainstream country-and-western performers such as Willie Nelson, Merle Haggard, and Red Steagall. Nel-

16 Robert Windeler, "Bio—Chet Atkins," *People Weekly,* December 16, 1974, p. 62.

son often spoke of his stylistic debt to Wills and performed such songs as "Stay All Night," while Haggard recorded a tribute album to Wills, learned to play the fiddle like his hero, added a former member of the Texas Playboys, Tiny Moore, to his band, and began referring to his music as "country jazz." Texas singer Red Steagall roamed all over the West with his Coleman County Cowboys playing his brand of western swing in dance halls and for rodeo dances. His popular version of "Lone Star Beer and Bob Wills Music" paid tribute to two cherished institutions of the Southwest.

The heightened interest in western swing inspired rediscovery of the veteran performers of the genre. At least two musicians, fiddler Jesse Ashlock (an alumnus of both Bob Wills' and Milton Brown's organizations) and Laura Lee McBride (Wills' first female singer) returned to Austin to perform with the young revivalists who were headquartered there. The Texas Playboys themselves were reconstituted under the leadership of Leon McAuliffe, while the Light Crust Doughboys, led by Jim Boyd and Smoky Montgomery, became active once again. As might be expected, Austin was a popular market for such groups, and they found an enthusiastic reception on the syndicated television show *Austin City Limits* and at Rod Kennedy's festivals in Kerrville.

The western swing renascence was paralleled by a revival of cowboy music. As we have already seen, the cowboy myth manifested itself in a variety of ways, most notably in the vogue of the Outlaws, but also in the brief flurry of interest in "urban cowboys" spawned by the movie of the same name. Real cowboy music—that is, songs about cowboys and the West—revived through the dedication of certain singers and songwriters who never abandoned their affection for this genre and the culture it represented. The grand masters of the romantic cowboy style, the Sons of the Pioneers, have never disbanded, although none of the original members remain. Through the years, and through successive personnel changes, the Pioneer sound, with its subtly nuanced vocal blend and rich harmonies, has remained remarkably intact. Marty Robbins maintained his commitment to cowboy songs until his death in 1983. Not only did he preserve such great old songs as "Streets of Laredo," he also contributed new and vital ones to the genre such as "El Paso City," a successor to his great hit of 1959, "El Paso." The ranks of the old movie cowboys have been thinned by death and retirement, but on occasion Roy Rogers and Rex Allen make special reappearances. Rex Allen, Jr., whose deep, resonant voice is almost as good as his father's, did much to revive interest in the old-time cowboy singers when he sang about them in "Can You Hear Those Pioneers."

The most dedicated crusade to resurrect the cowboy style came from a trio of young, urban-born musicians who called themselves Riders in the Sky (Fred "Too Slim" LaBour, Woody Paul, and Douglas B. Green). Green is a country music scholar and diversely talented musician from Michigan who turned a childhood fascination with Grade B cowboy movies into a profession. Combining musical virtuosity, replete with close harmony, yo-deling, and hot fiddling (done by Woody Paul), and kooky stage humor, Riders in the Sky filled a niche that no one else was exploiting. Their experiment won them a multitude of fans, a position on the *Grand Ole Opry*, and selection as hosts of *Tumbleweed Theatre* (old western movies) on the Nashville Network.

Country musicians have not been concerned solely with the Old West or with the cowboys of yesteryear. They also write and sing about cowboys who ride the range in pickup trucks, or who follow the rodeo circuit, or whose lifestyles suggest the independence once associated with the men on horseback. Bill and Sharon Rice spoke for millions of people when they wrote "My Heroes Have Always Been Cowboys" (sung by Willie Nelson in the movie *The Electric Horseman*). Ed Bruce, a Memphis singer and songwriter, on the other hand, was referring more to a lifestyle than to an occupation when he wrote "Mamas, Don't Let Your Babies Grow Up to Be Cowboys," but he demonstrated the timeless appeal of the image. Rodeo life spawned a fairly large body of songs. A few of them—such as Ian Tyson's "Someday Soon" and Doodle Owens' "Cowboys Ain't Supposed to Cry"—were quite poignant in their evocation of the loneliness and root-lessness that sometimes accompanied this unfettered but demanding existence. At least two singers, Moe Bandy and Red Steagall, both of whom had spent some time as bull riders, devoted major portions of their careers to performances at rodeos and rodeo dances.

The honky-tonk style survived into the eighties, but not with the universal appeal it had once enjoyed. The style that had once dominated country music ran counter to the crossover impulse and threatened the respectability that the country industry was trying to attain. Honky-tonk music was too "country" and too reflective of seamy barroom culture to attract that broad audience that country music was trying to win. Gradually, many of the founders of the style were being taken by death or retirement. Ernest Tubb's career finally ground to a halt, a victim of emphyzema, age, and endless miles; his death on September 6, 1984, brought to an end one of country music's longest and most respected careers. Floyd Tillman made infrequent appearances, and mostly in the Austin area, where he was treated as an elder statesman by the young musicians. He was named to the Country Music Hall of Fame in October 1984. Lefty Frizzell had died in 1974, but in the early seventies he recorded some of his greatest performances (e.g., "The Way Love Goes," "I Never Go around Mirrors") with a voice now richer, deeper, and more sensitive.

The most remarkable example of endurance shown by a honky-tonk singer has been that of George Jones. Few singers have achieved such artistic and commercial heights while descending to such personal depths of misery and self-abuse. From 1969 to 1975 he was married to Tammy Wynette, a dream pairing from the standpoint of fans, and once they began recording together they were described as "the president and first lady" of country music. Their years together were commercially rewarding for both singers—their duet performances were popular, and Jones made some of his best solo recordings—but he could not control his urge to drink, nor the violent outbursts that sometimes accompanied his drinking bouts. Jones' marital difficulties and alcohol binges were the stuff of soap opera, especially when accompanied by the periodic announcements of his "reform" and rehabilitation. His problems only made him more attractive to fans, and the lyrics of his heart-wrenching songs were often equated with the distress of his life.

In the years following his divorce in 1975, Jones' personal life deteriorated even further, his acute alcoholism being complicated by cocaine addiction. He became notorious for missing, arriving late, or showing up drunk for concerts ("No Show Jones" was a term often applied to him). But through it all, Jones remained intensely commercial and, in fact, began winning more music industry awards than at any previous time in his career. His resurgence is owed in large part to the skillful direction of Billy Sherrill, who became Jones' record producer in 1972. Jones, the traditionalist whose heart lay with the hard-core country music of his youth, and Sherrill, the sophisticated producer who seemed wedded to no particular style of music, constituted a highly unlikely, but successful, partnership. The son of an Alabama preacher, Sherrill served an apprenticeship with Sam Phillips in Memphis, but was working for Epic Records (a subsidiary of Columbia) in 1966 when he produced the first of a long string of hits, David Houston's "Almost Persuaded." Sherrill had a keen ear for commercial songs, many of which he wrote himself, and an acute perception of mass audience tastes. Many singers, including Charlie Rich, Tammy Wynette, Johnny Paycheck, Tanya Tucker, Johnny Duncan, and Janie Fricke, have profited from his direction. George Jones was no exception. While many fans and critics complained about the elaborate and lush instrumental and vocal arrangements that sometimes threatened to smother the singer's individuality, the Jones-Sherrill team produced some of modern country music's biggest hits and some of Jones' finest performances: "The Grand Tour," "If Drinking Don't Kill Me," "The Same Old Me," "Shine On," and the 1980 Grammy Award winner "He Stopped Loving Her Today."

Many singers have been nurtured on honky-tonk music, or have experimented with the style, but few have remained with it consistently. Several singers, in fact, debuted or established country music identities with honky-tonk style performances and then moved quickly to more popular forms of music. Ronnie Milsap ("I Hate You"), Johnny Rodriguez ("Pass Me By"), John Conlee ("Rose-Colored Glasses"), and Conway Twitty ("The Image of Me") began their country music careers with fine honky-tonk renditions, but then settled down into middle-of-the-road stylistic formats.

Mel Tillis made several superb honky-tonk recordings, such as "Heart over Mind," which were marked by the shuffle beat and twin fiddling borrowed from western swing instrumentation. He had also written many of the finest songs in the honky-tonk repertory, with Ray Price being a principal beneficiary of his genius. By the beginning of the eighties, though, Tillis had become an all-purpose entertainer—a comedian, actor, singer, and songwriter—and his honky-tonk hits became rarer as his appearances on the Johnny Carson show became more frequent.

Quite a few young singers exhibited a flair for the hard honky-tonk style. Wayne Kemp, the singer and writer of "Who'll Turn Out the Lights," was heard all too rarely and was scarcely known outside the industry, where he was recognized as a great writer of other people's hits. A few singers of superior caliber, such as Norman Wade in Louisiana and Johnny Bush in Texas, unfortunately had only local followings. Other singers, including Vern Gosdin, Leon Everette, and Gary Stewart, wore several stylistic hats but seemed most comfortable and convincing in the hard country camp. Gary Stewart, born a coal miner's son in Payne Gap, Kentucky, but reared in Fort Pierce, Florida, has never flirted with the country-pop sound, but instead has veered between rockabilly and honky-tonk, combining the zest and bounce of the former with the tortured lament of the latter. He learned both styles singing and playing the piano in the rough, blood-bucket beer joints in the area around Fort Pierce. A stint as pianist with Charley Pride's band introduced him to a wider public, but his 1974 recording of "Drinking Thing" earned him critical praise as a worthy heir to George Jones and other honky-tonk greats. Stewart's clear and pleading tenor voice, with its pronounced and breathy vibrato, was immensely appealing to hard-core country fans. He has also been one of the few country entertainers to draw the approval of *Rolling Stone* reviewers. Their endorsement, however, was triggered by the rockabilly in him—by the hedonistic abandon and "let the good times roll" qualities that characterized much of his music.

The most consistent of the new generation of honky-tonk singers, and major holdouts thus far against the pop impulse, have been George Strait, Mel Street, Moe Bandy, Gene Watson, and John Anderson. Strait is a genuine cowboy who grew up on a ranch near Pearsall, Texas. Although surrounded by country music during his youth, Strait did not sing publicly until his stint with the Army in Hawaii in the late seventies. Later, while pursuing a degree in agriculture and ranch management at Southwest Texas State University in San Marcos, Strait organized his Ace in the Hole Band and began playing in such clubs as Kent Finley's Cheatham Street Warehouse in San Marcos and at honky-tonks throughout Central and East Texas. Strait was never caught up in the Outlaw mania, even though Austin was only thirty miles up the road; instead, his music reflected the shuffle beat and Texas swing rhythms he had grown up with, as well as the singing of men like Ray Price, George Jones, and Merle Haggard. By 1982, music had become his full-time profession, and in the years that followed he put songs like "Let's Fall to Pieces Together," "You Look So Good in Love," and "Right or Wrong" (the Bob Wills standard) at the top of the country music charts. A happy combination of boyish good looks, skillful song selection, and vocal suppleness gave Strait the potential to become one of country music's superstars.

Mel Street was a Virginia mountain boy who was drawn to the music of Texas—and particularly to the singing of his hero, George Jones. He was living in West Virginia and working in an automobile body shop when "Borrowed Angel" was released on an obscure label in 1970. The song was somewhat unusual in that it not only spoke of illicit love without guilt or apology, but actually endorsed the practice. Listeners who responded positively to the record, however, did so because of its sound and not because of its content. Street's rich, melodic, and yet unadorned voice was beautifully complemented by the mournful strains of fiddle, dobro, and pedal steel guitar. In an age of increasing pop-country fusion, the sound heard on "Borrowed Angel" was, to most hard-core country advocates, a much-welcomed respite. Other big hits, such as "Smoky Mountain Memories" and the intriguingly named "Lust Affair," followed in Street's brief career, but success did not compensate for whatever problems led him to suicide on his forty-fifth birthday, October 21, 1978. George Jones sang "Amazing Grace" at his funeral.

Moe Bandy was born in Meridian, Mississippi, and reared in San Antonio. Like Mel Street, and probably most young people who leaned toward honky-tonk, Bandy was a disciple of George Jones. While working eight hours a day in his father's sheet metal and gutter shop, Bandy also sang nightly in local clubs with a little group called the Mavericks, and they were the opening act for most of the touring country groups who came to town. His first success at attracting attention outside of San Antonio came with "I Just Started Hating Cheating Songs." He became known after that for his "cheating and drinking songs," and he began a fruitful alliance with songwriter Whitey Shafer, who supplied him with other hits such as "Bandy the Rodeo Clown" and "The Biggest Airport in the World." Traditionalists waxed enthusiastic at the emergence of this hard country stylist who sang with remarkable clarity of tone, impeccable articulation, and emotional intensity. When he signed with his first big record company, Columbia, many people feared that the great corporation would tamper with his style and direct him toward the richer field of country-pop. His first Columbia release in 1975 was the cleverly written "Hank Williams You Wrote My Life" (by Paul Craft). Bandy's performance was thoroughly honky-tonk in style and content. Since that time he has never strayed far afield from the honky-tonk mold.

Gene Watson is still another Texan who perfected his art in the dance halls of that state. Born in Palestine and reared in Paris, both in the northeastern part of Texas, Watson moved to Houston in 1963 when he was about twenty years old. Watson soon became a popular local favorite, singing in the many clubs of Houston and recording on a variety of labels. His first major chart hit was a sultry, sexy song about illicit passion in New Orleans, "Love in the Hot Afternoon," which in arrangement was wholly within the country-pop framework. Watson, though, has been an outspoken advocate of "hard country" music, and his recordings since "Love in the Hot Afternoon" have generally been spiced with a honky-tonk flavor. Watson is the possessor of a strong, clear tenor voice, but with a hard-edged, slightly nasal sound that gives it a convincing country ring. Watson records also eschewed, for the most part, overarranged, country-pop instrumentation and instead let the pedal steel guitar set the dominant tone. Watson's "Farewell Party," a great hit for him in 1979, beautifully illustrates his basic approach and is one of the classics of modern honky-tonk music. The song itself is nothing more than a restatement of a very old theme, that of a self-pitying man who tries to make his cold lover feel guilty about his heartbreak. But Watson lifts the song above triteness with an utterly sincere and impassioned vocal that builds to a soaring finale.

The most commercially successful thus far of the modern honky-tonk singers, and the one whose ascent to superstardom seems most assured, is John Anderson of Apopka, Florida. Rock-and-roll first attracted the young Anderson to music, but he was converted to country music at the age of fourteen when he first heard Merle Haggard. By 1973 Anderson had drifted to Nashville and was singing, largely unnoticed, in the bars downtown near the old Ryman Auditorium. George Jones somehow heard about the singer and soon became his champion. At the end of the seventies, when his first records began to circulate, many people began to comment about the young man whose voice had an uncanny resemblance to that of Lefty Frizzell. The early eighties saw him recording his first big hits, with songs like "Your Lying Blue Eyes" and "I'm Just an Old Chunk of Coal," but even these were modest successes compared to his two blockbusters of 1983, "Swinging" and "Black Sheep." Anderson's repertory was somewhat analogous to that of Gary Stewart, in that it veered from slow, melancholy honky-tonk songs to rollicking, rockabilly-style tunes like "Black Sheep." Anderson differed markedly from Stewart, however, in his homage to the singers of the past. He often resurrected older songs such as "The Waltz You Saved for Me" and Frizzell's "I Love You a Thousand Ways," and was part of a small group of young musicians, including Emmylou Harris and Ricky Skaggs, who seemed genuinely respectful of older country music and dedicated to its preservation.

Musicians pursued several approaches to "tradition" in the eighties. The neo-honkytonk style favored by Anderson, Watson, and others was probably the most organic reflection of changes in country music and the culture which surrounds it, and therefore the most accurate representation of working-class values. The revivalists who consciously re-created older styles—such as the Hotmud Family and Red Clay Ramblers (old-timey string band music), Asleep at the Wheel (western swing), and Riders in the Sky (made-for-movies cowboy music)—made exciting music but worked in obviously limited milieus. Bluegrass musicians pursued their independent course by building new forms within the framework of a basically acoustic approach to music. Still another group of musicians, represented by Harris and Skaggs, made a virtue of the self-conscious employment of diversity, drawing upon many sources to create a music that was nevertheless "hard country" in its feel and ambience. Harris' and Skaggs' approaches seemed to augur well for country music's future. They were "traditional" in a modern and commercial context, and immensely appealing to a vast audience of both older and younger listeners.

Emmylou Harris was born in Birmingham, Alabama, but was an "Army brat" who traveled often and extensively with her parents. Her first venture into professional music came as an urban folk singer, singing in clubs in the Washington, D.C., area such as the Red Fox Inn. Her introduction to hard country music came through Gram Parsons, whom she met in Washington in 1972. She became his protégé, began listening to the Louvin Brothers, George Jones, Merle Haggard, and Ralph Stanley, and performed quite often with Parsons during the last several months of his life. Several of their best duets, such as "Hearts on Fire," "Love Hurts," and "We'll Sweep Out the Ashes," have fortunately been preserved on recordings.

Harris began her independent country music career in 1975 with the recording of a little-known Louvin Brothers song, "If I Could Only Win Your Love." She has since become a superstar, largely by cultivating a basic, uncomplicated country approach and by reviving a considerable amount of older material. She has done this, ironically, while other women country singers, such as Dolly Parton and Barbara Mandrell, have sought the pop-country middle ground. Harris' fresh, willowy beauty, of course, has not hurt her career, and neither has her clear, soprano voice which still shows a trace of Joan Baez and the other urban folksingers who influenced her early style. The clarity and wistful charm of her voice are sometimes clouded by muddied articulation and a tendency to sing before a too-loud background (her managers sometimes forget that she does not have the power of a Linda Ronstadt), but the overall mood of naturalness and seeming purity of her sound are enough to make most fans overlook any imperfections. Like many young performers who come to country music today, Harris is a true eclectic, borrowing from many styles. Her concerts and lps contain a mixture of contemporary and traditional material, rock-flavored songs and Appalachian-sounding ballads, and modern country-and-western numbers. Her band, the Hot Band, is capable of playing both acoustic and electric music, but when it breaks into an instrumental number, the results are loud, aggressively electronic, and rock-based (much to the dismay of the traditionalists in her audience). One of her greatest contributions to country music has been her encouragement, and employment, of other performers such as Delia Bell, the White Family, and Ricky Skaggs.

Skaggs was born in Cordell, Kentucky, on July 18, 1954. The precocious youngster was playing the mandolin by the time he was five years old, and had appeared on radio (WTCR, in Ashland, Kentucky) with his parents at about the same age. He and a friend, Keith Whitley (born in Sandy Hook, Kentucky, on July 1, 1954), played together often as teenagers and became skillful imitators of the Stanley Brothers. One night they went to hear Ralph Stanley at a small club in Louisa, Kentucky, and were asked to fill in until Stanley arrived. When Stanley walked into the club, he was surprised, and delighted, to hear the young men doing Stanley Brothers songs and in Stanley Brothers style. Ricky and Keith joined Stanley's band in 1970 when they were only fifteen years old, and they remained with him long enough to be part of nine lps. Stanley was greatly pleased with this band, and he sometimes talked of retiring and leaving his organization in the hands of these talented newcomers. Skaggs left Stanley, though, in 1972, and began playing in a succession of outstanding bluegrass bands such as Country Store, the Country Gentlemen, and the New South. He organized his own band, Boone Creek, in 1975 and became known in bluegrass circles for his proficiency with both traditional and progressive material. Beginning with an old-time/bluegrass perspective, Skaggs moved steadily toward progressive sounds and an eclectic repertory. His entree to a new and larger audience, however, came when he became a band member, and front man, for Emmylou Harris. In this first experience with an electric-based band, Skaggs played a variety of instruments and did some great duet singing with Harris, including "The Darkest Hour," which came from the repertory of his heroes, the Stanley Brothers.

In his journey toward an independent performing career, Skaggs took time to record a superb album (*Skaggs and Rice*) which paid tribute to both his family and his musical roots. The album featured Skaggs' mandolin and Tony Rice's guitar, and their soulful, close harmony. Skaggs and Rice beautifully recaptured the sound and mood of the brother duets on such songs as "Bury Me beneath the Willow" and "Will the Roses Bloom." It was one of modern country music's best moments.

Skaggs made his first venture into mainstream country music in 1981. He now combines such electric instruments as the takeoff guitar, bass, and pedal steel with drums, piano, dobro, and his own mandolin, fiddle, and acoustic guitar. His songs are also selected from many sources, including western swing, contemporary country, pop-rock, and bluegrass. His lps have been skillfully marketed, and singles have been periodically selected from them which became successive hits: "I Don't Care," "Heartbroke," "I Wouldn't Change You If I Could," "Highway 40 Blues." Audiences who attend Skaggs concerts are impressed more with his versatility than with his eclecticism. Skaggs is blessed with the clearest and most expressive tenor voice that has been heard in country music since Ira Louvin, and his instrumental virtuosity is breathtaking—he moves easily, and with mastery, from mandolin to fiddle to guitar. His selection as the CMA's Singer of the Year in 1982 and his nomination in several categories in the following years may or may not be a recognition of his extraordinary talents, but they do suggest that tradition-based country music still has a following in the United States.

Skaggs has been hailed as a traditionalist, and he still refers to his music as "bluegrass" and openly speaks of building a repertory that will appeal to hard-core country fans. He seems conscious, in fact, of filling a vacuum created by the country-pop impulse. But, of course, he is not purely a traditionalist, even though he does traditional material beautifully. His music is informed by the wide range of music that he and other young people have heard and played in today's world—and by the experiences of living in a society vastly different from that of their parents.

Skaggs has a versatile band that can play bluegrass, honky-tonk, western swing, or rock. Like Emmylou Harris' band, they sometimes go on extended jams that can last for several minutes, a legacy perhaps of such country-rock bands as those of Marshall Tucker and Charlie Daniels. This is no doubt disconcerting to bluegrass or old-time fans who go to hear Skaggs, but it is a concession to the rock-weaned younger listeners who also go to his concerts.

As this is written, it is impossible to know what Skaggs' future will be, or whether he portends a further traditionalizing impulse in country music. Both Skaggs and John Anderson, another successful young traditionalist, were among the five nominees for the CMA's Singer of the Year in 1983. Although one cannot predict whether other musicians will follow their lead in making stylistic choices, it is significant that these two great young stylists represent two divergent, and once regionally based, strains in country music: eastern bluegrass and western honky-tonk.

The country-pop emphasis nonetheless shows no sign of diminution, and the country side of the equation grows increasingly dim. The *Los Angeles Times* in September 1983 commented on the intermixing going on between black and country music.[17] While some black people dabble with country music, or express interest in it, the contrary impulse seems much stronger. Razzy Bailey and Earl Thomas Conley, among others, are very black-influenced. While this sort of amalgamation can be applauded, certainly on grounds of racial harmony or justice, and sometimes even in stylistic terms as a healthy fusion, the homogenization can also destroy the

17. Lee May, "Blacks Join the Country Music Surge," *Los Angeles Times* (August 30, 1983), pp. 1, 11.

identities of both forms of music. Country music still has room for tradition-oriented musicians, and an occasional Ricky Skaggs, John Anderson, Vern Gosdin, Gene Watson, Leon Everette, or Moe Bandy makes it on to the charts. But for every Ricky Skaggs there are a dozen pop-influenced performers who demonstrate great commercial appeal while also winning the country music industry's highest awards. Country music's future may very well be in the hands of such entertainers as Janie Fricke and Lee Greenwood, the CMA's choices in 1983 as the Female and Male Singers of the Year, both of whom came from non-country backgrounds and whose styles lie in the pop mainstream. The innovations represented by such singers may make country more commercial and more broadly appealing; they might also destroy it. Veteran country disc jockey Hugh Cherry is not alone when he warns of the music's loss of heritage and history: "Let us remember what happens when you kill the roots of a tree—it dies."[18] Country musicians also should never forget the admonition that so many of them grew up with: "What shall it profit a man if he gains the whole world and loses his own soul?"

18. Hugh Cherry, "Country DJs Carry Music to People," *Music City News* 18, no. 4 (October 1980): 19.

Garth Brooks. Photograph by Scott Newton/Austin City Limits.

12. Tradition and Change: Country Music, 1985–2002

Since this book was last revised in 1984, the country music industry has experienced, at varying times, both diminishing revenues and spectacular growth. In the decline that followed the urban cowboy craze, some commentators spoke ominously of the possible disappearance of the music. But by 1986 Randy Travis and other "neo-traditionalists" had generated a revitalization of hard country sounds and a new period of economic expansion. As exciting as the neo-traditionalist breakthrough had been, the early nineties saw a commercial burgeoning that went far beyond anything ever before experienced in country music, when singers like Garth Brooks, Clint Black, and Reba McEntire established sales records for CDs and concert box-office receipts that often surpassed those attained by entertainers in any other field of music. Popular culture is a fickle mistress, however. As this revision is prepared in early 2002, some observers and even a few music industry leaders in Nashville now speak balefully about the stagnation, and even the boring nature, of the products that they market. Stylistically and artistically, contemporary country music continues to evoke debates concerning its identity and authenticity. The resentment held by most traditionalists about the changes that have taken place in country music in recent years was graphically described in a song that was selected in 2000 as the International Bluegrass Music Association's (IBMA) Song of the Year and as the Country Music Association's Recorded Event of the Year (when recorded by George Strait and Alan Jackson). Entitled "Murder on Music Row," the song declared that "someone killed country music, cut out its heart and soul. They got away with murder down on music row."[1]

1. The song "Murder on Music Row" was included in Larry Cordle and Lonesome Standard Time, *Murder on Music Row* (Shell Point 1001), and in George Strait, *Latest Greatest Straitest Hits* (MCA 088170 102-2).

The word "country" endures as the description of a commercial genre of music, but the music that now dominates the playlists of "Top Forty" radio bears little resemblance to the styles that once prevailed on country radio and jukeboxes. The Country Music Association (CMA) and its long-time director, Bill Ivey (who also served in the second Clinton administration as chairman of the National Endowment for the Arts), have long followed a practice of recognizing as "country" any artist or form of music marketed as such by the recording companies. Consequently, partisans of "traditional" country styles have had to seek emotional and artistic solace in venues that lie outside the Top Forty milieu, or they have rejoiced when such "neo-traditionalists" as Randy Travis, Dwight Yoakam, Alan Jackson, Patty Loveless, and Brad Paisley have won recognition within the country mainstream.

The occasional prophets who have virtually predicted the commercial demise of country music have not reckoned with the enduring American impulse to go back to basics, to live at least vicariously a simpler life, and to find a form of music, with singable and easily understood lyrics and melodies, that connotes a wholesome lifestyle. Certainly, no one could have anticipated the emergence of Garth Brooks and his remarkable ability to fuse the dynamics of rock stage culture with the traditional postures of country music, nor could one have easily forecast the country line dance craze of the nineties, which brought thousands of people to the dance floor and reawakened an interest in "western" fashions. Although this work concentrates on the roles played by singers, singer-songwriters, and innovative instrumentalists, astute producers such as Jimmy Bowen, Tony Brown, Steve Buckingham, Emory Gordy, Jr., Jim Ed Norman, Allen Reynolds, and Randy Scruggs also have fueled country music's survival and commercial growth. They have managed to create a musical product that simultaneously suggests a sense of tradition and incorporates the most advanced techniques available in modern popular culture. Music industry leaders, however, sometimes lag far behind the tastes or expectations of the public. In early 2001, the soundtrack from a popular movie called *O Brother Where Art Thou?*, which included the old-time singing of such people as Dan Tyminski, Alison Krauss, Emmylou Harris, Gillian Welch, and Ralph Stanley, was released on a CD that quickly attained platinum status (the sale of one million copies). Nonetheless, Top Forty country radio stations were still reluctant to play selections from this very "hillbilly" sounding collection and did not do so until fans made their desires known through telephone calls and other communications. As a result, by mid-April 2001, Dan Tyminski's version of "Man of Constant Sorrow" had entered the *Billboard* popularity charts. By March 2002, sales of the *O Brother Where Art Thou?* soundtrack were approaching three million, and the CD had won five Grammy awards.

A traditionalist-modernist dialectic has animated country music since at least the late fifties in the wake of Elvis Presley's emergence and the country-pop resolution made by Nashville producers. It has only grown stronger in our own time.[2] Since the late eighties, a rash of young and generally photogenic entertainers, described variously as Young Country or New Country, have edged the older performers aside and consequently have renewed anxieties concerning the music's identity. Some musicians have attached themselves to country music because it is in vogue or because they were advised to do so, mainly as a marketing decision by promoters or recording executives who believed that their clients could "fit" the market niche and profit from country music's popularity with a "target" audience. Other performers had grown up in country households or otherwise had an intimate awareness of country's traditions. That is, they had heard country music at home or were aware of their parents' interest in such music. Performing country music was an easy decision for musicians like Mark Chesnutt, who grew up as the son of a local musician in the working-class musical environment of Beaumont, Texas, or for Sara Evans, who heard her family play bluegrass music on the tobacco farm where she was raised in New Franklin, Missouri, or for Dwight Yoakam, who equated the music with the songs and stories learned from his coal-mining grandfather in Pikeville, Kentucky. Most young musicians, though, like Trisha Yearwood, a banker's daughter from Monticello, Georgia, had little reason to identify the music with working-class culture, since their own lives and musical choices had been shaped in a media-obsessed suburban culture. These affluent origins, however, have not prevented Yearwood from becoming one of the most respected vocalists in country music.

Whether products of country music households, or new "converts" to country, virtually all of the Young Country acts had grown up listening to all of the popular music styles available in America—rock, blues, soul, salsa, rap, pop. Country's new musicians typically cite such pop acts as the Eagles, the Allman Brothers, Bon Jovi, Led Zeppelin, or U2 as influences, an affinity evidenced by various country musicians' tributes to the Beatles, Lynyrd Skynyrd, and other pop or rock music bands. In 1993 one of these collections, *Common Thread: The Songs of the Eagles*, featuring the singing of such country musicians as Travis Tritt, Clint Black, Vince Gill, and Trisha Yearwood, experienced spectacular commercial success.

On the other hand, Curtis Ellison has noted the tendency shown by contemporary country entertainers to conform to the music's time-honored

---

2. For a discussion of the historical roots of this argument, see James C. Cobb, "Rednecks, White Socks, and Pina Coladas? Country Music Ain't What It Used to Be . . . And It Really Never Was," *Southern Cultures* 5 (Winter 1999): 41–51.

rituals and to pay proper deference to the music's pioneers.[3] Even though
the venerable *Grand Ole Opry* no longer exerts the kind of influence that
it once had, it still exhibits a powerful attraction for both fans and musicians. Hal Ketchum, Garth Brooks, Alison Krauss, and Vince Gill are only
a few of country music's contemporary superstars who have accepted
membership in the show, and they make periodic appearances on its Saturday night programs. When a new performer is inducted into the *Opry*'s
cast, a veteran entertainer makes the announcement amidst a solemn
ceremony that stresses the enduring links between past and present.

The wearing of cowboy hats, jeans, and boots, of course, is well-nigh universal, even if the performers do not perform hardcore country music (and
they seldom do). Travis Tritt, who alludes to southern rock as the chief
musical influence in his life, apparently first used the term "hat acts" to describe these performers, suggesting that they were imitative singers who
had no real distinctiveness and that they were just playing at being cowboys (or merely emulating George Strait). The hat acts have included such
male singers as Garth Brooks, Clint Black, John Michael Montgomery,
Wade Hayes, Tim McGraw, Trace Adkins, Kenny Chesney, Mark Chesnutt, Tracy Byrd, Collin Raye, Sammy Kershaw, and Alan Jackson, and at
least one female, Terri Clark. However different in style, musical compe-
tence, and commitment to tradition, the proliferation of such musicians
made it quite clear that the music industry had become highly adept at
co-opting trends and fashions. Singers were being groomed to fulfill symbolic expectations about cowboys while also being encouraged to perform
contemporary styles that would appeal to a large audience that had little
or no experience with country music.

These new entertainers—"New Country"—fueled the greatest commercial boom that country music had ever enjoyed. Evidence of the
music's popular appeal and commercial strength became available in
May 1991 when *Billboard* magazine abandoned the imprecise practice of
obtaining data on CD sales from sales clerks and began relying on reports
gathered from a company named Soundscan. Through the scanning of
bar codes on CDs made at the time of purchase, Soundscan provided a
more accurate measurement of sales made in retail stores (including Wal-
Mart, K-Mart, Target, and Blockbuster). The charts that utilized Soundscan data indicated a significantly higher performance scale for country
singers than previously recognized. Country CD sales constituted 17 percent of the overall total for American music, a figure then second only to
that of rock. Statistics concerning radio listenership were even more favorable to country music. The Simmons Market Research Bureau, in a
1995 survey compiled for the CMA, disclosed that over 37 percent of the

3. Curtis W. Ellison, *Country Music Culture: From Hard Times to Heaven* (Jackson:
University Press of Mississippi, 1995).

American population (about 69,918,000 people) devoted some part of their time each week to listening to country music. The second-largest format, adult contemporary, claimed almost 19 million fewer listeners.

The musicians who contributed to country music's spectacular ascendance included performers who had been paying their dues long before the New Country acts appeared. Between 1985 and 1989, for example, Earl Thomas Conley—a Portsmouth, Ohio, singer who is regrettably forgotten today—recorded a staggering list of number one hits, such as "Once in a Blue Moon." On the other hand, George Strait, the direct inspiration for most of the hat acts, and the singer who did so much to usher in the era of neo-traditionalism, endures as a major presence in country music. In a career that has now spanned twenty years, the forever handsome and youthful Strait continues to make popular recordings that preserve the sound and flavor of western swing and other rhythms of his native state of Texas. The smooth and soulful blend of Alabama, a group whose career has been as long and successful as George Strait's, is still heard on country radio. The most obvious and enduring legacy of their career can be seen and heard in the music of scores of vocal groups such as the Mavericks, Exile, Diamond Rio, Shenandoah, Sawyer Brown, Confederate Railroad, Blackhawk, Little Texas, and Highway 101 who preserve the practice of good-time songs and close harmonies pioneered by Alabama twenty years ago.

The Judds (mother Naomi and daughter Wynonna) and Reba McEntire had also established thriving careers that reinforced the presence of women as self-directed stars in country music well before the great boom of the late eighties began. In 1984 the Judds' number one recording of "Mama, He's Crazy" introduced their fresh harmonies and acoustic sound to a national country music public. But as is often the case with overnight sensations, the Judds achieved this newfound success only after several years of hard work, sacrifice, and preparation (including several years in Hollywood and attempts at a movie career). With Naomi stressing their family orientation and Appalachian origins, the Judds were sometimes touted as traditionalists, particularly with songs like "Grandpa, Tell Me 'bout the Good Old Days." Their down-home values meshed easily with their adroit embrace of sophisticated methods of marketing and showmanship. Between 1985 and 1991, the Judds dominated most of the awards given to vocal groups, whether by the CMA, the Academy of Country Music (ACM), or *Music City News*. Their audience was understandably saddened when Naomi disclosed in 1991 that she had hepatitis C, and the act was disbanded. The Judds' exhausting farewell tour covered 116 cities between February and October 1991. Wynonna has carried on with a solo career and has been widely praised for her bluesy and soulful singing.

Reba McEntire also won widespread public attention in 1984 as a "new traditionalist" when she recorded an album called *My Kind of Country* (including such hit songs as "How Blue" and "Somebody Should Leave"). Her affecting Oklahoma twang, the knowledge that she grew up in a ranching and rodeo family, and her now-dissolved marriage to rodeo champ Charlie Battles inspired the mistaken belief that she was strongly wedded to hard country music. She began her public career as a child singing with her sister and brother, but her entree into show business came in 1974 when Red Steagall heard her sing the national anthem at the National Rodeo Finals in Oklahoma City. The resulting recordings made for Mercury soon impressed listeners with her powerful vocal range and distinctive manner of bending and extending notes. Reba was already an established star in 1985, then, when a new wave of neo-traditionalism began in country music. She profited from this renewed interest in hard country styles but soon moved far beyond them. Her career really peaked later in the decade with vocal and instrumental sounds that were closer to country-pop. McEntire had much going for her: good looks and a sparkling personality, a supple vocal style, a genius for recognizing good songs, and an astute business sense. These assets proved to be a great inspiration for women, not only because she stressed self-expression and identity, but also because, like earlier Oklahoma singer Gail Davies, she had taken firm control of the direction of her own career. Her assumption of the title role in Broadway's *Annie Get Your Gun,* presented in the year 2000, introduced her to an even larger audience.

The banner year 1986 saw the emergence of so many new young country artists that one could almost view the phenomenon as the changing of the guard. Surveying the list of people who debuted in that year, and in the years that immediately followed, it is hard to find an all-encompassing label that adequately defines their styles. Randy Travis was heralded as the bright new hope of traditionalism, presenting an unadorned style that seemed reminiscent of Lefty Frizzell. Other singers, such as Steve Earle and Lyle Lovett, flavored their country music with sounds that had origins in rock, blues, or sixties-style folk music. They were far from being traditional, but they brought fresh ideas and a sense of experimentation to country music. Whatever the style, the young musicians of the mid-eighties soon edged veteran performers like Cash, Haggard, Jones, Parton, Lynn, and Nelson off the popularity charts and out of the playlists of Top Forty radio. George Jones' hit of 1985, "Who's Gonna Fill Their Shoes," was more poignant and prophetic than he probably realized.

Randy (Traywick) Travis, from Marshville, North Carolina, seemed the likeliest candidate to fill the shoes of the old-timers when his first records appeared in early 1986. After a youthful brush with the law, Travis embraced country music and was singing in local clubs when he was only fourteen years old. With the support and management of Libby Hatcher, whom he later married, he moved to Nashville in 1981 and began making the rounds of the recording studios and publishing houses. Between May 1986, when "On the Other Hand" vaulted to the number one position on the *Billboard* country charts, and May 1990, when a new generation of country singers appeared, Travis enjoyed eleven number one songs and a couple that climbed to number two. His initial output garnered critical praise, the CMA's Horizon award for 1986 (given to the most promising newcomer), and the award for Male Vocalist of the Year from the CMA, Academy of Country Music, and *Music City News* in 1987 and 1988.

Like that of his contemporary Keith Whitley, Travis' clearly enunciated and deeply resonant baritone vocal style exhibited a strong indebtedness to Lefty Frizzell. Although perceived as a bearer of the honky-tonk tradition, with a pedal steel guitar driven sound that particularly suggested that influence, Travis actually sang few songs that carried the flavor of the barroom or bedroom. They sometimes conveyed sadness, but almost never a suggestion of drinking or cheating. More often, they expressed messages like that of the Paul Overstreet composition "Forever and Ever, Amen," an upbeat, affirmative view of life and relationships.

Dwight Yoakam proved that neo-traditionalism could flourish with a strong admixture of rock-and-roll. He was born in Pikeville, Kentucky, but grew up in southern Ohio amidst the throngs of expatriates from the Upper South who had traveled what Steve Earle described as "the hillbilly highway." By 1978 he had relocated in California, where he teamed with Pete Anderson, who became his guitarist and producer. There they found hospitable companionship among such West Coast cowpunks as Dave Alvin, Los Lobos, the Knitters, and Lone Justice. Yoakam and Anderson created a style that paid homage to traditional country music but brought to it the ambience and drive of rock. Above all, they incorporated the sound and sparkling electronic beat of Yoakam's heroes, Buck Owens and the Buckaroos, a source to which they eventually paid tribute in a 1988 performance with Owens called "Streets of Bakersfield."

In the mid-eighties, Yoakam became well known, if not always listened to, because of his outspoken criticism of Nashville and his passionate defense of hillbilly music and values. At first he was little more than a cult figure on the fringes of country music, but in 1986 two hit recordings, a remake of Johnny Horton's "Honky Tonk Man" and "Guitars, Cadillacs," carried him to the center. Yoakam's career has since been enhanced by his pouty good looks, sensuous stage movements (popularized through well-produced videos), appearances in movies, and charismatic presence.

Singer Keith Whitley carried not only a lifelong love of Lefty Frizzell and other classic honky-tonk stylists, but also a long apprenticeship in bluegrass music. Consequently, one could always hear a touch of Carter Stanley and Lefty in Whitley's soulful vocal stylings. This Sandy Hook, Kentucky, native was in fact singing Stanley Brothers songs with Ricky

Skaggs one night in 1970 when Ralph Stanley heard them for the first time. Whitley served two stints in Ralph's band but was playing with J. D. Crowe's great bluegrass unit when he made the transition to mainstream country music. He charted his first hit in 1986 with "Miami, My Amy," but the pinnacle of his career came in 1988 and 1989 with five number one recordings, including his most enduring song, "When You Say Nothing at All." Just when it seemed that Whitley had conquered every demon that blocked his path to success, he succumbed to the devil in the bottle that had plagued him since his teenage years. Neither the accolades of his fans nor his marriage to the beautiful singer Lorrie Morgan could save him. He died of alcohol poisoning on May 9, 1989, only three short months after "I'm No Stranger to the Rain" first entered the popular charts. The recording became the CMA's Single of the Year.

Ricky Van Shelton seemed to have one foot in the country-pop field and the other in the realm of hard country. The Grit, Virginia, native sang with a smooth voice and "easy listening" style but peppered his repertoire with rockabilly tunes, original numbers, and older country songs, some of which came from honky-tonk sources. His first number one recording, "Somebody Lied," was recorded in late 1986 and released in 1987. This and a string of similar successes that year, including his first album, *Wild-Eyed Dream,* won for him admission to the *Grand Ole Opry* and the CMA's Horizon award. In 1989 he was selected as the CMA's vocalist of the year. Shelton's boyish, handsome looks may have contributed to the efforts made by his producers to package him as a sex symbol. Early publicity photos sometimes showed him wearing not only the customary cowboy hat and jeans, but also an undershirt along with a languorous, bedroom look (a photo image also used more recently for singer Tim McGraw). While his packaging and diverse repertoire reflected efforts to make him broadly appealing, Shelton nevertheless took special pains to retain the affections of country music's traditional audience. He revived such classic songs as "From a Jack to a King," "Statue of a Fool," "Life Turned Her That Way," and "Somebody's Back in Town" that explicitly targeted older fans who needed reassurance that their brand of country music was still alive. By 1990 the emotional strain wrought by commercial insecurity, allegations of marital infidelity, and a problem with alcohol engendered a severe personal crisis. He made a religious renewal and in 1992 recorded a gospel album for his parents—*Don't Overlook Salvation.* The recording eventually won him a Grammy nomination and contributed to his popularity among Christian Contemporary fans (although he always insisted that he was first and foremost a country singer). Shelton now records infrequently and expends much of his energy writing popular children's books. Asserting the desire to have complete freedom in what he produces, he refuses to sign with a major company.

Neither k. d. lang, Lyle Lovett, nor Steve Earle could be described as a traditional performer, even though one finds elements in their styles that were once highly prized in country music. They were valued not for their traditionalism, but for their independence and cutting-edge styles. One of several Canadian performers (including Anne Murray, Terri Clark, and Shania Twain) who have attempted careers as country entertainers in the United States, and the first acknowledged lesbian in country music, k. d. lang (Katherine Dawn Lang) first came to country music through a fascination with the music of Patsy Cline. She promoted her first album, *Truly Western Experience,* made in Canada in 1984, with a stage show that featured the singer and her entourage dressed in cowboy attire. Lang, however, was essentially a torch singer with a sound best suited to blues and soul music. Her American-made recordings, such as *Angel with a Lariat* in 1987, generally received critical praise, and she won Grammy awards for her duet with Roy Orbison on "Crying" and for an album made in 1989, *Absolute Torch and Twang.* Lang nevertheless received little radio coverage in country music and eventually abandoned the field for a career in mainline pop music, a consequence of her musical experimentation and divergent lifestyle.

Lyle Lovett both impressed and confounded country listeners when his first album, *Lyle Lovett,* appeared in 1986. Folk revival fans, however, were familiar with his music because of his long tenure on the Texas club and festival scene where he collaborated and communed with such local legends as Guy Clark, Butch Hancock, Robert Earl Keen, Townes Van Zandt, and Nanci Griffith. He first discovered that he could write songs while working on degrees in journalism and German at Texas A&M University, as a classmate and soulmate of still another clever Texas songwriter, Robert Earl Keen (whose "Christmas from the Family" is simultaneously one of the funniest and most poignant songs in modern country music). Lovett first achieved acclaim as a winner at the Kerrville Folk Festival songwriters' contest (the venue that also introduced Nanci Griffith and Tish Hinojosa to music audiences). Lovett's angular looks and sky-high pompadour commanded attention, but his lyrics, delivered in a dry and droll, almost conversational manner, immediately captivated listeners and critics in fields far removed from country music. Four songs from his first CD, including the delightfully irreverent "God Will," moved on to the country charts. Since that promising debut CD, however, he has paid only occasional homage to traditional country music. His excellent double CD in 1998, *Step Inside This House,* honored Texas songwriters in particular. Lovett has remained a singular figure on the edge of mainstream country music, where he probably prefers to be.

Another talented Texan, Steve Earle, has similarly stayed on the fringes of country music but has profoundly impressed musicians both within that field and in bluegrass. He left his hometown of Schertz, just outside San Antonio, in 1973 to follow the rambling life of a folksinger popularized by his heroes Guy Clark and Townes Van Zandt. Unfortunately, he also shared Van Zandt's penchant for self-destruction, and the lure of drink and drugs almost permanently ruined his career in the mid-nineties. Earle arrived in Nashville in the mid-seventies, and by the time his first album appeared in 1986, he had crafted a body of songs that united the Texas tradition of storytelling with the verve and aggressiveness of rock. *Guitar Town* was a critical success, and one of its featured songs, "Hillbilly Highway," effectively combined autobiography with vignettes about the migrations of southern rural folk to Detroit and other cities. To many people Earle seemed to be the fulfillment of Gram Parsons' dream of fusing the styles and audiences of country and rock. That dream soon floundered, however, as Earle moved more insistently toward rock music and into an enslavement by cocaine and heroin. In 1994 he served a short jail term that was followed by a drug rehabilitation program. Earle happily turned his life around and has since recorded a series of CDs, including *El Corazon* and *Transcendental Blues,* that showcase his brilliant songwriting abilities and his fascination with bluegrass, blues, rock, Celtic, and country styles. His rough and sometimes profane concert style offends some listeners, including many of the bluegrass fans who attended his 1999 concerts with the Del McCoury Band, but no one has addressed contemporary issues with greater boldness, sensitivity, and compassion. Not only is he an outspoken opponent of the death penalty, he is also one of the rare country singers in this age of affluence and complacency who can embrace the memory of the radical anarchist Emma Goldman and assert "Come back, Woody Guthrie" (as he did in one of the songs recorded in *El Corazon*).

The parade of talented newcomers accelerated during the rest of the decade and on into the nineties. With Clint Black and Garth Brooks in the vanguard, this assemblage of entertainers took country music to the highest commercial plateau it had ever reached. Indeed, their success often surpassed that won by musicians in other forms of music. Like the singers of the early eighties, these musicians were also uncategorizable. Some of them were described as neo-traditional, but most were easily seduced by the allure of crossover success and were therefore more and more prone to dabble in the lucrative realm of pop. All the new singers played the game of being country, especially in their adoption of western attire. But they had also grown up in an era dominated by pop and rock, and, to a degree unprecedented in country music's history, their performances revealed those non-country styles. Consequently, while winning great acclaim for themselves and for country music, they also provoked the strongest urge for alternative, and presumably more authentic, sounds yet evidenced in the field.

Clint Black was born in Long Branch, New Jersey, but grew up in Houston, where he absorbed the sounds of pop rock and honky-tonk country. Blessed with dark hair and oriental eyes, and a strong resemblance to cowboy singer Roy Rogers, Black possessed a physical advantage that stood him in good stead in the unfolding age of music videos. Most important, he also had a powerful, wide-ranging voice that moved easily from romantic love songs to raucous barroom ditties. Black built an ardent following playing the clubs on the Houston-Galveston circuit, often with his songwriting partner Hayden Nicholas, but did not win national visibility until Bill Ham became his manager. Ham, the former manager of the rock group ZZ Top, signed Black to a contract with RCA in 1988. The following year he recorded one of the most successful debut albums in country music history, *Killin' Time,* which sold over three million copies and yielded four number one singles. This collection and the one that followed in 1990, *Put Yourself in My Shoes,* marked Black as a traditionalist in the honky-tonk vein, an identification that he quickly overcame. In the years that followed his first two CDs, Black built the style and image of a pop-country performer.

If Clint Black's ascent seemed meteoric, that of Garth Brooks was even more dramatic. His first song to appear on the country charts, "Much Too Young to Feel This Damn Old," rose modestly in May 1989 to the number eight position. But during the next three years he produced a string of number one songs and the best-selling country albums of all time—*No Fences, Ropin' the Wind,* and *The Garth Brooks Collection.* By 1996 Brooks' accomplishment of over sixty million album sales had been surpassed only by the Beatles and Billy Joel, but he had achieved this spectacular figure more rapidly than any other artist in any field of music.

Although Brooks exuded the rough if sometimes portly good looks of an athlete, physical appearance cannot explain his success. He has instead been a genius at merging musical styles and cultural symbols—rock and country, cowboy costuming, rock concert mannerisms and devices (including cordless microphones that permit him to roam freely on large stages, and ropes and pulleys that enable him to fly across the stage like Peter Pan), and a mastery of marketing (his major at Oklahoma State). His penchant for self-promotion enabled him to embrace a populist stance against the recording industry by offering his albums directly to his audiences at below-market prices. His energy-driven and rock-derived stage style (inspired in large part by his hero Chris LeDoux, a former rodeo champion who became a country-rock performer) lured to his concerts thousands who had not previously listened to country music. In part because of an ego that sometimes translates into arrogance, but more especially because of the flamboyant trappings that surround his music, Brooks has been the bane, or even the whipping boy, for country traditionalists. Kinky Friedman, for example, called him the "anti-Hank." Even though they may not have been the kind of fare that Hank favored, such songs as "The Dance," "If Tomorrow Never Comes," "Unanswered Prayers," and "Friends in Low Places" had memorable melodies and superb lyrics that spoke convincingly to a generation of suburban listeners who had few if any memories of, or ties to, working-class life. Abundant evidence proves the universal appeal of Brooks' music. His concert in New York's Central Park on August 7, 1997, played to an estimated 250,000 people and was seen and heard by additional multitudes that tuned in to HBO's *Garth Live from Central Park*.

Garth Brooks has been the most commercially successful country singer, but fellow Oklahoman Vince Gill is the most talented. Endowed with athletic good looks, extraordinary musical gifts (including a sweet, soaring tenor), and an affable personality that any diplomat would envy, Gill has accumulated more awards than any other country entertainer, including on two occasions the CMA's most coveted award, Entertainer of the Year, and at least twelve Grammies (for singing, instrumentation, and songwriting). Between 1989 and 1997, Gill virtually monopolized the Grammy award for best male country vocal performance. Born in Norman, Oklahoma, in the household of a lawyer who became a federal appellate judge, Gill hardly fits the profile of the suffering working-class musician. He first won recognition as a guitarist and only slowly blossomed as a vocalist. In fact, for a time he was less well known as a singer than his first wife, Janis Oliver, who sang with her sister Kristine as part of the duo Sweethearts of the Rodeo.

Gill's professional career was longer and more varied than those of most of his contemporaries, extending back to 1974, and included a lengthy stint in bluegrass with the Bluegrass Alliance, Boone Creek, and Byron Berline's Sundance band. He also played for a couple of years with the country-rock band Pure Prairie League and for an even shorter time with the Cherry Bombs, where he met fellow musician and future producer Tony Brown. Profiting from the experience of Ricky Skaggs, Gill entered mainstream country music in 1984, when he signed with RCA and eventually recorded three good but largely unrecognized albums. Superstardom came, though, when he joined MCA in 1989 and came under the direction of Tony Brown. *When I Call Your Name* (featuring a hit song with the same title) was the first of a series of CDs that illustrated his trademark mixture of pop-country, rock, bluegrass, and hard country material. Gill's professional generosity is exemplified by the numerous appearances he has made on other people's recordings, while the mutual love affair between him and the country music industry is evidenced each October by his service as the host of the CMA Awards Show.

The emergence of young, good-looking entertainers like Vince Gill, who combined the energy and flair of rock music with the ambience of country, clearly contributed to country music's massive commercial growth in the late eighties and early nineties. This expansion also owed much to the dance craze of the early nineties. The dance boom was, in part, a new phase of an interest that had been shown back in the Urban Cowboy era, when the Cotton Eyed Joe and Texas Two Step were prominently featured in new dance halls all across America. Country dancing's popularity also came in the context of a more general enthusiasm for dancing of all kinds in the United States, particularly swing, ballroom, and Cajun dancing. The dance craze also coincided with, and was in large part a consequence of, the burgeoning music video industry. Inspired by the precedent of MTV's rock music programming, the Oklahoma corporation Gaylord Enterprises introduced similar television venues for country music, TNN (The Nashville Network) and CMT (Country Music Television). Country music videos provided musicians instantaneous exposure among millions of viewers. The combining of young, good-looking entertainers and pulsating dance rhythms proved to be a potent and lucrative mixture.

The massive popularity of Billy Ray Cyrus' video and recording of "Achy Breaky Heart" in 1992 unleashed this new wave of dance interest. Within a year a spate of similar videos and recordings appeared, each featuring a line dance as an accompaniment for the song. Dance clubs appeared all over the nation; at least two television shows appeared on TNN that featured recordings of new songs and throngs of average folks dancing to them; and instructional videos and columns touting the new dance steps appeared in country music magazines. Initially recorded but not immediately released in 1991 as part of a proposed Mercury CD, Cyrus' performance was first introduced as part of a video replete with line dance choreography provided by Melanie Greenwood. After receiving massive exposure on TNN and CMT, the song and the album were greeted by an enthusiastic public on a CD called *Some Gave All* (which sold over five million copies). In his T-shirt or tank top, Cyrus seemed far removed from the cowboy image conveyed by the hat acts. His performances displayed the sexual energy and masculine aggressiveness of a rockabilly. In the wake of his success, other country entertainers with a wide variety of styles introduced their own popular dance videos, including Mary Chapin Carpenter's "Down at the Twist and Shout," Tracy Byrd's "Watermelon Crawl," Tim McGraw's "Indian Outlaw" (the song that really inaugurated his career as a superstar), and Brooks and Dunn's "Boot Scootin' Boogie." Leon Eric "Kix" Brooks and Ronnie Dunn moved quickly beyond the line dance identification to become the most popular duo in country music. They had pursued independent careers until 1991, when they joined to make the album *Brand New Man,* which contained "Boot Scootin' Boogie" (written by Brooks) and at least three other songs that vaulted to the top of the country charts. With Dunn doing most of the lead singing and Brooks chiming in with occasional harmonies, but more often energizing audiences with his strutting stage presence, the

duo brought thousands of people to the dance floor and secured a virtual monopoly in the award granted each year for Vocal Duo by the CMA
and ACM.

The country music made by Brooks and Dunn, Vince Gill, and others
is recorded with state-of-the-art precision. Enhanced by digital recording
techniques that permit the production of "perfect" recorded performances that can scarcely be recreated in live settings, the recordings are
then pitched to radio stations but are broadcast only if certain unnamed
"consultants" recommend them. Such recordings appear on increasingly
automated formats, played by disc jockeys whose patter and vocal mannerisms suggest an apprenticeship in rock-and-roll radio. The handful of
songs that manage to slip into these radio stations' "rotation" broadcasts
each day are often described as Top Forty Country but actually are even
fewer in number. The format does not differ substantially in any part of
the United States. A listener traveling anywhere in America will encounter
the same body of recordings played by similar-sounding announcers who
almost never give the names of either songs or performers. Critics dismiss
this music for its alleged suburban-mall lack of distinctiveness. But while
the music that now flows out of Nashville may not be "country" in any
meaningful sense as identified by traditionalists, its sales indicate that it
nevertheless fills the needs and expectations of millions of listeners who
think of themselves as fans of country music.

Bruce Feiler was the first observer to describe country music as "the
music of suburbia."[4] He argues that a large audience of people like himself—that is, well-educated, professional suburbanites who have a taste
for sushi bars and computers—have become attracted to the music because singers like Garth Brooks have divested the music of its earlier "dis-
tasteful" trappings. No fan of traditional country music can read Feiler's
analysis without being offended by some of his judgments and critiques—
particularly his negative allusions to hay bales, overalls, and other "dusty
old icons"—but he probably makes good sense in arguing that many
people have gravitated to country music because it conveys simple truths
and values shorn of hayseed or redneck characteristics. Country music
has profited commercially from the capitalistic-driven decision making
and stylistic compromises made by producers such as Jimmy Bowen and
artists who have created a product that successfully blends pop and country elements. And it has profited from the mood of social conservatism
that has emerged in the United States since the late sixties, and from the
"new patriotism" that has flourished in the wake of the tragedies of September 11, 2001. (Alan Jackson's Arista recording "Where Were You When

4. Bruce Feiler, *Dreaming Out Loud: Garth Brooks, Wynonna Judd, Wade Hayes, and
the Changing Face of Nashville* (New York: Avon Books, 1998).

the World Stopped Turning?"—a sensitive and deeply felt meditation about the disasters—was more than a masterpiece of compassion; it has also been a highly commercial item.) Although produced by men and women with thoroughly urbane sensibilities, and in studios equipped with state-of-the-art techniques, country songs tout small towns and insist that the good life is pursued most often in southern or western locales. Traditional morality holds sway. Often performed by entertainers who flaunt their sex appeal, contemporary country lyrics nevertheless stress family values with little consciousness of irony. In keeping with the over-all efforts to build a body of music that does not offend, partisan politics seldom intrudes into song lyrics (even though many country singers, like Travis Tritt, Michael Martin Murphey, and Lee Greenwood, often play prominent roles at Republican Party conventions and will make their views known in interviews and sometimes on stage). Some listeners may gravitate toward country music because it is a "safe" and "white" alter-native to Hip-Hop and other African American–derived styles, or because it still provides a musical forum where "good old boys" can trumpet their masculinity. But country music is popular, above all, not because of its politics, but because it speaks the language of millions of Americans in a simpler and more singable fashion than can be found in any other form of contemporary music. Its comprehensibility and its emphasis on tradi-tional values have, in a sense, made it the nation's new "adult" pop mu-sic (even though a horde of extremely young entertainers, such as Billy Gilman, Jessica Andrews, and LeAnn Rimes, have won spectacular suc-cess as country singers).

One of the most positive developments in modern country music has been the ascendance of women entertainers. Women have not only emerged as independent stylists and as architects of their own careers, they have also begun to comment more freely on issues that are relevant to their lives. Equally important, their growing presence as singers and fans has encouraged men to be more conscious of women's concerns. Garth Brooks, for example, might not have become emboldened to record "The Thunder Rolls," his controversial song about domestic abuse, had it not been for the commercial power demonstrated by women consumers. One might have reservations about *how* the women singers deliver their messages, but it is easy to applaud much of *what* they have to say. The women of country music clearly have been influenced in positive ways by the women's liberation movement, but few of them are overt feminists. They certainly have not attached themselves to the political arm of fem-inism. Instead, they live out the precepts of feminism in their career moves and lifestyles, and occasionally even in their song lyrics. One finds almost no one who defers to the authority of parents or husbands (even teenage sensation LeAnn Rimes broke bitterly with her father over a contractual dispute) and very few whose personalities are subsumed by membership in a group. The women assume equality as a natural right and have increasingly struck out to assert control over their careers.

Although women speak out often on "women's issues," increasingly they have gone beyond private or gender concerns to address larger public problems. Reba McEntire, for example, spoke for many women when the protagonist of "Is There Life Out There?" voiced the need to pursue education and an independent life, but her message was more universal when she warned about the danger of AIDS in "She Thinks His Name Is John." Several songs have commented on spousal abuse, such as Faith Hill's "A Man's Home Is His Castle," but none have been more graphic than Martina McBride's "Independence Day" and the Dixie Chicks' "Goodbye Earl." McBride's song speaks grimly of a fiery retribution, while the Dixie Chicks make a similar statement in a humorous song about an abused wife and her best friend who take the law into their own hands to deal with a cruel husband. A few songs, such as K. T. Oslin's "80's Ladies" and Deana Carter's "Did I Shave My Legs for This?," speak about the frustrations that often accompany efforts to be free, sexy, and domestic. Faith Hill's "I Can't Do That Anymore" (written by Alan Jackson) and Mary Chapin Carpenter's "He Thinks He'll Keep Her" express the need to live one's own life, even if it means defying other people's expectations or breaking the holy bonds of matrimony. The most positive message of all, however, came in Lee Ann Womack's award-winning song of 2000, "You Can Fly," a statement made to young girls that they should feel free to take chances and pursue their own dreams.

On the other hand, while listeners might applaud the independence asserted by women and their willingness to champion their causes in songs, traditionalists can hardly take heart from the sounds and styles featured by most female performers. Many women singers, such as Lee Ann Womack, Faith Hill, Sara Evans, and LeAnn Rimes, emerged from southern working-class homes, while others, such as Pam Tillis, Deana Carter, and Lorrie Morgan, grew up as the daughters of country musicians, but few of them exhibit the marks of those origins in their singing styles or choices of songs. Men are still free to play the roles of good old boys in country music (to be manly, to prize their trucks, and so on), and those emphases usually translate into what are perceived as southern style postures. Patsy Cline had earlier thrived commercially even though she was a tough-talking good old girl, and Kitty Wells had earned the title of "Queen of Country Music" while transmitting the aura of a faithful wife and homemaker. But the good old girl has no appeal to country women today. They increasingly ignore the roles once prescribed for their gender, and they look and sound like pop performers in both visual attire and vocal style.

Sexual equality and freedom also are taken for granted. One finds in country lyrics few bold statements concerning such matters as reproductive freedom, but women speak openly of their desire for sexual pleasure and fulfillment, and they are no longer reluctant to use their sexuality for commercial advantage. Such singers as Sara Evans, Faith Hill, and Shania Twain routinely appear in videos that present them in revealing costumes and suggestive poses. Faith Hill declared, in fact, that "sensuality is the most glorious gift a woman has,"[5] a conviction that animates her choice of wardrobe and the videos that she makes. The sexuality displayed by Evans, Twain, Hill, and other contemporary women performers is not a new phenomenon in country music—Dolly Parton and Tanya Tucker, for example, often appeared in provocative clothing—but in our post-Madonna era, Twain and Hill assert their sexuality much more aggressively. Both women have classic country music and working-class biographies. Born Eileen Edwards in Ontario, Canada, Shania Twain adopted the name of her stepfather, an Ojibwe Indian named Jerry Twain, who raised her after her father deserted the family. Jerry Twain and her mother were killed in an automobile accident, and Shania had to raise her younger siblings. As a child she appeared often on Canadian country music television shows, singing the songs of Emmylou Harris and other leading country performers. Her career and style, though, reveal nothing of the blue-collar world that had nourished her, and instead convey the glitter and packaging of urban show business. Possessing the looks and self-assurance of a fashion model, Shania was ripe material for the physical packaging that her husband and producer, Mutt Lange, lent to her career. Her stage performances have been marked by a playful and assertive sexiness, provocative songs, and costumes that take advantage of her physical attractiveness. She became famous, in fact, for her bare midriff. All these traits translated into one of the most commercially successful careers ever enjoyed by a woman performer. Shania's 1995 album, *The Woman in Me,* was said to be the best-selling album by a woman artist in country music history, selling nine million albums in the United States and twelve million worldwide.

Faith Hill grew up in the tiny town of Star, Mississippi, just south of Jackson, as the daughter of adoptive parents. She attended an all-white school but was fascinated with black gospel music, and she haunted black churches and soaked up as much of the music and style of Aretha Franklin as she could absorb. She relocated in Nashville when she was nineteen years old and worked at Opryland as a hostess and T-shirt salesperson until 1993, when her recording breakthrough came. Her first CD,

---

5. Quoted in Tamara Saviano, et al., "The Four Faces of Faith," *Country Music* (December–January 2001), p. 54.

Take Me As I Am, included the hit single "Wild One." Since that time, she has had immense commercial success, both as a solo artist and as a performer with her husband, Tim McGraw, as part of the Soul 2 Soul Tour. In the spring of 2000 her recording of "Breathe" (in an album of the same name) crossed over into pop music and won her a Grammy award.

Hill is country music's first true glamour queen, and her statuesque beauty has attracted as much notice as her music. Although in interviews she has occasionally expressed chagrin at the attention given such matters by the media, she has nevertheless carefully cultivated an aura of sensuality with an avalanche of videos and photographs. Journalist Geoffrey Himes noted that "it may be a bit disingenuous to pose for thousands of photos and then claim that your looks have had nothing to do with your career."[6]

Country traditionalists may be offended by the sexy personas projected by Twain and Hill, but one suspects that it is their vocal performance styles that inspire the strongest censure. Hard country fans would proclaim loudly that "they just ain't country." The Dixie Chicks, on the other hand, have proved that overt sexual posturing and traditional music are not necessarily incompatible. When this trio of young women first emerged in the mid-nineties, their platinum blonde hair, sassy personalities, and striking beauty seemed to mark them as country music's version of the Spice Girls. They soon proved, though, that they could sing fervently, write memorable songs, and play string instruments masterfully. In many ways their emergence was the best news that had happened to modern country music in a long time. Not only did they inject much hard country material into their performances, they also attracted hosts of young women to their shows, presenting evidence that women can play country string instruments as well as any man.

The Chicks came to mainstream country after a lengthy experience in Texas as bluegrass musicians. The Erwin sisters (Emily on five-string banjo and Martie on fiddle) had played bluegrass in Dallas since 1984, when they were teenagers, and in 1989 they joined with Laura Lynch and Robin Macy to create the first version of the Dixie Chicks (named for a song performed by the rock band Little Feat). Between 1989 and 1993 they moved from street-corner concerts to stints as opening acts for such major stars as Garth Brooks and a performance at President Clinton's inaugural ball.

The present incarnation of the Dixie Chicks emerged in about 1995 when Lynch and Macy left the band and Natalie Maines became lead vocalist. Natalie was the perky and strong-voiced daughter of Lloyd Maines, a well-known steel guitarist and record producer from Lubbock, Texas.

---

6. Geoffrey Himes, "Contradictions and Affirmations," *Country Music* (July–August 1996), p. 40.

Faith Hill. Photograph by
Scott Newton/Austin City
Limits.

Dixie Chicks. Photograph by Scott Newton/Austin City Limits.

The addition of Natalie Maines, a dropout from Boston's Berklee School of Music, gave the trio a modern mainstream sound and almost ensured a major broadening of their repertoire. They also divested themselves of the big hair and cowgirl attire they had once sported and began dressing in contemporary clothing that accentuated their physical assets. Most important, they signed a contract in 1997 with Sony Records and in 1998 recorded an album, *Wide Open Spaces,* that sold over four million units within a year of its production. Their second Sony album, *Fly,* which contained the comic murder ballad "Goodbye Earl," rose to the top of *Billboard*'s charts after selling almost 350,000 copies within one week of the CD's release. No country group had ever had such an auspicious beginning.

The Dixie Chicks' style and ambience are too broad-ranging to confine them to the neo-traditional category, but songs like "Goodbye Earl," "Tonight the Heartache's on Me" (a shuffle beat honky-tonk tune), and the heart-rending "Am I the Only One" satisfy a hunger that many people have for hard country material. The very characteristics that have made contemporary country music broadly appealing to millions of Americans have alienated many others. Narrow radio playlists and formulaic pop-rock sounds and arrangements may bring comfort to some listeners, but they have convinced others that the music is losing its soul, a quality that had reflected its working-class origins. In an effort to reach a larger public and to occupy that broad middle ground vacated by the disappearance of older forms of pop music, country music's producers have created a body of songs that have little grit or down-home vitality. Moralists and patrons of respectability may applaud the decline of cheating and drinking songs and the whole retinue of topics outlined by David Allen Coe in the Steve Goodman composition "You Never Even Call Me by My Name" (where Coe avers that "the perfect country song" would say something about drinking, Mama, prison, trains, and trucks), but such items had been the heart and soul of country music, and evidence of its working-class nature. Similarly, soothing songs of religious affirmation sometimes appear in the repertoires of country singers, but the older passion-filled and doctrinaire gospel songs almost never surface on Top Forty country radio or in the performances of country entertainers.

Sporadic manifestations of tradition—like those featured by the Dixie Chicks, or those occurring in Sara Evans' debut CD in 1995, *Three Chords and the Truth,* or in Patty Loveless' superb CD of 2001, *Mountain Soul*—do sometimes appear within mainstream country music. Neo-traditionalism surfaces from time to time because corporate country music breeds boredom and dissent, and younger singers and writers long for the sense of rootedness and working-class flavor that once prevailed in the music. In the nineties and early years of the twenty-first century such singers as Alan Jackson, Mark Chesnutt, Wade Hayes, Joe Diffie, Toby Keith, and

Brad Paisley have given renewed hope to those who like the old country sounds.

"Traditional," of course, is a highly relative or elastic term. None of the neo-traditionalists have been mere throwbacks to older styles of performance, and none of them can be described as "moldy figs," a term first used by jazz scholars to categorize musicians who were resistant to change. As Dwight Yoakam's, Joe Diffie's, and Marty Stuart's music suggests, rock-and-roll has exerted a strong, if ironic, influence among the neo-traditionalists. After all, rock-and-roll was the culprit that drove hard country music off the jukeboxes and radio playlists back in the late fifties, and it perennially attracted the scorn of both moralists and traditional country music fans. Larry Cordle spoke of its enduring and harmful legacy in "Murder on Music Row," when he opined that "drums and rock-and-roll guitars" were "shoved right up in your face." Rock-and-roll, however, strongly colored the styles of people like Travis Tritt, the Marietta, Georgia, native who often spoke fondly of his reverence for the southern rock varieties of the genre, and Marty Stuart, the multi-talented Mississippi musician who has been the most tireless champion of traditional country music. Stuart joined the Sullivan Family bluegrass band when he was twelve and became part of Lester Flatt's Nashville Grass at the age of thirteen. After Flatt's death, Stuart became a member of Johnny Cash's band for a time and was married to one of Cash's daughters. A lifelong collector, historian, and photographer of country music, he has passionately and eloquently defended traditional styles, illustrating his eclectic musical bent and willingness to combine seemingly disparate forms in such collections as *Hillbilly Rock* and *The Pilgrim*. Stuart was one of a small group in the eighties, including Steve Earle and Dwight Yoakam, who proudly used the term "hillbilly" to describe their music. If versatility were not enough to ensure his fame in country music history, he is also married to the beautiful and talented Connie Smith, a singer described by her contemporaries as one of the greatest vocalists in country music. About seventeen years younger than Smith, Stuart had had a crush on his future wife since he was a little boy.

Marty Stuart may be an uncompromising advocate of hard country styles, but most other musicians have been wary of firmly attaching themselves to the neo-traditional camp. No one has a voice that is more unmistakably country than Patty Loveless, a singer who communicates perfectly the inflections of her native Kentucky hills, but she has refused to identify with any specific stylistic label. A cousin of Loretta Lynn and Crystal Gayle, Loveless was born Patricia Ramey in Pikeville in eastern Kentucky, in the same hospital where Dwight Yoakam was born. Her father was a victim of black lung disease, the grim ailment that has taken the lives of many Appalachian coal miners. Country music has always been an integral and cherished part of her inheritance, but she has never hesitated to try her hand at other kinds of music. For instance, she sang rock-and-roll for a brief period and still injects songs with a rock flavor into her performances. Loveless first came to Nashville as a teenage employee of the Wilburn Brothers but did not figure prominently in that city's musical scene until 1987, when she joined MCA under the tutelage of producer Tony Brown. Brown directed her first album that year, which included her first chart single, "If My Heart Had Windows," a song learned from George Jones. Later recordings made for MCA and Epic, including the CMA's Best Country Album for 1995, *When Fallen Angels Fly,* often attained platinum status and won for her in 1996 the CMA's and ACM's prize as Female Vocalist of the Year. These recordings exhibited her eclectic tastes and only rarely ventured into the neo-traditional realm. If any question lingered, though, about her ability to sing traditional material, it was put to rest by her powerful performance (along with Ralph Stanley) of the great murder ballad "Pretty Polly" on Stanley's CD collection *Clinch Mountain Country,* and by her CD of 2001, *Mountain Soul,* a collection of hard country songs performed with acoustic backing.

Alan Jackson, in contrast, proudly wears the mantle of neo-traditional country singer. Jackson grew up Newnan, Georgia, as the son of an automobile mechanic whom he has commemorated in a fine song called "Working Class Hero." In vocal style, Jackson exhibits neither a Hank Williams nor a Lefty Frizzell influence but nevertheless has a believable and winning southern lilt and twang in his voice. Ever since his first major recordings for Arista in 1989, Jackson's advocacy of hard country music has been evidenced by his choice of songs and accompanying instrumentation. He knocked around Nashville for about four years, working in TNN's mailroom and making demos for other singers, before he recorded his first album, *Here in the Real World.* Since that time, Jackson has rarely strayed from his working-class roots or the hard country sound, with a long string of stellar recordings such as "Don't Rock the Jukebox," "Chattahoochie," "Mercury Blues," and "Midnight in Montgomery" (a tribute to Hank Williams). His music has often expressed a refreshing populist tinge and a reverence for his roots, a concern best heard in "Little Man" and "Working Class Hero." Jackson showed his disquietude about the nature of the music now being produced in Nashville in his decision to record (with George Strait) a cover version of "Murder on Music Row."

Other sometime country traditionalists, such as Mark Chesnutt, Travis Tritt, and Joe Diffie, have often spoken of their reverence for traditional country music but have frequently veered from the hard country format. Chesnutt came from one of the citadels of working-class country music, the area surrounding Beaumont, Texas, where his father, Bob Chesnutt, had been a local country singer and a collector of country records. Mark often joined his old friend Tracy Byrd in gigs in the local bar and honky-tonk circuit that had nourished their hero George Jones. No one was

Randy Travis. Photograph by Scott Newton/Austin City Limits.

George Jones (*with guitar*) and Alan Jackson. Photograph by Marty Stuart.

Earl Scruggs (*left*) and Marty Stuart. Photograph by Becky Johnson.

surprised when Mark quit school in the tenth grade to play music. His first commercial hit came in 1990 with the recording "Too Cold at Home" (for MCA), which was followed soon thereafter by such songs as the beautifully crafted "Brother Jukebox" (written by Paul Craft) and "Bubba Shot the Jukebox."

Travis Tritt began his ascent to stardom in 1990 with his first Warner Brothers album, *Country Club.* Tritt seldom claims to be neo-traditional but instead proudly identifies with such southern rock luminaries as Charlie Daniels, Lynyrd Skynyrd, and Hank Williams, Jr. Few country musicians, however, have been as gifted or as versatile as Tritt. He sometimes exhibits his skill on the five-string banjo and can speak of experience as a bluegrass musician, and he has recorded some of the finest examples of modern honky-tonk material, including "Here's a Quarter (Call Someone Who Cares)," "Lord Have Mercy on the Working Man," "The Whiskey Ain't Working" (with Marty Stuart), and "Out of Control Raging Fire," a duet with Patty Loveless and one of the strongest moments on her CD *Mountain Soul.* A series of engagements with Stuart in 1992, called the "No Hats" tour, indicated the two musicians' suspicion of the numerous "hat acts" and revealed their affinity for both rock-and-roll and hard country.

Joe Diffie carried genuine blue-collar credentials, having worked in a foundry and at other wage jobs while pursuing his dream of country music. He grew up in an Oklahoma family where Haggard, Jones, and Frizzell were gods. He followed his dream to Nashville in 1986 and, prospering from the burgeoning commercial scene that emerged that year, he became a much-sought-after singer on demo records. In 1990 he signed with Epic Records and recorded "Home," a song that immediately shot to the top of the charts. Widely heralded as a singer's singer and as a champion of hard country music, Diffie's music was, more accurately, an appealing synthesis of honky-tonk and rock, best exemplified in his CD of 1993, *Honky Tonk Attitude.*

The future of country neo-traditionalism is uncertain, but at the time of this writing, Brad Paisley, a devoted disciple of Buck Owens, seems to be the chief torchbearer of hard country sounds. He was born in 1972 in Glen Dale, West Virginia, an Ohio River town. Growing up in rural West Virginia, Paisley could hardly avoid hearing the sounds of genuine country music. His introduction came from his grandfather, who played Merle Travis–style guitar. He received further invaluable experience as a musician on the famous *Wheeling Jamboree,* where he played for eight years. Paisley moved to Nashville in the mid-nineties to enroll in the Belmont College music business program. Like Diffie, he soon began making music demos and writing songs. In 2000 he recorded his first Arista CD, *Who Needs Pictures,* on which he played all the guitar parts and for which he wrote all of the songs. Several of the album's songs received wide airplay, but the biggest hit has been the cleverly worded "Me Neither." He was enrolled in the *Grand Ole Opry* in early 2001.

While the weaknesses of Top Forty country music are apparent, the most glaring deficiencies are the virtual abandonment of veteran performers and the reluctance to promote the music of unorthodox entertainers. George Jones did succeed in breaking through country music's youth curtain in 1996 with a song called "Choices" that somehow managed to make it on to the charts. In general, though, Jones and other classic country singers such as Johnny Cash, Willie Nelson, Merle Haggard, Loretta Lynn, Emmylou Harris, Dolly Parton, Charley Pride, Ray Price, Hank Thompson, Vern Gosdin, and Gene Watson have had to seek new venues and audiences outside of mainstream country. A few of these musicians have become icons of youth pop culture, admired for their honesty and endurance and, in some cases, because they have rebelled against the Top Forty establishment. Johnny Cash, for example, has enjoyed the most remarkable career of any country musician. At least since his appearance at the Newport Folk Festival in 1964, Cash has preserved a following among young fans that seems only to be reinvigorated with each succeeding generation. Cultivating an air of mystery with his habit of dressing in black, exhibiting a receptivity to alternative styles and musicians, and clinging to a spare and almost austere acoustic sound, he has impressed listeners as a man of rugged and uncompromising integrity. Totally exiled from Top Forty radio, Cash has nevertheless maintained a commercial presence with a series of CDs (including the award-winning *American Recordings* in 1994) marketed to college and other independent radio stations. The aging Austin Outlaw, Willie Nelson, similarly preserved links to rock audiences through his well-publicized FarmAid concerts, where he collaborated with such socially conscious rock singers as John Cougar Mellencamp and Neil Young and won admirers among adult Americans with his albums of vintage popular songs. Merle Haggard has made fewer efforts to cultivate rock-culture youth and in fact had explicitly set himself apart from them in the early seventies with his anti-hippie anthem, "Okie from Muskogee." He nevertheless won much support among counterculture youth who admired the man who "wore his own kind of hat." He has been the subject of a fine tribute album, *Tulare Dust,* produced by the former cowpunk musician Dave Alvin and performed by a variety of alternative singers such as himself, Tom Russell, and Iris DeMent. This kind of patronage may have mellowed the outspoken country singer, because he now offers some regrets about the political positions he took back in the early seventies.

To its credit, the *Grand Ole Opry* still makes room each Saturday night for the music of such "old-timers" as Bill Anderson, Bill Carlisle, Little Jimmy Dickens, Jack Greene, Jimmy C. Newman, Jean Shepard, Connie Smith, Porter Wagoner, Billy Walker, and Charlie Walker. It is reassuring to traditionalists to see Porter Wagoner stride out on the stage still wearing his trademark Nudie costumes. Veteran musicians also find refuge in cities and venues outside of Nashville—in Branson, Missouri, in the clubs of Myrtle Beach, South Carolina, in the dance halls of Bandera, Texas, and in casinos and cruises that cater to Middle American tourists. The Statler Brothers, for example, may be banished from Top Forty radio, but they are assured evenings of capacity crowds when they appear at clubs like the Crystal Grand Theatre in the Wisconsin Dells resort town. Branson, Missouri, has long been a haven for entertainers who have either been ignored by Nashville or who do not want to stay on the road in order to make a living in the music business. Originating as an Ozark tourist mecca built around the theme park Silver Dollar City and the outdoor pageant "Shepherd of the Hills," the small city assumed country music overtones when a local hillbilly burlesque group called the Baldknobbers began playing old-time music in a local theater. Roy Clark was the first superstar who resettled in Branson, but he was soon followed by Mel Tillis, the late Boxcar Willie, Glen Campbell, Moe Bandy, and the most popular act of all, the Japanese fiddler Shoji Tabuchi, who had "converted" to country music in his native country after hearing Roy Acuff perform. The mile-long strip of road that runs through Branson is now dotted with glittering music clubs, and thousands of slow-moving automobiles and tour busses bring tourists to this phenomenon that is often described as "Las Vegas without the gambling."

Texas is still a thriving area for working-class country music, even though the scene is sustained more often than not by college students and other urban listeners who long to sample, at least for the moment, the laid-back life of Luckenbach along with "Willie, Waylon, and the Boys." Cowboy imagery and the Texas mystique—the conviction that the state has had a special legacy of freedom and innovation—continue to lure musicians to the region and to shape the kind of music they make. The popular television show *Austin City Limits,* of course, has fed such perceptions to a large audience each week for more than twenty years. Visitors to the Hill Country cowboy towns of Helotes and Bandera can always hear good local country music, but if they're lucky they might also hear the soulful sounds of Johnny Bush, Darrell McCall, Hank Thompson, Ray Price, or Gene Watson, all of whom make frequent appearances in the local clubs. In Austin, fans can always be assured of hearing a wide variety of country styles. Much of it is rock-inflected, but western swing and honky-tonk bands also make the city their prime area of activity. The performers who have passed through Austin include some of the most distinctive singers and songwriters in country music. Most of them, however, have never been heard on Top Forty radio stations, and regrettably remain unknown to most country music listeners. Austin is the locus for the music of a talented trio of friends from Lubbock, Butch Hancock, Joe

Ely, and Jimmie Dale Gilmore, who won regional notoriety and enduring cult status in the early seventies as the Flatlanders. For over thirty years they have made music, such as Hancock's "West Texas Waltz," that evokes the spirit of the Texas landscape and mirrors the dreams and anxieties of people everywhere. None of these performers has won great commercial success, but each has instead enjoyed critical praise for their recordings. While Ely's aggressive and high-energy style reflects his rockabilly roots, Gilmore's is more lyrical and country-based. He cuts a striking figure with his graying shoulder-length hair, high cheek bones, and dark Native American physical features, and he exhibits a gentle spirit that draws upon Buddhist meditative resources. It is his music, above all, that commands attention. Gilmore's clear, resonant, tenor voice and precise articulation are almost unique in country music, and his CD of 2000, *One Endless Night,* is a superb collection of songs written by his old friend Butch Hancock, Willis Alan Ramsey, Walter Hyatt, and other country poets. Gilmore made the ironic suggestion that the CD was too country for Top Forty radio, but for sheer lyric artistry and vocal interpretation, very little in that format could compete with it.

Junior Brown now lives in Tulsa, Oklahoma, but for many years was the headliner at Austin's Continental Club. For pure instrumental brilliance few musicians in country music can compare with him. Brown is not totally unknown to the average country music listener, because he made an award-winning video built around his song "My Wife Thinks You're Dead" that illustrated both his musicianship and his sense of humor. And he is certainly highly regarded by his fellow musicians. Nevertheless, Brown has had to pursue his career in alternative venues outside Nashville and among largely rock-oriented fans. The Arizona-born entertainer sings in a deep baritone reminiscent of Ernest Tubb, whose television shows he had faithfully watched as a kid. Although that influence appears in his song "My Baby Don't Dance to Nothing but Ernest Tubb," Brown's masterful artistry defies labeling. His guitar playing borrows from country, jazz, and rock sources, most notably the style pioneered by Jimi Hendrix, but he has introduced his own individualistic and idiosyncratic innovations. Brown is a performer who actually has to be seen to be fully appreciated. Playing an instrument that he invented, the guit-steel (a double-necked instrument that permits both electric guitar and steel guitar stylings), Brown dazzles his audiences with his rapid and flawless ability to move quickly from one style to the other in the course of an individual song.

Don Walser, a gentle giant born in 1934 in Lamesa, Texas, also commands physical attention from listeners with his size and bearing—he stands six foot six and weighs about 280 pounds. Most important, he sings country music the way it should be sung. Walser had always sung country songs and had been particularly enamored of the music of Bob Wills and

Doc Watson (*left*) and Mac Wiseman, 1997. Photograph by Becky Johnson.

Steve Earle, 1997. Photograph by Marty Stuart.

Lucinda Williams and Jim Lauderdale. Photograph by Becky Johnson.

Don Walser.
Photograph by Scott
Newton/Austin City
Limits.

the yodeling of Elton Britt, but he made no attempt at a full-fledged professional career until the age of sixty, when he retired from forty-five years of service in the National Guard. He brought to his new career an encyclopedic knowledge of country song lyrics, a desire to preserve authentic country sounds, a clear and powerful tenor voice, and a hair-raising yodel. Someone described him as the "Pavarotti of the Plains." Walser became a fixture in the dance halls of Austin and Central Texas, but neither his songs nor his style of singing were classic honky-tonk in nature. He has instead been highly diverse in his selection of songs, ranging from the soft pop-country tunes of Eddy Arnold to the hard country items of Ray Price and George Jones. Like Gilmore, Walser can be considered alternative because his pure country style seems anachronistic when measured against those that dominate Top Forty radio. He sang at the Summer Olympics in Atlanta in 1996 and participated in the Heritage tour along with Tish Hinojosa, but Walser has been heard by too few people. The bulk of his concerts have been confined to Texas, especially to the many clubs of Austin.

If Don Walser's vocal style cannot be defined by the clubs in which he plays, that of Wayne Hancock, another fine Texas singer, is very much a product of honky-tonk culture. Hancock exhibits the marks of a youth spent listening to rock-and-roll and hard country, and vocally he comes about as close to a Hank Williams sound as anyone in country music. Communicating easily with a hard-edged, nasally punctuated tenor, and cultivating the air of a rambler, the youthful Hancock has tried hard to link his music to the honky-tonk tradition. In "Juke Joint Jumping," for example, he speaks of experiences that he could not have known but probably learned about from his father—honky-tonking in the clubs that once lined the Gladewater highway in the East Texas oil fields. In songs like "Thunderstorms and Neon Signs," Hancock has also mined the terrain of loneliness and despair that Hank Williams explored in his songs. But like most young country musicians who venture into the realm of honky-tonk music, Hancock (and his chief disciple, Hank Williams III) seems most comfortable when he's belting out a good-time rock anthem or boogie tune.

The closest approximation of honky-tonk music, in all of its manifestations, can be found in the songs of Dale Watson. Born in Alabama and surviving a brief stint in California, Watson has become a fixture in the Austin musical scene. Watson's "Jack's Truck Stop and Café," an affectionate recollection of local music making in Tennessee, is not a literal account of a portion of the singer's life, but it evokes the kind of youthful experiences that shaped his music. Watson absorbed his values and music from his father, who was a truck driver and country singer, and he has remained passionately loyal to the culture that surrounded his father's life, preserving his fascination with trucking songs and with the music of that genre's greatest exponent, Dave Dudley. His concerts are essentially primers for his young fans, who are informed about the beauty found in the music of such "real" performers as Dudley, Merle Haggard, Wynn Stewart, and Conway Twitty. Watson has a strong, expressive baritone, and while he exhibits his debts to his honky-tonk mentors, he also infuses his concerts with the energy and drive of country-rock. Unlike other youthful honky-tonk revivalists, such as Wayne Hancock, Watson exhibits a fondness and affinity for slow sad songs, such as "Blessed or Damned," "I Hate These Songs," and "Every Song I Write Is for You" (a song written as a tribute to his sweetheart, who was killed in an automobile accident). Above all, he is an uncompromising hillbilly nationalist and never hesitates to express his contempt for the music of Top Forty. In "Play Me a Real Country Song" he pays tribute to the radio stations of his youth that played authentic country music.

Although Watson and the other Austin musicians usually have been writers as well as singers, few of them can be identified with the singer-songwriter culture that emerged from the folk revival. Embracing a tradition that began with Woody Guthrie and flowered in the sixties with Paul Simon, Joni Mitchell, and Bob Dylan, a contingent of musicians built a body of literate and often socially conscious music at festivals and in coffee houses throughout America. These musical poets generally adhered to acoustic instruments, preferring intimate environments where their music could be easily absorbed and appreciated. The most successful, though, such as John Prine, Steve Earle, Mary Chapin Carpenter, Shelby Lynne, and Lucinda Williams, have adopted electric instruments and the aggressive tone of rock music. Their relationship with country music has been problematic, and few have received more than minimal acceptance in Nashville or on Top Forty radio.

Although few of the Austin musicians are identified with the culture that emerged from the folk revival, Texas singers have made vital contributions to the singer-songwriter genre. Nanci Griffith, for instance, grew up in a musical household in Austin but was swept away by the music of the folk revival, particularly when she heard a local performer, Carolyn Hester, and the songs of the star-crossed troubadour Townes Van Zandt. Van Zandt always remained on the periphery of country music even though he recorded at least fifteen albums and introduced such songs as "Pancho and Lefty," "If I Needed You," and "Tecumseh Valley" to the permanent country music lexicon.

Griffith knew the songs of her colleagues in the folk movement, but she became highly regarded for the quality of her own songs, a talent first exhibited at the Kerrville Folk Festival in the Texas Hill Country. She found easy communion there with such festival regulars as Bill and Bonnie Hearne, the congenial and smooth-singing duo who also lent encouragement to Tish Hinojosa, Lyle Lovett, and other fledgling artists. Griffith had already had about eight years of music experience when she moved to Nashville in 1985 and made a critically praised album for Philo called *Once in a Very Blue Moon*. Although Kathy Mattea's 1986 version of Griffith's "Love at the Five and Dime" rose to number three on the *Billboard* charts, Griffith's tenure within the Nashville mainstream was neither happy nor commercially successful. Since that time she has kept the industry at arm's length but has continued to make first-rate recordings, including two tributes to other songwriters, *Other Voices, Other Rooms,* and *Other Voices Too,* and has cast her musical net more broadly by recording with the Nashville Symphony and the legendary Irish band the Chieftains. Along with Tim O'Brien, Steve Earle, and Ricky Skaggs, Griffith has experimented often with Celtic material and has won a large and devoted following in Ireland.

Leticia "Tish" Hinojosa is still another Austin-based singer-songwriter who can point to the experience of the Kerrville Folk Festival as the stimulus for her career. Her sensibilities as a songwriter, however, grew out of her experiences in San Antonio as the daughter of parents who had migrated from Mexico. As the youngest of thirteen children, Hinojosa clung closely to her mother, absorbing the lyrical love songs that she had transported across the border. Tish also heard the Tejano and Conjunto rhythms beloved by her father and, of course, the pop and country songs that came to her each day on the radio. Hinojosa spent two artistically productive, but commercially disappointing, periods in New Mexico and Nashville during the eighties, performing a mixture of country, rock, and folk tunes. Her first album, *Taos to Tennessee,* recalls that era. Her first major recording, however, came in 1989, when she reached into the cultural resources of her family and produced a CD called *Homeland*. There, in songs like "West Side of Town" and "Joaquin," she documented and paid tribute to the experiences of her family and other brave souls who had made the perilous journey across the Rio Grande. She followed these forays into family autobiography with powerful and sensitive songs, such as "Something in the Rain," that commented on the abuses visited on migrant laborers, children, and women. Social commentary has never vanished from her repertoire, but Hinojosa's most recent recordings, which have become increasingly bilingual, have been intensely introspective and mystical musings on her cultural heritage.

Iris DeMent was born in Arkansas but grew up in California surrounded by family and neighbors who still bore the accents, values, and music of her birthplace and the working-class South. With one of the most compelling, emotionally searing voices heard in modern American music, she has paid tribute to those origins in songs like "Mama's Opry" and "I'm Walking Home Tonight" (about the death of her father). DeMent grew up hearing the sounds of Jimmie Rodgers, the Carter Family, and Merle Haggard but forged her own personal and expressive style playing the coffeehouse circuit in Kansas City. After moving to Nashville in 1990 and coming under the tutelage of Emmylou Harris, she began singing backup vocals for other entertainers and in 1992 made her first solo record, *Infamous Angel,* for Philo. That album, and the two that followed (*My Life* in 1994, and *The Way I Should* in 1996), were critically acclaimed but seldom played on mainstream radio stations. She may have culled her intensely personal lyrics, in such songs as "Easy's Getting Harder" and "No Time to Cry," from autobiographical recollections, but she voiced the universal concerns of listeners with poignant lyrics and a penetrating emotional intimacy that few writers have achieved. DeMent has made frequent guest appearances on other people's albums (such as John Prine's great tribute to hard country music, *In Spite of Ourselves*) or on anthologies such as *Songcatcher,* where she reprised the beautiful ballad, "Pretty Saro," which she had sung in a movie of the same name. She also collaborated briefly with Merle Haggard, as a co-writer and opening act. Haggard's response to her third CD, *The Way I Should,* which contains biting political commentary about some of the nation's social ills, has not been disclosed.

Unlike Hinojosa and DeMent, Lucinda Williams cannot point to a working-class heritage. Born in Lake Charles, Louisiana, she grew up in a series of southern towns, the daughter of Miller Williams, a poet and university English professor (now at the University of Arkansas) who read a poem at Bill Clinton's second inauguration. While she undoubtedly absorbed certain literary sensibilities from her father and a love for music from her mother, she probably learned more from Hank Williams and other southern musicians who populated the family's radio. It would be an imaginative leap indeed to assert that she learned from still another southern poet who bore the name of Williams, but her preoccupation with the dark underside of human existence and evocations of loneliness do bear some resemblance to the insights of Tennessee Williams. Her best-known collection, the Grammy-winning *Car Wheels on a Gravel Road,* makes constant references to such southern towns as Lafayette, Baton Rouge, Jackson, and Greenville, each serving as a backdrop or context for her tales of sensuous longing, disappointment, and suicide.

Tim O'Brien is country music's renaissance man. The West Virginia native had first won the allegiance of bluegrass fans through his versatile musicianship with the Colorado-based band Hot Rize. By the time this colorful and award-winning group disbanded in 1990, O'Brien had already won some success as a songwriter and had seen two of his songs, "Walk the Way the Wind Blows" and "Untold Stories," become major hits for fellow West Virginian Kathy Mattea. A duet with Mattea, "The Battle Hymn of Love," recorded in 1990, reached the Top Ten lists and won for him a contract with RCA. Even though no material from that proposed album was ever released, O'Brien's artistic production has never slowed down (he in fact has combined his incessant musical performance with the presidency of the IBMA, a post to which he was appointed in January 2002). Albums made for Sugar Hill and other labels reveal a staggering musicianship and a catholicity of taste that seems unending. He has made fine duet albums with his sister Molly, has appeared as a singer and supporting musician on scores of recordings made by others, continues to write sensitive songs (such as the Nickel Creek hit, "When You Come Back Down"), and, of course, produces and performs ably on his own CDs. His wide-ranging receptivity to songs and his ability to move freely and convincingly from traditional to modern material is documented in an album of Bob Dylan songs, *Red on Blonde,* an album of old-time fiddle tunes and ballads called *From the Mountain* (inspired by the novel *Cold Mountain*), and two albums called *The Crossing* and *Two Journeys* that explore the presumed links between Appalachian music and Celtic culture.

O'Brien and the other musicians discussed above are, almost by definition, "alternative" entertainers. Either by choice or by necessity, they have had to pursue their careers outside the commercial channels controlled by Nashville. However, the term "alternative" (or "alt. country," a designation used on Internet websites) has been more often used to describe those musicians who have combined rock and country elements and who project an edge and vitality that seem absent from mainstream country music. In many cases, in fact, they have revived styles and themes that once lay at the heart of country music. Gram Parsons, of course, provided a central source of inspiration for such musicians, while the punk country (or cowpunk) bands on the West Coast and elsewhere (such as Jason and the Scorchers) contributed still another. A key event in the shaping of the alternative country movement came in 1990, when the country-rock band Uncle Tupelo recorded an album called *No Depression* (inspired by a Carter Family song from 1930). Performed in acoustic country style and sung by Jay Farrar with his typically pained and clenched-throat vocal delivery, the title song and album inspired a website and magazine called *No Depression.* By 1994 Uncle Tupelo had splintered into two new bands, Wilco (headed by Jeff Tweedy) and Son Volt (led by Jay Farrar). Neither act has remained committed to the style or approach promised by Uncle Tupelo. In fact, they have moved more closely to the rock mainstream, but they did much to unleash a broad movement of rock and country fusion. Such bands as the Old 97's, the Bottle Rockets, Jayhawks, Whiskeytown, and the Volebeats built styles that seemed derivative of, or analogous to, the music made by Uncle Tupelo.

The Bloodshot label in Chicago popularized still another term for alternative country groups when it described its own roster of talent as "insurgent" acts. Bloodshot musicians tended to be roots-oriented but iconoclastic in their choice of songs and styles. Most of the music on the Bloodshot label carried the aura, spirit, and sound of cowpunk music.

That is, it was designed to shock, arouse, or even offend. Bloodshot's own-ers and directors, however, seemed genuinely respectful of hard country music's past and contemptuous of contemporary Nashville's offerings. On a subsidiary label, Bloodshot Revival, they reissued recordings of clas-sic material performed by such people as Rex Allen, Johnny Bond, Spade Cooley, Jimmie Davis, Pee Wee King, Joe Maphis, Hank Penny, and Hank Thompson. The label also issued covers of older country material per-formed by Bloodshot acts on such anthologies as *For a Life of Sin* and *Straight Outta Boone County.*

Even though a roots emphasis defined the music produced by Blood-shot, the company marketed its product with an aggressiveness and swag-ger that seemed to come right out of rock culture. Furthermore, the "roots" that most appealed to Bloodshot's directors and artists were the presumed wild and hedonistic moments in country music's past (at best, the joys of drinking and dancing the night away and, at worst, recover-ing from a week-long binge). The Waco Brothers, who were virtually the Bloodshot house band, performed with an infectious abandon that was eminently suited for roadhouses and rock bars. Three members of the band—including its leader, the artist Jon Langford—came from England, and they tended to view and distill American country music into a dark kind of brew filled with whiskey, sex, and violence. Bloodshot's best-known artist, Robbie Fulks, discovered hard country music after earlier flirtations with rock, bluegrass, and folk but became an ardent student of the genre. Although Fulks performs with the frenetic spirit of punk country (reminiscent of Jason Ringenberg, who fronts a band called the Scorchers), he has exhibited an informed knowledge of, and appreciation for, older and often-obscure country entertainers (examples of this in-terest can be heard in his Bloodshot CD, *13 Hillbilly Greats*). His own compositions, though, tend to take jabs at some of country music's sacred cows (romantic love with "Tell Her Lies," religion with "God Isn't Real," and Nashville in "Fuck This Town").

Rock-derived musicians may have been the first to be labeled as alter-native country, but the description has since been so widely applied that it can no longer be defined in terms of style. The official journal of the movement, *No Depression,* often describes itself as the "alternative coun-try (whatever that is) bimonthly." As now conceived, alternative country might best be understood as any form of music that lies outside of, and in opposition to, Top Forty country music. It is inherently anti-Nashville, al-though a few musicians who have been identified as alternative artists, such as Tim O'Brien and Robbie Fulks, have tried and failed to make in-roads into the city's corporate recording machine. Some musicians, of course, resist being labeled as alternative and, in fact, fashion styles that are far different from those of the rock-country performers. For example, Mike Ireland, a Kansas City musician who had performed briefly with a rock-country group called the Starkweathers (named for a Midwestern mass murderer), went completely against the alternative grain with a CD called *Learning How to Live,* recorded for the SubPop label. The songs included in the album were unrelievedly somber in tone, reflecting the anguish and pain wrought by his then-recent marriage breakup, and in style were closer to the country-pop of Billy Sherrill's Nashville than anything done by the alternative country groups. In decided contrast, a young Chicago band called Freakwater often ventured into the realm of old-time country. Although they sometimes demonstrated that they could rock as hard as any alternative group, the principal singers in the band, Catherine Erwin and Janet Bean, sang songs like "Put My Little Shoes Away" with close, pristine harmonies that compared favorably with versions done earlier by pioneer hillbilly bands.

An assortment of swing and rockabilly groups also has flourished in the past fifteen years. This music had already been presaged in the seventies by such musicians as the Austin band Asleep at the Wheel, and Commander Cody and the Lost Planet Airmen. (One of the newer swing-rockabilly musicians, Bill Kirchen, had in fact been the guitarist on Commander Cody's famous version of "Hot Rod Lincoln.") Sometimes described as retro-country, because they dress in costumes that suggest the forties or fifties and play music from those years, members of a band known as BR5-49 were fixtures for years at Roberts Western Wear in downtown Nashville. Taking their name from the "phone number" used by Junior Samples in his car-salesman skit on *Hee Haw,* they won a large following because of their campy clothes, relentless energy, immense storehouse of songs, and shows that could extend for four hours and more. Out on the West Coast a band known as Big Sandy and the Fly Right Boys capitalized on the vogue for swing music that emerged in the early nineties. Led by vocalist Robert Williams (Big Sandy), the Fly Right Boys played an infectious mixture of rockabilly, rhythm-and-blues, and western swing. Still another West Coast band, the Derailers, made Austin their home and popularized a style and repertoire that owed as much to Buck Owens and the Buckaroos as it did to the rockabilly style with which they had begun.

Even though the Derailers and similar groups proudly acknowledge their debt to Owens and the Buckaroos, their sound and ambience are significantly different from the music made by their heroes and other honky-tonk pioneers. Honky-tonk country has been, in many ways, the most authentic expression of working-class country music culture, but it has been the least represented among young alternative musicians, even though such artists as the Derailers and BR5-49 are sometimes identified with the honky-tonk style, since their music is most often played in bars and dancehalls. But with rare exceptions, such as Jim Lauderdale and Dallas Wayne, who have recorded some good cry-in-your-beer shuffle songs, alternative country musicians do not present the full range of emotions heard in the classic performances of George Jones, Ray Price, or even Buck Owens. They can boogie or rock, but they find it difficult to wear their hearts on their sleeves. One should not expect to hear most alternative musicians sing a heartbroken lament like "He Stopped Loving Her Today" and certainly not a sentimental weeper like "Flowers for Mama." At its worst, the No Depression or insurgent style can seem like a form of slumming in a poor-white-trash neighborhood, but at its best, alternative country pays homage to styles that have been abandoned by mainstream country and often succeeds in recreating the gritty vitality and earthiness of working-class culture.

The most vital form of alternative country music, bluegrass, has flourished since 1984 with a paradoxical but complementary blend of tradition and innovation. On one hand, bluegrass continues to be a refuge for tradition-minded fans and musicians. On the other, it serves also as a seedbed for artistic experimentation within an acoustic context. Romantic evocations of traditional rootedness and pastoral simplicity achieve expression through superb and innovative musicianship. Finding it almost impossible to build a niche on Top Forty radio, bluegrass musicians have increasingly created their own infrastructure of promotion and exposure, including small record labels, radio shows, booking agencies, journals, festivals, and two promotional organizations, the IBMA and the Society for the Preservation of Bluegrass Music in America. Founded in 1985, the IBMA functions essentially as a chamber of commerce, clearinghouse, and showcase for bluegrass musicians. Thousands of people assemble each October in Louisville, Kentucky, to attend a trade show, awards ceremony, and dozens of concerts, or simply to jam night after night with fellow musicians. Since 1991, when Bill Monroe, Lester Flatt, and Earl Scruggs were selected, bluegrass immortals have been inducted into the IBMA's Hall of Honor. The music as a whole will eventually be commemorated in a museum and Hall of Fame located in Owensboro, Kentucky, not far from Bill Monroe's birthplace in Rosine.

Long before his death on September 9, 1996, Monroe had settled comfortably into the role of patriarch of bluegrass music and had established a mellow relationship with both fans and interviewers. Since his demise, the venerable Ralph Stanley has assumed the role of father figure (partly because Earl Scruggs has remained largely inactive). Joined in 1995 by his son Ralph II, Stanley has stayed on the road with his Clinch Mountain Boys, clinging to his traditional style and basking in such honors as a National Heritage Fellowship and an honorary doctorate from Lincoln Memorial University in Harrogate, Tennessee. "Dr. Ralph's" haunting voice and commitment to traditional values have been introduced to audiences well outside the bluegrass community through his presence on the soundtrack of the movie *O Brother Where Art Thou?* In 2002 his stark

Del McCoury Band (*left to right*): Ronnie McCoury, Jason Carter, Rob McCoury, Del McCoury. Photograph by Nancy M. Cutlip.

Alison Krauss, 1990. Photograph by
Becky Johnson.

Rhonda Vincent. Photograph by
Becky Johnson.

Nickel Creek (*top to bottom*): Sara
Watkins, Sean Watkins, Chris Thile.
Photographs by Nancy M. Cutlip.

interpretation of a song from the movie's soundtrack, "Oh Death," won for him the Grammy award for the best country vocal performance.

Bluegrass offered a different kind of refuge for some singers who could find little exposure elsewhere. The renewed commitment to bluegrass sounds, of course, was easy for veteran performer Ricky Skaggs, who took to the road in 1997 with a magnificent new band, Kentucky Thunder. Skaggs' marvelous versatility, clear tenor voice, and genuine devotion to traditional music immediately vaulted him into the front ranks of bluegrass musicians. Jim Lauderdale was no stranger to bluegrass, since he had performed the music early in his career before he became a valued Nashville songwriter. But two CDs recorded with Ralph Stanley exhibited his ease and familiarity with bluegrass. On the other hand, Dolly Parton and Steve Earle had almost no prior experience with the idiom when they ventured into their bluegrass experiments in the late nineties. Backed by an array of bluegrass' finest young musicians, Parton paid tribute to her Appalachian origins in two critically praised CDs, the Grammy-winning *The Grass Is Blue* and *The Little Sparrow*. Steve Earle also garnered much attention in 1999 when he recorded an album called *The Mountain* with the Del McCoury Band. Touting this partnership between country-rock and bluegrass as an attempt to erase the borders between the two audiences, Earle then toured with the McCourys for several months.

Virtually all bluegrass musicians have adhered to the central canon of the style, the reliance on acoustic instruments. But in their experimentation with a wide array of styles and songs, they have moved their music far beyond the classic parameters originally established by Monroe, Flatt, and Scruggs. As a result, bluegrass' innovators have generated debates concerning authenticity and direction that are similar to those encountered in the larger realm of country music. Karl Shiflett, a musician from Longview, Texas, has countered the work of the "progressives" with a delightful stage show that recreates the look and sound of Lester Flatt's classic bluegrass. Del McCoury, in contrast, demonstrated that classic bluegrass music could be popular and commercial without a mere recapitulation of older styles. He emerged as the leading heir of Bill Monroe's classic sound, with his own clear high tenor style and run-filled guitar playing, and with a band that included two of his sons, Ronnie and Robbie, fiddler Jason Carter, and bassist Mike Bubb. The combination of veteran believability, youthful good looks, outstanding musicianship, and a talent for working around a single microphone with almost-choreographed precision made the Del McCoury Band the most popular bluegrass band at the beginning of the twenty-first century.

Like the Del McCoury Band, the groups that win the highest accolades in bluegrass music are those that convey a traditional feel, or at least pay occasional homage to the music's roots, and are able to communicate that feeling with powerful, inventive musicianship and soulful vocal harmonies. The Nashville Bluegrass Band has had significant personnel changes since it was founded in 1984, but the central trio that created the group's distinctive vocal and instrumental sound—banjoist Alan O'Bryant, guitarist Pat Enright, and fiddler Stuart Duncan—have been present almost from the beginning. Capable of playing hard-driving instrumental tunes (featuring the smooth, clear tones of Duncan's fiddle), recreating sweet brother-style vocal harmonies, or rendering note-perfect a cappella versions of old gospel songs, the Nashville Bluegrass Band built a large following with a style that fused both traditional and progressive elements.

Other popular new groups, such as IIIrd Tyme Out and the Lonesome River Band, have been similarly middle-of-the-road in their styles and selection of songs but are even more popular than the Nashville Bluegrass Band among young fans. IIIrd Tyme Out—so called because its founding members, Russell Moore, Ray Deaton, and Mike Hartgrove, played in two previous bands—entered bluegrass competition in 1991. Since 1994 they have virtually owned the IBMA's Vocal Group of the Year award, and Moore (probably the finest singer in bluegrass) has won at least two awards as the Male Vocalist of the Year. The band has always featured bedrock bluegrass fare, including stellar a cappella performances of religious pieces (a universal convention in bluegrass since Ralph Stanley introduced the practice), but they have never been reluctant to venture into non-traditional territory. Russell Moore's virtuoso version of the Platters' song "Only You" has been one of their most popular numbers.

The Lonesome River Band, originally organized in Virginia in 1983, exhibits a similar mixture of tight, inventive vocal harmonies, dynamic instrumental patterns, and skillful retooling of old-time songs to fit contemporary tastes. The band is steeped in southern musical tradition. Their banjo player, Sammy Shelor, learned a variety of old-time styles from his grandfathers, and mandolin player and tenor singer Don Rigsby inherited from his family a large repertoire of lonesome religious pieces. Featured vocalist and bass player Ronnie Bowman brought to the band a lengthy prior experience as a gospel singer. Both individually and collectively, the Lonesome River Band has been one of the most commercially successful and critically rewarded groups in bluegrass music.

While the contributions made by these all-male bands have been immeasurable, the most important new trend in the music has been what Art Menius describes as the "feminization of bluegrass." Murphy Henry (who is herself a five-string banjo player and is the chief historian of bluegrass women) argues that women have been present in this vital genre since the days of Bill Monroe's pioneering band in the mid-forties. She cites Sally Forrester, accordion player and wife of fiddler Howard Forrester, and a member of Monroe's seminal mid-forties band, as the first "bluegrass woman," although women had rarely played leading or distinctive roles in this quintessentially good-old-boys style. Since the mid-eighties, however, women in growing numbers have fronted their own bands, have achieved distinction as singers and songwriters, and have demonstrated that they can play instruments as well as or better than men.

Alison Krauss was the real groundbreaker and one of the first true superstars to emerge in the bluegrass idiom. She began experimenting with bluegrass music in about 1983, when she was only twelve years old, playing the fiddle in and around her hometown of Champaign, Illinois. By 1986 she had formed her own band, Union Station, had recorded her first album, *Too Late to Cry,* for the Rounder label, and was beginning to realize that she could sing as well as she could play. Despite the strengths of her musicianship, her singing has been her ticket to fame. With a sweet, supple, and clear voice that begs comparison with the young Dolly Parton, Krauss has won recognition far outside the bluegrass community. Although she has been richly rewarded by the IBMA and the Society for the Preservation of Bluegrass Music in America, she has also garnered Grammy awards, was inducted into the *Grand Ole Opry* in 1993 (as the youngest member ever chosen and the first bluegrass performer since 1964), has been a successful producer of other people's recordings, and was selected in 1995 as the CMA's Female Vocalist of the Year. Krauss achieved these goals without ever abandoning her acoustic-based style and without the benefit of major record label support.

No other woman bluegrass performer has ranged quite as far as Krauss, nor been so richly rewarded, but many have nonetheless made crucial contributions to the music's development and popularity. Sara Watkins, the fine young singer and fiddler for Nickel Creek, whose singing bears strong resemblance to that of Alison Krauss, has become widely known to multitudes of country music fans through the popular videos made by her group. Missy Raines has not yet attained a similar genre-bending status, but she routinely wins the IBMA's award for best bass player each year, a talent exhibited through her far-flung tours with the sensational guitarist Jim Hurst. Lynn Morris organized her own band in 1988, but only after a lengthy apprenticeship with other bands in Colorado and Virginia. This Texas-born musician originally won plaudits as a five-string banjo player, but by 1996 had won the IBMA's Female Singer of the Year award and had recorded the poignant "Mama's Hand" (written by Hazel Dickens), which won the award for Best Song of the Year.

There has been no dearth of outstanding singers among the women of bluegrass. Some of them, like Dale Ann Bradley, Hazel Dickens, Carol Elizabeth Jones, Kathy Kallick, Katie Laur, Laurie Lewis, Claire Lynch, Kate MacKenzie, Valerie Smith, Suzanne Thomas, Rhonda Vincent, and Linda Williams, have versatile voices that can successfully interpret any style of music. None of them, however, are solely vocalists. Hazel Dickens, above all, has long been recognized as one of country music's greatest songwriters. Carol Elizabeth Jones, best known for her performances with her one-time husband James Leva, is a consummate songwriter who skillfully attains a traditional feel with lyrics that address the most pressing and sometimes painful current issues. Her "The Back of Your Hand," for example, is a sensitive and subtle comment on spousal abuse. Laurie Lewis has one of the sweetest voices in bluegrass music, as well as a soulful style of fiddle playing that easily compares with any other fiddler in the genre. Rhonda Vincent's musicianship is astonishing; she plays competently almost anything with strings on it. She won the Missouri State Fiddle Contest in 1973 when she was only eleven years old, and for the next twelve years or so toured with her family's band, the Sally Mountain Show. During the late eighties, Vincent occasionally made forays into mainstream country music and even toured with Jim Ed Brown for a brief period. By the end of the nineties she had returned full-time to bluegrass, and with a strong, passionate style of singing, a superb command of mandolin, fiddle, and guitar, and intelligent selection of songs, Vincent had become one of the major artists in the field. A CD released in 2000, appropriately entitled *Back Home Again,* was universally praised as the best bluegrass album of the year. Such songs as "Jolene" (from the pen of Dolly Parton), "Lonesome Wind Blues," and "Little Angels," a powerful song about child abuse, dominated the bluegrass charts throughout the year.

Progressive bluegrass, or what has often been described as "newgrass," continued to compete with more traditional varieties of the style. Bluegrass, in fact, has incubated a large and thriving body of acoustic musicians whose stylistic experimentations have stretched the limitations of anyone's definition of the form. Such musicians as Sam Bush, John Cowan, Bela Fleck, David Grisman, Edgar Meyer, Mark O'Connor, Tony Rice, Andy Statman, and Tony Trishka are as strongly identified with jazz, blues, and rock (and even classical music, as exhibited by recordings made by O'Connor and Fleck with the legendary cellist, Yo-Yo Ma) as with the bluegrass style that once commanded their loyalties. And even a musician like Tim O'Brien, whose affection for traditional rural styles has been apparent, is just as comfortable with the music of Stephane Grappelli or Miles Davis.

The defining progressive act, the Newgrass Revival, reached its artistic peak after 1981, when Sam Bush, John Cowan, Bela Fleck, and Pat Flynn combined their talents in a reconstituted version of the group. They stayed together until 1989, always eliciting positive reviews for their jazz-inflected acoustic music but never winning the kind of commercial success for which they hoped. Bush continued to be one of the most highly sought-after musicians in country music, leading Emmylou Harris' band for a brief period and eventually playing with virtually every acoustic musician in the business. Bela Fleck took the five-string banjo to new stylistic dimensions with his Flecktones, never completely abandoning bluegrass but moving far beyond the parameters of that form.

At the beginning of the new century, the chief standard bearers of the newgrass style are an ensemble of California-born musicians known as Nickel Creek—a brother and sister team, Sean and Sara Watkins (on guitar and fiddle respectively), their long-time friend, Chris Thile (on mandolin), and varying individuals on string bass. What is truly remarkable about these accomplished musicians is that, although their ages range from eighteen to twenty-three, Thile and the Watkins have been playing together for over ten years. They first encountered bluegrass at a San Diego pizza parlor frequented by their parents, and by the time Sara and Chris were only eight years old, they were sitting in with adult musicians. They may have originally attracted attention as "cute kids holding instruments," but few musicians have evolved as rapidly as these sophisticated master stylists. In 2000 they were selected by the IBMA as Emerging Artists of the Year, and in 2001 were chosen as the organization's Instrumental Group of the Year.

Recognition within the bluegrass community (which has met with the predictable skepticism of traditionalists) has been only one facet of the group's astounding ascent. Their first album, *Nickel Creek* (appropriately produced by Alison Krauss, and released by Sugar Hill in 2000), generated more positive response in the country music world than any bluegrass CD since Krauss' own recording of 1995, *Now That I've Found You.* Nickel Creek appeared in two popular videos on CMT, saw such songs as "Reasons Why" and "When You Come Back Down" enter the *Billboard* country music popularity charts, and embarked on a whirlwind period of personal appearances (topped off by enthusiastically received concerts in 2001 at the giant acoustic celebration in North Carolina, MerleFest).

Nickel Creek's emergence marked a major departure in bluegrass history and speaks volumes about the kinds of listeners who now respond to country music. Theirs is an almost wholly urban or suburban sound. Earlier newgrass musicians, such as David Grisman, Sam Bush, and even Bela Fleck, had sometimes exhibited the need to dip back into vintage bluegrass music, but the Nickel Creek musicians have as yet paid no homage to Monroe, Flatt, or Scruggs (they in fact have no banjo in their band). A few of their songs have won acceptance in mainstream country music, but one finds no songs that carry either a rural or a working-class ambience. Nickel Creek's music instead conveys the flavor and dynamics of a jazz string quartet, tempered by a New Age sensibility, and even a touch of Christian Contemporary aesthetics. In short, it seems to be ultra-California. Each musician demonstrates a mastery of his or her respective instrument. Traditionalists may blanche at the suggestion that Chris Thile is the best mandolin player in the world (he won the IBMA's mandolin award in 2001), but he will certainly do until the best comes along. Youth and charismatic stage presence enhance his appeal, but his mandolin playing is little short of astonishing, exhibiting a seemingly effortless ability to move from a high-powered fiddle tune to a soft and sweetly nuanced love song. The Nickel Creek musicians are still discovering and shaping their voices, but their harmonies on songs like "When You Come Back Down" are impeccable, and Thile's vocal performance of "The Fox" is a tour de force. This perfectly articulated performance of the old Burl Ives folk song is a vehicle for an extended jam that synchs seamlessly into a rendition of Bob Dylan's "Subterranean Homesick Blues" and then back to the original song.

Nickel Creek's emergence reminds us that what we have seen in the past fifteen years is a contest that not only questions the meaning of country music, but also asks to whom does this music belong? Nashville does not *own* country music, even though it shapes public perceptions of what that music is. It is a terrible condescension, however, for critics to dismiss out of hand the music that emanates from Nashville studios or the Top Forty format. That music is not simply the product of a handful of musicians and producers. It is sustained by millions of listeners. To cite only one example, Tim McGraw's album *Set This Circus Down,* which leaped to the number one position on the charts during the same week of its issuance in May 2001, did not generate that meteoric rise through some kind of capitalistic conspiracy that imposed it upon thousands of unwilling fans. The hosts of fans who buy McGraw's CDs, or who faithfully attend Nashville's Fan Fair each June, find something to listen to in contemporary country music that many of us reject or simply cannot hear.

On the other hand, a big wide world of country music exists outside of Nashville that many listeners never experience. Ironically, one often has to search the "folk" or "country-rock" bins at record stores, listen to National Public Radio's *Prairie Home Companion,* or attend venues that usually cater to rock or alternative musicians to hear the music of such compelling and roots-based entertainers as Iris DeMent, Steve Earle, Rosie Flores, Jimmie Dale Gilmore, Jim Lauderdale, Buddy and Julie Miller, Allison Moorer, Jim Watson, Gillian Welch, Kelly Willis, or Robin and Linda Williams. A diligent search, however, will introduce the curious listener to vital forms of country music alive and even thriving throughout America. Cowboy music, for example, is obviously no longer available in the movies made by Hollywood or in radio serials such as those once made by Gene Autry and Roy Rogers, but such singers as Don Edwards, Red Steagall, Ian Tyson, Michael Martin Murphey, the Sons of the San Joaquin, KG and the Ranger, and the irrepressible Riders in the Sky still spin their romantic magic in the milieu of rodeo dances, cowboy poetry gatherings, and western music conventions. Eddie Stubbs is not the only disc jockey who still plays classic country records, even though his programs probably reach more people through the powerful broadcasts of WSM in Nashville (fans of traditional country music, however, were alarmed in early 2002 by ominous reports that WSM might abandon its country music format). The marvelous syndicated television show *Austin City Limits* provides a national showcase for all kinds of roots musicians who find little exposure elsewhere. Folk and bluegrass festivals not only present the music of talented professionals, they also provide a context in which devoted amateurs can commune and make music with each other. For example, Rod Kennedy's Kerrville Folk Festival, about fifty miles west of Austin, still brings musical enjoyment to thousands of people each summer while also serving as a launching pad for new singers.

Visitors to still another festival, MerleFest (founded in memory of Doc Watson's son and held each April in Wilkesboro, North Carolina), will typically hear the cream of America's acoustic musical crop. Best of all, they will see and hear the music of the nation's greatest traditional musician, Doc Watson, who otherwise now makes only infrequent tours throughout the country. Watson has become virtually an icon in American popular culture, sustained not by the country music industry, but by legions of youthful fans who admire his musicianship and integrity.

MerleFest of course is not free, and the entertainers who gather there are talented professionals. But we need to be reminded of an additional truth: country music does not belong solely to the professionals. It endures anywhere that music is made for enjoyment, self-fulfillment, or diversion—in people's homes, at festivals and workshops, in churches, in the jam sessions held in VFW and American Legion halls and other public settings, in small-town oprys and jamborees, or in the dancehalls and honky-tonks where part-time musicians seek refuge from their day jobs. In these local settings we find earnest and enthusiastic amateurs trying hard to emulate what they saw and heard on the latest Shania Twain or Tim McGraw video, as well as musicians who can sing and play every song that Bill Monroe or Hank Williams ever made. If country music endures and preserves distinctiveness, it will do so through the devoted efforts of such loyal fans and local performers.

Bibliographical Essays

Abbreviations Used

BGU	*Bluegrass Unlimited*
CMA	Country Music Association
CMF	Country Music Foundation
CSR	*Country Song Roundup*
JAF	*Journal of American Folklore*
JCM	*Journal of Country Music*
JEMF	John Edwards Memorial Foundation
JEMFQ	*John Edwards Memorial Foundation Quarterly*
MCN	*Music City News*
OTM	*Old Time Music*
SFQ	*Southern Folklore Quarterly*

1. The Folk Background before Commercialism

My approach to country music's history is predicated upon several assumptions. Among these are the belief that the phenomenon is very old, having drawn upon many cultural and ethnic sources, some of which long predate the colonization of the United States. Carl Bridenbaugh's wonderful book, *Vexed and Troubled Englishmen, 1590–1642* (New York: Oxford University Press, 1968), suggests that many of the traits, such as restlessness and the ambivalent assertion of both hedonism and Puritanism, associated with the American character (and discussed in abundance in country lyrics) were part of the cultural baggage brought by the English to American soil. In the American environment, British folk culture, which was already a composite of the shifting ethnic and racial strains of the British Isles, came into immediate contact with the cultural resources of other peoples. Above all, the close and often intimate relationship between Africans and poor white southerners gave "southern music" a distinctiveness which set it apart from music in other regions of the United States (see my *Southern Music/American Music* [Lexington: University Press of Kentucky, 1979]).

My contention that country music bears a special relationship to the South has been challenged by some scholars. Simon Bronner has been the chief spokesman for the idea of "northern country music," as exemplified in his "Country Music Culture in Central New York," *JEMFQ* 13, no. 47 (Winter 1977): 171–182. Other useful studies of country music outside the United States include Peter Narvaez, "Country Music in Diffusion: Juxtaposition and Syncretism in the Popular Music of Newfoundland," *JCM* 7, no. 2 (May 1978): 93–101; two essays by Neil Rosenberg, "Folk and Country Music in the Canadian Maritimes: A Regional Model," *JCM* 5, no. 2 (Summer 1974): 76–83, and *Country Music in the Maritimes: Two Studies*, Memorial University of Newfoundland Reprint Series No. 2 (1976); and an interesting account of non-British music which resembles its southern hillbilly counterpart, Robert Coltman, "Habitantbilly: French-Canadian Old Time Music," *OTM*, no. 11 (Winter 1973–1974): 9–12.

While recognizing that commercial country music now has a following around the world and that rural-derived forms of music still show strength in various areas of the nation, I nonetheless remain convinced that country music has always received its most fervent support—as well as the bulk of its performing personnel—in the region extending southwestward from Virginia to Texas (or in what Richard A. Peterson and Russell Davis call "The Fertile Crescent of Country Music," *JCM* 6, no. 1 [Spring 1975]: 19–25). Southern white plain folk culture—the seedbed of commercial country music—has drawn little attention from scholars, a neglect that seems even more striking when compared to the wealth of material dealing with black Americans since World War II. Nothing in the area of poor white scholarship compares to Lawrence A. Levine's masterful *Black Culture and Black Consciousness* (New York: Oxford University Press, 1977). Levine's recognition that folk culture is dynamic rather than static (adapting but not succumbing to change) and his assertion that folklore and oral history are useful tools for perceiving folk consciousness are insights that scholars of other folk cultures should find relevant to their own work. The idea that the South as a whole has been a folk culture has been most persuasively argued by David Potter in "The Enigma of the South," in his *The South and the Sectional Conflict* (Baton Rouge: Louisiana State University Press, 1968), p. 15. Cultural conservatism and an organic interrelationship with the land have been shared by both black and white southerners and, to a certain extent, by rich and poor alike. W. J. Cash's classic work *The Mind of the South* (New York: Alfred A. Knopf, 1941) implies the existence of a common folk culture (although he does not use the term) when he talks of the subtle ways in which blacks and whites have influenced each other. He also convincingly demonstrates that the rich diversity of the South did not prevent southerners from sharing a set of assumptions and cultural traits that would have been familiar from Virginia to Texas. Many factors contributed to the shaping of this commonality of thought and behavior, but its preservation and extension were insured by the tendency of southerners to migrate to areas where their familiar way of life and the cultivation of cotton could be continued. This migration tended to be southwestward in nature, as demonstrated by Frank Owsley in "The Pattern of Migration and Settlement of the Southern Frontier," *Journal of Southern History* 19 (1945): 147–176, and by Barnes F. Lathrop in *Migration into East Texas, 1835–1860: A Study from the United States Census* (Austin: University of Texas Press, 1949).

Frank Owsley and the students who studied under him at Vanderbilt long held a monopoly on the study of southern plain whites. His *Plain Folk of the Old South* (Baton Rouge: Louisiana State University Press, 1949) contained excellent social portraits of plain people but was somewhat marred by a tendency to romanticize its subjects and by a strained effort to show that the plain folk were neither poor nor class-conscious (most of them, argued Owsley, owned land or otherwise had access to the bountiful southern public domain). George Pullen Jackson, in the best work yet written on southern folk music, *White Spirituals in the Southern Uplands* (Chapel Hill: University of North Carolina Press, 1933), does not address himself to the question of class consciousness or conflict, but he does demonstrate that urban-rural antagonisms have affected cultural/musical preferences in the South. Thomas D. Clark, in his impressively researched and fact-filled *Pills, Petticoats, and Plows: The Southern Country Store* (Norman: University of Oklahoma Press, 1944), comes closer than any other historian to re-creating the daily lives of nineteenth-century rural southerners. His study of the ubiquitous credit nexus, which governed southern economic relations throughout that century and much of the next, shows that an allegedly isolated rural South was in fact connected to the outside world in various insidious ways. Grady McWhiney and Forrest McDonald see unity in still another realm, and one which relates southerners not only to each other, but also to a dim and ancient historical past: Celticism. In a series of articles and public presentations, but most cogently in "The Antebellum Southern Herdsman, a Reinterpretation," *Journal of Southern History* 41, no. 2 (May 1975): 147–167, McWhiney and McDonald reaffirm Owsley's assertions of an abundant and classless folk society, but go a step beyond him to argue that the most binding ingredient of the Old South was the common Celtic heritage shared by most white southerners. Preponderantly Scotch-Irish, white southerners according to this theory were clannish, fiercely independent, given to rash and impulsive action, and slovenly in their agricultural practices (because they preferred open-range stock raising to husbandry). Celticism has obvious implications for the understanding of southern folk music, but thus far, although McWhiney and McDonald have promoted it often and with great passion, Celticism remains a theory in search of supportive data.

McWhiney and McDonald's Celtic theorizing is part of a reawakening of interest in the southern plain folk that gives promise of blossoming into a full-scale scholarly enterprise. Steven Hahn's provocative *The Roots of Southern Populism: Yeoman Farmers and the Transformation of the Georgia Upcountry, 1850–1890* (New York: Oxford University Press, 1983) and J. Wayne Flynt's *Dixie's Forgotten People: The South's Poor Whites* (Bloomington: Indiana University Press, 1979) will probably be catalysts in the investigation of all realms of poor white life and culture. Unlike Owsley's conservative orientation, their books are informed by the liberal consciousness of our own time and by the belief that scholarship can promote the cause of social justice. Flynt believes, for example, that many southern whites have been and still are poor, but that their culture (religion, music, folkways) has been a sustaining force for them and a phenomenon worthy of the respect of the rest of us. Flynt and his wife, Dorothy S. Flynt, have prepared a useful resource guide for students of plain folk culture: *Southern Poor Whites: A Selected, Annotated Bibliography of Published Sources* (New York: Garland Publishing, 1981).

Music has indeed been a constant presence in the lives of southern plain folk, or what we would now call the working class. A study of country music, then, should not begin in the 1920's when the first recordings were made, but instead should encompass the entire span of southern history. The pre-commercial and pre–twentieth-century manifestations of rural music should be studied with the same care devoted to other aspects of southern culture. Travel accounts will surely tell us something about revival singing, house parties, fiddle contests, or itinerant balladeers; country store ledgers, as Thomas Clark has already suggested, will provide information on the purchase of songbooks and musical instruments; plantation records and diaries, although generally the property of the upper classes, sometime make mention of rural musicians; deeds, wills, and property settlements might itemize fiddles and banjos; and newspapers will give occasional hints about music among the common folk. Newspapers, it is true, usually gave most of their attention to the polite music of the gentry (balls, soirées, recitals), but on occasion music of a plainer sort received at least brief coverage; the earliest accounts of fiddle contests in America, for example, were carried in the *Virginia Gazette* in the 1730's. Since rowdy behavior sometimes accompanied public performances of music, court and police records might pay unexpected dividends to music historians. The literary fiction that dealt with poor whites in the nineteenth century—

the Southwestern Humor of the antebellum period and the Local Color of the postwar years—should also be mined for the musical nuggets that might lie there. The most famous work in the genre, Augustus Baldwin Longstreet's *Georgia Scenes*, published in 1835 (but based upon earlier newspaper stories), describes a country dance in terms remarkably similar to accounts of such phenomena one hundred years later (reprinted, Atlanta: Cherokee Publishing Company, 1971). While fiction provides glimpses of rural/folk music, graphic representations may tell us even more. Archie Green has been reminding readers of the *JEMFQ* for several years, in his Music Graphics series, that placards, posters, handbills, genre art like that of William Sidney Mount, Currier and Ives lithographs, magazine illustrations, and a host of other popular arts forms will enhance our understanding of American folk music (see, for example, the sketch of a rowdy dance in Denison, Texas, accompanied by a fiddle and guitar, in *Scribner's Monthly*, July 1873, and reprinted in *JEMFQ* 14, no. 30 [Summer 1978: 84]).

When delving into the pre–twentieth-century history of southern music, it is difficult to separate "rural" from "urban" music, chiefly because few people then made those kinds of distinctions. One also finds that the border between "popular" and "folk" music was often tenuous and that commercialization has never been a stranger to folk music. Talented folk musicians have always sought audiences (or audiences have sought them), and their performances have always been rewarded in some manner. Accounts of English medieval fairs, public hangings, or any large event where large groups congregated, as well as of wayfaring people, circuses, puppet shows, equestrian exhibitions, medicine shows, and taverns, abound with references to pipers, fiddlers, dancers, balladeers, and broadside vendors. This is a rich area of research that awaits music historians, and I will list only a few of the works that have been useful to me: Bridenbaugh's *Vexed and Troubled Englishmen*, W. Chappell, *Songs from Olden Times* (London: Chappell, 1838); Charles Read Baskervill, *The Elizabethan Jig* (Chicago: University of Chicago Press, 1929); Vuillier Gaston, *A History of Dancing* (New York: D. Appleton and Company, 1898); George Speaight, *The History of the English Puppet Theatre* (London: George G. Harrap and Company, 1955); J. J. Jusserand, *English Wayfaring Life* (originally published in 1889, republished in New York, 1950); Isaac Greenwood, *The Circus: Its Origin and Growth Prior to 1835* (New York: Dunlap Society, 1898); and Julian Mates, *The American Musical Stage before 1800* (New Brunswick, N.J.: Rutgers University Press, 1962).

While some names are known to us, such as that of the great Philadelphia hornpipe dancer of the late eighteenth century, John Durang, or that of the famous English equestrian, John Bill Ricketts, who danced hornpipes on the backs of galloping horses, most of the dancers and musicians who roamed through antebellum America will always remain anonymous. Whether urban professionals or rural folk, they both absorbed and disseminated music in the American hinterlands, so much so that much of the music emanating from the eighteenth and nineteenth centuries has no clear folk or popular identity. Indeed, some of the music and much of the dancing came from upper-class and even courtly sources. The student of old-time fiddling will reap a rich harvest of information by exploring John Playford's *English Dancing Master* (first published in 1651), or Gaston's *A History of Dancing*, or even such "high-art" music magazines as *Etude* or *Musical America. Jacobs Orchestra Monthly*, an unlikely source for country music, contains some of the best explications of such items as "hoedown," "hornpipe," and "breakdown" that I have yet found (I have seen the issues for 1910 and 1911).

The traveling shows of course contributed immeasurably to the dissemination of songs and dances among rural Americans. Little published work has appeared on the equestrian acts, circuses, and puppet shows that traveled through America during the colonial and early national periods, but all of them featured music in the form of fiddlers, hornpipe dancers, and singing clowns. The ubiquitous medicine shows, however, which traveled the length and breadth of rural America by wagon and by flatboat, have found a chronicler in Brooks McNamara, *Step Right Up: An Illustrated History of the Medicine Show* (Garden City, N.Y.: Doubleday, 1976). Black-face minstrelsy, which contributed songs, dances, comedy, and instrumental styles to country music, has received extensive scholarly attention: an older work, Carl F. Wittke, *Tambo and Bones* (Durham, N.C.: Duke University Press, 1930), still has merit as a factual account of the phenomenon, but it has been superseded by Hans Nathan, *Dan Emmett and the Rise of Early Negro Minstrelsy* (Norman: University of Oklahoma Press, 1962); William W. Austin, *Susanna, Jeanie, and the Old Folks at Home: The Songs of Stephen C. Foster from His Own Time to Ours* (New York: Macmillan, 1975); and Robert C. Toll, *Blacking Up: The Minstrel Show in Nineteenth-Century America* (New York: Oxford University Press, 1974). Rural Americans who ventured into town in the late nineteenth and early twentieth centuries had an opportunity to absorb the music of the vaudeville shows, discussed by Gilbert Douglas, *American Vaudeville* (New York: Dover Publications, 1963), and Albert F. McLean, Jr., *American Vaudeville as Ritual* (Lexington: University of Kentucky Press, 1965), but they also encountered another approach to vaudeville in the traveling tent shows that came to rural America. The tent-repertory shows, or Toby shows (named after the red-wigged country boy character who appeared in many of them), have elicited much recent attention in the form of theses and dissertations, and at least two published works: Neil E. Schaffner, with Vance Johnson, *The Fabulous Toby and Me* (Englewood Cliffs, N.J.: Prentice-Hall, 1968), and William Lawrence Slout, *Theatre in a Tent* (Bowling Green, Ohio: Bowling Green Popular Press, 1972).

Sheet music was the source of much early country music (and in fact for many of the songs still heard today in bluegrass music). The collections of published music preserved in the Library of Congress and in other repositories, such as the New York Public Library and the William R. Hogan Jazz Archive at Tulane University, have been insufficiently utilized by scholars, but several published works suggest the utility of such research for the understanding of country music. Sigmund Spaeth often wrote with tongue in cheek when he discussed the sentimental songs of yesteryear, but in *Read 'Em and Weep* (New York: Doubleday, Page, 1926) and *Weep Some More My Lady* (New York: Doubleday, Page, 1927), he compiled valuable lists of many songs that not only made Americans cry but in many cases were eventually preserved in the country music repertory. Edward B. Marks, the cowriter of "My Mother Was a Lady," provides further insight into the reasons why such songs were written and tells how they moved out into the hinterlands in his memoir, *They All Sang* (New York: Viking Press, 1934). A few scholars have since begun to recognize the value of the "parlor songs" as a means of understanding the popular mind. Nicholas E. Tawa discusses the phenomenon for antebellum America in *Sweet Songs for Gentle Americans: The Parlor Song in America, 1790–1860* (Bowling Green, Ohio: Popular Press, 1980), but Norm Cohen has more clearly shown the relationship between nineteenth-century pop music and folk songs in "Tin Pan Alley's Contribution to Folk Music," *Western Folklore* 29, no. 1 (1970): 9–20. He and Anne Cohen also speculated on the way in which pop tunes were altered once they moved into the possession of the folk: "Tune Evolution as an Indicator of Traditional Musical Norms," *JAF* 86, no. 339 (January–March 1973): 37–47. Gene Wiggins conclusively demonstrated country fiddling's debt to turn-of-the-century pop music in "Popular Music and the Fiddler," *JEMFQ* 15, no. 55 (Fall 1979): 144–152, while William C. Ellis illustrated how one specific but powerful element of the sentimental tradition endured in country music: "The Sentimental Mother Song in American Country Music, 1923–1945" (Ph.D. dissertation, Ohio State University, 1978). A vast literature of printed material—on sheet music, in song folios or songsters, in magazines and newspapers (such as the *Dallas Semi-Weekly Farm News*, where old songs were printed at the request of readers)—still awaits the researcher, as does the music distributed on piano rolls, in music boxes, and on early phonograph recordings. Norm Cohen has made a valuable contribution to our understanding of the link between pop and country music in a record collection which he produced and annotated: *Minstrels and Tunesmiths: The Commercial Roots of Early Country Music* (JEMF 109), an assemblage of songs recorded between 1902 and 1923.

Another powerful source of country music, and one which has affected both its style and content, is religion. Our venture into religion should properly begin with the dissenting Protestant sects who began populating the southern backcountry before the American Revolution. Much of their history—and particularly their songmaking—will forever be lost to us, but Donald G. Mathews, in *Religion in the Old South* (Chicago: University of Chicago Press, 1977), and Rhys Isaac, in *The Transformation of Virginia, 1740–1790* (Chapel Hill: University of North Carolina Press, 1982), tell us how they came to command the allegiance of most black and white southerners. The institution which most effectively evangelized the South, while also giving it over to the Baptists and Methodists and contributing to its staunch orthodoxy, was the camp meeting. Every student of the meetings comments on the powerful appeal of the music heard there—Charles A. Johnson, *the Frontier Camp Meeting: Religious Harvest Time* (Dallas: Southern Methodist University Press, 1955); Bernard Weisberger, *They Gathered at the River: The Story of the Great Revivalists and Their Impact upon Religion in America* (Boston: Little, Brown, 1958); John Boles, *The Great Revival, 1787–1805: The Origins of the Southern Evangelical Mind* (Lexington: University Press of Kentucky, 1972); and Dickson Bruce, Jr., *And They All Sang Hallelujah: Plain-Folk Camp Meeting Religion, 1800–1845* (Knoxville: University of Tennessee Press, 1974)—but Bruce is the only historian who has tried to make music the central focus of his study. He argues that the choruses of the songs—improvised on the spot in order to encourage rapid learning and mass singing—are repositories of plain-folk theology.

The classic study of shape-note music and the singing schools which introduced the method to several generations of rural southerners is George Pullen Jackson, *White Spirituals in the Southern Uplands* (Chapel Hill: University of North Carolina Press, 1933). Every study of the shape-note style that has since been published is indebted to Jackson's pioneering work. Among the more significant of these works are Harry Eskew, "Shape-Note Hymnody in the Shenandoah Valley, 1816–1860" (Ph.D. dissertation, Tulane University, 1966), and Rachel Augusta Harley, "Ananias Davisson: Southern Tunebook Compiler" (Ph.D. dissertation, University of Michigan, 1972). The highly individualistic and conservative Sacred Harp tradition, named after one of the most famous of the shape-note songbooks, has been studied in Charles Linwood Ellington, "The Sacred Harp Tradition of the South: Its Origin and Evolution" (Ph.D. dissertation, Florida State University, 1969), and in Buell E. Cobb, Jr., *The Sacred Harp and Its Music* (Athens: University of Georgia Press, 1978).

Southern gospel music has been inadequately documented. James C. Downey touches upon the subject in "The Music of American Revivalism" (Ph.D. dissertation, Tulane University, 1968), and Jo Fleming has written an excellent account of the Vaughan Publishing Company, the Lawrenceburg, Tennessee, concern which pioneered in the use of traveling quartets: "James D. Vaughan, Music Publisher" (S.M.D. dissertation, Union Theological Seminary, 1972). The music of the Pentecostal movement has elicited no systematic study, a deficiency which progressively becomes more acute as the years pass and the founding fathers and mothers die. David Edwin Harrell, *All Things Are Possible: The Healing and Charismatic Revivals of Modern America* (Bloomington: Indiana University Press, 1975), is a superior study of Pentecostalism's resurgence since World War II, while Robert Mapes Anderson, *Vision of the Disinherited: The Making of American Pentecostalism* (New York: Oxford, 1979), is the best overall history of the phenomenon. Neither historian, though, says much about music. The deficiency may soon be rectified, because a doctoral candidate in music education at Kent State University, Larry T. Duncan, began a history of music in the Pentecostal movement in late 1983. There are also two short essays dealing with the influence of Pentecostalism on individual musicians: Van K. Brock, "Assemblies of God: Elvis and Pentecostalism," *Bulletin of the Center for the Study of Southern Culture and Religion* 3 (June 1979): 9–15; and Stephen R. Tucker, "Pentecostalism and Popular Culture in the South: A Study of Four Musicians," *Journal of Popular Culture* 16, no. 3 (Winter 1982): 68–81. (The four musicians discussed are James Blackwood, Tammy Wynette, Johnny Cash, and Jerry Lee Lewis). Except for Jo Fleming's study of James D. Vaughan, the history of the gospel quartet business has also been largely ignored. Lois Blackwell has written a much too brief and sketchy overview of the subject in *The Wings of the Dove: The Story of Gospel Music in America* (Norfolk, Va.: Donning Company, 1978), while the best academic treatment thus far has not been published: Stanley H. Brobston, "A Brief History of White Southern Gospel Music and a Study of Selected Amateur Family Gospel Singing Groups in Rural Georgia" (Ph.D. dissertation, New York University, 1977). A multitude of shape-note hymnals and revivalistic songbooks still await the investigation of some scholar who would explore them for an understanding of southern folk theology.

To find the sources of the songs that comprised the early country music repertory, we should therefore search the gospel hymnals, the sheet music and songsters of the nineteenth century, the phonograph recordings that became available at the turn of the century, and the vast panoply of folk resources that surrounded rural singers (we should be aware, however, that rural musicians sometimes learned songs from published folk music collections). In the realm of traditional ballads, scholars have usually begun with the magisterial collection of Francis James Child, *The English and Scottish Popular Ballads*, 5 vols. (Boston: Houghton, Mifflin, 1882–1898), a work which has influenced all subsequent collectors. Leslie Shepard, however, has probably come closest to explaining the type of British ballad which actually made the transit of the Atlantic in *The Broadside Ballad: A Study in Origin and Meaning* (London: Herbert Jenkins, 1962). The best attempts to assess the actual number of Child and broadside ballads which survived in America are Tristram P. Coffin,

The British Traditional Ballad in North America, rev. ed. (Philadelphia: American Folklore Society, 1963), and G. Malcolm Laws, Jr., *American Balladry from British Broadsides* (Philadelphia: American Folklore Society, 1957). Although the Child ballads are highly venerated by scholars, Norm Cohen and Guthrie Meade suggest that few of them wound up on early hillbilly records: "The Sources of Old Time Hillbilly Music, I: Child Ballads," *JEMFQ* 9, Part 2, no. 30 (Summer 1973): 56–61. Printed folksong collections abound, but the two general compendiums which come closest to reflecting the varied tastes of the folk (rather than that of the collector) are *The Frank C. Brown Collection of North Carolina Folklore*, edited by Henry M. Belden and Arthur Palmer Hudson, 7 vols. (Durham: Duke Unversity, 1952), and Vance Randolph, *Ozark Folksongs*, 4 vols. (Columbia: State Historical Society of Missouri, 1950); revised by Norm Cohen in a one-volume edition (Urbana: University of Illinois Press, 1982). Arthur Palmer Hudson reminds us that preferences for folk songs were pretty much the same throughout the rural South: "Folk Songs of the Southern Whites," in *Culture in the South*, edited by W. T. Couch (Chapel Hill: University of North Carolina Press, 1934). Alan Lomax, *The Folk Songs of North America* (New York: Doubleday and Company, 1960), is still the best one-volume collection available, and is distinguished by the provocative theorizing and annotations of its compiler. The old songs come alive in the field recordings made for the Archive of Folk Song at the Library of Congress. This collection has been insufficiently utilized, even though many of the recordings are offered for public sale.

Old versions of songs can be reproduced, but our understanding of the ways in which they were performed can never be anything more than speculative. No sound recordings were made until the 1880's, and folk musicians were not recorded in any substantial numbers until the 1920's— approximately two hundred years after the first tentative settlements were made in the southern backcountry. We might assume that some of the old people living in the deep and sheltered recesses of the southern mountains, and recorded in the decades after World War I, had preserved the singing styles of their ancestors, but we can never know conclusively. And most hypothesizing about vocal and instrumental styles has been based upon twentieth-century observations. Alan Lomax has made the boldest assertions about style in *The Folk Songs of North America* and in "Folk Song Style," *American Anthropologist* 61, no. 6 (December 1959): 927–955, where he stresses the conservatism of style and contrasts the repressed, tight-throat style of the whites with the expressive, open-throated singing of the blacks. Roger Abrahams and George Foss concentrate on white singing exclusively in *Anglo-American Folksong Style* (Englewood Cliffs, N.J.: Prentice-Hall, 1968), but none of these authorities, it seems to me, has sufficiently recognized that there are not one but many styles of folksinging. The best brief exposition of vocal and instrumental styles is a record anthology, *Going Down the Valley*, New World Records NW236 (edited and annotated by Norm Cohen).

D. K. Wilgus, in the record reviews he wrote for the *Kentucky Folklore Record* and *Journal of American Folklore*, and Norm and Anne Cohen, in "Folk and Hillbilly Music: Further Thoughts on Their Relation," *JEMFQ* 13, no. 46 (Summer 1977): 50–57, use the terms "domestic" and "assembly" to describe the two kinds of performance featured by folk musicians (home-centered and usually vocal music as opposed to the music performed instrumentally for a group of listeners or dancers). The assembly tradition, also called "display" by Richard Spottswood in vol. 14 of the record collection *Folk Music in America* (Library of Congress), has stimulated the interest of many scholars and enthusiasts. Fiddling, for example, is the central focus of a magazine called *The Devil's Box*, published in Madison, Alabama, by the Tennessee Valley Old Time Fiddlers Association, and is the subject of several good articles and academic theses: Linda C. Burman-Hall, "Southern American Folk Fiddle Tunes," *Ethnomusicology* 19 (January 1975): 47–65; Earl V. Spielman, "Traditional American Fiddling: An Historical and Comparative Analytical Style Study" (Ph.D dissertation, University of Wisconsin); Michael Mendelson, "A Bibliography of Fiddling in North America," which ran for several issues in *JEMFQ*, beginning with vol. 11, no. 38 (Summer 1975); John Burke, "Country Fiddling," *Bluegrass Unlimited* 6, no. 10 (April 1972): 17–20; and Barret E. Hansen, "The American Country Waltz," *JEMFQ* 5, Part 1, no. 13 (Spring 1969): 4–6. S. Foster Damon, "The History of Square Dancing," *Proceedings of the American Antiquarian Society* 62 (April 1952): 63–98, is not concerned with fiddling as such, but it does discuss one of the important milieus in which the fiddle held sway.

Other instruments and instrumental styles have not been quite as appealing to scholars as has the art of old-time fiddling. The mandolin, though, has been the subject of a doctoral dissertation by Scott Hambly, "Mandolins in the United States since 1880: An Industrial and Sociocultural History of Form" (Ph.D dissertation, University of Pennsylvania, 1977), and I have found some information on early Italian masters of the instrument in scattered music magazines such as *Etude* 61, no. 2 (February 1938): 127. The mandolin-banjo-guitar club craze early in the twentieth century inspired the formation of a few journals, such as *Gatcomb's Banjo and Guitar Gazette, Cadenza,* and *Crescendo,* which promoted the mandolin and other string instruments. Mail-order catalogues, like Sears-Roebuck and Montgomery Ward, made inexpensive brands available to the rural and small-town public.

Very little has been done on pre–twentieth-century string-band music as a whole, although Archie Green has made some interesting tentative observations in "String Bands," *JEMFQ* 15, no. 56 (Winter 1979): 215–224. The banjo has aroused the curiosity of Americans since at least 1784, when Thomas Jefferson referred to the "banjar" in *Notes on the State of Virginia*. Dena Epstein has documented the instrument's existence among American blacks, though, as early as 1754, in "The Folk Banjo: A Documentary History," *Ethnomusicology* 19 (September 1975): 347–371, and in *Sinful Tunes and Spirituals: Black Folk Music to the Civil War* (Urbana: University of Illinois Press, 1977), p. 36. The addition of the fifth string and Joel Walker Sweeney's alleged contribution to the innovation are explored in Jay Bailey, "Historical Origin and Stylistic Development of the Five-String Banjo," *JAF* 85, no. 335 (January–March 1972): 58–65. Robert B. Winans sees a direct link between the banjo styles favored by blackface minstrels and the early frailing techniques of country musicians: "The Folk, the Stage and the Five-String Banjo in the Nineteenth Century," *JAF* 89, no. 354 (1976): 423–428.

The discovery of southern folk music came about in the late nineteenth and early twentieth centuries, first with the vogue of spirituals in the 1870's, and later with the discovery of cowboy music and the romantic revelation of still-surviving ballad and folksong culture in the southern mountains. I have discussed these successive discoveries in *Southern Music/American Music*, pp. 18–41, while Henry Shapiro, *Appalachia on Our Mind: The Southern Mountains and Mountaineers in the American Consciousness, 1890–1920* (Chapel Hill: University of North Carolina Press, 1978), and, preeminently, David Whisnant, *All Things Native and Fine: The Politics of Culture in an American Region* (Chapel Hill: University of North Carolina Press, 1983), have explored more comprehensively the roots of our romantic fascination with mountain culture. No book surpasses Whisnant's in its discussion of the role played by settlement workers in the shaping of public perceptions of mountain music. This essay should not be concluded without mentioning the names of three men who contributed immeasurably to a national awakening to the immense wealth of southern folk music: John Lomax, with his *Cowboy Songs and Other Frontier Ballads* (New York: Sturgis and Walton, 1910); Cecil Sharp, *Folk Songs from the Southern Appalachians* (London: Oxford University Press, 1917); and Robert Winslow Gordon, whose early recording expeditions provided the nucleus for the Archive of Folk Song's great collection (a sampling of this material can be heard in Neil V. Rosenberg and Debora G. Kodish, eds., *Folk-Songs of America: The Robert Winslow Gordon Collection, 1922–1932*, Library of Congress, AFS L681 1978).

2. The Early Period Of Commercial Hillbilly Music

The study of country music's early commercial period has been much enhanced by the establishment of two impressive repositories: the Country Music Library and Media Center at the Country Music Foundation

(CMF) in Nashville, and the John Edwards Memorial Foundation (JEMF), once located on the campus of UCLA but now being transferred to the University of North Carolina at Chapel Hill. Both libraries contain enormous collections of phonograph recordings, tapes, videos, songbooks and folios, magazines, brochures, placards, assorted ephemera associated with the music industry, and interviews conducted with musicians and music industry people. These depositories, however, do not contain complete runs of certain journals; the Country Music Library's collection of *Billboard*, for example, begins only in 1939. Other issues dating back to the early 1900's must be sought in other libraries, such as that of the University of Texas in Austin where I did my own study, or purchased on microfilm. Other important early journals, such as *Talking Machine World*, can be found at the Library of Congress. In any event, the Union List of Serials should be consulted by anyone who seeks to run down an early music or entertainment publication.

Except for occasional picture-songbooks printed at private expense (usually by radio stations or by the entertainers themselves), or song folios of the type sold by Bradley Kincaid on WLS, virtually no magazines devoted to country music were published during the twenties. The researcher, then, must look for tidbits wherever they can be found, in *Billboard* or *Variety* (where hillbilly musicians were rarely mentioned), in *Talking Machine World*, in *Radio Digest* and other short-lived broadcasting journals, in popular magazines and newspapers (where radio logs were often carried), in record company brochures and advertisements, and in mail-order catalogues where records and musical instruments were advertised.

The best source for the music of the twenties, of course, is the old 78 rpm records themselves. Many of them are on deposit at the CMF Library and JEMF, and an extensive number have been commercially reissued by the phonograph companies, by foundations or institutions such as the Smithsonian, or by private collectors. (See Willie Smyth, *Country Music Recorded Prior to 1943: A Discography of LP Reissues,* JEMF Special Series, no. 13.) Printed versions can be found in surviving songbooks from the period, or in newly published versions transcribed directly from the old records. The New Lost City Ramblers, a folk revival band from New York City, reintroduced many of the songs in their concerts and also edited a fine collection of songs called *The New Lost City Ramblers Song Book,* edited by Mike Seeger and John Cohen (New York: Oak Publications, 1964). The English researcher Tony Russell has long been at work on a discography that will include every hillbilly recording made in America between 1922 and 1940. This ambitious project will be the greatest boon to country music scholarship yet made.

When scholars made their first hesitant entries into the field of country music, they found their work seriously hampered by the lack of readily available source material. Many of the old-time performers had died, and few, if any, had left any kind of papers or memoirs. The recording companies had maintained few files on their performing personnel and would disclose little information on the amount of record sales through the years. No reputable scholarly publication had considered country music worthy of attention. That the task of chronicling country music's significance and development has not been completely insurmountable is owed to a band of devoted hillbilly-music enthusiasts, unnoticed and unsung, who had been painstakingly gathering materials for decades. With little or no scholarly training, and with no motive other than a love for the music and a feeling that the older traditions should be memorialized, these individuals labored indefatigably to compile both discographical and biographical data on country performers. A veritable network of hillbilly-record collectors, not only in the United States but in countries such as England, Australia, Canada, and Japan, gathered the old records and songbooks and exchanged tapes and information with each other. Such people as Dave Wylie, Doug Jydstrup, Harlan Daniel, Joe Bussard, Gus Meade, Joe Hickerson, Will Roy Hearne, Peter Kuykendall, Joe Nicholas, Lou Deneumoustier, Eugene Earle, John Edwards, Garth Gibson, Fred Hoeptner, Bob Pinson, and Richard K. Spottswood, who were in no sense trained folklorists, used their private funds and all the available time at their disposal to search through radio stations, record shops, flea markets, and junk stores for the out-of-print records of earlier years. They conducted the same kind of diligent, and often fruitless, search for information about the lives and careers of the old-time performers. They maintained contact with each other through newsletters and auction lists, and through such mimeographed journals as *Disc Collector, Country Directory, Blue Yodeler*, and *Country and Western Spotlight* (a New Zealand publication). These magazines are treasure troves of recording data and biographical sketches.

Scholars had never totally ignored hillbilly music, but they had devoted most of their attention to uncommercialized folk music, not realizing that many of their collected items had begun life on hillbilly records, or had been picked up by hillbilly singers from folk sources. Although much more work needs to be done on this important subject, Ed Kahn, in an excellent exploratory article, "Hillbilly Music: Source and Resource," *JAF* 78, no. 309 (July–September 1965): 257–266, has pointed to the limited, but pioneering, scholarship done by such folklorists and scholars as Herbert Halpert, Guy B. Johnson, and Howard Odum on the relationship between traditional song and commercial recordings. Alan Lomax has done similar work. As early as 1934 he and his father (John A. Lomax) began transcribing and publishing texts and tunes from commercial records, many of which were included in *American Ballads and Folk Songs* (New York: Macmillan Company, 1934). Not until 1947, however, did a discographic appendix appear in a standard folk song collection: John A. Lomax and

Alan Lomax, eds., *Folk Song, U.S.A.* (New York: Duell, Sloan and Pearce, 1947). Alan Lomax had earlier recognized the importance of commercial recordings and in 1940 had issued what was intended to be merely an introductory guide to the subject: *List of American Folk Songs on Commercial Records,* in *Report of the Committee of the Conference on Inter-American Relations in the Field of Music, William Berrien, Chairman* (Washington, D.C.: Department of State, September 1940). In 1948, Charles Seeger reviewed in the *Journal of American Folklore* a number of hillbilly and race recordings that had been released in previous years, marking the first time that the country's major scholarly folk publication had admitted the existence, or relevance, of commercial country music: "Reviews," *JAF* 61, no. 240 (April–June 1948): 215–218.

D. K. Wilgus was probably the first folklorist to make hillbilly records the subject of an academic thesis, "A Catalogue of American Folksongs on Commercial Records" (M.A. thesis, Ohio State University, 1947). In the late fifties Wilgus, as editor of the *Kentucky Folklore Record* at Western Kentucky State College, and later as director of the Center for the Study of Comparative Folklore and Mythology at UCLA, continued to stress the relationship between folk and hillbilly music. His record reviews in Kentucky and for *JAF* made the study of phonograph records a respectable aspect of folklore scholarship. John Greenway, anthropologist and folklorist at the University of Colorado, made scattered comments about a few hillbillies like Jimmie Rodgers, Merle Travis, and the Carter Family in his *American Folk Songs of Protest* (Philadelphia: University of Pennsylvania Press, 1953), and in 1957 his essay on Jimmie Rodgers became the first article on hillbilly music to appear in a scholarly journal: "Jimmie Rodgers—a Folksong Catalyst," *JAF* 70, no. 277 (July–September 1957): 231–235. In the late fifties Archie Green, who was then Associate Professor of Labor and Industrial Relations at the University of Illinois and an authority on labor/protest music, also moved into the study of hillbilly music, recognizing that commercial recordings were valuable repositories of working-class life and lore. Since that time the indefatigable and insatiably curious Green has become America's most authoritative scholar of country music. Wilgus, Greenway, Green, and Ed Kahn (who was then preparing a doctoral thesis on the Carter Family at UCLA), constituted the nucleus of a small but growing fraternity that recognized country music's distinctive position within American folk music, and one whose ranks was enlarged by the enthusiasm generated by the folk revival of the early sixties. One of the most impressive results of their intellectual labors, and for the student the most important introduction to the scholarly study of country music, is the "Hillbilly Issue" of the *Journal of American Folklore: JAF* 78, no. 309 (July–September 1965). This landmark issue, specially edited by John Greenway and D. K. Wilgus, was devoted exclusively to country music and included articles by each of the scholars previously mentioned along with two by new researchers to the field, Norm Cohen and L. Mayne Smith.

Country music scholarship has definitely blossomed since the early sixties, and has moved away from the domain of ephemeral and mimeographed journals. Three journals with scholarly orientation now provide outlets for writers and historians: the *JEMF Quarterly, Old Time Music,* (edited by Tony Russell in England), and the *Journal of Country Music,* the organ of the CMF in Nashville. Each journal accepts articles from both popular and academic sources, but *JEMFQ* is most catholic in its receptivity to non-country music scholarship (much to the dismay of some of its subscribers). *JCM* and *JEMFQ* accept material on both old-time and modern country music, while *OTM* rarely moves past the World War II era.

When my research began in 1961 for the first edition of this book, no repositories were yet in existence, and no scholarly journal made country music its area of concern. Only a relative handful of works on country music had been published: Ruth Sheldon's biography of Bob Wills, *Hubbin' It: The Life of Bob Wills* (Tulsa: privately published, 1938); Carrie "Mrs. Jimmie" Rodgers, *My Husband Jimmie Rodgers* (San Antonio: Southern Literary Institute, 1935); George D. Hay, *Story of the Grand Ole Opry* (Nashville: privately published, 1953); William R. McDaniel and Harold Seligman, *Grand Ole Opry* (New York: Greenberg, 1952); and Linnell Gentry, ed., *A History and Encyclopedia of Country, Western, and Gospel Music* (Nashville: McQuiddy Press, 1961). Apart from the occasional articles which appeared in popular magazines and newspapers, as well as the rather light and journalistic accounts found in song magazines and fan journals (almost none of which dated back to the twenties), little reliable material was available. I depended heavily on *Disc Collector, Country Directory, Country and Western Spotlight* (especially the articles written by John Edwards), and on the advice freely granted by Bob Pinson and Archie Green. The Sears-Roebuck and Montgomery Ward catalogues were useful compendiums of records, songbooks, and musical instruments. Record catalogues and brochures, records and liner notes, newspaper radio logs, *Billboard* magazines, publications that issued forth from the folk revival (such as *Sing Out* and *Little Sandy Review*), and Gentry's assemblage of reprinted articles in *A History and Encyclopedia of Country, Western, and Gospel Music*, constituted the bulk of my original research.

The discussion that follows reflects the scholarship that appeared both before and after the first edition of this book. If it is more extensive than some of the other chapter bibliographical essays, it is because the "folkness" of the early commercial music has generated more scholarship than the more recent manifestations of country music.

The social context of the twenties, which encouraged both the exploitation and the rejection of rural culture, is discussed in a variety of works.

Frederick Lewis Allen's *Only Yesterday* (New York: Harper and Brothers, 1931), though dated in some respects, is still a useful introduction to the period. A study which appeared in the early thirties, President's Research Committee on Social Trends, *Recent Social Trends in the United States* (New York: McGraw-Hill Book Company, 1933), documented some of the lasting innovations of the era. George Tindall, on the other hand, concentrated on the Ku Klux Klan and other negative factors which gave the South a bad reputation during the decade in "The Benighted South: Origins of a Modern Image," *Virginia Quarterly Review* 40 (Spring 1964): 281–294, and in *The Emergence of the New South, 1913–1945* (Baton Rouge: Louisiana State University Press, 1967). No one better epitomized the ambivalence of the era than Henry Ford, who propelled the nation into a new industrial age with his wonderful machine while simultaneously clinging to the values and prejudices of an earlier rural society. Ford, the fundamentalist and conservative farm boy, is discussed by Allan Nevins and Frank Ernest Hill, *Ford: Expansion and Challenge, 1915–1933*, vol. 2 (New York: Charles Scribner's Sons, 1957), pp. 323, 492. His anti-Semitism and the belief that jazz was a Jewish invention are reflected in his magazine the *Dearborn Independent* (see the issues of August 6 and 13, 1921, for examples). Ford's championship of fiddling and old-time dances was discussed quite often in the popular magazines of the twenties. "Fiddling to Henry Ford," *Literary Digest* 88, no. 1 (January 2, 1926), is a representative example. Recent discussions of the phenomenon include Estelle Schneider and Bob Norman, "The Henry Ford Dance Movement," *Sing Out* 25, no. 4 (November–December 1977): 24–27, and Don Robertson, "Uncle Bunt Stephens: Champion Fiddler," *OTM*, no. 5 (Summer 1972): 4–7.

Henry Ford's automobile was at the center of much of the social and technological change of the period, but the radio and phonograph contributed more to the discovery and expansion of hillbilly music. Leroy Hughbanks, *Talking Wax, or the Story of the Phonograph* (New York: Hobson Book Press, 1945), Roland Gelatt, *The Fabulous Phonograph* (New York: J. B. Lippincott Company, 1955), and Oliver Read and Walter L. Welch, *From Tin Foil to Stereo: The Evolution of the Phonograph* (New York: Bobbs-Merrill, 1959), are still the best discussions of that medium. Eric Barnouw is the acknowledged authority on the radio, but one will learn nothing about country music programing from him. Much more pertinent to our purposes is William Mckinley Randle, "History of Radio Broadcasting and Its Social and Economic Effects on the Entertainment Industry, 1920–1930" (Ph.D dissertation, Western Reserve University, 1966), vol. 1. Most of my statistics on radio stations in the twenties come from Frederick Lewis Allen, from *Recent Social Trends*, and from such contemporary magazines as *Literary Digest* 75, no. 6 (November 11, 1922): 29.

The recording of hillbilly music was, in part, a phase of the discovery and exploitation of racial and ethnic music in the twenties. Useful introductions to this material are Pekka Gronow, "A Preliminary Check-list of Foreign Language 78's," *JEMFQ* 9, Part 1, no. 29 (Spring 1973): 24–32, and Richard K. Spottswood, "Ethnic Music in America: First Progress Report on a Discography," *JEMFQ* 15, no. 54 (Summer 1979): 84–91.

Since phonograph records are relatively easy to find, catalogue, and preserve (in contrast to the extremely scarce material dealing with radio in the twenties), scholars have been much preoccupied with them. The relationship between the recording industry and early hillbilly music has been the central concern of Charles Wolfe in several fine essays: "Toward a Contextual Approach to Old-Time Music," *JCM* 5, no. 2 (Summer 1974): 65–75; "Ralph Peer at Work: The Victor 1927 Bristol Sessions," *OTM*, no. 5 (Summer 1972): 10–16; and "Columbia Records and Old-Time Music," *JEMFQ* 14, no. 51 (Autumn 1978): 118–125, 144. Additional insights concerning Ralph Peer's role and methods are found in Nolan Porterfield, "Mr. Victor and Mr. Peer," *JCM* 7, no. 3 (December 1978): 3–21, and in Porterfield's *Jimmie Rodgers* (Urbana: University of Illinois Press, 1980), while Norm Cohen, in *Long Steel Rail: The Railroad in American Folksong* (Urbana: University of Illinois Press, 1981), tells us much about record sales in the twenties, and in the process demolishes a number of myths about alleged million-sellers.

My understanding of the repertory found on early hillbilly records was enhanced by such record company catalogues as Brunswick's *Songs from Dixie* (1926–1928), *Catalog of Victor Records* (1925–1934), and *Columbia Record Catalogue* (1923–1941). The JEMF has also reprinted *Gennett Records of Old Time Tunes: A Catalog Reprint*, JEMF Special Series, no. 6. I of course have listened to as many of the old records as possible, both on the original 78's and on lp's of reissued material. Probably the best single discussion of the type of material found on the early records is Anne and Norm Cohen, "Folk and Hillbilly Music: Further Thoughts on Their Relation," *JEMFQ* 13, no. 46 (Summer 1977): 50–57, although Norm Cohen and Guthrie Meade, "The Sources of Old Time Hillbilly Music: Child Ballads," *JEMFQ* 9, no. 30 (Summer 1973): 56–62, is a useful corrective to some of the assumptions that many people once held about the hillbilly repertory.

The songwriters who began moving country music away from its traditional moorings in the twenties have not been properly studied or appreciated. Carson Robison, for example, receives some attention in articles devoted to his associate Vernon Dalhart, but only one article, and that in a popular magazine, concentrated on his writing: Mrs. Henry Parkman, "Now Come All You Good People," *Colliers* 84 (November 2, 1929): 20–24, 58–59. Record reissues have also slighted Robison, but good selections of his material can be found on two albums: *Carson J. Robison: Just a Mel-*

ody, Old Homestead OHCS-134, which includes such self-penned songs as "Barnacle Bill the Sailor" and "Little Green Valley" and several duets with Frank Luther and Vernon Dalhart, and *The Immortal Carson Robison*, Glendale Records GL 6009, which includes such famous Robison compositions as "Carry Me Back to the Lone Prairie" and "I Left My Gal in the Mountains." Dick Burnett, the most traditional of the early song-writers, is discussed by Charles Wolfe in successive issues of *OTM*, nos. 9 and 10 (Summer and Autumn 1973) and in *Kentucky Country: Folk and Country Music of Kentucky* (Lexington: State University Press of Kentucky, 1982). Blind Andy Jenkins is discussed also by Wolfe in "Frank Smith, Andrew Jenkins, and Early Commercial Gospel Music," *American Music* 1, no. 1 (Spring 1983): 49–60. Jenkins had earlier been evaluated by D. K. Wilgus in *A Good Tale and a Bonnie Tune*, edited by Mody C. Boatright et al., Publications of the Texas Folklore Society (Dallas: Southern Methodist University Press, 1964), pp. 227–237. Blind Alfred Reed was the subject of an article by certain unnamed members of the Rounder Record Company: "The Life of Blind Alfred Reed," *JEMFQ* 7, no. 23 (Autumn 1971): 113–115. For information on the most sophisticated of the early hillbilly composers, Bob Miller, I am indebted to Joe Dan Boyd, who supplied me with information from the *Memphis Press-Scimitar*, May 5, 1939, and the *Memphis Commercial-Appeal*, February 7, 1953. Like Carson Robison, Miller is deserving of much better scholarly treatment than he has received.

The literature on the singers and musicians of the early commercial period is large and growing. The logical place to begin is with Norm Cohen's essay "Early Pioneers," in *Stars of Country Music*, edited by Bill C. Malone and Judith McCulloh (Urbana: University of Illinois Press, 1975), pp. 3–42, which discusses Eck Robertson, Henry Whitter, Fiddlin' John Carson, Ernest Stoneman, Charlie Poole, Gid Tanner, Riley Puckett, Clayton McMichen, and Carl T. Sprague. Early women performers have been generally neglected, but Robert Coltman has done much to redress the problem in "Sweetheart of the Hills: Women in Early Country Music," *JEMFQ* 14, no. 52 (Winter 1978): 161–181. Three of the pioneer women performers (Roba Stanley, Zora Layman, and Sara Carter) are anthologized in the Time-Life Collection *The Women*, but the best recorded introduction to the early women is *Banjo Pickin' Girl*, Rounder 1029 (notes by Charles Wolfe and Patricia A. Hall), which includes Eva Davis, Samantha Bumgarner, Roba Stanley, Louisiana Lou (Eva Conn), Billie Maxwell, Moonshine Kate (Rosa Lee Carson), and the Bowman Sisters (Gennie and Pauline). The recognition of Eck Robertson's contributions began when Mike Keasler, a student in Roger Abrahams' folklore class at the University of Texas, interviewed the master fiddler in Amarillo, December 30, 1962. Other interviews followed, and that of John Cohen appeared in *Sing Out* 14, no. 2 (April–May 1964): 55–59. I found the reference to Robertson's early radio performance on WBAP in the *Fort Worth Star-Telegram*, March 30, 1923. All of Robertson's recorded fiddle tunes have been reissued on Sonyatone Records STR 203, with extensive notes by Peter Feldman.

Fiddlin' John Carson has received considerable attention from country music scholars. Gene Wiggins is now preparing a full-scale biography, but the article that first publicized the account of Carson's pioneer recording was Kyle Crichton, "Thar's Gold in Them Thar Hillbillies," *Colliers* 101 (April 30, 1938): 24 ff. Archie Green corrected the errors in this original version, and supplied missing data, in his superb and oft-quoted "Hillbilly Music: Source and Symbol," *JAF* 78, no. 309 (July–September 1965): 204–228. Fuller biographical accounts of Carson are found in Bob Coltman, "Look Out! Here He Comes! Fiddlin' John Carson," *OTM* 9 (Summer 1973): 16–22; Norm Cohen, "Fiddlin' John Carson: An Appreciation and a Discography," *JEMFQ* 10, no. 36 (Winter 1974): 138–157; and Gene Wiggins, "John Carson: Early Road, Radio, and Records," *JCM* 8, no. 1 (May 1979): 20–39.

Ernest Stoneman, the patriarch of the Stoneman Family bluegrass band and a performer whose career spanned over forty years of country music history, was discussed by Norm Cohen, Eugene Earle, and Graham Wickham, in *The Early Recording Career of Ernest V. "Pop" Stoneman: A Bio-Discography*, JEMF Special Series, no. 1, 1968, and in Cohen and Earle, "An Ernest V. Stoneman Discography," *JEMFQ* 16, no. 57 (Spring 1980): 36–50.

Charlie Poole and the North Carolina Ramblers have been treated well by modern scholars and enthusiasts. Much of their material has been reissued with great success by David Freeman on his County record label in Floyd, Virginia. Kenny Rorer, a relative of both Poole and his first fiddler, Posey Rorer, has compiled two fine works on this wonderful North Carolina band: "Leaving Home: Charlie Poole's Early Years," *JCM* 9, no. 1 (1981): 82–86, and a book, *Rambling Blues: The Life and Songs of Charlie Poole* (London: OTM, 1982).

That other great, but dissimilar, band, the Skillet Lickers, has also received much attention, as have two of its stellar members, Clayton McMichen and Riley Puckett. Norm Cohen's essay "Early Pioneers" in *Stars of Country Music* is again the place to begin, but Cohen has also written on McMichen in "Clayton McMichen: His Life and Music," *JEMFQ* 11, no. 39 (Autumn 1975): 117–124. Both Cohen and Charles Wolfe, in "Clayton McMichen: Reluctant Hillbilly," *Bluegrass Unlimited* 13, no. 11 (May 1979): 56–63, stress the great fiddler's complexity and the conflict in his art between tradition and modernity. Norm Cohen's "Riley Puckett: King of the Hillbillies," *JEMFQ* 12, no. 44 (Winter 1976): 175–185, is probably the best capsule treatment of that influential guitarist and singer.

The man who took southern ballad and parlor singing to northern audiences—Bradley Kincaid—has had his story well told by Loyal Jones, an authority on the politics and culture of Appalachia. Jones first wrote on the "Kentucky Mountain Boy" in the *JEMFQ* 12, no. 43 (Autumn 1976): 122–138, and again in a small book called *Radio's "Kentucky Mountain Boy" Bradley Kincaid* (Appalachian Center: Berea College, 1980). Kincaid's famous songbooks are also discussed in this work, as well as in Archie Green, "Bradley Kincaid's Folios," *JEMFQ* 8, no. 45 (Summer 1977): 21–28. The best collection of his recordings is Bradley Kincaid, *Mountain Ballads and Old-Time Songs*, Old Homestead OHCS 107.

Some musicians clearly elicited research and publication because they were rediscovered during the folk revival of the sixties. Clarence Ashley, Dock Boggs, and Buell Kazee each enjoyed renewed careers; each was newly recorded; and each received written recognition. The great Kentucky ballad singer Buell Kazee told some of his story in an lp called *Buell Kazee Sings and Plays*, Folkways FS3810. Loyal Jones told more of it in his notes to a later album, *Buell Kazee*, June Appal 009. Kazee also told his story to me in Stillwater, Oklahoma, April 7, 1972. Clarence Ashley was properly appreciated in Ralph and Richard Rinzler's notes to the album *Old-Time Music at Clarence Ashley's*, Folkways FA2355, and was the subject of an essay in *Tennessee Traditional Singers*, edited by Thomas C. Burton (Knoxville: University of Tennessee Press, 1981). Dock Boggs was discussed briefly by Michael Seeger in the notes to the album *Dock Boggs*, Folkways FA 2351, and by himself in "I Always Loved the Lonesome Songs," *Sing Out* 14, no. 3 (July 1964): 32–37.

Boggs is not the only important musician who has received minimal attention, in some cases, one supposes, because they recorded only a few songs, or did not live long enough to be rediscovered during the folk revival. Charles Wolfe wrote a short but good account of George Reneau in *JEMFQ* 15, no. 56 (Winter 1979): 205–208. Tony Russell did brief sketches on "Frank Hutchison: The Pride of West Virginia," *OTM*, no. 1 (Summer 1971): 4–7, and on "Kelly Harrell and the Virginia Ramblers," *OTM*, no. 2 (Autumn 1971): 8–11.

When the first edition of this book was prepared, my discussion of Vernon Dalhart relied principally on the research of the vaudeville music collector/historian Jim Walsh: "Favorite Pioneer Recording Artists: Vernon Dalhart," Part I, *Hobbies: The Magazine for Collectors* 65, no. 3 (May 1960): 33–35, 45; Part II, no. 5 (July 1960): 34, 36–37, 55; Part III, no. 6 (August 1960): 33–35; Part IV, no. 8 (October 1960): 34–36, 44; and "Death of Three Recording Artists," *Hobbies* 53, no. 10 (December 1948): 32. Although these articles still have great value, I have supplemented them with information garnered from Walter Darrell Haden, "Vernon Dalhart," in *Stars of Country Music*, pp. 69–93. Norm Cohen, in *Long Steel Rail*, also clarifies much of the murky data dealing with the origins and sales figures of "The Prisoner's Song" and "The Wreck of the Old 97." After many years of neglect, Dalhart material began to reappear on recordings at the end of the 1970's. Representative lp's include *Old Time Songs*, Davis Unlimited DU 33030; *Ballads and Railroad Songs*, Old Homestead OHCS 129; and *Original Edison Recordings: First Recorded Railroad Songs*, Mark 56 Records 794.

The Carter Family has certainly not suffered from scholarly inattention. I talked briefly wtih Maybelle Carter in Nashville on August 26, 1961, and with Joe Carter in Meridian, Mississippi, on March 24, 1978, but received no information that differs substantially from that found in the published works. Ed Kahn was the first person to do research on the Carter Family, but his dissertation, "The Carter Family: A Reflection of Changes in Society," UCLA, was not completed until 1970. I profited greatly from his aid and encouragement. The closest thing to primary materials are the articles written by June Carter, "I Remember the Carter Family," *CSR* 17, no. 90 (October 1965): 16–17, and 17, no. 91 (December 1965): 16–20—both reprinted in *Sing Out* 17, no. 3 (June–July 1967): 6–11. Probably the best secondary account of the Carters, because it combines a survey of their recorded material with a biographical sketch, is the Time-Life Collection devoted to the family (notes by Tony Russell). Another excellent record/ biography collection is "The Carter Family on Border Radio," JEMF 101 (with extensive notes by Archie Green, Norm Cohen, and William H. Koon). Green's "The Carter Family's 'Coal Miner's Blues,'" *SFQ* 25, no. 4 (December 1961): 226–237, was a fine piece of work on a selected aspect of their career, and John Atkins' essay in *Stars of Country Music*, pp. 103–131, was a good factual survey of the famous family's career.

I am grateful for the support given to me by Dave Wylie and George Biggar on the *National Barn Dance*. Wylie corresonded with me frequently in 1967, supplying me with the results of his research on the Chicago barn dance, and putting me in touch with Biggar, who also provided me with an extensive amount of material. It is regrettable that neither Wylie nor Biggar ever converted their research into a book. Biggar, who was also associated with other midwestern barn dances, did write an article, "The WLS National Barn Dance Story: The Early Years," *JEMFQ* 7, no. 23 (Autumn 1971): 105–112. I learned much about the WLS performers from Sears-Roebuck catalogues and also profited greatly from two books which dealt, at least indirectly, with WLS and the *Barn Dance*: James F. Evans, *Prairie Farmer and WLS: The Burridge Butler Years* (Urbana: University of Illinois Press, 1969), and Boris Emmet and John E. Jeuck, *Catalogues and Counters: A History of Sears, Roebuck and Company* (Chicago: University of Chicago Press, 1950).

I learned about other barn dances and assorted hillbilly radio shows through newspaper research (as in the case of WBAP in 1923: *Fort Worth Star-Telegram*) and through a perusal of *Radio Digest* from 1929 to 1933. Information on the *WSM Barn Dance*, which ultimately became the

Grand Ole Opry, came from a variety of published sources and interviews. I talked with Harry Stone in Nashville on August 28, 1961; Sam McGee in Franklin, Tennessee, on August 14, 1973; Deford Bailey in Nashville on July 20, 1974 (Russell Stockard, a former student of mine at Tulane University, also talked with Bailey on October 6, 1973). George D. Hay wrote his own recollection of the show, *A Story of the Grand Ole Opry* (privately published in Nashville, 1953). Hay's daughter, Margaret Hay Daugherty, wrote a short account of her father for *Bluegrass Unlimited* 17, no. 1 (July 1982): 28–34. William R. McDaniel and Harold Seligman wrote *Grand Ole Opry* (New York: Greenberg, 1952), and Jack Hurst compiled a large-format, lavishly illustrated account of the show, *Nashville's Grand Ole Opry* (New York: Abrams, 1975). Richard Peterson explains the interrelationship between the National Life and Accident Insurance Company, WSM, and the *Grand Ole Opry* in "Single Industry Firm to Conglomerate Synergistics: Alternative Strategies for Selling Insurance and Country Music," in *A Growing Metropolis: Aspects of Development in Nashville*, edited by James Blumstein and Benjamin Walters (Nashville: Vanderbilt, 1975). Although all of these works are useful, the acknowledged authority on the *Opry* is Charles Wolfe. He has written several articles on the institution, including "Nashville and Country Music, 1925–30: Notes on Early Nashville Media and Its Responses to Old-Time Music," *JCM*, no. 4 (Spring 1973): 2–16, and several essays on musicians identified with the show (to be described later). But the obvious place to begin reading about the great country music institution would be Wolfe's *The Grand Ole Opry: The Early Years, 1925–35*, OTM Booklet 1 (London, 1973). (Wolfe is now preparing a thorough revision and enlargement of this book.)

The most prominent of the early *Opry* performers have been discussed in various publications, including Wolfe's previously cited books on Tennessee music and the *Grand Ole Opry*. One of the *Opry* pioneers, the talented fiddler Sid Harkreader, wrote a memoir of his experiences, *Fiddlin' Sid's Memoirs: The Autobiography of Sidney J. Harkreader*, edited by Walter D. Haden, JEMF Special Series, no. 9; and Alton Delmore, who joined the show in 1933 with his brother Rabon, left an unfinished autobiography which was published in 1977 (to be discussed in the bibliographical essay for Chapter 4). The story of Sam McGee has been told in a number of places: in Jon Pankake's notes to *The McGee Brothers and Arthur Smith*, Folkways FA2379; in Marvin Clemons, "Sam McGee from Tennessee," *Bluegrass Unlimited* 10, no. 4 (October 1975): 28–32; in an interview conducted by Bob Krueger for *Guitar Player* 10, no. 6 (June 1976): 16 ff; and by Charles Wolfe in *Tennessee Traditional Singers*. Deford Bailey was rediscovered in the mid-seventies, and he received some long overdue attention: David Morton, "Every Day's Been Sunday," *Nashville* 1, no. 12 (March 1974): 50–55; Frye Gaillard, "An Opry Star

Shines On," *Country Music* 3, no. 6 (March 1975): 38–40; and Jon Hartley Fox, "I Was a Humdinger—Deford Bailey," *Bluegrass Unlimited* 17, no. 6 (December 1982): 68–70.

Finally, as might be expected, the irrepressible Uncle Dave Macon has drawn much attention from modern-day researchers. The best of this material includes Ralph Rinzler's notes to *Uncle Dave Macon*, Decca DL4760; Rinzler and Norm Cohen, eds., *Uncle Dave Macon: A Bio-Discography*, JEMF Special Series, no. 3; and Charles Wolfe's essay in *Stars of Country Music*, pp. 43–69.

3. The First Country Singing Star: Jimmie Rodgers

My original research on Jimmie Rodgers included a series of interviews with relatives and friends of the Blue Yodeler: Rodgers' sisters-in-law, Pearl Rodgers and Elsie McWilliams; his stepbrother, Jake Smith; a brother-in-law, Nate Williamson (all in Meridian, Mississippi, August 23–25, 1966); and his half-sister, Lottie Mixon, in York, Alabama, on August 25, 1966. I also talked with a friend of Rodgers', Claudia Rigby Vick, on August 23, 1966; and with Bill Bruner, one of Rodgers' earliest singing disciples, on August 24, 1966.

Since these original interviews, I have also talked with a few musicians who either played with or had some association with Jimmie Rodgers. These include Billy Burkes in Meridian, May 26, 1978; Wilbur Ball in Meridian, May 24, 1978; Dwight Butcher in Meridian, May 25, 1978; Raymond Hall in Memphis, Tennessee, June 24, 1978 (I also had considerable correspondence with him); and Claude Grant (of the Tenneva Ramblers) in Bristol, Virginia, September 2, 1970.

I also explored *Billboard* carefully, from 1928 through Rodgers' death in May 1933, and found numerous accounts of his tent-rep and vaudeville appearances. Research in selected newspapers, such as the *Houston Post-Dispatch*, December 1931–February 1932, and the *New Orleans Picayune*, 1928–1929, also provided accounts of his theater performances and occasional radio appearances.

Few published accounts on Jimmie Rodgers existed in 1961 when I began my research. However, I did find Carrie "Mrs. Jimmie" Rodgers' remembrance of her husband, *My Husband Jimmie Rodgers* (San Antonio: Southern Literary Institute, 1935), to be useful despite the romanticized and sanitized view presented of Rodgers. Especially helpful was John Greenway's pioneering article "Jimmie Rodgers—A Folksong Catalyst," *JAF* 70, no. 277 (July–September 1957): 231–235, even though I thought he placed too much emphasis on Rodgers' blues songs. Greenway's "Folk Song Discography," *Western Folklore* 21, no. 1 (January 1962): 71–76, is a much more satisfactory evaluation of the Blue Yodeler. Ralph Peer wrote a short statement of his first meeting with Rodgers—"Discovery of the First Hillbilly Great," *Billboard* 65, no. 20 (May 16, 1953): 20–21, but certain details of his story have since been corrected or amplified by Charles Wolfe in "Ralph Peer at Work: The Victor 1927 Bristol Sessions," *Old Time Music*, no. 5 (Summer 1972): 10–16, and by Nolan Porterfield in his biography. Former Ranger William W. Sterling provided a few interesting glimpses of Rodgers' relationship to his adopted state of Texas in *Trails and Trials of a Texas Ranger* (privately published, 1959).

For my understanding of the blues tradition in which Jimmie Rodgers worked, I originally relied upon Samuel Charters, *The Country Blues* (New York: Rinehart and Company, 1959); Paul Oliver, *Blues Fell This Morning* (London: Cassell and Company, 1960); and Jerry Silverman, *Folk Blues: One Hundred and Ten American Folk Blues* (New York: Macmillan Company, 1958). Since the original publication of my book, there has been an explosion of scholarship in the blues field: Lawrence Levine, *Black Culture and Black Consciousness* (New York: Oxford University Press, 1977); Jeff Todd Titon, *Early Downhome Blues: A Musical and Cultural Analysis* (Urbana: University of Illinois Press, 1977); William Ferris, Jr., *Blues from the Delta* (Garden City, N.Y.: Doubleday, 1978); Robert Palmer, *Deep Blues* (New York: Viking Press, 1981); and David Evans, *Big Road Blues* (Berkeley: University of California Press, 1982).

Jimmie Rodgers too has received new and extended treatment, both popular and scholarly, since the first publication of my book. Two short statements on Rodgers appeared in *Country Music* magazine: Townsend Miller, "Anita Remembers Her Daddy, Jimmie Rodgers," 1, no. 9 (May 1973): 32–38; and John P. Morgan, "Jimmie Rodgers Remembered, Part II," 1, no. 10 (June 1973): 38–42. Morgan, a medical doctor, contributed an unusual slant on Rodgers in another article, "Famous Persons Who Have Had Tuberculosis: Jimmie Rodgers and Dow Pharmaceuticals," *JEMFQ* 15, no. 54 (Summer 1979): 80–82. Robert Coltman looked for the origins of Rodgers' famous blue yodel in "Roots of the Country Yodel: Notes toward a Life History," *JEMFQ* 12, no. 42 (Summer 1976): 91–94; Dave Samuelson tried to clarify the incident that led to the original breakup of Rodgers and the Tenneva Ramblers in his notes to the lp, *The Tenneva Ramblers*, Puritan LP 3001; Henry Pleasants included Rodgers in *The Great American Popular Singers* (New York: Simon and Schuster, 1974), pp. 111–125; and Johnny Bond compiled *The Recordings of Jimmie Rodgers: An Annotated Discography*, JEMF Special Series, no. 11.

Most important, full-scale biographies and assessments of Rodgers have appeared. Two English writers and Jimmie Rodgers buffs, Chris Comber and Mike Paris, wrote the essay on Rodgers for *Stars of Country Music*, edited by Bill C. Malone and Judith McCulloh (Urbana: University of Illinois Press, 1975), pp. 131–155, and later followed that with a biography,

Jimmie the Kid (London: Eddison Press, 1977). The Comber and Paris book was a sympathetic and reasonably accurate account of Rodgers, but it did not proceed from the kind of meticulous and exhaustive research that Nolan Porterfield poured into his biography, *Jimmie Rodgers: The Life and Times of America's Blue Yodeler* (Urbana: University of Illinois Press, 1979). The result is a milestone in country music scholarship. Soon after I became involved in my original research, two friends then living in Cape Girardeau, Missouri—Ray and Kay White—told me about a young English professor there at Southeast Missouri State who was quite a disciple of Rodgers. This was Porterfield. Periodically in the years that followed, other reports from other quarters issued forth about his proposed Jimmie Rodgers biography, and much of his research provided the basis for Robert Shelton's discussion of Rodgers in *The Country Music Story* (New York: Bobbs-Merrill Company, 1966). It has been well worth the wait. Porterfield has given us a fine biography of Jimmie Rodgers and an excellent account of the early country music industry.

4. Country Music during the Depression

An excellent place to begin the study of country music in the thirties is Bob Coltman, "Across the Chasm: How the Depression Changed Country Music," *OTM*, no. 23 (Winter 1976–1977): 6–13. This is a thoughtful essay, concentrating on the years 1930–1934, that stresses the transitional nature of the period, when "amateurs gave way to professionals" and their music became more mellow and more geared toward novelty.

The reorganization of the record business inspired by hard times is illuminated somewhat by John Edwards, "The Old Labels—No. 2," *Country and Western Spotlight* (Special John Edwards Memorial Edition, September 1962), pp. 14–15, but the indispensable work on record labels is Brian Rust, *The American Record Label Book* (New Rochelle, N.Y.: Da Capo Press, 1978). Archie Green has compiled a useful chronology of the Okeh-Columbia relationship in Appendix III of "Hillbilly Music: Source and Symbol," *JAF* 78 (July–September 1965): 228. The crucial role played by the new Decca company in the thirties is described in "Platter War," *Business Week*, November 10, 1934, p. 14, and in *Time* 36, no. 10 (September 2, 1940): 45. Paul Cohen also provided me with information on this subject in an interview in Nashville, August 29, 1961. An almost complete listing of Decca's early hillbilly recordings made from 1934 to 1945 (the 5000 Series) is in *Record Research*, no. 23 (June–July 1959): 13–16, while a shorter listing is in *Country and Western Spotlight*, no. 42 (June 1963): 4–6. Although they are now extremely hard to obtain, a Japanese researcher, Toru Mitsui, compiled and annotated eleven lp's of Decca hillbilly material which were released in Japan under the general title of *From the Southeast to the Southwest: 1930's Decca Hillbilly Records.* Nothing comparable to this has been issued in the United States.

Despite the extraordinary popularity of radio during the thirties, the medium has still not received the kind of study that the country music researcher would hope for. A few histories of individual radio stations, however, do exist: James F. Evans, *Prairie Farmer and WLS: The Burridge Butler Years* (Urbana: University of Illinois Press, 1969); C. Joseph Pusateri, *Enterprise in Radio: WWL and the Business of Broadcasting in America* (Washington, D.C.: University Press of America, 1980); and Lillian Jones Hall, "A Historical Study of Programming Techniques and Practices of Radio Station KWKH, Shreveport, Louisiana, 1922–1950" (Ph.D dissertation, Louisiana State University, 1959).

Information on the *Grand Ole Opry* during the thirties can be obtained from Wolfe's history of the radio show: *The Grand Ole Opry: The Early Years, 1925–35, OTM* Booklet 1 (London, 1973; a revised version is now in preparation by Wolfe); from Alton Delmore's autobiography, *Truth Is Stranger Than Publicity* (Nashville: Country Music Foundation Press, 1977); and from Elizabeth Schlappi, *Roy Acuff, the Smoky Mountain Boy* (Gretna, La.: Pelican Publishing Co., 1978). I also picked up some information on this subject from Harry Stone (interview, Nashville, August 28, 1961) and from Herald Goodman, (interview, Carrollton, Texas, December 29, 1967).

The bulk of my information on WLS and the *National Barn Dance* came from correspondence with Dave Wylie and George Biggar, as cited in notes to Chapter 2. James F. Evans' history of WLS was also very helpful, as was Lewis Atherton, *Main Street on the Middle Border* (Bloomington: Indiana University Press, 1954), which commented on the *Barn Dance*'s popularity among rural and small-town midwesterners. John Lair gave me some additional information in an interview at Renfro Valley, Kentucky, August 18, 1973. *Billboard* issues provided some statistics concerning attendance and receipts at *Barn Dance* road shows. An interesting article on Bob Atcher in *Country Style* shed some interesting light on the differences between the *National Barn Dance* and the *Grand Ole Opry*. According to Atcher, union scales hurt the Chicago show and contributed to its eventual demise (Matt Huff, "Smilin' Bob Atcher, Back on the Circuit," *Country Style*, no. 22 [July 28, 1977]: 35).

Other radio barn dances of the thirties have not been nearly so well documented as have the *Opry* and the *National Barn Dance*. A couple of good accounts of other shows, however, do exist: Willie J. Smyth, "Early Knoxville Radio (1921–41): WNOX and 'Midday Merry Go-Round,'" *JEMFQ* 18, nos. 67–68 (Fall–Winter 1982): 109–116; and Timothy A. Patterson, "Hillbilly Music among the Flatlanders: Early Midwestern Radio Barn Dances," *JCM* 6, no. 1 (Spring 1975): 12–18, which stresses the high percentage of nonsoutherners on these shows. Some information on radio shows can be gleaned from the studies of individual musicians (see Ivan and Deanna Tribe, "The Doc Williams Reunion," *Bluegrass Unlimited* 7, no. 9 (March 1983): 61–65, which also comments on WWVA, Wheeling, West Virginia). I found numerous references to radio barn dances in *Broadcasting and Broadcast Advertising* (Washington, D.C.), which I checked for the years 1934–1939. Such magazines as *Billboard* and *Radio Digest* also make occasional mention of such shows. The area of hillbilly radio research is clearly still wide open.

The alliance between advertising and country music became most strongly marked in the thirties. Pusateri, in *Enterprise in Radio*, talks about the "P.I. accounts" which accompanied hillbilly broadcasting all over the country and which made the subject of his book, WWL, known far and wide as the "aches and pills" station. I found *Broadcasting and Broadcast Advertising* to be an extremely fruitful source for references to Aladdin Mantle Lamps, Drug Trade Products, Alka-Seltzer, Garrett Snuff, and scores of other items that were intimately associated with country radio programming. Stewart H. Holbrook, *The Golden Age of Quackery* (New York: Macmillan Co., 1959), has a section on Black Draught and Wine of Cardui, products made by the Chattanooga Medicine Company, and long staples of the hillbilly radio trade. Don R. Jason, "WSM and Its 3,000 Salesmen," *The Advertiser* 5, no. 9 (October 1934): 23–24, gives an interesting account of how National Life and Accident Insurance salesmen sold premiums to working-class people by stressing the company's interrelationship with WSM and the *Grand Ole Opry*.

The largest advertiser of hillbilly music, Crazy Water Crystals, received a lot of attention in the thirties because of its notoriety. It deserves similar attention from scholars today because of the role it played in making country music a national phenomenon. I am deeply indebted to Pat Ahrens for information which she supplied, and also for her article "The Role of the Crazy Water Crystals Company in Promoting Hillbilly Music," *JEMFQ* 17, no. 19 (Autumn 1970): 107–109. I also interviewed the former president of the company, Carr P. Collins, in Dallas, April 20, 1962, and Hubert Fincher, the son of the company's southeastern manager, J. W. Fincher, by phone from Columbia, South Carolina, October 17, 1970. Dorothy Neville, *Carr P. Collins: Man on the Make* (Dallas: Park Press, 1965), was also helpful, as were such contemporary accounts as Ruth deForest Lamb, *American Chamber of Horrors* (New York: Farrar and Rinehart, 1936); Morris Fishbein, "Modern Medical Charlatans," *Hygeia* 16, no. 1 (January 1938): 21–25; and Richard Lee Strout, "The Radio Nostrum Racket," *Nation* 141 (July 17, 1935): 65–66.

One of the most notorious of the "medical charlatans," John R. Brinkley, played a crucial role in the emergence of the famous Mexican border stations. At least one doctoral dissertation has concentrated on Brinkley's influence on American radio programming: Ansel Harlan Resler, "The Impact of John R. Brinkley on Broadcasting in the United States," (Ph.D. dissertation, Northwestern University, 1958). Brinkley also received considerable published treatment, in contemporary periodicals and by more recent popular historians: Richard Hughes Bailey, "Dr. Brinkley of Kansas," *Nation* 135 (September 21, 1932): 254–255; J. C. Furnas, "Country Doctor Goes to Town," *Saturday Evening Post* 212, no. 43 (April 20, 1943): 12–13, 44ff; and Gerald Carson, *The Roguish World of Dr. Brinkley* (New York: Rinehart and Company, 1960). More pertinent to the study of country music are Ed Kahn, "International Relations, Dr. Brinkley, and Hillbilly Music," *JEMFQ* 9, Part 2, no. 30 (Summer 1973): 47–55, and Mike Paris' account of a long-time performer on border radio, "The Jesse Rodgers Story," *OTM*, no. 13 (Winter 1974–75): 5–8. I obtained additional information on Mexican border programming from Carr P. Collins (April 20, 1962) and from the Rev. Sam Morris, who preached his temperance sermons on border stations for many years (interview, San Antonio, July 14, 1973).

When we turn to the country musicians of the thirties, we find a wealth of published material. The white blues singers of the period were merely the most recent manifestations of a very old fascination with black music and culture (see Tony Russell, *Blacks, Whites, and Blues* (New York: Stein and Day, 1970). Stephen Ray Tucker organized and annotated an excellent collection of "Blues and Boogie Music" within the white country tradition (including several of the musicians discussed in this chapter), but it remains buried somewhere within the Smithsonian Institution. One of the finest country-blues singers, Jimmie Tarlton, was rediscovered during the folk revival. He is discussed by Norm and Anne Cohen in "The Legendary Jimmie Tarlton," *Sing Out* 16, no. 4 (September 1966): 16–19, and by Graham Wickham, *Darby and Tarlton* (special edition of Doug Jydstrup's *Blue Yodeler*, 1967). The Allen Brothers were little known until Donald Lee Nelson found them in 1971: "The Great Allen Brothers Search," *JEMFQ* 7, Part 3, no. 23 (Autumn 1971): 126–129. Nelson followed that with "The Allen Brothers," *JEMFQ* 7, part 4, no. 24 (Winter 1971): 147–151. Tony Russell soon thereafter discussed them in "Chattanooga Boys: The Allen Brothers," *OTM*, no. 4 (Spring 1972): 12–13, and in the notes to an lp, *The Allen Brothers: The Chattanooga Boys*, Old Timey LP-115. They also receive a brief mention in John P. Morgan and Thomas C. Tulloss, "The Jake Walk Blues," *JEMFQ* 13, no. 47 (Autumn 1977): 122–126. Cliff Carlisle has received scandalously little attention, even though he was one of the superb singer-yodelers of the period, and a pioneer in the performance of the Dobro guitar. A good summary of his career, though, is Gene Earle, "Cliff Carlisle," *Folk Style* (Bromley, England), no. 7 (1960): 3–26, while Charles Wolfe provides the best interpretation of his style and musical contributions in *Kentucky Country* (Lexington: University Press of Kentucky, 1982), pp. 62–65. Carlisle's clear, sparkling style can be sampled on two lp's of reissued material: Old Timey 103 and 104. Frank Hutchison is much less documented than Carlisle. Tony Russell did a short sketch on him called "Frank Hutchison: The Pride of West Virginia," *OTM*, no. 1 (Summer 1971): 4–7, while Mark Wilson provided the notes for Hutchison's reissue album, *The Train That Carried My Girl from Town*, Rounder 1007.

Of all the entertainers who experimented with the blues idiom in the thirties, only two, Gene Autry (who will be discussed in the notes to Chapter 5) and Jimmie Davis, went on to weather successive stylistic changes in the country music industry. I interviewed Davis in Baton Rouge, Louisiana, August 15, 1977, and Stephen Ray Tucker (Tulane University) interviewed him in Baton Rouge, February 12, 1980. Tucker, who is preparing a history of country music in Louisiana, has graciously provided me with some of the fruits of his research. I learned some additional information about Davis in an interview with one of his long-time musicians, Joe Shelton (Yantis, Texas, July 31, 1974), and from a little article by Floy Case, "Jimmie Davis," *Mountain Broadcast and Prairie Recorder*, n.s., no. 2 (December 1944): 3, 5, 6. Country music historians tend to be more interested in Davis' risqué-blues repertory than in his later and more varied offerings. Eric Wadin compiled a list of Davis' early material in "A Rare List of Jimmie Davis Recordings," *Country and Western Spotlight*, no. 41 (March 1963): 7–8, and Tony Russell (*Blacks, Whites, and Blues*) and Nick Tosches (*Country: The Biggest Music in America* [New York: Stein and Day, 1977], pp. 118–128) concentrated on this phase of Davis' career.

For an introduction to the duet tradition in country music, one might begin with the Time-Life Collection *Duets*, edited by Charles Wolfe. This collection surveys the style from 1927 (Mac and Bob) to 1972 (George Jones and Tammy Wynette). Wolfe also discusses "The Delmore Brothers" in *Pickin'* 2, no. 8 (September 1975): 4–12, and is the editor of Alton Delmore's autobiography, *Truth Is Stranger Than Publicity* (Nashville, Country Music Foundation Press, 1977). The latter is a rare autobiography by a country singer, and though it is sketchy for the post-1950 period, it evokes well the unsteady, barnstorming atmosphere of the thirties and forties. Delmore is candid in his remarks about other musicians and the music business and has some unflattering things to say about the *Grand Ole Opry*.

Interest in the music of the Dixon Brothers was revived during the urban folk period, and Dorsey Dixon enjoyed a brief second career. Archie Green was drawn toward the Dixons because they had worked in textile mills since childhood and had written songs about their factory experiences. Green wrote "Minstrel of the Mills" (about Dorsey) for *Sing Out* 16, no. 3 (July 1966): 10–13, and then produced and annotated Dixon's fine lp, *Babies in the Mill*, Testament T-3301. In addition to these sketches by

Green, Mike Paris has written "The Dixons of South Carolina," *OTM*, no. 10 (Autumn 1973): 13–17.

I have always had a warm spot in my heart for the Callahan Brothers, having grown up with their music which I heard over KRLD in Dallas. Homer "Bill" Callahan has since been extremely helpful to me and has graciously supplied me with information and photographs on several occasions. I interviewed him twice, the first time with Bob Pinson in Dallas, August 23, 1963, and the second time in Dallas, July 10, 1978. I have also talked to him frequently by telephone. Another interview with Paul Buskirk, the great mandolin player, provided additional information on the Callahans and Gus Foster (Houston, July 8, 1976). Of the printed material on the Callahan Brothers, two essays deserve special recognition: Bob Pinson, "The Callahan Brothers," *Country Directory*, no. 2 (no date): 5–13, and Ivan Tribe, "Bill and Joe Callahan: A Great Brother Duet," *OTM*, no. 16 (Spring 1975): 15–22.

Lester McFarland and Robert A. Gardner (Mac and Bob) are sorely in need of a biographer. Their roles in popularizing the mandolin and in introducing such classic songs as "Twenty-one Years" should earn them much more than the slender documentation they have thus far received. Dave Wylie and George Biggar told me most of what I know about Mac and Bob, although John Edwards provided a skeleton outline of their career in "McFarland and Gardner," *Country and Western Spotlight* (September 1962): 15. Mac and Bob are also seldom anthologized in record reissues, although the Time-Life duet collection includes their version of "When the Roses Bloom Again." Dave Wylie did produce a good, but now out-of-print, lp of some of their most representative recordings: "*Mac and Bob*," Birch Records 1944.

Charles Wolfe has pointed out that Karl Davis and Harty Taylor, another influential duet, has also suffered from historical neglect: "Whatever Happened to Karl and Harty," *Bluegrass Unlimited* 18, no. 4 (October 1983): 26–32. The Time-Life duet collection, though, does include three of their songs as well as a brief biographical sketch. My own knowledge of Karl and Harty had originally come from Dave Wylie, and particularly from a short account he had supplied to me from *Stand By* magazine, November 2, 1935, p. 9.

The Blue Sky Boys and the Monroe Brothers, on the other hand, have been well anthologized and documented. Much of my information on the Blue Sky Boys (the Bolick Brothers) came from two interviews with Bill Bolick: the first in Greensboro, North Carolina, August 24, 1965, and the second by phone to Greensboro on September 3, 1970. Several excellent published accounts of the Bolicks exist. In the first edition of this book I made use of William A. Bolick, "Bill Bolick's Own Story of the Blue Sky Boys" (Introduction and commentary by William A. Farr), *Sing Out* 17, no. 2 (April–May 1967): 18–21, and the notes to *The Blue Sky Boys*, Camden CAL797, by Archie Green. David Whisnant challenged some of the earlier conclusions about the Blue Sky Boys—particularly the idea that they retired from music because of stylistic inflexibility—in his notes to the lp *The Blue Sky Boys*, JEMF 104 (a reissue of *Presenting the Blue Sky Boys*, Capitol ST2483). Douglas B. Green supplied full and sensitive notes for the RCA reissue, RCA Bluebird AXM2-5525, and Wayne W. Daniel wrote a very good summary of the Blue Sky Boys' career in "Bill and Earl Bolick Remember the Blue Sky Boys," *Bluegrass Unlimited* 16, no. 3 (September 1981): 14–21. One of the most significant insights into the Bolicks' relationship with their fans is Douglas B. Green, ed., "The Blue Sky Boys on Radio, 1939–40: A Newly Discovered Log of Their Daily Program Kept by Ruth Walker," *JCM* 4, no. 4 (Winter 1973): 108–158. These notes, kept faithfully by a loyal fan, tell us much about the Bolicks' repertory and remind us of the importance of radio to country entertainers.

The Monroe Brothers have received much attention, not only because of their vital and exciting performances, but also because of their anticipation of bluegrass. Bill Monroe's story has been well told by several writers, and that bibliography will be discussed later in the notes to Chapter 10. Particularly relevant, though, for the Monroe Brothers is Ralph Rinzler's essay on Bill in *Stars of Country Music*, edited by Bill C. Malone and Judith McCulloh (Urbana: University of Illinois Press, 1975), pp. 221–243. Charlie Monroe has not been so fully treated, but Ivan Tribe's short essay "Charlie Monroe" in *Bluegrass Unlimited* 10, no. 4 (October 1975): 12–21, is a good place to begin. Douglas B. Green conducted a good and long interview with Charlie which is excerpted as "The Charlie Monroe Story" in *Muleskinner News* in three successive issues: 4, no. 1 (January 1973); 4, no. 2 (February 1973); and 4, no. 3 (March 1973). Green also organized and wrote the notes for the outstanding anthology of Monroe Brothers recordings, *Feast Here Tonight*, RCA Bluebird AXM2-5510 (thirty-two selections).

Women began to achieve a certain prominence in country music during the thirties, and in some cases even established independent identities. The Time-Life collection *The Women* (edited by several unnamed staff members) contains recordings by several entertainers who were active during the decade: Lulu Belle Wiseman, Zora Layman, Sara Carter, Patsy Montana, Girls of the Golden West, Coon Creek Girls, Dezurik Sisters, Louise Massey, Judy Canova, Texas Ruby, and Cousin Emmy. Published accounts, however, are still few and far between. All of my information on Grace Wilson came from Dave Wylie, particularly in a letter dated March 24, 1967. George Biggar supplied me with some material on Lulu Belle Wiseman, but I obtained more from Scott Wiseman in a telephone interview to Spruce Pine, North Carolina, on August 19, 1973. Lulu Belle's performances and tours were also described frequently in *Billboard* and various radio-oriented magazines during the thirties. The best accounts of Cousin Emmy and the Coon Creek Girls are in Wolfe's *Kentucky Country*. The zestful performing style of Cousin Emmy is hinted at in the transcript of her performance given at the Ash Grove in Los Angeles in 1967: John Cohen, ed., "Cousin Emmy by Herself," *Sing Out* 18, nos. 2–3 (June–July 1968): 26–27. The best presentation of her style, of course, comes in the recorded performance anthologized in the Time-Life collection. I obtained additional information on the Coon Creek Girls through a telephone interview with Lily May Ledford (Pennington), in Lexington, Kentucky, August 12, 1973, and from a short sketch in *Stand By* magazine, April 3, 1937, p. 12. I talked to Millie Good McCluskey by phone (Cincinnati, August 11, 1973), and learned the basic details of the career of the Girls of the Golden West. I learned among other things that they came, not from Muleshoe, Texas, but from Southern Illinois.

Individual musicians of the thirties have been discussed in a wide array of scattered sources. The extremely popular radio team of Asher Sizemore and Little Jimmy is discussed in Wolfe's *Kentucky Country*, pp. 60–61. Lew Childre, an alumnus of the tent-rep vaudeville circuit and an itinerant radio performer during the decade, is discussed by Wolfe in "Doc Lew: The Life and Times of Lew Childre," *Bluegrass Unlimited* 13, no. 5 (November 1978): 26–30, and in the notes to *Lew Childre: On the Air, 1946*, an lp produced by Old Homestead (OHCS-132) and taken from radio transcriptions. The record captures some of the informality and ebullience that characterized his live performances. Two other performers who were best known for their radio work, Doc Williams and Buddy Starcher, have been poorly documented on recordings. Williams, however, is the subject of two articles which I have found useful: Barbara Kempf, "Meet Doc Williams, Country Music Star, Country Music Legend," *JEMFQ* 10, Part 1, no. 33 (Spring 1974): 1–7, and Rex Rutkoski, "Doc Williams," *Bluegrass Unlimited* 12, no. 11 (May 1978): 25–32. Buddy Starcher's life and career have been capsuled by Ivan Tribe in "Buddy Starcher—Mountain State Favorite," *Bluegrass Unlimited* 13, no. 9 (March 1979): 46–52.

Clyde Moody and Grandpa Jones, on the other hand, made many recordings, but most of their work came after the thirties. During that decade they were also best known for their radio performances. I interviewed Moody on August 15, 1973, in Nashville, but also learned much from Ivan Tribe and John Morris, "Clyde Moody: Old-Time, Bluegrass and Country Musician," *Bluegrass Unlimited* 10, no. 1 (July 1975): 28–34. The versatile Grandpa Jones, whose career has been one of the longest in country music, has been the subject of several good articles. With the assistance of Charles Wolfe, he is also writing his autobiography. Wolfe has discussed "The Music of Grandpa Jones," *JCM* 8, no. 3 (1981): 47–48, 65–88.

Alanna Nash, in *Frets* 2, no. 9 (September 1980): 22–25, and Don Rhodes, in *Country Music* 3, no. 4 (January 1975), have written short evaluations of Jones' career.

Several fiddlers made names for themselves in the thirties, independently of bands. Discussions of Clayton McMichen have already been cited in the notes to Chapter 2. Curly Fox is described briefly in Mary Morgan, "Curly Fox: A Living Legend," *Bluegrass Unlimited* 11, no. 10 (April 1977): 12–16. The greatest fiddler of all, Arthur Smith, has received biographical treatment and stylistic evaluation from Charles Wolfe in two essays: "Fiddler's Dream: The Legend of Arthur Smith," *Devil's Box* 11, no. 4 (December 1977), 26–67, and "The Odyssey of Arthur Smith," *Bluegrass Unlimited* 13, no. 2 (August 1978): 50–57. Twenty-eight of Smith's performances have been reissued on two lps, *Fiddlin' Arthur Smith*, vols. 1 and 2, County 546 and 547 (taken from the period 1935–1940).

A few of the string bands from the southeastern states have elicited popular or scholarly treatment. The most "rural" of these bands, Mainer's Mountaineers, is discussed by Ivan Tribe and John Morris, in "J. E. and Wade Mainer," *Bluegrass Unlimited* 10, no. 5 (November 1975): 12–22, and by Brad McCuen, in "Mainer's Discography," *Disc Collector*, no. 24 (May 1973): 8–24. Two "graduates" of the Mainer band, Wiley and Zeke Morris, are discussed by Wayne Erbsen, in "Wiley and Zeke, the Morris Brothers," *Bluegrass Unlimited* 15, no. 2 (August 1980): 40–50. Roy Hall's string band, the Blue Ridge Entertainers, possessed some of the raw, rustic vitality of Mainer's Mountaineers, but in other ways, such as their use of the dobro, they anticipated the sound of the forties. The band's story is told by Ivan Tribe in "Roy Hall and His Blue Ridge Entertainers," *Bluegrass Unlimited* 13, no. 3 (September 1978): 44–50. The Prairie Ramblers, who began their existence as the Kentucky Ramblers, were even more transitional in their sound and choice of songs, sometimes sounding like an old-time band but more often reflecting the western swing sounds that were filtering in from the West. Bob Healy discusses the group in "The Prairie Ramblers," *Country Directory*, no. 3 (1962): 4–14, and Charles Wolfe evaluates their contributions to country music in *Kentucky Country*. Hank Penny did not identify with the rural musicians of the Southeast; his Radio Cowboys consequently were not transitional at all, but were strongly marked by the rhythms of western swing. I interviewed Penny by phone at his home in Chatsworth, California (January 17, 1981), but also obtained relevant information from Rich Kienzle, "The Checkered Career of Hank Penny," *JCM* 8, no. 2 (1980): 43–78, and from Ken Griffis, "Hank Penny: The Original Outlaw," *JEMFQ* 18, nos. 65–66 (Spring–Summer 1982): 5–13.

The early history of the steel guitar has been one of the special research interests of Rich Kienzle (see his "Steel," *Country Music* 4, no. 4 [January

1976]: 35, 38, 61–62). Robert Gear discusses the pre-American origins of the style in "Hawaiian Music: Styles and Stylists of the Islands," *Frets* 3, no. 5 (May 1981): 34–36. Early recorded examples of the musicians who brought the instrument and style to the United States can be heard on *Hula Blues* (Rounder 1012). Early hillbilly exponents of the style are anthologized on an Old Timey lp, *Steel Guitar Classics* (Old Timey 133). The special contributions made by the Dopera Brothers with their famous Dobro are discussed in Duncan G. Robertson, "Dobro," *Guitar Player* 2, no. 5 (October 1968): 20–21, 50, and by Ed Dopera, as told to Michael Brooks, "The Story of the Dobro," *Guitar Player* 5, no. 8 (December 1971): 29–31, 39–40, 49. Jerry Byrd's seminal contributions to the art of steel guitar playing are explored in an interview with him conducted by Tom Bradshaw: "Jerry Byrd," *Guitar Player* 6, no. 2 (March 1972): 25, 45–48.

The rediscovery and romanticization of the folk in the context of the Great Depression have been touched upon by many writers, and several scholars have commented upon the ways in which the government touched the lives of the plain folk, distributing relief, providing economic protection, and documenting and commemorating their culture. Although several government agencies, such as the Library of Congress, the WPA cultural projects, and the Farm Security Administration, strove to preserve folklore and folk music, no scholar has attempted to study all of these various campaigns in any comprehensive or systematic manner. Representative articles which discuss selected aspects of the government's approach to folk music include Harold Spivacke, "The Archive of American Folk-Song in the Library of Congress, *SFQ* 2, no. 1 (March 1938): 31–35; Herbert Halpert, "Federal Theatre and Folksong," ibid., pp. 81–85; and B. A. Botkin, "WPA and Folklore Research: Bread and Song," ibid. 3, no. 1 (March 1939): 7–14. A more extended discussion of the Archive of American Folk-Song is provided by Debora Kodish, "A National Project with Many Workers: Robert Winslow Gordon and the Archive of American Folk-Song," *Quarterly Journal of the Library of Congress* 35 (October 1978): 218–233.

Southern labor unrest during the thirties is discussed in several fine works, including Thomas Tippett's contemporary treatment of the Piedmont textile strikes, *When Southern Labor Stirs* (New York: Jonathan Cape and Harrison Smith, 1931); Liston Pope's sociological study of the failure of unionism in North Carolina, *Millhands and Preachers: A Study of Gastonia* (New Haven: Yale University Press, 1942); John Hevener's study of the bloody struggle for economic justice in the Kentucky coal fields, *Which Side Are You On? The Harlan County Coal Miners, 1931–1939* (Urbana: University of Illinois Press, 1979); George B. Tindall's *The Emergence of the New South, 1913–1945* (Baton Rouge: Louisiana State

University Press, 1967); and Irving Bernstein's superb general labor history, *The Lean Years: A History of the American Worker, 1920–1933* (Boston: Houghton Mifflin, 1960).

The music inspired by textile work is surveyed by Archie Green in "Born on Picketlines, Textile Workers' Songs Are Woven into History," *Textile Labor* 21, no. 4 (April 1961): 3–5, and in his notes to *Babies in the Mill*, Testament T-3301. David McCarn, the greatest of the textile-worker songwriters, is discussed by William Henry Koon in "Dave McCarn," *JEMFQ* 11, Part 4, no. 40 (Winter 1975): 167–176. McCarn's songs can be heard on a couple of lps: *Singers of the Piedmont*, Bear FV12505, and *Poor Man, Rich Man: American Country Songs of Protest*, Rounder 1026 (Mark Wilson, annotator).

Coal-mining and balladry are the subjects of Archie Green's *Only a Miner: Studies in Recorded Coal-Mining Songs* (Urbana: University of Illinois Press, 1972), a work which is valuable not only for the subject it emphasizes but also for its understanding of the whole field of commercially recorded country music. Green addresses himself more directly to the conflicts in the eastern Kentucky coal fields during the early thirties in his notes to Sara Ogan Gunning, *Girl of Constant Sorrow*, Folk-Legacy FSA-26. Gunning was a labor union activist, as was her half-sister Aunt Molly Jackson, and both of them were protest singers who eventually took their songs north. Aunt Molly was eventually memorialized in an entire issue of *Kentucky Folklore Record*, 7, no. 4 (October–December 1961).

The Okie migration, which contributed greatly to the transplantation of hillbilly culture in California, has been well studied in both fiction and history. Walter J. Stein concentrated on California's reaction to the great horde of migrants in *California and the Dust Bowl Migration* (Westport, Conn.: Greenwood, 1973). Jacqueline Gordon Sherman, on the other hand, discussed the ways in which the Okies adjusted to their new home: "The Oklahomans in California during the Depression Decade" (Ph.D dissertation, UCLA, 1970). Charles Todd and Robert Sonkin collected music among the Okies and deposited their research in the Archive of American Folk-Song. They wrote of their experiences in "Ballads of the Okies," *New York Times Magazine*, November 17, 1940, pp. 6–7, 18.

The great Okie balladeer and hillbilly singer Woody Guthrie has inspired an enormous amount of print, including his own self-justification, *Bound for Glory* (New York: E. P. Dutton and Company, 1943). Richard Reuss compiled much of this material in *A Woody Guthrie Bibliography* (New York: Guthrie Children's Trust Fund, 1968), and wrote his own assessment of the singer in "Woody Guthrie and His Folk Tradition," *JAF* 83, no. 329 (July–September 1970): 273–304. Guthrie finally found his biographer, though, in Joe Klein: *Woody Guthrie* (New York: Alfred A. Knopf, 1980), a superbly written and meticulously researched piece of scholarship. Guthrie's relationship to hillbilly music and culture is more convincingly discussed there than in any other work. Furthermore, Klein's book explores with great detail and deftness the role played by the Communist Party in promoting the idea of the folk song as a weapon in the class struggle. Klein's *Woody Guthrie*, John Greenway's *American Folk Songs of Protest* (Philadelphia: University of Pennsylvania Press, 1953), and R. Serge Denisoff's *Great Day Coming: Folk Music and the American Left* (Urbana: University of Illinois Press, 1971) should be utilized to understand the concept of "protest song" and the way in which music has been used to promote radical causes.

5. The Cowboy Image and the Growth of Western Music

I have written an article, "Country Music in the Depression Southwest," for *The Depression in the Southwest*, edited by Donald W. Whisenhunt (Port Washington, N.Y.: Kennikat, 1980), pp. 58–75, stressing the innovative styles that emerged during the period, while also mindful that the region was an heir to the musical traditions of the older South. Texas' debt to southern folk tradition is discussed in Alan Lomax's notes to *Texas Folksongs*, Tradition Records, TLP 1929; by Norman L. McNeil, "The British Ballad West of the Appalachian Mountains" (Ph.D. dissertation, University of Texas, 1956); and in William A. Owens, *Texas Folk Songs* (Dallas: Texas Folklore Society, 1950; 2d ed., 1977) and his *Tell Me a Story, Sing Me a Song* (Austin: University of Texas Press, 1983). Francis E. Abernethy, folklorist and English professor at Stephen F. Austin State University in Nacogdoches, Texas, has waged a lifelong campaign—as a singer and often as editor of *Publications of the Texas Folklore Society*—to remind us of Texas' rich folk traditions. His most recent venture into this subject has been the excellent *Singin' Texas* (Dallas: E. Heart Press, 1983). Abernethy can recall, as can most Texans of rural origin, the "Young People's Page" of the *Dallas Semi-Weekly Farm News*, where old songs were printed on request, indicating that rural Texans' song preferences were no different from those in other rural southern areas (the Texas State Library has some scattered copies from the pre–World War I period). William W. Savage, Jr., has written a useful survey of Oklahoma's folk and popular music traditions, *Singing Cowboys and All That Jazz: A Short History of Popular Music in Oklahoma* (Norman: University of Oklahoma Press, 1983). Similar studies of other states should be written.

The phenomenon that contributed greatly toward making Texas, Oklahoma, and Louisiana different from other southern states—oil—is discussed by Coke Rister, *Oil! Titan of the Southwest* (Norman: University of Oklahoma Press, 1949). Too little has been done on the social consequences of the oil boom (particularly on the clash between rural folkways and this new industrial power), but a few writers have compiled some of the folklore that grew out of the oil discoveries: Alice Cashen, "Boom-Town Tales," in *Tales from the Big Thicket*, edited by Francis E. Abernethy (Austin: University of Texas Press, 1966), pp. 137–154; Mody Boatright, *Folklore of the Oil Industry* (Dallas: Southern Methodist University Press, 1963); and Boatright and William A. Owens, *Tales from the Derrick Floor* (Lincoln: University of Nebraska Press, 1970). The reader, however, should not be expecting a collection of oil songs; almost none emerged from the culture of oil work.

The other great phenomenon that set Texas and Oklahoma apart from the South–cowboy culture—has been subjected to a massive and unending documentation. The Library of Congress' great exhibition in 1983, "The American Cowboy," is a dramatic visual reminder of the romantic appeal exerted by this universal American hero. A large library exists which discusses the effects of the western and cowboy image on American life, but among the more instructive works are George Bluestone, "The Changing Cowboy: From Dime Novel to Dollar Film," *Western Humanities Review* 14, no. 3 (Summer 1960): 331–337; David B. Davis, "Ten Gallon Hero," *American Quarterly* 6, no. 2 (Summer 1954): 111–126; Kenneth Munden, "A Contribution to the Psychological Understanding of the Cowboy and His Myth," *American Image* 15, no. 2 (Summer 1958): 103–147; and Joe B. Frantz and Julian Ernest Choate, Jr., *The American Cowboy: The Myth and the Reality* (Norman: University of Oklahoma Press, 1955).

On the subject of singing cowboys and their relationship to country music, good places to begin one's research would be Stephen Ray Tucker, "The Western Image in Country Music" (M.A. thesis, Southern Methodist University, 1976), and Douglas B. Green's lengthy survey, "The Singing Cowboy: An American Dream," *JCM* 7, no. 2 (May 1978): 4–62. Green continues to remind audiences of this tradition in another vital and entertaining way, as Ranger Doug, the singer-yodeler-guitarist of the revivalist-cowboy singing trio Riders in the Sky. Tucker and Green concentrate on the professionalization of cowboy music, but William R. Smith discusses music among real cowboys in "Hell among the Yearlings," *OTM*, no. 5 (Summer 1972): 16–19.

Several of the pioneer singing cowboys who made the first recordings in the twenties have been anthologized in *Authentic Cowboys and Their Western Folksongs*, RCA Victor Vintage Series LPV-522 (notes by Fred G. Hoeptner). The songs they sang had earlier been collected, for the most part, by the first two great compilers of cowboy songs: Nathan Howard Thorp, *Songs of the Cowboy* (Estancia, N.M.: New Print Shop, 1908), and John A. Lomax, *Cowboy Songs and Other Frontier Ballads* (New York: Sturgis and Walton, 1910). The John A. Lomax Family Papers, a massive collection housed at the Eugene C. Barker Texas History Center, the University of Texas at Austin, has been insufficiently utilized by country music scholars, but I have found much useful information relating to the early commercialization and artistic exploitaton of cowboy and other kinds of folk music. At least two of the "original singing cowboys," Jules Verne Allen and John White, wrote their own recollections of cowboy life and song: Allen, *Cowboy Lore* (San Antonio: Naylor Company, 1933), and White, *Git Along, Little Dogies: Songs and Songmakers of the American West* (Urbana: University of Illinois Press, 1975). Both books brought a strong note of realism into the study of cowboy music, by reminding us that (according to Allen) guitars and good voices were rare among cowboys, and (according to White) most cowboy songs began in the fertile minds of individuals—usually as poems in newspapers or magazines—and not in some romantically communal fashion.

When I was compiling information on the early singing cowboys, Archie Green reminded me of the early Charles Nabell recordings (letter, February 6, 1967). I interviewed Carl Sprague in Bryan, Texas, on August 4, 1963. Most of my scanty knowledge of Jules Verne Allen and the Cartwright Brothers came from the RCA Victor Vintage collection and from Allen's book. Since that time William Koon and Carol Collins have written "Jules Verne Allen, the Original Singing Cowboy," *OTM*, no. 10 (Autumn 1973): 17–19, and Bill Rattray (with the assistance of Jack Cartwright) has written "The Cartwright Brothers Story," *OTM*, no. 9 (Summer 1973): 10–14. Most of the extant knowledge of Goebel Reeves is possessed by Fred Hoeptner, whose findings were originally published in Robert Shelton, *The Country Music Story* (New York: Bobbs-Merrill, 1966), pp. 149–151. More recently, Hoeptner has published "Goebel Reeves, the Texas Drifter," *OTM*, no. 18 (Autumn 1975): 10–17. Nolan Porterfield has also speculated on Reeves' alleged relationship with Jimmie Rodgers in *Jimmie Rodgers: The Life and Times of America's Blue Yodeler* (Urbana: University of Illinois Press, 1979), p. 43. John Edwards also briefly discussed Reeves in "The Mystery of the Texas Drifter," *Country and Western Spotlight*, September 1962, p. 31. The other cowboy-Wobbly, Harry McClintock, told much of his story to Joe Nicholas in a long letter published in *Disc Collector*, no. 12, pp. 1–2, and no. 13, pp. 11–13.

The most professional of the original "singing cowboys," Otto Gray and Ken Maynard, have been better documented largely because they excelled in other realms: Gray as a businessman and Maynard as a Hollywood actor. Gray, of course, was not a singer at all, but as an effective organizer and promoter, he obtained recognition for his group in media that were usually hostile to any kind of country music. I found several references to Gray and his band in issues of *Billboard* dating from 1928 to 1932. Contemporary trade accounts can be well supplemented by Leslie A. McRill, "Music in Oklahoma by the Billy McGinty Cowboy Band," *Chronicles of Oklahoma* 38, no. 1 (Spring 1960): 66–74, and by Savage, *Singing Cowboys and All That Jazz*. Ken Maynard, of course, appears in any history of Hollywood Westerns, but he has also been discussed by Ken Griffis in

"The Ken Maynard Story," *JEMFQ* 9, Part 2, no. 30 (Summer 1973): 67–70. His songs are discussed by William H. Koon in the same issue, pp. 70–76.

The greatest Hollywood singing cowboy, Gene Autry, still has not received the kind of critical and comprehensive biographical treatment that students of country music and western films would desire. Autry has been resistant to in-depth interviews, and his autobiography (written with the assistance of Mickey Herskowitz) is sketchy on many of the areas of musical performance that historians are interested in: *Back in the Saddle Again* (New York: Doubleday, 1978). One of his sidekicks, Johnny Bond, collected material on Autry for many years, but did not convert it into a biography. Bond did, however, provide assistance to Douglas B. Green, who compiled the best short biography and evaluation of Autry that is available: the chapter on Autry in *Stars of Country Music*, edited by Bill C. Malone and Judith McCulloh (Urbana: University of Illinois Press, 1975), pp. 155–171. Green also did a short sketch, "Gene Autry: The Pre-Singing Cowboy Years," for *Pickin'* 2, no. 1 (December 1975): 22–26. The interview with Arthur Satherley, "'I'm a Record Man'—Uncle Art Satherley Reminisces," *JEMFQ* 8, Part 1, no. 25 (Spring 1972): 18–22, sheds some light on the early Autry years, as does Archie Green's "The Death of Mother Jones," *Labor History* 1, no. 1 (Winter 1960): 1–4. As in so many other areas, I found the Sears-Roebuck catalogues to be very helpful in building a profile of Autry's early commercial preferences.

Douglas B. Green's article in *JCM*, "The Singing Cowboy: An American Dream," is the best introduction to the whole retinue of actors who followed in the wake of Autry's success (and the best place to see and hear these men is in the old cowboy movies shown on *Tumbleweed Theatre*, a show hosted by Green and Riders in the Sky on the Nashville Network). Johnny Bond is a good source for the cowboys who came to Hollywood as part of Autry's organization, and also for those who were hired by other studios to compete with Autry (see his *Reflections: The Autobiography of Johnny Bond*, JEMF Special Series 8). Bond's biography of Tex Ritter, *The Tex Ritter Story* (New York: Chappell, 1976), is the best account available on that singer. Douglas B. Green did a short appreciation of Ritter for *Frets* 1, no. 5 (July 1979): 10–12. Archie Green also came up with an interesting item about Ritter, a 1927 concert of cowboy songs which he performed with pianist Oscar Fox at the University of Texas: "Commercial Music Graphics," *JEMFQ* 12, no. 41 (September 1976): 29.

The prolific writer-researcher Ken Griffis (who is fast becoming the leading authority on California country music) has written on several of the Hollywood singing cowboys: "The Ray Whitley Story," *JEMFQ* 6, Part 2, no. 18 (Summer 1970): 65–68; and "I've Got So Many Million Years: The Story of Stuart Hamblen," *JEMFQ* 14, no. 49 (Spring 1978): 4–22. He has also given us the best account of the Sons of the Pioneers that has yet been written.

The Sons of the Pioneers' movie appearances, their popular radio transcriptions, and their fifty-year longevity in the music business made them known to a multitude of fans, and consequently has made them attractive to researchers. I originally drew upon a biography of Roy Rogers by Elise Miller Davis, *The Answer Is God* (New York: McGraw-Hill, 1955), and a short sketch by John Edwards on the Sons of the Pioneers in *Country and Western Spotlight*, September 1962, p. 34. The best history now available is Ken Griffis, *Hear My Song: The Story of the Celebrated Sons of the Pioneers*, JEMF Special Series No. 5. Griffis has also written shorter essays on individual members of the group, including "The Early Career of Tim Spencer," *JEMFQ* 8, Part 1, no. 25 (Spring 1972): 4–7; "The Hugh Farr Story," *JEMFQ* 7, Part 2, no. 22 (Summer 1971): 68–73; and "The Bob Nolan Story," *JEMFQ* 16, no. 58 (Summer 1980): 63–65. An extensive number of Sons of the Pioneers records have been reissued, and the JEMF has issued an lp composed of material taken from radio transcriptions: *The Sons of the Pioneers*, JEMF LP102.

Several of the movie cowboys were also radio cowboys and, like Stuart Hamblen, had their own radio shows for many years, or, like the Sons of the Pioneers, were heard widely on transcriptions. The distinctions drawn in this chapter and bibliographical essay were therefore not always precise. We do not know enough about the transcription business, but Linda Painter has enhanced our understanding with "The Rise and Decline of Standard Radio Transcriptions," *JEMFQ* 17, no. 64 (Winter 1981): 194–201. Douglas Green has also ventured into this area of research with his article "Foy Willing and the Riders of the Purple Sage: Teleways Transcriptions, 1946–1948," *JCM* 6, no. 1 (Spring 1975): 28–41. (The Riders of the Purple Sage were the chief competitors of the Sons of the Pioneers, and were active in both radio and the movies.) The Beverly Hillbillies, who combined the cowboy and hillbilly images, were extremely popular radio personalities in California. Their story has been told by Bob Healy in *Country Directory*, no. 23 (1962): 31, and by Ken Griffis in *JEMFQ* 16, no. 57 (Spring 1980): 3–17. For three of the most active cowboy/cowgirl radio acts of the thirties, I relied on interviews: Red River Dave McEnery, in San Antonio, Texas, June 19, 1973; Millie Good McCluskey (Girls of the Golden West), telephone interview in Cincinnati, August 11, 1973; and Patsy Montana, telephone interview in West Covina, California, August 20, 1973. Additional information on Patsy Montana can be found in Chris Comber, "Patsy Montana: The Cowboy's Sweetheart," *OTM*, no. 4 (Spring 1972): 10–11, and in Robert K. Oermann and Mary A. Bufwack, "Patsy Montana and the Development of the Cowgirl Image," *JCM* 7, no. 3 (1981): 18–33.

The New York cowboy singer phenomenon of the thirties is deserving of at least an article. Previously cited material on Tex Ritter and Ray Whitley would be good places to start, but additional pertinent sources would be the tapescript on Dwight Butcher in *JEMFQ* 5, no. 13 (Spring 1969): 10–22, and Jay Taylor, "Montana Slim: Canada's Legendary Wilf Carter," *JEMFQ* 13, no. 47 (Autumn 1977): 118–121. I picked up some information on the New York scene from Red River Dave and Bobby Gregory (interview in Nashville, August 30, 1971). Although she was not a cowgirl singer, Ethel Park Richardson gave encouragement and exposure to the cowboys who came to New York. Her story is told by Jon G. Smith in "She Kept On A-Goin': Ethel Park Richardson," *JEMFQ* 13, no. 47 (Autumn 1977): 105–115.

One final word about the radio cowboys: their ranks were large, and their performance territory was immense, ranging from New York to California and from California to the Mexican border. I heard many of them, such as Cowboy Slim Rinehart, J. R. Hall, and Texas Jim Robertson, as I was growing up. Other names like Tom Murray, Tex Owens, and Marc Williams, have become familiar to me as I read through *Radio Digest* and old country music publications. I hope that students of country music will find some way of documenting their existence and evaluating their contributions.

Texas was characterized by more than cotton, cowboys, and oil; it was also a cosmopolitan mixture of racial and ethnic groups whose musical forms often intertwined while yet maintaining some distinctiveness. One interesting example of this musical fusion is discussed by Clifton Machann, in "Country-Western Music and the 'Now' Sound in Texas-Czech Polka Music," *JEMFQ* 19, no. 69 (Spring 1983): 3–7. No one, of course represents this hybridization better than the Czech-country musician Adolph Hofner, as I discovered in my interview with him in San Antonio, July 24, 1973. His musical eclecticism can be sampled on the lp *South Texas Swing—Adolph Hofner, 1935–55*, Arhoolie 5020 (notes by Tony Russell).

Texas' honky-tonk culture, which was nurtured by Prohibition repeal, the oil boom, electrical amplification, and the region's cosmopolitan musical mixture, is deserving of a major scholarly study. To my knowledge, I was the first writer to affix the term "honky-tonk" to a subgenre of country music (in the doctoral dissertation which preceded this book, 1965). The origin of the term has still not been tracked down, although Nick Tosches, in *Country: The Biggest Music in America*, has found a usage of it in Ardmore, Oklahoma, in 1894 (p. 24). I contributed to the selection of material, and wrote the notes, for a Time-Life collection called *Honky Tonkin'* (forty recordings including Al Dexter's "Honky Tonk Blues"—the first country song to carry the term in its title—plus other singers, such as Ernest Tubb, Floyd Tillman, and Ted Daffan, who contributed to the shaping of the style). I also wrote an article called "'Honky Tonk': The Music of the Southern Working Class," for *Folk Music and Modern Sound*, edited by William Ferris and Mary Hart (Jackson: University Press of Mississippi, 1982), pp. 119–129. Jukeboxes, which were constant accoutrements of the honky-tonk world, have not been properly documented or evaluated. *Billboard* issues provide some statistics on their numbers and circulation, and the popular press occasionally alludes to their significance (see, for example, Lewis Nichols, "The Ubiquitous Juke Box," *New York Times Magazine*, October 5, 1941, p. 22). More recently, John Morthland has commented on the music machine's significance for country music: "Jukebox Fever," *Country Music* 6, no. 8 (May 1978): 35–36.

Ernest Tubb, the first great singer to take his honky-tonk-nourished style to the stage of the *Grand Ole Opry*, has been the subject of a master's thesis: Ronnie Pugh, "The Texas Troubadour: Selected Aspects of the Career of Ernest Tubb" (Stephen F. Austin State University, 1978). Pugh has since written two illuminating articles on Tubb: "Ernest Tubb's Performing Career: Broadcast, Stage, and Screen," *JCM* 7, no. 3 (December 1978): 67–93; and "The Recording Career of Ernest Tubb," *JCM* 9, no. 1 (1981): 21–82. The best published biographical sketch of Tubb is that of Townsend Miller in *Stars of Country Music*, pp. 243–259. Of the many articles on Tubb in popular country music journals, the best include Townsend Miller, "Ernest Tubb's Early Recording Career," *JEMFQ* 8, Part 2, no. 26 (Summer 1972): 58–62; Peter Guralnick, "Ernest Tubb: Still the Texas Troubadour," *Country Music* 5, no. 8 (May 1977): 38ff; and Patrick Carr, "Ernest Tubb," ibid. 8, no. 8 (May 1980): 30–34. The story of Tubb's decision to add electric instrumentation to his recordings came from an interview with him in Austin, March 24, 1962.

Electrification, an essential ingredient of the honky-tonk sound and a major force for change in country music, has only recently begun to attract much scholarship. My interview with Bob Dunn in Houston, July 17, 1966, marked the beginning of an understanding of the way that the electric guitar became a part of country instrumentation. Since that time, Rich Kienzle has done most to clarify the process through which electrification became the norm in country music: "Steel," *Country Music* 4, no. 4 (January 1976): 37–38, 61–62, and "The Electric Guitar in Country Music: Its Evolution and Development," *Guitar Player* 13, no. 11 (November 1979): 30, 32–34, 36–37, 40–41. Alvino Rey's pioneering role in guitar electrification is mentioned in *Who Is Who in Music*, 5th ed. (1951), p. 346, and Lloyd Loar's contributions are described in Roger Siminoff, "Lloyd Loar," *Frets* 1, no. 5 (July 1979): 38–44. Ted Daffan's early experiments were described to me in various interviews: November 20, 1971; May 31, 1974; and July 7, 1976 (all in Houston, and the last two by telephone). The influence exerted by the black guitarists Eddie Durham and Charlie Christian is described in Leonard Feather, *The Book of Jazz* (New York: Meridian Books, 1960), pp. 112–115, and in Joachim E. Berendt,

The New Jazz Book: A History and Guide (New York: Hill and Wang, 1962), pp. 190–193.

Since the early seventies, western swing has become one of the most active research areas in country music and a fertile field for record reissues, most of them coming out of California. Some of the earliest collectors and discographers of country music, such as Bob Pinson, Glenn Healy, Glenn White, and Fred Hoeptner, were avid western swing specialists. Their ranks have been joined in recent years by such authorities as Rich Kienzle, Cary Ginell, Tony Russell, Chris Strachwitz, and Charles Townsend (the biographer of Bob Wills), who have been actively involved in the reissuance of old recordings and in the writing of informed liner notes and articles.

The early Texas fiddle bands have been much appreciated, but only rarely anthologized or historically documented. Charles Faurot and Bob Pinson probably know more about Oscar and Doc Harper, Solomon and Hughes, and Prince Albert Hunt than any other researchers, but they have written very little about them (Charles Faurot, though, produced and wrote the notes for the important album *Texas Farewell*, County 517, an anthology covering the years from 1922 to 1930, and Pinson has periodically shared some of his knowledge with me, particularly in Dallas, on August 23, 1963). I have since talked with Ona (Mrs. Doc) Harper in Terrell, Texas (by phone on July 11, 1978), but have not been able to follow up with a more extended interview. My knowledge of the Humphries Brothers comes from interviews with Jess Humphries' daughter, Katherine Russell, in Burnet, Texas, July 6, 1976; Cecil Humphries' daughter, Mertice Pogue, in the same city on the same date; and the Humphries Brothers' sister, Velma Whitted, in Liberty Hill, Texas, July 6, 1976.

The East Texas Serenaders are the only early Texas fiddle band who have had an entire album reissue devoted to them: County 410. They were also the subjects of an early sketch by Fred Hoeptner: "The Western Style—East Texas Serenaders," *Disc Collector*, no. 17 (May 1961): 8–11. I have since interviewed the band's guitarist, Cloet Hamman, in Lindale, Texas, July 5, 1978. Johnny Gimble told me that Huggins Williams was an early influence on his own style (interview in Kerrville, Texas, July 2, 1976).

My information on the Light Crust Doughboys and their controversial announcer, W. Lee O'Daniel, originally came from Bob Healy, "The Light Crust Doughboys," *Country Directory*, no. 3 (1962): 21–29; from Healy, "W. Lee O'Daniel and His Hillbilly Boys," ibid., no. 4 (1963): 6–11; and from Bob Pinson, "The Musical Brownies," ibid., pp. 11–17. My knowledge has since been amplified by Charles Townsend, who wrote of the group in his essay on Bob Wills in *Stars of Country Music*, pp. 171–195, and in his larger biography of Wills. I have also learned more about O'Daniel from Seth S. McKay, *W. Lee O'Daniel and Texas Politics, 1938–42* (Lubbock: Texas Tech Press, 1944). Much more needs to be done on O'Daniel and his exploitation of country music for political purposes.

Bob Pinson is responsible for most of the information that country music specialists have on Milton Brown and his seminal band, the Musical Brownies. Pinson wrote a short sketch of the group in *Country Directory*, no. 4 (1963): 11–17, and then again for *OTM*, no. 1 (Summer 1971): 14–17. He later supplied a complete discography of the group for *OTM*, no. 5 (Summer 1972): 21–22. I learned more about the Brownies in interviews with Roy Lee Brown (Milton's brother) and Fred "Papa" Calhoun, both in Fort Worth on May 24, 1963; Bob Dunn in Houston, July 17, 1966; and Cliff Bruner in League City, Texas, June 19, 1976, and Dickinson, Texas, January 31, 1982 (by phone).

Most of the western swing bands that appeared after 1935 either were influenced by the Musical Brownies or were spinoffs from them (groups founded or led by former Brownies). The above-mentioned interviews with Dunn and Bruner provided information on some of the spinoff groups. Bob Healy wrote about Ocie Stockard in "Ocie Stockard and the Wanderers," in *Disc Collector*, no. 18 (no date given): 19–20, and he made brief mention of Dunn's Vagabonds in "The Ted Daffan Story," *Country Directory*, no. 4 (1963): 27–31.

Garna Christian provides a good survey of the western swing scene in Houston in "It Beats Picking Cotton: The Origins of Houston Country Music," *Red River Valley Historical Review* 7 (Summer 1982): 37–50. The Swift Jewel Cowboys are described in Tony Russell's notes to *Chuck Wagon Swing—Swift's Jewel Cowboys*, String STR806. I learned some facts about Shelly Lee Alley in an interview with his widow, in Houston, August 10, 1966. Bob Healy contributed a "Shelly Lee Alley Discography" to *JEMFQ* 9, Part 1, no. 29 (Spring 1973): 33–34. Other Houston musicians are able to provide bits and pieces of information on Alley, and Nolan Porterfield adds still more in his biography of Jimmie Rodgers. I learned about the Bar-X Cowboys from Garna Christian (cited above), and from interviews with Ted Daffan and Jerry Irby (in Houston, June 4, 1977). The extremely influential Blue Ridge Playboys (which included, at one time or another, Leon Selph, Ted Daffan, Floyd Tillman, and Moon Mullican) have not received the kind of academic or popular attention that their stellar membership should warrant. My knowledge of them has come mostly from interviews: Leon Selph, Houston, June 4, 1977; Ted Daffan, Houston, November 20, 1971; Floyd Tillman, Austin, October 21, 1971; and Gordon Baxter, Silsbee, Texas, June 27, 1978. The Baxter interview was particularly helpful on Moon Mullican as well as the East Texas honky-tonk scene of the forties and early fifties. Baxter also wrote an interesting article on Mullican called "Pop Never Wanted Me to Be a Musician," *MCN* 4, no. 8 (February 1967): 27.

The San Antonio western swing scene has received very little attention from country music specialists. My limited knowledge comes totally from the interview with Adolph Hofner (San Antonio, July 24, 1973) and from Tony Russell's notes on Hofner's Arhoolie lp (5020) and Cary Ginell's notes to *The Tune Wranglers, 1936–38*, Texas Rose TXR2703.

The literature on the Dallas scene is a bit fuller, primarily because two very popular groups, Bill Boyd and the Cowboy Ramblers, and the Shelton Brothers, worked in that environment. I talked to Jim Boyd in Dallas on April 20, 1962 (by phone), but the fullest account—biographically and musically—of the Cowboy Ramblers is supplied by Bob Pinson in his notes to the RCA Bluebird reissue, AXM2-5503. A complete discography of the Cowboy Ramblers, compiled by Brad McCuen, is in *Country Directory*, no. 3 (1962): 15–21. My understanding of the Shelton Brothers came from interviews with the three brothers: Merle, Dallas, October 20, 1963; Bob, Seven Points, Texas, July 3, 1971 (actually a short conversation between performances at a country festival); and Joe, Yantis, Texas, July 3, 1971.

In the first edition of this book I complained about the "paucity of written material" on Bob Wills. That deficiency has been more than remedied in the last eight years or so. The revival of interest in Bob Wills' music, and in the whole field of western swing, has been paralleled by a proliferation of published works on Wills and his music. Charles Townsend profited from the western swing revival, but he may have also contributed to its expansion in his biography of Wills. The first fruits of his research came in the essay on Wills which he wrote for *Stars of Country Music*, pp. 171–194, but the crowning achievement was his highly praised biography, *San Antonio Rose: The Life and Music of Bob Wills* (Urbana: University of Illinois Press, 1976). The book is the product of several years of research and is bolstered with an impressively long list of interviews. One can quarrel with some of Townsend's interpretations, as I do—such as the assertion that Wills learned his music "directly" from blacks (and was the only country musician to do so), that he somehow derived his musical freedom and spontaneity from his exposure to the open Texas range country, and that he was essentially a jazz musician—and still recognize it as a major and impressive contribution to our understanding of one of the giant figures of both country and popular music.

In addition to Townsend's book, other significant contributions to the Bob Wills story include the Time-Life collection devoted to his music (with notes by Rich Kienzle); *The Bob Wills Anthology*, Columbia KG32416 (notes by Bill Ivey); Danny Hatcher's "Bob Wills: Discography of the Columbia Years, 1935–47," *JCM* 3, nos. 3–4 (Fall–Winter 1973): 114–134; a diary kept by some unknown fan, "Bob Wills and His Texas Playboys on Radio, 1942," *JCM* 5, no. 4 (Winter 1974): 135–193; Al Stricklin, with Jon McConal, *My Years with Bob Wills* (San Antonio: Naylor Company, 1976);

The War Years 511

and, of course, Ruth Sheldon's pioneering biography of Wills, *Hubbin' It: The Life of Bob Wills* (Tulsa: privately printed, 1938).

My own comprehension of Wills' music has been augmented by interviews with Johnny Gimble, Leon McAuliffe, and Al Stricklin (all in Kerrville, Texas, on July 2, 3, and 4, 1976), and with Cindy Walker (Mexia, Texas, August 12, 1976), Hoyle Nix (Kerrville, July 1, 1978), and Laura Lee McBride (Houston, November 2, 1978).

Finally, a note about the recordings of western swing. The number of reissued lps is beginning to be too large to be listed comprehensively. Therefore, I will note only a few of the most important ones. In addition to the Bill Boyd and Bob Wills anthologies which have already been mentioned, *Okeh Western Swing*, Epic EG37324 (notes by John Morthland) is a collection well worth owning. The series produced by Chris Strachwitz includes a good sampling of virtually all of the western swing groups (Old Timey 105, 116, 117, 119, 120, 121). And because of their seminal importance, at least two collections devoted to Milton Brown and His Musical Brownies should be mentioned: *Milton Brown and His Brownies*, MCA 1509, and *Milton Brown and His Musical Brownies*, String STR804 (notes by Tony Russell).

6. The War Years: The National Expansion of Country Music

Historians are gradually beginning to explore the social and cultural consequences of World War II for America (see Geoffrey Perrett, *Days of Sadness, Years of Triumph: The American People, 1939–45* (Baltimore: Penguin, 1973), but no one has yet concentrated on the revolutionary changes in southern society wrought by that conflict. The war really gave a deathblow to farm tenantry, as poor southerners, white and black, moved by the millions into the cities and to the North and West. The overall dimensions of this migration are touched upon by Jack Temple Kirby, "The Southern Exodus, 1910–1960: A Primer for Historians," *Journal of Southern History* 49, no. 4 (November 1983): 585–601. A need still exists for scholars to examine the ways in which the migrants and their descendants were changed by the experience (and, indeed, the way in which their new homes were changed), but excellent preliminary investigations include Lewis Killian, *White Southerners* (New York: Random House, 1970) and his "The Adjustment of Southern White Migrants to Northern Urban Homes," *Social Forces* 32, no. 1 (October 1953): 66–70; Harry Schwarzweller, James S. Brown, and J. J. Mangalam, *Mountain Families in Transition: A Case Study of Appalachian Migration* (University Park, Pa., 1971); and an unpublished paper by John Hevener, "Appalachians in Akron, 1914–45: The Transfer of Southern Folk Culture" (delivered at the Northern Great Plains History Conference, October 1975). The effects that the migration had on the expansion of country music—the emergence of "hillbilly bars" and the growing appearance of hillbilly records on jukeboxes—is noted in *The Billboard Music Year Book* for 1944 and in various *Billboard* issues during the war years, as well as in Killian's article in *Social Forces*. An excellent description of the movement of southern hillbilly music into northern border areas is Charles Camp and David Whisnant, "A Voice from Home: Southern Mountain Musicians on the Maryland-Pennsylvania Border," in *Long Journey Home, Southern Exposure* (Chapel Hill, N.C.), Summer–Fall 1977, pp. 80–90. Although these studies are necessary and useful, scholars now need to explore the movement of southern rural people into *southern* cities. In what ways were the migrants, and the cities, changed—and what were the consequences for the style and popularity of country music?

Writers have often commented on the popularity of country music among American military personnel, and have noted the influence exerted by southern boys and girls who took their musical tastes into the barracks, service clubs, and military theatres. No one, though, has really examined such military magazines as *Yank* and *Stars and Stripes* to find documentation for such presumptions, nor have ex-servicemen been interviewed in any kind of systematic way. Most of my information about servicemen's tastes (other than the impressionistic knowledge gained from relatives and friends who served in the military) comes from *The Billboard Music Year Book* for 1943 and 1944, and from *Movie-Radio Guide* 11, no. 1 (October 11–17, 1941): 1, and from selected issues of *Billboard*, such as 57, no. 10 (March 10, 1945), which quoted unnamed Army Special Service officers as saying that country music was "the most popular of all music with the services" (p. 29). My information on the Camel Caravan came from the above-mentioned issues of *Billboard* and *Movie-Radio Guide*, and from an interview with Minnie Pearl in Nashville, July 28, 1972, and from her autobiography, *Minnie Pearl*, written with Joan Dew (New York: Simon and Schuster, 1980).

The music industry controversies which affected country music's wartime growth—such as the BMI-ASCAP conflict, the American Federation of Musicians' strike, and shellac rationing—were discussed in *The Billboard Music Year Book*, 1943 and 1944 (and reviewed in the same publication in 1961); Roland Gelatt, *The Fabulous Phonograph* (New York: J. B. Lippincott Company, 1955); David Ewen, *Panorama of American Popular Music* (Englewood Clifs, N.J.: Prentice-Hall, 1957); Hazel Meyer, *The Gold in Tin Pan Alley* (New York: J. B. Lippincott Company, 1958); and Renfro Cole Norris, "The Ballad on the Air" (M.A. thesis, University of Texas, 1951). A strong indication of country entertainers' resentment of ASCAP and their receptivity to BMI is found in the testimony that several of them (including Gene Autry, Jimmie Davis, and Roy Acuff) gave to a U.S. Senate subcommittee in 1958: Hearings before the Subcommittee on

Communications of the Committee on Interstate and Foreign Commerce, U.S. Senate, 85th Congress, 2d Session, on S. 2834 (March 11–July 23, 1958).

In order to learn the extent of country music growth and expansion during the war—personal appearances, club appearances, record and jukebox activity, and radio barn dance activities—I combed through *Billboard and Billboard Year Book* issues for the years 1941–1945. Additional insights on the *Renfro Valley Barn Dance* were obtained from interviews with John Lair in Renfro Valley, Kentucky, August 18, 1973, and Harry Mullins (Little Clifford) in Mt. Vernon, Kentucky, August 18, 1973. The burgeoning western ballroom scene of California is discussed in Ken Griffis, "The Harold Hensley Story," *JEMFQ* 6, Part 4, no. 20 (Winter 1970): 146–151, and in Gerald F. Vaughan, "Foreman Phillips: Western Swing's Kingmaker," *JEMFQ* 15, no. 53 (Spring 1979): 27–28. *The Billboard Music Year Book* (1944) gives statistics about attendance at Foreman Phillips' dances and concerts. Gene Autry's wartime popularity (before he volunteered for military service) is described in *Billboard* and in his autobiography.

The *Grand Ole Opry*'s rise to preeminence was described to me by Harry Stone (interview in Nashville, August 18, 1961) and Minnie Pearl (interview, Nashville, July 28, 1972). One of the most illuminating sources concerning the wartime *Grand Ole Opry* is "The Grand Ole Opry, 1944–45: A Radio Log Kept by Dick Hill, of Tecumseh, Nebraska," *JCM* 5, no. 3 (Fall 1974): 91–122. Hill corresponded with me frequently during the sixties and seventies and provided an early xeroxed copy of the log, along with other memorabilia dealing with midwestern barn dances and performers. Students of country music should be immensely grateful to people like Hill who faithfully preserved such material, and we should be on the lookout for other data of this kind.

Before discussing the singers and songs of the war years, mention should first be made of a development that not only contributed to country music's commercial and national expansion but also adds a dimension in the historical understanding of the music: the appearance of journals devoted to country music. Only scattered copies of these magazines still remain, mostly in the possession of collectors or older musicians, but the Country Music Library and Media Center and JEMF are gradually adding to their files. Archie Green did a preliminary study of these magazines, based upon those in the Joe Nicholas collection donated to the Country Music Library: "Early Country Music Journals," *JEMFQ* 16, no. 59 (Fall 1980): 141–147. His findings were amplified and clarified to a certain extent by Eddie Nesbitt, a veteran performer from the Washington, D.C., area, in "A History of the Mountain Broadcast and Prairie Recorder," *JEMFQ* 13, nos. 65–66 (Spring–Summer 1982): 23–30. The earliest country music magazines (such as *Song Exchange News, The Jamboree, Cowboy Radio Guide,* and *The Mountain Broadcast and Prairie Recorder*) all seem to date from the early years of the war or from the immediate pre-war period. According to Nesbitt, *The Mountain Broadcast and Prairie Recorder* was the first to appear (in 1939), and one can easily agree with him that no better source exists for live country music radio programming of that era. Some of the country music columnists, such as Floy Case, still live; they should be interviewed in order to deepen our understanding of the "nationalization" of country music.

Pertinent articles and books on several musicians who were prominent during the war (such as those on Gene Autry, Bob Wills, Ernest Tubb, Roy Hall, and Charlie Monroe) have been discussed in the bibliographical essays for Chapters 4 and 5. My main concentration here will be on the dominant personality of the war period: Roy Acuff. Four interviews proved helpful in obtaining insights into Acuff's stylistic preferences and song sources: two with Acuff (Nashville, August 26, 1961, and Marthaville, Louisiana, 1981); one with Wesley Rose, Nashville, August 28, 1961; and one with Beecher Kirby, Nashville, July 27, 1972. Elizabeth Schlappi, however, has spent more time than anyone else researching the life and career of Acuff, and she has always freely provided assistance to me and to other historians. Her chief works are *Roy Acuff and His Smoky Mountain Boys Discography* (Country Research Series, *Disc Collector*, no. 23, 1966); the essay on Acuff in *Stars of Country Music*, edited by Bill C. Malone and Judith McCulloh (Urbana: University of Illinois Press, 1975), pp. 195–221; and a book, *Roy Acuff, the Smoky Mountain Boy* (Gretna, La.: Pelican Publishing Company, 1978). Acuff is the subject of an excellent Time-Life collection, organized and annotated by John Rumble (this collection is the best available selection of Acuff's recordings). A. C. Dunkleberger's *King of Country Music: The Life Story of Roy Acuff* (Nashville: Williams Printing Company, 1971), contains useful factual information but is completely uncritical in its approach. The story about Acuff's decision to claim that Rachel Veach and Brother Oswald were brother and sister is in the notes (p. 2) of Time-Life's *Women* collection. Original stanzas of "The Wabash Cannon Ball" are printed in George Milburn, *Hobo's Hornbook* (New York: Ives and Washburn, 1930). The sources of Acuff's songs should be a good research project for someone, but at least one of the lesser-known writers who supplied songs for him has been the subject of a couple of short sketches: "Jim Anglin: I Wanted to Be a Novelist" (no author listed), *MCN* 5, no. 2 (August 1967): 17, and Ivan M. Tribe and John W. Morris, "The Story of the Anglin Brothers," *Bluegrass Unlimited* 13, no. 5 (November 1978): 30–33. Another source, Fred Rose, is far from obscure. My original sketch of him came from *The ASCAP Biographical Dictionary of Composers, Authors, and Publishers*, p. 421, and from an interview with Wesley Rose (Nashville, August 28, 1961). The definitive treatment of Rose now is John W. Rumble, "Fred Rose and the Development of the Nashville Music Industry, 1942–1954" (Ph.D. thesis, Vanderbilt University, 1980). Finally, the source of the famous quote "To hell with Roosevelt; to hell with Babe Ruth; to hell with Roy Acuff!" is still unknown. One of its earliest appearances in print is in Dickson Hartwell, "Caruso of Mountain Music," *Colliers* 123, no. 10 (March 5, 1949): 26. Acuff told me that the original source of the story was war correspondent Ernie Pyle (interview, August 26, 1961).

The songs of the World War II period have not been collected or anthologized in any systematic way. *Billboard* began making its first tentative listings of "hillbilly hits" (as judged by jukebox play) in 1940, when it included such songs with "foreign" numbers (ethnic recordings), and was still lumping hillbilly and "race" recordings together at the end of the war. Broadcast Music, Inc. (BMI), did not publish its lists of "country hits" until 1944, and only a few songs were mentioned (the BMI-licensed country songs which had "gained national acceptance as measured by consistent appearance in the music business trade press"): *BMI Country Hits, 1944–1968* (New York: Broadcast Music, Inc., 1968), p. 2. BMI, though, can supply author and publishing data for most of the songs which appeared during the earlier war years. Some of the songs from the forties have been anthologized in books published by various companies (for example, *Forty Country and Western Hits of Our Times* (New York: Leeds Music Corporation, 1955) and *One Hundred Great Country and Western Songs*, vol. 2 (New York: Hill and Range Songs, 1964). Dorothy Horstman's *Sing Your Heart Out, Country Boy* (New York: E. P. Dutton, 1975), contains a large number of the songs which appeared between 1941 and 1945. Horstman's fine book (currently being revised and enlarged) is unique in its attempt to explain the origins of songs in the composers' own words (as much as possible).

The country songs that commented on the war would comprise a small volume by themselves. Horstman includes seven of the best in a section called "Songs of War and Patriotism," pp. 232–251, and Jennie A. Chinn quoted several others in her article, "There's a Star-Spangled Banner Waving Somewhere: Country-Western Songs of World War II," *JEMFQ* 16, no. 58 (Summer 1980): 74–80. The article only scratches the surface, however, and much more work needs to be done on the subject. One can envision, for example, a long article called "Country Music Goes to War: Songs of War and Patriotism, 1922–1984."

The songs of the forties, of course, did not all deal with the war by any means. Except for an occasional patriotic song such as "There's a Star-Spangled Banner Waving Somewhere," the songs which really signaled country music's growing national acceptance dealt with lost love, nostalgia, self-pity, or romance—time-honored themes that harked back to country's folk roots, Rex Griffin, the writer of the perennial favorite, "The Last Letter," still remains much less known than his great song. I learned a few things about him in interviews with musicians who knew or worked with him (Red River Dave, San Antonio, June 19, 1973; Hank Penny, January 17, 1981) and with his brother, Buddy Griffin, Dallas, July 6, 1973. Wiley Walker and Gene Sullivan, whose recordings of the lonesome "Live and Let Live" and "When My Blue Moon Turns to Gold Again" remained on jukeboxes throughout the war period, have been largely forgotten in recent years. My knowledge of them comes from interviews with Mrs. Wiley Walker in Oklahoma City, January 25, 1982; Wiley Walker, Jr., Oklahoma City, January 23, 1982; and Gene Sullivan, Oklahoma City, January 26, 1982 (all by phone). Wiley and Gene are richly deserving of a reissue album.

Al Dexter, whose "Pistol Packin' Mama" took the country by storm in 1943 (particularly in a "cover" version by Bing Crosby and the Andrews Sisters), received a considerable amount of publicity during the war. A couple of contemporary articles which commented on Dexter and his song were an unsigned sketch in *Life* 15, no. 11 (October 11, 1943): 55, and Maurice Zolotow, "Hillbilly Boom," *Saturday Evening Post* 216 (February 12, 1944): 22–23. Dexter supplied me with biographical information in a letter dated September 21, 1973 (from Denton, Texas), and in a phone interview on August 26, 1973. He also sent me an article by John W. Moody called "Wine, Women, and Song," *Denton Record-Chronicle*, February 11, 1973. Nick Tosches tells the story of "Pistol Packin' Mama's" origins in *Country: The Biggest Music in America* (New York: Stein and Day, 1977), pp. 192–195.

7. The Boom Period: The Emergence of a Big Business, 1946–1953

When country music demonstrated its powerful commercial appeal after the war, the entertainment trade journals began to pay it a respect that had long been absent. Indeed, the whole world of show business began to take it into account. Consequently, *Billboard*'s "top ten" listings of country songs dates from 1948. The first summary listings of this material, covering the years from 1948 to 1963 and compiled by the Record Market Research Division of *Billboard*, appeared in *The World of Country Music* (New York: Billboard, 1963), pp. 187, 189–199. *Country Song Roundup*, founded in Derby, Connecticut, in 1947, began its existence as the most enduring song-and-news magazine in country music history. The magazine still thrives in 1984.

Information on record releases, country radio shows (both live and DJ-directed), and personal appearances fills the pages of *Billboard* during these years, as well as the occasional yearbooks and encyclopedias distributed by the journal (see, for example, *The Billboard Encyclopedia of*

Music, 8th annual edition (1946–1947). I found additional information on record companies in Paul S. Carpenter, *Music: An Art and a Business* (Norman: University of Oklahoma Press, 1950), pp. 72–73, and on radio barn dances in Linnell Gentry, ed., *A History and Encyclopedia of Country, Western, and Gospel Music* (Nashville: McQuiddy Press, 1961), pp. 168–175 (unfortunately, this material was removed from Gentry's revised edition in 1969).

The exciting postwar California scene deserves a full-scale study, and one that Ken Griffis will probably write. In the meantime, a number of smaller articles have been helpful to me. Gerald F. Vaughan comments on Foreman Phillips' active role in "Foreman Phillips: Western Swing's Kingmaker," *JEMFQ* 15, no. 53 (Spring 1979): 27–29, but Hank Penny presents a much more negative view of Phillips in Rich Kienzle, "The Checkered Career of Hank Penny," *JCM* 8, no. 2 (1980): 63 (this is the best survey of Penny's career, although Ken Griffis, "Hank Penny: The Original Outlaw," *JEMFQ* 18, nos. 65–66 [Spring–Summer 1982]: 5–13, is also useful). Vaughan also adds to our knowledge of California's western ballroom circuit with "That Ozark Playboy: Red Murrell," *JEMFQ* 17, no. 61 (Fall 1981): 119–122, while Ken Griffis reminds us that Ray Whitley was more than a singing cowboy; he was also a popular band leader: "The Ray Whitley Story," *JEMFQ* 6, Part 2, no. 18 (Summer 1970): 65–68.

The great impact made by Spade Cooley and Tex Williams is discussed by Griffis in "The Tex Williams Story," *JEMFQ* 15, no. 53 (Spring 1979): 5–19, and by Rich Kienzle, in "When a Country Star Turns Murderer: The Strange, Tragic Case of Spade Cooley," *Country Music* 5, no. 10 (July 1977): 34, 36, 38, 64. I also found a contemporary biographical sketch on Williams in the *National Hillbilly News* 3, no. 2 (December 1947). The best introduction to Cooley and Williams is in the exciting music they made, a good sampling of which is *Spade Cooley*, Columbia FC37467 (a reissue of ten selections recorded from 1944 to 1946).

Merle Travis, the all-purpose musician who performed as a solo act and as an accompanist for musicians throughout California, receives his most serious treatment from Archie Green, in *Only a Miner: Studies in Recorded Coal-Mining Songs* (Urbana: University of Illinois Press, 1972). Here we find a discussion of how his classic "Sixteen Tons" and "Dark as a Dungeon" came to be written. The other and more prominent side of his performing nature—the good-natured, honky-tonk impulse—is portrayed in the Time-Life collection, *Honky Tonkin'*. Two articles based on interviews demonstrate the man's versatility and intelligence: Dorothy Horstman, "Merle Travis," *Country Music* 4, no. 1 (October 1975): 31–34, and Bob Baxter, "Merle Travis: The Man, the Music," *Guitar Player* 10, no. 9 (September 1976): 20–21, 28–36. It is a shame that Travis never wrote his autobiography, or a history of the California music scene. He was a walking library of country music history (see Merle Travis, "Recollections of Merle Travis, 1944–55," *JEMFQ* 15, no. 54 (Summer 1979): 107–114; and ibid., no. 55 (Fall 1979): 135–143.

Merle Travis and other California musicians played central roles in the development of the solid-body guitar and other electric instruments. In addition to the Rich Kienzle articles mentioned on p. 459, one should also read a couple of articles in *Guitar Player.*which expound upon the role played by Leo Fender: 5, no. 6 (September 1971): 9, 38; and 12, no. 5 (May 1978): 32ff. (both based on interviews).

Nudie the Tailor's influence in country music was as pervasive as that of Leo Fender. Two short sketches of the man which I have found helpful are Bill A. Wheeler, "Nudie the Tailor," *Country Music Review* (March–April 1965): 40–41, and Jan Otteson, "Nudie Is the Original 'Rhinestone Cowboy,'" *MCN* 15, no. 8 (February 1978): 13.

Despite the dynamic influence exerted by California musicians and personalities, the *Grand Ole Opry* had become, at least symbolically, the most important country music institution in the world. A couple of magazine articles suggest the reverence that most fans had for the show: Rufus Jarman, "Country Music Goes to Town," *Nation's Business* 41 (February 1953): 44–51, and Don Eddy, "Hillbilly Heaven," *American Magazine* 153 (March 1952): 29 ff. The most illuminating material for me, however, was the transcripts of the *Prince Albert Shows* (the thirty-minute segments carried on NBC). The transcripts listed the songs as well as the dialogue between comedians Minnie Pearl and Rod Brasfield and host Red Foley. Regrettably, Foley has been almost forgotten since his glory days in the fifties. Record reissues have almost completely passed him by, and writers have seldom discussed him. Charles Wolfe, however, does discuss him in *Kentucky Country: Folk and Country Music of Kentucky* (Lexington: State University Press of Kentucky, 1982), and at least one journal writer, John Pugh, has commemorated him: "The Late, Great Red Foley," *Country Music* 5, no. 9 (June 1976): 53–56.

The chief challenger of the *Grand Ole Opry*—the *Louisiana Hayride*— has found its historian in Stephen Ray Tucker, a doctoral candidate at Tulane University who is writing a general history of Louisiana Cajun and country music. He has already published "The Louisiana Hayride, 1948–54," in the *North Louisiana Historical Journal* 8, no. 5 (Fall 1977): 187–201, and the subject will constitute at least a chapter in his dissertation. I have obtained additional information on the show in interviews with Homer Bailes (Jennings, Louisiana, August 16, 1974), Paul Howard (Shreveport, Louisiana, August 26, 1974), and Pappy Covington (Shreveport, July 27, 1974). I have also seen a brief sketch by Frank Page and David Kent entitled "The Louisiana Hayride," *Country Gazette* 1, no. 5 (August 1976): 3.

The world of recording in the immediate postwar years has received scattered attention from writers, but no one has brought all the disparate threads together into one compact article or book. That crucial agent of country music dissemination, the disc jockey, has received only minimal historical treatment. The best article I have seen is by Hugh Cherry: "Country DJ's Carry Music to People," *MCN* 18, no. 4 (October 1980): 18–19. The small record labels have not been much better documented, and the most attention given to them, in fact, is in books devoted to black music. I obtained some information on the Gold Star and Starday labels from Pappy Daily (interview, Houston, August 19, 1977). Syd Nathan and his King label are discussed in Richard L. Gordon, "The Man Who Is King," *Saga* (January 1951), reprinted in *JEMF Newsletter* 4, no. 10, Part 2 (June 1968): 63–66, while the Bullet label's history is described by Martin Hawkins in "Bullet Records: A Shot in the Dark," *JCM* 8, no. 3 (1981): 33–41. And one must not overlook John Broven's enthusiastic and marvelously detailed *South to Louisiana* (Gretna, La.: Pelican Publishing Co., 1983), which discusses J. D. Miller and other Louisiana recording men who recorded an abundance of country, Cajun, and blues artists.

Nashville's rise to prominence as a recording center for country music should not cause one to forget that much recording went on in Louisiana, Dallas, Cincinnati, and other places. Jim Beck's Studio in Dallas, for example—where people like Lefty Frizzell, Ray Price, and Marty Robbins made some of their best recordings—has not been properly studied. The minimal amount of knowledge I have of Beck comes from Bill Callahan (interview, Dallas, February 8, 1982) and from Buddy Griffin (interview, Dallas, July 6, 1973).

Nashville's early ventures into the recording field are well described in John Rumble, "The Emergence of Nashville as a Recording Center: Logbooks from the Castle Studios, 1952–53," *JCM* 7, no. 3 (December 1948): 22–42. The original Nashville sessions musicians are discussed in Time-Life's *Hank Williams* collection, and in Charles Wolfe, "Tommy Jackson: Nashville Fiddler," *Bluegrass Unlimited* 15, no. 3 (September 1980): 42–47. Chet Atkins' rise to prominence is discussed in Bill Ivey's "Chet Atkins," in *Stars of Country Music*, edited by Bill C. Malone and Judith McCulloh (Urbana: University of Illinois Press, 1975), pp. 301–316, and in Atkins' autobiography (written with Bill Neely), *Country Gentleman* (Chicago: Henry Regnery Co., 1974).

My discussion of song writing and publishing in the early fifties owes much to interviews with Jim Denny (Nashville, August 25, 1961) and Cindy Walker (Mexia, Texas, August 12, 1976) and to a short article on songwriters in Billboard, *The World of Country Music*, pp. 146, 162–163. Sketches of individual songwriters that have been useful to me include "Jim Anglin: I Wanted to Be a Novelist," *MCN* 5, no. 2 (August 1967): 17; Ivan M. Tribe, "Mac Odell: The Ole Country Boy," *Bluegrass Unlimited* 11, no. 4 (October 1976): 30–34; and two on Felice and Boudleaux Bryant,

"Country Music Is What You Make It" (by Boudleaux Bryant), *Nashville Sound*, 1, no. 1 (September 1975): 8–10, and Lee Rector, "Writers Felice and Boudleaux Review Thirty Years," *MCN* 17, no. 8 (February 1980): 7.

When we venture into the area of performers, we find a proliferation of both musicians and publicity sketches that is almost impossible to discuss. The material that follows will not be definitive by any means. Some performers who were treated in earlier chapter notes—like Grandpa Jones— will not be discussed again. Others will be omitted because little has been written on them. Jimmy Dickens, for example, has been named to the Country Music Hall of Fame, but no serious articles have been devoted to him, and only one record reissue (it is to be hoped that his Hall of Fame honor will generate his rediscovery).

The brother duet and family tradition of singing lingered in the performances of such musicians as the Bailes Brothers, the Louvin Brothers, Johnny and Jack, the Maddox Brothers and Rose, and in bluegrass (which will be discussed in Chapter 10). Most of my knowledge of the Bailes Brothers comes from a long interview with Homer Bailes (Jennings, Louisiana, August 16, 1974) and a shorter one with Clyde Baum (Pollock, Louisiana, October 19, 1974). Ivan Tribe also supplied me a tape of an interview he conducted with Johnnie Bailes (August 18, 1974). Tribe's two short essays on the groups are indispensable: "The Bailes Brothers," *Bluegrass Unlimited* 9, no. 8 (February 1975): 8–13, and "West Virginia Homefolks: The Bailes Brothers," *OTM*, no. 19 (Winter 1975–1976): 17–20. Don Rhodes, "Remembering the Bailes Brothers," *Pickin'* 4, no. 2 (March 1977): 6–14, provides a good summary of their career, and *National Hillbilly News* 3, no. 3 (January–February 1948): 7, tells about them at the time they joined the *Louisiana Hayride*. The most interesting items of all, though, on the Bailes Brothers are the lps composed of material taken from their transcribed radio shows on KWKH in the late forties. Complete with commercials, songbook pitches, and personal appearance announcements, the albums are wonderful introductions to the Bailes Brothers style and to the era of live radio: *The Bailes Brothers*, Old Homestead OHCS 103 and 104.

The Louvin Brothers are also featured on an album composed of transcribed radio shows: *Songs That Tell a Story*, Rounder 1030 (notes by Douglas B. Green). Taken from programs presented on WZOB in Fort Payne, Alabama, in 1952, the lps capture the Louvins at their best, when they were gospel singers performing with only mandolin and guitar. This is an important album to have, not only because it re-creates the atmosphere of old-time radio shows but also because it stresses a side of their performing approach which is neglected in other big reissue projects: both the *Smithsonian Collection of Classic Country Music* and the Time-Life *Duet* project feature only the "secular" songs of the Louvins. I obtained some biographical information from Charlie Louvin (interview, Meridian, Mississippi, May 25, 1977), who later supplied me with tapes of most of the Louvin Brothers' recordings. Two of the better articles on the duo are Don Rhodes, "Looking Back on the Louvin Brothers," *Pickin'* 3, no. 2 (March 1976): 4–12, and Suzy Lowry Geno, "Charlie and Ira—The Louvin Brothers," *Bluegrass Unlimited* 17, no. 9 (March 1983): 12–18.

Johnny and Jack have been the subject of many scattered references and sketches but are seldom discussed in any extended fashion. Ivan Tribe and John Morris give some information about their origins (particularly Jack Anglin) in "The Story of the Anglin Brothers," *Bluegrass Unlimited* 13, no. 5 (November 1978): 30–33, and Dixie Deen writes a very good summary of the two singers in "Johnny Wright: Again the Bugle Blows," *MCN* 5, no. 1 (July 1967): 3–6, 24.

Rose Maddox did much to clarify my understanding of her family in an interview on January 23, 1982 (by telephone to Ashland, Oregon), but the best introduction to the Maddox Brothers and Rose is the two albums of reissued material released on the Arhoolie label (5016 and 5017). Keith Olesen's notes give us a good summary of the group's lives and career, while the recordings convey the zest and vitality of their performances.

Rose Maddox was one of several women who began to compete favorably with men in the postwar years. She, Texas Ruby, Cousin Emmy, Molly O'Day, Wilma Lee Cooper, Kitty Wells, and Goldie Hill are anthologized in Time-Life's *Women* collection along with brief written biographies. I learned the outline of Martha Carson's career in an interview with her in Nashville, August 16, 1973. Information on her earlier career as part of the duet of James and Martha Carson is provided in Ivan Tribe, "James Carson Roberts," *Bluegrass Unlimited* 14, no. 11 (May 1980): 66–72. Wilma Lee Cooper has drawn the attention of researchers because of her unwavering commitment to tradition. Sue Thrasher conducted a good interview with her in *Long Journey Home, Southern Exposure,* Summer–Fall 1977, pp. 90–97, while Douglas B. Green, in "Wilma Lee and Stoney Cooper," *Bluegrass Unlimited* 8, no. 9 (March 1974): 25–27, and Wayne W. Daniel, "Wilma Lee Cooper: America's Most Authentic Mountain Singer," ibid. 16, no. 8 (February 1982): 12–17, present good summaries and evaluations of her career.

Molly O'Day's story has been well told by Ivan Tribe and John Morris: "Molly O'Day and Lynn Davis," *Bluegrass Unlimited* 9, no. 3 (September 1974): 10–15, and *Molly O'Day, Lynn Davis and the Cumberland Mountain Folks: A Bio-Discography,* JEMF Special Series, no. 7 (1975). References to O'Day also show up in material devoted to Hank Williams, the Bailes Brothers, and Mac Wiseman, because she influenced these and other singers in dramatic ways.

As might be expected, published material on Kitty Wells is not hard to find. Representative articles include Geoff Lane, "The Queen of Country Music," *Country Music* 3, no. 3 (December 1974): 40–45; Mary Ellen

Moore, "Kitty Wells: The One and Only Queen of Country Music," ibid. 5, no. 6 (March 1977): 47–48; Douglas B. Green, "The Queen Still Reigns," ibid. 8, no. 9 (June 1980): 41–44; and an article that should put to rest any idea that Kitty was a woman's liberationist, "Woman Put on Earth for Man to Look After, Kitty Wells Says" (unsigned), *Country Style*, no. 3 (August 1976): 17. The previously mentioned article on Johnny Wright (by Dixie Deen) also contains interesting material on Kitty Wells. The best introduction to her quiet, soulful singing is in the music of two fine lps: *Country Hall of Fame*, MCA CDL8504, and *The Golden Years*, Rounder Special Series 13.

There is a great need for a major article on the comedy-singing acts of country music, as well as an anthology of their recorded material. Bill Carlisle is discussed by Dixie Deen in "Woman behind the Man," *MCN* 4, no. 1 (July 1966), and in Wolfe's *Kentucky Country*, pp. 64–65. Lonzo and Oscar receive brief attention in Aline Miller, "Lonzo and Oscar," *Pickin'* 4, no. 4 (May 1977): 32–33, while Homer and Jethro are discussed by David Grisman in "Jethro Burns," *Frets* 1, no. 8 (October 1979): 38–41. Douglas B. Green has a section called "Comedy" in *Country Roots: The Origins of Country Music* (New York: Hawthorn, 1976), pp. 65–87, in which Carlisle, Lonzo and Oscar, Homer and Jethro, and other comedians are briefly discussed. Brief biographical sketches of these men are also found in Gentry, *A History and Encyclopedia of Country, Western, and Gospel Music*.

The boogie craze in country music and its origins are best described in Nick Tosches, *Country: The Biggest Music in America* (New York: Stein and Day, 1977), pp. 29–31. Stephen Ray Tucker has organized and annotated an excellent collection of "blues and boogie" material for the Smithsonian Institution as part of their proposed series of reissued country recordings. The release date is unknown to both Tucker and me.

The mainstream country singers of the early fifties—such as Carl Smith, Hank Locklin, and George Morgan—largely remain undocumented, and their music remains unreissued. Norm Cohen has suggested why: "The country music of the years immediately after the second world war has fallen between the cracks of the reissue business. Too late to catch the interests of the old-timey enthusiasts, too old for contemporary country fans, too country for bluegrassers, it has been neglected by almost everyone" (*JEMFQ* 15, no. 56 [Winter 1979]: 244). Although sketches and occasional interviews with such musicians appear in *Country Song Roundup*, *Music City News*, and various short-lived country magazines, the reader is advised to consult Gentry for basic biographical data.

Several of the honky-tonk stylists, however, have been justly appreciated. I participated in the organization and wrote the notes for Time-Life's *Honky Tonkin'*. Here one will hear the music of, and read sketches about, such performers as Floyd Tillman, Ernest Tubb, Hank Thompson, Webb

Pierce, and Lefty Frizzell. These musicians, and more, are also in the *Smithsonian Collection of Classic Country Music*. Interviews have been helpful in obtaining knowledge about several of the honky-tonk performers. I interviewed Floyd Tillman in Austin, October 21, 1971; in Bacliff, Texas, May 31, 1974; and in Austin, February 15, 1982. As mentioned in the notes to Chapter 5, my June 27, 1978, interview with Gordon Baxter in Silsbee, Texas, proved most helpful in understanding Moon Mullican. Special mention, though, should be made of an album devoted to Mullican: *Moon Mullican: Seven Nights to Rock*, Western 2001, an assemblage of several of his King recordings from 1946 to 1956, and with complete and discerning notes by Rich Kienzle. Relevant material on Ernest Tubb is also given in Chapter 5, although the reader should be reminded of an excellent lp which concentrates on the music of the postwar period, *Ernest Tubb: Honky Tonk Classics*, Rounder Special Series 14 (notes by Ronnie Pugh). An interview with Hank Thompson in Kerrville, Texas, July 3, 1977, provided me with insights about his long and important career. John Broven, in *South to Louisiana*, has much to say that is good and enlightening about Harry Choates, particularly in pages 29–35. Mike Leadbitter had earlier discussed the singer-fiddler in "Harry Choates: Cajun Fiddle Ace," *OTM*, no. 6 (Autumn 1972): 20–22. I learned something about Choates' early performing years, and about the possible sources of his style, in an interview with Leo Soileau in Ville Platte, Louisiana, June 15, 1974.

A strong revival of interest in Lefty Frizzell occurred after his death, and more will come now that he has been elected to the Country Music Hall of Fame. One entire lp side (seven songs) of Time-Life's *Honky Tonkin'* collection album was devoted to Frizzell, and other reissues of his material have appeared frequently. Bill Callahan and Alice Frizzell supplied me with information about Lefty's early life and career on February 18, 1982, and March 2, 1982 (both by telephone). Geoff Lane has written one of the best of the popular articles on Frizzell: "The Last of Lefty Frizzell," *Country Music* 4, no. 2 (November 1975): 38–42, 63.

The great gap between Webb Pierce's immense popularity in the early fifties and his current almost total neglect is hard to understand. He should already be in the Country Music Hall of Fame. In the meantime, several articles provide glimpses of his personality, style, and contributions. These include Scott Cohen, "Webb," *Country Music* 3, no. 5 (February 1975): 34–37; "Pierce—a Leader Then, a Leader Now," *MCN* 13, no. 9 (March 1976): 16; Jack D. Johnson, "The Webb Pierce Story," *Country Music Review* 1, no. 6 (February 1964): 5; and a very favorable review of a Pierce concert in Austin, Texas, by John Bustin, "Pierce Has Solid Hold on Country Music Fans," *Austin American*, October 7, 1964. Pierce's role in popularizing the pedal steel guitar is discussed in Jean-Charles Costa,

"The Country Guitar: The Mysterious Pedal Steel," *Country Music* 1, no. 1 (June 1973): 42–44, and John Haggard, "Bud Isaacs," *Guitar Player* 10, no. 11 (November 1976): 31, 78, 80.

Eddy Arnold, the first great crossover stylist in country music, has never suffered from media neglect. Dixie Deen wrote an interesting sketch of him called "Eddy Arnold: His World," *MCN* 3, no. 10 (April 1966): 1, 4, 23. Arnold's autobiography, *It's a Long Way from Chester County* (New York: Pyramid Books, 1969), gives the basic facts of his life and career but says too little about the country music world that provided the context for his rise to fame. Arnold says nothing, for example, about Roy Wiggins, the steel guitarist who created the original Eddy Arnold instrumental sound. Douglas B. Green corrects that imbalance somewhat in "Roy Wiggins Stays 'In' with Ting-a-Ling Style," *MCN* 14, no. 4 (October 1976): 21. *Billboard* issues in the mid- and late forties provide all the evidence one needs of Arnold's powerful commercial appeal, and *The World of Country Music*, which summarized all the "top ten" listings from 1948 to 1963, shows that no other country singer equaled him in the recording of hit songs.

One of my greatest disappointments as a researcher has been my inability to arrange an interview with Hank Snow, one of my all-time favorites. I have instead relied on a handful of printed sources and, of course, his very large recorded output. *The Hank Snow Twenty-Fifth Anniversary Album* (Nashville: privately printed, 1961) is a good compendium of biographical and discographical information. "Country Song Roundup Talks with Hank Snow," *CSR* 20, no. 112 (November 1968): 11–13, is a fairly substantial interview, while two *Country Music* essays provide good discussions of him: Marshall Fallwell, "Hank Snow Moves On in the Old Tradition," *Country Music* 2, no. 3 (November 1973): 66–71, and Peter Guralnick, "The Singing Ranger: Hank Snow," ibid. 7, no. 2 (November–December 1978): 28–32.

Another great stylist of the fifties, Slim Whitman, has received extensive media attention in the last several years because of the remarkable success of his "television special" records. I have not seen Kenneth L. Gibble, *Mr. Songman: The Slim Whitman Story* (Elgin, Ill.: Brethren Press, 1982), but have instead used some of the popular accounts that have appeared in music or commercial magazines. Kelly Delaney, "Slim Whitman Is Loved around the World," *MCN* 17, no. 7 (January 1980): 13, is fair and objective, but Richard Sanders, "Slim Whitman," *Us* 5, no. 12 (June 9, 1981): 72–74, calls him "the throaty thrush of the Moral Majority" and says that he "epitomizes all that is hokey and heartfelt in the American dream."

When writing on Hank Williams for the first edition of this book, I relied most heavily upon Eli Waldron, "Country Music: The Death of Hank Williams," *Reporter* 12, no. 10 (May 19, 1955): 35–37; Waldron, "Country Music: The Squaya Dansu from Nashville," *Reporter* pp 12, no. 11 (June

2, 1955): 39–41; *CSR* (Special Hank Williams Memorial Issue) 1, no. 24 (June 1953): 5–14; Rufus Jarman, "Country Music Goes to Town," *Nation's Business* 41 (February 1953): 44–51; Bernard Asbell, "Simple Songs of Sex, Sin, and Salvation," *Show: The Magazine of the Performing Arts* 2, no. 2 (February 1962): 88–91; various issues of *Billboard*; and interviews with Audrey Williams (Austin, July 2, 1962) and Wesley Rose (Nashville, August 28, 1961).

Since then, the story of Hank Williams has been broadened and clarified by the appearance of two major biographies, at least one solid reminiscence by a Drifting Cowboy (Jerry Rivers), a wealth of reissued recordings, and a few fine articles. The single best approach to Williams is the Time-Life collection *Hank Williams*, with notes by Roger M. Williams. Roger Williams (no relation to Hank) also wrote the best-balanced and most solidly researched biography of Hank: *Sing a Sad Song: The Life of Hank Williams* (Garden City, N.Y.: Doubleday, 1970; republished by University of Illinois Press, 1981). One of the great virtues of the University of Illinois Press edition is its inclusion of a Hank Williams Discography compiled by Bob Pinson. The most recent biography—Chet Flippo, *Your Cheating Heart: A Biography of Hank Williams* (New York: Simon and Schuster, 1981)—presents an uglier and more tragic picture of Hank than does Roger Williams. The book is troubling to many people because of its use of fictionalized dialogue and because of its assertion that Hank did not write some of the songs attributed to him. Jerry Rivers, on the other hand, gives an affectionate account of Williams in *Hank Williams: From Life to Legend* (Denver: Heather Enterprises, 1976). Among the best popular articles which touch upon Hank Williams are Ed Linn, "The Short Life of Hank Williams," *Saga* 13, no. 4 (January 1957): 8–11, 86–91; Tom Ayres, "Son, Can You Play That Thing," *Country Rambler*, no. 4 (November 4, 1976): 42–43 (about steel guitar player Felton Pruitt, but very good on Hank and the early *Louisiana Hayride*); and "Remembering Hank" (interviews with several people conducted by Hank Williams, Jr.), *Country Music* 3, no. 6 (March 1975): 24–27. My understanding of Hank's second marriage and his last years on the *Louisiana Hayride* was enhanced by my interview with Paul Howard in Shreveport, July 26, 1974.

Two final items of interest should be mentioned, Hank's mother's reminiscence of her son (which I have not seen), and the 1964 movie of his life (which I have seen). Lilly Williams' book (actually written by ghostwriter Allan Rankin), *Our Hank Williams* (Montgomery, Ala.: privately published, 1953), should tell us much about the mother if not the son. The movie, *Your Cheating Heart* (with George Hamilton in the title role), was Hollywood's sanitized version of the Williams legend. Produced by MGM in 1964, the film completely omitted Hank's second wife, presented him at the end as a reformed drunkard, made no reference to drugs, and featured a style of country instrumentation that was more representative of the sixties than of Hank's own time. The movie's chief saving grace was the singing of Hank, Jr., on the soundtrack.

8. The Development of Country-Pop Music and the Nashville Sound

A short sketch of Mitch Miller, the producer who did most in the early fifties to move country songs into the repertories of pop singers—along with a list of such songs which made the transition—is in *The World of Country Music* (New York: Billboard, 1963), p. 145. But proof that "traditional" country singers such as Hank Snow were continuing to thrive on down to 1955 is in *Number One Country Singles* (New York: Billboard Publications, 1980). Further evidence of country music's burgeoning financial status is the appearance of two new country music journals, *Country and Western Jamboree* in 1955 and *Rustic Rhythm* in 1957, both with slick covers and attractive formats, and each boasting national circulation. Before long, though, each became filled with stories about the new rockabilly sensations, and neither survived long after the rock-and-roll explosion.

The books and articles that describe rock-and-roll's roots and its early development are beginning to constitute a rather large library. Arnold Shaw's *Honkers and Shouters: The Golden Years of Rhythm and Blues* (New York: Colliers Books, 1978) is a detail-filled account that concentrates on the singers of the forties and fifties. Tony Glover, "R&B," *Sing Out* 15, no. 2 (May 1965): 7–13, is a good short survey which comments on the way rhythm-and-blues was watered down by rock-and-roll musicians. Nick Tosches, in *Country: The Biggest Music in America* (New York: Stein and Day, 1977), pp. 29–33, talks about the hillbilly boogie exponents of the late forties and early fifties who may have influenced the early rockabillies. The most complete general histories of rock-and-roll are Carl Belz, *The Story of Rock* (New York, Oxford University Press, 1969), and Charles Gillett, *The Sound of the City: The Rise of Rock 'n' Roll* (New York: Dell, 1972). Jim Miller, ed., *The Rolling Stone Illustrated History of Rock 'n' Roll*, 2d rev. ed. (New York: Random House/Rolling Stone Press, 1981), is an anthology of articles dealing with all aspects of rock music, from Elvis to the present. One of the best modern writer-critics of rock and popular music, Peter Guralnick, has written two provocative books of essays dealing with blues, rock-and-roll, and country musicians: *Feel like Going Home: Portraits in Blues and Rock 'n' Roll* (London: Omnibus Press, 1978), and *Lost Highway: Journeys and Arrivals of American Musicians* (Boston: David R. Godine, 1979).

The most comprehensive account of the company which introduced the rockabilly sound to the world is Colin Escott and Martin Hawkins, *Sun Records: The Brief History of the Legendary Record Label*, 2d rev. ed.

(New York: Quick Fox, 1980). John Pugh contributes a shorter chronicle of the famous label in "The Rise and Fall of Sun Records," *Country Music* 2, no. 3 (November 1973): 26–32, and Barbara Sims tells what it was like at the beginning in "Sun Records: An Insider's View," *JEMFQ* 12, no. 43 (Autumn 1976): 119–121. Although Michael Bane touches on the subject in *White Boy Singin' the Blues: The Black Roots of White Rock* (New York: Penguin Books, 1982), the best compact account of rockabilly music is Nick Tosches, "Rockabilly," in *The Illustrated History of Country Music*, edited by Patrick Carr (New York: Country Music Magazine Press, 1979), pp. 217–237.

Elvis Presley has inspired a vast and proliferating literature, some of which is reviewed in Mark Crispin Miller, "The King," *New York Review of Books* 24, no. 20 (December 8, 1977): 38–42. Jerry Hopkins, *Elvis: A Biography* (New York: Warner Books, 1972; originally published in 1971) is still the most reliable and objective book-length treatment of Presley, and his *Elvis: The Final Years* (New York: St. Martin's Press, 1980) is a balanced, and yet sobering, account of his subject's tragic decline and demise. Albert Goldman's best-selling and widely publicized biography, *Elvis* (New York: McGraw-Hill, 1981), contains many fascinating vignettes, including the story of Colonel Parker's Dutch origins, but one can hardly escape the conclusion that Goldman despises Elvis, the South, and the hillbilly culture that gave the singer birth. The best interpretation of Presley, and a brilliant exposition of the tensions in southern culture that gave rise to both country music and rock-and-roll, is Greil Marcus, *Mystery Train: Images of America in Rock 'n' Roll Music*, 2d rev. ed. (New York: E. P. Dutton, 1982). A more extended effort to relate Presley to southern culture is Jac Tharpe, ed., *Elvis: Images and Fancies* (Jackson: University Press of Mississippi, 1979), a series of essays by such writers as Stephen Ray Tucker, Linda Ray Pratt, Van K. Brock, Charles Wolfe, and myself.

The published accounts dealing with other rockabillies are also beginning to be quite extensive. Women have not been neglected, and Robert K. Oermann and Mary A. Bufwack have written a fine study, including a discography, of such singers as Wanda Jackson, Brenda Lee, and Janis Martin: "Rockabilly Women," *JCM* 8, no. 1 (May 1979): 65–94. Carl Perkins (with Ron Rendleman) has written an autobiography, *Disciple in Blue Suede Shoes* (Grand Rapids, Mich.: Zondervan, 1978), which stresses his religious conversion. Further insight into Perkins' music, though, can be found in Michael Lydon, *Rock Folk: Portraits from the Rock 'n' Roll Pantheon* (New York: Dial Press, 1971), and in Patrick Carr, "Carl Perkins, Livin' Legend," *Country Music* 2, no. 1 (September 1973): 65–71. John Goldrosen, *The Buddy Holly Story*, 2d rev. ed. (New York: Quick Fox, 1979), is an excellent biography, but one can also learn much from William J. Bush, "Buddy Holly," *Guitar Player* 16, no. 6 (June 1982): 64–66, 74–82, 86, 90–108. The Everly Brothers are discussed in one essay in Philip

Norman, *The Road Goes On Forever* (New York: Fireside Books, 1982), but their country background is best described in an essay written by their father: Ike Everly, "Father Calls Mother Secret of Amazing Success," *Country and Western Jamboree* 3, no. 5 (August 1957): 15, 34, and ibid. 4, no. 1 (Summer 1958): 10–16, 33, 38. Of course, no better example of their country roots can be cited than the album *Songs Our Daddy Taught Us*, Cadence CLP3016.

Jerry Lee Lewis has been fascinating to writers, and several of them have written books or long articles about him. Nick Tosches talks about him at great length in *Country: The Biggest Music in America* and has written a biography of Lewis with the provocative title *Hellfire: The Jerry Lee Lewis Story* (New York: Delacorte, 1982). *New York Times* music critic Robert Palmer wrote a good article called "The Devil and Jerry Lee Lewis," *Rolling Stone* 13 (December 1979), and later followed that up with a biography, *Jerry Lee Lewis Rocks* (New York: Delilah Books, 1981). A former wife, Myra Gail Lewis (with Murray Silver), wrote still another book on the controversial singer, *Great Balls of Fire: The Uncensored Story of Jerry Lee Lewis* (New York: Quill Books, 1982). When writing about Lewis, the subject of religion can hardly be avoided. One of the best short expositions of the impact made by Pentecostalism on Lewis is Stephen Ray Tucker, "Pentecostalism and Popular Culture in the South: A Study of Four Musicians," *Journal of Popular Culture* 16, no. 3 (Winter 1982): 68–80.

Marty Robbins was the first mainstream country singer to jump on the rockabilly bandwagon. A couple of short articles give the main outlines of his story, "Marty Robbins," *Rustic Rhythm* 1, no. 1 (April 1957): 20–21, and "Alias Marty Robbins," *Hoedown* 1, no. 2 (June 1966): 8–12, but the best introduction to his life and music is the Time-Life collection *Marty Robbins* (with notes by Patricia Hall). The forty reissued recordings show just how versatile he was, but the fullest exposition of his rockabilly leanings is a German reissue, *Rockin' Rollin' Robbins*, Bear Family BFX15045 (seventeen recordings made between 1954 and 1958).

Two other singers who were able to adjust to the new accent on youth generated by rock-and-roll were Sonny James and Johnny Cash. The remarkably enduring James deserves more attention than he has received from writers. Two articles suggest why he has not been more appealing to publicists: Robert Adels, "Sonny James: At All Times, in All Ways, the Southern Gentleman," *Country Music* 2, no. 1 (September 1973): 46–49, and Michael Bane, "Sonny James Sticks to Ice Cream," *Country Music* 5, no. 5 (February 1977): 42–46. Johnny Cash, on the other hand, has always demonstrated a superb mastery of media exploitation. He has been the subject of popular newsstand biographies, the best of which is Christopher Wren, *Winners Got Scars Too: The Life and Legends of Johnny Cash* (New York: Dial Press, 1971), and he has written an autobiography, *Man in Black* (Grand Rapids, Mich.: Zondervan, 1975), which is largely designed as an "inspirational" tract. John Grissim comments on Cash in *Country Music: White Man's Blues* (New York: Coronet Communications, 1970), and Tom Dearmore notes that Cash's protest and social activism tend to ignore contemporary questions of war, poverty, and racism: "First Angry Man of Country Singers," *New York Times Magazine*, September 21, 1969, pp. 32–49, 54–58. The most serious student of Cash has been Fred Danker, who has written on him in several forums: an essay in *Stars of Country Music*, edited by Bill C. Malone and Judith McCulloh (Urbana: University of Illinois Press, 1975), pp. 317–337; articles such as "The Repertory and Style of a Country Singer: Johnny Cash," *JAF* 85 (October–December 1972): 309–329; and the notes to the Time-Life collection *Johnny Cash*. John L. Smith adds further to our knowledge of Cash's recorded output with *Johnny Cash's Discography and Recording History, 1955–1968* (JEMF Special Series, no. 2).

The country-pop impulse is well defined in Eddy Arnold's autobiography, *It's a Long Way from Chester County* (New York: Pyramid Books, 1969) and in Chet Atkins' autobiography, *Country Gentleman* (Chicago: Henry Regnery Co., 1974). Charlie Lamb gave me his personal testimony as to how country music publicists adjusted to the desire for pop recognition (interview, Nashville, August 28, 1961). The forging of Chet Atkins' "compromise" is best described in Bill Ivey's essay on Atkins in *Stars of Country Music*, pp. 301–316, and Atkins' reflections about what he had done are discussed in John Gabree, "Chet Atkins: Story of a Quiet Man," *Country Music* 2, no. 8 (April 1974): 24–31. Atkins expresses some regrets about the role he played in introducing sophisticated arrangements to country music in Robert Windeler, "Bio—Chet Atkins," *People Weekly*, December 16, 1974, p. 62.

The artists-and-repertoire men who engineered the country-pop fusion are discussed in *The World of Country Music*, pp. 58–72, and in several *Billboard* issues extending from 1957 to the early sixties—for example, 69, no. 46 (November 11, 1957): 42, and 72, no. 28 (July 11, 1960): 29. Popular articles which commented on the phenomenon and indicated its commercial fruits include Goddard Lieberson, "Country Sweeps the Country," *New York Times Magazine*, July 28, 1957, pp. 13 ff.; Clarence B. Newman, "Homespun Harmony," *Wall Street Journal* 37, no. 141 (May 3, 1957): 1, 6; Bernard Asbell, "Simple Songs of Sex, Sin, and Salvation," *Show: The Magazine of the Performing Arts* 2, no. 2 (February 1962): 88–91; and Richard Warren Lewis, "Thar's Gold in Them Thar Hillbillies," *Show Business Illustrated* 2, no. 2 (February 1962): 32–38.

I do not know who coined the term "Nashville sound," but I first heard it used by Tommy Hill, who was then a recording engineer for Starday Records, in an interview in Nashville, August 23, 1961. The sessions musicians have been often mentioned in popular and trade magazines, but

Rich Kienzle has written two of the most discerning articles about them: "Hank Garland: Country Jazz Pioneer," *Guitar Player*, January 1981, pp. 76–86, and "The Piano Is a Stringed Instrument," *Country Music* 9, no. 7 (March 1981): 10, 12–13. Alice M. Gant wrote a heavily sociological article on the Nashville musicians which mentioned no one by name; however, in the midst of her long exposition (pp. 29–30) she did explain the "number system" used by the performers: "The Musicians in Nashville," *JCM* 3, no. 2 (Summer 1972): 24–44. Bill Ivey gives a twenty-five-year retrospective look at the Nashville sound in "Commercialization and Tradition in the Nashville Sound," in *Folk Music and Modern Sound*, edited by William Ferris and Mary Hart (Jackson: University Press of Mississippi, 1982), pp. 129–141.

The literature on the country-pop singers of the late fifties is not extensive, but Linnell Gentry, ed., *A History and Encyclopedia of Country, Western, and Gospel Music* (Nashville: McQuiddy Press, 1961; rev. ed., 1969), has brief biographical blurbs on all of them, and *BMI Country Hits, 1944–1968* (New York: Broadcast Music, Inc., 1968) and Billboard's *Number One Country Singles* give evidence of their popularity (particularly in 1957 and 1958). Dixie Deen wrote a very good four-part article on Skeeter Davis: "Skeeter Davis: Born to Sing," *MCN* 4, no. 7 (January 1967): 3–4; no. 8 (February 1967): 6, 8–9; no. 9 (March 1967): 6, 9; no. 10 (April 1967): 30. Skeeter Davis claimed in an interview with Archie Campbell on the program *Yesteryear in Nashville* that the 1953 recordings of the Davis Sisters influenced the style of harmony that came to prevail in country music (such as that of the Everly Brothers) while also popularizing the pedal-steel guitar (from a taped, syndicated presentation on the Nashville Television Network). Davis' colleague on RCA, Don Gibson, was discussed in an article whose title is a bit exaggerated: "Don Gibson: An Exclusive In-Depth Interview," *CSR* 21, no. 124 (November 1969): 12–13, 40. Ferlin Husky received brief treatment in Frieda Barter, "Ferlin Husky—What's in a Name," *Country and Western Jamboree* 1, no. 12 (February 1956): 8–9. Faron Young has received more coverage than most, partly because of his enduring commercial appeal, but also because he has been good copy with his humor and salty language. See Hubert Long, "Faron Young," *Rustic Rhythm* 1, no. 2 (May 1957): 16–20; Bob Allen, "Faron Young: Live Fast, Love Hard and Keep On Cussin'," *Country Music* 9, no. 1 (September 1980): 28–31; and Jerry Bailey, "The Singing Sheriff Shoots from the Hip," ibid. 3, no. 2 (November 1974): 58–66.

Three of the country-pop singers have continued to generate extensive written coverage, while also being the subject of numerous record reissues. Although each is deceased, Marty Robbins, Jim Reeves, and Patsy Cline continue to demonstrate enormous commercial appeal. Robbins has been discussed earlier. My knowledge of Jim Reeves comes mainly from interviews with his mother, Beulah Reeves (DeBerry, Texas, September 7,

1966), and Tom Perryman (Henderson, Texas, September 7, 1966). A good recent summary of Reeves is Rich Kienzle, "Jim Reeves: The Undying Legacy," *Country Music* 7, no. 9 (July–August 1979): 19–21. Patsy Cline is honored with three songs in the Time-Life collection *The Women* (more than any other performer), has been discussed in numerous articles, such as Donn Hecht, "I Remember Patsy Cline," *Country Music* 2, no. 2 (October 1973): 42–47, figures prominently in Loretta Lynn's autobiography, *Coal Miner's Daughter* (New York: Warner Books, 1976), and has been the subject of a biography: Ellis Nassour, *Patsy Cline* (New York: Tower Publications, 1981).

The founding and purposes of the Country Music Association are discussed in *Billboard* 66, no. 46 (November 13, 1954): 14; and 70, no. 26 (June 30, 1958): 9; and by Harry Stone, "The Country Music Association," in *The Country Music's Who's Who* (first annual edition, 1960), p. 79. *CMA Close-Up* (a monthly publication of the association) has since then been a continuing source of information on the active trade organization.

The establishment of the Country Music Hall of Fame and Museum is described in *Billboard Music Week*, November 6, 1961, p. 52, and November 17, 1962, p. 5; and in *MCN* 4, no. 10 (April 1967): 8, 15, and 5, no. 4 (November 1967): 32. Dixie Deen also provides a good history of the Hall of Fame and its official opening in "Country Music Hall of Fame Opens," *MCN* 4, no. 10 (April 1967): 4, 8, 15–16.

The phenomenon of the all-country-music radio stations is discussed in *CMA Close-Up*, February 1967, p. 7, and in scholarly fashion in George Carney, "Spatial Diffusion of the All-Country Music Radio Stations in the United States, 1971–74," *JEMFQ* 13, no. 46 (Summer 1977): 58–66, and in Richard P. Stockdell, "Early Country Radio: Dispelling a Myth," ibid. 15, no. 55 (Fall 1979): 152–156.

9. The Reinvigoration of Modern Country Music, 1960–1972

Country music's commercial resurgence in the sixties was accompanied by a burgeoning of publicity and journalistic coverage. *Music City News*, originally owned by Faron Young, began its existence in July 1963 and is still being published in 1984. This monthly newspaper has been heavily fan-oriented and is rarely critical of any entertainer or any trend in country music. Its policy seems to be, "If you can't say something good about somebody, then don't say anything." Nevertheless, the newspaper is a good source for the basic facts concerning country music, and its "Letters to the Editors" section sometimes contains evidence of the dissatisfaction felt by many fans about the growing pop emphasis in country music. Of the many writers who have been associated with the publication, Dixie

Deen (the wife of Tom T. Hall) was the most historically conscious. Her feature articles have been very helpful to me.

I obtained some information about the appearance of country entertainers on early television experiments from interviews with Bobby Gregory (Nashville, August 30, 1971) and Red River Dave McEnery (San Antonio, June 19, 1973). At least two general articles concentrate on the subject: John Scott Colley, "The Sound Seen: Country Music on Television," *JCM* 3, nos. 3–4 (Fall–Winter 1973): 107–113; and Douglas B. Green, "Country Music's Big on the Tube Again," *Country Music* 5, no. 4 (January 1977): 42, 45–47. Two of the most popular hosts of syndicated television shows in the sixties—the Wilburn Brothers and Porter Wagoner—have received only minimal attention from writers (and both have been greatly overshadowed by their "girl singers," Loretta Lynn and Dolly Parton). Dixie Deen wrote good articles on both the Wilburns and Wagoner: "The Woman behind the Man," *MCN* 3, no. 10 (April 1966): 5, 14, 19 (about Mom Wilburn and her sons); and "Purely Porter Wagoner," *MCN* 4, no. 9 (March 1967): 3–4. Paul Soelburg wrote a two-part article on Wagoner, "The Porter Wagoner Story," for *CSR* 24, nos. 23 and 24 (February and March 1972), but the best article on this singer is Dave Hickey, "Porter: The Last Great Hillbilly?" *Country Music* 3, no. 8 (May 1975): 22–27, 60–63.

The prime-time country television shows are described by Colley and Green (articles mentioned above). I found some description of Jimmy Dean's early shows in *Variety* 206, no. 3 (March 20, 1957): 35, and in *Billboard* 69, no. 21 (May 20, 1957): 146. Ellis Nassour's *Patsy Cline* (New York: Tower Publications, 1981) also contains information on Dean's television interests and on Connie B. Gay. Glen Campbell and his popular television show evoked responses from all the popular magazines of the day, but one of the best articles which concentrates on his Arkansas origins is John Fergus Ryan, "They Knew Glen Campbell before He Was a Superstar," *Country Music* 2, no. 7 (March 1974): 68–73. Campbell's fellow Arkansas native Johnny Cash—still another of the major television personalities—was discussed in the bibliographical essay for Chapter 8, but information more pertinent to his later career is in the *Sunday Showcase* of the *Nashville Tennessean*, April 20–26, 1969, pp. 4–7 (by Kathy Sawyer) and in *Newsweek*, February 2, 1970, pp. 84–85. One should not ignore Tom Dearmore, "First Angry Man of Country Singers," *New York Times Magazine*, September 21, 1969, pp. 32–34, 36–39, 42, 49, 54–58; this is the best available critical analysis of Cash. My information about the computerized nature of *Hee Haw* comes from John Fergus Ryan, "Press a Button and Out Comes 'Hee Haw'," *Country Music* 2, no. 1 (September 1973): 28–34. One of the gifted mainstays of the show, Roy Clark, has been much written about. The article that I have found most useful is Jon Sievert, "Roy Clark: An Entertainer since Age Four, America's Most

Visible Guitarist," *Guitar Player* 12, no. 11 (November 1978): 54–56, 120, 124, 126–136.

Country music's popularity and expansion abroad are subjects worthy of extended academic treatment. A good beginning has been made by Richard C. Helt in "A German Bluegrass Festival: The Country Boom and Some Notes on the History of American Popular Music in West Germany," *Journal of Popular Culture* 10, no. 4 (Spring 1977): 821–832. Sources which were helpful to me include Omer Anderson, "Fifty Million Europeans Can't Be Wrong," *Billboard* 72, no. 28 (July 11, 1960): 1; *Billboard Music Week* 73, no. 33 (September 25, 1961): 3; ibid., no. 39 (October 2, 1961): 11; and "Country Music Goes International," in *The World of Country Music* (New York: Billboard, 1963), pp. 165–167, 171–173. Three interviews also provided some knowledge of foreign interest in country music: Martin Haerle, Nashville, August 23, 1961; Charlie Walker, Kerrville, Texas, July 1, 1977; and Bill Clifton, Baltimore, June 10, 1976.

The urban folk revival still awaits a definitive treatment. Until such a study is undertaken, Oscar Brand's *The Ballad Mongers: Rise of the Modern Folk Song* (New York: Funk and Wagnalls, 1962) will serve as a good introduction. Folk music's left-wing identification is discussed by R. Serge Denisoff, *Great Day Coming: Folk Music and the American Left* (Urbana: University of Illinois Press, 1971). Contemporary magazines which documented the revival, while also printing many of its songs, included *Broadside, Little Sandy Review, Hootenanny,* and *Sing Out.* Articles on the urban folk movement appeared in prodigious numbers in other magazines. Among the best are Nat Hentoff, "Folk Finds a Voice," *Reporter* 26, no. 1 (January 4, 1962): 39–42; Hentoff, "The Rise of Folkum Music," *The Commonweal* 75, no. 4 (October 20, 1961): 99–100; and John McPhee, "Folk Singing," *Time* 80, no. 21 (November 23, 1962): 54–60.

The best place to begin for an understanding of the ways in which urban folk music and hillbilly music intersected are the albums of the New Lost City Ramblers (see, for example, *The New Lost City Ramblers,* Folkways FA2396). The leader of the group is discussed by Jon Pankake in "Mike Seeger: The Style of Tradition," *Sing Out* 14, no. 3 (July 1964): 9–10, while many of the songs reintroduced by the Ramblers are collected in *The New Lost City Ramblers Song Book,* edited by Mike Seeger and John Cohen (New York: Oak Publications, 1964). A powerful catalyst that contributed to the stimulation of interest in hillbilly music among urban folk fans was the *Anthology of American Folk Music,* produced by Folkways in 1952, and made up of hillbilly, blues, gospel, and Cajun material originally recorded between 1927 and 1933 (from the collection of Harry Smith). The greatest new discovery inspired by the folk revival, Doc Watson, is discussed in such articles as Michael Bane, "A Chat with Doc Watson," *Country Music* 4, no. 11 (August 1976): 57, 59; Chet Flippo,

"Doc Watson and His Tall Drink o' Water Merle," *Rolling Stone*, no. 137 (June 21, 1973): 24; H. Lloyd "Stretch" Whittaker, "Doc Watson," *BGU* 5, no. 5 (November 1970): 4–5; and Don Rhodes, "Doc Watson," *BGU* 12, no. 7 (January 1978): 10–14 (the best of the group). Svare Forsland and I also interviewed Watson for WWOZ-FM in New Orleans (1982).

As far as I can determine, my discussion of the saga song craze in the original edition of this book (*Country Music U.S.A.: A Fifty-Year History* [Austin: American Folklore Society/University of Texas Press, 1968], pp. 300–303) is about the only published recognition of this phenomenon. I depended on *Billboard* issues extending from late 1958 through 1959, and on such lps as *Jimmie Driftwood Sings Newly Discovered Early American Folk Songs* (RCA Victor RPM 1635); Johnny Cash, *Songs of Our Soil* (Columbia 1339); *Johnny Horton Makes History* (Columbia 1478); and Marty Robbins' *Gunfighter Ballads* (Columbia 1349).

The hard country resurgence of the sixties is documented in material dealing with such performers as George Jones, Ray Price, Buck Owens, and Merle Haggard—and above all in their recordings. Dolly Carlisle's biography *Ragged but Right: The Life and Times of George Jones* (Chicago: Contemporary Publications, 1984), is an honest and sympathetic treatment of the singer, but the best introduction to the durable Jones is the Time-Life collection devoted to him. Pepi Plowman wrote a long biographical sketch of him in the inelegantly titled "A Singin' Fool," *Texas Monthly*, June 1982, pp. 144–149, 232–239. One of the best older sketches of Jones is Dixie Deen, "The Crown Prince of C-W Music," *MCN* 4, no. 2 (August 1966): 1, 31. Interviews which were helpful to me include a short one with Jones in Austin, August 16, 1962, and a longer one with Pappy Daily in Houston, August 19, 1977.

I also talked with Ray Price in Austin on March 2, 1962, and learned a few biographical details about him from an unsigned article called "Hit Maker—Ray Price," in *Rustic Rhythm* 1, no. 2 (May 1957): 11–15. More recent articles which have been extremely helpful are "Cherokee Cowboys Reunion" (which lists many of his musicians over the years) in *Country Gazette* 1, no. 1 (February 1977): 4; Dave Hickey, "Hillbilly Heaven," *Country Music* 5, no. 6 (March 1976): 40–42, 61–64; and Tom Ayres, "Ray Price Remembers Hank Williams," *Country Music* 5, no. 12 (September 1977): 41–44, 56.

Although much ink has been expended on its major participants, no full-scale study has yet been done on the hard country scene in California since the sixties. One of the father-figures of Bakersfield country music, Bill Woods, is discussed by Lee Rector in "Bill Woods Helps Others to Stardom," *MCN* 15, no. 12 (June 1978): 34. Buck Owens was a giant of country music in the early sixties, but he has received only scattered attention. The Time-Life collection *Honky Tonkin'* includes one song by Owens and a very brief biographical blurb. Most of my original information came from sketches in the contemporary music magazines, such as Harris Martin, "Buck Owens Riding All Time Height of Popularity," *MCN* 2, no. 12 (June 1965): 1, 4.

Merle Haggard has inspired so much writing that it is difficult to single out that which is best. The following includes only a sampling of such material. The best place to start would be his autobiography, written with Peggy Russell, *Sing Me Back Home* (New York: Quadrangle, 1981). Haggard is generally honest and candid about his life and career, almost to a fault, but he strangely says nothing about "Okie from Muskogee," the most controversial song in his repertory and the one which really catapulted him to the top of the music business. A good example of the approval shown by some liberal critics for his music—before "Okie from Muskogee"—is Alfred G. Aronowitz, "New Country Twang Hits Town," *Life*, May 3, 1968, p. 12. Paul Hemphill also wrote from a liberal perspective in his essay on Haggard in *Stars of Country Music*, edited by Bill C. Malone and Judith McCulloh (Urbana: University of Illinois Press, 1975) pp. 357–373. This is a good and sensitive assessment of Haggard (written after "Okie"), but is somewhat strained in its efforts to explain away his conservatism. Haggard does talk about "Okie" in an interview in *Penthouse* 8, no. 3 (November 1976): 126–128, 178–184. Another good short discussion of Haggard, stressing his eclectic musicianship, is Peter Guralnick, "Merle Haggard: In the Good Old Days (When Times Were Bad)," *JCM* 8, no. 1 (May 1979): 39–46, 63–64. Haggard's jazz inclinations are the subjects of Tim Schneckloth, "Merle Haggard: Country Jazz Messiah," *Down Beat* 47, no. 5 (May 1980): 16–19, 63 (one of the rare times that this magazine has ventured an appreciation of a country artist), and John Morthland, "Merle Haggard's Country Jazz," *International Musician and Recording World*, November 1980, pp. 38–39, 104.

The country writers who did so much to rejuvenate country music in the modern period are discussed singly and collectively in a variety of places; nevertheless, they still have not been given their proper due. The best overall discussion of country lyrics, which also includes material on the writers themselves, is Jimmie N. Rogers, *The Country Music Message* (Englewood Cliffs, N.J.: Prentice-Hall, 1983). *Music City News* runs periodic "Songwriters Special" issues which include vignettes on leading writers. These include 16, no. 8 (February 1979); 17, no. 8 (February 1980); and 18, no. 8 (February 1981). I interviewed Bill Anderson in Nashville on August 22, 1961, and Harlan Howard in Nashville on August 24, 1961. Among the extensive number of sketches on writers found in various music journals, I have found the following to be of particular interest: "An Exclusive CSR Interview" (with Curley Putman), *CSR* 22, no. 129 (April 1970): 34–35; "Harlan Howard (in His Own Words)," *CSR* 22, no. 130 (May 1970): 30–32; Mira Smith and Margaret Lewis, "The Country Music Writer" (on Liz Anderson), *CSR* 27, no. 193 (August 1975): 27–29;

and Fred Abdella, "John D. Loudermilk: From 'A Rose and a Baby Ruth' to a Grammy," *Acadiana Profile* 5, no. 4 (August–September 1976): 59–61.

The best place to begin for further insights into Tom T. Hall would be his autobiography, *The Storyteller's Nashville* (Garden City, N.Y.: Doubleday and Company, 1979). The book is much like Hall's songs; it is witty, sensitive, and conversational in tone. The most discerning portrait of Hall, as well as the most critical assessment of his songs, is William C. Martin's essay in *Stars of Country Music*, pp. 391–415. I talked to Hall in Nashville on July 27, 1972, but also learned much from Dixie Deen, "Tom T. Hall's 'Touch of Greatness,'" *MCN* 5, no. 2 (August 1967): 3–4; Noel Coppage, "Tom T. Hall," *Stereo Review* 33, no. 2 (August 1974): 58–61; and Ken Stambaugh, "The Storyteller: Tom T. Hall," *Nashville West* 1, no. 3 (November 1975): 8–9, 26–28.

John Hartford, the man who did much to give country songwriting a new direction, is well treated in two good articles: Tom Hill, "John Hartford: Riverboats and Music," *Pickin'* 5, no. 4 (May 1978): 21–26, 64–67; and Barry Silver, "John Hartford," *BGU* 14, no. 4 (October 1979): 12–16. The most famous representative of country music's "new breed" of writers—Kris Kristofferson—has been much written about. Representative articles include David Rensin, "King Kristofferson," *Country Music* 2, no. 13 (September 1974): 25–32; Jack McClintock, "Just a Good Ole Rhodes Scholar," *Playboy* 22, no. 3 (March 1975): 120, 122, 170–175; Paul Hemphill, "Kris Kristofferson Is the New Nashville Sound," *New York Times Magazine*, December 6, 1970, pp. 54–55, 137–142; and Tom Burke, "Kris Kristofferson's Talking Blues," *Rolling Stone*, no. 159 (April 25, 1974): 40–46.

The few academic treatments of women country singers concentrate on the period before Kitty Wells. Several popular writers, however, have written overviews of the post-1960 generation of women singers. The best of these accounts is Joan Dew's *Singers and Sweethearts: The Women of Country Music* (Garden City, N.Y.: Doubleday and Co., 1977). Representative articles include Noel Coppage, "Country Music's Traipsin' Women," *Stereo Review* 33, no. 6 (December 1974): 84–89; Roy Blount, "Country's Angels," *Esquire* 87, no. 3 (March 1977): 62–66, 124–126, 131–132; and Lynn Kellermann, "It Wasn't God Who Made Honky Tonk Angels," *Music Gig* 2, no. 11 (June 1976): 15–18. *Country Music* magazine also devoted a special issue to the subject—"The Women in Country Music," 2, no. 11 (July 1974)—but only Dolly Parton received any kind of extended treatment. The Time-Life collection devoted to women is oriented toward the pre–Kitty Wells era, but several modern performers are included (Loretta Lynn, Tammy Wynette, Dolly Parton, Tanya Tucker, Lynn Anderson, Jeanne Pruett, Barbara Mandrell, Jessi Colter, and Emmylou Harris).

Discussions and sketches of individual women singers fill the pages of *Music City News* and *Country Music*, and on occasion a performer even draws the interest of a rock-oriented magazine such as *Rolling Stone* or a man's magazine like *Playboy*. Crystal Gayle, for example, received very approving treatment from Chet Flippo in "The Problem with Crystal," *Playboy*, November 1981, pp. 131–132, 156, 202–205, 209. She is also discussed by Kelly Delaney, in "Crystal Gayle Takes Time to Become a Mother," *MCN* 20, no. 11 (May 1983): 8–9, and by Laura Eipper, in "Crystal," *Country Music* 8, no. 6 (March 1980): 30–36, 68. Jeannie C. Riley's religion and regrets about her early brazen image are discussed by Michael Bane, in "Jeannie C. Riley Lowers Her Hemline and Raises Her Hopes," *Country Music* 5, no. 3 (December 1976): 34–38, 71. Tanya Tucker has never suffered from neglect. *Country Music* magazine, for example, has devoted considerable attention to her: J. R. Young, "Tanya Tucker: Country's Youngest Superstar," 1, no. 10 (June 1973): 32–36; Mary Ellen Moore, "Tanya: Ballad of a Teenage Queen," 5, no. 10 (July 1977): 22–26; and Dolly Carlisle, "Tanya: Daddy's Little Girl Grows Up," 7, no. 7 (May 1979): 34–37.

The three great women superstars, Loretta Lynn, Tammy Wynette, and Dolly Parton, have elicited extensive discussion and critical treatment. Lynn and Wynette have written autobiographies, and Parton has been the subject of popular "newsstand biographies." Lynn's autobiography, written with George Vecsey, is as charming and candid as the singer: *Coal Miner's Daughter* (New York: Warner Books, 1976). It is especially good on her early Appalachian years, but predictable when it discusses the problems that a simple country girl encounters once she finds show business success (marital tension, illness, difficulties in balancing her career with home duties). She was on the cover of *Newsweek* and was the centerpiece of that magazine's extensive coverage of country music: Pete Axthelm, "Lookin' at Country with Loretta Lynn," *Newsweek* 81, no. 25 (June 18, 1973): 65–72. Sally Quinn wrote a good, brief sketch of Loretta, "Country Girl," for the *New York Post*, August 16, 1975, p. 13, while Martha Hume concentrated on the singer that the fans never see in "The Strange and Private World of Loretta Lynn," *Country Music* 4, no. 4 (January 1976): 30–33, 54. Sharon Rowlett wrote a profile of Loretta's husband in "Mooney Lynn," *Country Style*, no. 27 (January 1978): 25, 68, and Robert Windeler did a sketch of her most controversial song in "Loretta Lynn's 'Pill' Is Hard for Some Fans to Swallow," *People Weekly* 3, no. 12 (March 31, 1975): 23–25.

Tammy Wynette is the only woman country singer who has had a Time-Life collection devoted to her. The writer of the collection's notes, Joan Dew, was also Tammy's collaborator in her autobiography, *Stand By Your Man* (New York: Simon and Schuster, 1978). Wynette is honest about her failed marriages and disappointed loves and physical problems. Despite the heavy soap opera treatment, the book can still be read with profit as an introduction to southern lower-class life in the years following World War II and as a glimpse of the modern country music industry. The ever-dependable Dixie Deen wrote one of the best short articles on Wynette, not long after her career began, in "Tammy Finds Elusive Dream," *MCN* 5, no. 6 (December 1967): 3, 9. Tammy has been one of the few country singers who has been fascinating to rock journalists; consequently, her records have been reviewed in *Rolling Stone*, and she was the subject of a lengthy article in that magazine—condescending, sarcastic, and generally contemptuous—by Michael Thomas: "Tammy Wynette: A Little Tear in Every Word," *Rolling Stone*, no. 108 (May 11, 1972): 44–47. Tammy was also interviewed in *Penthouse* 12, no. 1 (September 1980): 117–119, 172–176.

Dolly Parton has not only been written up in *Rolling Stone*, she has probably received more press coverage than any other country entertainer (with the possible exceptions of Willie Nelson and Kenny Rogers). Her famous anatomy has certainly inspired more jokes than any other country entertainer has provoked. Alanna Nash's *Dolly* (Los Angeles: Reed Books, 1978) is about the best of the popular biographies, but Chet Flippo wrote two admiring articles for *Rolling Stone*: "Dolly Parton: Tennessee Mountain Home-Grown," no. 198 (October 23, 1975): 24; and "Dolly Parton," no. 246 (August 15, 1977): 32–38. Chris Chase also did a good journalistic piece on Dolly called "The Country Girl," *New York Times Magazine*, May 9, 1976, pp. 17, 60, 71–73. The most discerning insights into Dolly's personality are provided in the interview she did for *Playboy* 25, no. 10 (October 1978): 81–84, 88–91, 95–98, 101–110. The frankness and humor of her replies confirms the belief that she should write her autobiography.

The movement of non-Anglo, non-Protestant, and nonwhite performers into country music is a subject worthy of extended treatment. The vital tradition of Cajun music, which has maintained an independent identity while also often interrelating with country music, is best documented by Barry Jean Ancelet, with photographs by Elemore Morgan, Jr., *The Makers of Cajun Music/Musiciens cadiens et créoles* (Austin: University of Texas Press, 1984). Other useful works include Tony Russell, *Blacks, Whites and Blues* (New York: Stein and Day, 1970); Nick Tosches, *Country: The Biggest Music in America* (New York: Stein and Day, 1977), esp. pp. 167–229; Nicholas Spitzer, "Cajuns and Creoles: The French Gulf Coast," in *Long Journey Home: Folklife in the South*, edited by Allen Tullos (Chapel Hill, N.C.: Southern Exposure, 1977), pp. 140–155; John Broven, *South to Louisiana: The Music of the Cajun Bayous* (Gretna, La.: Pelican Publishing Company, 1983); Dan Dickey, "The Development of *música tejana: Guitarreros, conjuntos* and *orquestas tejanas*" (unpublished paper presented at the annual meeting of the Texas State Historical Association, Austin, March 2, 1984); and Kay Council, "Exploratory Documentation of Texas *Norteño-Conjunto* Music" (Master's thesis, University of Texas at Austin, 1978).

Doug Kershaw, Jimmy C. Newman, Al Terry, and other Cajuns who have played country music are discussed in John Broven's book. Douglas B. Green wrote a good short sketch of Newman for *Country Music*: "Jimmy C. Newman and His Cajun Country Roots," 7, no. 7 (May 1979): 20, 66, 68. John Grissim devotes a chapter to Kershaw in *Country Music: White Man's Blues* (New York: Coronet Communications, 1970), but Kershaw's own short autobiography is the best introduction to the man: *Lou'siana Man* (New York: Collier Books, 1971).

The best account of Johnny Rodriguez is the essay by Bill C. and Ann Malone in *Stars of Country Music*, pp. 415–437. Since Freddy Fender was active in Louisiana, he draws some attention from John Broven. One of the best single essays on Fender, however, is Roxy Gordon, "Wasted Days, Wasted Nights?" *Country Music* 5, no. 6 (March 1976): 22–26, 64.

My information on black country singers came mainly from short sketches in the music magazines, although I did have an interview with Stoney Edwards in Nashville, October 15, 1971. Examples of the magazine sketches include Paula Becker, "Linda Martel: New Look, New Sound, New Star," *CSR* 22, no. 133 (August 1970): 12–13; "O. B. McClinton: The Black Country Irishman," *Soul* 6, no. 24 (March 27, 1972): 12; Mike Kosser, "Cotton Picker McClinton Walked Long Road to Stardom," *Country Style*, no. 7 (December 1976): 53; Mark Schwed, "Black Country Music Singer, Big Al Downing, Breaking the Industry's Color Barrier," *New Orleans Times-Picayune/States-Item*, December 16, 1982 (a UPI story); "Stoney Edwards: A Very Special Person," *CSR* 27, no. 189 (April 1975): 10–11, 44; and Peter Guralnick, "Stoney Edwards: Black Man Singing in a White Man's World," *Country Music* 7, no. 7 (May 1979): 42–44, 68.

The best synthesis of Charley Pride's career is Ann Malone's essay in *Stars of Country Music*, pp. 373–389. Examples of the rapport he established with white audiences, along with an introduction to his early style, can be heard in the lp recorded in 1969 at Fort Worth's Panther Hall: *Charley Pride in Person—Recorded Live*, RCA ANL1-0996. An appreciative evaluation of the man, and a critical review of several of his records, can be found in Charlie Burton, "Charley Pride," *Rolling Stone*, no. 83 (May 27, 1971): 52–53. Other representative articles included Melvin Shestack, "Charley Pride and the Chicken Ladies," *Esquire* 75, no. 3 (March 1971): 102–105, 60, 66; Patrick Carr, "What Now, Charley Pride," *Country Music* 3, no. 4 (January 1975): 58–59; and "No. 1 Country Singer," *Sepia* 21, no. 5 (May 1972): 35–42.

The political preoccupations exhibited by some country singers and writers in the late sixties and early seventies, along with country music's identification with first George Wallace and then the "silent majority," inspired a rash of both good and poor writing. Paul Hemphill's *The Nashville Sound: Bright Lights and Country Music* (New York: Simon and Schuster, 1970), clearly profited from the music's political notoriety, and it received prominent reviews in such periodicals as *Life*. Hemphill alluded to the George Wallace identification, but placed more stress on the music's working-class orientation. Two liberal writers saw only destructive consequences arising from country music's burgeoning commercial growth: Florence King, "Red Necks, White Socks, and Blue Ribbon Fear," *Harper's* 249 (July 1974): 30–34; and Richard Goldstein, "My Country Music Problem—and Yours," *Mademoiselle* 77, no. 2 (June 1973): 114–115, 185. Radical writer Irwin Silber let the pro–Vietnam War songs speak for themselves, but he quoted their lyrics alongside reports of atrocities in the war: "A Study in Illusion and Reality," *Sing Out* 17, no. 4 (August–September 1967): 20–25. Selected contemporary articles which commented on country music's conservative politics include Paul Dickson, "Singing to Silent America," *Nation*, February 23, 1970, pp. 211–213; Earl C. Gottschalk, Jr., "Love It or Leave It: New Patriotic Music Wins Fans, Enemies," *Wall Street Journal*, August 18, 1970, pp. 1, 12; and Neil Maxwell, "The Bigotry Business: Racist Records, Books Are Hits in the South," *Wall Street Journal*, April 20, 1967, pp. 1, 12. At least one conservative song, "Welfare Cadilac," received extensive, and generally favorable, discussion in *Music City News*: 'Welfare Cadilac' Touches a Nerve," *MCN* 7, no. 11 (May 1970): 1, 25, 30. President Nixon's favorable response to the song and his request that Johnny Cash sing it at the White House, are discussed in *Time* 95, no. 15 (April 13, 1970): 16. A good example of the rousing reception which northern audiences gave to "Okie from Muskogee" can be heard on Merle Haggard's lp, *The Fightin' Side of Me*, Capitol ST451, recorded live in Philadelphia. Scholar Patricia Averill, however, denies the ideological emphasis attributed to "Okie" and argues that Haggard's record company selected "the aspect of audience reaction which reinforced its own exoteric view of what the audience liked" (p. 36) in "Esoteric-Exoteric Expectations of Redneck Behavior and Country Music," *JCM* 4, no. 2 (Summer 1973): 34–38. Three other scholars also deny that country music was simply "right-wing know-nothingism": Paul DiMaggio, Richard A. Peterson, and Jack Esco, Jr., "Country Music: Ballad of the Silent Majority," in *The Sounds of Social Change*, edited by R. Serge Denisoff and Richard A. Peterson (Chicago: Rand McNally, 1972), pp. 38–55.

Country music's alleged working-class identification has often been commented upon, but no study has fully explored the idea, either from the standpoint of the fans, or from that of the musicians. There are good collections and critiques of certain types of occupational songs (such as those of Archie Green on cotton mill and coal-mining songs, and Norm Cohen's on railroad pieces—each of which has been previously discussed), but almost nothing exists on worker attitudes as expressed in songs. The one area of worker subculture that has attracted country singers—trucking— is actually a gray area, because many truck drivers (the independent owner-operators) think of themselves as small businessmen rather than

workers. Truck drivers, though, do like country music, and country sing-
ers have responded with a multitude of songs about their profession. Fred
E. H. Schroeder made a good beginning in explaining the appeal of the
truck driver in "A Bellyful of Coffee: The Truckdrivin' Man as Folk Hero,"
Journal of Popular Culture 2, no. 4 (Spring 1969): 679–687, but Joyce
Gibson Roach is superficial and condescending in "Diesel Smoke and
Dangerous Curves: Folklore of the Trucking Industry," in *Hunters and
Healers: Folklore Types and Topics*, edited by Wilson M. Hudson, Publica-
tions of the Texas Folklore Society, no. 35 (Austin: Encino Press, 1971),
pp. 45–53.

Robert Shelton was one of the first music critics to recognize the emergence of the truck-driving song genre: "Meet a New Folk Hero, the Truck
Driver," *New York Times*, December 4, 1966. Neville Raymond does a good
job in showing the interrelationship between trucking and country music
in "Hitch Your Truck to a Country Star," *Country Music* 1, no. 1 (September 1972): 41–44, and the same magazine devoted several pages to
the CB and trucking craze which accompanied C. W. McCall's great hit
"Convoy" in 1976: 5, no. 3 (December 1976): 48–55, 71. Sketches of singers who have specialized in truck-driving songs appear in the various
country music magazines. For example, the man who began the modern
craze for such music is discussed by Dixie Deen in "'Six Days on the
Road' Puts Ravin' Dave Dudley on Country Music Map," *MCN* 4, no. 1
(July 1966): 11, 20.

10. Bluegrass

Bluegrass is the best-documented genre of country music. It has drawn
the loving attention of dedicated fans and the meticulous analysis of scholars (largely because it reached its commercial peak during the folk revival
and the subsequent rediscovery of hillbilly music). Most of this documentation, though, resides in short articles and discographies, many of
which are not easily accessible to the general reader. Scott Hambly provides a good bibliographical survey of bluegrass material in the notes to his
"San Francisco Bay Area Bluegrass and Bluegrass Musicians: A Study
in Regional Characteristics," *JEMFQ* 16, no. 59 (Fall 1980): 118–120.
Hambly notes the existence of three book-length historical surveys of
bluegrass: Toru Mitsui, *Burugurasu Ongaku* [Bluegrass Music] (Toyo-
hashi, Japan: Traditional-Song Society, 1967; rev. ed., 1975); Steven D.
Price, *Old as the Hills: The Story of Bluegrass Music* (New York: Viking
Press, 1975); and Bob Artis, *Bluegrass* (New York: Hawthorn Books, 1975).
Mitsui's book, however, is unavailable to American readers; Price's is
too superficial; and, while Artis' is good and reliable, it is far from being
comprehensive. For several years folklorist and bluegrass musician Neil

Rosenberg has been preparing a full-scale history of bluegrass for the University of Illinois' Music in American Life series. If Rosenberg's previous writings on bluegrass are any indication, his book will be the definitive treatment of the subject.

The best short discussions of bluegrass, both in the *Journal of American Folklore*, concentrate on stylistic evolution: L. Mayne Smith, "An Introduction to Bluegrass," *JAF* 78, no. 309 (July–September 1965): 245–256; and Neil Rosenberg, "From Sound to Style: The Emergence of Bluegrass," *JAF* 10, no. 316 (April–June 1967): 143–150. Two academic studies of individual musicians also shed light on bluegrass' origins and development: Ralph Rinzler's essay on Bill Monroe, pp. 221–243, and Rosenberg's essay on Flatt and Scruggs, pp. 279–301, both in *Stars of Country Music*, edited by Bill C. Malone and Judith McCulloh (Urbana: University of Illinois Press, 1975). The music has drawn little of the contextual and cultural analyses which it needs, but Robert Cantwell has mapped out a fruitful route that might be followed in two thoughtful and provocative essays: "Believing in Bluegrass," *Atlantic* 229, no. 3 (March 1972): 52–54, 58–60; and "The Lonesome Sound of Carter Stanley," *BGU* 10, no. 12 (June 1976): 10–16. Cantwell has also written a book, which I have not seen, called *Bluegrass Breakdown: The Making of the Old Southern Sound* (Urbana: University of Illinois Press, 1984) which promises to be controversial and stimulating.

At least four magazines, *Frets, Muleskinner News, Pickin'*, and *Bluegrass Unlimited*, have been devoted fully or in part to bluegrass music. *Frets* and *Pickin'* took all kinds of string instrumentation into their purview and provided technical information for musicians. *Muleskinner News*, founded by promoter Carlton Haney in January 1970, and *Bluegrass Unlimited*, established in July 1966 by Peter Kuykendall and Richard Spottswood, were almost exclusively oriented toward bluegrass (except for occasional items on old-time musicians) and were aimed principally at fans. *Muleskinner News* is now defunct, but *Bluegrass Unlimited* has had a continuous existence since 1966 and is a gold mine of information on every phase of the music it promotes (biographical articles, discographies, record and book reviews, concert and festival dates, interviews, classified ads, and songs).

Although *Bluegrass Unlimited* prints song lyrics periodically, the best sources for bluegrass songs are Bill Clifton's *150 Old-Time, Folk, and Gospel Songs* (privately printed sometime in the 1950's), and Peter Wernick's *Bluegrass Songbook* (New York: Oak Publications, 1976). The Wernick book also contains excerpts from interviews with bluegrass singers giving advice on how to sing bluegrass music.

The recognition of Bill Monroe's seminal contributions to bluegrass music is largely a product of Ralph Rinzler's scholarship. Rinzler wrote a short essay called "Bill Monroe: The Daddy of Blue Grass Music," in *Sing*

Out 13, no. 1 (January 1963): 5–8, and the notes to some of Monroe's albums (such as *The High Lonesome Sound of Bill Monroe*, Decca DL4780). Rinzler's most complete overview of Monroe is the essay in *Stars of Country Music*, pp. 221–241, a preview of the much larger biography that he has long been preparing for the University of Illinois Press.

Other useful works on Monroe include Alice Gerrard Foster, "Growing Up in Rosine, Kentucky: An Interview with Bill Monroe," *Sing Out* 19, no. 2 (July–August 1969): 6–11; Steve Rathe, "Bill Monroe," *Pickin'* 1, no. 1 (February 1974): 4–8; James Rooney, *Bossmen: Bill Monroe and Muddy Waters* (New York: Dial Press, 1971), and Neil Rosenberg, *Bill Monroe and His Blue Grass Boys: An Illustrated Discography* (Nashville: Country Music Foundation Press, 1974). Many of the classic Columbia recordings made by Monroe and the Blue Grass Boys between 1945 and 1949 have been reissued on the County label: vol. 1, CCS104, and vol. 2, CCS105 (with notes by Douglas B. Green).

The prolific Neil Rosenberg has also contributed the best summary and evaluation of Flatt and Scruggs, in his notes to the Time-Life collection *Flatt and Scruggs* and in his essay on the duo in *Stars of Country Music*, pp. 279–299. Musician and songwriter Jake Lambert (with the assistance of Curly Sechler) wrote a biography of Lester Flatt which, though anecdotal and sketchy, is nonetheless informative and candid about the singer: *The Good Things Outweigh the Bad* (Hendersonville, Tenn.: Jay-Lyn Publication, 1982). Interviews with Lester Flatt and Earl Scruggs in Nashville on August 23, 1961, and again with Scruggs in Austin on November 6, 1971, were extremely helpful. The Scruggs banjo style is described by Rinzler in the notes to *American Banjo Scruggs Style*, Folkways FA2314; by James D. Green, Jr., "A Musical Analysis of the Banjo Style of Earl Scruggs: An Examination of *Country Music* (Mercury MG20358)," *JCM* 5, no. 1 (Spring 1974): 31–37; by Thomas Adler, "Manual Formulaic Composition: Innovation in Bluegrass Banjo Styles," *JCM* 5, no. 2 (Summer 1974): 55–64; and by Scruggs himself in *Earl Scruggs and the 5-String Banjo* (New York: Peer International Corp., 1968). A vital and unique ingredient of the Flatt and Scruggs sound, Burkett "Uncle Josh" Graves, is discussed in Bob Krueger's "Josh Graves: 35 Years of Dobro," *Guitar Player* 11, no. 4 (April 1977): 28–29, 68, 72, 76. The post-separation careers of Flatt and Scruggs are discussed in Pete Kuykendall, "Lester Flatt and the Nashville Grass," *BGU* 5, no. 7 (January 1971): 3–6, and in Bill Littleton, "Earl Scruggs Still Wants to Break New Ground," *Country Music* 1, no. 2 (October 1972): 50–52. The best discography of Flatt and Scruggs is R. J. Ronald, "Lester Flatt and Earl Scruggs Discography," *BGU* 2, no. 7 (January 1968); 2, no. 8 (February 1968): 5–9.

All of the old-timers have been well covered by the bluegrass magazines, although only a few—such as Monroe, Flatt and Scruggs, and the Osborne Brothers—have received additional exposure in other magazines or media journals. Most of the printed material on Reno and Smiley is centered around the versatile musician Don Reno; the best is Bill Vernon's long interview, "The Don Reno Story, Part 1: Early Years," *Muleskinner News* 4, no. 6 (June 1973): 8–11; "The Don Reno Story, Part 2: Bill Monroe and Beyond," ibid. 4, no. 8 (August 1973): 8–11; and "The Don Reno Story, Part 3: The Years with Red Smiley," ibid. 4, no. 9 (September 1973): 8–11. Both men are discussed by Bob Artis in *Bluegrass*, pp. 59–67, and Reno's career is brought up to date to the beginning of the eighties in Linda Stanley's "Don Reno: A Bluegrass Family Tradition," *BGU* 15, no. 2 (August 1980): 17–23.

Much of my basic information on the Stanley Brothers came from interviews with Carter and Ralph in San Marcos, Texas, on February 6, 1964. The best critical analysis and appreciation of Carter Stanley is by Bob Cantwell, "The Lonesome Sound of Carter Stanley," *BGU* 10, no. 12 (June 1976): 10–16. Because of his longevity as a performer and his commitment to tradition, Ralph Stanley has inspired several good essays. These include Fred Bartenstein, "The Ralph Stanley Story," *Muleskinner News* 3, no. 3 (March 1972): 6–18; Ralph Rinzler, "Ralph Stanley: The Tradition from the Mountains," *BGU* 8, no. 9 (March 1974): 7–11; Larry Mitchell, "'Dr.' Ralph Stanley," *Pickin'* 4, no. 7 (August 1977): 4–9, 12, 14; and Jack Tottle, "Ralph Stanley: The Stanley Sound," *BGU* 15, no. 11 (May 1981): 14–21. Other articles which shed some light on the Stanley Brothers are Joe Wilson, "Bristol's WCYB: Early Bluegrass Turf," *Muleskinner News* 3, no. 8 (October 1972): 8–12; Robert K. Oermann, "Rickey Skaggs Remembers the Stanley Brothers," *BGU* 15, no. 11 (May 1981): 26–29; and Pete Kuykendall, "Curly Ray Cline," ibid., pp. 32–37.

Because of his dabblings in other areas of country music, Mac Wiseman has generated a considerable amount of print in the journals devoted to the country field. The following articles concentrate on his bluegrass involvement: Douglas B. Green, "Mac Wiseman—Remembering" (based on interviews), *Muleskinner News* 3, no. 5 (July 1972): 2–8; Don Rhodes, "Mac Wiseman," *BGU* 16, no. 2 (August 1981): 16–22; and Tom Henderson, "Mac Wiseman," *Pickin'* 2, no. 7 (August 1975): 4–14.

Jimmy Martin is inevitably discussed in any work dealing with Bill Monroe, the Osborne Brothers, or any other entertainer with whom he has played. We get some inkling of his origins in Jimmy Martin, "My Childhood," *CSR* 17, no. 91 (December 1965): 30. The single best discussion of Martin, however, is by Peter Kuykendall, "Jimmy Martin: Super King of Bluegrass," *BGU* 14, no. 3 (September 1979): 10–18.

Jim and Jesse McReynolds are unique in being the first bluegrass musicians to have a book-length biography devoted to them: Nelson Sears, *Jim and Jesse: Appalachia to the Grand Ole Opry* (Lancaster, Pa.: privately printed, 1976). This is an idealized portrait of the two men written by a faithful fan, although one does get a good sense of both the problems and joys inherent in the lives of professional performers. (Scott Hambly's evaluation of the book, "Jim and Jesse: A Review on Fan Historiography," *JEMFQ* 13, no. 46 [Summer 1977]: 96–99, is strongly recommended.) I interviewed Jim McReynolds in Biloxi, Mississippi, on October 31, 1981, and obtained additional information from Dixie Deen, "'Diesel on My Tail'—Jim and Jesse," *MCN* 4, no. 11 (May 1967): 6, 8, 10; and Bill and Bonnie Smith, "100,000 Miles Away from Home: Jim and Jesse on the Road," *BGU* 10, no. 2 (August 1975): 8–18.

Since the Osborne Brothers experienced considerable success in mainstream country music, their names appeared often in *Music City News*, *Country Music*, and other journals that were usually not very receptive to bluegrass entertainers. The articles I have selected come from bluegrass-oriented periodicals: Neil Rosenberg, "The Osborne Brothers," *BGU* 6, no. 3 (September 1971): 5–10; and "The Osborne Brothers, Part 2," ibid. 6, no. 8 (February 1972): 5–8; Peter Kuykendall, "The Osborne Brothers— From Rocky Top to Muddy Bottom," ibid. 12, no. 6 (December 1977): 10–16; Don Rhodes, "The Osborne Brothers: Progressive, Innovative Bluegrass," *Pickin'* 6, no. 9 (October 1979): 20–28; and Bill Emerson, "The Osborne Brothers: Getting Started," *Muleskinner News* 2, no. 4 (July–August 1971): 2–11.

The Osborne Brothers won a larger following for themselves and for bluegrass with a progressive approach. The Lilly Brothers, on the other hand, took a very traditional sound into the North. Introductions to them, and to the Boston bluegrass scene, are found in Tom Heathwood, "The Lilly Brothers," *Muleskinner News* 1, no. 6 (November–December 1970): 4–5, 15, and Bill Vernon, "Tex Logan Remembers the Lilly Brothers," ibid., pp. 6–7. The most complete account of the Lillys, stressing their West Virginia experiences as well as their years in Boston, is Ivan M. Tribe, "Pros Long before Boston: The Entire Career of the Lilly Brothers," *BGU* 9, no. 1 (July 1974): 8–17. James J. McDonald gives some biographical information, but concentrates more on musical style and repertory, in what seems to be the only article on a bluegrass group ever written for a major folklore journal: "Principal Influences on the Music of the Lilly Brothers of Clear Creek, West Virginia," *JAF* 86, no. 342 (October–December 1973): 331–344.

If the Lilly Brothers carried the gospel of bluegrass and old-time country music north, Bill Clifton took it around the world. He also built bridges to the urban folk community which changed the nature and direction of bluegrass. Most of my knowledge came from a lengthy interview with Clifton in Lutherville, Maryland, on June 9, 1976. A short account of his influence in Great Britain (along with a discography of most of his recordings) is given by Ron Petronko, "Bill Clifton in Britain," *BGU* 6, no. 4 (October 1971): 10–15. Clifton's re-emergence on the American bluegrass scene in 1978, as part of the First Generation (with Red Rector and Don

Stover), is discussed in "A Bluegrass Experiment," *BGU* 13, no. 2 (August 1978): 22–27, and in John Atkins, "Bill Clifton and Red Rector," *Pickin'* 6, no. 4 (May 1979): 24–26.

Bluegrass music's expansion to the North is touched upon in many of the previously mentioned articles dealing with Flatt and Scruggs, the Osbornes, Jimmy Martin, the Lillys, and Bill Clifton. The role played by lesser-known musicians is described by Charles Camp and David Whisnant in "A Voice from Home: Southern Mountain Musicians on the Maryland-Pennsylvania Border," in *Long Journey Home: Folklife in the South*, edited by Allan Tullos (Chapel Hill, N.C.: Southern Exposure, 1977), pp. 80–90. Studies of bluegrass music in such cities as Detroit and Cincinnati would be very helpful. Ivan Tribe has provided us a glimpse of the way that records circulated among northern fans in "Jimmie Skinner: Country Singer, Bluegrass Composer, Record Retailer," *BGU* 11, no. 9 (March 1977): 34–38.

The interrelationship between bluegrass and the urban folk revival, which was partly a product of the music's expansion north, is documented in several articles and in the liner notes of a few record albums which were marketed among urban folkies. D. K. Wilgus introduced bluegrass to the academic audience through his record reviews in the *Kentucky Folklore Record* after 1957 and in the *Journal of American Folklore* after 1962. Folk fans learned about the music in a variety of magazines such as *Caravan: The Magazine of Folk Music, Hootenanny*, and *Little Sandy Review*; in Robert Shelton's folk music column in the *New York Times*; and through the songs and notes of such lps as Earl Taylor's *Folk Songs from the Blue Grass*, United Artists 3049 (notes by Alan Lomax), *American Banjo Scruggs Style*, Folkways FA2314 (notes by Ralph Rinzler), *Mountain Music Bluegrass Style*, Folkways FA2318 (notes by Mike Seeger), and *The Greenbriar Boys*, Vanguard VRS-9104 (notes by Rinzler). That larger world outside the folk-music audience learned about bluegrass through the popular television series *The Beverly Hillbillies*, the theme of which was Earl Scruggs' version of "The Ballad of Jed Clampett," and through brief articles in popular magazines: "Pickin' Scruggs," *Time* 77, no. 27 (June 30, 1961): 53; Peter Welding, "Music from the Bluegrass Roots," *Saturday Review* 44 (June 10, 1961): 48; and Alan Lomax, "Bluegrass Background: Folk Music with Overdrive," *Esquire* 52, no. 4 (October 1959): 103–109.

The Washington, D.C., bluegrass scene deserves a comprehensive history and analysis. Part of the story is found in Peter Kuykendall, "Bluegrass on the Air," *BGU* 6, no. 4 (October 1971): 3–8 (concentrating on WKCW in Warrenton, Virginia). Other references to the Washington scene show up in articles or liner notes pertaining to people who have played there. Buzz Busby, for example, is discussed in the notes to *Honky Tonk Bluegrass*, Rounder 0031 (no author listed). Articles on the Stoneman Family generally tell of their role in popularizing bluegrass in the nation's capital; see, for example, Don Rhodes, "Roni Stoneman," *BGU* 11, no. 11 (May

1977): 13–17, and Ivan Tribe, "The Return of Donna Stoneman: First Lady of the Mandolin," ibid. 17, no. 12 (June 1983): 16–26. Bob Artis devotes a chapter to the Washington sound and to the band, the Country Gentlemen, which did most to create that sound (*Bluegrass*, pp. 107–121). I gained some insights into the Gentlemen in an interview with Charlie Waller in Hugo, Oklahoma, on August 10, 1974, and from such articles as Bill Evans, "Good Music, Good Friends: The Country Gentlemen," *BGU* 12, no. 12 (June 1978): 18–25, and Roland Leiser, "Country Gentlemen: Tradition, Style, Humor," *Pickin'* 5, no. 11 (December 1978): 24–28.

Bluegrass' retreat to the festivals is treated at great length by Artis, especially on pp. 122–140, and Carlton Haney, the man who did most to popularize the festival format, is discussed in Fred Bartenstein, "The Carlton Haney Story" (an interview), *Muleskinner News* 2, no. 4 (September 1971): 8–10, 18–21; and in "Carlton Haney: True Great," *BGU* 18, no. 3 (September 1983): 22–25. Festival schedules and advertisements are carried in *Bluegrass Unlimited*.

The "newgrass" phenomenon is documented in the lives and music of many musicians, including some, such as Don Reno, who are considered to be exponents of "classic" bluegrass. The chromatic style banjo player Bill Keith is discussed in Tony Trischka, "Bill Keith," *BGU* 10, no. 6 (December 1975): 12–15, and Roger H. Siminoff, "Bill Keith: Yesterday, Today, and Tomorrow," *Pickin'* 4, no. 11 (December 1977): 4–17. The chromatic style is explained by Thomas Adler in "Manual Formulaic Composition: Innovation in Bluegrass Banjo Styles," *JCM* 5, no. 2 (Summer 1974): 55–64. Frank Wakefield's contributions to "progressive" mandolin playing are discussed in Jack Tottle, "Bluegrass Mandolin, 1/3rd Century Later," *BGU* 6, no. 9 (March 1972): 5–9, and Dix Bruce, "Frank Wakefield," ibid. 18, no. 1 (July 1983): 14–22. The fiddler who has moved farthest into the realms of jazz and rock, Vassar Clements, is discussed by Barry Silver in "Vassar Clements Out West," *BGU* 12, no. 11 (May 1978): 18–23. The marvelous musician Tony Rice, who is as much at home in jazz as he is in the traditional bluegrass in which he was reared, is discussed by Jack Tottle in "Tony Rice: East Meets West," ibid. 12, no. 4 (October 1977): 10–16. Mike Auldridge, the dobroist who has done much to define the sound of the Seldom Scene, has drawn extensive interest because of his session work in many areas of music. Two of the better articles on him and his music are Michael J. Weiss, "Mike Auldridge: Cruising on a Dobro," *Pickin'* 5, no. 3 (April 1978): 12–17, and Roger H. Siminoff, "Mike Auldridge," *Frets* 3, no. 5 (May 1981): 26–31.

The great band of which Auldridge is a part—the Seldom Scene—is discussed in several articles, including Bill Vernon, "The Seldom Scene," *Muleskinner News* 4, no. 3 (March 1973): 6–8; Robert Kyle, "The Seldom Scene: Bluegrass Super Group," *Pickin'* 5, no. 10 (November 1978): 20–24,

30; Don Rhodes, "The Stability and Versatility of the Seldom Scene," *BGU* 15, no. 1 (July 1980): 14–19; and Jack Tottle, "Don't Wait for Them to Buy, Sell It: John Duffey and His Music," ibid. 9, no. 5 (November 1974): 8–13.

Much scattered material exists on the newgrass, or progressive, bands. The following is merely a sampling of articles which would be helpful to the interested fan or scholar: H. Lloyd Whittaker, "Cliff Waldron and the New Shades of Grass," *BGU* 5, no. 10 (April 1971): 51; Mary Jane Bolle, "Happy Medium: J. D. Crowe and the New South," ibid. 8, no. 8 (February 1974): 7–9; Marty Godbey, "A Conversation with J. D. Crowe," ibid. 16, no. 1 (July 1981): 14–21; Tom Henderson, "On the Cuttin' Edge with Eddie Adcock," *Pickin'* 2, no. 9 (October 1975): 4–12; Pete Kuykendall, "II Generation," *BGU* 9, no. 9 (March 1975): 10–15; Jack Tottle, "Doyle Lawson and Quicksilver," ibid. 15, no. 5 (November 1980): 16–22; Jack Tottle, "The Country Gazette: Keep on Pushing," *Muleskinner News* 5, no. 7 (July 1974): 6–11, 16; Douglas B. Green, "Country Gazette: Alive and Well," *BGU* 14, no. 2 (August 1979): 12–15; Richard Smith, "Rodney Dillard: California Hillbilly," *Muleskinner News* 6, no. 1 (January–February 1975): 6–9; Marty Godbey, "Spectrum," *BGU* 15, no. 6 (December 1980): 14–21; and Ronni Lundy, "The New Grass Revival," ibid. 13, no. 5 (November 1978): 10–15.

Gospel bluegrass is almost a genre by itself. There are scores of bands, mostly in the South and Midwest, which perform nothing but religious music. A full-scale study of such music, concentrating on the more obscure groups, would be very useful. Until such work is completed, an article by Howard Wight Marshall will serve as a good introduction to the field: "'Keep on the Sunny Side of Life': Pattern and Religious Expression in Bluegrass Gospel Music," *New York Folklore Quarterly* 30, no. 1 (March 1974), reprinted by the John Edwards Memorial Foundation, Inc. (Los Angeles) as Reprint No. 31. The pioneer of gospel bluegrass, Carl Story, is discussed by Don Rhodes in "Carl Story," *Pickin'* 4, no. 12 (January 1978): 6–13. Douglas B. Green discusses the Sullivan Family in "The Sullivan Family—Goodwill Ambassadors of Bluegrass Gospel," *BGU* 15, no. 4 (October 1980): 11–15, while Don Rhodes concentrates on the Lewis Family in "On the Hallelujah Turnpike with the Lewis Family," ibid. 14, no. 12 (June 1980): 18–24.

The young traditionalists have elicited as much print as have the newgrass people. I have had short interviews with four of these musicians: Charlie Moore in Reidsville, North Carolina, September 5, 1970; Del McCoury in Hugo, Oklahoma, August 10, 1974; Roy Lee Centers in McKinney, Texas, July 6, 1973; and Larry Sparks in McKinney, Texas, July 6, 1973. Charlie Moore received the attention of Pete Kuykendall in "Charlie Moore," *BGU* 7, no. 7 (January 1973): 5–9 (the article also includes a discography by Nick Barr), and of Kathy Kaplan in "Charlie Moore," *Pickin'* 2, no. 4 (May 1975): 4–6, 8, 10. Del McCoury's life and career are adequately described by Gwen Taylor in "Del McCoury," *BGU* 7, no. 12 (June 1973): 17–19, and by Eugenia Snyder, in "Del McCoury, Low Key but Powerful," ibid. 16, no. 11 (May 1982): 17–24. As a master guitarist and soulful singer, Larry Sparks has drawn more attention than any of the other young musicians and has graced the cover of *Pickin'* once and that of *Bluegrass Unlimited* at least three times: Terry Lickona, "Going to the Top with Larry Sparks," *Pickin'* 4, no. 4 (May 1977): 4–9; Douglas B. Green, "Larry Sparks," *BGU* 7, no. 6 (December 1972): 7–8; Thomas Cook, "Larry Sparks—I'm Giving It All I've Got," ibid. 12, no. 2 (August 1977): 14–18; and Bill Vernon, "Larry Sparks," ibid. 17, no. 10 (April 1983): 13–18.

Other traditionalists have not been nearly so well documented as Sparks, but the following is a sampling of some of the more representative articles: Ivan M. Tribe, "The Shenandoah Cutups: Classic Bluegrass from a Newer Group," *BGU* 11, no. 6 (December 1976): 8–12; Frank Godbey, "Who in the World Are the Bluegrass Cardinals?" ibid. 10, no. 11 (May 1976): 12–17; Brett F. Devan, "The Bluegrass Cardinals," ibid. 15, no. 12 (June 1981): 20–28; Kathy Kaplan, "The Pinnacle Boys," ibid. 11, no. 4 (October 1976): 10–14; Mike Greenstein, "Joe Val and the New England Bluegrass Boys," ibid. 12, no. 1 (July 1977): 14–16; Judith A. Feller, "The Boys from Indiana," ibid. 17, no. 2 (August 1982): 14–20; Ralph Dice, "Bill Grant, Oklahoma Bluegrass Man," ibid. 16, no. 7 (January 1982): 8, 10–11, and Don Rhodes, "Delia Bell: The Way It's Supposed to Be Sung," ibid., pp. 9, 12–13; Herschel Freeman, "Dave Evans," ibid. 15, no. 7 (January 1981): 10–14; and Don Rhodes, "Band on the Run—The Johnson Mountain Boys," ibid. 16, no. 6 (December 1981): 12–17.

Buck White and his daughters are really in a class by themselves—part bluegrass, part country, part folk—but they have carried their version of the bluegrass gospel to an audience larger than that commanded by any other bluegrass musicians. Two good articles which assay different stages of their careers are Douglas Green, "Buck White and the Downhomers," *BGU* 7, no. 11 (May 1973): 7–10, and Boris Weintraub, "Buck White and the Down Home Folks," ibid. 16, no. 5 (November 1981): 9–13.

This essay should not be concluded without some reference to a few of the talented youngsters who have worked within the bluegrass context. Marty Godbey discusses one such group in "The McLain Family Band," *BGU* 15, no. 8 (February 1981): 12–16. Although his subjects are now grown up, Mike Carpenter discussed three of the best-known bluegrass prodigies in "Those Incredible Youngsters: Jimmy Henley, Jimmy Gyles, and Mark O'Connor," *Pickin'* 2, no. 11 (December 1975): 4–12. Barry Silver discusses another multi-talented youngster in "Stuart Duncan: Bluegrass in Miniature," *BGU* 12, no. 5 (November 1977): 14–17. One of the young musicians discussed in the above-mentioned article by Mike Carpenter—Mark O'Connor—has gone on to great success in jazz, folk-rock, and mainstream country; see Bonnie Smith, "Mark O'Connor: Winning It All by 14," ibid. 10, no. 10 (April 1976): 34–40; and Mitchell Feldman, "Mark O'Connor: From the Dawgs to the Dregs," *Downbeat* 49, no. 6 (June 1982): 16–18.

11. Country Music, 1972–1984

A new magazine appeared in late 1972—*Country Music*—which contributed some of the most honest and objective criticism that the country field had ever received. The magazine attracted a number of excellent journalists, such as Dave Hickey, Nick Tosches, Rich Kienzle, Peter Carr, John Morthland, and Paul Hemphill, who were knowledgeable about most forms of popular music and who also had a thorough understanding of American popular culture. Some of the writers had experience in rock journalism, and a tinge of the *Rolling Stone* style (sarcastic, irreverent, salacious) intruded into their essays. Above all, several of the writers (such as Rich Kienzle in his "Retrospectives" column) had a genuine appreciation for and an understanding of older forms of country music.

Rolling Stone itself occasionally ventured into the discussion of country music, although most of its applause went to musicians such as Gary Stewart, Waylon Jennings, and Willie Nelson who had an appeal to youthful and "hip" audiences. Chet Flippo was the magazine's most knowledgeable country music expert, and one of its best writers. Other rock magazines, such as *Creem* and *Crawdaddy*, only rarely dealt with country music, but they did carry occasional stories on such country-rock musicians as Gram Parsons and the Nitty Gritty Dirt band.

Newspaper columnists have played increasingly important roles in popularizing and documenting country music. Townsend Miller, for example, did much to make the Austin musicians known far and wide through his weekly columns in the *Austin American-Statesman* in the seventies. Jack Hurst, a *Chicago-Tribune* columnist whose weekly articles are widely syndicated, is the most influential of all the newspaper country-music specialists. Although he rarely says anything negative about the musicians whom he describes and whose records he reviews, he is always scrupulously fair and objective in his treatment of country music's varied styles. His personal preferences clearly lean toward hard-core forms of country music.

The affairs of the country music industry itself, as well as occasional tidbits about performers and performances, are discussed in the official publication of the Country Music Association, *CMA Close-Up* (published monthly in Nashville). The evidence of country music's commercial burgeoning is found in the pages of this little journal and in the rash of popular magazine articles that have appeared in the last decade and a half (two of the most significant were *Newsweek*, June 18, 1973, and *Time*, May 5, 1974—both cover stories).

Another dramatic indication of country music's "arrival" in American popular culture was the success of the movie *Nashville* in 1975. The movie was widely, and favorably, reviewed, but the most important discussions of its relationship to country music (real and imagined) were Noel Coppage, "And Then There's 'Nashville,'" *Stereo Review*, October 1975, pp. 55–56, and Patrick Anderson, "The Real Nashville," *New York Times Magazine*, August 31, 1975, pp. 10–11, 36, 40–42. *Urban Cowboy*, the promoter of cowboy chic, was inspired by Aaron Latham's "The Ballad of the Urban Cowboy," *Esquire* 90 (September 12, 1978): 21–30. The singer who profited most from the movie's popularity, Mickey Gilley, has been discussed in several articles, the most important of which are Peter Guralnick, "Mickey Gilley's Piano Roll Blues," *Country Music* 6, no. 6 (March 1978): 40–42, 63–66; Bob Claypool, "Just Ol' Mickey," ibid. 4, no. 7 (April 1976): 54–58; and Lee Rector, "Mickey Gilley," *MCN* 20, no. 7 (January 1983): 16–17. Michael Bane concentrated on another movie phenomenon which made heavy use of country music—and country musicians—in "Burt Reynolds: Smokey and His Country Music Bandits," *Country Music* 9, no. 2 (October 1980): 77–80. The politics of country music was discussed in the notes to Chapter 9, but a couple of other articles deserve mention which comment on the music's relationship to presidential politics in the late seventies: Ed Kiersh, "What's Jimmy Carter Doing in This Magazine, Anyway?" *Country Music* 5, no. 3 (December 1976): 40–42; and Bob Allen, "Haggard's a Working Man at Heart," *MCN* 19, no. 12 (June 1982): 12.

Information on the Association of Country Entertainers (ACE) can be extracted from the music journals of the day, but the organization promoted its own cause in a plethora of mimeographed material which included a newsletter called "The Booster Bulletin."

The country-pop singers have not suffered from inattention. Barbara Mandrell is discussed approvingly by John Fergus Ryan, "A Visit with Barbara Mandrell," *Country Music* 2, no. 5 (January 1974): 32–34, 68–73; and by Genevieve Waddell, "Barbara Mandrell: Little Miss Versatility," *CSR* 26, no. 181 (August 1974): 8–9. The pop-rockabilly and sometimes-honky-tonk singer Joe Stampley is discussed by Neil Pond in "Joe Stampley Keeps Versatile," *MCN* 21, no. 4 (October 1983): 40, 49. Anne Murray has been much discussed, as in John Gabree, "Anne Murray: The Girl Next Door Grows Up," *Country Music Beat* 1, no. 1 (January 1975): 43–45, and Lee Rector, "Canada's Anne Murray Brings Styles Together," *MCN* 17, no. 7 (January 1980): 16–17. John Lomax III conducted a very good interview with Don Williams in *JCM* 8, no. 1 (May 1979): 2–19, and Harry Morrow did a sympathetic portrait of Williams in "Whispering Thunder," *Country Music* 6, no. 6 (March 1978): 24–26, 65. Two of the best assessments of Larry Gatlin are in *Country Music*: Dolly Carlisle, "Larry Gatlin:

Straight Ahead," 8, no. 7 (April 1980): 20–25, and Laura Eipper, "Larry Gatlin," 7, no. 4 (January–February 1977): 46–48, 95. Most articles on Gatlin stress his sometimes troubled relationship with fans; material on Conway Twitty, on the other hand, concentrates on his close rapport with his intensely loyal audience: John Pugh, "Conway Twitty: Sexy Songs and Good Deeds Keep Him on Top," *Country Music* 5, no. 6 (March 1977): 39–40; Patrick Carr and Marshall Fallwell, "Introducing Harold Jenkins," ibid. 2, no. 9 (May 1974): 25–32; Charlie Burton, "Country Music Interviews: Conway Twitty," ibid. 1, no. 1 (September 1972): 47–52; Dixie Deen, "Conway Rocks Right into Country Success," *MCN* 4, no. 8 (February 1967): 3–4; and Sonia L. Nazario, "Country Music Fans Pay Tribute to Idols at Big Theme Parks," *Wall Street Journal*, December 12, 1983, p. 1. Kenny Rogers, of course, is a darling of the media, and is known to millions through his movies and television specials. Two magazine pieces which have been particularly helpful are Bob Allen, "Kenny Rogers' Second Edition," *Country Music* 7, no. 1 (October 1977): 22–26, 58–59, and "Playboy Interview: Kenny Rogers," *Playboy* 30, no. 11 (November 1983): 65–69, 72–77, 80–82.

Country music's three great vocal groups, the Statler Brothers, the Oak Ridge Boys, and Alabama, have been often discussed. The Statlers have had a Time-Life collection devoted to them (with notes by Charles Wolfe), and several articles, among which are Patrick Carr, "The Statler Brothers: "How the Class of '57 Buys a Schoolhouse, Wins Eight CMA Awards in an Air of Complete Calm," *Country Music* 9, no. 7 (March 1981): 38–45, and Lee Rector, "The Statler Brothers Shore Themselves with Fans," *MCN* 20, no. 12 (June 1983): 32–33. As a group with a gospel past and an approach that appeals to a broad spectrum of fans, the Oak Ridge Boys have shown up in a wide variety of periodicals. These include an interview, "The Oaks: Acorns, Roots and Branches," in *Performance* 8, no. 38 (January 19, 1979): 50–56; Todd Everett, "The Oak Ridge Boys Go Secular," *High Fidelity and Musical America* 29, no. 4 (April 1979): 107–110; and Bob Anderson, "Crossing Over from Canaan: The Oak Ridge Boys Go Country," *Country Music* 6, no. 5 (February 1978): 34–38. The literature devoted to Alabama will eventually be enormous, but for the time being I have depended on Suzan Crane, "Alabama: Southern-bred and Stardom Bound," *Country Music* 9, no. 2 (October 1980): 30–33, and Barry Bronson, "Alabama: A Day in the Lives," *MCN* 21, no. 4 (October 1983): 28–29, 45.

The youth-country fusion of the seventies and the consequent emergence of country-rock are deserving of a lengthy study. Bud Scoppa did a preliminary survey of one aspect of the phenomenon in "The L. A. Turnaround," *Country Music* 2, no. 13 (September 1974): 58–65, and Jan Reid discussed the manifestations of country-rock in Austin in *The Improbable Rise of Redneck Rock* (Austin: Heidelberg, 1974). Bob Dylan's contributions to the mating of country music and the youth audience are discussed in Neil V. Rosenberg, "Bob Dylan in Nashville," *JCM* 7, no. 3 (December 1978): 54–66. Such Dylan lps as *John Wesley Harding* and *Nashville Skyline* are important documents of the youth/rock flirtation with country music, but the most significant milestones are the Nitty Gritty Dirt Band's *Will the Circle Be Unbroken*, United Artists UAS 9801; the Byrds' *Sweetheart of the Rodeo*, Columbia CS9670; the Flying Burrito Brothers' *The Gilded Palace of Sin*, A&M SP4175; and Gram Parsons' *GP*, Warner Brothers 0598. Noel Coppage wrote an excellent review of *Will the Circle Be Unbroken* for *Stereo Review* 30, no. 3 (March 1973): 104–105, and Jerry Leichtling conducted an insightful interview with the Nitty Gritty Dirt Band in *Modern Hi Fi and Music* 5, no. 9 (November 1975): 23–26. Gram Parsons' crusade to fuse country and rock, and his often bizarre lifestyle, are discussed in such articles as Judson Klinger and Greg Mitchell, "Gram Finale," *Crawdaddy*, October 1976, pp. 43–58; Patrick Sullivan, "Gram Parsons: The Mysterious Death and Aftermath," *Rolling Stone*, no. 146 (October 25, 1973): 12, 14; Jimmy Cornelison, "Gram Parsons' Music Continues to Live On," *MCN* 21, no. 2 (August 1983): 12; and Ben Fong-Torres, "Gram Parsons: The Spirit of Country," *Esquire* 96, no. 6 (December 1981): 96–98.

The southern rock musicians were reviewed and discussed in such magazines as *Creem*, *Crawdaddy*, and *Rolling Stone*. The most country-oriented of the group, Charlie Daniels, also appeared frequently in country publications (for example, Stan Sucher, "Charlie Daniels Reacts to His Sound," *MCN* 14, no. 9 (March 1977): 4; Russell Shaw, "Charlie Daniels: The Pride of Tennessee," *Country Music* 5, no. 6 [March 1977]: 42–43; and Bob Allen, "Charlie Daniels: Double Platinum Fiddle Player," ibid. 8, no. 7 [April 1980]: 28–30, 39–42).

The best introduction to Hank Williams, Jr., aside from his music, is his autobiography (written with Michael Bane), *Living Proof* (New York: Dell, 1979). Although one can question the reliability of the information concerning his father and mother, Hank, Jr., is very frank about his own life. His account should be supplemented with John Escow, "Oedipus Rocks: The Rise and Fall of Hank Williams, Jr.," *New Times* 10, no. 11 (May 29, 1978): 38–43, 47–50, and Chet Flippo, "Hank Williams Jr's Hard Road," *Rolling Stone*, no. 266 (June 1, 1978): 8, 17.

The Austin musical scene was touted euphorically by Townsend Miller in his weekly columns for the *Austin American-Statesman*, and only slightly more dispassionately by such southwestern-based magazines as *Country Gazette* (published in Austin by Buster Doss), *Buddy Magazine* (named in honor of Buddy Holly and published in Dallas), *Austin Sun* (a counterculture organ), and *Picking Up the Tempo* (published in Albuquerque, but heavily oriented toward Austin). Jan Reid wrote the only book-length study of the Austin musicians in *The Improbable Rise of Redneck Rock*, and followed that up with a eulogy for the phenomenon, "Who Killed

Redneck Rock," *Texas Monthly* 4 (December 1976): 112–113, 209–216. The most scholarly assessments of Austin music, each of which concentrates on the symbols and images surrounding and shaping the musicians, are Archie Green, "Austin's Cosmic Cowboys: Words in Collision," in *And Other Neighborly Names: Social Process and Cultural Image in Texas Folklore*, edited by Richard Bauman and Roger D. Abrahams (Austin: University of Texas Press, 1981), pp. 152–194; Green's "Michael Adam's Honky-Tonk Paintings," *JEMFQ* 18, nos. 67–68 (Fall–Winter 1982): 155–165; David Perry, "Cosmic Cowboys and Cosmetic Politics," ibid. 15, no. 53 (Spring 1979): 38–43; and Nicholas Spitzer, "Bob Wills Is Still the King: Romantic Regionalism and Convergent Culture in Central Texas," *JEMFQ* 2, Part 4, no. 4 (Winter 1975): 191–197. Travis Holland is far from scholarly in his impressionistic and stream-of-consciousness-style *Texas Genesis* (Austin: B. F. Deal, 1978), but he provides a considerable amount of useful inside information on the early Austin scene. Holland played bass and guitar for many of the Austin musicians, and he may be right on target when he asserts that their music was not country, but was instead a fusion of rock and urban folk.

I had the good fortune to know Kenneth Threadgill, and to have been an active participant in the musical sessions held at his famous bar in the early sixties. I interviewed him in Austin on July 8, 1971. Among the more useful short articles on him are Greg Olds, "Threadgill," *Austin American-Statesman Show World*, July 5, 1970, pp. T26–T29; Prissy Mays, "Old Is Beautiful—in Music or on Threadgill," *Alcalde*, May 1973, pp. 13–15 (the magazine of the University of Texas Alumni Association); and Wayne Oakes, "Thousands Turn Out for Threadgill," *Texas Observer* 62 (August 7, 1970): 17–19.

My knowledge of the origins of the Armadillo World Headquarters came mostly from an interview with its founder and proprietor, Eddie Wilson, in Austin on June 5, 1974. Among the most helpful articles dealing with the club are Ed Ward, "There's a Little Bit of Everything in Texas," *Creem* 5, no. 4 (April 1974): 46–48, 76; and Henry Staten, "Armadillo World Headquarters," *Texas Observer* 63 (February 12, 1971): 18–19.

Articles on individual Austin musicians are plentiful. The man who coined the term "cosmic cowboy," Michael Murphey, is described by Lydia Dixon-Harden, "Michael Murphey Finally Gets Settled in Country Music," *MCN* 21, no. 4 (October 1983): 23, 45. The best songwriter to drift through Austin, Guy Clark, is evaluated by Kelly Delaney, "Guy Clark: A Songwriting Craftsman," ibid., pp. 20–21. Marcia Ball reveals that her heart was never really with country music in Bunny Matthews, "Irma's Still the Queen but Tall Texan Marcia Ball Is Heir Apparent to the New Orleans Musical Throne," *Wavelength*, no. 40 (February 1984): 18–20. The self-styled Texas Jewboy, Kinky Friedman, has been fascinating to writers as much for his irreverent humor as for his music: Kaye Northcott,

"Kinky Friedman's First Roundup," *Texas Monthly* 1, no. 4 (May 1973): 95–96; Larry Sloman, "Kinky and the Money Changers," *Crawdaddy*, April 1975, pp. 30–31; and Lester Bangs, review of *Sold American*, Vanguard VSD 97333, in *Rolling Stone*, no. 137 (June 21, 1973): 63. Except for Willie Nelson, Jerry Jeff Walker has inspired more print than any other Austin-based musician, including articles by Douglas Kent Hall, "Mr. Bojangles' Dance: The Odyssey and Oddities of Jerry Jeff Walker," *Rolling Stone*, no. 176 (December 19, 1974): 9, 20; John Moulder, "Jerry Jeff Walker, Hell-Raising Poet," *Country Rambler*, no. 2 (October 7, 1976): 8–10; and John Morthland, "Jerry Jeff Rides Again," *Country Music* 6, no. 6 (March 1978): 28–32. In addition to the above-mentioned articles, I also profited from interviews with Marcia Ball in Kerrville, Texas, July 2, 1978; Alvin Crow, Kerrville, July 4, 1977; and Steve Fromholz, Kerrville, July 4, 1977.

The articles on Willie Nelson cannot all be mentioned. The best place to begin would be Rich Kienzle's excellent notes to the Time-Life Collection on Nelson. Of the many interviews with Nelson, among the best are Bob Allen's in *JCM* 8, no. 2 (1980): 3–14; David Breskin's in *Musician*, no. 45 (July 1982): 40–48, 84–85; and Alanna Nash's in *Stereo Review*, no. 5 (November 1979): 68–70. Other articles which are commendable in their summary and/or evaluation of Nelson's career are Chet Flippo, "Willie Nelson," *Rolling Stone*, no. 269 (July 13, 1978): 45–49; Roy Blount, Jr., "Wrasslin' with This Thing Called Willie Nelson," *Esquire*, August 1981, pp. 78–80, 83–87; and William C. Martin, "Growing Old at Willie Nelson's Picnic," *Texas Monthly* 2 (October 1974): 94–98, 116–124. Nelson's movie career is discussed by Bob Allen, "Willie Nelson: Being a Movie Star Sure Beats Working," *Country Music* 9, no. 2 (October 1980): 34–36, 45–47; Michael Bane, "Willie: The Gypsy Cowboy Goes Hollywood," ibid. 7, no. 7 (May 1979): 24–28; and John Pugh and Bill Oakey, "Willie Goes to the Movies," ibid. 8, no. 6 (March 1980): 56–58.

Willie's fellow "Outlaws" are discussed in a variety of places. Probably the best short summary of the group (and one which was influential in naming them) is Dave Hickey's "In Defense of the Telecaster Cowboy Outlaws," *Country Music* 2, no. 5 (January 1974): 90–95. The fullest history and critique is Michael Bane, *The Outlaws: Revolution in Country Music* (New York: Doubleday, 1978). Individual Outlaws receive attention in such essays as Mickey Lane, "Tompall—the Outlaw with Style and Flavor," *Nashville Sound* 2, no. 8 (November 1976): 18–21, 36; Kelly Delaney, "Billy Joe Shaver: Cowboy in His Soul," *Country Music* 9, no. 1 (September 1980): 76; Larry L. King, "David Allan Coe's Greatest Hits," *Esquire* 86 (July 1976): 71–73, 142–144; and Neil Pond, "David Allan Coe Polishes His Image," *MCN* 20, no. 12 (June 1983): 24–25.

Waylon Jennings has had a full-scale biography devoted to him: R. Serge Denisoff, *Waylon* (Knoxville: University of Tennessee Press, 1983). The book has received mixed reviews, but it does present the basic facts (and discography) of Jennings' life and career. It should be supplemented with John L. Smith, "I Ain't No Ordinary Dude—a Bio-Discography of Waylon Jennings," *JCM* 6, no. 2 (Summer 1975): 45–95; Bob Campbell, "Waylon: An Interview," *Country Music* 7, no. 4 (January–February 1979): 50–55; and Lee Rector, "An Inside Look at the Real Waylon Jennings," *MCN* 20, no. 6 (December 1982): 16–17.

The hard country revivalists have received scattered attention. The western swing and rodeo singer Red Steagall is discussed by Cindy Kent, "Red Steagall Attests to Bob Wills Music," *MCN* 14, no. 3 (September 1976): 8. I also talked to Steagall in Kerrville on July 3, 1977. Lee Rector did a short sketch of Riders in the Sky, "Western Music Comes Alive with Riders," in *MCN* 18, no. 4 (October 1980): 42. The honky-tonk–rockabilly singer Gary Stewart received extensive press coverage in 1976 (his peak year) because of his expertise in two different styles of expression. The best of these articles are Patrick Carr, "Goodtime Gary," *Country Music* 5, no. 9 (June 1976): 34–41, and Kit Rachlis, "Honky-Tonkin' Blues in Rock-and-Roll Shoes," *Rolling Stone*, no. 209 (March 25, 1976): 56, 58. A glimpse of the obscure honky-tonk singer Vernon Oxford and of his remarkable popularity abroad is provided by John Pugh in "The Vernon Oxford Conspiracy," *Country Music* 9, no. 2 (October 1980): 59–62. George Strait is gradually beginning to receive the attention he deserves, with the best article being that of Bob Millard, "Strait Leaves Ranch for Music Career," *MCN* 20, no. 6 (December 1982): 10. Gene Watson deserves more coverage than he has received, but two of the better sketches on him are Bill Oakey, "Gene Watson," *Country Music* 9, no. 3 (November 1980): 60–61, and Tom Robinson, "Gene Watson: A New Look, but the Same Sound," *MCN* 20, no. 7 (January 1983): 10, 20. I interviewed Moe Bandy in Kerrville on July 3, 1977, and learned additional information about him from Bob Allen, "Moe Bandy: Honky Tonk Hero, Hardcore Country Survivor," *Country Music* 7, no. 4 (January–February 1979): 42–44, and from Nick Tosches, "Honky Tonk Lives," ibid. 3, no. 7 (April 1975): 35–38. The most commercially successful of the young honky-tonk singers—John Anderson—has not yet attained the kind of magazine exposure that seems commensurate with his immense public popularity. One brief article, though, which I found helpful was Bob Allen, "Country John," *US* 5, no. 5 (March 3, 1981) (pages not numbered).

Material dealing with George Jones was described in the notes for Chapter 9, but two additional articles which shed light on his remarkable endurance in the seventies are Bob Allen, "The Decline and Fall of George Jones," *Country Music* 7, no. 4 (January–February 1979): 28–30, 32–34, and Richard Nusser and Patrick Carr, "George Jones: Problems, Problems, Problems," ibid. 4, no. 3 (December 1975): 30–34, 59.

As might be expected of someone with both beauty and talent, Emmylou

Harris has been a favorite of magazine writers. The following list of articles is certainly not exhaustive: Bill Littleton, "Emmylou Gives 'Piece of the Sky,'" MCN 13, no. 2 (August 1975): 9; Bud Scoppa, "Emmylou Harris's Quiet Country Sky," *Rolling Stone,* no. 184 (April 10, 1975): 60, 62; Dave Hickey, "Emmylou Harris: Stardom Hasn't Gone to Her Head," *Country Music* 4, no. 12 (September 1976): 23–26, 59; Ben Fong-Torres, "Emmylou Harris: Whole-Wheat Honky Tonk," *Rolling Stone,* no. 259 (February 23, 1978): 8, 10, 18, 21; Joyce Maynard Bethel, "Emmylou Harris—Heart Is Still in Country Music," *New York Times,* March 12, 1978, p. 241; Jas Obrecht, "Pro's Reply: Emmylou Harris," *Guitar Player* 12, no. 11 (November 1978): 8, 152, 154, 158–159; Lee Rector, "Emmylou Harris, Doing the Music She Likes," *MCN* 17, no. 11 (May 1980): 16–17; and Rip Kirby, "Emmylou," *Country Music* 9, no. 1 (September 1980): 36–44.

Harris' one-time partner and fellow traditionalist Ricky Skaggs has not been so well publicized. His accelerating commercial success, though, will inevitably be documented in a rash of books and magazine articles. For the time being, I have relied on such articles as Jack Tottle, "Ricky Skaggs: Clinch Mountain to Boone Creek," *BGU* 11, no. 7 (January 1977): 8–16; Robert K. Oermann, "Ricky Skaggs Remembers the Stanley Brothers," ibid. 15, no. 11 (May 1981): 26–29; and Robert Kyle, "Ricky Skaggs: Moving beyond Bluegrass," *Pickin'* 6, no. 1 (February 1979): 51–54.

The article which comments on the growing interchange between soul and country music is Lee May, "Blacks Join the Country Music Surge," *Los Angeles* Times, August 30, 1983, pp. 1, 11. The concern about country music losing its own "soul" is voiced by Hugh Cherry in "Country DJs Carry Music to People," *MCN* 18, no. 4 (October 1980): 18–19; and by Bobby Bare in Lydia Dixon's "Bobby Bare: The Songwriter Speaks Up for the Soul of Country Music," ibid. 20, no. 11 (May 1983): 10A.

Suggestions for Additional Reading and Listening, Post-1985

Anyone who wishes to explore the current state of country music will find copious detail on the Internet. Every performer has an "official" website and, usually, several unofficial ones conducted by fans or followers of country music. *Country Weekly,* a magazine that appears on supermarket shelves, provides a steady diet of gossip about country entertainers along with news about the latest CD or video releases. *Close Up* (the newsletter of the Country Music Association) conveys information from a Nashville music industry perspective. Virtually any current performer can also be seen and heard on music videos shown by Country Music Television or the Nashville Network (recently renamed the National Network). Furthermore, many of the entertainers who work outside of Nashville's orbit can be seen on such syndicated television shows as *Austin City Limits.*

A variety of encyclopedias also provide basic information. These include Kurt Wolff, ed., *Country Music: The Rough Guide* (London: Rough Guides Ltd., 2000); David Goodman, ed., *Modern Twang: An Alternative Country Music Guide and Directory* (Nashville: Dowling Press, 1999); Barry McCloud, ed., *Definitive Country: The Ultimate Encyclopedia of Country Music and Its Performers* (New York: Berkley, 1995); and Paul Kingsbury, ed., *The Encyclopedia of Country Music: The Ultimate Guide to the Music* (New York: Oxford University Press, 1998). The Kingsbury volume, sponsored by the Country Music Foundation, is probably the most authoritative and includes articles and biographical vignettes written by an assortment of academicians, journalists, and freelance writers.

Several journals survey country music from a variety of perspectives. *Country Music* magazine still exists, and while it has not preserved the excellence once given to it by such perceptive and hard-hitting writers as Dave Hickey, Patrick Carr, Rich Kienzle, and John Morthland, it nonetheless provides reliable information on most active musicians. The *Journal of Country Music* presents lengthy, well-researched articles and reviews on both historical and contemporary issues. Many of the journal's best essays and reviews have been excerpted in Paul Kingsbury, ed., *The Country Reader* (Nashville: Country Music Foundation Press and Vanderbilt University Press, 1996). *Bluegrass Unlimited* has always been a thorough compendium of material on both bluegrass and old-time music. *Old-Time Herald,* however, is the best source of information on traditional styles of country music, particularly the string bands and other acts that sprang from the folk revival. The best current journal devoted to country music and other roots-expressions is *No Depression* (published in Seattle, Washington). It is exhaustive in its coverage of classic country, bluegrass, country-rock, and other "alternative" forms. *The Oxford American,* a bimonthly magazine published in Oxford, Mississippi, runs a special issue each year dealing with the various styles of southern music.

General Studies and Histories

Most academic histories ignore the role played by country music in southern and American life. Surveys of the 1920's, for example, almost always comment on jazz as a musical expression that helped to define that age, but they miss the opportunity to talk about country and old-time music as a voice of tradition-minded Americans (or even of those who merely welcomed an exotic alternative to urban popular styles). Similarly, neither Hank Williams nor Merle Haggard makes it into most contemporary studies of American culture, even though these musicians voiced the aspirations, values, or frustrations of millions of people. A few historians of the South, however—such as Edward Ayers, Numan Bartley, John Boles,

James Cobb, Thomas Connelly, Pete Daniel, Charles Joyner, Jack Temple Kirby, Melton McLaurin, Ivan Tribe, and Charles Reagan Wilson—have either written directly on country and other grass-roots music forms or have incorporated observations of music into their historical analyses. Edward Ayers, *The Promise of the New South: Life after Reconstruction* (New York: Oxford University Press, 1992), is an indispensable history of late-nineteenth-century southern culture and of the role played by music. Jacquelyn Dowd Hall, et al., *Like a Family: The Making of a Southern Cotton Mill World* (Chapel Hill: University of North Carolina Press, 1987), masterfully shows how music helped to define and sustain the lives of rural people who adapted to industrial regimentation. Ted Ownby, *Subduing Satan: Religion, Recreation, and Manhood in the Rural South, 1865–1920* (Chapel Hill: University of North Carolina Press, 1990), does not address music specifically but provides a perceptive study of the context out of which country music grew. John Shelton Reed, the leading sociologist of the South, comments frequently on country music, particularly in such books as *Southern Folk Plain and Fancy: Native White Social Types* (Athens: University of Georgia Press, 1986) and *My Tears Spoiled My Aim and Other Reflections on Southern Culture* (Columbia: University of Missouri Press, 1993). All of Charles Joyner's works on the South are informed by training in folklore, music, and history. A good summary of his views is found in the book of essays *Shared Traditions: Southern History and Folk Culture* (Urbana: University of Illinois Press, 1999). Pete Daniel, *Lost Revolutions: The South in the 1950s* (Chapel Hill: University of North Carolina Press, 2000), talks about the interrelationship of southern working-class culture, rock-and-roll, and other forms of music. James N. Gregory presents the best available study of the transplantation of southern and southwestern culture (particularly music and religion) in California in *American Exodus: The Dust Bowl Migration and Okie Culture in California* (New York: Oxford University Press, 1989). Two of the finest analyses of country music and southern life have been provided by journalists: Peter Applebome, in *Dixie Rising: How the South Is Shaping American Values, Politics, and Culture* (New York: Times Books, 1996), and Rick Bragg, in his memoir of growing up in northeastern Alabama, *All Over but the Shoutin'* (New York: Pantheon Books, 1997).

A number of general histories or interpretations of country music also have become available in the past fifteen years, including my *Don't Get Above Your Raisin': Country Music and the Southern Working Class* (Urbana: University of Illinois Press, 2002). I somehow inadvertently omitted from the earlier revision a reference to one of the greatest works on folksong scholarship, Norm Cohen, *Long Steel Rail: The Railroad in American Folksong* (Urbana: University of Illinois Press, 1981), which has much to say about early commercial country music. John Lomax III, from the "first family" of American folklore scholarship, concentrates on the rise of the contemporary country music industry in *Nashville, Music City USA* (New York: Harry M. Abrams, 1985). Bob Oermann, a respected Nashville music journalist, has contributed *A Century of Country: An Illustrated History of Country Music* (New York: TV Books, 1999), written as an accompaniment to the Turner Broadcasting System's thirteen-part television history of country music. Bob Millard's *Country Music: 75 Years of America's Favorite Music* (New York: Da Capo Press, 1999) is basically a listing of country music events and personalities arranged chronologically by decades. Patrick Carr, ed., *The Illustrated History of Country Music* (New York: Random House, 1995), is a well-written body of essays contributed by such music authorities as Charles K. Wolfe, Douglas B. Green, and Bob Pinson. Historical essays on country music are also included in Robert Santelli, Holly George-Warren, and Jim Brown, eds., *American Roots Music* (New York: Harry N. Abrams, 2001), a companion volume to the PBS documentary series of the same name. Brian Hinton, *Country Roads: How Country Came to Nashville* (London: Sanctuary Publishing Ltd., 2000), is a highly detailed but breezy survey of country music written by an English rock journalist. It's hard for me to resist a book that refers to *Country Music, USA* as "magisterial" and as "the Old Testament of country music history."

Interpretive and Specialized Studies

A large and growing body of literature deals with country music from a broad range of perspectives. My *Singing Cowboys and Musical Mountaineers* (Athens: University of Georgia Press, 1993) grew out of a series of lectures presented at Mercer University in Macon, Georgia, and is composed of essays dealing with country music's pre-commercial origins, its indebtedness to nineteenth-century popular music, and the influence of romantic symbols on its development. Cecelia M. Tichi, in *High Lonesome: The American Culture of Country Music* (Chapel Hill: University of North Carolina Press, 1994), argues that country musicians explore the same themes, such as home, the lure of the open road, and spirituality, that our greatest poets have addressed. Richard A. Peterson challenges the idea of country music's working-class origins in *Creating Country Music: Fabricating Authenticity* (Chicago: University of Chicago Press, 1997). Laurence Leamer and Bruce Feiler have written the best broad interpretive surveys of contemporary Top Forty country music. Leamer's *Three Chords and the Truth: Hope, Heartbreak, and Changing Fortunes in Nashville* (New York: HarperCollins, 1997) is a non-sentimental but perceptive and sympathetic study, and it contains good biographical portraits of such people as Shania Twain and Mary Chapin Carpenter. Feiler's *Dreaming Out Loud: Garth Brooks, Wynonna Judd, Wade Hayes and the Changing Face of Nashville* (New York: Avon Books, 1998) also has perceptive studies of the musicians named in its title and is the best available critique and defense of the music that now emanates from Nashville.

Nicholas Dawidoff's beautifully written *In the Country of Country: People and Places in American Music* (New York: Pantheon Books, 1997) is my favorite book among the recent interpretive studies of country music (probably because he and I tend to like the same kind of country singers). Dawidoff presents a jaundiced view of contemporary Nashville and sympathetic portraits of such "roots performers" as Iris DeMent, Doc Watson, Ralph Stanley, and Merle Haggard.

Between November 1991 and August 1993, Curtis W. Ellison traveled over five thousand miles, including trips to Nashville's Fan Fair and every other conceivable type of performing venue, to write *Country Music Culture: From Hard Times to Heaven* (Jackson: University Press of Mississippi, 1995). It is the best account of country music as a community or "family" consisting of fans and musicians. Alanna Nash, *Behind Closed Doors: Talking With the Legends of Country Music* (New York: Knopf, 1988), presents an insider's view of her subject based on twenty-seven interviews with stars ranging from Roy Acuff to Hank Williams, Jr.

Mary A. Bufwack and Robert K. Oermann, *Finding Her Voice: The Saga of Women in Country Music* (New York: Crown, 1993), is the best general survey of a topic that has been too long neglected. Murphy Henry edits a quarterly newsletter, *Women in Bluegrass* (published in Winchester, Virginia), and has written a master's thesis at George Mason University in Fairfax, Virginia, on a pioneering woman performer: "'Come Prepared to Stay. Bring Fiddle.' The Story of Sally Ann Forrester: The Original Bluegrass Girl" (1999). The thesis has been reprinted with the same title in Charles K. Wolfe and James E. Akenson, eds., *Country Music Annual, 2001* (Lexington: The University Press of Kentucky, 2001). The *Country Music Annual*, which has appeared in two volumes (2000 and 2001), grew out of the International Country Music Conference, held each year at Belmont University in Nashville.

Bluegrass music has elicited some fine scholarship, much of it found in biographies that will be discussed later. The most comprehensive survey of this exciting musical genre is Neil V. Rosenberg, *Bluegrass: A History* (Urbana: University of Illinois Press, 1985), a work that needs to be updated and reissued. Barry R. Willis, *America's Music: Bluegrass* (Franktown, Colo.: Pine Valley Music, 1998), is loaded with all kinds of interesting and recent details, but it lacks the narrative and analytical strength found in the Rosenberg book.

The best available studies of rockabilly music are only incidentally concerned with country music, but they indicate the ways in which country inspired and presaged rock-and-roll: Michael Bertrand, *Race, Rock, and Elvis* (Urbana: University of Illinois Press, 1999), and Craig Morrison, *Go*

Cat Go! Rockabilly Music and Its Makers (Urbana: University of Illinois Press, 1996).

Robert Cantwell's purview is similarly broader than country music in *When We Were Good: The Folk Revival* (Cambridge: Harvard University Press, 1996), but he discusses a phenomenon that provided a new audience for bluegrass music and altered the direction and scope of country music in general. This impressive book would be an excellent text for a college course on the 1960's.

The popular syndicated television show *Austin City Limits* also introduced a multitude of Americans to country music and informed them of the large contingent of entertainers who work outside the Nashville mainstream. Its story has been well told by Clifford Endres, *Austin City Limits* (Austin: University of Texas Press, 1987), and John T. Davis, *Austin City Limits: 25 Years of American Music* (New York: Billboard Books, 2000). Both books include a wealth of photographs, mostly from the camera of Scott Newton.

Several excellent studies of country songs and songwriters have become available. Kathleen Hudson, director of the Texas Heritage Music Foundation in Kerrville, provides thirty-four interviews with such talented tunesmiths as Willie Nelson, Lyle Lovett, and Tish Hinojosa in *Telling Stories, Writing Songs: An Album of Texas Songwriters* (Austin: University of Texas Press, 2001). Dorothy Horstman's perspective is unique in *Sing Your Heart Out, Country Boy* (Nashville: Country Music Foundation Press, 3d rev. ed., 1996). She presents the lyrics of more than three hundred songs in fifteen categories (such as home, unrequited love, and prison), and attempts to explain the songs' meaning and context in the words of the songwriters. Jimmie N. Rogers quotes only a few lyrics directly, but evaluates 1,400 songs and their themes in *The Country Music Message: Revisited* (Fayetteville: University of Arkansas Press, 1989). Although Rogers found that "nearly three of every four popular country songs are about love," a large number were concerned with the various aspects of living. Melton A. McLaurin and Richard A. Peterson, eds., *You Wrote My Life: Lyrical Themes in Country Music* (Philadelphia: Gordon and Breach, 1992), is a well-researched and cogently argued collection of essays on the themes of class, region, and religion in country music. Peterson's essay on "class unconsciousness" is particularly trenchant. Cecelia Tichi, ed., *Readin' Country Music: Steel Guitars, Opry Stars, and Honky Tonk Bars* (special ed. of *South Atlantic Quarterly* 94, no. 1 [Winter 1995]), includes essays by sixteen scholars whose interests range from lyric meaning to questions of gender identity and visual symbolism (as portrayed, for example, in the music paintings of Thomas Hart Benton). Gene Edward Veith and Thomas L. Wilmeth in *Honky-Tonk Gospel: The Story of Sin and Salvation in Country Music* (Grand Rapids, Mich.: Baker Books,

2001) explore the contending allures of the flesh and spirit as manifested in country songs. Charles K. Wolfe covers virtually every realm of country music, from old-time styles to the Nashville Sound, in *Classic Country: Legends of Country Music* (New York: Routledge Press, 2000), a collection of his essays written over a period of thirty years and more.

Local and Regional Studies

A fairly extensive list of publications provides reminders that country music exists outside of Nashville. For example, Joe Carr and Alan Munde, musicians and instructors in the Commercial Music Program at South Plains College in Levelland, Texas, discuss West Texas as an incubus of many important musicians: *Prairie Nights to Neon Lights: The Story of Country Music in West Texas* (Lubbock: Texas Tech University Press, 1995). Wayne W. Daniel contributes a fine account of a city that once rivaled Nashville as a country music center: *Pickin' on Peachtree: A History of Country Music in Atlanta, Georgia* (Urbana: University of Illinois Press, 1990). With Bill Sloan's help, Horace Logan talks about his own important career as a radio announcer and promoter, while also discussing the once-thriving country music scene in Shreveport, Louisiana, in *Elvis, Hank, and Me: Making Musical History on the Louisiana Hayride* (New York: St. Martin's Press, 1998). Johnny Horton's bass player and confidant, Tillman Franks, also talks about the *Hayride* and more in *I Was There When It Happened* (Many, La.: Sweet Dreams Publishing, 2000). Popular comedian Pete Stamper similarly entwines his own story with that of an important radio show in *It All Happened in Renfro Valley* (Lexington: University Press of Kentucky, 1999). Reta Spears-Stewart talks about Red Foley and the regional show he hosted in *Remembering the Ozark Jubilee* (Springfield, Mo.: Stewart, Dillbeck, and White Productions, 1993). One of my favorite country music historians, the prolific Ivan Tribe, discusses the Wheeling radio scene and much more in *Mountaineer Jamboree: Country Music in West Virginia* (Lexington: University Press of Kentucky, 1984). In many respects, Gerald W. Haslam has written the best regional study of country music, *Workin' Man Blues: Country Music in California* (Berkeley: University of California Press, 1999). The book is important, not merely because it is well written and well researched, but also because it surveys a crucial topic that has been too long ignored. Gene Fowler and Bill Crawford's engaging story of the powerful Mexican border broadcasts (the X-Stations), *Border Radio* (Austin: Texas Monthly Press, 1987; rev. ed., University of Texas Press, 2002), is actually more than a regional study. It shows how these stations transmitted the music of regional performers to virtually every nook and cranny of the United States. Finally, Nashville must be given its due. Concentrating on the period from 1925 to 1940, Charles K. Wolfe, in *A Good-Natured Riot: The Birth of the Grand*

Ole Opry (Nashville: Country Music Foundation Press and Vanderbilt University Press, 1999), explains how a regional broadcasting phenomenon became a national treasure.

Biographies and Autobiographies

Personal narratives and reminiscences of country entertainers have flourished since 1985, and a few of them have landed on the *New York Times* best-seller list: Ralph Emery, with Tom Carter, *Memories: The Autobiography of Ralph Emery* (New York: Simon and Schuster, 1991); Reba McEntire, with Tom Carter, *Reba: My Story* (New York: Bantam, 1994); and Peter Guralnick's splendid two-volume biography of Elvis Presley, *Last Train to Memphis: The Rise of Elvis Presley* and *Careless Love: The Unmaking of Elvis Presley* (Boston: Little, Brown and Company, 1994, 1998). Tom Carter, an Oklahoma-born journalist, has collaborated with several performers: George Jones, in *George Jones: I Lived to Tell It All* (New York: Villard, 1996); Glen Campbell, in *Rhinestone Cowboy: An Autobiography* (New York: Villard, 1994); and Merle Haggard, in *Merle Haggard's My House of Memories* (New York: Cliff Street Books, 1999). Carter also has been the subject of a profile by Bob Allen, "What Hath Tom Carter Wrought?" in *The Country Reader,* pp. 306–312. What he and other journalists and freelance writers (including Bob Allen) had "wrought," of course, was a veritable industry of drugstore—and supermarket—rack "biographies" of country superstars. Although the actual input made by the country entertainers, as well as the quality of the books, varies greatly, the worth of these books should not be discounted. They tend to be predictably formulaic in approach, stressing the hard early lives of their subjects, the redemptive role of music, and, often, the saving grace of religion in their lives. The books are often significant for what they choose to omit, but nevertheless they provide insights about working-class people, mostly southern, who otherwise would have had little voice in American culture. A college course built around country music autobiographies would be much more useful than some of the subjects that make it into the curriculums.

The above-listed autobiography of Ralph Emery is illuminating because he has been involved intimately with country entertainers (he even married one) since the late 1950's as a Nashville radio and television personality. The book's presence on the *New York Times* best-seller list suggests the importance that country music television programming now assumes in American culture. Emery has followed up that book with other recollections, written with Patsi Bale Cox, including *The View from Nashville* (New York: William Morrow, 1998) and *Fifty Years Down a Country Road* (New York: William Morrow, 2000). The reader will receive an alternative view of Emery in the candid and engaging autobiography written by his ex-wife, Skeeter Davis: *Bus Fare to Kentucky: The Autobiography of Skeeter Davis* (New York: Birch Lane Press Book, 1993).

Much can be learned about contemporary country music in Naomi Judd, with Bud Schaetzle, *Love Can Build a Bridge* (New York: Fawcett Crest, 1993), and Lisa Rebecca Gubernick's biography of Trisha Yearwood, *Get Hot or Go Home* (New York: St. Martin's Paperbacks, 1993), but my favorites in this genre are the frank and revelatory accounts of some of country music's most wizened or colorful performers: Johnny Cash, with Patrick Carr, *Cash: An Autobiography* (San Francisco: Harper, 1997); Waylon Jennings and Lenny Carr, *Waylon: An Autobiography* (New York: Warner Books, 1996); Willie Nelson, with Bud Shrake, *Willie: An Autobiography* (New York: Simon and Schuster, 1988); and Dolly Parton, *Dolly: My Life and Other Unfinished Business* (New York: HarperCollins, 1994). These books tend to be disarming in their honesty and illuminating for what they have to say about other performers and the music business.

Biographies of country music entertainers have become plentiful, but few of them have been written from a scholarly perspective, and even fewer have concentrated on contemporary performers. As noted earlier, the Guralnick biography of Elvis Presley is definitely the best of the lot, but others deserve commendation. Nick Tosches tells an intriguing story in his search for the influential white minstrel and blues singer Emmett Miller: *Where Dead Voices Gather* (Boston: Little, Brown, 2001). Old-time country music has been well served by Charles K. Wolfe in *The Devil's Box: Masters of Southern Fiddling* (Nashville: Country Music Foundation Press and Vanderbilt University Press, 1997); *DeFord Bailey: A Black Star in Early Country Music,* written with David Morton (Knoxville: University of Tennessee Press, 1991); and *In Close Harmony: The Story of the Louvin Brothers* (Jackson: University Press of Mississippi, 1996). Gene Wiggins takes us back to the very beginnings of country music history with *Fiddlin' Georgia Crazy: Fiddlin' John Carson, His Real World, and the World of His Songs* (Urbana: University of Illinois Press, 1987).

Our understanding of country music in the crucial twenty years or so following World War II has been much enlarged by biographies that chronicle the lives of the first major country-pop performer, three seminal honky-tonk singers, a versatile Canadian singer who rose to the top of the American country music business, the first great independent woman singer, and the first African American superstar: Don Cusic, *Eddy Arnold: I'll Hold You in My Heart* (Nashville: Rutledge Hill Press, 1997); Michael Streissguth, *Eddy Arnold: Pioneer of the Nashville Sound* (New York: Schirmer Books, 1997); Daniel Cooper, *Lefty Frizzell: The Honky-Tonk Life of Country Music's Greatest Singer* (Boston: Little, Brown, 1995); Colin Escott, with George Merritt and William MacEwen, *Hank Williams: The Biography* (Boston: Little, Brown, 1995); Bill Koon, *Hank Williams, So Lonesome* (Jackson: University Press of Mississippi, 2002); Ronnie Pugh, *Ernest Tubb: The Texas Troubadour* (Durham: Duke University Press, 1996); Hank Snow, with Jack Ownbey and Bob Burris, *The Hank*

Snow Story (Urbana: University of Illinois Press, 1994); Margaret Jones, *Patsy: The Life and Times of Patsy Cline* (New York: Da Capo, 1999); and Charley Pride, with Jim Henderson, *Pride: The Charley Pride Story* (New York: William Morrow, 1994).

Western Swing, a close companion of honky-tonk music, is documented in Cary Ginell, *Milton Brown and the Founding of Western Swing* (Urbana: University of Illinois Press, 1994), and Wade Hall, *Hell-Bent for Music: The Life of Pee Wee King* (Lexington: University Press of Kentucky, 1996). Ginell reminds us that Bob Wills was not the sole creator of this vital Texas-style dance form, and Hall surveys the life of a former Polish Milwaukee polka king named Frank Kuczynski who altered the sound of country music when he took western swing, electric guitars, and drums to the stage of the *Grand Ole Opry*.

The pivotal roles played by West Coast musicians are discussed in a couple of biographies about innovative southerners who took their talents to California: Ben Fong-Torres, *Hickory Wind: The Life and Times of Gram Parsons* (New York: Pocket Books, 1991), and Jonny Whiteside, *Ramblin' Rose: The Life and Career of Rose Maddox* (Nashville: Country Music Foundation Press and Vanderbilt University Press, 1997). Parsons' influence is still felt and heard in the music of Emmylou Harris and the whole retinue of alternative country performers. The Maddox biography includes a lengthy, and previously unpublished, letter of endorsement of Rose Maddox and her brothers written by the legendary Woody Guthrie.

Bluegrass music is the central thread that links another cluster of biographies, but these distinctive personalities are colorful in their own right: in *The Stonemans: An Appalachian Family and the Music That Shaped Their Lives* (Urbana: University of Illinois Press, 1993), Ivan Tribe has chosen to document Pop Stoneman and his talented children who span virtually the entire history of country music. Their story also chronicles the emergence of women performers in bluegrass. Tom Piazza deals with the cantankerous but brilliant musician Jimmy Martin in *True Adventures with the King of Bluegrass* (Nashville: Country Music Foundation Press and Vanderbilt University Press, 1999). John Wright tells the story of the venerable keeper of the flame of tradition, Ralph Stanley, in *Traveling the High Way Home: Ralph Stanley and the World of Traditional Bluegrass Music* (Urbana: University of Illinois Press, 1993). Tom Ewing helps to illuminate the world of "the father of bluegrass music" with *The Bill Monroe Reader* (Urbana: University of Illinois Press, 2000). Richard D. Smith, however, has contributed one of country music's most eagerly embraced biographies, *Can't You Hear Me Calling: The Life of Bill Monroe* (Boston: Little, Brown, 2000). Monroe emerges from these pages with major flaws and virtues but still endures as one of the giants of American music.

Cowboy music has found its chronicler in Douglas B. Green, *Singing in the Saddle: The History of the Singing Cowboy* (Nashville: Vanderbilt University Press, 2002). Jim Bob Tinsley has contributed two impressive books that present histories, biographies, and songs (with words and music) from this distinctive genre: *He Was Singin' This Song* (Orlando: University Press of Florida, 1981) and *For a Cowboy Has to Sing* (Orlando: University Press of Florida, 1991).

The visual history of country music has been chronicled by an extensive array of photographers, illustrators, and costume makers. Some of the finest photographers, and samples of their work, include Becky Johnson, *Inside Bluegrass: Twenty Years of Bluegrass Photography* (Madison, North Carolina: Empire Publishing, 1998); Marty Stuart, *Pilgrims, Sinners, Saints, and Prophets* (Nashville: Rutledge Hill Press, 1999); Carl Fleischhauer and Neil Rosenberg, *Bluegrass Odyssey: A Documentary in Pictures and Words, 1966–86* (Urbana: University of Illinois Press, 2001); and the dean of country music photographers, Les Leverett, *Blue Moon of Kentucky: A Journey into the World of Bluegrass and Country Music as Seen through the Camera Lens of Photo-Journalist Les Leverett* (New York: Empire Publishers, 1996). In *Hillbilly Hollywood: The Origins of Country and Western Style* (New York: Rizzoli International Publications, 2000), Debby Bull recalls the wonderful world of country music costuming pioneered by the Los Angeles tailors, Manuel Cuevas and Nudie Cohen, who inaugurated the flamboyant tradition of sequins, spangles, and beads.

One final word should be said about those music writers whose work seldom appears in monographs or biographies, but who nevertheless have enriched and broadened our understanding of country music. Unfortunately, if readers ignore the rich body of literature encompassed by CD liner notes, music magazine articles and reviews, encyclopedia items, and newspaper columns, they will generally be unaware of people like Jack Hurst, the dean of newspaper country music columnists, who since the 1960's has been documenting the world of country music in the *Chicago Tribune* and other newspapers. Readers probably know about Nat Hentoff through his extensive writings on civil liberties and other political and constitutional topics, but they may be unaware of his free-ranging critical commentary on all forms of American popular music for the *Village Voice* and other journals. These and other writers, such as Chet Flippo (the long-time Nashville representative for *Rolling Stone* magazine), Jon Weisberger (the most productive and informed writer on bluegrass), Grant Alden, Bob Allen, Peter Blackstock, David Cantwell, Patrick Carr, Kevin Coffey, Daniel Cooper, Bill Friskics-Warren, Geoffrey Himes, Rich Kienzle, and Alanna Nash bring more than a relentless energy and sharply honed critical acuity to their chosen profession, they also write the best prose that can be found in country music scholarship.

I will conclude with a note about recordings but will resist the temptation to give a comprehensive list of available material. Readers might want to consult my discography in *Don't Get Above Your Raisin',* but no assurance can be given that items listed there will still be in print by the time this book is published, or that they will not have been outmoded by more relevant items. Serious researchers in old-time, or pre–World War II, country music will need to visit the two major repositories for such material, the Country Music Foundation Library in Nashville and the Southern Folklife Collection at the University of North Carolina in Chapel Hill, where they will be permitted to hear "listening copies" of relevant recordings. Eventually, data for all country recordings made before 1941 will be available in books being prepared by Tony Russell and Richard Spottswood. The Spottswood volume will be the fruit of labors made by the late Guthrie T. "Gus" Meade, whose voluminous collections of instrumental and vocal music are housed at the Southern Folklife Collection.

Students and fans of postwar country music should be aware of Joel Whitburn, *The Billboard Book of Top 40 Country Hits* (New York: Billboard Books, 1996), a valuable listing of recordings that since 1944 have made the charts in that journal. Tom Roland, *The Billboard Book of Number One Country Hits* (New York: Billboard, 1991), concentrates on the years since the 1960's and provides detailed discussions of 848 songs. David Cantwell and Bill Friskics-Warren are more subjective and ambitious in *Heartaches by the Number: A Critical Guide to Country Music's 500 Greatest Singles* (Nashville: Country Music Foundation Press and Vanderbilt University Press, 2002). Their book will be an indispensable source for music historians but is certain to evoke spirited and needed debate. Some collected reviews of CDs are available, such as Kurt Wolff, *Country: 100 Essential CDs, The Rough Guide* (London: Rough Guides Ltd., 2000), and Paul Kingsbury, ed., *Country on Compact Disc: The Essential Guide to the Music* (New York: Grove Press, 1993). The Kingsbury volume provides reviews of more than two thousand CDs by twenty-six critics but is obviously incomplete. No compiler is likely to keep up with the avalanche of recordings that continue to flow into the channels of American musical commerce.

Since 1985 the major recording labels have reissued much older country material, either as anthologies or as boxed collections devoted to single performers. Most of these recordings come from the decades after 1960 and tend to be repetitious in nature. Pre-1960 items more often show up as leased recordings on such labels as Time-Life, Rounder, County, Sugar Hill, Shanachie, Yazoo, Razor and Tie, Rhino, Bloodshot Revival, CMF (Country Music Foundation), Document, Trikont, Bear Family, and Smithsonian Folkways. Bear Family, located in Hambergen, Germany, has the most impressive library of reissued vintage country music. Interested purchasers can obtain the "complete" recordings of a staggering list of such musicians as Roy Acuff, Cliff Bruner, the Carter Family, Johnny Cash, Bill Clifton, Jimmie Davis, Lefty Frizzell, Ray Price,

Marty Robbins, Jimmie Rodgers, Hank Snow, Ernest Tubb, and Bob Wills in boxed sets that include full biographical and discographical notes and reams of photographs. The Smithsonian Institution now owns Moe Asch's massive Folkways catalogue and has gradually been re-releasing these items as CDs under the Smithsonian Folkways imprint. The most epochal consequence of this merger has been the reissuance of Harry Smith's *Anthology of American Folk Music,* my choice as the most significant body of roots recordings made in the twentieth century. Pirated material, of course, also appears frequently on labels located in the United States, Europe, and Japan. A large market for older recordings definitely exists. Some of the Time-Life anthologies, for example, have experienced vigorous sales and have appeared on *Billboard*'s popularity charts. The availability of this material, along with ordering information, can easily be obtained by consulting the websites of County Sales in Floyd, Virginia, Old Homestead in Brighton, Michigan, or Downhome Music in El Cerrito, California.

Finally, fans of contemporary country music can easily find information on desired recordings by checking the pages of *No Depression, Bluegrass Unlimited,* or *Old-Time Herald* (for alternative, bluegrass, and traditional music), or by consulting *Billboard, Country Weekly,* or the computer listings at Tower Records, Barnes and Noble, and other local record stores, or Amazon.com (for mainstream country items).

Guide to Recordings

$\mathbf{R}$ecordings are listed throughout the bibliographical essays, so no attempt will be made here to present a definitive discography. The purpose of this list is to provide a core sampling of some of the best general collections of recorded country music, and to suggest outlets through which much of this material might be obtained.

The best mail-order sources for bluegrass and old-time country music, and for reissues of all kinds, are Down Home Music, 10341 San Pablo Avenue, El Cerrito, California 94530 (the leading outlet for imports); Old Homestead Records, Box 100, Brighton, Michigan 48116; Roundhouse Records, 186 Willow Avenue, Somerville, Massachusetts 02144; and County Sales, Box 191, Floyd, Virginia 24901. County Sales sends out a monthly newsletter, compiled by Dave Freeman, which reviews lps in the bluegrass, old-time, and reissue categories. The publication can generally supply information on records which it does not review.

Record reviews, of course, can be found in such journals as *Music City News*, *Country Song Roundup*, *Old Time Music*, *Country Music* (with Rich Kienzle's "Retrospectives" column providing excellent coverage of older material), *Bluegrass Unlimited*, and in such syndicated newspaper columns as those of Jack Hurst. Listings of "the best" country albums are generally impressionistic surveys, and usually reflect merely the personal tastes of the reviewers, what they happen to have in their private collections, or what is currently in print. Martha Hume, for example, in her chatty *You're So Cold I'm Turnin' Blue* (New York: Viking Press, 1982), describes "Eighty Essential Albums for a Country Music Record Collection," pp. 152–171. Douglas B. Green lists without comment close to 300 lps in *Country Roots: The Origins of Country Music* (New York: Hawthorn Books, 1976), but John Morthland undertakes the ambitious task of describing and evaluating the "750 greatest albums" in *The Best of Country Music* (Garden City, N.Y.: Doubleday and Company, 1984). He does not succeed, but he does provide a useful guide for people wishing to compile a collection. Morthland's work is marred somewhat by rather idiosyncratic selections and some highly questionable judgments. For example, he discusses the Bailes Brothers, the Louvin Brothers, Jimmie Skinner, and Doc Watson in a section called "The Depression Years," and says of Roy Acuff that the singer "milked the same two or three melodies far too often to ever sustain a productive recording career" (p. 78). This judgment is both unfair and untrue.

The single best guide to reissued recordings, and a landmark in country music scholarship, is Willie Smyth's *Country Music Recorded Prior to 1943: A Discography of LP Re-Issues* (JEMF, 1984). This work includes every known album of reissued material, both American and foreign, and a complete listing of all pre-1943 song titles which have appeared on reissue lps!

Suggested Collections:

1. *Smithsonian Collection of Classic Country Music* (compiled and annotated by Bill C. Malone, 1981): A boxed collection of eight lps including 143 songs spanning the years from 1922 to 1975 (or from Eck Robertson to Willie Nelson). It can be purchased only at the Smithsonian shops in Washington, D.C., or from Smithsonian Recordings, Box 10230, Des Moines, Iowa.

2. Library of Congress, Archive of Folk Song Recordings: These are field recordings made in the 1930's and 1940's, and many can be obtained directly from the Library of Congress, Washington, D.C. 20540.

3. Library of Congress, *Folk Music in America* (edited by Richard K. Spottswood, 1976). This collection was a Bicentennial project, and is designed as a sampler of all of America's folk music traditions, from Indian and Tex-Mex to Cajun and country. The fifteen albums are arranged into such categories as "Religious Music: Congregational and Ceremonial" and "Songs of Labor and Livelihood."

4. *Anthology of American Folk Music*, Folkways FA2951-53 (compiled and edited by Harry Smith). This collection is organized in three boxes containing two records each: Vol. 1, "Ballads"; Vol. 2, "Dances and Religious"; Vol. 3, "Songs." Introduced in the mid-fifties, these recordings of hillbilly, blues, gospel, and cajun songs from the twenties and thirties influenced at least a generation of "folk singers."

5. JEMF Sound Documents: These are lps of reissued country, blues, and gospel recordings, each of which includes a well-annotated booklet.

Especially noteworthy are *The Carter Family on Border Radio*, *Presenting the Blue Sky Boys*, and *Minstrels and Tunesmiths*.

6. Time-Life Collection of Country Music (edited by Charles K. Wolfe). Fourteen lps devoted to such topics as "The Women," "The Duets," and "Honky Tonkin'," and such prominent individuals as Hank Williams, Johnny Cash, Bob Wills, Marty Robbins, the Statler Brothers, Flatt and Scruggs, Roy Acuff, Tammy Wynette, Willie Nelson, George Jones, and the Carter Family. Each collection includes three records and forty songs, and is edited by an expert in the field (like John Rumble for Roy Acuff, and Neil Rosenberg for Flatt and Scruggs). Unfortunately, the collection was available only by subscription and is now discontinued.

7. Several small commercial labels have specialized in the reissuance of older material. These include Rounder, County, Old Homestead, Old Timey, Texas Rose (Western Swing), Shasta (Cowboy), Vetco, and at least two German concerns, Cattle and Bear Family. Some of the most ambitious reissue projects of American country music have been undertaken in foreign countries. Such performers as Jimmie Rodgers, the Carter Family, and Hank Williams have been anthologized in Japan in massive ten-lp record sets, and Toru Mitsui (a scholar and record collector) has produced eleven lps of material taken from 1930's Decca recordings. Titles of American-produced lps, and some of the foreign-made albums, can be obtained from the sources mentioned at the beginning of this essay.

8. The big commercial corporations also occasionally release older recordings from their files. However, these items usually go out of print quickly, and the reader is advised to obtain them as soon as they appear. As of this writing, the best available collection is Columbia's Historic Edition Series. Beautifully organized and engineered, and well annotated by members of the CMF staff, the albums are devoted to Gene Autry, Sons of the Pioneers, Lefty Frizzell, Spade Cooley, Flatt and Scruggs, Jimmie Dickens, Bob Wills, Carl Smith, Bill Monroe, Roy Rogers, Patsy Montana, and Leon McAuliffe.

Index

Index of Song Titles

"I've Got the Kansas City Blues," 108
"I've Ranged, I've Roamed, and I've Travelled," 85
"I Walk the Line," 254
"I Want to Be a Cowboy's Sweetheart," 145
"I Want to Be Loved," 214
"I Was Country When Country Wasn't Cool," 376
"I Was Sorta Wondering," 230
"I Wonder How the Old Folks Are at Home," 338, 359
"I Wonder Where You Are Tonight," 124, 144, 234
"I Wouldn't Change You If I Could," 413

"Jack's Truck Stop and Café," 447
"Jake Walk Blues," 105
"Jambalaya," 243
"Jealous Lover, The," 132
"Jerusalem Ridge," 324
"Jesse James," 139, 140
"Jesus Hits like an Atom Bomb," 216
"Jimmie Brown the Newsboy," 67
"Joaquin," 449
"Joe Turner Blues," 163
"John Henry," 123
"Johnny Reb," 284
"Jolene," 461
"Johnson's Old Grey Mule," 123, 125
"John T. Scopes Trial, The," 46
"Jole Blon," 152, 230, 231, 399
"Jordan Is a Hard Road to Travel," 44
"Joshua," 311
"Juke Joint Jumping," 447
"Just a Closer Walk with Thee," 206, 225
"Just a Friend," 192
"Just Because," 169
"Just Because I'm a Woman," 311
"Just between You and Me," 316
"Just Get Up and Close the Door," 307
"Just Me and the Jukebox," 350

"Just One More," 288
"Just Tell Them That You Saw Me," 16, 337
"Just When I Needed You," 229

"Katie Dear," 110
"Kaw-liga," 392
"Keeper of the Key," 293
"Keep My Skillet Good and Greasy," 74
"Keep on the Firing Line," 12
"Keep on the Sunny Side," 67
"Kentucky," 113, 213
"Kentucky Waltz," 211
"Kinnie Wagner," 48
"Kisses Sweeter than Wine," 279, 282
"Kitty Wells," 72, 223
"Knock Three Times," 378
"Knot Hole Blues," 170
"Knoxville Girl, The," 215
"Korea, Here We Come," 317

"Ladies Love Outlaws," 400
"Lady Gay, The," 57
"Lass of Roch Royal, The," 14
"Last Date," 258
"Last Letter, The," 154, 195, 515
"Last Roundup, The," 150
"Lawdy Miss Clawdy," 247
"Leather Breeches," 18
"Leave It There," 131
"Leaving Home," 51
"Leaving Louisiana in the Broad Daylight," 385
"Lee Highway Blues," 36
"Legend in My Time," 259
"Legend of Bonnie and Clyde," 294
"Legend of John Henry's Hammer, The," 282
"Legend of the Dogwood Tree," 223
"Legend of the Rebel Soldier, The," 364
"Legend of the Robin Red Breast, The," 56
"Leonard," 295